£14.95

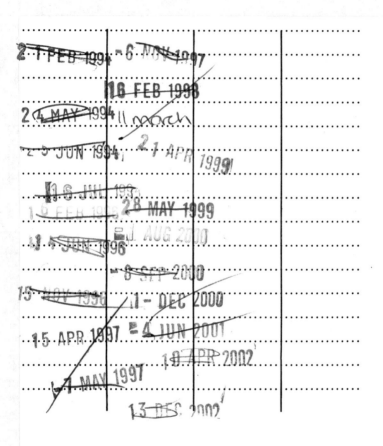

"Me? I'm just one of those shadowy figures who inhabit the mysterious twilight world where the medical and legal professions meet."

Drawing by Handelsman; © 1986
The New Yorker Magazine, Inc.

TREAT ME RIGHT

Essays in Medical Law and Ethics

IAN KENNEDY

CLARENDON PRESS · OXFORD

Oxford University Press, Walton Street, Oxford OX2 6DP

Oxford New York Toronto
Delhi Bombay Calcutta Madras Karachi
Petaling Jaya Singapore Hong Kong Tokyo
Nairobi Dar es Salaam Cape Town
Melbourne Auckland

and associated companies in
Berlin Ibadan

Oxford is a trade mark of Oxford University Press

Published in the United States
by Oxford University Press, New York

British Library Cataloguing in Publication Data
Kennedy, Ian
Treat me right: essays in medical law and ethics.
1. Medical ethics   2. Medical laws and legislation
I. Title
174'.2   R724
ISBN 0-19-825559-4
ISBN 0-19-825558-6 (pbk)

Library of Congress Cataloging in Publication Data
Kennedy, Ian, 1941-
Treat me right: essays in medical law and ethics / Ian Kennedy.
p.   cm. Bibliography: p.   Includes index.
1. Medical laws and legislation—Great Britain.   2. Medical
ethics—Great Britain.   I. Title.
[DNLM: 1. Ethics, Medical—Essays.   2. Jurisprudence—essays. W 32.6
K35t]
KD3395.A75K46 1988   344.41'041—dc19
[344.10441]   DNLM/DLC
for Library of Congress   87-28141   CIP
ISBN 0-19-825559-4
ISBN 0-19-825558-6 (pbk)

Phototypeset by Dobbie Typesetting Limited, Tavistock, Devon
Printed and bound in
Great Britain by Biddles Ltd,
Guildford and Kings Lynn

To Jack

Preface to the Paperback Edition

In preparing this edition I decided to resist the temptation to tinker even further with the essays which appeared in the 1988 edition. Enough is enough! Instead, I have simply added two papers I have written since. One concerns what I think will be a problem of increasing importance in the 1990s: what I have called maternal–fetal conflict. Medical technology more and more enables us to monitor the progress of a fetus. But, with knowledge come choices, in this case, whose interests should prevail, the mother's or the fetus's when these do not coincide. There are so many layers to such a dilemma, philosophical, political, religious, legal, that it commands interest not only in its own right but as a paradigm for so many other issues in reproductive medicine. And, it is undoubtedly reproductive medicine which will hold centre stage in bioethics in the 1990s. The second paper allows me to rehearse the view I have been seeking to advance for some time now: that medical law is best understood and analysed as part of human rights law. I say this for two reasons. First, resort to the language of rights assists in the attempt to develop law which redresses the disequilibrium of power between doctor and patient. To argue that patients have rights ensures that they will be taken seriously as partners in the enterprise of health. It is no part of this argument, of course, that patients should take power over the relationship, only that they be empowered. The second reason is more abstract. I have for some time been urging that if medical law is to find its identity (or justify its existence) it needs to break out of the traditional English approach to legal categories. These are almost universally fact-based or contextual. Fact situations are shovelled under the heading of, for example, tort, or contract, or property almost as if by acccident. The horrible questions of why these facts are considered and those are not, or if this is covered then why not hang-gliding, or sex, or mushroom collecting, are not asked. The search for an underlying conceptual framework is ignored as an empty exercise, something for idle hands. Continental Europeans shake their heads in disbelief. In my view this general challenge to English law can be met as regards medical law by stating that medical law is a part or sub-set of human rights law. It is the contextual application of the over-arching framework of human rights. Obviously, there is a lot of work to be done. By including the new chapter on human rights, I hope both to contribute to the process and to show the richness of analysis such an approach can bring.

Having eschewed a moment ago amending the rest of the essays any more, there are a couple of developments since 1988 that I really ought to mention. First, there is the case of *Re J* [1990] 3 All ER 930 in which Lord Donaldson,

Master of the Rolls, having refused the opportunity to do so in *Re C* [1989] 2 All ER 782, spells out in more considered detail the law governing the case of the severely handicapped new-born baby. Those seeking a definitive guide to the criteria relevant in determining best interests will still be disappointed. But the case is undoubtedly a step forward. First, it confirms the view I express in chapter 8 that doctors may under certain circumstances 'treat for dying' (not 'treat to die' as Ward J. unhappily put it in *Re C* [1989] 2 All ER 787). Second, it expands somewhat on the rather cryptic criterion of Templeman LJ (as he then was) in *Re B* ([1981] 1 WLR 1421, 1424) that treatment for dying may be justified if the life of the child 'is demonstrably going to be so awful . . .'.

Second, in discussing the possible sale of kidneys in chapter 11 I noticed the furore which followed the report in 1985 of the sale of kidneys by Turkish donors. The Government at the time of writing had not decided what course of action to take. Surprisingly, the Human Organ Transplants Act, 1989 making such sales a criminal offence, was introduced and passed in double quick time to echoes of righteous indignation from all corners of Parliament. No one had the bad taste to remark that trafficking in kidneys was only necessary because of the dire shortage, and this shortage was in large part due to the Human Tissue Act 1961 which all Governments have steadfastly refused to touch for the past thirty years. Nor was anyone bold enough to remark on the oddity of a Government committed to free enterprise and the market place jumping like scalded cats to ban people from trading in tissue, when they are exhorted daily to trade their lives in unwholesome working conditions regulated (if that is the right word) entirely by market forces.

My thanks are due again to Richard Hart at OUP.

I.K.
April 1991

Acknowledgements

Chapter 1.   Reprinted from The Cambridge Lectures 1983, ed. E. Baldwin by permission of Butterworths Law Publishers Ltd.

Chapter 3.   Reprinted from *Postcoital Contraception: methods, services and prospects*, (1983) by permission of Pregnancy Advisory Service.

Chapter 4.   Reprinted from 42 *Modern Law Review* (1979) by permission of the *Modern Law Review*.

Chapter 5.   Reprinted from *Moral Dilemmas in Modern Medicine*, ed. M. Lockwood (1985) by permission of Oxford University Press, and from *Medicine in Contemporary Society*, ed. P. Byrne (1987) by permission of King's Fund.

Chapter 6.   Reprinted from *King's Counsel* (1985) by permission of King's College London.

Chapter 9.   Reprinted from 47 *Modern Law Review* (1984) by permission of the *Modern Law Review*.

Chapter 11.   Reprinted from 16 *Medicine Science and the Law* (1976) by permission of the British Academy of Forensic Sciences.

Chapter 12.   Reprinted from 5 *Journal of Medical Ethics* (1979) by permission of the Institute of Medical Ethics.

Chapter 13.   Reprinted from 2 *Anglo-American Law Review* (1973) by permission of Barry Rose Periodicals Ltd.

Chapter 16.   Reprinted from *The Continuing Care of Terminal Cancer Patients*, ed. R. Twycross (1980) by permission of Pergamon Books Ltd. and from *The Management of Terminal Malignant Disease*, ed. C. Saunders (1982) by permission of Edward Arnold (Publishers) Ltd.

Chapter 17.   Reprinted from the *Criminal Law Review* (1976) by permission of Sweet & Maxwell Ltd.

Chapter 18.   Reprinted from the *Criminal Law Review* (1977) by permission of Sweet & Maxwell Ltd.

Chapter 19.   Reprinted from *Ethics & Law in Health Care & Research*, ed. P. Byrne by permission of John Wiley & Sons, Ltd.

Chapter 20.   Reprinted from *Human Rights for the 1990s*, ed. R. Blackburn by permission of Mansell Publishing Ltd.

Contents

Table of Cases

British Cases

xiii

United States Cases

Canadian Cases

Decisions of the European Commission and
Court of Human Rights

Miscellaneous Cases from Other Jurisdictions

1

Emerging Problems of Medicine, Technology, and the Law*

I have been invited to discuss emerging problems in technology, medicine, and the law. I take 'technology' in this context to mean the application of know-how and skill in the practice of medicine. Many problems exist for the practice of law in this area, and more are appearing. Just on Monday and Tuesday of this week I sat in on a case in the High Court in London. Mrs Victoria Gillick was asking for a declaration that National Health Service doctors in the area in which she lives would be acting unlawfully if they put into effect a Memorandum of Guidance issued by the Department of Health addressed to local health authorities stating that it was permissible to give contraceptive advice and treatment to girls under the age of 16 years without the consent of their parents. Mrs Gillick claimed standing to bring the action on the ground that she is the parent of children in the area. She asked for a declaration that no child of hers be given such contraceptive advice or treatment without her consent. Indeed, she said that no child under 16 years may be given contraceptive advice or treatment, because that would aid and abet the criminal offence of unlawful sexual intercourse by a man with a girl under the age of 16.[1] This is only one example of the recent spate of cases which are coming up for decision in the United Kingdom.

Such litigation is still relatively unusual. In the United States, there seems to be a case in medical law every other hour; but we in the United Kingdom have had very few. However, suddenly, in the last five years or so, there have been several. For example, there was recently a case on voluntary euthanasia after the publication of a booklet advising people how, if they were so minded, they could take their own lives.[2] The booklet was published by the Voluntary Euthanasia Society as an exercise of the so-called right to

* A lecture delivered to the Canadian Institute for Advanced Legal Studies, Cambridge, 1983. Subsequently, it was published in *The Cambridge Lectures* (Butterworths, 1985), pp. 99–114. The text here has been revised slightly.
[1] The court at first instance denied Mrs Gillick the declarations sought; [1984] 1 All ER 365. Her subsequent appeal, however, was successful. The DHSS appealed to the House of Lords, and the appeal was allowed by a majority of 3 to 2, *Gillick* v. *West Norfolk and Wisbech AHA* [1986] AC 150, and see Chapter 5.
[2] *Attorney-General* v. *Able* [1984] 1 All ER 277.

die. The Attorney-General sought a declaration that the publication of the booklet would be a violation of the criminal law, because it would be aiding and abetting the commission of suicide by someone who read and acted upon it, or at least would be an attempt to do so. The judgment was at best equivocal on the issue. The declaration was denied, but the court indicated that the publication could, in certain circumstances, amount to a crime.

We have also seen two cases which raised the question of what treatment a doctor may legally be required to deliver to severely handicapped newly born babies. One was a civil law case.[3] The other was a criminal law case in which a doctor, whose management of such a baby resulted in the child's death, was prosecuted for murder, the charge later being reduced to attempted murder.[4] You can imagine the concern in the community when a doctor who was otherwise highly respected suddenly ended up in the dock on a charge for which the sentence is mandatory life imprisonment. This happened as a result of his carrying out what he thought was appropriate treatment for a severely handicapped baby. I shall return to this case later.

In addition, we have seen a so-called wrongful life case.[5] We have also had proposals in Parliament for amendments to the law on abortion, and have had cases regarding the interpretation of the existing Abortion Act before our courts.[6] We have had failed sterilization cases, where damages have been sought.[7] We have had significantly more medical negligence cases than we used to have.[8] In short, the past five years have seen a considerable growth of activity in the area of medical law.[9]

Clearly, problems of medical law are emerging, and clearly they must be solved. I would have thought — and I am sure all of you will agree — that it is not fair to doctors, doctors' insurers, patients, parents, relatives — indeed any of us — to have problems which touch us all, as these do, with no apparent solution. But although it is clear that we ought to solve them, it is by no

---

[3] *Re B* [1981] 1 WLR 1421. [4] *R.* v. *Arthur, The Times*, 6 Nov. 1981.
[5] *McKay* v. *Essex AHA* [1982] 2 All ER 771.
[6] *Royal College of Nursing of the UK* v. *DHSS* [1981] AC 800.
[7] See, e.g., *Udale* v. *Bloomsbury AHA* [1983] 2 All ER 522; *Thake* v. *Maurice* [1986] 1 All ER 497; *Emeh* v. *Kensington AHA* [1984] 3 All ER 1044; *Gold* v. *Haringey HA* [1987] 2 All ER 888.

[8] See e.g. *The Times*, 19 Aug. 1986, reporting an increase in subscriptions to the Medical Defence Union of around 70 per cent (from £336 to £576), which was attributed to an increase in litigation, as well as to the cost of meeting claims.

[9] Indeed, since delivering this paper, there have been a number of cases concerning the law relating to consent to medical treatment. *Freeman* v. *Home Office* [1984] 1 All. ER 1036 is a decision of the Court of Appeal on the voluntariness of consent. *Sidaway* v. *Governors of the Bethlem Royal Hospital* [1985] AC 871 is a most important case on informed consent which was decided by the House of Lords (see further, chapter 9). July 1984 saw the publication of the Report of the Committee of Enquiry into Human Fertilization and Embryology (the Warnock Report; Cmnd. 9314, HMSO), followed by the Surrogacy Arrangements Act 1985 and bills such as the Unborn Children (Protection) Bill, so far unsuccessful, aimed at outlawing research on early embryos (see further, chapter 6).

means clear how we ought to do it, and what solutions should be adopted. It is those questions which I am going to address.

MEDICAL LAW—A CATEGORY

These issues and cases, whether they concern sterilization, medical negligence, the Abortion Act, or whatever, all fall within what I would call 'medical law'. I would suggest to you that there is a discrete area of law which can properly be called 'medical law', though it has by no means yet been marked out or accepted as having its own territory. It is, in my view, a discrete area, concerned with the interactions between doctors and patients and the organization of health care. There are common issues which permeate all the problems and the doctor–patient relationship: respect for autonomy and self-determination in the context of consent, truth-telling, and confidences, respect for dignity, respect for life, and respect for justice. All these ethical precepts run through the area involved. But the issues still tend to be seen in terms of traditional legal categories; for example, as problems of family law, tort law, or contract law in the area of private law, or as problems of administrative law, constitutional law, or criminal law in the area of public law. This prevents them from being understood as problems having certain things in common which mark them off from others. And, until that happens, I do not think that we are going to have a coherent approach to the emerging problems in medical law, an approach which recognizes these common themes and seeks to develop a body of doctrine which has coherence and some internal consistency.

DEVELOPMENTS—WHAT'S NEW?

It is a trite observation that developments will always be taking place in medicine. In one sense there is nothing new in recent events such as *in vitro* fertilization, the freezing of embryos, genetic engineering, or kidney transplants and kidney dialysis. After all, there is a continuum of development and refinement of medical technology and medical skills, from the knife, the leech, and the potion to surgery, antiseptics, and anaesthesia. Anaesthetics, I am sure, posed as many problems when they were first introduced as, for example, transplants have recently. After all, you very often did not recover from the process of being put to sleep for an operation. Vaccines emerged for the most part at the end of the nineteenth century; then came drugs, blood transfusions, skin grafts, and tissue transplants. And, in treatment not involving physical intervention, the movement has been from hypnosis to psychoanalysis to psychotherapy and beyond to include such practices as transcendental meditation, and even 'sexual dysfunction counselling' in its various forms.

What, then, is new about what is happening now? Is there anything which warrants giving special attention to recent developments in medical technology?

I think there may be. All the developments mentioned have brought moral and legal questions in their wake. But it was arguably only recently that they were recognized as legal questions. The idea that consent, for example, was ordinarily required before treatment could legally be justified appears very late in legal writings dealing with medical practice. Indeed, the perception that a patient had any rights or, if there were rights, that they amounted to a legal claim, or that if it was a legal claim, it was worth pressing before a court; all these various thresholds had to be crossed before there was an issue for the courts to decide and before law emerged on which to build and to mark out the limits of the legally permissible such that doctors and patients became aware that their relationship was subject to legal regulation. Legal, as well as moral, problems were, therefore, always involved in medical developments; but only recently, perhaps, have they been perceived as such, as questions which could be taken to the courts for decision.

LAW LAGGING BEHIND DEVELOPMENTS

As regards some of the problems posed by medical technology, however, it is hardly surprising that the law has said little. The great legal commentators of the eighteenth and nineteenth centuries, Blackstone or Stephen, cannot be condemned for having nothing to say about embryo transfer. It was not exactly part of their concept of reality. And to the lack of any legal tradition in this area must be added the fact that, in any event, it is normal for the law to fail to keep pace with developments of any kind. The law is usually somewhat behind the introduction of new techniques.

This is particularly the case with medical developments, because they are happening so quickly, and because of what I have called elsewhere the 'technological imperative' often felt by doctors and those engaged in medical research—the imperative that if you *can* do something, you *must* do it. The moment you find out what you can do, you do it and let other people pick up later the intellectual, legal, and moral tangle which you may have left in your wake.

So, despite the fact that matters such as freezing embryos, or turning off ventilators, or questions such as whether haemophiliacs should be entitled within the National Health Service to receive a particular blood factor which is very expensive, pose extraordinarily difficult legal and moral problems, it is unfortunately the case that the law is not very clear.

Given this uncertainty in the law and the moral implications of their actions, doctors and those engaged in medical research have sometimes sought legal advice before proceeding with some new technique or innovation or research. But the imprecision of the law has often meant that the legal advice given has been conservative. For example, the legal advice given by leading counsel in 1965 to the Medical Research Council in the United Kingdom as to whether non-therapeutic medical research could legally be carried out on children was that experiments on children under the age of 12 were unlawful. The reason given was that the law permitted only what was in a child's best interests. And since such experiments could never been in a child's *best* interests, they could not therefore be carried out lawfully. As a consequence, such research was not conducted for a considerable number of years. Eventually, however, it was decided that this particular legal advice was too conservative, as well as impeding research. A revised view gained acceptance: that such research, if it posed only a *minimal* risk to a child, could properly be carried out, and that a parent, therefore, could properly consent.[10] So such research was begun, albeit with great care.

But once a new technique is employed, even after suitable reflection, entirely new problems are sometimes thrown up which had not been envisaged when the technique was introduced, and so are even less likely to be subject to legal or moral resolution. Here we are even less likely to have a clear idea of what the law requires. Furthermore, there may be another reason why the law has not caught up with rapid medical developments. The moral debate about the circumstances under which we should, for example, turn off the ventilator of a terminally ill patient or intervene when a baby is born severely handicapped, as well as the social evaluation of what it may cost in spiritual, emotional, and political terms, takes a long time. We have to know about the nature of the development and the possibilities it opens up; we have to reflect on it, and allow time for public discussion and debate. This need for an intellectual breathing space, when seen against the background of the technological imperative, has meant that the law, which inevitably comes after the public and social evaluation, is even more behind. We may not know what is happening, what we want to do about it, or what is right. A lag— indeed, a hiatus—in the law is inevitable.

Finally, we in the United Kingdom, and I think this is equally true in Canada, have had a tradition of leaving the regulation and control of medical practice largely to the medical profession. Regarding the problems as merely technical, we have trusted the profession, and been unwilling to interfere too closely in the decisions arrived at. You can see this, for example, in the nature of the civil law's involvement in medical practice, to the extent that it has been involved at all. The civil law has said that a doctor's conduct falls to be judged by reference to how a reasonable doctor would behave in similar circumstances. How a reasonable doctor would, in fact, behave is then

---

[10] See R. Nicholson, ed., *Medical Research with Children* (Oxford University Press, 1986).

regarded as a matter of expert evidence, on which only the medical profession is competent to speak.[11] In other words, it has been left to the medical profession to set the legal standard of care. That has been the traditional legal approach, to leave difficult questions to the medical profession. And in the case of criminal law, it is rare in the extreme to see a doctor prosecuted for practising what other people regard as valid treatment. If responsible, reputable doctors are prepared to say that some procedure is adequate or proper treatment, then that is normally sufficient for the law.

ARE TODAY'S DEVELOPMENTS DIFFERENT?

Let me return to the question I posed earlier. Is there anything significantly different in recent developments in medicine? Although the history of medical developments forms a continuum, are the problems that have been emerging in the last two or three decades, the sort of problems I have put before you, of a different nature from those before? Certainly they are happening more rapidly. Certainly there are many more of them, and they are tumbling over each other to get into the popular press every day. For example, a new 'breakthrough' in cancer treatment can be found in one newspaper at least once a week. Certainly because the issues touch such matters as life and death and procreation, they are very taxing and very troubling.

But, as I have said, this was just as true of developments in the nineteenth century, such as anaesthesia, or of earlier twentieth-century developments, such as antibiotics. For example, when penicillin was introduced, a particular difficulty confronted the American armed forces in North Africa. There was a limited supply of penicillin, and many people needed it. Therefore, the United States Surgeon-General issued an order. Two classes of patient were defined: those suffering from various forms of venereal disease, and those suffering from major war injuries: wounds, loss of limbs, and the like. The Surgeon-General issued an order that those wounded in brothels were to receive the penicillin and those wounded in war should not. How, you may ask, could that possibly be the case? Yet it is defensible on the proposition that those with venereal disease would be back at the front fighting the enemy after two or three injections, whereas those with massive wounds would go back to the United States, perhaps to recover, but never to fight again. Given that the greater goal was the defeat of the enemy, one can begin to understand that decision. So the problems which touch life, death, and procreation are by no means novel in the area of medical development.

Perhaps what has changed is the social climate in which these developments are taking place and in which medicine is now practised. Until recently, such

[11] See e.g. *Whitehouse* v. *Jordan* [1981] 1 All ER 267.

matters have been left for private treaty, if you will, between the doctor and his professional organization, between the doctor and the relative, and between the doctor and the patient. Imagine, for example, the following. Doctor and relative come together. The relative says, 'I think Granny has had enough. If she gets pneumonia, let her go.' The doctor says, 'I am not entirely sure about that. I think antibiotics may still be appropriate.' The relative says, 'Granny and I talked it over some time ago, and she said that if she was ever in this position she would rather not be treated.' Should we be concerned that in the private agreement between the parties, Granny is allowed to depart this world? I think there is a very real sense that we are no longer prepared to leave such matters merely to private agreement and regulation.[12]

Compare the development of a rather unusual form of treatment introduced in the United Kingdom some 30 years or so ago, surgery for transsexuals. Transsexuals claim that they are really of the opposite gender, whatever their biological sexual characteristics may indicate; and they plead for appropriate 'reassignment surgery', so that they can pass in what they regard as their proper and true gender. No one raised the question of whether such surgery could amount to the crime of mayhem (or maim), whereby the Sovereign is deprived of the services of a fighting soldier. Removing surgically various parts of the body such that the patient is thereafter irreparably changed, and some would say disabled, seems to me to be basically a question of maim. It certainly persuaded centres in a number of jurisdictions in the United States to cease surgery on transsexuals. In the United Kingdom, however, this legal issue seems hardly to have been raised, and the surgery has been regarded as if it were simply a technical matter for private discussion within the medical profession. The possible relevance of criminal law, the vexed question of what may be consented to, and the administrative difficulties posed for the legal system by requests for new passports or birth certificates went largely unremarked.[13]

More recently, by contrast, the mother of an 11-year-old daughter who suffered from Soto's syndrome, whereby, for her age, she was physically overdeveloped, but mentally somewhat retarded, wanted the daughter to be sterilized.[14] The mother was concerned that the daughter's friendly nature and her intellectual backwardness, combined with her apparent physical voluptuousness, might persuade someone to take advantage of her, and that she might become pregnant. The mother certainly did not want to have to worry about a grandchild when her daughter was only 11 or 12 and already demanded a great deal of attention. So she consulted her local, caring doctor, who agreed to sterilize the girl. But the climate of opinion was changing.

[12] For an excellent review of the issues, see *In re Claire C. Conroy*, 190 NJ Super 453; 464 A.2d 303 (1985).
[13] See further, chapter 13. [14] *Re D (a minor)* [1976] 1 All ER 326.

The child's teacher discovered the mother's intentions and immediately sought the advice of the court as to whether or not the surgery would be lawful. In other words, it was no longer accepted that such a decision was just for the doctor and the parent to make. Larger issues were at stake, on which, it was said, only a court could decide. Remarkably, the case came before one of the very few female judges in the High Court, Mrs Justice Heilbron. She held that to sterilize the girl at such an early age would be a violation of a fundamental right to reproduce, and that, therefore, the sterilization should not take place.

Notice the contrast. In the past, the assumption was made that, if something was described as treatment, it was *ipso facto* justified. The word 'treatment' was enough. And treatment was what the doctor said was treatment. The law did not enquire any further. Obviously, this seems now to be changing.

Let me give you one last example. Sexual dysfunction counselling, which I referred to earlier, is, perhaps, slightly bizarre, but very worth analysing. In San Diego three years ago, I saw a report in a local newspaper[15] of a centre where someone could have counselling and 'treatment'—that was the term used—whereby he or she would be introduced to a member of the opposite sex who would help to resolve the particular sexual problem complained of. Such help might well—and, of course, usually did—involve sexual intercourse. The important question for analysis is why the person who organized the centre was not guilty of the crime of living off immoral earnings. Does it not sound like prostitution by another name? But if you call it 'treatment' and 'counselling', do you thereby embellish it with a ring of apparent respectability, whereby it jumps over the legal hurdle which would otherwise be in the way? That is the sort of question I am putting to you. Are we now prepared to accept this argument? After all, the word 'treatment' is not only descriptive, it is also prescriptive; it has a normative quality. The change may be that, now, we are not as ready as we once were to accept the doctor's, or the doctor's and patient's, words, or simply the use of the word 'treatment', as conclusive of the propriety of any particular form of conduct.

CHANGING ATTITUDES

In attempting to explain this change, we must examine a number of factors. First, there is a greater preparedness to question the implications of medical developments, and hence much more extra-professional debate. Second, there is a more informed and educated population. Third, the mass media have become greatly interested in scientific and medical developments. Fourth, there is a consequent change in the relative status of the profession. More

[15] 'Love with a Proper Stranger', *San Diego Reader*, vol. 8, 11 Oct. 1979.

people are willing to ask why, or what is going to happen to them, or do you think we should do this or that. Fifth, hand in hand with this, has been a change in the nature of the doctor–patient relationship, such that the patient is no longer a supplicant (or even a mendicant). Now he is better perceived as a consumer or client. The patient may no longer be given commands for his own good, but rather, advice which he can take or leave. Sixth, the government's involvement in the supply of medical services and in research, and the consequent demands for public accountability, have had their effect on this change in social relations. Seventh, the more widespread use of the language of human rights is important, bringing with it the idea that we have certain rights which apply to medical practice just as to other areas. Finally, there is a recognition of the need to separate out the moral and value-laden aspects of medical development, and then debate them and try to get them right, which involves a certain amount of accountability and responsibility. I perceive a call for solutions to the problems of medical developments by reference to criteria set by non-medical, as well as medical, people. Indeed, this very demand for solutions to be arrived at by society is itself one of the emerging problems of medical technology. This is because, notwithstanding the demand, it is very hard to find the appropriate mechanism for arriving at proper solutions.

While there is, quite properly, an increasing public interest in medical developments, we must take care to treat this interest seriously. There is something very attractive about these medical problems; they bring out the voyeur in all of us. There is a danger that we may simply spot the problem, rub our hands, say how interesting it is, and then move quickly on before someone asks the hard question of what to do about it. We have a public responsibility as lawyers, judges, and writers, as well as a private self-interest, to try to be more than voyeurs as we seek to solve these problems.

MEDICAL DEVELOPMENTS AND LEGAL PROBLEMS

What sort of problems are we up against? And what is the best way to solve them, bearing in mind the demand for public solutions and the danger of what I have called 'voyeurism'? I will mention a few examples, simply to indicate the wide spectrum of problems confronting us.

First there is the apparently very simple question regarding when someone is dead. This concerns all of us in one sense, but none of us in another. When the final determination is made, the issue will be moot as regards our own intellectual pursuit of the issue! The problem of when a person is dead is clearly very significant for lawyers. For example, property passes on death; the crime of murder connotes the taking of a life; the Fatal Accidents Act only comes into operation if there is an accident which leaves someone dead; and there are the various tax implications.

The problem of the definition, or meaning, of death is clearly a very difficult philosophical question. It is both a normative and a descriptive question. To say someone is dead is to make a very profound statement about life. Dying may be said to be a process, while death is an event. The question then becomes where in the process of dying, death shall be judged to occur. There are a number of choices. You can wait until every cell has degenerated to the point where all that is left of us is some kind of smelly porridge. You can opt for some earlier stage, such as when an old person has become senile. Or you can choose somewhere else along the spectrum represented by the process of dying. Clearly, no one is going to opt for a definition of death which regards as dead someone who is merely senile or incapable of communication or unconscious. And, as if the problem were not hard enough, modern medical technology has produced the ventilator, which has, in turn, created its own problems. Questions have been raised as to when it is permissible in law to declare someone to be dead, if he is on a ventilator and continues to breathe, even though he will never breathe again unaided.

We have arrived at a solution in this country which seems to be palatable to most people. The definition of death is the same as it has always been. What have changed are the criteria for recognizing it (or the operational definition) now that we have ventilators which mimic life by making people breathe, thanks to the Electricity Board, rather than their own vital functions. We have had to identify that part of the body which drives the heart and lungs—that is, the brain-stem. This has allowed us to conclude that if the brain-stem has been completely destroyed, the person can be declared dead, even though he may still be breathing and his heart beating because of the ventilator. Even with the aid of the ventilator, he will cease to breathe and to have a pulse within 10 to 14 days. Once this intellectual problem is solved, there still remains a problem of communication with the public, to allay its fears that people are being improperly declared dead and their organs used for transplants while they are still alive.

The problem of the definition of death has been resolved in this country without any statute or case-law, unlike what has happened in a number of jurisdictions in the United States. Indeed, confidence in the definition is such that we are now moving to the position that it may well be unethical to take organs for the purpose of transplant except in cases in which the donor's heart was still beating at the time of removal, because that increases the chances that the kidney or other organ is in a healthy state. Death will have been determined, and the ventilator will have been left on until the relevant organ has been removed for transplant. This is the so-called beating-heart cadaver.

Likewise, in the United Kingdom, we have had to deal with another medical-legal problem posed by technological developments, the problem of sterilization. Except in the case of the young girl whom I have already mentioned,[15a] the law seems to have become clear. It was only in 1954, however, that Lord Justice Denning, as he then was, in one of his more than common *ex cathedra* statements on the law, declared—although it was irrelevant to the case at issue, thereby, perhaps, contriving to give himself authority in the next case that came along—that sterilization was against the law unless it was done on good medical grounds for reasons of illness or health.[16] Well, by the National Health Service (Family Planning) Amendment Act 1972, provision was made for sterilization services to be provided by the National Health Service. But there had been no statute saying sterilization was not unlawful. It was just made available for social or birth control purposes. It is one of the wonderful examples of the fudge-and-nudge development of English law. There was no town crier. It was not really written up in the books. The whole legal attitude towards sterilization simply had changed.

Another example of developed medical law is that relating to transplants. At the very least, we have a legal framework for it. I do not think the framework is very good, but at least we have a statutory regime. The circumstances under which tissue and organs may be removed for the purposes of transplant are contained in what is a somewhat venerable piece of legislation, the Human Tissue Act 1961.[17]

UNSOLVED PROBLEMS

These examples point to circumstances in which we have solved, at least for the time being, the problems posed by medical technological development, either directly through law or interstitially without the need to have recourse to law. But there are many more problems which have not been solved and which press urgently for resolution.

I mention straightaway the question I mentioned at the outset, that of what the law says may be done in the treatment of a severely handicapped newly born baby. There is some law, in the form of a couple of cases. But the cases are very difficult to reconcile with each other and, therefore, to use for the purposes of advice or predicting future judicial behaviour. The case of *Re B*[18] involved a baby born with Down's syndrome and with what is called 'duodenal atresia'. This means that the small intestine is blocked and that if the blockage is not removed surgically, the baby will die. The parents in this case were asked if they wanted the baby to undergo surgery. They said that they did not. The doctor was prepared to accede to this. But the director

[15a] And see now, *Re B (a minor) (wardship: sterilisation)* [1987] 2 All ER 211.
[16] *Bravery* v. *Bravery* [1954] 3 All ER 59.
[17] See further, chapters 11 and 12.
[18] See *supra* n. 3.

of the local Social Services Department, on being advised of this by a member of his staff, asked the court either to make the child a ward of the court or to allow the local authority to take the child into its care, so that it, *qua* parent, could give consent for surgery. At first instance, the court was much persuaded by the views of the parents and refused the local authority's application. But Lord Justice Templeman (now Lord Templeman), speaking for the Court of Appeal the next day, declared that the views of the parents had been too much relied upon by the judge at first instance. Although they were relevant, Templeman LJ held that they were not conclusive as to what should happen to the child, particularly where a child's life or death was involved. He decided that if a surgeon was prepared to carry out the necessary operation, the Court would give consent on behalf of the child. He went on to say that there may be circumstances in which life is so 'demonstrably awful' that one ought not to consent to such surgery. But he decided that this was not one of those cases. He suggested that the law might be that there comes a point in what is loosely, and rather unhelpfully, called the 'quality of life' argument — I say 'unhelpful' because it does not mean anything: it begs the question of what quality is *the* quality — when you may say, let the child die. But he did not articulate what that point was. That remains to be done. And, in the interim, of course, those who must advise doctors must do so, conscious of both the importance of the issue and the lack of clear guidance.

Then came the case of *R. v. Arthur*.[19] A doctor was charged with the murder of a baby. The child was born with Down's syndrome. There was no atresia. It was, as far as the doctor knew at the time, a case of uncomplicated Down's syndrome. Later, pathological tests showed that there was some brain and heart damage; but this is not uncommon in children with Down's syndrome, and it is not incompatible with their surviving. After consultation with the parents, the doctor wrote in the notes 'Nursing Care Only'. The baby was given doses of a drug which would tend to make it sleep. Of course, if a baby is encouraged to sleep and then fed only on demand, it tends not to be fed. On the other hand, some children do not need to be fed for a while, and the notes did indicate that this particular baby had received some milk and water. But after three days the baby died.

The doctor was prosecuted. The original charge was murder; but during the trial this was reduced to attempted murder, since the prosecution experts could not say, on being shown pathological findings under a microscope, precisely what the baby had in fact died from. Mr Justice Farquharson's direction to the jury as to the relevant law was at the very least equivocal, or, more accurately, unclear. He seems to have regarded it as part of the criminal law that a doctor could, under certain circumstances, lawfully engage in 'a holding operation' to see whether 'nature would take its course'. The

---

[19] See *supra* n. 3.

difficulty with such a proposition is that nature may take its course in many circumstances if you do not intervene, but that it is the nature of medicine that you *do* intervene. Indeed, normally the law imposes on a doctor a duty to act, once the relationship of doctor and patient has been established: and it is not usually open to the doctor thereafter to argue that there is no liability for an omission. Clearly, the baby was not in the same condition as the baby in the *Re B* case, in that its life was not threatened by atresia; but, in *Re B*, Templeman LJ said that the baby ought to receive the necessary treatment. If *Arthur* is to be reconciled with *Re B*, it can only be on the basis that in both cases the court is saying that in some circumstances the law allows the doctor not to intervene. The problem concerns the facts. The baby in *Arthur* would not fall in the *Re B* category; yet the judge seems to have instructed the jury that nature could legally be left to take its course. I think therefore that the law is inching towards the notion that there are some circumstances under which doctors do not have to strive officiously to keep a child alive. What those precise circumstances are, however, is still very hard to say.

Another new area is that of *in vitro* fertilization (IVF). So-called test tube babies are with us; and there is no use saying it ought never to have happened. You cannot put the genie back in the bottle. All you can do is try to tame him and make sure he does not grant any old wish. We desperately need good workable law to deal with artificial insemination by donor (AID) and other forms of artificial conception. Equally pressing is the need for law to deal with the inevitable corollaries of IVF, especially surrogate-mother agreements, womb-leasing, and most problematical of all, research on embryos not intended for implantation.[20]

Consider another problem. Within five years it will be possible, in the view of most, to intervene *in utero*, to operate surgically on a foetus, even to the extent of altering its genetic make-up. Let us imagine, for example, a mother who has been carrying a child for seven months, at which point it is discovered that the child is suffering from a congenital disability which could be corrected by foetal surgery. Imagine further that the mother refuses to consent to surgery on the foetus. There you have the makings of a most difficult conflict of interests. Is the mother entitled to refuse the surgery, because, after all, it is *her* body that the doctor must operate on? If she does, can the child be taken from her if he is born disabled because of her neglect? There are already cases in some jurisdictions in the United States in which mothers have been forced—ultimately they would have agreed—to undergo treatment because they were carrying babies who would otherwise have died.[21] Here is an area ripe for controversy and for legal analysis and resolution.

---

[20] See Surrogacy Arrangements Act 1985 and chapter 6.
[21] See e.g. *Raleigh Fitkin–Paul Morgan Memorial Hospital* v. *Anderson*, 42 NJ 421, 201 A. 2d 537 (1964), cert. denied, 377 US 985. [And see, *D (a minor)* v. *Berkshire County Council*

My last brief example is something I was involved with in the correspondence columns of *The Times*, which, as you know, is where we usually solve our legal problems in this country. I gave advice to the Pregnancy Advisory Service that what is called 'postcoital birth control' did not in law amount to abortion.[22] This technique of postcoital birth control involves giving a woman who has had unprotected sexual intercourse a much larger than usual dose of the female hormones contained in the normal contraceptive pill. It means that if the woman's ovum has been fertilized, it will be prevented from developing further. The woman ordinarily will present herself at the Pregnancy Advisory Service, say that she has had unprotected intercourse, and ask for this treatment. Is this patient seeking an abortion? If so, the terms of the Abortion Act 1967 must be complied with. Two doctors must certify that the circumstances specified by the law exist. Alternatively, can the pill just be given by the doctor in the clinic without further enquiry? The answer turns on whether or not the doctor is procuring a miscarriage for the purposes of sections 58 and 59 of the Offences against the Persons Act 1861. I gave the opinion that a *miscarriage* cannot be procured unless the woman is *carrying*. I went on to argue that until the fertilized egg is implanted in the womb, a woman was not carrying for the purpose of the law, with the consequence that if, in the period of time before the egg is implanted in the womb, implantation is prevented, this would not be a violation of the Abortion Act. A number of legal scholars thought I was wrong. There was heated correspondence in *The Times*.[23] In the end the Attorney-General stood up in Parliament and, in reply to a written question, essentially adopted my position, and said that no prosecutions would be brought against those prescribing the so-called morning-after pill. But the Attorney-General is not a judge. The question has still not been answered to the satisfaction of all.

RESOLVING THE PROBLEMS

How on earth do we deal with these questions? There is no doubt, in my view, that the population at large is both aware and concerned, and is demanding that answers be provided by the legal system. Some may say that the problems are often so novel that they are outside the law, that they do not come within any line of legal development. They are different from problems concerning exemption clauses or exclusion clauses or leases. But I do not think that the problems, however complex or novel they may be, are *outside* the law. Rather, there is an area in which we do not have any clear law.

[1987] 1 All ER 20, *Jefferson* v. *Griffin Spalding County Hospital Authority*, 274 S.E. 2*d*. 457 (1981), and J. Robertson and J. Schulman, 'Pregnancy and Pre-natal Harm to Offspring', 17 *Hastings Center Report* 23 (1987)].

[22] See chapter 3.

[23] See *The Times*, 11 Apr. 1983.

As regards some of the problems, there may be some legal regulation, but it is imperfect regulation, as we have seen. Others can be regulated only by the use of analogies from other areas of law, which are more or less strained. In Scotland, for example, the law on AID was developed by pronouncing that AID was analogous to adultery. This is an analogy that can be drawn, but it is not the one that I would choose.

Some problems, however, seem to beggar the search for an appropriate analogy. They seem genuinely to be in a state of no law. But if you accept the notion of a gapless system of law, it may be that everything which is not forbidden by law must be allowed. This means that we must consider whether the various activities discussed are unlawful, or whether, alternatively, they are apparently licit, but ought to be subject to legal regulation. Of course, in determining whether they are unlawful, what we are doing, in fact, is making a prediction as to what a tribunal faced with the problem would hold. We must analyse when analogies may be used and what they would be, or go back to first principles. We must even develop the keenest of noses to detect the moods of the courts. This is not a particularly satisfactory state of affairs. Doctors are not terribly impressed when you say that the advice which you are giving them is a function of your ability to sniff the judicial air or smell the Court of Appeal!

Everyone — doctor, patient, citizen — ought to know where he or she stands. But what is so special about medical law? Surely, these doubts and uncertainties occur in every area of law. The difference may lie in the absence of any tradition in this area of law, the mass of unanswered questions, the concern that the public and the media genuinely have, and the nature of this concern. Medical law may have a direct effect on health and illness, in that harm can flow from a decision not to treat because of doubtful legality, or equally, from a decision to treat, where the law is unclear and where such treatment may medically be less than desirable. Furthermore, in many of the situations discussed, it is the criminal law which is involved. It is generally thought to be of crucial importance that people should know where they stand as regards the criminal law. Finally, it seems to me quite clear that the law has a chilling effect in this area, in so far as doctors may be discouraged from embarking on developments or initiatives because conservative lawyers, who, after all, are there to be conservative, very often say that the law is unclear, and that it would be safer not to go ahead.

CLARIFYING THE LAW

So how can we make the law more certain? There are several possibilities. Let me enumerate them very quickly before I dismiss several of them. We can leave it to the doctor and the patient, as if the law were not relevant, or as if the doctor lived in some law-free zone and need not be responsible for his actions. We can leave it to the profession to draw up some sort of code. We can have a code drawn up by non-professionals as well as professionals. We can leave it to the court. We can legislate. We can have a departmental circular which, of course, has no legislative force, although such documents are often regarded as if they were delegated legislation. Or we can go to the European Court of Human Rights.

There are objections to all of these. I do not even want to discuss the idea of leaving it to the particular doctor or the medical profession in general. Doctors do not have any particular monopoly of expertise on the moral and legal issues under discussion, or on what we ought to do about them. They have a monopoly of expertise on what can be done, on what can be called the medical-technical, but not on the medical-moral and medical-legal.

Let me briefly mention development of the law through case-law. Getting the law clear through case-law has all the usual objections. If it is the civil law which is involved, you need the right facts and a willing and persevering party prepared to invest the time, effort, and money necessary for litigation. If the criminal law is involved, you have to wait for a doctor to do something about which the law is not clear and then prosecute him. This seems extremely unfair to doctors. Furthermore, any law which would develop from this case-by-case method would be at best spotty, and in the case of criminal prosecutions would inevitably, to a great extent, turn on the particular facts. Thus, leaving things to case-law in the normal run of things is simply to rely on happenstance. What about declaratory judgments? Could they be a better way of developing a body of case-law? As in medicine, preventive action, solving a problem by seeking a declaration before it arises in an acute case, may seem the most attractive approach. But the English courts, with the greatest respect, seem reluctant to use such declaratory judgments. There may be some argument for this reluctance in the context of criminal law, because a judge is being invited to make general propositions of law without reference to anything but hypothetical facts, which may never be encountered precisely in real life. He is being asked to act as a mini-legislator, and the English courts are loath to act in this way. This was clear in the euthanasia case which I mentioned earlier. In that case, the court said that the publication of the booklet by the organization called Exit might or might not amount to the crime of aiding and abetting suicide, depending, *inter alia*, on whether the person read it and was really motivated by it so that a cause or link could be shown. So, although I would like to see more medical law cases taken before the courts for declaratory judgments to determine whether, on the facts, a particular practice is lawful, there is still the problem that this is, at best, an interstitial form of law-making.

Declaratory judgments may not be the answer, therefore, in this country. They may be a more satisfactory way of developing law in Canada, given the new Charter of Rights. It may be necessary to declare what the law is because of the possible constitutional implications of certain medical practices — for example, the treatment of those detained as being mentally ill. It is possible to mount a constitutional argument about most medical practices if you try hard enough.

In the United Kingdom, some way that is better than case-law needs to be found. Legislation is the answer, you may think. But, frankly, there is absolutely no chance of the legislature descending into these detailed problems. The legislature has enough difficulty in terms of time passing the Finance Act each year. Furthermore, can you imagine a legislature in this country, or indeed any country, passing a law saying that under certain circumstances you may let babies die? Imagine the headlines in the local papers the next day! So, to look to the legislature to solve many of these agonizingly difficult medical-legal problems is simply unrealistic. and, in any event, it would take a terribly long time.

I think a better way has to be found than an occasional prosecution of a doctor by some self-appointed keeper of the world's conscience, or some civil suit brought after the event, given the knowledge that the legislature does not seem to want to become involved. One fascinating route is that used by Larry Gostin, the brilliant ex-director of the organization called MIND (the National Association for Mental Health). Gostin knew that the law was not clear in many areas of mental health law, such as the circumstances under which treatments such as electro-convulsive therapy (ECT) and psycho-surgery may be carried out and the whole question of the role of consent in treatment. He knew also that to succeed in individual cases before the English courts would be very difficult. So he went to the European Commission on Human Rights and subsequently to the European Court, to establish certain principles.[24] The effect of a decision in Europe is that English law and departmental practice then has to be brought into line. This was a brilliantly effective device. It was effective in another sense, I might add, because the European Court on Human Rights tends to speak in more general terms than our courts do and therefore laid down general principles which could apply in more than one particular situation.

That is one route; but it may not always be available or appropriate, and again, it is time-consuming, as all domestic administrative procedures must have been exhausted. For my part, I have argued for some time that, rather than look forlornly to the courts or legislature, a Standing Committee should be set up by Parliament or by the Lord Chancellor's Office, charged with constantly reviewing and clarifying the law and, if necessary, drafting new law. It would have appointed members and a permanent secretariat, rather like the now defunct President's Commission for the Study of Ethical

[24] See e.g., *X* v. *United Kingdom* (1981) 4 EHHR 188.

Problems in Medicine in the United States,[25] Such a Standing Committee would issue opinions, publish working papers, seek opinions, and then propose law if necessary. I must report, however, that the Law Commission, when I met its Chairman, seemed at best mildly disinterested, and at worst very disinterested; and elsewhere the idea has been greeted with a deafening silence.

An alternative route, because I do not think I will get my Standing Committee, is to leave the law alone, to give up any hope of formal legal solutions. Instead, the aim would be to try to create a Code of Practice, or a set of guidelines, to be worked out by professionals and non-professionals, the non-professionals to be drawn from all relevant constituencies. They would tackle the various issues on the basis of agreed priorities and would be able to do the work relatively quickly because they would already have the relevant expertise. Any Code would be drafted in general terms, accompanied by a commentary. The Committee would offer solutions after proper reflection and consultation. There are precedents for such an approach. The British Code of Practice for transplants, for example, emerged out of just such a process.

Once the proposed Code was published, it would serve as the guide for conduct. If a doctor were challenged as to the propriety of a particular practice, he could say that he had complied with the Code. Compliance should, in my view, be regarded as prima facie evidence of lawfulness. If a court subsequently decided that something in the Code was unlawful, the doctor who had complied would not be subject to sanction. Conversely, non-compliance would be prima facie evidence of unlawfulness, and the doctor who had deviated from the Code would have the onus of proving that he had, in the event, behaved lawfully.

This approach involves adopting an extra-legal, or meta-legal, institutional mechanism. In my view, it would be more likely to bring about solutions to the many emerging problems posed by developments in medical technology than any other approach considered. The Code could be kept constantly under review, and thereby avoid problems often associated with formal legal mechanisms, which are usually unable to address emerging problems in an appropriately prompt and coherent way.

[25] But now, perhaps, resuscitated; Health Research Extension Act 1985 (PL 99–158), and see 16 *Hastings Center Report*, no. 2, p. 2 (1986).

2

What is a Medical Decision?*

It is a distinct honour and privilege to deliver this year's Astor Lecture, an institution created to honour the memory of Viscount Astor and his benefaction to the School. I was kindly warned by the Dean that my audience would range from eminent doctors to beginning medical students to interested non-medical observers. I have tried to respond to this warning by choosing a topic on which we all have our views. If I can reciprocate and issue a warning myself, it is to remind you that I am a lawyer. You need to be warned of this, not only so that those of you who have previously fallen foul of lawyers may reach for your hypertension tablets or switch off your hearing-aids, but also because, since I am an outsider, I may say things which are rarely heard in the hurly-burly of medical life. I have chosen to consider what I regard as a very complex topic. Many—indeed, perhaps most of you—will not agree with what I have to say. I hope, however, that I may give you food for thought, even though it may not entirely suit everybody's palate. I conclude these opening remarks by saying that I am thankful that, even though I am a lawyer among doctors, we have not, and will not, I hope, ever reach that state of undeclared war between our two professions which exists in the United States, particularly in California. We can still talk to each other, and have much to learn from each other. The state of affairs in the United States puts me in mind of the anecdote of an English doctor taking a visiting American doctor to his local village fête. Many of the village worthies were there, doing the usual things: Punch and Judy, conjuring for children, and so on. There was a man playing a barrel-organ, with a monkey on a chain collecting money in a cup. 'Oh! Isn't that just quaint', said the American doctor. 'Who is that guy?' 'Oh, he's the local solicitor,' replied his host. 'Solicitor? That's a lawyer, isn't it? Gee, I hate lawyers. I detest them,' the American doctor fumed. The two carried on walking, and as they drew near to the barrel-organ, the monkey eagerly proferred the cup for some money. The American

---

* This paper was originally delivered as the Astor Lecture at the Middlesex Hospital Medical School on 3 July 1979, and was subsequently published in the School's journal. It appears here in an amended form. The views expressed were subsequently expanded in the Reith Lectures, particularly Lecture 4 (*The Listener*, 4 Dec. 1981). This may be of interest, therefore, as being 'a dry run' (albeit somewhat crude) at what remains a central issue of medical ethics. In particular, the distinction between medical-technical and medical-moral runs through all of these essays.

doctor smiled and took out a fifty-pence coin which he dropped into the monkey's cup. His host was intrigued. 'How is it' he asked, 'that you hate lawyers so much, yet you drop fifty pence into the monkey's cup?' 'Well, I may hate lawyers,' was the reply 'but they're so cute when they are young!'

Let me turn to my topic, in the spirit, I hope, of mutual enquiry.

The title I have chosen, 'What is a medical decision?' is in the form of a question. The question may better be framed: what decisions are within the specific competence of a doctor to make? Put another way, what is appropriate for a doctor to decide (and thereafter to do)? Still further, it can be turned around to the question: are there decisions which should not be made by doctors alone? Let us stay with this last formulation for a moment. Of course there are. Examples are many and obvious: they concern what rate of income tax we should have, what form of education system we should have, whether we should have a Welfare State and, if we should, how it should be operated. Some other examples, picked not entirely at random, might concern what the law on homicide should be, whether we should all be honest, or, finally, how children should be raised. But this, you may think, is banal. Of course, such decisions are not for the doctor alone. No one, least of all the doctor, would argue that they were. Well, we will see. But even if it does appear banal, it may be that we do have to begin our enquiry far away from what is thought to be traditional doctoring, at the outer edges of what may be the sphere of their decision making, and then work inwards until we reach the point at which we can begin to hear the answer, yes, that is a medical decision.

Perhaps, before going further, I should explain why I ask the question. There are a number of reasons. First, it is intellectually very intriguing, and very hard to answer. Second, the answer is vital to an understanding of the role of a doctor; or, put another way, of the proper competence of a doctor. Third, the conviction exists in my mind that failure to examine the question has resulted in decisions being taken by doctors which may not properly be within the unique or special competence of a doctor *qua* doctor to make.

To return to my question, then, an easy answer would be that a medical decision is a decision made by a doctor. But this falls foul of what we have seen already; that is, that some—indeed, most—decisions made by doctors— for example, to vote Conservative—would not be considered medical decisions. So we could say that a medical decision is a decision made by a doctor in a medical context. But this is obviously circuitous. It merely says that what is medical is what is medical. So, let us approach it from a different angle and say that doctors are competent to decide upon issues of health and ill health. Notice at this stage that I say issues of 'health and ill health', which, I hope, is a neutral proposition and includes such things as recognition of conditions, diagnosis, and prognosis. This brings us a little closer to what may satisfy you, though it still will not satisfy me, as a basis for further analysis. Why? Because I want to know what health and ill health are; and, of course, the mere substitution of other words, such as 'disease' or 'illness', does not throw any further light. I do not need to tell you that the concepts of health and its opposite, ill health, are exceedingly hard to tackle. But equally, I think you will see that our apparently simple opening question leads us inexorably to the point where we must tackle them; and I shall do so, albeit briefly, conscious of the fact that this must be familiar ground to many of you.

I suppose the notion of ill health is most manageable if defined in purely physical terms, in terms of abnormality or impairment of function. You do not need to be told that, even if it is so defined, there still exist considerable problems related, for example, to what is the norm. A couple of good examples are perhaps the question of what is high blood-pressure, and what impairments of function are such as to warrant being described as ill health. For example, a man whose thumb has been severed in an accident is thereafter permanently disabled and his manual function is impaired, but can he be considered unhealthy for ever? Once you expand ill health to include the mental as well as the physical condition, the problem of definition becomes, in my view, virtually unmanageable. Attacks on the imprecision and unscientific nature of psychiatry do not need to be repeated here. It is well known that there are whole schools of thought which call into question the very notion of mental illness or mental disease, quite apart from the often huge differences between those who accept the notion of mental health, but differ in ascribing it to X or Y. The notions of health and ill health become completely unmanageable as concepts when you take the final step and define health as the World Health Organization (WHO) defines it as 'not the mere absence of disease, but total physical, mental and social well-being'. Indeed, it is this sort of analysis which led Illich[1] to conclude that the whole of medicine is a moral enterprise, since it defines what is normal and, in behavioural terms, what is proper. Thus, he says, medicine has acquired the authority to label one man's complaint a legitimate illness, to declare another man sick though he does not complain, and to refuse to recognize another as being ill, so that his pain must be borne alone.[2]

So, reminding ourselves of our journey, if we say that doctors are equipped to make decisions on issues of health and ill health, we can see that, depending on our definitions, we are forced to the conclusion that a doctor's unique competence — what he alone is qualified to do — extends from making decisions concerning the management of a broken leg to the management of our comfort and happiness, our social well-being. We would all accept the former. Few, if any, would accept the latter. Thus, put another way, if we accept the proposition that doctors are equipped to make decisions on issues of health and ill health, the breadth and meaning we give to health

[1] Illich, *Limits to Medicine* (Penguin, 1977).   [2] Ibid. 53.

and ill health determine the breadth of the range of decisions deemed to be within the unique competence of doctors. It is my contention that, just as the concepts of health and ill health have been expanded enormously without rigorous intellectual examination, so, as a concomitant of that, the sphere of alleged unique competence of the doctor has correspondingly expanded, as if by reflex, with little reflection until recently of the implications.

It may be interesting *en passant*, before I go on, to speculate as to the reasons for this process of expansion. There may be many; but three appeal to me as significant, each interlocking with the others. The first is that the National Health Service has created the promise of health in its widest form. As the typical physical scourges of infectious diseases have been eliminated, other scourges have taken their place as conditions to be overcome. In terms of patient contact with doctors, perhaps the principal scourge is unhappiness, in all its forms. If people are told that they need not be unhappy and that others are happy, then they will seek to be happy, defining their unhappiness in terms not only of abnormality but also as ill health, encouraged in this view by many forces, not least the advertising of drug companies. Then, if the normalizing of abnormality is the job of the doctor, it is easy to understand why his consulting rooms and hospital wards are filled with unhappy people. The figures are truly astonishing. Dunlop estimated that 10 per cent of all sleep was induced by hypnotic drugs. The amount of aspirin and tranquillizers swallowed each day is astronomically high — 1,500 tons of aspirin a year and about 2–4 million tranquillizers (on prescription) every day. An estimated one in three hospital beds are occupied by the mentally ill, and one in nine of the whole population will spend some time in a mental hospital. Without ever really being examined, the situation has become virtually out of control, and probably cannot be reversed. In fact, there seems little doubt that the single largest cause of illness, however defined, is poverty and what it brings in its wake, as Doll at Oxford has shown, and as Muir Gray makes clear in his recent book.[3] Yet we continue to ride the same tired whirligig of disease identification, exchanging one problem for a new one. And we do so, notwithstanding the fact that, by comparison with the effects produced by sanitation and clean water, medicine's advances are really rather limited.

The second reason for the expansion I referred to is that the doctor himself has encouraged the process whereby he is seen as the purveyor of panaceas, though, if pressed, he would be the first to deny that he has any panaceas. But it is gratifying to his self-esteem, his perception of himself as a helper. Realistically and, I hope, objectively, it guarantees that if one problem area is overcome, another will surely take its place, so that he will never cease to be wanted. Quite simply it gives the doctor power. Indeed, the analysis of the doctor–patient relationship in terms of power offers revealing insights.

[3] M. Gray, *Man against Disease* (Oxford University Press, 1979).

Although I would not necessarily endorse the views of Ivan Illich, I regard his description of the doctor's attitude to his patient as one of infantilization as striking. The third reason I mention for this expansion of the notion of health and the doctor's role is that, in an age of secularism, people have lost faith in established religions. Yet there seems to be a need in all of us for something spiritual, for a belief in, or at least a flirtation with, magic. The doctor has become, among other things, the modern magician, able, through potions and laying-on of hands, to heal the body and the spirit. To those of you who doubt this, consider whether the so-called placebo effect has not some magical properties, a contention which I do not consider to be invalidated by recent work on endorphins. And, given the power and status that this role of magician imparts, it is not surprising that the doctor has taken on the mantle, protesting the while that these responsibilities are irksome. So they are; but ask him to give them up (or engage in the contentious analysis I am proposing), and he will cling to them with limpet-like tenacity. It puts me in mind of the story of the doctor and the priest travelling in a car together when it crashed into a tree. The priest's last words were 'Get me to a doctor'; the doctor's last words, for he was wiser, were 'Get me to a priest.'

It is important at this point to make it clear that I am not criticizing doctors or attacking them or purporting to sit in judgment over them. Far from it. I am trying to analyse what I think is a reality and what produces that reality. I am not allocating blame, because even if I could, I am sure that it is an irrelevant and unprofitable exercise. Too often, the moment this debate is opened, the floodgates of vitriol are opened also. I think of the learned editor of the *New England Journal of Medicine* who, following good military advice of 'l'audace, toujours l'audace', has confused the debate by attacking courts and judges and, by implication, lawyers,[4] since it is they who lead the debate in the United States. I have no brief for lawyers, but it seems an irrelevance which only muddles the debate.

So, to repeat, the scope of the alleged unique competence of the doctor has become as wide, as imprecise, and as flexible as the meaning given to the notions of health and ill health. I want now to propose a rethinking of this sphere of competence. I want to do so for two complementary reasons: first, because, as an observer, I see many decisions being taken by doctors which I would not categorize as medical, and which therefore I am not happy to leave to them alone; and second, because I think it unfair that responsibility in many areas of human concern has been improperly shifted on to doctors by the rest of us, simply because we are happy to have others bear this responsibility, and because the doctor, at least initially, seems prepared to

---

[4] A. Relman, 'The Saikewicz Decision: Judges as Physicians', 298 *New England Journal of Medicine* 508 (1978).

take it on. Of course, as an outsider proposing this rethinking, I will encounter opposition. This is inevitable. One of the greatest ironies of my position is that I am constantly confronted by doctors complaining, quite rightly very often, that they have to make too many hard decisions which it is not really their job to make, that they are too often expected to do society's 'dirty work', and that they need guidance. But the moment I try to analyse the problem and offer guidance or suggest what should be done, I am immediately met by a chorus of cries, all variations on the theme that I do not really understand, that these are medical matters after all, that I should not trespass on the professional competence of others, that these are matters of professional judgment, and so on.

Now, let me put my contention baldly and clearly. It is that there are a large number of decisions being made by doctors which I would not categorize as medical or wholly medical. And, that being so, they are not for doctors alone to make. Perhaps I ought to make it crystal clear what I mean by 'not for doctors alone to make'. I mean that although doctors may have to take them in the sense that they are 'in the field', as it were, decisions taken 'in the field' must conform with standards set by others. They may not be at the discretion of the particular doctor, group of doctors, or even the medical profession as a whole. Expanding on my contention, I will put it to you that there are countless decisions taken by doctors which are not medical, but rather involve questions of morality or philosophy or economics or politics. And by not being medical, I repeat, they are not, in my view, for doctors alone. Now you may say that, of course, a doctor's decisions have moral implications or economic implications; but this is intrinsic in any decision making.

That must be right. So let me explain my point in more detail. An elderly patient has a form of illness which is potentially fatal, but which can be treated. If it is treated, she will live a somewhat restricted life, but one which may well be tolerable and will allow her to continue to do a number of things which she enjoys. The treatment, however, is very expensive. The diagnosis, prognosis, and range of available treatments are technical-medical matters. Whether her life will be worth living subsequently and who is to judge are moral issues. Whether the National Health Service should spend money on her, and thereby not spend it on another, and who is to judge are issues calling for economic analysis, political judgments, and moral theory. All are involved in the medical decision, but our question is whether they are for the doctor alone to assess.

I hasten to add that doctors make what I am calling moral or philosophical decisions not only as regards issues on the outer circle of those vague things called health and ill health, but also as regards issues right at the core of what has always been regarded as ill health. I hope to demonstrate this by three or four examples. These will illustrate both my point and what I have in mind as being a medical decision, since I am aware that, so far, I have drawn the distinction without illustrating the difference. The examples I have chosen are concerned as you will see with morality. But lest you think my contention is limited to this, let me begin by mentioning a decision which I would call social or political. We have seen how commonly doctors prescribe tranquillizers when faced with unhappiness. Further thought must provoke the question asked by the Oxford physician Muir Gray: is it right to prescribe drugs to damp down symptoms produced by social tensions, when the tension causing them, if unchecked, might be able to bring about social changes which would then deal with the underlying social problems, not just the symptoms.

The first example I take is the treatment of severely handicapped newly born babies. Some of you may have heard an analysis of this problem that I attempted on the radio some time back.[5] It did not altogether meet with approval, but I do not shrink from repeating it, notwithstanding the appearance of yet another paper by Duff and Campbell, this time in the *Journal of Medical Ethics*, dismissing the argument.[6] They do not explicitly bracket me among those castigated as half-baked, semi-informed 'troglodytes', but they drop a strong hint! Accept the following facts for the sake of argument. A baby is born with spina bifida. An assessment is made of the severity of the handicap. A decision is taken that the baby should not be operated upon, but be given analgesics or sedatives. The baby subsequently dies. But the baby was not born dying. It was born ill, and if established forms of therapy, including surgery, had been extended to it, it would have survived. But it would have survived paralysed in the lower limbs, incontinent, and with the prospect of numerous surgical interventions. It was because of this that the doctors did not operate and allowed, or encouraged, the baby to die. The baby had no reasonable quality of life ahead of it, it was said; hence it was better that it should die. But a decision as to what quality of life is worth living is not, in my view, a medical decision, and thus not for doctors alone to make. It is a decision of great moral weight which cannot and should not be left to the discretion of the particular doctor or team of doctors. There is nothing in the training of a doctor which makes him specially or uniquely competent to make such a decision. Equally, it is not a decision for parents alone, though many would argue that it is. It has never been part of our morality or our law that parents have discretion as to whether their child lives or dies. Since I use this as an illustrative example only, here is not the place to set out *in extenso* my view on how the decision should be taken, though it is fair to say that a doctor who fails to carry out an operation in the circumstances described above could well be in violation

---

[5] 'The Defect', BBC Radio, 18 and 25 Oct. 1978.
[6] A. G. M. Campbell and R. S. Duff, 'Deciding the Care of Severely Malformed or Dying Infants', *Journal of Medical Ethics* 65 (1979).

of the criminal law.[7] Suffice it to say that, though the decision may be taken by a doctor, it is not, in my view, a medical decision, a decision resting on medical criteria of what a reasonable life is, since there are none. It is instead a moral decision, resting on moral principles which are not established by doctors alone, but with which doctors must conform.

My second example concerns truth-telling. I shall concentrate on the often considered issue of whether a patient with a cancer which is likely to prove fatal should be told of this. There is a wide body of opinion among doctors which has it that the decision, whether to tell the patient the truth, is a medical one—that is, that it is within the doctor's unique competence to decide. The idea has developed that there are circumstances which justify withholding the truth, or even plain lying to the patient. This is purportedly justified by a number of arguments, which effectively boil down to what some call 'the therapeutic privilege', the privilege to withhold information when, in the specialized view of the doctor, to relate such information to the patient would not be in the patient's best interests. Now it is, of course, a basic moral principle—and, I interject, a legal principle—of our society that we should tell the truth. Moral philosophers have analysed circumstances in which this moral principle may be modified or may give way to another. But there cannot, in my view, be any doubt that the decision as to whether or not the principle of truth-telling should be breached is a moral one. This is particularly so in the context of the relationship between a doctor and his patient, in which the basis of the relationship is alleged to be confidence and trust. To accept the doctor's argument is to accept that the doctor is the sole guardian of that confidence and trust, and the sole arbiter of whether he ought to observe the trust or breach it. Trust thus becomes a chimera, a phantom, a myth. The decision whether to tell the truth seems quintessentially a moral one, and therefore, once again, one not to be made by reference only to the standards or views of doctors, since they are neither the repositories of moral wisdom nor necessarily trained in moral analysis. That there may be circumstances in which the truth need not be told and in which the therapeutic privilege may be justified is conceded; but what these circumstances might be is subject to moral debate, a debate which is not appropriately conducted only among doctors. I might add one rider to this problem. There is now a growing body of evidence regarding whether patients in fact want to be told the truth in the context of the example I gave. The nearly overwhelming evidence is that they do—notwithstanding the doctor's argument that it would be against their interests. Yet the debate about, and the practice of, withholding the truth continues. An explanation I find intriguing surfaces if the assumption is reversed; namely, that it is the doctor, not the patient, who cannot bear the truth; and so the doctor develops appropriate justifications

---

[7] But see now *R* v. *Arthur*, *The Times*, 5 Nov. 1981, and chapter 8.

to defend himself. There is much of value, in this and other contexts, in the brilliant insights of Jay Katz, a psychiatrist and lawyer at Yale, who brings the concepts of psychoanalysis to bear on these problems.[8] He concerns himself with the psychodynamics of the doctor–patient relationship, and wonders whether here, as elsewhere, we are not witnessing a classic example of countertransference from the doctor to the patient.

My next example relates to AID. Of course, AID is outside the mainstream of medical practice, but it does offer some interesting insights, none the less. Why do we have AID? So that a woman may become pregnant. Traditionally it is associated with the situation in which there is a married couple and the husband cannot, for whatever reason, impregnate his wife. Is AID a matter for doctors at all is my first question? It merely involves the collection of sperm and the introduction of this sperm into the woman. Just because it involves touching a woman and has to do with reproduction, the automatic response is to think of it as a medical matter. Doubtless there is technical expertise involved, but such expertise may quite readily be acquired, and the risks involved are low. Why is AID not accomplished through the organization of sperm banks, either state-operated or commercially run, and then either by self-administration by the woman or administration by some adequately trained technician? It may be that the answer lies in a species of that circular argument I noted before: that AID is done by doctors, therefore it is a medical matter, therefore it *must* be done by doctors. Arguments as to alternative ways of meeting a need get lost, as does the question of whether the wish to achieve pregnancy, other than by intercourse with a partner, is within the exclusive jurisdiction of doctors to satisfy. I ask this preliminary question because it is a necessary introduction to the specific point I want to make. Once AID is seen as a matter for doctors, there is the chance or likelihood — indeed an inevitability — that the doctor will establish criteria which must be met before this service is provided. These criteria will be alleged, quite spuriously in my view, to be medical, again if for no other reason than that they are what a doctor or doctors stipulate. Thus we have the recent debate about whether lesbians should be able to obtain AID, a rather esoteric debate, but one which serves to make my point. The Ethical Committee of the British Medical Association considered this long and hard, it was reported the other day, and decided that, yes, doctors are free to offer AID to lesbians. The decision was reached by a very narrow majority, and on the basis of 'the freedom to practice medicine as the doctor thought right'. But first, this assumes what has not been shown convincingly, namely, that supplying AID need necessarily be defined as practising medicine; and second, in invoking 'the freedom to practise medicine as thought right', it allows the argument that a doctor has the unique and exclusive right to exercise his discretion

[8] See J. Katz, *The Silent World of Doctor and Patient* (Collier Macmillan, 1984).

as to whether he provides this service or not, on the basis of his particular moral value system, regardless of the moral values of others. But this assumption, that we are dealing here with a medical matter, is challenged if one refers to what was actually said in the debate, or to what one can gather happens in practice. For, the arguments in the debate turned on such points as its being wrong for lesbians to bring up children, or that the doctor had to make the moral decision whether the child would be brought up as part of a loving family unit. This, I submit, makes my point. I readily concede that it is a moral issue. What I ask, however, is: since when did doctors have the unique competence to determine what is right and wrong, or what is a stable or loving family? It might be said parenthetically that judges do this every day in our Family Courts, and that they have no unique competence either, to which I would reply that the judges may not impose their own values willy-nilly, but must operate within guidelines established by Parliament, after proper debate of the rights and wrongs. One final point: Dr Thomas, Chairman of the BMA's Ethical Committee, is reported as saying at the end of the debate on AID: 'This is not a moral issue. This is the protection of your right to practise medicine as we have always practised it in this country.' One blushes for him if he cannot see the irony of the remark, since assertions of rights tend to involve invoking a moral principle.

My last example concerns abortion. I want merely to look at one small, usually neglected corner of the debate. I am concerned here with the so called conscience clause which allows a doctor to refuse to carry out an abortion if such an act would offend his conscience. Let us clear the ground for the debate. First, in 1967, Parliament decided, after appropriate debate, that abortion should be available lawfully under certain conditions. Second, apart from abortion, under the NHS generally, doctors are obliged to make available to someone presenting him- or herself the services offered by the NHS: that is, they must ordinarily see someone who is registered as a patient or who needs help and does not have a doctor. It does not follow, of course, that they must provide a particular service; but they may not ordinarily refuse to offer a service on grounds other than the health needs of the patient as judged by a reasonably competent member of the profession. But then there is the conscience clause, the effect of which is that a doctor employed and paid by the taxpayer is entitled to opt out of providing a service voted for and paid for by the taxpayer if he does not think it right. I compare the doctor here with a member of another profession which provides a service, and whose relationship with the client—and this is crucial—is also, as with the NHS doctor, not one of contract, that is, it is not one in which the parties themselves establish the basis of their relationship, namely the barrister. It is a first principle of the code of ethics of a barrister that he may not refuse a case. Of course, in practice he may not be free, or may even contrive not to be free; but the principle stands. An Irishman alleged to have thrown one of the bombs in Birmingham in 1973 will be granted legal aid, notwithstanding the universal abhorrence of his deed, and a barrister briefed to represent him cannot, all other things being equal, say, 'I do not represent terrorists. I do not think they deserve representation.'

Yet the doctor, obliged to provide a service, when confronted by someone who wants—indeed, needs—that service, can say, 'I am not giving it because of my abhorrence of abortion,' notwithstanding the lack of any universal abhorrence, as evidenced by the fact that the democratically elected Parliament has voted to include abortion as a service available through the NHS. Parliament, in allowing the conscience clause, has been persuaded to accommodate the doctor's moral values and allow him to make a moral decision when, in my view, it is no part of a doctor's role *qua* doctor to legislate morality for others and impose his views on others. Compare, if you will, the doctor in the NHS who said that he did not treat black people because they were feckless. I fully appreciate the fact that the Abortion Act might not have passed without this concession; but that merely indicates the extent of the concession. I also appreciate that a law which did not have a conscience clause, so that a doctor could not, all things being equal, refuse to abort, might not create the best environment for doctor–patient relations. But it is never said that a barrister who votes Conservative may refuse to represent a squatter, or will give bad representation if he does (although, of course, it may be true). To the doctor who complains that he wants to practise medicine without abortions, the answer must be that he can choose to engage in private practice, and thereby arrange his affairs by agreement with his patients. If he joins the NHS, he should remember the last word of the three, 'service', and serve. Membership of the profession would seem to demand this. Another quite radical option is to allow abortions, at least in the very early weeks of pregnancy, to be carried out by people other than doctors. This, of course, is resisted by arguments having to do with health risks and dangers. Again, the doctor closes the circle on the argument by saying doctors need only perform abortions if they do not think it wrong. This is a moral decision taken by them, but nobody else's moral values are relevant, because abortion is a medical matter and, being a medical matter, is *ex hypothesi* only for doctors. It is no surprise that there grew up a market for abortions to fill the need unsatisfied by the NHS, or that feminists, particularly in the United States, are devoting time, money, and expertise to developing do-it-yourself abortion advice. To the doctor who scoffs at this or regrets the risks it creates, the response can be made that it is a development which is the direct result of doctors making themselves moral, as well as medical, arbiters.

Let me now remind you that we began by saying that decisions about the law of homicide, whether we should be honest, or how children should be raised were obviously not medical decisions. The examples I have chosen—the spina bifida baby who dies, truth-telling, and AID only in the context of a loving family — show how doctors have in fact come to make them so.

What is left for me to say? First, what a medical decision is. Second, what we should do about the situation I have described. I do not have an easy answer to the first part. I believe, however, that a doctor's special competence lies in, first, the knowledge which allows him to make a diagnosis and prognosis of what is generally accepted as being ill health; second, the knowledge of what therapies, if any, are available in the context of a particular condition of ill health; third, the judgment of which therapy or response to adopt so as to produce, to the best of his ability, an end result deemed appropriate not by him but by the patient, one approved by society at large. No more, no less. To make this concrete, in the case of an elderly man with a fractured hip who develops pneumonia, the doctor's competence is to diagnose the pneumonia and be aware of its prognosis, to know what can be administered, and then to judge what should be done in the light of his patient's wishes and general moral principles as to what ought to be done, not his own. He may believe that the old man should be allowed to die, but his particular values, though relevant, are not decisive. If he complains that society has no view or does not understand or has not ever had to care for such a patient, this is no answer. It certainly gives him no warrant for following his own views alone, or even those of doctors in general. Rather, it is his job to call attention to all the relevant facts, so that appropriate moral debate can be conducted by all of us. He may find that the rest of us endorse his views; but that does not mean that we should not be able to consider the matter first.

So what do I call for, albeit as a voice crying in the wilderness? A two-way traffic of debate: first, in one direction, a realization by doctors of the nature of the decisions they take and a greater reflectiveness. First steps on the way to this can be made by ensuring that medical students are properly exposed to medical ethics and moral debate. The eyebrows rise. We have no time in medical school for such niceties, with all that anatomy, physiology, biochemistry, and so on to teach, some doctors argue. But this does not prevent the same doctors from arguing in the next sentence that doctors are more than technicians, and must make judgments and hard decisions. When asked where the skill to embark on an analysis necessary for such judgments to be made is acquired, they will doubtless reply, relying on a theory of education by osmosis, that if you had seen as many patients as they have or done as many operations, you would understand that they get their training on the job, not contemplating their navels. The transparent weakness of this argument is obvious. If you go to Africa thinking that a lion has stripes, you will see striped lions, though you may not see what everyone else would regard as lions or zebras. If you enter medical practice, thinking for example, that life is sacred, without ever having examined the proposition rigorously, you will give the old man antibiotics and claim not only that you are right, but that this is a medical decision for you alone to take, regardless of the views of others. I have even heard the argument by doctors that if you want to 'interfere', then you can do the work yourself. This is not debate. It is defensive hostility. It cannot seriously be maintained that because you choose to be a doctor, it must be your way or not at all. If that argument were good, miners would be driving Rolls Royces!

Incidentally, mention of the argument that the doctor is more than a technician calls for close examination. A doctor may say that he is a member of a distinguished and learned profession in which the making of judgments is part of the professional skill. But, as I understand it, membership of a profession brings increased obligations and duties because of the greater skill and knowledge possessed. There is nothing, in my view, which says that being a member of a profession confers privileges vis-à-vis the public; yet this, on examination, is what the doctor claims. The same argument applies to the question of whether medicine is a science or an art. If it is a science, it involves accountability, defensible taxonomy, and demonstrable causality. It may also attract the derogatory cachet 'technician'. So the move is made to art. But if it is an art, what is the doctor claiming unique competence for, since art cannot, at bottom, be the preserve of one group.

There are some signs that the debate which I call for is beginning to take place. My presence here may prove the point, even if it has not enhanced the debate! Still, the formal teaching of medical ethics is a desultory exercise. Only this week I visited my own medical school and asked, 'Where are the medical ethics books kept?' 'Medical ethics?' replied the librarian, 'We don't have any. Try the Theology Library.' The growth in interest in the BMA and elsewhere is indeed welcome, and one hopes it will be sustained.

The other direction of the debate I am asking for calls for doctors to involve others in the dilemmas they face, to give up their closely guarded professional secrecy, and hence some of their power, and to indicate just what it is that they do and have to decide, so that we may all discuss it, and assist in deciding what is right.[9]

---

[9] The growth in interest has, of course, been very considerable since this paper was written, both within and outside medical schools and the medical profession. As for books on medical ethics, the library of the Centre of Medical Law and Ethics at King's College London now has over 700 titles, together with a dozen or more specialist journals. Medical ethics has come a. long way in 7 years. And, most important, it has, by and large, retained a commitment to vigorous analysis and debate, in which the only currency is ideas, free from any sense of moral or political orthodoxy. The *Journal of Medical Ethics* is an excellent example of this.

3

The Legal and Ethical Implications of Postcoital Birth Control*

The purpose of this important symposium, as I understand it, is to make more widely known the form of birth control called 'postcoital birth control'. Perhaps we should recall that it is exactly a year since the Pregnancy Advisory Service opened its first clinic offering this service, in April 1981. Some of you in the audience will have heard the BBC radio interview that Helene Grahame, PAS press and information officer, gave this morning. In it she set the scene for the symposium by pointing out that, despite the fact that services have been offered for a year now, there is still a considerable lack of awareness among doctors, especially GPs, and the public of these services, so much so that women quite often have to travel long distances to get help. Ms Grahame made the important point, to which I shall return later, that what we are talking about is a form of emergency birth control. We are not, at present at least, discussing something which can be looked upon as a regular method of birth control.

The radio interviewer drew attention to the rather difficult questions concerning the legal and ethical propriety of postcoital birth control. There are, indeed, some difficult problems, and some people and groups are sorely exercised by them. This is the purpose for which I have been invited today: to explore with you the legal and ethical implications of this technique of birth control. By now, you have already been more than well informed as to the technical nature of the exercise; that what we are discussing is the use of a high dose of combined oral contraceptives or IUDs or prostaglandin pessaries. The risks of the procedure seem slight as carried out in practice, at least according to the review of its first nine months' activity which PAS has carried out, and which Ms Grahame has written up.[1] This low risk factor is, of course, subject to the proviso, as she points out, that appropriate care is taken in interviewing and counselling the applicant and in prescribing for her.

---

* This paper was originally read at a symposium held by the Pregnancy Advisory Service on 15 April 1982 in London. It was subsequently published in *Postcoital Contraception: methods, services and prospects* (PAS, 1983), pp. 62–70.

[1] H. Grahame, 'Postcoital birth control: a significant addition to family planning services', *Postcoital Contraception*, previous note, 77.

THE LAWFULNESS OF THE PROCEDURE

The present practice, as you know, is to offer this service if the woman presents herself within 72 hours of unprotected intercourse. The question I have to ask, and then try to answer, must be, is this lawful? In correspondence to which I will refer more fully later, the Department of Health and Social Security (DHSS) has taken the view that postcoital birth control is unobjectionable, both ethically and legally, if performed within 72 hours. It is in the light of this correspondence that PAS adopted its 72-hour time-limit. Of course, a letter emanating from the DHSS is not law. Indeed, even circulars of the DHSS must not be regarded as law, despite the authority they appear to have. The recent test case brought by the Royal College of Nursing over the Abortion Act demonstrated this, even though the DHSS was, in the end, vindicated in its view by the House of Lords.[2] Certainly there exist groups willing to challenge the view taken by the DHSS. Nualla Scarisbrook, a spokeswoman for Life, was reported in '*Pulse*', 17 October 1981, as saying that in her view the procedure was unlawful. 'We would very much like to have a test case on this,' she is reported to have said, 'but we haven't got the money.'

The lawfulness of the procedure as it is now practised depends, simply, on what form of birth control it is. It may not, logically speaking, be *contra*ception, since conception may already have taken place. But, if it is not abortion, then it is quite lawful. But alternatively, it could be abortion. Professor Glanville Williams points out that no clear line is drawn by the law between contraception and abortion. 'The legislation', he notes laconically, 'is unspecific.'[3] If postcoital birth control is a form of abortion, then it is unlawful by sections 58 or 59 of the Offences Against the Person Act 1861, unless justified under the provisions of the Abortion Act 1967. It may be, of course, that in particular cases, or even generally, the procedure could be justified under the Abortion Act; but having to satisfy the Act's requirements would mean that the type of service now available could not be offered. It would mean, in effect, the end of the procedure as we know it; and this is recognized by all. This is not only because the Abortion Act demands that certain criteria be met, but also because it is surrounded by formal trappings, requiring, as it does, the certification of two registered medical practitioners and the filling-in of forms, all of which involve expense and time.

So, to take the discussion a step further, let us remind ourselves that the Offences Against the Person Act 1861 talks, in sections 58 and 59, of a 'woman with child' and of 'procuring a miscarriage'. The Abortion Act talks

---

[2] *Royal College of Nursing of the UK* v. *DHSS* [1981] 1 All ER 563.
[3] G. Williams, *Textbook of Criminal Law*, 1st edn. (Stevens, 1978), p. 262.

of 'pregnancy' and at one point, in section 1(1)(b) uses the phrase 'the child'. The long title of the Abortion Act, which represents in summary form the intention of the Parliament in enacting the law, reads: An Act to amend and clarify the law relating to the termination of pregnancy by a registered medical practitioner'. These, then, are the words we have to look at and interpret in deciding on the law.

When is a woman 'pregnant', or 'with child', so that a 'miscarriage' cannot be procured except under the circumstances envisaged by the Abortion Act? One view is that expressed informally by the DHSS, as I have already mentioned, that a woman is not pregnant until a fertilized egg has been implanted in her womb. You will recall that, on this basis, the DHSS intimated that postcoital birth control was not unlawful as practised now by PAS, and could properly be regarded as contraception if performed within 72 hours of intercourse. The choice of 72 hours as the time-limit seems somewhat odd if implantation is taken as the moment at which a woman becomes pregnant. Certainly it cannot be justified on this basis on any rational, scientific grounds, since implantation may well take longer than 72 hours. Perhaps it reflects an abundance of caution, or is chosen as reflecting an average period of time during which the fertilized egg is in the fallopian tube before descending.

LEGITIMATE AND SERIOUS DIFFERENCES OF VIEW

There is, of course, another view as to when a woman can be said to be pregnant. In correspondence with the Minister of Health, which was made public in the autumn of 1981, Father McGuire, Chairman of the Sheffield branch of Life, argued that human life begins at fertilization. This means, he maintained, that postcoital birth control is a form of abortion, because a woman is 'with child' in that she has conceived. As I have indicated, the Minister, through his officials in the DHSS, rejected this view in a spirited exchange which is excellently reported in the *Sunday Times* of 27 September 1981. I too am unpersuaded by the argument of Life, though I readily concede that this is not an area where there are certainties, and that there is room for legitimate and seriously held differences.

I would reject the view taken by Life principally from the point of view of the language and spirit of the law. But it is fair to say that there is also a perfectly respectable philosophical argument which I will mention briefly before I turn to the law. On a philosophical level some may argue that biological life may not be owed any duty as a human life until some point is reached in its development. This was the view taken in the well-known Report of the British Council of Churches in 1962.[4] The point at which

---

[4] *Human Reproduction* (British Council of Churches, 1962).

biological life is owed a duty of protection as human life, is, the Report concluded, the point of implantation of the fertilized egg in the womb. 'A woman cannot abort', says the Report, 'until the fertilized egg has nidated and thus become attached to her body.' Therefore, the British Council of Churches found 'nothing objectionable' in the use of techniques to prevent implantation. This view was expressed, of course, in the context of the pill and the IUD; but it is equally applicable to postcoital birth control. It suggests that ethically good arguments exist to justify the practice. As I have said, however, those who begin from different premisses will remain unconvinced. My own position is somewhere in between. It is that an early embryo is owed a duty of protection, but that this duty is not absolute. It may have to give way to the claims of another (the mother) for good reason.[5]

THE LEGALITY OF ANY PROCEDURES AIMED AT PREVENTING IMPLANTATION

Let me now turn to my reasons for regarding the view taken by Life as being wrong in law. Remember that, in interpreting what the law may be, I am really attempting to predict what a court would decide if called upon to resolve the dispute, by interpreting the words of the Offences Against the Person Act and the Abortion Act. I am not here concerned with what the law ought to be, with what a court ought to decide, but rather with what the law is, with what a court is likely to decide. The first point is linguistic. In the ordinary use of language, we do not think of a fertilized egg as a 'child'. Nor would we think of a woman as 'pregnant' until implantation has taken place. As the officials in the DHSS argued, you cannot procure a miscarriage until you have a carriage, and you would not ordinarily use the notion of 'carrying' a child until it was implanted in the womb. This argument finds favour with Professor Williams who, after noting, as I have said, that the language of the Acts is unspecific, suggests that there is no reason why a court should not decide that 'the word "miscarriage" in the section on abortion means the miscarriage of an implanted blastocyst.'[6] Thus, on the basis of the language used, it would, in my view, be extremely unlikely that a court would find that the present procedure, performed within 72 hours, was an abortion, with all that this implies.[7] I am fortified in this view by a second point. The use of IUDs as a regular form of contraception has become so widespread that its lawfulness cannot seriously be disputed. If

---

[5] See further, chapter 6. [6] Williams, *supra* n. 3.

[7] Notice that the prosecution would not need to prove that a woman was in fact pregnant. When performed by a doctor, the offence consists in doing something 'with intent to procure the miscarriage of a woman, whether she be or be not with child' (s. 58).

the law allows the use of IUDs as contraception in ordinary circumstances, then, to be consistent, it must allow the use of IUDs and the other procedures in the context of postcoital birth control, because the effect is the same in all cases, the prevention of a fertilized egg being implanted in the womb. Thus, for reasons based on ordinary use of language and on consistency and established acceptance of IUDs, any procedure of postcoital birth control aimed at preventing implantation, certainly in the first 72 hours after intercourse and probably (as I will suggest) during the whole of the period of time known to be required for implantation, is not an abortion as a matter of law. It follows that the present procedure does not, in my view, offend against the law; nor is it an unethical procedure. I have already admitted, however, that others may (and do) not agree. It is to be regretted, therefore, that we do not have in this country well-established methods for clarifying the law by asking the courts to issue declaratory judgments. And while there remain those who argue that the law forbids postcoital birth control, it behoves all those who favour and promote it to observe a proper caution both in what they do and in what they say. Just to mention one, apparently trivial example, Ms Grahame, in the paper to which I referred earlier, speaks at one point of distances travelled by those seeking help, and says that, 'despite this 61.7% were treated within 48 hours of exposure to pregnancy'.[8] 'Exposure to the risk of pregnancy' may be a preferable expression in the context.

ISSUES ARISING FROM THE USE OF POSTCOITAL CONTRACEPTION

Having considered the present 72-hour practice, I want now to move on to examine some other issues which arise, or could arise, from the use of postcoital birth control. Perhaps it ought to be said at the outset that it is clear that the need it serves is a very real one. Ms Grahame reports that in the first nine months of offering the service, 554 women were seen, of whom 516 were treated. Eighty per cent of the women were over 24 years of age. They were often conscientious family-planners whose lives had become disrupted or who had been advised against using the pill and whose alternative precautions had failed. Against this background, the need is felt to extend the service to women who fall outside the 72-hour limit which, at present, PAS feels obliged to observe. The question is whether it is lawful to extend the time-limit within which either a combination of hormones is given or an IUD is fitted. If the aims of this symposium are to make this form of birth control more widely known to GPs and to maximize its benefits, this question has to be both raised and answered. Hormones can undoubtedly

---

[8] Grahame, *supra* n. 1, 78.

be effective after far more than three days have elapsed since intercourse; so, equally, can IUDs.

In answering this question it is important to notice the background against which the answer is given. The courts are undoubtedly conservative in their interpretation of the Abortion Act, which is the relevant law. This was clearly illustrated in the recent case brought by the Royal College of Nursing. Lord Wilberforce in the House of Lords went out of his way, albeit in dissent, to indicate that the Abortion Act is to be strictly construed. 'In my opinion', he wrote, 'this Act should be construed with caution . . . the Act is not one for "purposive" or "liberal" or "equitable" construction.'[9] With this caution in mind, I still hold to my view that postcoital birth control is lawful as contraception, rather than abortion, up to the maximum period before implantation, whatever the official view of the DHSS may be. The question is then one of what this maximum time period may be. My answer is that it is that time period which the consensus of informed medical scientific opinion states is the maximum time after intercourse before implantation takes place. This may be anywhere between 7 and 10 days. This is a matter of expert opinion, and, I repeat, depends on what constitutes the consensus of informed opinion. The crime under section 58 consists, however, of doing certain acts 'with intent to procure the miscarriage' of a woman. Is not a doctor who thinks that a fertilized egg may be implanted and gives the pill 'just in case' guilty of the crime since, by the doctrine of conditional intent, he intends to procure a miscarriage? The response must be that up to the maximum time for implantation, he is entitled to believe that there is no implantation and can justify his prescription of the pill as being done with the intention of preventing carriage rather than procuring miscarriage.

If, however, the number of days after intercourse is greater than this agreed maximum time-limit, it follows that prescribing hormones or fitting an IUD is unlawful, unless done in accordance with the provisions of the Abortion Act, beause the woman would be deemed pregnant by our definition. As Williams put it, 'Even dating the prohibition of abortion from implantation would not establish the legality of the gel and prostaglandin preparations now being developed [nor the late insertion of the IUD, I would add], which expel the fetus at an early stage after implantation.'[10] This, I submit, is the present reality against which those who wish to think of the future and do what they can to develop postcoital birth control, must plan. It is best regarded as an emergency treatment, but its widest possible use may be encouraged, provided the appropriate time constraints are adhered to. To those who would advocate that its use be extended beyond the period of 7 to 10 days which, I have suggested, may be the maximum, the reply must be that the law as it is written at present forbids this as a form of contraception rather

[9] *Supra* n. 2, 565.   [10] Williams, *supra* n. 3.

than abortion. The only way to change this state of affairs is, of course, to get the legislation changed. Quite frankly, the recent history of public and Parliamentary debates on abortion persuades me that this is a very remote possibility. This must be accepted as a social fact, a legitimate expression of public will. Given the vigilance with which certain groups scrutinize decisions about abortion and contraception, everyone working in this field is well advised to accept this or risk prosecution.[10a]

QUESTIONS OF LEGAL LIABILITY

Finally, let me raise two points which deserve attention and which arise out of the previous discussion. The first is a lawyer's point, but it is one which should be borne in mind by all those involved in this area. Is there any question of legal liability on the part of the individual doctor or the agency if postcoital birth control is used but is not effective? And, if it proves not to have worked, what risk is there of foetal damage, and would there be any legal liability if it occurred?

These questions will be dealt with in turn. First, no guarantee is (or should be) offered that the procedure will always prevent pregnancy. Clearly, women should always be informed of this and of the imperative need for anyone who has been treated to go back to the agency or to go to her doctor to discover whether the treatment has been successful. PAS and all responsible doctors do, of course, already urge women to return for a check-up.[11] According to Ms Grahame's figures, however, only some 60 per cent do so. This may be inevitable, given the nature of the service, but it is hardly ideal. It seems to me that it is important for agencies and doctors to use, and be seen to use, all measures which time and resources allow to ensure that women return for check-ups. Clearly, the ultimate decision is the woman's. But only by showing a scrupulous concern for the future welfare of the woman will agencies or doctors fulfil the duty to their patients which the law and ethics impose on them.

If, when a woman presents herself for a check-up, she is found to be pregnant, what then? Is abortion justified? It is, I understand, the common practice to offer abortion in those cases in which the procedure has proved

---

[10a] Notice now section 1(b) of the Surrogacy Arrangements Act 1985 which provides that a woman who carries a child in pursuance of an arrangement to do so, 'is to be treated as beginning to carry it at the time of the insemination or . . . embryo insertion that results in her carrying the child'. If this provision is of general application it threatens the whole basis of the argument I have advanced. I think it unlikely, however, that the provision was intended to render, for example, the use of IUDs unlawful by a side-wind.

[11] The information sheet prepared by PAS for women having postcoital treatment urges a follow-up visit as 'essential'; *Postcoital Contraception, supra* n. 1, Appendix III.

ineffective. This seems to me to be a lawful and appropriate course of action. The justification can be found in sections 1(1)(a) or 1(1)(b) of the Abortion Act. It may happen, however, albeit rarely, that the woman changes her mind, and decides that since the procedure has failed and she is pregnant, she will have the child. At this point the legal and ethical duty of the agency or doctor is to ensure that the woman receives all appropriate care during her pregnancy. This includes not only physical care, but also counselling, given the circumstances of the pregnancy and the possible risk of foetal damage. Clearly, it would not be good enough for the agency or doctor just to give the woman a check-up and then send her on her way with generalized advice about antenatal care. Rather, their obligation would be to explain the need for and, indeed, make arrangements for, access to facilities such as ultrasound and amniocentesis.

Now let us turn to the woman who does not return for a check-up, and subsequently discovers that she is pregnant. Can she allege that the agency or doctor is legally liable to her because she is now pregnant? The simple answer is that if the proper procedure was followed when she first came for help, it would have been made clear to her that the procedure is not guaranteed to be successful and that, in any event, she should return for a check-up. In such circumstances there should be no question of legal liability. But what if she not only finds that she is pregnant, but subsequently is delivered of a disabled baby and claims that the disability is due to the treatment she received to avoid the pregnancy? The first point to be made is that any legal liability will depend on showing that it was the procedure employed which caused the baby's disability. There is some unease among researchers that foetal damage may be a consequence of ineffective treatment, such that some doctors practising in the field routinely evacuate the womb after 14 days if the procedure has failed. So let us assume that a causal link could possibly be established between the procedure and the disablement. Any legal liability would then depend on showing that the doctor or the agency has been negligent. We have already seen that if proper care was taken at the time of first treatment to advise the woman that the procedure was not guaranteed and of the need for a check-up, she can hardly complain later that she became pregnant and was delivered of a disabled baby. The very point of the check-up is to alert all concerned of the risk of this happening, and there would be no negligence if this had been made clear to the woman. What if she said that the procedure or the hormones used were unsafe or had not been tested adequately, such that it was negligent to employ them on her. This argument would doubtless fail. There is a large body of evidence which suggests that the procedures are safe, provided they are properly administered, and proper instructions and information are given to the woman. If these safeguards are observed, there is no risk of legal liability, given the present state of knowledge.

SELF-ADMINISTRATION AN UNLIKELY PROSPECT

The second and last point I want briefly to consider is of a different nature. To some, postcoital birth control represents a further step towards a desired state of affairs in which the control of reproduction can be a matter of self-help or self-medication, without the need to have recourse to doctors. Clearly, the elimination or reduction of the need for medically performed terminations can be seen this way. The point is one of women's self-determination, of the extent to which they can wrest control over their bodies, and particularly their reproductive system from the hands of professionals, namely doctors, mostly male doctors, and take it over themselves. The point, in short, is one of women's liberation. It is not an unimportant point.

It seems to me of the utmost importance that two trends of thought, which are complementary to each other, are translated into practice to the extent that it is possible. The first is that, to the greatest extent possible, women should be involved in making decisions about the medical care they receive. This, of course, implies that they are properly informed as to the available options, and that they are treated as partners in a joint enterprise which has as its goal their care and their fulfilment. In large part, they are still expected to behave as passive recipients of beneficence, and are treated to obloquy if they behave otherwise. Nowhere is this more true than in the medical response to pregnancy and childbirth. The second trend in thinking is that, to the extent that it is possible, procedures having to do with birth control, pregnancy, and childbirth should be 'demedicalized'. This is an ugly word which is intended to convey the notion that, whenever possible, individuals or groups should be allowed and encouraged to look after themselves. No doubt this can be carried too far: but the fact that sometimes the arguments are somewhat stridently put is due, in no small measure, to the sense of dominion that many women feel doctors exercise over their lives. To these women, there is little distinction between medical care and moralizing, since they see in the form of medical care offered, and in the way it is offered, an overlay of moral strictures and fiats which they find not only offensive, but which also subverts their power to determine their own futures.

That said, can postcoital birth control properly be regarded as fitting into this scheme of development towards self-help, self-reliance, and self-administration of remedies? My view is that it cannot. The principal reason is that at present the selection of which procedure to use, the careful assessment and judgment of the appropriateness of hormones or other means, must be made by a doctor. This is because the treatment is, and ought to remain, an emergency measure, and should not be embarked on without assessment of, for example, medically identifiable counter-indications. But, it may be argued, this is the very point. It leaves women at the mercy of their doctors. There are two responses to this. First, if women find their doctors unhelpful, then this is where agencies such as PAS should assist. Their role, as I see it, is, first, to persuade doctors to incorporate postcoital birth control into their ordinary practice; and second, in cases where women nevertheless cannot obtain it, to meet the need through the service they offer. The second response must be that any argument in favour of women's self-determination should not prevail at the expense of ignoring legitimate concerns as to the medical consequences of this form of birth control. Indeed, to ignore such concerns is to undermine this self-determination by encouraging women to engage in behaviour which poses risks for their future well-being. This would be irresponsible. And, I might add, any self-administration would at present be a criminal offence, that of procuring an illegal abortion contrary to section 58 of the Abortion Act, if performed outside the time-limit which I have described as the limit of the legal notion of contraception. I add this point because some of the argument in favour of self-administration arises out of an irritation with the existing time-limit set by doctors and agencies.

It could be argued that these objections could, and will, be overtaken by the gradual movement towards making the substances required for the procedure—hormones or prostaglandins, in particular—available for sale without restriction. I think this development is most unlikely. Two changes would be needed. First, the law on self-administration and abortion would have to be changed. Although I would, in principle, be in favour of this, at least as regards the first trimester of pregnancy, there is little possibility of Parliament enacting such a change. Second, the stipulation that the various drugs be available only on prescription would have to be changed to make them available over the counter. Given the undoubted risks which attend the use of such drugs, I think it inadvisable that such a change be contemplated; nor do I think that the Committee on Safety of Medicines would for a moment consider it.

4

A Husband, a Wife, and an Abortion*

It is rare that a completely novel issue falls for determination by the High Court. *Paton* v. *Trustees of BPAS*[1] was just such an occasion. It fell to Sir George Baker P., sitting as an additional judge of the Queen's Bench Division in Liverpool. A husband petitioned the court to enjoin the British Pregnancy Advisory Service and his wife from terminating her pregnancy by abortion. The wife was pregnant by her husband, but wished to have an abortion despite his opposition. Counsel for the husband conceded the novelty of the claim.[2] At the end of counsel's submission, Sir George Baker P. held that the 'claim for an injunction is completely misconceived and must be dismissed'.[3] In his short judgment, he brushes aside the legal arguments made on the husband's behalf. Indeed, it is a classic English common-law judgment, long on common sense and respect for the realities of life and short on the various tempting nice points of law. Sir George Baker P. took as his starting-point the proposition that an injunction may be granted only if the claimant can show he has a legal right enforceable at law or in equity. Thus the question was: did the husband have any right? This argument already, by implication, closes off another possible approach, namely, whether the foetus has any rights which the husband, as father, can assert for him. The husband does not seem to have made this claim; but in any event, Sir George Baker P. expressly stated that the foetus has no rights in English law, and thus no standing to assert any claim.[4] English law is, indeed, clear; a foetus has no rights; or, put another way, is not a legal person until born alive.[5]

---

* First published as 'Husband Denied a Say in Abortion Decision', 42 *Modern Law Review* 324 (1979).　　　　　　　　　　　　　　　　　　　　　　　[1] [1978] 2 All ER 987.

[2] The Court referred to an unreported Ontario decision as the only case known. See, however, *Doe* v. *Doe*, 314 N.E. 2*d* 128 (Mass. 1974), which held that a husband had no right under the Constitution to be a father or to protect his unborn child. Compare *Rothenberger* v. *Chasalow, Los Angeles Times*, 22 April 1977, in which the New Jersey Supreme Court granted a man a temporary injunction restraining his girl-friend (not wife) from having an abortion since it would, 'violate his right to fatherhood'. The next day the girl-friend rendered further argument moot by having an abortion! See further J. P. Witherspoon, 'Impact of Abortion Decisions upon the Father's Role', 35 *The Jurist* 32 (1975).

[3] *Supra* n. 1, 992.　　　　　　　　　　　　　　　　　　　　　　　　　　[4] Ibid. 990.

[5] Apparent exceptions—e.g. succession rules concerning a child *en ventre sa mère*—prove not to be, since they all demand that a child be born alive before any rights may attach.

42

So, did the husband have any rights? It is not entirely clear what right he was claiming. It seems, however, that the basis of his claim was that his wife's abortion could only be carried out if he consented; that he had, in other words, a right to veto by withholding his consent. This was easy to deal with. Once it was accepted that the abortion would be otherwise lawful, all that the court needed to do was to refer to the Abortion Act 1967. The Act makes no provision for a husband's consent. The only parties involved are the pregnant woman seeking the abortion and the doctors certifying that the necessary circumstances exist to meet the requirements of the Act. Doubtless, the total exclusion of the husband's involvement did not, and does not, please everyone;[6] but lawful abortion is a creature of statute, and the statute has no place for the husband's wishes or consent.

Could the husband have based his claim on any other legal grounds? Claims invoking fundamental rights, whether to parenthood or whatever, are, of course, justiciable in the United States by reference to the Constitution. Such an approach is still unfamiliar to English courts. Some support could be gained, however, from two sources, though for the reasons offered later, neither could be regarded as very fruitful. First, in the case of *Re D*,[7] Heilbron J. held that to sterilize an 11-year-old girl would violate a basic human right, her right to reproduce. No source is identified from which this fundamental right is drawn; and it is perhaps arguable whether reference to such is necessary for the decision, which could have rested merely on what view the court took of the best interest of the girl. Certainly, little could be built on it by way of analogy. Second, and alternatively, the husband could have pointed to the European Convention on Human Rights as conferring on him the right to parenthood. In a sense, however, any success on this ground would be a hollow victory. Babies, like the tide, waiteth for no man, and certainly will not wait for a decision that would take many months to arrive at. Nor is there any power to issue any form of interim order. The abortion would have been carried out long since. And, even if the court found for him, the finding would be merely declaratory of an incompatibility between the Convention and English law, calling, perhaps, for legislation incorporating the court's view. It would not offer any specific remedy for the husband.[8]

Another possibility would have been for the husband to have framed his action in the form of a claim to custody of the unborn child. Such a claim

---

[6] P. T. O'Neill and I. Watson, 'The Father and the Unborn Child', 38 *MLR* 174 (1975).

[7] [1976] Fam. 185.

[8] Article 2, The Right to Life, and Article 12, The Right to Marry *and Found a Family* (my emphasis), could be invoked. See F. Jacobs, *The European Convention on Human Rights* (Oxford University Press, 1975), pp. 21–2, and Application 7045 of 1975. Contrast, further, the holding in *Paton* that any right the husband might have, he would have *qua* husband and father, with the possible position of the illegitimate father under the Convention since the effective removal of the stigma of illegitimacy; Jacobs, 134–5.

is considered at length by Bradley in a paper written before *Paton* was decided, but published subsequent to it.[9] There is, of course, no precedent for a court considering—let alone granting—custody in respect of an unborn child. It would require more than a little departure from existing law, and perhaps more judicial creativity than most judges would contemplate. Note, however, that here the illegitimate father would be on an equal footing with the husband-father if the argument succeeded, by virtue of section 14 of the Guardianship of Minors Act 1971. Doubtless, Bromley's view is to be preferred that, 'if it is desirable that the father's consent be obtained [to abortion] . . . this should be made explicit by Parliament and not left to the judge to achieve by a very dubious extension of the law of custody.'[10]

Could the husband have used any argument based on a notion of property? The foetus is biologically, in part, the product of his genetic material. Expressed in terms of property, the claim may seem odd; but such a claim perhaps most closely reflects the natural reaction of the husband that 'the baby is half mine.' To say that human beings, born or unborn, have not been subject to property rights since the abolition of slavery is too easy an answer. It begs the question. If property is the congeries of rights which may be asserted by one against all comers, the question is whether there is any such right which the husband can claim. Put this way, however, it is clear that the property argument dissolves into an examination of the various rights already discussed.

It may be that there are more arguments which the husband could have used. Indeed, the issue is ideally suited for exercises in all sorts of legal sophistry. And, law apart, it is, of course, as Sir George Baker P. pointed out, an issue highly charged with emotion. For example, some will see it as yet another battle in the war for women's liberation; others as affecting the future stability of homes and marriages; others as justifying abortion on demand in view of the stark alternative of forcing a woman to carry a child; and others as a matter of profound moral and theological weight. Indeed, Sir George Baker P. adverted to the 'great emotions and vigorous opposing views'[11] aroused by such an action. The temptation to be led by these considerations into making nice legal or philosophical points would, of course, be fatal if given in to. For all arguments of principle have to be weighted against the one reality, the consequences of finding in the husband's favour. A moment's thought is enough to realize that no court would admit the husband's claim.

It is trite law that a court will exercise its discretion to issue an order only when there is a good chance that the order will be enforceable. This is the nub of the case, and was recognized as such by Sir George Baker P.: 'Personal

---

[9] D. C. Bradley, 'A Woman's Right to Choose', 41 *MLR* 365 (1978).
[10] P. M. Bromley, *Family Law*, 5th edn., p. 308.   [11] *Supra* n. 1, 989.

family relationships in marriage cannot be enforced by the order of a Court; to issue an injunction would be, adopting the words of a Florida judge, "ludicrous".'[12] Admittedly, it is possible to object that the examples given of 'personal family relationships' involve individual, personal choices without any questions of a third party, a foetus, being involved, and that this is a crucial distinction. Also, arguably, it is not a question of 'cannot' but 'should not', since a normative, moral stance has to be taken by a court. Such objections carried little weight with the Court, and, it is submitted, rightly so. To say that the presence of the foetus makes a difference is to assume that which must be proved. The fact that English law has consistently refused to attribute legal personality to a foetus, and that in the context of abortion there is simply no room for compromise, since to favour the mother's claim to an abortion *ex hypothesi* means the destruction of the foetus, suggest that this is, as Sir George Baker P. said, an example of a family relationship where a court would not and should not grant an injunction.

As for the second point, the normative choice to be made by the court must always be conditioned by what is possible and practicable, as well as by some sense of transcendental justice. Sir George Baker P. asked himself what could be the remedy if an injunction were ordered and disobeyed. He persuaded himself that no remedy existed: 'No judge could even consider sending . . . a wife to prison for breaking such an order.'[13] And, he went on, once it was conceded that the abortion was lawful, the Court did not have the power to enjoin a doctor from performing it.

A further point, not made in the judgment, is that if the mother encountered difficulty in obtaining her abortion in England, she could go abroad or even resort to self-help—or the back-street abortionist, thereby ushering in again the era which the Abortion Act was designed to bring to an end for ever. Even more compelling is the obvious common-sense argument that even to contemplate requiring a mother to remain pregnant against her will for a further six months or more is to realize that it is a nonsense. Once society, through its legislature, has made the moral choice that abortion under certain circumstances is socially acceptable, to deny a woman a lawful abortion is to flout Parliament's wishes, and, some would say, to reintroduce a form of bondage by denying the woman the right to deal with her body as she wishes (provided she meets certain criteria). If more practical arguments are needed, mention could be made of the potential damage to the mother's health (physical and psychological) in enduring an unwanted pregnancy and the undoubted damage to the child, born to a resentful and reluctant mother and a shattered home, regulated only by court injunctions and hostility.

It has been assumed until now that the contemplated abortion would be lawful. The issue left undecided by *Paton* is the rights, if any, of the husband

---

[12] Ibid. 990.   [13] Ibid. 991.

if the contemplated abortion were to be unlawful, in that the requirements
of the Abortion Act were not satisfied. Counsel for the husband had initially
suggested that he might argue this, but it was not pursued, allowing Sir George
Baker P. to conclude that 'it is not necessary for me to decide that question
or to consider *Gouriet* v. *Union of Post Office Workers* further.'[14] This
unanswered question warrants further examination.

The first point to consider is how it might be alleged that an abortion,
if performed, would be unlawful. The Act places the responsibility for
certifying that the required conditions are met on two registered medical
practitioners. If evidence appeared subsequent to an abortion that some fraud,
in the sense of unwarranted certification, had been perpetrated by the doctors,
then a criminal prosecution could be mounted. But that is only after the
abortion. The question here is whether anything could be done beforehand.
Sir George Baker P. expressed his view 'that it would be quite impossible
for the courts to supervise the operation of the 1967 Act'.[15] He cited in
support Scarman LJ's words in *R.* v. *Smith (John)* that 'a great social
responsibility is firmly placed by the law on the shoulders of the medical
profession.'[16] But, Scarman LJ went on to say, in a case in which the
conviction of a doctor was upheld, that 'Although the 1967 Act has imposed
a great responsibility on doctors, it has not ousted the function of the jury.
If a case is brought to trial which calls in question the bona fides of a doctor,
the jury, not the medical profession, must decide the issue.'[17] But the
question is, can a judge play the role before abortion that Scarman LJ saw
a jury playing after the abortion? Sir George Baker P. insisted that it would
be 'a foolish judge who would try to do any such thing unless, possibly, there
is clear bad faith and an obvious attempt to perpetrate a criminal offence'.[18]
Well, the exception contemplated by Sir George Baker P. effectively swallows
up most of his alleged principle, since lack of good faith is the primary
basis on which prosecutions against doctors would be brought. Thus, it is
submitted, a civil court could, in principle, take jurisdiction to admit a
complaint that a contemplated abortion, if carried out, would be unlawful.[19]

The next question is more difficult. At whose suit could the court take
jurisdiction? Obviously the remedy sought, since the complaint is about future
conduct, is an injunction. Thus, although on the facts before him Sir George
Baker P. was able to avoid considering *Gouriet*,[20] clearly it is central to the
question now posed. First, it is, and always was, clear that the Attorney-
General may bring an action either of his own motion or at the instance of

---

[14] Ibid. 989.   [15] Ibid.   [16] [1974] 1 All ER 376, 378.
[17] Ibid. 381.   [18] *Supra*, n. 1, 992.
[19] The court seems to have overlooked the fact that the husband could also invoke the
criminal law. An agreement to perform an abortion contrary to the provisions of the Abortion
Act 1967 is a criminal conspiracy. The wife would be both an inciter and a conspirator, and
thus liable to arrest.   [20] [1977] 3 All ER 70.

a husband (and, query, even an illegitimate father) who 'relates' the facts to him. The law is not so clear, however, if, for whatever reason, the Attorney-General declines to bring an action; and decline he may, since the Attorney-General's power is, per Lord Diplock in *Gouriet*, 'anomalous' and 'to be used only in the most exceptional circumstances'.[21] None the less, the issue should be pursued, not merely for the sake of completeness, but because it is by no means unlikely that it will come before the courts at some time or other. *Gouriet* indubitably decides that a private citizen has no standing to bring an action to restrain another from engaging in a threatened criminal act. Only the Attorney-General may do so. But, equally clearly, all the Law Lords recognized an exception to this, namely, when that which is the crime also constitutes an infringement of a private right vested in the plaintiff. This does not avail the husband in the case under consideration, since, as we have seen, he apparently has no private right to prevent his wife's abortion.

There may, however, be a second exception in *Gouriet*. It appears rather blandly in the headnote of the report in the *All England Law Reports* as follows: 'A private person could only bring an action to restrain a theatened breach of the law if his claim was based on an allegation that the threatened breach would constitute an infringement of his private rights *or would inflict special damage on him*'.[22] None of the Law Lords expresses the exception in italics in quite those terms. Lord Wilberforce endorses the notion, but in a part of his speech apparently devoted to declaratory judgments,[23] Lord Dilhorne states that a private individual '*may* be able to do so [prevent public wrongs] if he will sustain injury as a result of a public wrong',[24] but his speech is somewhat equivocal on the point. Lord Edmund-Davies is equally equivocal, at one point apparently contemplating only one exception to the *Gouriet* principle,[25] yet at others mentioning this second exception.[26] Lord Fraser's is the most clear endorsement of this second exception.[27] Lord Diplock makes no mention of it, however, and indeed, is categorical and unequivocal in his view that only where a private right exists may the plaintiff have standing.[28] Indeed, a reading of the case as a whole leaves a rather confusing impression.[29]

---

[21] Ibid. 97.   [22] Ibid. 72; my emphasis.   [23] Ibid. 85.
[24] Ibid. 94; my emphasis.   [25] Ibid. 107.   [26] Ibid. 104, 114.
[27] Ibid. 114.   [28] Ibid. 99.

[29] Compare Lord Denning, MR, in *Ex parte Island Records* [1978] 3 All ER 824; a private individual has standing if he can show: (1) 'that he has a private right which is being interfered with by the criminal act, *thus* causing . . . him special damage over and above the generality of the public' (p. 829; my emphasis); (2) 'that his private rights *and interests* are specially affected by the breach' (p. 830; my emphasis); (3) that his 'rights *or* interests' are threatened (p. 830; my emphasis). [But see now the rejection of Lord Denning's view by the House of Lords in *Lonrho Ltd.* v. *Shell Petroleum Co. Ltd.* (No. 2) [1982] AC 173, per Lord Diplock; and see further, *RCA Corpn.* v. *Pollard* [1982] 3 WLR 1007.]

The fact remains, however, that the possibility of a second exception to the *Gouriet* principle is absolutely critical for the husband in the case under consideration. If it does indeed exist, a way may be found, after all, for the husband to prevent his wife's abortion under certain circumstances. The argument would not be without difficulties, but would be, it is submitted, very strong. A public right exists to have the provisions of the Abortion Act obeyed. Breach of these provisions is a public wrong. That being so, it is indisputable that the husband suffers special damage, over and above that suffered by the public at large, since it is 'his child' (more precisely the result of his union with the mother) which is being aborted. Thus the husband, on the assumption that the Attorney-General chose not to act, would be able to side-step Gouriet and to seek an injunction if he had evidence of bad faith on the part of the doctors (and query, how strong it would have to be before he could ask the court to grant an injunction). Of course, it would still be open to the court in its discretion to refuse the application, although, it is submitted, the court would be unlikely to do so if the evidence were strong enough. Also, of course, it would depend on the husband's knowing the doctors involved so that an attack could be made on the bona fides of their medical judgment. The reality would still be, however, that the wife, if determined enough, would be able to obtain an abortion somewhere. So[30] once again, any success for the husband would be a phyrrhic victory. For there is no escape from the common sense reflected in Sir George Baker P.'s judgment that, if the wife wants an abortion, she will have it, husband's consent or not, court or no court, and that a court is best advised to recognize this and not interfere. Indeed, perhaps the real import of *Paton* is the cynical advice to a wife: 'If you want an abortion and you think your husband will object strenuously, go ahead and have it without telling him!' If the husband does not know of the wife's intention, he cannot even begin to take action, civil or criminal. This may not be a recipe for marital concord, but neither is the resort to courts for injunctions.

POSTSCRIPT

Not content with the High Court's decision, the husband applied to the European Commission of Human Rights.[31] He alleged that the denial of an injunction constituted a violation of his rights under Articles 2 and 8 of

---

[30] In fact, Lord Diplock seems to have delivered a death-blow to the argument in *Lonrho* (*supra* n. 29). He insisted that for the second exception to apply, there must be more than a public wrong which affects the plaintiff more seriously than others. There must also be a public right, i.e. a legal right enjoyed by all who wish to avail themselves of it. No such right exists as regards the Abortion Act, and thus the argument advanced here must be regarded now as lost.

[31] *Paton* v. *United Kingdom*, 3 EHRR 410 (1980).

the European Convention on Human Rights. The Commission rejected his application on both grounds.

As for Article 2, the husband relied on the first sentence: 'Everyone's right to life shall be protected by law.' The Commission decided that it did not have to resolve the problem of whether the word 'everyone' included an unborn child, such that a foetus would have a 'right to life'. Instead, it rested its decision on the ground that the authorization of an abortion by English law, at least in the initial stages of pregnancy, served to protect the life and health of the woman, and that this served to limit whatever right to life a foetus might have.

In invoking Article 8, the husband asserted a right of his own, rather than a right of the unborn child—namely, the right guaranteed under paragraph 1 to respect for his family life. The Commission decided, however, that, since the pregnancy was terminated to avoid harm to the woman's health, this was a permissible interference with the husband's rights under paragraph 1, as being necessary for the protection of the rights of another person pursuant to paragraph 2.

It might have been thought that this was the end of the matter, but in February 1987, in the case of *C.* v. *S.* [32] another application for an injunction to restrain a woman from having an abortion was made to the High Court, this time by the woman's erstwhile boy-friend. The court rejected the application, following *Paton*, stating again that the man had no standing to bring an action, whether on behalf of the unborn child or on his own behalf as putative father. On appeal to the Court of Appeal, the case took a curious turn. Counsel for the man, while appealing against the High Court's ruling on the issue of standing, invited the court to reach a decision on a third ground, which had also been rejected in the High Court. This was that, because the unborn child's gestational age was between 18 and 21 weeks, any abortion would contravene the provisions of the Infant Life (Preservation) Act 1929, and thus be the crime of child destruction. By section 1, the offence is committed if a person 'with intent to destroy the life of a child capable of being born alive, by any wilful act causes a child to die before it has an existence independent of its mother'. The critical words for the court were 'capable of being born alive'. Surprisingly, the court allowed counsel to develop the argument, and did not invoke the *Gouriet* principle.

The Court of Appeal then decided that a foetus at 18 to 21 weeks of gestational age was not 'capable of being born alive' within the proper meaning of the Act, since on agreed medical evidence its lungs would not be sufficiently developed to support life, even with the aid of a ventilator. The court rejected the husband's argument that because the foetus had a

[32] [1987] 1 All ER 1230.

beating heart and a central nervous system it was indeed capable of being born alive. Although the court did not give its reasons, this must, with respect, be right. The point is not, however, without difficulty. Certainly, the foetus *is* 'alive' *in utero*. So, in one sense, it is 'capable of being born alive', if it does not die in the process of birth. But, if this interpretation was adopted, no abortion would be lawful, however young the foetus or embryo. The Abortion Act 1967 would thereby be nullified by a judicial interpretation of the Infant Life (Preservation) Act. It is not surprising that the Court of Appeal chose an alternative interpretation which avoided this consequence. The court chose to interpret the words to mean capable of sustaining independent existence, with any necessary and appropriate medical care. Specifically, the court stated that the foetus must be capable of breathing, either independently or with the aid of a ventilator. Without this capacity, it was not capable of being born alive within the meaning of the Act.

While apparently clarifying the law, the Court of Appeal's decision does, however, raise further problems. If I am right in my understanding of the effect of the decision, the criterion for determining whether a proposed abortion violates the Infant Life (Preservation) Act 1929 is whether the foetus has reached that stage of gestational development at which, if born, it would be capable of sustaining its own life with or without reasonable medical care. But this raises immediately the question of *how long* the baby, if born, must be capable of sustaining life. The law of murder would say that a moment of life is enough, in that if a child's life was extinguished, it would be of no consequence that it was on the brink of death already. But this analysis may not be appropriate when what is being considered is a decision about a child's chances of survival while it is still *in utero*. Instead, the better view may be that the medical evidence should be that the child, if born, would be capable of sustaining life for a reasonable period of time—in other words, that the child would have a reasonable chance of survival.

Clearly, the impact of this decision is considerable, given the court's interpretation of the words 'capable of being born alive'. The reality of modern neonatal care is that a child of around 24 weeks gestational age may well survive in a centre of excellence. Consequently, the traditional view that no offence would be committed under the Infant Life (Preservation) Act until the child was 28 weeks old cannot now be regarded as good law if it ever was. For, all that the Act stipulates is that at 28 weeks the child will be presumed to be capable of being born alive. It does not state that a child is not so capable until 28 weeks. It follows, therefore, that an abortion carried out when a foetus has reached, for example, 25 weeks would be unlawful in the absence of clear evidence that the foetus was so severely disabled as to be incapable of sustaining itself. A prosecution brought in the case of an abortion of a 25-week-old foetus could well, therefore, result in a judicial limitation of abortions under the Abortion Act 1967 through the interpretation of the Infant Life (Preservation) Act 1929, when all attempts to revise or reform the Abortion Act itself in Parliament have met with failure. Some may well regret such a development, taking the view that on a matter of such public importance and controversy, policy is better made by the legislature than by the courts.

5

The Doctor, the Pill, and
the 15-year-old Girl*

In this article I shall investigate the ethical and legal implications of prescribing oral contraceptives to young girls. This is a matter both of topical interest and of great concern. It is part of a wider debate about the relationship between parents and their children, particularly in their dealings with others. I have chosen to examine it here, however, because, in addition to its intrinsic importance, it is an issue which demonstrates how law and moral philosophy may intersect and interact with medicine.

I hardly need to say that this is an issue on which people have strongly held views. My aim here is to present a scheme for understanding and analysing the problems involved, and to explore ways of arriving at answers. Since the answers must be ones we can live with, this will also mean, of course, that I shall have to explore the implications of some of the answers that others advocate.

The hypothetical case I want to consider is as follows. A girl of 15 approaches her doctor, and asks him to prescribe contraceptive pills. The girl, in making her request, makes it clear to the doctor that she does not want her parents to be told that she has consulted him on this matter. The doctor knows that the girl is 15 years old. He is the family doctor and knows the girl's parents. He also knows that the girl is asking for the pill because she is contemplating having sexual intercourse, rather than for any other medical reason.

Let me quickly add a couple of comments about these assumptions. I have assumed that the doctor knows the girl's family, because this is the hard case. The problems are different, and perhaps easier to solve, if the girl has run away from home or has gone to another town and, for example, registered with a GP on a temporary basis. I am also prepared to assume throughout that the doctor tries to persuade the girl to involve her parents, but that she adamantly refuses. Finally, you will notice that I say that the girl is thinking of having intercourse. I will consider in due course what significance, if any, should be attached to the fact that she may already have had intercourse.

* First published in M. Lockwood, ed., *Moral Dilemmas in Modern Medicine* (Oxford University Press, 1985). The part of the Postscript dealing with confidence was first published in P. Byrne, ed., *Medicine in Contemporary Society* (King's Fund, 1987).

The first question that has to be considered before we proceed further is whether, given all the circumstances, the pill would be appropriate treatment for the girl. 'Treatment', of course, is a concept which has moral and social, as well as technical, dimensions. That a doctor describes something within his technical competence as 'treatment' does not necessarily make it so. The term 'treatment' connotes something which not only *can* be done, but is also morally and socially warranted. Here, however, the question being asked is whether, simply in medical-technical terms, the pill is appropriate treatment. I will assume for the sake of argument that it is, and that there are no counter-indications or medical-technical reasons which argue against prescription.

A second question then arises. Are there any relevant factors of a non-medical-technical nature which the doctor is obliged to consider before he responds to her request? Can the doctor, having decided that the pill is appropriate, all things being equal, then go ahead and prescribe or refuse to prescribe without further ado? I will return to the issue of refusal at a later stage. I merely point out here that some would argue that the doctor is under no obligation to prescribe the pill, and may refuse to do so, since the girl is not ill in the accepted sense. As an alternative, it is suggested that the doctor can impose a condition that the girl agrees to her parents being involved, even when it is clear that she does not want this; so that the condition is tantamount to a refusal. It is by no means clear that these arguments are sound; whether they are or not is something that I shall consider later. But for the moment, I will assume that the doctor wishes to prescribe the pill.

Rephrasing the question slightly, are there any necessary preliminary conditions which have to be satisfied? Clearly, the answer must be that there are both ethical and legal conditions to be met. I will consider these in turn.

ETHICS

The girl has said that she wants the contraceptives; but is this ethically sufficient? Ought the doctor to prescribe them on her say-so, given the assumptions made above? Can the doctor, in other words, rely and act upon this purported exercise of authority by the girl?

Any attempt to answer these questions must be by reference to principles and to the analysis that follows from these principles. This is the traditional mode of thinking and analysis in both ethics and law. I suppose that, for me, the relevant starting-point in any ethical analysis must be the principle of respect for persons as persons. What this means here is that a doctor has a duty to respect the integrity and individuality of the person before him. A more specific duty derived from this is the duty to respect the person's autonomy. Respect for autonomy in turn forms a basis for the derivation of further, yet more specific, principles, the most important of which, in the present context, is the principle of consent.

It is consent and respect for autonomy that I shall be concentrating on. Here, the girl has purported to act autonomously, and has given her consent for the doctor to treat her. (It should be borne in mind that the doctor must, *inter alia*, take the girl's blood-pressure, so there will, in legal language, be a *touching* for which consent is needed.) In the language of principles, therefore, the questions can be posed as follows. Must the doctor respect this purported exercise of autonomy? Can he act on the basis of the girl's consent?

To pose these questions at all is implicitly to admit that there may be circumstances in which it would be wrong to act on the girl's say-so. She may not, as the expression goes, know her own mind. This gives the clue as to what the analysis must focus on. Consent is valid (that is, ethically to be relied upon) only if it is genuinely an expression of autonomy. It will be an expression of autonomy only if the girl is capable of being, or is competent to be, autonomous. The girl must be someone who is capable of weighing rationally her decision and its consequences for her and her way of life and values. Notice that this is not the same as saying that she *has* weighed them in this particular decision, since it is the prerogative of all of us to be irrational. It is an unsolved problem, however, and one to which I shall return, how irrational a person can be and still be judged competent or capable.

This is because capacity is judged by others. In the context of medical care, autonomy is, in effect, a status granted by other people. They have to decide whether paternalism is called for, or whether a person shall be allowed to rule his own life. In our example, the person doing the judging is the doctor. And, clearly, being in a position to make such a judgment vests the doctor with very great power, a power which is virtually beyond regulation or control. For it will be very hard subsequently to challenge whatever decision the doctor may make, if only because he may insist that, on the facts available to him *at that moment*, his decision was justified. There would normally be no evidence to the contrary, save, of course, the patient's own account, which, ordinarily, can be argued away by the doctor as being necessarily partial, the product of illness or perhaps of anger or confusion.

We have argued that consent requires autonomy, but that autonomy need be respected only if the person is judged capable. Given the implications of such a judgment, in terms of the power it vests in the doctor to grant or deprive the patient of the right to self-rule, it is clearly of crucial importance to identify the criteria by which capacity is to be judged. Various criteria or sets of criteria can be extracted from the literature on consent and capacity. Probably the best recent (1982) discussion is the report in the United States of the President's Commission for the Study of Ethical and Legal Problems in Medicine and Biomedical and Behavioral

Research, entitled *Making Health Care Decisions*.[1] I will consider each proposed criterion in turn.

The 'content' or 'outcome' approach

This view has it that a person's capacity to decide for himself depends upon, and is to be judged by reference to, the content of his decision, or the outcome which will follow any particular decision made in purported exercise of autonomy. The effect of this approach is that if the content or outcome is of a particular nature, the person is judged to be lacking capacity, with the consequence that his consent (or refusal of consent) must (not may) ethically be ignored. Of course, everything turns on what content or outcomes are to be taken to be indicative of incapacity. In analysing this question, it should be borne in mind that the question of the patient's capacity almost always arises because the doctor or the patient's relatives disagree with the patient's decision. You will not see arguments about capacity when the doctor and relatives, on the one hand, and the patient, on the other, are in full agreement. But merely disagreeing with the content of a decision or not approving the consequences of it cannot by themselves serve as criteria for determining capacity. It may be, of course, that the likely consequences of the decision are so bad, as judged by others, that they cause the doctor to doubt the patient's ability to weigh the various factors involved. But putting the point this way suggests that it is not the particular consequences, or the content, of the decision, but rather the patient's ability to weigh these up for him- or herself, which is being relied upon as the criterion of capacity. I shall return to this point later.

Suffice it to say here that it is a dangerous confusion to regard the outcome or content of a decision as *in itself* a criterion of capacity, as opposed to being merely evidence regarding the satisfaction of some other criterion. Such an approach purports to respect each person's autonomy. In effect, however, it serves as a blueprint for undermining that autonomy on any occasion when a person with power, in our case a doctor, thinks that the patient's decision is bad or unreasonable. While masquerading as respectful of autonomy, it provides a recipe for substituted judgment (that is, the supplanting of the patient's judgment by that of the doctor) or paternalism. It means that a patient who opts for a decision which is inconsistent with widely held values, or is otherwise unconventional, runs the risk of being labelled as *ipso facto* incapable of knowing his or her own mind and reaching his or her own decisions.

---

[1] President's Commission for the Study of Ethical and Legal Problems in Medicine and Biomedical and Behavioral Research, *Making Health Care Decisions*, Washington DC, US Government Printing Office, 1982.

The invalidity of this criterion becomes apparent as soon as it is examined thoughtfully. It is perhaps important to remember, therefore, that it is an approach which is very commonly resorted to by all professionals, not only doctors. There is a natural tendency for the doctor and others to believe that they know best, and therefore to think that if a decision on the part of a patient or client seems to them unwise or uncalled-for, they need not regard it as binding on them. Unless the patient is correspondingly determined and articulate, the reality of medical practice, as with other client–professional contacts, can be that the outcome test is what the doctor actually acts on. That this is unethical, an abuse of power, has still to enter the thinking of very many doctors.

If the outcome or content approach is invalid, then it cannot be used by our doctor to determine whether the 15-year-old girl knows her own mind. Her capacity cannot, therefore, be made to depend on whether the doctor thinks sexual intercourse is something young girls in general, or she in particular, should engage in.

The status approach

The basis of this approach is the argument that a particular status carries with it, by necessary implication, a lack of capacity. A familiar example of this form of argument is the assertion that if someone is mentally ill, he is, by virtue of belonging to the class of mentally ill people and having the corresponding status, incapable of arriving at considered decisions which may properly be relied upon. Another, equally familiar, example is the status of minority. Leaving aside for a moment the question of what constitutes minority, the view is that, by being a minor, a person *ipso facto* lacks capacity.

The invalidity of this approach is equally obvious. Merely to belong to a given class does not entail incapacity, except and unless that class is defined by reference to lack of capacity. The question to be asked, therefore, is whether all mentally ill persons or minors, once they are so categorized, must be considered to be incapable of making autonomous decisions on any matter, at any time. Unless the answer is yes, it will be clear that the class is not defined in terms of capacity, but by other factors with, at best, a merely contingent connection with capacity, such as symptoms of illness or number of birthdays. Clearly, someone may be mentally ill or be only 15 years old, yet still have the capacity to decide and to act autonomously. The mental illness may only affect certain aspects of behaviour or feeling or thought, or may coexist with periods of lucidity. A 15-year-old's decision not to go to the cinema with her parents, for example, or to go to her school counsellor for advice would be regarded as hers to make.

The fundamental flaw in the status approach is that it takes no account of the individuality of each person. Respect for autonomy, however, involves respect for each person's individuality. It demands, therefore, that any criterion intended to determine when someone is incapable of being autonomous should, equally, be respectful of that person's individuality. The test must look at, and be sensitive to, the qualities of the individual. Merely placing him in a class is far too gross a test of capacity. It denies respect to the individual as an individual, and must therefore be rejected.

There is a further, supplementary objection to the status approach. Minority as a status is usually associated with being below a certain fixed age, whether it be 16, 18, or 21. While it is clearly necessary, for legal purposes, to choose a definite age, even though it is bound to some extent to be arbitrary, there is no such necessity in the case of ethical analysis. Ethics need take account only of the fact that there is such a thing as minority, that there is, for every individual, a stage of development at which that individual is immature. This immediately makes it clear that it is, in fact, maturity that is the criterion, not minority. And since maturation is a process that will necessarily vary from individual to individual, to adopt one particular age or date as the bench-mark of maturity in all persons is clearly untenable. Indeed, even the law, which must, for the sake of certainty, adopt some fixed point of reference for minority, defines it differently for different purposes. For example, the age of consent for the purposes of volunteering for the armed services is not the same as the age at which someone may vote. Equally, the age at which a person may marry without parental consent is not the same as the age at which the same person may consent to sexual intercourse.

As regards consent to medical treatment, the picture is sometimes muddied by those who argue, first, that the *law* requires the consent of a parent(s) or of someone *in loco parentis* before a doctor may treat someone under 16 years of age, and, second, that since it is ordinarily morally obligatory to uphold the law, it is therefore *ethically* wrong for a doctor to treat someone under 16, save in an emergency, in the absence of parental consent (or some legally acceptable substitute). Now I concede that ordinarily one ought to obey the law. But it is as well to get the law straight! It is not the law, nor in my view has it ever been, that a doctor may not treat a person under 16 without another's authority. I shall be arguing this point more fully later on, when I come to examine the law. Suffice it to say now that once the legal argument is shown to be spurious, the ethical argument built on it, that 16 is the magic age for consent, can safely be ignored. (But see now the first postscript.)

It follows, then, that in our case the fact that the girl asking for the pill is only 15 years old cannot ethically be regarded as settling the question of whether she has the capacity to act autonomously. Evidence it may be; but evidence of maturity or lack thereof, since maturity is the key.

The individual's capacity to comprehend

It should be clear from what has been said so far that the only valid criterion of capacity is the ability of the particular individual to comprehend the nature and consequences of the proposed procedure. This is a test which is specific to each individual and thus maximizes respect for each person's autonomy. It makes maturity the crucial determinant, the maturity that consists in having a stable set of values and outlook on life and the ability to weigh the proposed procedure in the light of these so as to arrive at a considered decision. As a criterion, it differs from the outcome or content approach in that the content of the decision has to conform to the girl's set of values, rather than those of her doctor or some other, allegedly objective scale. It is the approach that the President's Commission refers to as the 'functional approach', because it 'focuses on an individual's actual functioning in decision-making situations'.[2]

If, however, it is suggested that capacity must not be measured by reference to whether any decision is reasonable, or objectively acceptable, the objection may be made that this is to err too much on the side of subjectivity. By so doing it may, in effect, reduce the autonomy of the girl. This would be so if it meant that a decision which, by any account, would entail harm for the girl was to be respected because it accorded with her world-view or scheme of values. Acting on this decision, it is said, may not further the girl's autonomy, since, if it flows from ill-considered premises or a skewed perception of the world, it could mean that she exposes herself to avoidable and irreparable harm, and thereby reduces her ability to enjoy autonomy in the future.

There is obviously some force to this argument. It is as valid here as it is in the case of the mentally ill person whose decision is the product of a rather strange perception of the world. But equally, there is force in the counter-argument, that this could usher in through the back door what has already been refused formal admittance, namely the outcome or content approach. Clearly, we are not far from the content approach if we say that the girl's present decision should be overridden because it is unreasonable or may have dangerous consequences. One should bear in mind the power vested in the doctor, in that it is he who is the arbiter of capacity, and he who is likely to wish most strongly that the girl would opt for a course other than the one she has in fact chosen. Given this, we can see that the doctor may well pay lip-service to the test of her ability to comprehend the procedure proposed, and yet judge her incapable by virtue of the decision she arrives at. Of course, this would be done for what the doctor, at least, would regard as the best possible motives. But it would, for all that, be strongly paternalistic.

---

[2] Ibid. 170.

It would also mean that the proposed criterion of capacity is, in the event, unworkable, since it provides insufficient safeguards for the individual. As the President's Commission put it:

The fact that a patient belongs to a category of people who are often unable to make general decisions for their own well-being or that an individual makes a highly idiosyncratic decision should alert health professionals to the greater possibility of decisional incapacity. But it does not conclusively resolve the matter.[3]

Thus, something more must be added to this criterion. The first additional factor must be that, in enquiring whether the girl before him comprehends the nature and consequences of the procedure proposed, the doctor must act with total integrity. He must recognize and accept the reason for the enquiry, namely his obligation to respect the girl's autonomy, and must devote an appropriate amount of time and care to pursuing it. He must use language which is comprehensible, and must be conscious of the imbalance of power, which is a feature of virtually all doctor–patient relationships.

The second thing that needs to be added is that any enquiry into capacity must take account of certain presumptions. The President's Commission recommends that if a minor patient is over 14, it should be presumed that she is capable of deciding for herself, so that evidence would have to be adduced to rebut the presumption. In practical terms, this would mean that the doctor would have to note carefully, and be prepared to stand by, whatever evidence persuaded him that a girl over 14 lacked capacity. Such a presumption would not decide the issue of capacity, but would provide the starting-point for an enquiry about whether it could be rebutted on the strength of the facts in the particular case.

I find the Commission's recommendation attractive, with respect to its use of this notion of presumptions. The difficulty, however, lies in the way it rejects status, in the form of under or over 16, only to readopt an age criterion later, in the form of under or over 14. The difference, it will be said, lies in the fact that the first criterion is arbitrary and inflexible, the second flexible and merely the first stage in a necessary enquiry. Accepting this, it is none the less arguable that, in practice, there is a danger of the one age simply supplanting the other as a hard and fast cut-off point. On balance, this may be a necessary risk that proponents of the criterion must run. Ultimately, they can only place their faith in the doctor's integrity, and hope that the presumptions will operate as intended.

The final element that should be incorporated into this criterion, to make it as sensitive as possible to the principle of respect for autonomy, is some sort of mechanism to maximize the chances of the doctor actually pursuing the necessary enquiry into capacity. What I have in mind is some sort of

---

[3] Ibid. 171–2.

formalized testing device which would be available to doctors, and which they would be instructed to make use of. Such a suggestion is made by the President's Commission, which recommends the adoption of a standardized test, appropriately designed to measure capacity. The Commission refers to this as the 'mental status examination':

The 'mental status examination' is perhaps the best example of how professional expertise can be enlisted in making assessments of incapacity. Such an evaluation is intended, among other things, to elicit the patient's orientation to person, place, time, and situation, the patient's mood and affect, and the content of thought and perception, with an eye to any delusions and hallucinations; to assess intellectual capacity, that is, the patient's ability to comprehend abstract ideas and to make a reasoned judgment based on that ability; to review past history for evidence of any psychiatric disturbance that might affect the patient's current judgment; and to test the patient's recent and remote memory and logical sequencing.[4]

This sort of test would have the merit of emphasizing that judgments of capacity are not really medical-technical, but rather matters of common sense. A test designed by those having some knowledge of maturity could, then, ensure that the question of capacity was not left to be decided entirely on the basis of the doctor's own, possibly idiosyncratic, judgment. This is not to say that such a procedural device would supplant the exercise by the doctor of his own judgment. But it might serve to constrain it within limits set by others.

If this criterion of capacity, the ability to comprehend the nature and consequences of the proposed procedure, is accepted, subject to the suggested provisos, it means that the 15-year-old girl can give valid consent to the prescription of the pill, provided she meets the criterion. The doctor, therefore, once satisfied of this, is entitled to prescribe the pill as a matter of good medical ethics. The fact that she is 15 years old would, all other things being equal, be neither here nor there. As to whether she meets the necessary criterion of maturity, it could be said that the very act of consulting a doctor to obtain contraceptives is an act of maturity. It would then be for the doctor to put before the girl the various disadvantages involved in her decision (asuming her to be aware of the advantages). Notice that it is for the doctor to do so. It is not open to him to object that she is incapable of deciding because she is ignorant of the relevant implications. Once a relationship of doctor and patient has been created between them, it is the doctor's duty to place before her that information which will allow her to reach an informed and considered decision.

At this point, it may be objected that all the emphasis has been on respect for autonomy, and that I have ignored at least two other relevant

---

[4] Ibid. 172, n. 8.

considerations. They are the claim of the parents to be involved in the decision, and the need to consider the interests of the family and the possible effect on the family of a decision to prescribe. I will consider these in turn.

The parents' claim

The parents' claim to be informed by the doctor if their daughter should seek contraceptives is often presented in an unattractive manner, as if it were really a property issue. 'She is our daughter. Therefore we have a right to be consulted.' This is how it is often put. Clearly, it is not, when properly formulated, a property claim. Rather, it is an assertion that, since the parents have responsibilities towards their daughter, so they are entitled to be consulted, and to be involved in her decisions. But does this latter proposition flow from the former? In the recent case of *Gillick* v. *West Norfolk and Wisbech Area Health Authority*,[5] in which these issues were aired, Mrs Gillick argued that she had rights in respect of her children by virtue of being their parent and custodian. What are these rights? They are, I submit, only those rights necessary to perform parental obligations. A parent is, in my view, the trustee of the interests of the child. This being so, the primary obligation of the parent is to bring the child to an enjoyment of autonomy, as free as possible from constraints on this enjoyment. In short, parental obligations are to be understood as being primarily autonomy-enhancing. This means that the parent has an obligation initially to protect the child, while she is still immature, and thereafter, as the child acquires maturity, to leave her to make her own decisions and her own mistakes.

If this is correct, and the girl is judged to be capable of making her own decisions, on the criterion proposed above, there would seem to be no justification for the parent insisting, as did Mrs Gillick, on being informed and consulted until her daughter reaches the age of 16. As we have seen, the age of the girl does not suffice to determine her capacity to make decisions. Someone might retort that it is a crime for a man to engage in sexual intercourse with a girl under 16 years of age, and that, once supplied with contraceptives, the 15-year-old girl may, by engaging in intercourse, become a party to a crime in the non-legal sense. The fact that it is a crime, however, does not mean that the parents are entitled to be consulted in circumstances where it is conceded that the girl is autonomous. As I shall argue later, I believe that the doctor is under a legal obligation to treat the girl, assuming her to be autonomous. That a male partner may subsequently commit a crime would, presumably, be a matter of regret for the doctor; but it is not necessarily a reason for forsaking his commitment to her autonomy or his pledge of confidentiality.

[5] [1984] 1 All ER 365 (now, [1985] 3 All ER 402.)

This is not to say that the parents have no claim at all. It is to suggest only that their claim may not weigh heaviest on the scale. A doctor may wish to involve the girl's parents. Indeed, the girl herself may wish to do so, but be deterred by her belief that they would not understand. In such circumstances, the girl's claim, assuming that she has been judged capable of making her own decisions, is, I submit, to be given precedence over that of the parents. To argue otherwise involves saying one of two things, neither of which can seriously be sustained. The first is what Mrs Gillick said, that until her daughter reaches 16, she has a right to be consulted (and presumably a right of veto) over *any* decision her daughter may make concerning medical treatment. Such a conclusion falls foul of the objections to the status approach outlined earlier. Taken to its extreme, it implies that, on the girl's sixteenth birthday, some magical process takes place whereby maturity and the capacity to make decisions are suddenly visited upon her. It ignores all the arguments concerning the process of gaining maturity.

Alternatively, one would have to say that, despite being capable of making her own decisions (as I am assuming that she is), the girl is somehow unable to act responsibly, and that her parents must, for that reason, be consulted. This is clearly contradictory. If autonomy is self-enhancing, then I submit that the girl's autonomy is to be preferred for at least three reasons. First, pregnancy, which is a likely consequence of her failing to obtain contraceptives, can hardly be described as self-enhancing in these circumstances. Second, denying the girl the right to act autonomously, when it is granted that she is capable of doing so, is clearly autonomy-reducing. Third, exercise of the power to make her own decisions is, by contrast, autonomy-enhancing, and consequently to be preferred.

The interests of the family

The second consideration which it may be said that I have overlooked is the interests of the family. Here I assume that the doctor, being the family doctor also, would wish to take account of the interests of the family, considered as a unit. He may decide that the girl's wishes are in conflict with the best interests of the family as a family. This could persuade him not to accede to the girl's request, even though he accepted that she was capable of making her own decisions.

There are several obvious objections to giving greater weight to the claims of the family than to the principle of respect for autonomy. The first is that there is no reason to think that the doctor is the best judge, or indeed any judge, of where the family's true interests lie. The doctor may decide on a given course of conduct, for example, because it seems to him to be the best way of keeping the family together. But the underlying assumption may be invalid. Maybe it would be better for this particular family to break up. And whether it should break up or not is, surely, a matter exclusively for members of that family to decide, unless or until others, perhaps including the doctor, are consulted. For the doctor to interfere, unasked, on the basis of limited information and irrelevant personal preference is wholly unwarranted.

The second objection is that the family includes the daughter. Thus, the family's interests must include her interests. Where her views do not, or may not, coincide with those of other members of the family, it is a false antithesis to contrast her views with the interests of the family. It is a case, rather, of there being a division of opinion within the family. In such circumstances, there is no obvious reason why the doctor should prefer the views (or what he imagines to be the views) of other members of the family to those of the girl. The only argument that one could advance is, assuming the doctor's views of what the rest of the family wanted to be correct, that they know best. But if it has already been granted that the girl is capable of acting autonomously, such an argument must fail, unless it means that they know best who agree with the doctor. And to say that is to substitute the exercise of power for respect for principled analysis.

The final objection to preferring the alleged interests of the family is a more pragmatic one. The girl, in approaching the doctor, has stipulated that he may not consult or involve her parents. This is at least prima facie evidence that the family is not an integrated unit with a common set of interests which can be identified and served. If the doctor persists in thinking that it is, the major casualty will be the girl herself, who will lose faith in her doctor or seek help elsewhere or even abandon efforts to get help from any doctor.

This concludes my discussion of capacity. If the girl, on proper enquiry by the doctor, is found to understand the nature and consequences of taking the pill, including, obviously, its risks, then she must be judged capable of making her own decisions, and the doctor may act on her request. It only remains to say that if the doctor decides, on the criterion I have proposed, that the girl is not capable of making her own decisions, then he may not treat her on her say-so alone. Ethically speaking, he is bound to ignore her consent. Doing so is entirely in keeping with the principle of respect for autonomy, since it is autonomy-enhancing to protect the immature from their ill-considered decisions. It is also in conformity with the principle of beneficence, in that the doctor is, under the circumstances, acting for the girl's own good and to protect her from harm.

Confidentiality

Let me turn now to a separate ethical issue raised by the girl's request that her parents not be informed that she is asking for contraceptive pills. The question can be simply put. Is the doctor, if he proceeds to prescribe the pills, having satisfied himself, therefore, that the girl is competent to act autonomously, ethically entitled thereafter to inform the parents, despite the girl's request to the contrary?

It may well be that the doctor should try to persuade the girl to involve her parents. In so doing, the doctor pays proper heed to the interests of the parents and the family, and also gives the girl the opportunity to reflect further on her decision. In some cases the girl may change her mind, persuaded, for example, that her parents may be more understanding than she had supposed. In our case, however, she remains unmoved.

One principle derived from the general obligation of respect for each person is that of respect for promises. An essential feature of respect for another is honouring his trust; and keeping promises is one example of observing this trust. Implicit in the doctor–patient relationship is the promise that information imparted to the doctor *qua* doctor will not be divulged. There are, obviously, good pragmatic, as well as principled, reasons for this, since the patient will not otherwise confide in the doctor, and the doctor will then be unable to do his job. Thus, without the need for it to be made explicit, the doctor is obliged to keep his patient's confidences. It follows, *a fortiori*, that he is obliged to do so if the patient explicitly demands it, as in our case, where the girl makes it a condition of the relationship.

There are those, however, who argue that, despite obligations of confidence, the doctor is entitled, or even obliged, to tell the parents. Can there be any justification for this, if the girl forbids it, and it is conceded that she is capable of acting autonomously? The only argument one could give is that the parents have an interest in knowing, and that this interest transcends any duty the doctor might have towards the girl. But the first difficulty with this argument is that, if this is what the doctor believes, he is under an obligation to make it clear at the outset of the consultation that he cannot agree to the girl's conditions. This would give the girl the opportunity to end the consultation and go elsewhere. But there may be nowhere else that it is feasible for her to go, or else the mere fact of discussing the issue before going elsewhere will have alerted the doctor to what the girl is contemplating.

Further difficulties in the argument that the parents have a right to know then appear. The doctor may prefer the interests of the parents because of what he assumes (or knows) them to want. Alternatively, he may do so out of respect for the principle of beneficence. I shall take the latter point first. For the doctor to assume that he knows what is best for the girl would, I submit, be an unwarranted act of strong paternalism, whereby the doctor merely substitutes his judgment for hers. If it is granted that the girl knows her own mind, then the presumption must be that she knows what is best for herself. The fact that the doctor happens to disagree with her is not a sufficient reason for him to ignore or override her wishes; for, if it is, it gives rise to the general principle that the doctor should always be the final arbiter of the best interests of his patient. This principle has only to be stated to be seen to be unacceptable; it would be rejected unhesitatingly by patients and doctors alike. Clearly, it has no place in sound medical ethics.

As regards the first point, there are powerful pragmatic, as well as principled, reasons why the doctor should not prefer the presumed interests of the parents. It would mean that any trust between the girl and the doctor would be destroyed, possibly for ever. It might even lead to a loss of confidence in doctors in general, with consequent risks to the girl's future health and well-being. Moreover, if it became generally known that it was considered ethically acceptable for doctors to inform on girls to their parents, girls in the future might be deterred altogether from consulting doctors to get contraceptive advice or treatment, with all that this could entail.

For all these reasons, therefore, I submit that there is no good case for the doctor to breach the girl's confidence and inform her parents.

LAW

As with many other aspects of the relationship between a doctor and his patients, it is not only ethics that would seek to regulate the prescription of contraceptives to the 15-year-old. The law is also involved. Some argue rather forlornly that the law has no place in the practice of medicine. It is, they say, far too blunt an instrument to deal sensitively with the complexities of the doctor–patient relationship. The answer, of course, is that there is nothing intrinsically to distinguish the relationship between a doctor and his patient from that of any other professional and his client. Moreover, there are things that a doctor is allowed by law to do, which others are not; and this privilege must be the object of proper regulation and scrutiny. And if some of the things that a doctor may do to another involve conduct that society takes very seriously—for example, touching, cutting, and restraining—then clearly the regulation and scrutiny must take the form of law.

It is one thing to say that the law is involved. Unfortunately, it is quite another to say precisely what the law requires. The reasons for this are not hard to understand. For example, new procedures and new technology have posed new problems for which the law, looking backwards for guidance as it inevitably does, has no immediate answers. Also, there has been a growing tendency in the past few years for issues to be tested in the courts, either because of a lack of confidence in other less formal methods of resolution, or because of a desire to clarify the respective rights and duties of the parties involved. Such litigation does not always serve to clarify the law. Frequently the resolution of an issue before the courts serves rather to bring into sharper focus the unsolved legal questions which remain; indeed, it may itself prompt such questions. And, of course, such a legal minefield is a heaven-sent opportunity for commentators and academics confidently to map the ways out (all different!), knowing that they will not have to leave the safety of their own rooms. If anyone is to be blown up, metaphorically speaking, it will be the doctor or the patient. It will come as no surprise to discover that doctors cannot, generally speaking, muster the same sang-froid. They have to get their hands dirty in their day-to-day practice, and, if there is to be law, it should, they protest, at least give them clear guidance as to what is permissible.

The plea seems entirely just. But, sadly, there are relatively few ways within the English system of making the law clear. Parliament appears to be unwilling to provide any leadership in clarifying medical-legal issues, important though they are. The only other lawmakers are the courts, and they depend on having a case brought before them, a case, moreover, the facts of which are such as to allow the laying down of rules of more general applicability. The fundamental drawback to relying on the courts, apart from the inter-stitial nature of the process (*ad hoc* and random, filling in gaps as they are encountered), is its unfairness. Ordinarily it involves suing a doctor or putting one in the dock so as to test the lawfulness of what he has done. It cannot be right that society's method of developing its medical law should be at the expense of some doctor, who up till then may well have thought — and indeed have been assured — that he was acting lawfully.

There is one other role that the courts could play, that of making declaratory judgments. A declaratory judgment is one in which a court is invited to say what the law would be if someone decided to embark on a particular course of conduct. It is a device commonly employed in the United States, where, for example, courts have been asked to rule on whether it would be lawful for a doctor, under certain specified circumstances, to discontinue certain forms of life-sustaining treatment. The attraction of this procedure notwith-standing, English courts have been slow to adopt it, being reluctant to solve hypothetical disputes, as opposed to real ones.

What has been true of lawmakers has been true equally of law-reformers. The Law Commission has studiously avoided all dealings with medical law. The various Royal Colleges have taken their professional preference for self-regulation to the point where they have often tended to oppose any proposed reform of the law, even where its aim is clarification for the benefit of their members. All in all, it is a rather sorry state of affairs, a vacuum in legal leadership. The contrast with Australia and Canada, with their energetic and helpful Law Reform Commissions, and with the United States and its President's Commission (now admittedly defunct) is a depressing one.

There is no alternative, therefore, but for me to try to take to heart my own strictures against academics, and to try to offer an analysis of what, in my view, the law currently provides in the way of guidance on the issue of prescription of contraceptive pills to 15-year-old girls.

[When I first wrote this essay, in September 1984, all that we had to go on was the decision of Woolf J. in *Gillick*. Since then, the case has been heard and decided by both the Court of Appeal and the House of Lords. What I intend to do, therefore, is to repeat, in a somewhat amended and abbreviated form, what I had to say on Woolf J.'s judgment and on the decision of the Court of Appeal, which I added as a postscript, asking you to bear in mind that my comments were made before the House of Lords' decision. I shall then offer a further postscript with some observations on the House of Lords' decision and on subsequent developments.]

It would be comforting if the law reflected what I have argued are good medical ethics. As will become clear, however, things may not be quite that simple. I take as a point of reference throughout my analysis the judgment of Woolf J. in *Gillick*. Mrs Gillick brought an action against the local Area Health Authority. She sought a declaration from the court that a Health Service Notice issued by the DHSS in December 1980[6] had no authority in law. The Notice in question outlined arrangements for the organization and development of NHS family-planning services. It was accompanied by a Memorandum of guidance which, in its revised version, suggested that a doctor was entitled, albeit only in exceptional circumstances, to prescribe contraceptives to girls under 16 without consulting their parents.

There were what Woolf J. called 'two principal limbs'[7] to Mrs Gillick's case. The first was that the Notice and accompanying Memorandum advises doctors, in effect, to commit a crime, as being accessories to unlawful sexual intercourse with a girl under 16, contrary to section 6 of the Sexual Offences Act 1956. Notice that the offender under section 6 is the male partner. The section is intended to protect young girls, who are considered to be the victims of the offence, and cannot themselves be held guilty of any offence. The doctor, therefore, would have to be the accessory of the male partner.

The second limb of the case was that, in authorizing doctors to give advice and treatment to girls under 16 years of age, without their parents' consent, the guidance, if it did not advocate a criminal offence, was nevertheless inconsistent with the rights of parents over their children. For our purposes, this can be reduced to the proposition that a girl under 16 may not in law give a valid consent to treatment (save, perhaps, in certain cases of emergency).

Consent to treatment

This second argument is the more easily countered, and I shall therefore deal with it first. Woolf J. found it 'most surprising that there is no previous authority of the courts of this country whether a child under 16 can consent

---

[6] HN (80) 46.   [7] *Supra* n. 5, 370.

to medical treatment'. His conclusion, however, was in line with the analysis I offered earlier, thereby suggesting that on this issue ethics and law coincide. He declared:

The fact that a child is under the age of 16 does not mean automatically that she cannot give consent to any treatment. Whether or not a child is capable of giving the necessary consent will depend on the child's maturity and understanding and the nature of the consent which is required. The child must be capable of making a reasonable assessment of the advantages and disadvantages of the treatment proposed, so the consent if given can be properly and fairly described as a true consent.[8]

Woolf J. referred to the fact that the Health Service Notice specifically states that it 'would be most unusual to provide advice about or methods of contraception without parental consent'. This indeed is a salient feature of the Notice, that it says this should be done only in exceptional circumstances. Woolf J. went on to say, however, that 'in the exceptional case there remains a discretion for the clinical judgement of the doctor whether or not to prescribe contraception.'[9] The supposed parental right to be involved in the treatment and care of a child under 16, regardless of that child's level of maturity, was, therefore, rejected by the court. All that the court was prepared to concede was that the doctor should try to persuade the child to involve her parents, and that the capacity (or, in legal terms, the competence) of the child varied with her understanding and maturity and the seriousness of the procedure involved. Thus Woolf J. was prepared to suggest that 'it is unlikely that a child under the age of 16 will ever be regarded by the courts as being capable of giving consent to sterilisation.'[10]

One final point ought to be made. Once the child is over 16, then, in law at least, she is prima facie competent to give consent, by virtue of section 8(1) of the Family Law Reform Act 1969. The doctor, of course, is still ethically and legally obliged to ensure that the 16-year-old before him is *actually* capable of making her own decisions.

Accessory to crime

I turn now to the other legal issue, the question of whether the doctor, in prescribing the contraceptive pills, is an accessory to a crime. If he were to be so judged, all the previous analysis would be irrelevant. It would be of no consequence that the girl was capable and competent to consent and that the doctor could rely on her consent without reference to her parents. Much, therefore, hangs on the answer we arrive at. If Mrs Gillick were successful in this argument, she would achieve her objective, albeit by what, from her point of view, would be a less satisfactory route, since it would not rest on

---

[8] Ibid. 373.   [9] Ibid. 375.   [10] Ibid. 374.

parental rights. Indeed, if the courts were to find that the doctor would be guilty of a crime, the question of parental consent would be irrelevant. For, if it were a crime, the fact that the parents had consented to their daughter's being treated would be neither here nor there, since they may not waive the operation of the criminal law. This rather obvious point seems to have been lost on Mrs Gillick's legal advisers, since the form of declaratory relief they sought included both the proposition that no child under 16 should be treated without parental consent, and the somewhat contradictory proposition that, if the doctor were to treat any girl under 16, he would be guilty as an accessory.

In law, a person is liable as an accessory if he aids, abets, counsels, or procures the commission of a crime. On some occasions, a person may be charged with engaging in only one of these forms of behaviour; on others, he may be charged in what Williams calls 'the blunderbuss' way,[11] which includes all of them. It has sometimes been considered correct law to combine aiding with abetting and to regard these as committed by an accessory who is present at the scene of a crime, whereas counselling and procuring are combined to describe an accessory who is not present. Smith and Hogan, the leading commentators on criminal law,[12] suggest that such an approach may not always be appropriate, and that, in any event, although these words mean different things, 'all four words may be used together to charge a person. . . . So long as the evidence establishes that D's [the accused's] conduct satisfied one of the words, that is enough.'[13] Williams comments: 'Any one of the four verbs may be charged, or all four may be charged together (with the conjunctive "and") and in the same count [of the indictment]. Charging all four is the safest thing to do, because the shades of difference between them are far from clear.'[14]

I propose, therefore, to take each of these words in turn, and consider whether the doctor's prescription of contraceptives falls within the meaning of any of them. If it does, then he will be guilty of a crime. In seeking to identify the meaning of these words, it must be remembered that they are legal terms. This means that, for the most part, they carry their ordinary meaning, but that there is also some accretion of technical usage, since they are employed in the context of a system which has its own rules. I might add that I will confine myself to the legal analysis necessary to solve the problems before us. There are, not surprisingly, a host of subsidiary issues which are tempting to the analyst, but I will endeavour to resist the temptation to become embroiled with them.

---

[11] G. Williams, *Textbook of Criminal Law*, 2nd edn. (Stevens, 1983), p. 338.
[12] J. C. Smith and B. Hogan, *Criminal Law*, 4th edn. (Butterworths, 1978).
[13] Ibid. 114.
[14] *Supra* n. 11, 331.

I begin with the word 'procure'. According to Lord Widgery CJ,[15] 'to procure means to produce by endeavour'. What this means is that there must be 'a causal link between what you do and the commission of the offence'.[16] 'Procure' does not, however, connote any agreement or consensus between the parties. The *Attorney General's Reference* case provides an example in which a man who admitted having 'laced' his friend's drinks without the friend's knowledge was found guilty of procuring his friend's offence of driving with an excess of alcohol in his blood.

Next, there are the words 'abet' and 'counsel'. I take these together, since they have a common core of meaning. This lies in the fact that a person is guilty if he encourages another to commit a crime or incites him or instigates the crime. There must, in other words, be a consensus between the abettor or counsellor and the perpetrator of the crime. There need not, however, be any causative link between the encouragement and the crime. The encouragement must have been operative on the mind of the offender. But it does not have to be the reason why the crime was committed; it may well be that the offender would have committed it anyway.

Finally, there is the word 'aid'. This has its natural meaning of giving help or support, or assisting. Lord Simon in *Lynch* v. *D.P.P. for Northern Ireland*[17] identified the *actus reus* of aiding as 'the supplying of an instrument for a crime or anything essential for its commission'.[18] As will become clear, these words are very important. The *mens rea* of aiding was identified by Devlin J. in *National Coal Board* v. *Gamble*[19] as being the 'intention to aid as well as knowledge of the circumstances'[20]—that is, the circumstances which amount to the crime. Devlin's view was cited with approval by Lord Simon in the *Lynch* case.

A number of propositions can be derived from this definition. The first is that motive must be distinguished from intention. To establish liability as an aider, one need not show that the accused desired the end result. Second, there is no need to show encouragement by the aider or any consensus between him and the perpetrator of the crime. Third, the definition establishes that it is not necessary to show that the aider, by his assistance, caused the perpetrator to commit the crime. Indeed, the aider could be guilty even if the perpetrator would have committed the crime in any event. Finally, it may be of help to point out that cases in which someone has been found guilty of aiding have usually involved his having helped in such matters as how to commit the crime—for example, by supplying a plan of a bank—or what to do it with—for example, by providing the means of breaking into a safe—or how to commit the crime more easily—for example, by supplying the

---

[15] *Attorney General's Reference (No. 1 of 1975)* [1975] 2 All ER 684.
[16] Ibid. 686. [17] [1975] AC 653. [18] Ibid. 698.
[19] [1959] 1 QB 11. [20] Ibid. 20.

combination of the safe — or more safely — by keeping a look out — or finally, how to get away — by driving the get-away car.

It is clear from this analysis of what counts as an accessory that the doctor *could* be guilty as an accessory. If he prescribes the contraceptive pills with the intention of encouraging the girl to have sexual intercourse, then he will obviously be guilty as an abettor or counsellor. This will be so whether he sees the girl alone or sees her with her male partner. And if the doctor does see both of them, he could also be guilty of the crime of conspiracy, and possibly of incitement. To be guilty of conspiracy, the doctor must have acted 'in pursuance of a criminal purpose held in common'[21] between him and the male partner. He cannot be guilty of conspiracy if he sees only the girl, since he cannot, by section 2(2) of the Criminal Law Act 1977, conspire with her, as she is the intended victim of the crime. To be guilty of incitement, the doctor must not only intend that the crime be committed, but also use some persuasion or pressure in an effort to bring it about.

It will presumably be very rare, however, for a doctor to encourage a young girl to engage in sexual intercourse. It will be even rarer for him to incite or conspire with her male partner to do so. To say that a doctor may be guilty of a crime as an accessory by abetting or counselling is to be analytically accurate, but somewhat other-worldly. Ordinarily a doctor will not encourage sexual intercourse. Indeed, he will probably seek to discourage it in one so young.

What is quite certain is that the doctor will not be guilty of abetting or counselling if he follows the spirit of the Memorandum of Guidance issued with the Health Service Notice, which was the object of Mrs Gillick's displeasure. For he will, in that case, have gone through a process of discussion with the girl, and will have assessed the situation and explained to her the unwisdom of sexual intercourse at her age. Then, and only then, will he have reached the conclusion that she is one of the 'exceptional cases' envisaged in the Notice, where professional counselling and the prescription of contraceptive pills may be called for, a conclusion that the doctor is likely to have arrived at with regret. In such circumstances, it cannot be argued that the doctor is guilty of encouraging, that is, abetting or counselling.

Equally, given the established meaning of 'procuring', it is hard to see how the doctor can ever be guilty, as an accessory, of procuring unlawful sexual intercourse. He cannot be said to have produced the intercourse by his endeavour. For his prescription of the contraceptive pills is not the cause, the *sine qua non*, of the unlawful intercourse. The male partner can have intercourse with the girl regardless of whether she has been to her doctor or not. Moreover, a charge of procuring would fail on proof that the couple planned to have intercourse in any event, with or without contraceptives.

---

[21] *R. v. Meyrick* (1929) 21 Cr. App. Rep. 94, 102.

Even if it could be shown that the girl told the doctor that she would not have intercourse if he did not prescribe contraceptives, this would still not be procuring. It might, however, be encouraging, because, in such circumstances, whatever the doctor may have said, it could be argued that, by the very act of prescribing contraceptives, he was encouraging the girl to have intercourse, and was therefore an accessory. Encouraging, however, requires more than the mere provision of assistance or advice. There must also be an *intention to encourage*, and it may be that the doctor could still escape liability on this ground.

The conclusion, therefore, is that, setting aside the obviously very rare case in which a doctor encourages a girl or a couple to engage in unlawful sexual intercourse, he does not, by prescribing contraceptive pills, abet, counsel, or procure an offence.

The doctor is thus free to prescribe unless it can be shown that he *aids* in the commission of the offence of unlawful sexual intercourse. The exasperated non-lawyer, having seen the other words defined away, may insist that of course the doctor was guilty of aiding: the other words may have technical meanings, but surely everyone would accept that the doctor lent assistance to the male partner. The doctor knows why the girl wants the pill, and that, if he prescribes, the chances are that she will have sexual intercourse. Knowing this, as he must, whether he tries to encourage or discourage the girl is irrelevant. His prescription serves as a green light which furthers intercourse, removing as it does whatever inhibitions the girl or her male partner may have had as a result of their fear of impregnation. Surely, therefore, the doctor must be guilty of aiding and, as such, be an accessory.

You may recall my saying earlier that words such as 'aid' should, as far as possible, carry their ordinary meaning. But you may also recall my pointing out that words are subject to interpretation by the courts, and that, within the legal system, each interpretation serves as a precedent. It is part of the tradition of the legal system that precedents are followed, or are at least treated with great respect, as carrying authority. An obvious reason for this is the certainty and predictability thereby engendered. Citizens are thus enabled to know where they stand; they can order their lives confident that they understand what the rules mean. There may be the occasional novel interpretation and new precedent, but, by and large, certainty is cultivated. The very fact, however, that the law uses words as its tools means that there is a certain inherent uncertainty — or flexibility, at least — in meaning. In one way this is a good thing. For it allows the law to develop and change in response to new, or newly perceived, needs. In criminal law, however, by contrast, say, with commercial law, certainty is regarded as the more important goal, even if secured at the cost of inflexibility. Reasons for this are not hard to find. The most obvious one, perhaps, is the fact that liberty is at stake. Every citizen, one might say, is entitled to know the proper limits of permissible conduct *before* he acts, if the consequence of overstepping them may be loss of liberty.

With this in mind, it is for you to judge, in the light of the considerations I am about to raise, whether it would be desirable to subsume the doctor's conduct under the word 'aid'. Let me begin by saying that the ordinary legal meaning of the word would, in my view, at present not be applicable to the doctor's prescription of contraceptive pills. He would not be an accessory, since the prescription does not amount to 'the supplying of an instrument for a crime or anything essential for its commission'.[22]

If you wish to see the doctor regarded as guilty, in law, as an accessory, then I would urge you to reflect on the consequences of defining 'aiding' in the way necessary to achieve this. You could well be embarrassed by the precedent it would set. Other conduct, which you would not wish to categorize as criminal, might turn out to be indistinguishable in this respect from the doctor's conduct, and might therefore leave the persons involved open to prosecution. In the past, as I have said, aiding has been confined to such matters as how to do a crime, what to do it with, how to do it more safely or easily, and how to get away. And when I say 'more safely', actual cases have been concerned with helping the perpetrator(s) avoid detection. The doctor's conduct fits none of these categories. Before deciding to extend the meaning of 'aid' so as to make him guilty as an accessory, consider the following examples.

A college tutor is visited by one of his students, who says that he is one of a group of students who periodically climb spires in the university to put up flags in support of rag week. Inevitably, in the course of the climb, the stonework of some of the spires is slightly chipped, and sometimes lightning-conductors are damaged. (This would amount to criminal damage, under the Criminal Damage Act 1971.) The tutor tells the student that it is an extremely silly thing to do, and advises him not to do it (thus not encouraging the student). 'But', the tutor goes on, 'if you insist on climbing spires, for Heaven's sake wear this crash helmet.'

Second, suppose that a college tutor is told by one of his rugby-playing students that he intends to settle off the field an old score, arising out of an incident on the field when he was fouled by an opposing player. Again, the tutor points out the folly of such behaviour and the demeaning nature of brawling. But the student insists that he will have his fight. The tutor then says, 'I think you are a damned fool, but it might help if you wear these' and hands him some shin-guards.

There are, of course, many other examples one could cite. I have chosen these two because a tutor has some sort of special responsibility for a student and is thus in a position somewhat analogous to that of a doctor. The

[22] *Supra* n. 17, 698.

examples both have to do with mitigating any harm which may come to the student if he insists on doing what he says he is going to do in a context in which the tutor may have some duty to help. They do not involve supplying an instrument for a crime or anything essential for its commission.

It can be argued that the doctor's conduct is very similar. He provides the contraceptive pills after urging a different course of action, out of a sense of a duty to help. The pills are not an instrument for the crime of unlawful sexual intercourse; nor are they essential for its commission. If, despite that, you find the doctor guilty as an accessory, you will have to find the tutors in our two examples guilty also, and many other people in similar circumstances. It is doubtful if anyone, even Mrs Gillick, would really wish criminal liability to extend that far.

Woolf J.'s decision in Gillick

Let me now turn to Woolf J.'s judgment in *Gillick*.[23] Woolf J. made it clear that there *were* circumstances in which a doctor could be guilty as an accessory if he encouraged the girl or the couple, but regarded such occasions as likely to be very rare. 'I accept', he stated, 'that a doctor who is misguided enough to provide a girl who is under the age of 16, or a man, with advice and assistance with regard to contraceptive measures with the intention thereby of encouraging them to have sexual intercourse is an accessory. . . . However, this, I assume, will not usually be the attitude of the doctor.'[24] He agreed with counsel for the DHSS, however, that he could grant the declaration sought by Mrs Gillick only if compliance with the Health Service Notice would *always* constitute a crime. In his judgment, by contrast, the doctor would not commit a crime if he complied with the terms of the Notice and prescribed contraceptive pills only in exceptional cases.

Woolf J. offered three reasons for his judgment. The first is the one that I set out, albeit in a different form, above. Woolf J. decided that the contraceptive pills do not directly assist in the crime of unlawful sexual intercourse. 'The analogy of providing the motor car for a burglary or providing poison to the murderer . . . are not true comparisons.' He admitted that the provision of the pills could 'increase the likelihood of a crime being committed'; but this, he decided, did not constitute aiding; nor did it amount to encouraging, since encouraging has a subjective, rather than objective, meaning (requiring as it does the appropriate intention). Woolf J. concluded on this point that the prescription of the pill was 'not so much "the instrument for the crime or anything essential to its commission" but a palliative against the consequences of the crime'.[25]

[23] See *supra* n. 5.   [24] *Supra* n. 5, 371.   [25] Ibid. 372.

The second reason offered by Woolf J. was that the girl commits no crime, so that for the doctor to be guilty as an accessory, he would have to act through her as an innocent agent. This is not, given the present state of legal authorities, an insurmountable difficulty. Woolf J. was concerned first with the case in which the doctor saw the girl alone, and it was alleged that he encouraged her to engage in unlawful sexual intercourse. Since she is the victim of the crime, Woolf J. seems to have taken the view that it is the male partner who would have to be encouraged in order for there to be a crime. Even if this is so, there are cases—for example, *R. v. Cogan and Leak*,[26] in which it has been held that counselling an *actus reus* through an innocent agent can suffice for liability as an accessory. Alternatively, if it were alleged that the doctor aided the commission of the crime, the same authorities suggest that a person may be guilty as an accessory by assisting in the commission of the crime through an innocent agent. Making a child deliver a jemmy to a burglar-friend is an obvious example. If, then, the doctor could otherwise be guilty as an accessory, either by encouraging or aiding, the innocent agency argument with respect, probably would not save him.

The third ground for Woolf J.'s decision is as follows:

There will be situations where long-term contraceptive measures are taken to protect girls who, sadly, will strike up promiscuous relationships whatever the supervision of those who are responsible for their well-being. . . . In such a situation the doctor will prescribe the measures to be taken purely as a safeguard against the risk that at some time in the future the girl will form a casual relationship with a man when sexual intercourse will take place. In order to be an accessory, you normally have to know the material circumstances. In such a situation the doctor would know no more than that there was a risk of sexual intercourse taking place at an unidentified place with an unidentified man on an unidentified date, *hardly the state of knowledge which is normally associated with an accessory before the fact.*[27]

The difficulty with this part of the decision is that it does not seem to accord with the view of the law taken by previous authorities or with the view set out by Woolf J. himself three months previously in his judgment in *Attorney General v. Able*.[28] Smith and Hogan summarize the law, which is admittedly complex, as follows, relying on the case of *R. v. Bainbridge*.[29] 'It seems clear that if he [the alleged accessory] knows the type of crime which is contemplated, that would be enough, even if he did not know the person or thing which was to be the subject of it or time, place or other circumstances in which the crime was to be carried out.'[30] In the case of *Able*, Woolf J. had to consider whether supplying a booklet entitled 'A Guide to Self-Deliverance' could constitute a crime, as aiding, abetting, counselling, or procuring the suicide of another, contrary to section 2(1) of the Suicide Act 1961. Turning

---

[26] [1976] 2 QB 217.   [27] *Supra* n. 5, 372; my emphasis.   [28] [1984] 1 All ER 277.
[29] [1960] 1 QB 129.   [30] *Supra* n. 12, 124.

to the question of knowledge of the material circumstances, Woolf J. stated: 'They would not know precisely when, where or by what means the suicide was to be effected, if it took place, *but this does not mean that they cannot be shown to be accessories.*'[31] All that was needed was knowledge of the type of crime, Woolf J. concluded, citing *R. v. Bainbridge.*[32]

Thus, two of the three grounds on which Woolf J. bases his decision seem, with all due respect, to be less than convincing. The first ground, the interpretation of the word 'aid', provides the only really sound basis for his judgment that a declaration, in the form required by Mrs Gillick, should not be granted.

To some, this may seem like a rather unsatisfactory conclusion. For those who support the decision, it may seem a fragile basis for the doctor's planning of his future conduct, depending as it does on the interpretation of one word. The opponents of the decision will also feel dissatisfied, having been thwarted, in their eyes, by one word, when everyone knows that words can be put to a number of different uses. In the concluding part of this analysis, I will therefore offer a way out of the legal problem of the possible criminal liability of the doctor which does not rely on this approach.

An alternative legal analysis

I will state my conclusion at the outset. A doctor is never committing an offence when he is acting as a reasonable doctor. What the reasonable doctor should do, in the sphere of medical ethics, is for all of us to discuss and have our say in determining. Ultimately, it should be set out as the product of a thoughtful and appropriately representative procedure. An example of such a procedure, or at least something that approximates it, is the publication of the Health Service Notice and accompanying Memorandum. It is part of the democratic process, in that it can be challenged and responsible ministers can be called to account for it. It has been drafted only after consultation with the range of groups and individuals concerned with such matters. Of course, it is not ideal, in that civil servants within any ministry tend to be secretive about whose advice they seek, and tend to take power to themselves and thus become unrepresentative and unresponsive, to the extent that this is allowed (a phenomenon that will be familiar to devotees of 'Yes Minister'). That said, I would suggest that the publication of Codes of Practice, or Guidelines, is a practice much to be encouraged. In a perfect world, these would be produced by a body adequately representative of the moral and social views of the community. In the interim, a departmental circular open to public scrutiny and challenge is a workable alternative.

Once such a Health Service Notice or Code of Practice or Memorandum is published, those to whom it is addressed, in our case doctors, are expected

---

[31] *Supra* n. 28, 285; my emphasis.   [32] *Supra* n. 29.

and entitled to observe it. To do so, the argument goes, would be to act as a reasonable doctor. The Notice would be conclusive on what it is socially and morally permissible for the doctor to do. Those who wish to change the Notice must use the political process and the market-place of ideas. Unless it contains references to law that are contentious, change should not be available through the legal process, if the proper procedures leading to the formulation of the Notice can be shown to have been observed. For the courts to be granted the power to effect change would, within our constitutional system, be an unwarranted departure from their traditional role as, at best, interstitial legislators unwilling to interfere with or challenge the exercise of properly constituted democratic power. In other words, Mrs Gillick would have to go to the newspapers and the politicians to change the Health Service Notice, and would not be able to go to the courts. The issue would be simply non-justiciable.

The legal way of stating the conclusion just offered is to say that the doctor commits no crime because he has a lawful excuse, derived from his duty to treat. But, of course, the doctor is allowed to deliver only that treatment which is authorized by law. So the argument is in danger of becoming circular. The doctor may treat. But he may treat only if entitled to treat. There is still a need to break out of this circularity and decide whether the doctor's conduct is legally permissible or renders him an accessory.[33]

The way out is to recognize that the doctor's prescription of the pill does fall within the concept of treatment, assuming that there is no intentional encouragement of sexual intercourse. I have suggested already that, as regards the social and moral aspects of treatment, as opposed to the medical-technical, it is for society to mark out the bounds. The basis on which the prescription of contraceptive pills may be justified is as follows. Good public policy requires doctors to treat patients for perceived and well-recognized health needs. We are not talking here of any old request from a young girl. What we are considering is a request for contraceptive pills from a girl capable of acting autonomously. One recognized health need relates to the consequences to a girl's health of unprotected sexual intercourse. This health need, and health risk, is an acknowledged fact of life. The doctor, then, is under a duty to treat the girl for this health need by, *inter alia*, prescribing contraceptive pills. It may be that, if he does so, a few girls will be led to engage in sexual intercourse, or to do so more often, when otherwise they would not. But this is simply the inevitable price to be paid for the much greater benefit of maintaining the health of young girls, through a reduction (or at least no increase) in the number of abortions and unwanted pregnancies, and a corresponding reduction in the accompanying ill health and social cost.

---

[33] Williams captures the problem with two propositons which are opposing and each of which is circular. 'The law compels the performance of this duty; therefore doing it cannot be a crime. To do this would be a crime; therefore doing it cannot be a legal duty.' *Supra* n. 11, 344.

This analysis allows us to solve a problem I posed at the outset, about whether the doctor was entitled to refuse to prescribe the pills or impose unacceptable conditions. If it is accepted that the doctor has a duty to treat, he should be slow to refuse to do so. The duty is one imposed and approved of by society. If there is a genuine health risk to the girl, the duty to treat must apply here also. This would mean that the doctor who turned the girl away could well be guilty of neglect, should untoward consequences ensue.

Granted, then, that the doctor has this legal duty, and assuming that treatment is understood in the way I have suggested, it will follow that he will not be guilty of any crime. He will be behaving as a reasonable doctor, and this for two reasons: first, the reasonable doctor will be the doctor whose sole concern is for the legitimate health needs of, and risks to, his patient; second, the Health Service Notice and Memorandum set out what a reasonable doctor should do, and they accord with what I have suggested concerning the doctor's duty to avoid health risks. The doctor who follows the Notice, therefore, would not be guilty of a crime.

Some authority for the approach I have advocated can be found in Woolf J.'s judgment, even though he does not himself adopt it. He speaks of the case in which the doctor may prescribe contraceptive pills to a girl under 16 as that in which, 'despite the fact he was firmly against unlawful sexual intercourse taking place . . . [the doctor] felt nevertheless *that he had to prescribe the contraceptives* [as being] *in the best interests of the girl* in protecting her from an unwanted pregnancy and the risk of a sexually transmitted disease'.[34]

Williams also lends authority to my approach when he argues that 'if a person acts in pursuance of a legal duty (or what would be one but for the law of complicity), . . . he should not be accounted an accomplice.'[35]

The conclusion I arrive at is the same as that reached by Woolf J. The method chosen is very different, however, and in my view is to be preferred. It allows for a legal analysis of the doctor's conduct based on the central legal and ethical concept of duty, rather than on the meaning of the 'four traditional verbs'.[36] It allows one to conclude that the doctor should, in matters of moral and social conduct, be guided by documents emanating from properly accountable bodies; and that if he does so, he will, quite properly, be insulated from legal liability.

POSTSCRIPT (FEBRUARY 1985): ENTER THE COURT OF APPEAL

I said earlier that it would be nice if the law coincided with what I have proposed as good medical ethics. I then took comfort from the fact (as it

---

[34] *Supra* n. 5, 371; my emphasis.   [35] *Supra* n. 11, 346.   [36] Ibid. 334.

seemed to me) that it does. The confidence with which I was then able to state the law has, however, received a cruel blow. Mrs Gillick appealed against Woolf J.'s decision. After a hearing of five days, the Court of Appeal unanimously allowed her appeal (on 20 December 1984). Woolf J. was wrong, the court decided. The law relating to consent and the rights of parents was not as he stated it.

Not surprisingly, there was much commotion. The Press and television were full of stories praising the decision as reasserting important moral principles or heralding the doom of the unwanted pregnancies and venereal disease which would follow. Many doctors, particularly those involved in family-planning medicine, were dumbstruck and anxiously sought advice on the precise import of the court's decision.

The dust has not yet settled. Nor will it for a while. The DHSS has decided to appeal to the House of Lords for a final and definitive statement of law.

Without attempting to predict what the House of Lords will decide — this is one occasion when it would be wiser to hold back with the angels! — it may be helpful to examine analytically the Court of Appeal's judgment. (By the Court of Appeal's judgment, I mean the judgment of Parker LJ, which was the leading judgment).

Clearly, this is not the place for a detailed exegesis. All I shall attempt is the briefest outline. It is important, however, to look critically at the reasons offered by the Court for disagreeing with Woolf J. and for reaching a decision which few, if any, commentators thought open to them.

The decision

Put baldly, the Court of Appeal opted for an approach to the issue of prescribing contraceptives to young girls which was couched in the language of parental rights. Parents have rights as regards their children, rights which last at least until a child reaches the age of 16. Others may not meddle with these rights. Except in an emergency, only a court can come between a parent and a child. In particular, a parent has a right to be told of any request a child may make for treatment by a doctor, so as to be able to give or withhold consent. Without such authorization, the doctor is a mere meddler, interfering with the legitimate rights of parents, albeit for the best of motives. If he believes that a girl needs care and that the parents are unjustifiably standing in the way, or would do so if asked, his only recourse is to petition the court. The court can then enquire into the welfare of the child and make whatever decision seems best, which may mean overriding the parents' wishes. The girl cannot give valid consent on her own behalf. The doctor who treats her without her parents' consent is therefore not only violating her parents' rights; he is actually assaulting her.

There is obviously a lot to chew on here. What I shall do is divide the argument into its separate components. In so doing, I shall ignore various points concerning administrative and public law, which need not detain us.

Ethical analysis

The Court of Appeal was, of course, at pains to make clear that its concern was exclusively with the law, and not with moral or social questions. It could not, however, totally avoid taking a view, implicitly or, at times, explicitly, on the rights and wrongs of the issue. For when the law is open (just about) to differing interpretations, the one you choose is the one which best accords with your sense of what is morally right. The court was clearly persuaded that the interests of family stability, and of the wishes of parents in particular, should prevail over any arguments about a girl's autonomy. That the parents may be perverse or, as evidenced by the child's refusal to involve them, alienated from their child is no reason for denying them their legitimate moral claims as the child's parents. The court's model of the parent–child relationship—the child remaining at home until the age of 16, firmly under the parents' influence and control—clearly bears little relation to the realities of modern life in many households. But the court, if it was aware of this fact, was quite undeterred by it. Its position appears to have been this: where there is a conflict between what *ought* to be the case and what, as a matter of fact, *is* the case, then it is the facts that must be changed. Reality must be brought into line with what is right. The point that children might have rights too was scarcely even raised, much less conceded. Parents (such was the court's view) are normally the best arbiters of the interests both of their family and of their children.

This, then, was the ethical base from which the court proceeded to state the law. It is an approach which is enjoying a certain vogue at present, representing as it does a reaction against what some see as an over-permissive liberalism.

The capacity of the girl

The legal test of capacity propounded earlier and reflected in Woolf J.'s judgment was rejected by the court. They decided that a child under 16 (and possibly until she reaches majority at 18) is under the control of her parents. Consequently, she cannot validly consent to medical treatment; nor can a doctor treat her without parental authority, since otherwise parental rights (on which, more later) are violated.

Why, you may ask, did the court take 16 to be the crucial age? Well, as regards medical treatment section 8(1) of the Family Law Reform Act 1969 provides that someone over 16 may give valid consent. (One has the strong impression that, had that not been the case, parental control would have been said by the court to last until 18.) If the girl over 16 *can* consent, then, the court decided, the girl under 16 cannot. They purported to derive this from section 8(3) of the same Act, which provides that 'Nothing in this section shall be construed as making ineffective any consent which would have been effective if this section had not been enacted.' This somewhat Delphic utterance had always been assumed to preserve the power at common law of the person under 16 to give valid consent. The court, however, tended to the opposite view, that it preserved the common-law power of parents to consent on behalf of their children, even if the child were over 16, and to consent on a child's behalf if she were under 16.

The enquiry then turns to the common-law position apart from statute. As I have suggested, virtually every commentator, including me, had no doubt that at common law a person had the capacity to consent, if able to understand what was being consented to. The court decided otherwise. The common-law rule, it said, was that a child could not give valid consent until she had reached the 'age of discretion', which in the case of a girl was 16. In the case of a boy, they said, it was 14, apparently unembarrassed by the discriminatory nature of such a rule and the swipe it takes at section 29 of the Sex Discrimination Act 1975, which forbids discrimination between sexes in the provision of, *inter alia*, goods and services (including, one might argue, family-planning services).

A number of observations are in order. First, an analysis of the judgment suggests that it might have either of two implications. Contraceptive treatment involves contact and conversation between doctor and girl of such a nature that it calls for special rules, different from all the normal rules governing medical treatment and other forms of touching consented to by a girl. Its nature is such that a girl under 16 is intrinsically incapable of validly consenting to it, whatever her capacities in other matters. This proposition has only to be stated to be shown to be completely untenable, both in fact and in law. There is nothing in the nature of contraception which makes it different in principle from, for example, vaccination or treatment for vaginal infections or varicose veins, save for the fact that reproductive functions are involved. But this is also true of hormone therapy or the treatment of dysmenorrhea. The judgement cannot, therefore, sensibly be interpreted as making a special case of contraceptive treatment.

Alternatively, the implication goes much further. I have suggested that there is no difference in principle between contraceptive treatment and other medical treatment. Nor can there be a distinction between medical treatment and other circumstances in which a girl might be touched with her apparent consent, as in the case of a handshake, a kiss or embrace, or in a game of netball. If this is right—and it must be in principle—and assuming that the premiss is accepted, then if a girl under 16 cannot in law consent to contraceptive treatment, it must follow that she cannot in law give valid consent to *any* touching. The kiss and cuddle, the handshake, and so on would equally be unlawful, as being contrary to parental rights, unless consented to by the parent, despite, or regardless of, the girl's consent in fact.

Such a conclusion, however, is contrary both to law and to common sense. Young girls can and do consent to have shoes fitted on them, to have their hair done, or to have cosmetics applied by a shop assistant in a department store. No one, I submit, is breaking the law if he shakes a 15-year-old girl's hand, knowing that she has been forbidden to see him. Indeed, the law specifically recognizes a young girl's progressive emergence as a person in her own right, as she gains in maturity and understanding. Thus, a girl can be held to her contract, if the contract was for something necessary, such as education, clothes, food, and, significantly, 'physic', as the old writers call it—that is, medical care. The criminal law holds a child responsible for her actions at 10; and under the law of evidence, a child may give evidence if capable of understanding the oath and its significance. Interestingly, the common law requires the enquiry about capacity to be conducted in open court, the judge making the determination after examination.

To argue, therefore, that in none of these cases is a girl of 15 able validly to consent because she is, by virtue of age alone, disabled from doing so, is to ignore great areas of the common law which say that a girl's capacity to make her own decisions (and mistakes) depends on her understanding, maturity, and intelligence, *not* her age.

Second, the age of discretion has always been a rather shadowy notion. It was rather surprising to see it appear, bursting with vitality, in the court's judgment. Even more surprising was the central importance given to it, such that the court appeared to regard it as the crucial or clinching argument. It was the age of discretion, the court said, that the law recognized as the point at which a girl could consent for herself, and that age was 16. The difficulty with this, which did not seem to trouble the court, is that, historically, the age of discretion was not 16 for a girl and 14 for a boy, but 12 for a girl[37] and 14 for a boy. Until 1929, after all, 12 was the age at which a girl could consent to marry. The age of 16 is derived from a particular statute passed in 1549 making it a crime to take girls under 16 out of the possession of their fathers. It was an anti-fortune-hunters' statute. The consent of the girl was no defence under the statute.

But this statute, which remains law in a revised form as section 20 of the Sexual Offences Act 1956 did not state that a girl could not consent to *anything* before she was 16. Indeed, if she left her father of her own free will and went off with a man, the man committed no offence, and any

---

[37] On one reading of the old authorities; but I am now persuaded that the better view is 14 for a girl.

marriage they subsequently contracted was valid, provided she was over 12. That a later statute was passed, providing that, in such circumstances, she disinherited herself, further proves her capacity to consent. So, leaving aside the lack of any real relationship in law or fact between the abduction or seduction of a girl by a man and her treatment by a doctor seeking only to protect her from health risks, the statutes and cases provide no basis for the court's conclusion regarding consent and the age of discretion.

Furthermore, in the quite recent case of *R. v. D.*,[38] Lord Brandon, in the House of Lords, specifically decided that, on a charge of kidnapping a child, the prosecution had to show that the child had not consented to go with the person charged. The capacity of the child so to consent was, Lord Brandon went on, dependent not on age, but on whether the child was of sufficient understanding and intelligence to decide for herself. No fixed age, let alone 16, got a look-in, though Lord Brandon agreed that at some point the tender age of the child would entitle the court to assume a lack of capacity. Parliament has since passed the Child Abduction Act 1984, whereby it is an offence to take a child under 16 out of the lawful control of a parent, with no mention of consent. But this only confirms that at common law the position was as stated by Lord Brandon.

A further reason for fastening on the age of 16 was the court's view that the flexible criterion advanced by Woolf J. (and assumed to be the law by the rest of us) was unworkable. First, a doctor would have to make an enquiry of a girl whom he might not know well and whose assurances might not be truthful. He might not, therefore, be in any position to judge. Parents could lose control of their children, and their children's interests could be harmed, on the assessment of some outsider. There would be no certainty in the law, with the result that parents, doctors, and society at large would not know where they stood.

The most obvious response, I suppose, is to point out that, every day, doctors have to assess the capacity of people of whatever age to make decisions, and are trusted to do so. Whether a person is mentally ill, confused, affected by pain, or grief or drugs, or is simply uncomprehending is something doctors are already expected and obliged to assess. So the young girl poses no special problem to those trained in family planning and general practice. (Compare, if you will, the assumption that the judge is quite competent when it comes to assessing a young person's capacity to take the oath!) Furthermore, a flexible criterion of capacity works in other areas of the law and in other legal systems, such as the Scottish system, which embraces it with no obvious harmful side-effects. In short, it has worked as a criterion in the past, and could presumably continue to work. It cannot, therefore, be its lack of apparent certainty that made it objectionable in the eyes of

[38] [1984] 3 WLR 186.

the court. It must, rather, have been the court's desire to assert its view of parental rights.

Parental rights

The view of the court was that a parent has the right to control a girl, even to control her *completely*, at least until she reaches 16, and perhaps until the age of majority. This, the court decided, flows from the right to custody which all parents have over their children. No one may interfere with this right except in emergencies or by order of a court. It follows that a doctor may not treat a girl under 16 without parental consent, because to do so violates parental rights. A girl may not on her own give a valid consent, as she lacks the requisite legal capacity. The parental right to control entails a lack of capacity in the child, presumably because of some assumed incapacity to know her own best interests until the clock strikes midnight on the eve of her sixteenth birthday.

The court's decision, I submit, is dubious both as a description of the law and as a description of many (if not most) parent–child relationships, for the following reasons. First, the basic objection based on parental rights is that it has always been assumed (and correctly so) that parents have duties towards their children. Whatever rights they have are instrumental only, allowing for the fulfilment of these duties, the primary one being that of bringing a child to maturity and autonomy, free from avoidable harm. If the assertion of a right to control a child's behaviour, in this case her access to a doctor, could result in harm to the girl, due to her refusal to involve her parents and the doctor's consequent refusal to treat her, this seems completely at odds with the purpose for which a parent has rights in the first place. Yet this is the necessary consequence of the court's decision. To those who argue that the court's decision strikes a blow not for parental rights, but for family stability, by requiring the girl to involve her parents if she wants the doctor to see her, the only answer is to ask them to step back into the real world. Anyone who thinks that family stability can be re-established by *forcing* a girl to talk to her parents, as a condition for receiving treatment, when her resistance to attempts by the doctor to involve them has already shown that family communications are badly damaged is living in cloud-cuckoo-land.

Second, the court placed particular emphasis on the right physically to control a child. In doing so, they chose to be guided by a couple of nineteenth-century cases and to ignore the changes in law and social attitudes since then, marked both in case-law and in statute. Lord Denning put it well in *Hewer* v. *Bryant*,[39] when he described the right to control as 'a dwindling right. . . . It starts with a right and ends with little more than advice.'

[39] [1970] 1 QB 357.

Ever since the nineteenth century, and particularly since 1925, when the Guardianship of Infants Act was passed, statute law has always been concerned to protect not parents' rights, but the best interests and welfare of the child. Furthermore, it is beyond doubt that the idea of a legal right to control must be understood against a background of reality. The law never likes to make itself look silly, by saying you have a right to do what you plainly cannot do — for example, chastise your son who happens to be a junior boxing champion. The legal right to control must be understood, therefore, as being subject to the extent to which it can be exercised in fact. Thus, as a girl grows up and away from her parents, or the parents lose interest in or neglect the girl (which is often the case as regards contraception), so the legal right to control is lost. It is lost because the duty to bring the child to maturity has either already been fulfilled or else has effectively been abandoned.

This brings us to a central objection to the decision. The court decided that the parents' right to control meant that no one — for example, a doctor — could interfere with that right without first approaching a court, which would then determine the girl's best interests. If parental duties are properly analysed, however, it can be seen that it is the parent who must seek the aid of the court in matters of control of the child. The parent does not have some presumptive right over a child until 16, such that all others must keep their distance. Instead, the parent has the duty to care for the girl, and if he feels that he cannot carry it out because, for example, the girl is turning to someone else, the parent can ultimately ask the court for help. But, significantly, a court will not necessarily side with the parent. It is bound by statute, the Guardianship of Minors Act 1971, to make the welfare of the child the paramount consideration.

A further objection to the Court of Appeal's analysis is that it overlooks the fact that others besides parents may have duties to the girl. The teacher is one example. His responsibility to the girl may involve doing that which a parent expressly disapproves of, ranging from teaching a subject in a particular way to encouraging her to take an examination to detaining her for bad behaviour. The doctor, equally, has responsibilities to a girl who is otherwise capable of consenting to treatment. To give the parental right to control precedence over the various responsibilities of others, particularly when the parent may not be exercising that right properly is to neglect the welfare of the girl and so violate the policy which has guided family law for more than half a century. To reply that the doctor can always apply to a court if he feels that a girl is in need of care is to propose a solution which in practice is no solution at all. Doctors have no time for this, far less the knowledge or appetite. Girls told that they must wait and then go to court will vote with their feet, and the back-street abortionists will rub their hands.

It is the final objection in this brief appraisal that is perhaps the most telling. The Court of Appeal introduces into the law the notion of a child as a chattel, an objoot of posserrion and control. This is hardly the posture that a court, a legal system, or a society committed to the welfare of children would ordinarily adopt. That it gives serious consideration to a parent who refuses consent to treatment which a competent young girl wants and a doctor thinks appropriate is, frankly, alarming.

The doctor's duty to treat

The idea that a doctor might have a duty to treat, quite apart from parental views, was not raised before the court. It was, however, implicitly rejected, in that the court found that a girl had no capacity to give a valid consent until 16. Since the doctor needs consent, it therefore follows that he must ask the parent, save in an emergency. Some would like to see this word 'emergency' interpreted very widely—so widely, in fact, that it would give back to doctors the discretion that the court has otherwise denied them. It could be argued quite plausibly that every time a girl consults her doctor about contraceptive treatment, it is something of an emergency, since the risks of sexual intercourse and possible pregnancy are very real. Certainly, what I have suggested as good medical ethics could justify giving 'emergency' the widest possible meaning, going far beyond the obvious case of the 'morning-after' pill, after unprotected intercourse. Aside from this, however, the court appears to give no support to the notion of a duty to treat.

The criminal law

Arguments about possible criminal liability, which were canvassed so vigorously in the High Court, were not greatly pressed or relied upon before the Court of Appeal. What did strike the court as important was what they took to be the policy reflected in the criminal law's prohibition against sexual intercourse with girls under 16. The various crimes set out in the Sexual Offences Act 1956 were, the court said, clearly intended to protect a girl from harm, and were a clear indication by Parliament that girls were to be protected even from themselves, since, although they might consent to sexual intercourse, this consent was no defence for the man. How could it be, the court asked, that a girl under 16 was deemed by Parliament to be incapable in law of consenting to sexual intercourse, and yet capable of consenting to contraceptive treatment? The criminal law statutes do exist to protect girls. But the prescription of contraceptives can be seen as entirely in keeping with this Parliamentary policy of protecting them from harm. If sexual intercourse has already taken place or is inevitable, the provision of contraceptives is the only way to protect girls from any consequent danger or health risk. To say that a girl should desist from sexual intercourse may show commendable consistency and commitment, but it ignores the well-recognized fact that sexual intercourse will take place, contraception or no.

Conclusion

All I have offered are a few brief comments on the Court of Appeal's decision. There are many other things that could be said, but I have chosen to concentrate on an analysis of the issues of principle. Clearly, there is a host of arguments that could be advanced concerning consequences, social, medical, political, and so on. Such arguments might serve to focus attention on the practical implications of our analysis; but they cannot compel any conclusion, although they might help to tip the scales if the analysis and arguments were otherwise finely balanced.

The court has clearly adopted an ethical stance different from the one I proposed, and has moulded the law accordingly. For the reasons I have indicated, I find the result unsatisfactory on analytical grounds. The case now goes to the House of Lords. Their Lordships have to choose. Clearly, much hinges on their choice; not merely contraceptive treatment and advice, but the whole question of the legal and ethical status of the relationship between parents, children, and others. By the time you read this, the choice will have been made. The House of Lords will have handed down its decision. I, meanwhile, must wait, firmly convinced that the Court of Appeal's view is wrong, and that it deserves to be rejected.

FURTHER POSTSCRIPT (SUMMER 1986):
THE HOUSE OF LORDS' DECISION

The DHSS appealed to the House of Lords. The hearing occupied two weeks of their Lordships' time in late June and early July 1985. It was October before the judgment was handed down.[40] The appeal was allowed by a majority of 3–2. Lords Fraser, Scarman, and Bridge formed the majority, with Lords Brandon and Templeman in dissent. Mrs Gillick was not granted the declaration she sought. The Court of Appeal's view was ruled wrong and was rejected.

Decisions of the House of Lords, because they represent a final view — for the time being anyway! — of the law, are traditionally fallen upon by commentators and treated to the most minute scrutiny. Obviously careful analysis of a case is important if responsible advice is to be given to those who may be affected by its conclusion. It must be remembered, however, that a case is not a tax statute, with each word to be pulled apart. Instead,

---

[40] *Gillick* v. *West Norfolk and Wisbech AHA* [1985] 3 All ER 402.

it is part of a dynamic process of law. What is decided in a particular case, what it means, therefore, can only be arrived at sensibly by looking back to see how the law previously developed and forward to how the law may continue to develop as a consequence of what their Lordships have said, and how this fits into the ever-changing mosaic of the law. Irritatingly, there are some legal commentators who see each case as existing in its own, separate world, to be analysed only in its own terms and then fitted into the known and unchanging corpus of the law. And if it will not fit, then it is probably wrong!

It is with these thoughts in mind that I begin what I fear will be a lengthy exegesis of the decision of the House of Lords. My justification for treating the decision at length is that it is not only important as a case on a controversial social issue, but that it also has implications which go beyond this issue and are relevant to medical law generally. It is perhaps proper, therefore, to both record the basis on which the legal arguments were finally settled and to identify some questions which remain.

It would, of course, be simpler if the House of Lords had spoken with one voice. But on such an important and controversial issue, each Law Lord wished to have his say. The consequence is that while Lords Fraser and Scarman decided the case more or less on the basis of the analysis that I have advanced so far, their speeches show some differences, and that Lord Bridge, who joined them in the majority, dealt with the case on a wholly different footing. Nor were the dissenting judges, Lords Brandon and Templeman, to be outdone. They agreed in the conclusion. Their reasons for doing so, however, were quite different.

Faced with such diversity, it may be helpful to take the issues previously examined and see how each of their Lordships dealt with them; also to notice any additional grounds which were relied on. It should be said at the outset that Woolf J.'s 'two principal limbs' of the case had grown into something rather larger (a body of law, a hydra, or whatever metaphor appeals to you) by the time the House of Lords were done with it.

Parents' rights

Speaking for the majority, Lords Fraser and Scarman both stated — or, better put, restated, after the distraction of the judgment of the Court of Appeal — two fundamental principles. The first is that, on a proper understanding of the law, both historically and in the context of the modern growth of legislation regulating the family, parents have duties to, rather than rights over, their children. This is not to say that parents have no rights. Rather, it is to make clear that these rights are instrumental only, so as to enable parents to carry out their duties, and must, as a consequence, always be exercised with the interests of the child, rather than the parent, in mind. As

Lord Scarman put it, 'the principle is that parental right or power of control of the person and property of his child exists primarily to enable the parent to discharge the duty of maintenance, protection and education until he reaches such an age as to be able to look after himself and make his own decisions.'[41]

The second is that the law should seek always to respond appropriately to changes in social attitudes. While this does not mean that a court should follow every fashion or whim, it does mean that a court ignores at its peril, in terms of the respect and acceptance its decisions will command, any changes in society which challenge the premisses on which the law has hitherto been based.

The conjunction of these principles led Lords Fraser and Scarman to reject the view expressed by the Court of Appeal, and to reinstate the view of Woolf J. In particular, they rejected the nineteenth-century cases on which the Court of Appeal had relied in suggesting that a parent had in law the right completely to control the activities of a child until the child reached the age of 16, or even until she ceased to be a minor at the age of 18. Lord Scarman described the case of *Agar-Ellis* as 'horrendous'.[42] Lord Fraser's language was somewhat more diplomatic, in that he described it as 'a historical curiosity'.[43] To rely on these cases was, in the view of Lords Fraser and Scarman, to fail to recognize the enormous changes which had taken place both in the family and in society. Fathers were no longer a law unto themselves. Children were the responsibility of all of us, and parents enjoyed them on trust. And, just as important, children grow up and away from their parents as they mature, and the law should recognize this. It must strike a proper balance between protecting the vulnerable and allowing the rest to take their first tentative steps as full citizens.

Consequently, it was the law as expressed in *Hewer* v. *Bryant* which was to be followed. Parental rights certainly were recognized by the law, but they were 'dwindling rights', their decline corresponding to the law's recognition of the growing entitlement of a child to manage his or her own affairs. For Lord Scarman, 'the parental right to determine whether or not their minor child below the age of 16 will have medical treatment terminates if and when the child achieves a sufficient understanding and intelligence to enable him or her to understand fully what is proposed.'[44]

Lord Templeman, in his dissent, did not share this view. While appearing to recognize the 'dwindling right' of parents to control their children in circumstances other than those involving the provision of contraceptive advice and treatment, he was firmly of the view that where contraception was concerned, parental rights of control remained until the girl reached the age of 16. A doctor who gives contraceptive advice or treatment to

[41] Ibid. 421.   [42] Ibid. 419.   [43] Ibid. 412.   [44] Ibid. 423.

a girl below the age of 16 would be behaving unlawfully. The principal justification for this position was to be found, in Lord Templeman's view, in Parliament's prohibition of sexual intercourse with a girl below the age of 16. This, to him, represented a clear statement of public policy, that girls below that age were not capable of knowing their own minds about sexual matters. As Lord Templeman put it, in typically robust language, 'There are many things which a girl under 16 needs to practise, but sex is not one of them.'[45]

Children's rights

Intrinsic in the analysis of parental rights and duties was the recognition by the House of Lords that what was really at stake was the rights of children. This can be seen most clearly in the speech of Lord Scarman, who remarks at one point: 'Nor has our law ever treated the child as other than a person with capacities and rights recognised by the law.'[46] It is also in keeping with the more general view that medical law is, at least in part, an aspect of human rights law, in that there are certain rights recognized or guaranteed as fundamental which are at stake in the practice of medicine. In this case, it is the basic right of children to be entitled or empowered to come to an enjoyment of autonomy. But this is only a particular example of the more general right to autonomy, increasingly protected by the law through the doctrine of consent, as was recognized by Lord Scarman in his speech in *Sidaway* v. *Governors of the Bethlem Royal Hospital*.[47] As John Eekelaar writes, 'Children will now have, in wider measure than ever before, that most dangerous but most precious of rights: the right to make their own mistakes.'[48]

Once it is recognized that what is at stake are the rights of a growing child, the question for the law is to identify the circumstances in which a parent should be entitled to exercise those rights on behalf of the child, and when the child may do so him- or herself. This led the House of Lords to examine the issue of capacity, to which we must now turn.

Capacity to consent

The issue before the House was, of course, the criteria to be applied in law to determine the capacity of a child below the age of 16 to consent to contraceptive treatment. (You will notice that I refer only to *treatment*, while the Memorandum of Guidance and the Law Lords talk of *advice and*

---

[45] Ibid. 432.   [46] Ibid. 420.   [47] [1985] 2 WLR 480.
[48] J. Eekelaar, 'The Emergence of Children's Rights', 6 *Oxford Journal of Legal Studies* 161 (1986).

treatment. I shall not consider the issue of advice in my analysis because, whatever view of the law is taken, it cannot, I submit, be seriously argued that the doctor merely by giving advice to a young girl behaves unlawfully, except in the circumstances specifically indicated.) Analytically, the question before us concerns the criteria for capacity. You will notice that I now draw a distinction between the criteria for capacity and the test to establish satisfaction of these criteria. I am now persuaded that there are only two criteria: status and understanding.[49] Once understanding is recognized as the correct legal criterion, the focus shifts to the identification of the relevant test required by the law to establish understanding; or, more simply put, what understanding means. I shall return to the matter of the test later.

In essence, the majority in the House of Lords agreed with Woolf J. and with the analysis offered earlier. The criterion of capacity to consent in law, they decided, is not a matter of age, but of the ability of the person to understand what is involved in any particular transaction or procedure, which in turn involves a combination of maturity, intelligence, and understanding. The age of discretion, resurrected, or exhumed, by the Court of Appeal as the correct legal criterion of capacity, was returned to the shadows or laid to rest again, for the last time, it is to be hoped.

In applying these legal principles to the specific issue at hand, Lord Scarman held that a girl below the age of 16 could give valid consent to receive contraceptive and other medical treatment. Conscious, however, of the great sensitivity of the issue, he was at pains to emphasize that the determination of a girl's competence by a doctor was a matter of great responsibility, particularly in the context of contraception. Before she could be regarded as entitled to make her own decisions and, consequently, as free of parental control, Lord Scarman made it clear that:

it is not enough that she should understand the nature of the advice which is being given: she must also have a sufficient maturity to understand what is involved. There are moral and family questions, especially her relationship with her parents; long-term problems associated with the emotional impact of pregnancy and its termination; and there are the risks to health of sexual intercourse at her age, risks which contraception may diminish but cannot eliminate.[50]

Lord Fraser expressed the criterion of capacity somewhat differently at different stages during his speech. First, he spoke of the girl being 'capable of understanding what is proposed'.[51] Later, he spoke of the necessity for the girl to have 'sufficient understanding and intelligence'.[52] Later still, however, he made it a requirement 'that the girl (although under 16 years of age) will understand his [the doctor's] advice'.[53] Lord Fraser was equally

---

[49] I am obliged to Andrew Grubb, of Fitzwilliam College, Cambridge, for this conversion.
[50] *Supra* n. 40, 424.   [51] Ibid. 409.   [52] Ibid. 410.   [53] Ibid. 413.

anxious, however, to emphasize the great care which must be taken in translating the principle of legal capacity into practice in the case of any particular young girl. To this end he laid down five requirements on which the doctor must be satisfied if he is to be entitled to act upon the girl's consent and treat her without involving others. They are:

(1) that the girl (although under 16 years of age) will understand his advice; (2) that he cannot persuade her to inform her parents or to allow him to inform the parents that she is seeking contraceptive advice; (3) that she is very likely to begin or to continue having sexual intercourse with or without contraceptive treatment; (4) that unless she receives contraceptive advice or treatment her physical or mental health or both are likely to suffer; (5) that her best interests require him to give her contraceptive advice, treatment or both without the parental consent.[54]

It is these five requirements which have come to be regarded as the principal ruling in the case, even though Lord Scarman makes no mention of them and may, as we shall see, have contradicted at least one of them. The importance they have acquired can be gauged by the fact that they form the central part of the redrafted Memorandum issued by the DHSS in the light of the case.[55]

For his part, Lord Bridge, while basing his decision on quite different grounds, expressed his agreement with the speeches of Lords Fraser and Scarman on the issue of capacity to consent.

It will come as no surprise, however, that the views of Lords Fraser and Scarman are not wholly free of difficulties. In particular, it is important to enquire whether the criterion of capacity set out is one which is relevant only to contraception or whether it applies to medical treatment in general, and indeed all other transactions. This is particularly relevant with regard to Lord Fraser's five requirements, since most, if not all, seem specifically intended to refer to consent to contraceptive treatment. I will defer any comment on this and other questions until later, however, since at this point, I am concerned only to note what was decided. For the sake of completeness, Lord Templeman's dissenting view should be mentioned. He denied that a girl below the age of 16 was, in law, capable of consenting to contraceptive advice or treatment, on the basis of public policy. He was prepared to concede, however, that in other cases of medical treatment, the criterion of capacity was 'the age and understanding of the infant'.[56]

Public policy

As has been seen, the Court of Appeal relied in part on what it took to be public policy, as reflected in the criminal law, to find in Mrs Gillick's favour.

---

[54] Ibid.   [55] Appendix HC (86) 1.   [56] *Supra* n. 40, 432.

The approach of the majority in the House of Lords was more subtle. While recognizing the capacity to consent of a girl below the age of 16, they appreciated that the lawfulness or otherwise of a doctor's conduct in prescribing the pill to the girl might not rest solely on her capacity to consent. Such consent might be a necessary, but not a sufficient, condition of lawfulness, if it could be demonstrated that public policy demanded that the consent be legally inoperative in this particular case, if not generally. The offence of unlawful sexual intercourse with a girl below the age of 16, contrary to section 6 of the Sexual Offences Act 1956, makes this very point. The girl's consent may be valid; otherwise the man would be charged with rape, as was made clear in *R. v. Howard*.[57] But Parliament has determined that girls of such an age should be protected, not least, from themselves. Thus, their consent is legally inoperative and provides no excuse for the man.

Should the same argument apply in the case of prescribing the pill? For both Lord Brandon and Lord Templeman, the answer was that it should. The majority, however, decided otherwise. As Lord Bridge put it:

On the issue of public policy, it seems to me that the policy consideration underlying the criminal sanction imposed by statute on men who have intercourse with girls under 16 is the protection of young girls from the untoward consequences of intercourse. Foremost among these must surely be the risk of pregnancy leading either to abortion or the birth of a child to an immature and irresponsible mother. In circumstances where it is apparent that the criminal sanction will not, or is unlikely to, afford the necessary protection it cannot, in my opinion, be contrary to public policy to prescribe contraception as the only effective means of avoiding a wholly undesirable pregnancy.[58]

This does not entirely dispose of the question of public policy. The recital by Lord Fraser of the five requirements which the doctor must satisfy before he may lawfully treat a young girl presents some difficulties. For a start, the statement clearly raises questions concerning the true criterion of capacity, and what, if any, legal consequences follow if the doctor ignores some or all of these points. I shall return to these questions later. What is important here is whether Lord Fraser intends to say that consent validly given is a necessary condition of lawful treatment, but that, as a matter of public policy, it is not a sufficient one, since other conditions have also to be satisfied. Three of the other conditions seem to apply only to the circumstances surrounding contraceptive treatment, and do not touch on capacity. But the fifth may be of more general application. So, it is this fifth condition which is important for us here.

On one view, Lord Fraser can be taken as saying that the girl's consent is not enough. The final arbiter of whether to treat or not is the doctor, since,

[57] [1966] 1 WLR 13.   [58] *Supra* n. 40, 428.

you will recall, the doctor must be satisfied 'that her best interests require him to give contraceptive advice, treatment or both without the parental consent'. Surely, the argument goes, if the girl is competent and exercises her autonomy, it would follow that the doctor would be entitled to, and should, rely on this without more, since she would be deemed to be a competent judge of her own interests. By stipulating that the doctor must *also* judge what is in her interests, Lord Fraser could be saying that public policy demands that the final decision be the doctor's, not the girl's.

Two possible (and mutually exclusive) answers suggest themselves. When Lord Fraser talks of the girl's 'best interests', he could be referring to *medical* interests. This would accord with the general tenor of his speech, and may be borne out by his reference in the next paragraph of the speech to their being 'nothing strange about investing them [doctors] with this further responsibility which they alone are in a position to discharge satisfactorily'.[59] Arguably, the only thing that doctors are uniquely in a position to discharge is medical expertise. Such a conclusion could equally be arrived at if the word 'therefore' were implied after the words 'best interests'. One weakness in this view, of course, is that if this is what Lord Fraser meant, quite apart from the fact that it is not what he said, it is entirely superfluous, since doctors always have to act in the best medical interests of their patients. Why, therefore, would Lord Fraser make it one of his points which the doctor in this particular context must observe?

The alternative view is the one already noted: namely, that public policy requires the doctor to exercise *his* judgment of what is in the girl's best interests. This would be a disconcerting view, in the light of Lord Fraser's apparent general acceptance that the law respects the autonomous decisions and choices of a person, provided that the person is properly competent. It would also lead to unfortunate confusion, since Lord Scarman makes no such proviso in his speech.

The importance of the point cannot be overstated. If Lord Fraser intended by these words to make the doctor the final arbiter of the girl's best interests, the case cannot be regarded as authority for the proposition that with understanding and maturity comes the capacity to make legally binding decisions, at least as regards contraceptive treatment, and perhaps as regards medical treatment in general. In fact Lord Fraser would merely have replaced the parent by the doctor. As it happens, this is how Lord Templeman saw the case in his dissenting judgment. He saw the case as a contest between parent power and doctor power, since he rejected the idea that, as regards contraception, a girl below the age of 16 will ever be capable in law of deciding for herself. But the approach for which I have argued throughout and which Woolf J. adopted involves a rejection of *both* these alternatives, in favour

---

[59] Ibid. 413.

of the right of the girl to decide for herself if competent to do so. Certainly, it is also the view adopted by Lord Scarman.

So, does Lord Fraser grant capacity to the girl with one hand and take it away with the other? If so, it would seem to make his reasoning concerning the acquisition of capacity somewhat otiose. It would also extend the power of doctors in an area which is not specifically one of medical expertise, namely, the assessment of what is in a person's best interests generally, when that person is accepted as being capable of making her own judgments. Unfortunately, it does not help to look to Lord Bridge, the third member of the majority, to resolve this question. His speech is concerned almost entirely with whether the matter should be decided by the courts at all. When it comes to the question of consent and capacity, he is content merely to 'agree with the reasons expressed by *both* of my noble and learned friends'.[60]

For what it is worth, I take the view that, on balance, Lord Fraser may indeed have intended to replace parent power with doctor power, at least as regards contraception, though probably not otherwise. I have already referred to the counter-argument that, in speaking of 'interests', he was referring only to medical interests, and that his speech should not be read as allowing or requiring doctors to second-guess their young patients, who, they have already decided, are competent to consent to treatment. Some support for this view can be gained from what Lord Fraser says a little earlier, namely, that 'there may be circumstances in which a doctor is a better judge of the *medical advice and treatment* which will conduce to a girl's welfare than her parents.'[61] But, the evidence for the other view may be stronger. Of particular significance are the following words of Lord Fraser:

There may well be other cases where the doctor feels that because the girl is under the influence of her sexual partner or some other reason there is no realistic prospect of her abstaining from intercourse. If that is right it points strongly to the desirability of the doctor being entitled in some cases, in the girl's best interest, to give her contraceptive advice and treatment if necessary without the consent or even the knowledge of her parents. The only practicable course is, in my opinion, to entrust the doctor with a discretion to act in accordance with his view of what is best in the interests of the girl who is his patient.[62]

Reference to the doctor's being 'entitled' and to the necessity 'to entrust the doctor with a discretion' suggests strongly that Lord Fraser intended to leave the last word to the doctor; and this is further borne out by his statement that 'the medical profession have in modern times come to be entrusted with very wide discretionary powers going beyond the strict limits of clinical judgement and, in my opinion, there is nothing strange about entrusting them with this further responsibility which they alone are in a position to discharge satisfactorily.'[63]

[60] Ibid. 428; my emphasis.   [61] Ibid. 412; my emphasis.   [62] Ibid. 413.   [63] Ibid.

The truth of the matter may be that Lord Fraser, unlike Lord Scarman, was directing his attention primarily to contraceptive treatment. It may be, therefore, that the real answer to the question posed is that Lord Fraser intended to say that the doctor must consider the young girl's interests generally as regards contraceptive treatment, but only 'medical' interests as regards medical treatment in general. The result, however, is most unsatisfactory. It means that on one view, and the more persuasive view at that, the two judges who spoke for the majority on this issue arrived at significantly different conclusions, though purporting to agree with each other. From my point of view, it is clear that if Lords Fraser and Scarman are in fact in disagreement, Lord Scarman's view is to be preferred as representing a more appropriate and more analytically sustainable statement of law.

Criminal law

The argument that the doctor, by following the advice contained in the Memorandum, is an accessory to a crime under the Sexual Offences Act 1956, which was largely ignored by the Court of Appeal, was advanced with renewed vigour before the House of Lords. Lords Fraser, Scarman, and Bridge were unpersuaded. They were all content to adopt the reasoning of Woolf J. Lord Scarman summed up the majority's position somewhat pithily. 'It would depend, as my noble and learned friend Lord Fraser observes, on the doctor's intention, a conclusion hardly to be wondered at in the field of the criminal law.'[64]

Lord Templeman, although in dissent, appears also to have adopted the view of the majority and of Woolf J. in this regard. To him too, it is a matter of the doctor's intention. Where contraceptive treatment is given because the girl cannot be deterred from sexual intercourse or it is otherwise judged to be in her best interests, Lord Templeman takes the view that it is provided 'not for the purpose of aiding and abetting an offence under s. 6 but for the purpose of avoiding the consequences, principally pregnancy, which the girl may suffer from illegal sexual intercourse'.[65] As we have seen, Lord Templeman's disagreement with the majority lay elsewhere. In his view, the Court of Appeal was right. A girl below the age of 16 is not in law capable of consenting to contraceptive treatment. Only a parent may give valid consent, save in exceptional circumstances. Consequently, a doctor who seeks to give contraceptive treatment without parental consent is interfering unlawfully with the rights of parents.

Lord Brandon's speech is in marked contrast. For him, the case called for answers to two questions. The first was whether the provision of contraceptive

---

[64] Ibid. 425.   [65] Ibid. 431.

advice[66] and treatment to a girl below the age of 16 can ever be lawful. The second concerned the relative rights and powers of the girl and her parents if no unlawful conduct was committed. Clearly, if the answer to the first question is that it can never be lawful to provide contraceptive advice and treatment, the second question is irrelevant, since it remains unlawful whether the girl or her parents consent or not.

Lord Brandon's answer to the first question was that it is unlawful. He was, therefore, in a minority of one in not accepting the majority's and Woolf J.'s view of the criminal law. He was also in a minority of one in deciding the case on the narrow point of criminal law, without any reference to the multitude of other issues raised.

Despite the lack of enthusiasm for Lord Brandon's views shown by the other members of the House, it may be worthwhile to examine briefly the reasons he advanced. After all, his is a view which many sympathize with.

Lord Brandon's view is as follows:

> On the footing that the having of sexual intercourse by a man with a girl under 16 is an unlawful act, it follows necessarily that for any person to promote, encourage or facilitate the commission of such an act may itself be a criminal offence, and must, in any event, be contrary to public policy. The question again arises whether the three activities to which I referred earlier should properly be regarded as, directly or indirectly, promoting, encouraging or facilitating the having, contrary to public policy, of sexual intercourse between a man and girl under 16. In my opinion there can be only one answer to this question, namely that to give such a girl advice about contraception, to examine her with a view to her using one or more forms of protection and finally to prescribe contraceptive treatment for her, necessarily involves promoting, encouraging or facilitating the having of sexual intercourse, contrary to public policy, by that girl with a man.[67]

There are thus two propositions. The first is that to provide contraception *may* be a criminal offence. Two comments are in order here. First, you will notice that in addition to 'promote' and 'encourage' Lord Brandon uses the word 'facilitate'. It can only be that he is using it as a substitute for the word 'aid'. But 'facilitate' is not a term of art ordinarily used in the criminal law. Indeed, an indictment framed simply in terms that a defendant 'facilitated' a particular crime would probably be declared by a court to be bad in law.[68] And since it is not a term of art, the only meaning 'facilitate' can have in law is 'aid'. This being so, all the case-law concerned with 'aiding' must apply equally to 'facilitating'. If Lord Brandon takes the view that the law on aiding is other than that expressed by Woolf J., then, with respect, it should have

[66] Lord Brandon included the giving of advice in the conduct he regarded as being in breach of the criminal law.   [67] *Supra* n. 40, 429.

[68] Section 8 of the Accessories and Abettors Act 1861 uses the four words 'aid', 'abet', 'counsel', and 'procure'; and these are now to be found incorporated into the Criminal Law Act 1977, schedule 12.

been set out for all to see. If, on the other hand, Lord Brandon sought to avoid the implications of this case-law on aiding — and he does not consider it or Woolf J.'s reasoning in his speech — he cannot, with great respect, do so simply by substituting another word. Undoubtedly, as I have argued earlier, the word 'aid' could cover the doctor's conduct in certain circumstances. But to do so, it would need rather more careful analysis than is offered by Lord Brandon. And, as regards 'promoting' or 'encouraging', this, surely, must be a matter of intention.

The second comment is more fundamental. All that Lord Brandon says is that it *may* be a criminal offence. But this is what Woolf J., the Court of Appeal, and the rest of the House of Lords all agreed. Indeed the DHSS conceded the point. The issue before the House was not whether there *may* be a criminal offence, but whether the doctor, by following the Memorandum of Guidance, *inevitably* committed a crime, regardless of his intention or purpose. By using the word 'may', Lord Brandon seems to have conceded the point. It is hard to understand, therefore, how his conclusion that the doctor giving contraceptive advice or treatment to a girl below the age of 16 is behaving unlawfully can be justified on this ground.

I turn now to the second proposition in the extract from Lord Brandon's speech set out earlier. This is that 'to promote . . . *must*, in any event, *be contrary to public policy*' (my emphasis) and that if a doctor gives contraceptive advice or treatment, this '*necessarily* involves promoting . . . ' (my emphasis). Logically, the word 'necessarily' should be considered first, since if it can be shown to be an untenable view, Lord Brandon's proposition fails, even if the public policy point is good. In my submission, the conclusion reflected in the word 'necessarily' cannot be supported, for the following reasons. If, on the one hand, Lord Brandon means that, as a matter of logic, giving a girl advice about contraception, examining her, or prescribing contraceptive treatment, all *necessarily* entail encouraging or aiding, this is clearly wrong. The advice may take the form that she should abstain from all sexual contact. The examination may persuade the doctor to inform the girl that only barrier methods of contraception are suitable, and, of course, these are promoted and readily obtainable from slot-machines and shops without the need for any intervention by the doctor. Finally, the treatment may be given to a girl below the age of 16 who intends to marry, with her parents' approval, on her sixteenth birthday and wishes to establish what level of dosage of contraceptive pills is appropriate to avoid unpleasant side-effects and yet be likely to give her protection against pregnancy once she is married. In none of these cases does the doctor's conduct *necessarily* involve encouraging or aiding unlawful sexual intercourse. Far less is it contrary to public policy.

If, alternatively, Lord Brandon was using the word 'necessarily' in a factual sense, as a description of what in fact will happen, this also is clearly wrong.

There was no evidence before the House concerning the relationship between what a doctor may do or say and the subsequent behaviour of young girls. In the absence of such evidence, Lord Brandon is not, with all due respect, entitled to draw conclusions of fact of his own, to take judicial notice, as it were, of what *necessarily* happens. It may be that unlawful sexual intercourse is often the sequel to the doctor's intervention. This, however, is not enough. Unless it is an *inevitable* consequence of a doctor's intervention, as a matter of fact, that unlawful sexual intercourse takes place, the alternative justification for the use of the word 'necessarily' also fails, and with it fails one of the two planks in the second proposition I identified earlier.

The other plank in Lord Brandon's second proposition is that the intervention of the doctor *must* be contrary to public policy. We have already seen that Lords Fraser, Scarman, and Bridge take a quite opposite view of what public policy calls for. For them, protection of the girl from further victimization was justification enough for the doctor to act in appropriate circumstances. Lord Brandon appears not to be persuaded by this. But, more important, he seems to be going much further. He seems to be saying that if some conduct is, in the view of the courts, against public policy, it may, for that reason alone, be categorized as unlawful.

The significance of this view depends on the meaning to be attached to the word 'unlawful'. One meaning is well recognized by the law. It arises in circumstances in which the courts state that a particular transaction between parties is so contrary to public policy that the court will not allow any party to use the law to enforce or give effect to the transaction. Surrogacy agreements were undoubtedly one such example before the introduction of legislation.[69] Clearly, Lord Brandon is not using 'unlawful as being contrary to public policy' in this sense. He is not saying merely that the law will not help or come to the aid of the parties. He is saying that the law makes it unlawful for the parties to enter into such a transaction and will punish them if they do.

The only other meaning that 'unlawful' can have in this context is, in my view, that the conduct complained of is a crime, and that it is a crime for the reason that it is contrary to public policy, and for that reason alone. This is the only plausible explanation of Lord Brandon's view, since he specifically concludes that the provision of contraceptive advice and treatment cannot be 'carried on lawfully in any circumstances whatsoever', which must mean that the doctor is barred by law from providing such treatment. Such a bar *in limine* can only be founded on the criminal law.

The obvious difficulty with this view is that it forces Lord Brandon into a logical inconsistency. He cannot conclude that the provision of treatment *may* be a crime and then assert that it *must* be one, which is the only sensible

[69] Surrogacy Arrangements Act 1985.

reading of the language he uses. And there is a further difficulty. Such a view as Lord Brandon's raises the most fundamental questions. As has been made clear by the House of Lords, most recently in *D.P.P.* v. *Knuller Ltd.*[70] it is not the proper task of the court to create new crimes. This is the job of Parliament. To allow judges to develop the criminal law by declaring something to be a crime if they think it ought to be one is more than undesirable; it is constitutionally improper. It may violate the principle *nulla poena sine lege*—no one may be punished except by reference to already existing law. It may introduce a wholly unacceptable degree of uncertainty into the criminal law. It certainly usurps the role of Parliament. For these reasons, therefore, it is submitted, with respect, that Lord Brandon's approach to the case may be rejected, resting as it does on a view of the criminal law which cannot be supported in theory or in its application to actual cases.

The duty of the doctor

The suggestion was made earlier that the law may recognize a duty in a doctor to care for a girl's health needs, including, if need be, the provision of contraceptive treatment. The imposition by the law of such a duty would, it was argued, give the doctor a legal justification if he provided contraceptive treatment. Although aired before the House of Lords, this view was not adopted by their Lordships. The majority were content to rely on an analysis which was less onerous for the doctor, since this was all that was necessary to allow them to reach the conclusion they sought. The effect of the speeches of the majority is to recognize that the doctor has in law, not a duty, but a power to treat, subject to the consent of the girl.

It might be thought that one of the implications of this mode of analysis is that the House recognized the need to allow the doctor a discretion whether to exercise his power or not, a discretion to be exercised by reference to the health needs and interests of the girl. But such a view would not be justified in my view. For, if by 'power' what is meant is that it is always for the doctor to decide what treatment to give, this is no different from when the doctor is under a *duty* to treat, since to argue that there is a duty to treat does not carry any conclusion about what form the treatment should take.

If, on the other hand, 'power' is used to suggest that the doctor may choose whether or not to treat, regardless of the circumstances of the girl, this, in my view, would be quite wrong in law. Provided that a relationship of doctor and patient is established, in that the girl is competent and sees the doctor in a context which gives rise to such a relationship, the doctor is under a legal duty to render all proper care. Should she, therefore, on any reasonable view of the facts, be in need of care, the doctor would not be entitled or

[70] [1973] AC 435.

empowered in law to choose not to treat her. If he did so choose, he would be liable in negligence. For this reason, I still hold the view that there is some advantage to be gained from speaking in terms of the duty of the doctor.

The role of the court

Although Lord Bridge agreed in general terms with Lords Fraser and Scarman and thereby formed the majority for the decision, his analysis of the case was radically different from those of the other four Law Lords. He dealt with the case as a matter of public law and asked a deceptively simple question: should the courts really have become involved in the case at all? The other members of the House also asked the question, but did not find themselves particularly troubled in answering it. They certainly did not regard it as a hurdle which presented any particular difficulty. For Lord Bridge, things were not so straightforward.

The last few years have seen a very great extension by the courts of their power to review the decisions of Government. Indeed, this is one of the most important legal developments since the Second World War. In grand terms, it can be seen as part of the continuing process whereby the estates of the realm jockey for power in a democracy conscious of the need, especially in the case of the courts, to go slowly and tread lightly. In more mundane terms, it means that the courts are more prepared than ever to assert that, in reaching decisions which are apparently political in nature, there are legal criteria which governments have to meet, if they are to avoid the risk of their decisions being overturned, for lack of fairness or reasonableness, for example. And, in tandem with this extension of jurisdiction, have come developments in procedure broadening the class or range of persons who can petition the court, or 'have standing', as the lawyers put it.

Lord Bridge surveyed the Gillick litigation, and saw it as raising the central question of where the courts should draw the line and limit their self-created power of review. Should Mrs Gillick have been granted standing to bring her case? And if so, was it proper to review and pronounce on a Memorandum of Guidance addressed to doctors and issued by the DHSS?

Lord Bridge was prepared to assume that Mrs Gillick had standing to contest the lawfulness of the Memorandum. But had the courts jurisdiction to review the lawfulness of the Memorandum? On this issue, Lord Bridge declared himself deeply troubled. Here was a piece of advice. 'Only in a very loose sense'[71] could it be said that the Memorandum was issued pursuant to any statutory power or responsibility. It was just sent out as guidance. Doctors could take it or leave it. Hitherto, the courts had confined their jurisdiction to review to circumstances in which Government purported to

---

[71] *Supra* n. 40, 426.

exercise statutory powers and that exercise could be examined by reference to a specific statutory background. 'Here', Lord Bridge stated, 'there is no specific statutory background'[72] against which the court could ask the question of whether any statutory authority had behaved unreasonably. He continued:

The issue by a department of government with administrative responsibility in a particular field of non-statutory guidance to subordinate authorities operating in the same field is a familiar feature of modern administration. The innumerable circulars issued over the years by successive departments responsible in the field of town and country planning spring to mind as representing a familiar example. The question whether the advice rendered in such non-statutory guidance is good or bad, reasonable or unreasonable cannot, as a general rule, be subject to any form of judicial review.[73]

Lord Bridge admitted that in the well-known recent case of *Royal College of Nursing of the UK* v. *DHSS*,[74] the court had assumed jurisdiction to review a circular issued by the DHSS. The circular advised that it was lawful within the provisions of the Abortion Act 1967 for nurses to perform certain functions during the course of terminating a pregnancy. This case, he urged, was exceptional. It raised a pure point of law which it was in the public interest to resolve. But, Lord Bridge went on:

The occasions of a departmental non-statutory publication raising, as in that case, a clearly defined issue of law, unclouded by political, social or moral overtones will be rare. In cases where any proposition of law implicit in a departmental advisory document is interwoven with questions of social and ethical controversy, the court should, in my opinion, exercise its jurisdiction with the utmost restraint, confine itself to defining whether the proposition of law is erroneous and avoid either expressing *ex cathedra* opinions in areas of social and ethical controversy in which it has no claim to speak with authority or proferring answers to hypothetical questions of law which do not strictly arise for decision.[75]

With respect, Lord Bridge captures more clearly and more precisely what I had sought to argue previously: namely, that Parliament, not the courts, was the forum to which Mrs Gillick should have appealed.

Problems arising from the decision

The criterion of capacity

The majority, as we have seen, accepted as the criteria of legal capacity the capacity to understand and maturity. Since it is the doctor who has to judge whether the young girl who consults him without parental knowledge is capable of understanding, it is critically important to know exactly what the criterion means, or, to put it another way, what the law requires of the

[72] Ibid.   [73] Ibid.   [74] [1981] AC 800.   [75] *Supra* n. 40, 427.

doctor. In the abstract, there are at least three possibilities regarding what is intended here. First, he must take all reasonable steps to ensure that she is put in a position in which a reasonable person such as she could understand what is being proposed. Or, second, he must take all reasonable steps to ensure that the girl before him *can* (in the sense of 'is capable of') understand what is being proposed. Or, third, he must take all reasonable steps to ensure that she *does* understand what is proposed.

On the face of it, only the second option is tenable. The first defeats the very purpose for which the criterion exists: namely, to determine the competence of the particular girl whom the doctor is dealing with. The third is impossible to achieve. The doctor cannot *make* someone understand.[76] Furthermore, in seeking to discover whether a girl *does* understand, the doctor may find himself locked in an endless and fruitless cross-examination of the girl.

Unfortunately, the members of the majority in the House of Lords do not appear to have given their minds to this question. Thus the speeches of Lord Fraser and Lord Scarman contain language which favours first one interpretation, then another. Of particular importance is what Lord Fraser says in his recital of the five matters on which the doctor must be satisfied before he may treat. He puts as his first point, you will recall, that 'the girl . . . *will* understand his advice' (my emphasis). This would suggest that the third of the options set out above is the law, despite its unworkability. It seems clear, however, from other passages in his speech, that Lord Fraser did not intend this interpretation. On other occasions he speaks of a girl as having capacity if she is 'capable of understanding'[77] or 'has sufficient understanding and intelligence'[78] or 'can understand'.[79]

Lord Scarman's view seems clearer. He adopts with Woolf J. the view expressed in the Canadian case of *Johnston* v. *Wellesley Hospital*,[80] that the girl must be 'capable of appreciating'. To this extent, he and Lord Fraser seem to be in agreement. But, just as Lord Fraser sows the seeds of doubt with one form of words which differs in import from the others, so does Lord Scarman. At one point he is anxious to assert that maturity, as well as understanding, is a crucial criterion in assessing capacity. In doing so, he states that 'it is not enough she *should understand* the nature of the advice.'[81] It may be argued that the word 'should' suggests that the criterion is whether the girl *does*, rather than *can*, understand. Such a conclusion should not, in my view, be read into Lord Scarman's speech, particularly in the light of what he says elsewhere.

---

[76] See, however, the flirtation with this notion in the Canadian case of *Kelly* v. *Hazlett* (1977) 75 DLR (3*d*) 536, 556, and the discussion in *Consent to Medical Care* (Law Reform Commission of Canada, 1980).

[77] *Supra* n. 40, 409.   [78] Ibid. 410.   [79] Ibid. 414.

[80] (1970) 17 DLR (3*d*) 139.   [81] *Supra* n. 40, 424; my emphasis.

Thus I have no doubt that the meaning of capacity is that accepted by Woolf J. The girl must be capable of appreciating, or understanding. Thus, the duty of the doctor is to show that he has taken all reasonable steps to satisfy himself of this. A way of testing the validity of this conclusion is to consider whether a court would hold that a doctor was in breach of his duty merely on the assertion by a girl, supported, let us say, by evidence, that she did not, as a matter of fact, understand what was said to her. In my view, a court would need more than this. It would need to be satisfied that the doctor had failed to present the relevant information in a form she was capable of understanding, quite apart from whether she did or did not understand.

The subordinate question of what 'capable of understanding' means must be raised and answered, because of what Lord Scarman said at different stages in his speech. First, he states that a child must achieve 'a sufficient understanding and intelligence to enable him or her to understand fully what is proposed'.[82] Subsequently, he endorses what was said in *Johnston* v. *Wellesley*, that 'an infant who is capable of appreciating fully the nature and consequences of a particular operation or of particular treatment can give an effective consent thereto.'[83] And, you will remember, Lord Scarman, in discussing capacity generally, said: 'there is much that has to be understood by a girl under the age of 16 if she is to have legal capacity to consent to . . . treatment.'[84]

The following questions arise. First, what significance can be attached to the word 'fully'? Two interpretations are possible. It can mean that the girl is only legally capable of deciding for herself if she has a complete grasp of all the technical information surrounding the proposed treatment and all the relevant moral and social considerations. Alternatively, it can mean that she is fully capable of understanding whatever is in general imparted by doctors to their patients in these circumstances. It can, therefore, be read as qualifying either the information to be grasped or the capacity to be brought to bear on the information.

If the first of these two alternatives were correct, it would set a standard for capacity unknown elsewhere in the law and impossible to meet. It would mean that a girl is only to be regarded as having capacity in law when she has the same knowledge and expertise as the doctor advising or treating her. For only then would she be in possession of all the relevant information— that is, be 'fully' in possession. This would make a nonsense of the law, and particularly of Lord Scarman's speech, since it would mean that in the act of recognizing a young girl's autonomy, the law sets a standard for recognition which is unattainable. It can only be, therefore, that Lord Scarman intended the word 'fully' to have the second of these two meanings. And this conclusion

[82] Ibid. 423.   [83] Ibid. 424.   [84] Ibid.

is borne out by noticing that when he applies his general view to contraceptive treatment, he stipulates only that 'a doctor will have to satisfy himself that she is *able to appraise* these factors.'[85]

This view of the meaning of 'fully' leaves undecided, however, the precise content of the information that the girl must be given. In my view, this must be governed by the general law. This I take at present to be that the girl must be put in possession of all relevant, material information which doctors generally, subject to review by the courts to ensure that the patient's right to information was not violated, would deem it proper to give.[86]

A second question which arises from Lord Scarman's analysis is whether, in requiring that the girl have 'sufficient maturity' and be 'able to appraise' the various factors he enumerates, he is setting a standard of capacity which is more demanding than that ordinarily required in law and in practice. For, it may be said, many adult patients do not always display maturity; nor are they always able to make the appraisals he calls for. In my submission, the standard should not be different. What is different is the care to be taken in complying with the standard. In the case of adults, maturity may properly be assumed in the absence of evidence to the contrary, as may be the ability to weigh and appraise the relevant factors. But in the case at hand, in which what is being discussed is contraception or, indeed, any medical treatment for a young girl, no such assumption may be made, and the factors which go to satisfy the legal standard must be spelled out.

Lord Scarman is not, therefore, giving 'capacity' a different meaning in the case of young persons. Instead, he is demanding that the relevant criterion be satisfied, both in general in the context of any medical care and in particular as regards contraceptive treatment for young girls. Given that Parliament has indicated through the Sexual Offences Act 1956 that a girl may not be presumed to know her own mind when consenting to intercourse, Lord Scarman is making it clear that the onus on the doctor to satisfy himself of the girl's capacity to consent to contraceptive treatment is that much greater.

The third and final question to arise is the *test* the law lays down, which the doctor must, therefore, apply, to determine whether in fact a girl is capable of understanding. Their Lordships are silent on this point. Consider the options. To be judged capable, must the girl's decision be rational (in whose view?), or reasonable (to whom?), or sensible (to whom?), or correct (in whose view?), or measured and considered? In view of what was said earlier concerning respect for autonomy, the law ought only to insist, and the doctor need only satisfy himself, that the girl's decision is a measured and considered one. Any other test, with the vexed exception of rationality,[87] allows, to a

---

[85] Ibid.; my emphasis.
[86] *Sidaway* v. *Bethlem Royal Hospital Governors*; *supra* n. 47.
[87] See the discussion in chapter 9.

greater or lesser extent, the reintroduction of paternalism, and must for that reason be rejected if the general thesis of the case is to be maintained.[88]

Notice that I am suggesting that the test of capacity to understand is the capacity to reach a measured decision, not an informed one. This distinction is important, since it may otherwise be argued that a girl lacks capacity because she expresses to the doctor a view of contraception which is ill informed — for example, that she can fail to take up to ten pills in any given cycle and remain safe from impregnation. Of course, some ignorance would be so basic as to warrant — indeed, demand — a conclusion of incapacity. But by and large, it is the capacity to understand relevant information, not the prior possession of it, with which the law is concerned. It is the *doctor's* duty to provide this information by responding to any observation she may make, so as to put the girl in a position to decide. That, after all, is what informed consent is about.

Next we must consider whether the 'capacity to understand' is a criterion of general application. Both Lords Fraser and Scarman regarded the capacity to understand as having general application as the criterion of legal capacity. They did not see themselves as laying down a rule limited to contraceptive treatment. Rather, they saw the case as an opportunity to bring the law concerning consent to contraception and medical treatment into line with the general law. Fixed age limits (the status approach) may be desirable in some areas of law, but, in Lord Scarman's view:

the law relating to parent and child is concerned with the problems of the growth and maturity of the human personality. If the law should impose on the process of 'growing up' fixed limits where nature knows only a continous process the price would be artificiality and a lack of realism in an area where the law must be sensitive to human development and social change.[89]

Thus, he concluded, 'parental right yields to the child's right to make his own decision when he reaches a sufficient understanding and intelligence to be capable of making up his own mind on the matter requiring decision.'[90]

Lord Templeman, in the minority, also endorsed capacity to understand as the general legal criterion of capacity. His dissent was based on his view that, although this may be the law generally, contraceptive treatment presented an exception. As has been said, to him, a girl below the age of 16 is never competent to understand what contraception and contraceptive treatment involve. As a proposition of fact, however, this cannot be so, since, to invalidate it, it is only necessary to find some girl somewhere who can understand. The proposition must, therefore, be one of policy; and, as we have seen, as such, it is not one which found favour with the majority.

---

[88] Compare the use of the word 'balanced', used by Lord Templeman in describing the patient's decision, in *supra* n. 47, 666.

[89] *Supra* n. 40, 421.

[90] Ibid. 422.

Remedies

When the man in the street thinks about the law, he, not unnaturally, thinks in terms of what will happen if the law is broken. It is disconcerting, therefore, to realize that this apparently simple question, when asked of the House of Lords' decision in *Gillick*, admits of no easy answer. Let me see if I can unwrap the issues here.

We must assume that a doctor has not complied — or does not intend to comply — with the law as stated by the majority. Let us discount the criminal law aspect, since that is relatively straightforward, in that, if the relevant intention can be established and it is accompanied by unlawful conduct, the doctor would be criminally liable. Is there, otherwise, any legal remedy available? The two parties who may, in theory, seek a remedy are, of course, a girl and her parents.

First, let us take the girl. Let us assume that she says that the consent she supposedly gave was invalid because, in fact, she was at the time and in the circumstances incapable in law of consenting. Leaving aside questions of fraud in obtaining consent, which need not detain us here, she would then appear to have an action against the doctor in the tort of battery if she was examined or treated. As has been said, no action would appear to lie if she was merely advised, save if the advice was negligently given and, in reliance on it, she suffered harm. Any action would be hers, even though it would have to be brought by her parent or guardian acting as best friend.

But let us assume that the doctor asserts, as he is likely to do, that she was competent. How is the issue to be resolved? Obviously, the easy answer is that it is a matter of evidence. But this is not enough. Assume, if you will, that there are a number of friends and members of the family of the girl prepared to testify that, in their view, she could not reasonably have been said to be capable in law of consenting. Can the doctor respond that the judgment of capacity is a matter of clinical judgment and for a doctor alone to decide, acting, of course, as a reasonable doctor, such that the views of non-doctors are inadmissible? In my view, the answer, in principle, is that the judgment of a girl's capacity to understand is not one uniquely within the competence of the doctor to make. The informed view of others would in law be entitled to a hearing. As a practical matter, however, it would be hard to persuade the court to reject the doctor's judgment, since he and only he was there at the time of the consultation with the girl, and so only he can be entitled to judge what passed between them. Perhaps the only circumstance in which a doctor's judgment of competence would be overturned would be in the unlikely event of there being evidence that the doctor had behaved in a reckless or improper way. It would not be enough, on this view, to urge that he was probably mistaken, if the mistake was both reasonable and honest. Once the question of whether the girl was in fact competent was resolved of course, the girl's action in battery would either succeed or fail, all things being equal.

We can now turn to the situation in which the girl admits that she was competent, but complains that the doctor did not satisfy himself as to one or other of the four other requirements called for by Lord Fraser (though not by Lord Scarman). You will recall the view taken earlier that, while Lord Fraser seemed to have intended that all the requirements should apply to contraceptive treatment, perhaps only the first (capacity) and the last (interests, meaning perhaps medical interests) apply to medical treatment in general. If, then, she complains that the treatment given was not in her best *medical* interests, this is merely to allege negligence, and would be dealt with as a normal negligence action. Thus, as regards medical treatment in general, Lord Fraser is saying nothing remarkable, and the ordinary remedy of a negligence action would be available if the doctor were in breach of his duty, and she suffered harm as a consequence.

So, the question of the relevance of Lord Fraser's other four requirements to any remedy the girl may have in law appears only to arise as regards contraceptive treatment. So what if she complains, for example, that the doctor did not try to persuade her to involve her parents or could have talked her out of contraceptive treatment if he had really tried? This raises a most troubling question. Are the requirements set out by Lord Fraser *legal* requirements or merely exhortations addressed to doctors, included in Lord Fraser's speech to reflect the exhortations contained in the Memorandum of Guidance which was the subject-matter of the case?

The lawyer's way of answering this question is to ask what legal action she could bring. An action in battery would not appear to be open to her, since she gave a valid legal consent. But what of an action in negligence? She would have to allege that the obligation to satisfy the four other requirements forms part of the legal duty owed her by the doctor, such that failure to satisfy them amounts to a breach of duty. She would also have to prove that she suffered some harm as a consequence of this breach, a task which would not be easy to accomplish. But let us assume this can be shown, so as to deal with the central question.

Lord Fraser, for his part, does not seem to regard the obligations he imposes on the doctor as legal obligations. He appears to see them as merely ethical in nature, since he concludes that his recital of the five requirements:

ought not to be regarded as a licence for doctors to disregard the wishes of parents on this matter whenever they find it convenient to do so. Any doctor who behaves in such a way would, in my opinion, be failing to discharge his professional responsibilities, and I would expect him to be disciplined by his own professional body accordingly.[91]

---

[91] Ibid. 413.

Lord Scarman, although he does not explicitly adopt Lord Fraser's five requirements, also looks to the profession, rather than the courts, to ensure that the doctor behaves appropriately. 'Abuse of the power to prescribe contraceptive treatment for girls under the age of 16 would render a doctor liable to severe professional penalties. The truth may well be that the rights of parents and children in this sensitive area are better protected by the professional standards of the medical profession.'[92]

This, you may think, is a strange view for a court to take. It lays down standards which, at least prima facie, are legal standards, and then appears to eschew responsibility for the supervision and enforcement of them. I too think it strange. Indeed, with great respect, I think it is also a view which may not necessarily be followed by a court if asked directly to decide the issue at the suit of a girl. I take the view that a court could well hold that a doctor's duty of care in law involves, *inter alia*, that he satisfy himself as to each of Lord Fraser's requirements. It would be a matter of evidence in each case whether in fact he has done so. But if a court decides that he has not, and that a girl has suffered harm as a consequence (which admittedly may be difficult to show), a court could well find him negligent.

If I am right, it would, of course, carry very considerable implications for any view that the law obliges the doctor to respect autonomy. Indeed, it would, on one view, reintroduce paternalism because of the very nature of the tort of negligence. To succeed in an action in negligence, the girl must show harm suffered as a consequence of the doctor's breach of duty. But here the harm would be that she was not protected from herself by the doctor. Ordinarily, we do not regard it as the law's job to oblige other people to protect us from ourselves, when the potential harm is the consequence of our own choices. Here, however, the law would be doing precisely that, if Lord Fraser's requirements have the effect I suggest. I would prefer, as I have said, that Lord Fraser's fifth requirement be interpreted otherwise, even as regards contraceptive treatment; but, failing that, I would urge that Lord Scarman's more straightforward approach to the law be adopted. By his approach, the doctor has no additional duties to satisfy once competence is established, so that none of these complications would arise.

The argument may, of course, be put that regulation by the profession, rather than by the law, is better in such delicate and complex matters as this. There may be some force in this, but I have never been persuaded that its delicacy or its complexity should take medical practice outside the law; nor should the fact that it is practised by responsible professionals. All these points apply equally well to, for example, solicitors and the practice of law, yet the law regulates these. Further it must be said that Lord Fraser is a Lord

92 Ibid. 425.

of Appeal in Ordinary. He is not a member of the General Medical Council. His views on medical ethics, if that is what they are, must, of course, be most helpful. But whether they ought to form a major (to some, central) part of his speech in a legal action is another matter. Equally, while the General Medical Council should pay proper attention to what Lord Fraser says, it does not follow that it should, without more ado, endorse all that he says.

So far, we have considered the remedies which may be available to a girl. We must now consider whether her parents or guardian may also, or alternatively, have any redress for failure by the doctor to comply with the law as stated by the majority. What we are asking here is whether a parent has any legal redress *as a parent*, not as someone acting on behalf of a child. To have any legal action, the parent must be able to assert a legal right which has been violated by the doctor in treating the girl. Putting it this way gives the clue to what is, analytically, the appropriate response. A parent would have to assert that he has a right of action for damages or for an injunction for a wrong done to *him*, for interference with the parental rights he has over his child. This, you will realize, is where we started!

Certainly, the Court of Appeal's judgment and, it seems, the speech of Lord Templeman can be read as recognizing or creating such a cause of action at the suit of parents. But the whole thrust of the majority's decision is to make it clear beyond doubt that parents do not have rights of their own as parents, but only contingently, to allow them to fulfil their duties to their children. This being the case, it must follow that the purported right of action available to parents in their own right contemplated by the Court of Appeal is a creature unknown to—indeed, rejected by—the law. The law will not listen to a parent who claims that *he* has been wronged by what the doctor has done. In this context, the law's concern is only with the child. The only role the parent has is to assert and protect the rights of that child, and this role ceases when the child becomes competent to make his or her own decisions.

Thus, it follows that if a doctor has already treated a girl, her parents may not bring any legal action alleging breach of a *parental* right, even if the doctor has failed to satisfy the requirements set out by Lord Fraser and these are judged to be legal requirements. The requirements *may* have legal force, as has been suggested, but only at the suit of and for the protection of the girl. If the parents discover that the girl is contemplating treatment, it also follows that they may not bring an action for an injunction to prevent the doctor from interfering with *their* rights. They do not have any such right. If the girl is competent, she may consent to treatment without their permission. And, in any event, even if their intention is to protect what they see as the girl's rights, their view may not prevail since, as is clear from section 1 of the Guardianship of Minors Act 1971, it is the child's welfare which is paramount when any question concerning the care and upbringing of a child is before a court.

Confidence

Although it was barely touched on by the House of Lords, the issue of confidence has attracted more attention than any other since the case was decided. The issue can be stated briefly. Under what circumstances is a doctor bound in law or ethically by the obligation of confidence to a girl who comes to see him? I use the term 'obligation of confidence', since this is the way it is traditionally put in the law. Its advantage is that it makes it clear that it is an *obligation* which is imposed on the doctor. It is more accurately perceived as a duty, however, since it vests in another a right to claim that it be observed.

Here is not the place for the careful analysis of the obligation of confidence in the context of medical practice which is long overdue, particularly as far as the law is concerned. For much is said about confidentiality. To listen to some doctors, you would think it the most important issue in medical ethics, an absolute principle admitting of no exception, even if, in the next breath, these same doctors will justify discussing a patient's condition with his family without his knowledge or consent. Indeed, it often seems that the principle of respecting the confidences of others is one of the last great unanalysed myths in medicine. That said, I will try to confine my remarks to the circumstances surrounding the *Gillick* case.

Ethics. In the General Medical Council's blue pamphlet entitled 'Professional Conduct and Discipline', there is a section headed 'Professional Confidence'. It was in this section that one of the issues which arose in the *Gillick* case had traditionally been dealt with: namely, the circumstances under which a doctor may treat in confidence a young person without the knowledge of her parents. The central issues of the *Gillick* case—capacity, consent, and the rights of parents and children—had previously been perceived to be legal issues on which the General Medical Council's 'blue book' was best advised to keep quiet. Clearly, such a view is unfounded and ought to be remedied, but we are talking of what was the case.

Traditionally, the General Medical Council's guidance had been that, in treating young girls, doctors were to observe the rule of professional confidentiality. However, no detailed analysis of what this might entail was offered. When the Court of Appeal handed down its judgment, the General Medical Council, conscious that, ordinarily, it ought not to give advice which may be unlawful, revised its guidance. The Council issued interim guidelines advising doctors that they may not give contraceptive advice or treatment to girls below the age of 16 without parental permission. The issue of confidence as between the girl and the doctor could not, therefore, arise.

Once the House of Lords' decision was made known, the General Medical Council issued a further revision of its guidelines. It advised that 'if the doctor is satisfied of the child's maturity and ability to understand', and the child:

refuses to allow a parent or such other person to be told, the doctor must decide, in the patient's best medical interest, whether or not to offer advice or treatment. He should, however, respect the rules of professional confidentiality. . . . If the doctor is not so satisfied, he may decide to disclose the information learned from the consultation; but if he does so he should inform the patient accordingly and his judgment concerning disclosure must always reflect both the patient's best medical interest and the trust the patient places in the doctor.[93]

It is the part of the advice which refers to the incompetent girl which has attracted criticism, most noticeably from the British Medical Association, whose Secretary, Dr John Havard, condemned it both in *The Times*[94] and in the *British Medical Journal*.[95] The adjectives 'confused', 'muddled', and 'woolly' were just some of those used. The view advanced by Dr Havard was, and remains, that even in the case of the incompetent girl, the fact that she has consulted the doctor and, presumably, what he has learned in the process of assessing her competence must be kept secret from others, including her parents, if she so wishes.

If this is intended to be a rule of general application—and it appears to be so—it only has to be stated to be seen to be untenable. If it were valid, it would mean that a girl however young and immature can bind her doctor to secrecy and that, thereafter, the doctor must observe this secrecy, on pain of being judged to have behaved unethically. Imagine that a 9-year-old girl, for example, finds her way to the family doctor's surgery and tells him not to inform her parents, but that she would like some of the contraceptive pills which her older girl-friends have, as she is going to play 'husbands and wives' with them that evening. Anyone who seriously argues that the doctor *must* not tell a soul about this visit is living in fairyland. Of course he may tell others, particularly, in most cases, the parents, whether he thinks she is in danger or just needs a good talking-to. Indeed, many would argue that the doctor *must* tell the parents in such circumstances. The licence or, to some, the duty to tell others arises from the moral obligation of the doctor to put those who are responsible for the girl in a position in which they can properly exercise their responsibility.

Once this argument is conceded, it is clear that there must be some point at which the doctor will ordinarily owe an obligation of confidence to a young girl; but until that point is reached, he will not. That point must be whether the girl is competent to know her own mind and to reach a competent decision,

---

[93] General Medical Council, *Annual Report*, Mar. 1986, p. 4.
[94] *The Times*, 26 Feb. 1986.   [95] *British Medical Journal*, 22 Feb. 1986.

for example, to ask the doctor not to tell her parents about a consultation. Indeed, Dr Havard himself seems to have conceded as much in an earlier article on the *Gillick* saga, written after Woolf J.'s judgment. He wrote that 'the experience of other countries suggests that the medical profession may have a hard struggle on its hands to preserve *the right of competent minors* to confidentiality and privacy in medical treatment in the face of parental counter-claim.'[96]

This common-sense position can also be reached by a more formal analysis, if we ask the question of what gives rise to a doctor's obligation to respect a girl's confidence. As Dr Gillon points out, 'medical confidentiality cannot readily be seen as a moral end in itself, but as a means to some morally desirable end, whether this is the general welfare, respect for autonomy, or respect for privacy.'[97] For my part, I regard the end as being respect for autonomy. And once this is understood, that the obligation is a contingent one, it becomes clear that it needs a relationship of autonomous persons to come into existence. It follows that no obligation of confidence can be owed to a girl who is incompetent, since she is, by that token, not capable of exercising autonomy. Indeed, to insist that what she says *must* be kept secret, while admitting her incompetence, may be said to violate the principle of respect for autonomy, in that it may result in preventing her from coming to autonomy free from harm. Dr Gillon makes this very point: '[W]ith children the question must always arise: is this patient sufficiently autonomous for the principle of respect for autonomy [the end served by confidentiality] to apply?'[98] It is, of course, true that there are various levels of competence, such that competence to understand contraception may not be the same as competence to understand and bind someone to secrecy. This is why the duty is placed on the doctor to assess each girl's competence individually. It is, however, the case that, as regards requests for contraception without parental involvement, the request and the secrecy are so closely connected as ordinarily to call for the same approach.

Thus, I submit, the guidance given by the General Medical Council is entirely in keeping with good medical ethics. Those who criticize it are confused in their understanding of both the nature and the meaning of the obligation of confidence. Furthermore, many critics have simply misunderstood what the guidance says. It does not say that a doctor *must* tell her parents when an incompetent girl comes to see him. It merely advises him that he *may* do so, but that he must be prepared to justify doing so, since he must always be conscious of the need not to undermine the trust which patients, including young patients, put in their doctors.

---

[96] J. Havard, 'Confidentiality—a major issue in medical ethics', 11 *Journal of Medical Ethics* 8 (1985); my emphasis.
[97] R. Gillon, editorial, 'Medical Confidentiality', 10 *Journal of Medical Ethics* 3 (1984).
[98] Ibid. 4.

Before leaving the General Medical Council's guidance and the criticism it attracted, it is fair to say that the real basis of the criticism may not rest on ethical analysis but on what some fear may be the consequence of the guidance. Some, especially those involved in family-planning services, argue that the effect of the guidance will be that girls who need advice and help will be deterred from seeking it, out of fear that a doctor may judge them to be incompetent and then tell their parents of their visit. I have no doubt that this fear is very real and deeply felt. But however real it is, it does not serve as a reason for giving different guidance. For, if the girl is incompetent and the doctor judges it proper to tell her parents or others, this, we have seen, is not only proper, but desirable. If, however, the girl is not incompetent, but the doctor behaves improperly and labels her as such for some idiosyncratic reason of his own, it is not the guidance which is bad. Instead, it is the doctor. Thus, to those who argue that the guidance should be framed to take account of what may, quite improperly, be done, the answer must be that it is no part of the General Medical Council's role to write codes of conduct to accommodate bad doctors. The General Medical Council's task is to write good medical ethics. It is the task of all of us to expose doctors who act contrary to good ethics.

Law. Although there may be some doubt as to the formal legal basis of the obligation of confidence owed by a doctor to his patient, there can be little doubt that such an obligation exists.[99] The general law on confidentiality talks variously in terms of binding someone to the obligation or entrusting someone with secret information.[1] On the specific nature of the obligation owed by a doctor to his patient, the law as yet offers no guidance. What follows, therefore, is necessarily an analysis from first principles. I will seek to take the analysis step by step, as a series of propositions.

First, since there will not usually be a contract between a young girl and a doctor, it is probable that the obligation of confidence arises, if it arises at all, in equity, through her entrusting him with information about herself, on condition that he keep it secret. For the girl to be able in law to put the doctor in a position of trust, it must be, therefore, that she has the legal capacity to entrust. Equally, to bind the doctor in law requires the legal capacity to bind. It is submitted, therefore, that for an obligation of confidence to be owed in law by a doctor to his patient, the patient must have the necessary legal capacity to bind the doctor to such an obligation, which, in turn, must mean the capacity to understand what a relationship of confidentiality entails.

---

[99] See *Hunter* v. *Mann* [1974] QB 767.
[1] See, generally, F. Gurry, *Breach of Confidence* (Oxford University Press, 1984).

Second, the obligation of confidence entails that one party has the right to control the dissemination of whatever information she makes available, and that the other party to the obligation has no right to disseminate any information, except for some major reason of public policy. Thus, the key to confidentiality is the right to control access to information as against third parties. In the case of a competent young girl, her parents are third parties, and she may legally exercise control over the information she gives the doctor by binding him to secrecy. In the case of an incompetent young girl, her parents can exercise control over information which the doctor learns from her, in that they, on her behalf, can prevent him from disseminating it to third parties, such as the Press. This right to control arises from the more general right which parents have so as to be able to carry out the duties they owe to their children. In this case, the duty is to protect the child's privacy and welfare. But this is not the important issue here. The question we are concerned with is, as between the incompetent young girl and the doctor, is the parent a third party? Can the incompetent girl purport to exercise a right of control over information given to the doctor so as to bind him not to disclose it to her parents? The answer, I submit, is that she cannot.

Third, there are several ways to justify the conclusion just arrived at. The first is that it is in the public interest that matters of importance for the welfare of a young child be disclosed to those responsible for the welfare of that child, so as to allow them to carry out their obligations to the child. These, ordinarily, are the parents. The girl is incompetent to exercise any right to control any information. The doctor has no such right, save as regards trivial information which he judges unimportant for the welfare of the child. His exercise of such judgment is, of course, subject to review, whether by an action in negligence at the suit of the child (or parents on her behalf) or by a complaint of unethical conduct should the child be harmed as a consequence of an improper exercise of judgment.

This, I submit, would be the mode of analysis which a court would follow if an incompetent young girl sought through a friend to enjoin a doctor from telling her parents certain information. An alternative legal analysis might be that, while it is the young girl who is the patient, it is the parent also who enters into the legal relationship with the doctor, and it is only through the parent that duties owed to the child can be fulfilled. It is the parents who in law may consent to or refuse treatment, who give relevant information for the purposes of taking a history, are legally entitled to information for the purposes of giving consent, and receive instruction for subsequent care of the child. Their entitlement to all this is a necessary concomitant of their duty to safeguard the welfare of the child. It follows that information imparted to or learned by a doctor in the absence of the parents must be passed on to them if, in the judgment of the doctor, it touches on the welfare of the child and is not trivial.

But, fourth, a parent has no claim *in his own right as a parent* to information which the doctor has acquired. The right is contingent on his parental duty and, therefore, can be exercised only for such purposes. Thus, if a parent sought an injunction requiring a doctor to disclose certain information—whether, for example, he had treated a young daughter—the court would apply section 1 of the Guardianship of Minors Act 1971, which requires that a court make the welfare of the child the paramount consideration when it has before it a question as to the care and upbringing of a child.

Thus, a prima facie right to control information is vested by operation of law and good sense in the doctor, a right he must exercise for the welfare of his young patient, one which means that he will pass on all but trivial information to the parents. It is not the young girl who binds the doctor. It is public policy which is regulating him. And, it follows that it is equally public policy that a doctor treating an incompetent young girl may in law and ethics (and, at least in ethics, must sometimes) disclose information to parents. If he does, he will not be exposed to any action for breach of confidence at the suit of the girl, since he owes no legal obligation of confidence to her. If he fails to do so in circumstances in which it is judged that he should, he may be exposed to liability at the suit of the girl if she suffers harm as a consequence of his failure.

In a recent paper,[2] Lord Scarman briefly mentions the issue of confidentiality. When the doctor has judged a girl incompetent, 'is he', Lord Scarman asks, 'under an obligation to tell the parents that the girl has been to see him?'[3] He takes the view that the doctor owes the girl the duty of respecting her confidence such that 'the law would not . . . require the doctor to break confidence'.[4]

In such a brief comment, Lord Scarman obviously did not intend to review the law *in extenso*. As far as the more straightforward question goes, it will be seen that the view I reach entirely accords with that of Lord Scarman. There is no question that the doctor *must* tell others, outside public policy considerations, and the law will not 'require' him to do so. This is the view both of ethics and of law which I adopt. Lord Scarman does not, however, consider the more difficult question of whether the doctor *may* tell others. I submit that there is nothing in what he says which invalidates the view I have expressed. His use of the words 'duty of respecting confidence' does, however, warrant comment. I have sought to argue that such a duty does not, and should not, arise as between the doctor and the incompetent patient and, with respect, continue to hold this view.

[2] Lord Scarman, 'Law and Medical Practice', in P. Byrne, ed., *Medicine in Contemporary Society* (King's Fund, 1987).
[3] Ibid. 6.   [4] Ibid. 7.

I am further fortified in this view by the analysis of United States law by Angela Holder.[5] She writes that:

There have been no decisions in which a minor sued a physician for revealing information to his parents. However, it would seem that if the physician does not feel the need to obtain consent of the parents to treat the child, he is by that decision assuring the child that the normal physician–patient relationship that would obtain if he were an adult has begun to apply. . . . *By accepting the child as a responsible patient who has the right to consent to treatment* the physician has implicitly accorded that child the normal rights of a patient.[6]

After noting that the 'Model Act of the American Academy of Pediatrics apparently does not regard confidentiality as to parents as a right of a minor patient,' she observes that the Act:

seems to approve *acceptance of a minor for treatment* without parental consent when the patient does not want them to be informed and then, later, abrogating that acceptance and the implicit terms of the relationship. In addition to the clear deceit involved, if the circumstances are such that the parents' consent is legally necessary at all, it is necessary for the institution of treatment, not at a later time or after treatment is concluded.[7]

Holder concludes by preferring as 'more ethical and responsible' the approach of the Pediatric Bill of Rights of the National Association of Children's Hospitals. This 'makes clear that the child's treatment is to be conducted according to normal rules of physician–patient confidentiality if consent from the parent is not required *at the time the relationship commences*.'[8] For a relationship to commence, the parties must agree to enter into it, either themselves or by proxy (except in the case of an emergency). To agree entails the capacity to agree. Without such capacity, no relationship can be embarked on, and thus no question of an obligation of confidence arises.[9]

---

[5] A. Holder, *Legal Issues in Pediatrics and Adolescent Medicine*, 2nd edn. (Yale University Press, 1985).   [6] Ibid. 143; my emphasis.
[7] Ibid.; my emphasis.   [8] Ibid. 144; my emphasis.
[9] In a recent paper J. Montgomery argues against the view advanced here. First, he asserts that at least in private practice a duty to observe confidence arises from contract, since a contract for medical care is one which the law recognizes as being enforceable against a minor. Unfortunately, this seems to confuse legal incapacity with actual incapacity. If a child lacks actual capacity to enter into a contract, the law of contract is irrelevant. Second, Montgomery looks to equity. He concludes that, 'Any child who approaches a doctor without telling his or her parents that he is doing so *ex hypothesi* expects the consultation to be confidential. The very action evidences the maturity required before the law will recognize this expectation'. Here, Montgomery clearly overstates the case. I am sure he is right in many cases, but to adopt a hard and fast rule against disclosure would, particularly given the flexible approach of equity, be quite wrong in others. 'Confidentiality and the Immature Minor'; 1987] Fam. Law, 101 *et seq.*

CONCLUSION

As we have seen, the *Gillick* case settles some questions (at least for the present) and poses some others. I have tried to show that the questions are important for medical law, are often extremely complex and can only be approached properly by the application of careful and rigorous analysis. It may be that some do not accept the conclusions reached. But at this stage of medical law, the approach is nearly as important as the answers. At least, if analysis takes the place of opinion or bias, we can all talk the same language.

6

The Moral Status of the Embryo*

You cannot put genies back into bottles. You can, however, try to make sure that the genies do not go around granting any old wish. You can give the genies some rules.

In vitro fertilization, as a method of dealing with infertility, is probably here to stay. But we can still, just about, ask whether the possibilities created by IVF should become practice. I say 'just about' because theory is becoming reality with great rapidity, and reality has the habit of becoming practice. 'The thrust of scientific curiosity in laboratories seems to be outpacing Society's ability to ask questions' is how the *Times* leader of 24 May 1984 put it.

It has not only been the speed of developments which has affected the questions asked. For some time, such debate as there was about where it was all leading us was characterized by epithet. Medical scientists were harbingers of a brave new world. Cautious commentators were Luddites. Researchers invoked 'the right to know'. Critics invoked the Third Reich. In the middle was the general response of 'Gee whiz', coupled with centre-page photographs of mother and child (or, more recently, children). Reports from a number of working parties have raised the level of debate, but not surprisingly, have shown considerable disagreement.

In effect, then, the debate is just beginning. And we ought not to let ourselves be hustled into making hasty decisions by the doctor or researcher anxious to get on with things. Science seems to be in a hurry, but we can properly ask for time to catch our breath and consider. We are not interfering. It is our right to deliberate on issues which touch the deepest values of our culture. And public opinion needs time to prepare and educate itself.

---

* This paper first appeared in a shorter version in *The Times*, 26 May 1984. Since then the *Report of the Committee of Inquiry into Human Fertilisation and Embryology*, chaired by Baroness Warnock, has been published (Cmnd. 9314, HMSO), and I have added a brief comment on the relevant part of the *Report*. The whole was then published in *King's Counsel* (King's College London, 1985), p. 21. The paper was written for the general reader and appears here in an amended form. It seeks to argue from first principles. Obviously, there is much recent scholarship of relevance. See e.g. M. Lockwood, 'When does life begin?', in Lockwood, ed., *Moral Dilemmas in Modern Medicine* (Oxford University Press, 1985); M. Warnock, *A Question of Life* (Blackwell, 1985); J. Mahoney, *Bioethics and Belief* (Sheed and Ward, 1984).

Helping the childless or adding to our understanding of immunology are noble aims. But they must not be used as trumps. There is no reason why they should be paramount among our aims if we find the moral price of pursuing them too high. The question then boils down to how we determine and assess the relevant moral arguments so that some sort of public guidance as to what is morally proper can be offered to the doctor and the researcher.

Two issues stand out as particularly taxing: the use of a woman's womb to bring to term the fertilized egg of some other couple and the use of embryos for research. I do not wish to say more on womb-leasing (sometimes called 'surrogate motherhood') save to make two points. First, the fundamental moral question must be whether the procedure could harm the interests of the future child, rather than whether it satisfies the wishes of the couple to have a family, or whether the woman voluntarily and knowingly agrees to it. Second, it must not be thought that the procedure, if permitted, will necessarily be limited to situations in which the woman in the couple cannot bear her own child. It would clearly be attractive to some women not to have to go through pregnancy. Womb-leasing could dramatically challenge cultural perceptions of and attitudes to the family and familial responsibilities. These issues, which are somewhat deeper than questions of commercialization or exploitation, deserve the most careful consideration.[1]

I wish to concentrate on research on embryos. I do so because it makes us confront an issue which is basic to much of the thinking about IVF and which goes to the heart of our humanity. When I use the term research here, I exclude therapeutic research aimed at assisting an embryo to survive. I am concerned only with non-therapeutic research which ends in the embryo's destruction. As you know, doctors commonly fertilize more eggs than they subsequently implant in the woman. May they conduct research on these 'spare' embryos? To ask whether they may is to ask what is the moral status of such an embryo. Another, arresting way of putting it is: what, if anything, is the difference between an early embryo and a hamster?

THE EMBRYO'S CLAIM TO PROTECTION

What may legitimately be done with embryos 'excess to need'? This is not some factual enquiry concerning 'when life begins'. The enquiry is as follows: granted that the researcher has this entity—and I use this abstract term intentionally—and granted that its coming into being as an entity and its ceasing to exist as an entity involve a process with no sure beginning or end, what characteristics would the entity need to possess in order to have some

---

[1] See, now, the Surrogacy Arrangements Act 1985.

moral claim to respect (such respect ordinarily taking the form of a claim to protection), such that we have some moral duty to it.

In answering this question, it may be conceded that whatever claim it has—or duties we owe it—may increase as it progresses towards that point at which its claim to respect, and usually protection, is greatest. This may be when it has been born alive, and does not fall into that class of severely handicapped babies whom we may think it morally right to allow to die.

If this entity's claim on us becomes greater as time goes on, it follows that the claims of others, or our perceived duties to others, whose circumstances are closely associated with the entity, though they may still outweigh the entity's claims, will have to be shown to be increasingly strong. It may be for this reason that, for example, a compromise is struck on abortion, such that the mother's claim to do with her body as she wishes may outweigh any claim to protection the foetus may have in the early stages of foetal development, but may not do so the nearer the foetus progresses towards birth. The justification offered for this may well be a rather simplistic notion that the foetus is more recognizably like us, or the more thoughtful suggestion that if the acquisition of those qualities which create the greatest claim to protection (or the greatest duty of respect in us) is a gradual process, then it follows that the further along in the stage of development towards maturation the foetus is, the greater its claim.

THE CRITERION OF HUMANNESS

The point in the development of the entity at which it *begins* to make a claim to protection on us has then to be chosen. It is, of course, a choice, a selection of a significant point. One view is that it should be that point at which the entity takes on some minimal quality of humanness. I am using the term 'humanness' here with the intention of capturing the notion that there is a difference between the mere factual question of being a member of a species and the mixed factual and moral question of whether there are specific qualities which the member of the species must demonstrate before it can be regarded as *counting* as a person or individual. It may help to give an example. Dying is a process. Death is an event. The determination of when death occurs involves choosing a point in the process of dying. Involved in that choice is a mixed moral and factual statement of what it means to be a person, such that, if certain physiological phenomena are absent, the person is said to have died. The current view is that a person dies as an integrated, self-sustaining system when the brain-stem ceases irreversibly to function. Thereafter, parts of the body may continue to survive, for example, hair may grow, or cells may emit electrical charges and some parts may intentionally be kept alive—for example, organs for transplant or cells in a supporting environment—but it could not be said that the person is alive.

Thus, imagine a body that used to go by the name of Brown. It is not a wholly factual enquiry as to when Brown died. It is also a moral question as to what he has to become so as to cease to count as a human person. This is what I call the issue of 'humanness'. It is not the same as the issue of membership of the species *Homo sapiens*.

Since, in identifying a minimal quality of humanness sufficient to make a claim on us, we are talking of a moral commitment, we could say that this is a matter of faith, or an unarguable premiss. This would block further argument. But, if *reasons* are to be offered to justify choosing one point rather than another, the reasons must be defensible. One Catholic position, for example, talks of the point of fertilization as being the significant point at which a claim accrues, because at that point you have an entity which has the necessary genetic encoding to develop towards maturity. I will return to this position later.

Of the various reasoned arguments offered, the one which at present attracts the most attention is that which states that, in choosing the significant point, we should draw on the analogy of the definition of death. Dr Robert Edwards in particular favours this approach. After all, the definition of death is, in effect, a statement about life, since it is concerned with determining when those factors and qualities which amount to humanness are absent, such that the person may be pronounced dead, though, of course, the organism continues to live in parts. If we accept as relevant criteria for determining death the irreversible absence of pulse, respiration, and the capacity for consciousness and sentience, then it could be said that, on the basis of symmetry, it is rationally defensible to use the first appearance of these faculties as marking the beginning of humanness. It would then be a matter of technical expertise to discover when these faculties, particularly those associated with sentience, were developed, although it would still call for a choice as to what stage of development was sufficient to count.

Such an analysis is not without considerable difficulties. Principal among these is the difficulty associated with sentience. If it is the laying-down of those structures responsible for sentience which is crucial, this may lead inevitably back to the moment of fertilization, since one stage of development depends on and leads to another. Furthermore, since sentience is such a complex notion, it is by no means clear that it can be stated with authority which, among many, structures may be responsible for it.

If it is the *development* of the capacity for sentience which is crucial, then the embryo could simply be kept anaesthetized. This would allow experiments to be carried out without moral objection for as long as was desired. If, however, as is likely, this would attract widespread objection, sentience alone cannot be the significant criterion. If, on the other hand, it is the *capacity* to be sentient that is crucial, then very great difficulties exist. Not only would this allow anaesthetizing the embryo even after the capacity had developed; it would also make it difficult to distinguish between the embryo which could not feel pain and the patient who is comatose or in a vegetative state, or even one who is sedated or anaesthetized. Objections which would undoubtedly be raised as to the use of the latter for research would seem equally to apply to the former.

None the less, if this basis for analysing the acquisition of a minimal quality of humanness and its gradual development thereafter is relied upon, it could be argued that after the developmental stage judged relevant by those who propose it was reached—for example 25 + days of embryonic life—the entity can be called 'human'. Once called 'human', it has some claim to respect and protection, though not, as we have seen, an absolute claim. Given such a notion of humanness, would it be licit to conduct experiments once the embryo had reached the relevant state of development? Some would say that even then, though it has a claim to respect and protection, research which could enhance understanding and/or improve the health or the lot of others could still be justified on some utilitarian basis. I find this argument unpalatable. It involves violating what many would see as a fundamental principle, that we may not use humans as means to an end, but must respect them as ends in themselves. This principle entails that once the entity is judged to have even the most limited form of humanness, it is entitled to respect and protection from being the object of research.

THE CLAIM OF THE EARLY EMBRYO

Clearly, if you accept the Catholic position mentioned earlier, that fertilization is the significant point for humanness, then research on embryos at any stage of development is morally wrong. But, if you accept, for the sake of argument here, that there is a stage at which humanness is acquired, does it follow that research on entities which have not reached that stage of development is morally permissible? All the working parties which have reported so far have suggested it should be permissible.[2] I would ask you to suspend judgment for a while. I will divide the question into two parts.

If the development of the entity which is now available for research has not been facilitated by the doctor with the primary intention of using it for research purposes, then, prima facie, there may be no objection in principle to its being used for research. Its availability would be fortuitous and, as in the case of tissue available after abortion, it could be said that it is

---

[2] See e.g. Council for Science and Society, *Human Procreation: Ethical Aspects of the New Techniques* (Oxford University Press, 1984).

justifiable to take advantage of such a fortuitous occurrence so as to enhance knowledge and improve treatment of others. Even this reasoning, though persuasive, may, however, have to give way to the qualifying view arising from a community sense of moral repulsion which I consider later.

THE RELEVANCE OF INTENTION

But what of the situation in which the development of the entity available for research has been facilitated by the doctor (or research scientist) with the primary intention of using it for research and then discarding it? Here there may be considerable difficulty in condoning such research as morally permissible. (Intention is used here, I ought to add, in the sense of doing something for the purpose of achieving a particular result, or with knowledge that such a result will take place as a matter of substantial certainty).

Any moral objection may at first blush seem hard to defend, if it is granted that the entity in question has not developed to that stage at which it acquires those characteristics consonant with the current view of humanness. But in reaching any moral judgment, I am concerned with the intention of the moral agent, the researcher. If the intention is, as stipulated, to facilitate the development of an entity only so as to do research, then it is proper to enquire whether this intention is morally defensible. Clearly, if one were a straight-forward consequentialist, there would be few problems, since it is not difficult to argue that the benefits to be gained from such research outweigh any costs, particularly since the entity does not have any of the characteristics of humanness, and is, in other words, of no more moral worth than a hamster or a piece of mouse tissue.

But such an analysis is far from satisfactory. More compelling are those arguments which suggest that the research is morally wrong because the intention of the researcher is morally repugnant. In arriving at such a conclusion, it is important to notice at the outset that our genuine, conscience-searching agonizing over the issue arises precisely from the fact that intuitively we do not equate a fertilized human egg with a hamster or a piece of mouse tissue. If we did, there would be no debate. It is because we do not, and emphatically, if only intuitively, we do not, that we agonize over the moral propriety of research on embryos.

But why is the intention of the researcher in this case morally repugnant? Let us take the argument in stages. The first point to notice is that the doctor or researcher facilitated the development of more embryos than were needed for implanting in the woman. He could have settled for one or two embryos, but chose not to do so. Had he done so, the question of what to do with 'spare' embryos would not have arisen. Admittedly, the woman's chances of becoming pregnant would have been reduced, from about 33 per cent to

16 per cent; but to say that this justifies the development of more embryos than are needed for implanting assumes what has to be proved, namely, that the woman's claim to have her chance of pregnancy doubled 'and to avoid further laparoscopies outweighs any other claims which moral principles or intuitions may convince us of.

Secondly, the doctor has deliberately chosen not to implant the 'spare' embryos. There was a time when IVF continually failed to lead to any pregnancy. Then the procedure was improved, and successful implantation became a real possibility. So, in the case we are considering, what the doctor has chosen to do is to deny this entity the possibility of developing further, so that he can do research on it. He has, therefore, by his intervention, caused it to be used and, thereby, to be caused to cease to exist. This can be asserted to be morally wrong.

The moral wrongness cannot, of course, be based simply on the fact that a choice was made not to implant it, although some seem to be content to rest their case on this. They argue that this is another example of hubris, in that man chooses which entity shall continue to live (or join the lottery which may result in birth) and which shall not. But, such an argument is question-begging, in that it is only hubris or morally wrong if the entity chosen not to live deserves greater moral respect than such a choice entails.

The argument must lie elsewhere. Some rely on the idea that although the entity lacks what have been advanced as the necessary features of humanness, which would give it a claim to protection, it does have a certain feature which sets it apart. This is its *potentiality* to become human.

TWO ARGUMENTS ABOUT POTENTIALITY

One form of the potentiality argument is hard to sustain, however. What has to be argued is that the mother's egg, once fertilized, has acquired the necessary and sufficient characteristics, namely the genetic coding, which will allow it, without anything more, to become human. The difficulty with this position is that the evidence does not bear it out. Scientists will point to examples of embryonic development after abnormal fertilization (such as the hydatidiform mole) and to genetic changes subsequent to fertilization. Also the fertilized egg will need a sympathetic womb; thus its mere existence does not entail that it has the necessary and sufficient conditions for development to humanness.

There is, however, an alternative form of the potentiality argument which may be sustainable. To assert that something has the potentiality to develop into something else is not necessarily to assert that it has the necessary and sufficient conditions to do so. It may merely mean that it has a good chance of becoming that thing, that it has the opportunity to do so. In the context of the fertilized egg, it means that it meets certain criteria, it has the necessary genetic material, to enable it to participate in the lottery which Nature contrives for the continuation of existence until birth. The exceptional cases, such as genetic changes after fertilization, can then be discounted as exceptions which prove the rule. They do not embarrass this form of the potentiality argument, since it does not rest on the notion of necessary and sufficient conditions. Equally, that the fertilized egg may not succeed in Nature's lottery or that Nature contrives to waste many such eggs are not arguments against this form of the argument, for the following reason. We do not argue that everything which occurs naturally is necessarily good, otherwise killing would be even more widespread! Indeed, it is the chosen aim of medical science to allow man to come to terms with Nature, rather than be subject to its whims. Thus, it follows that, just because something happens in nature is no argument for causing it to happen by our intervention, when we have the choice to do otherwise.

This form of the potentiality argument leaves open the question of whether the fertilized egg, being only potentially human, can make a claim on us for protection, and whether its claim would be so strong as to make research on it morally wrong. One way of responding, which may demonstrate the plausibility of the argument, is to notice that we are sufficiently concerned and exercised about the early embryo to feel the need to justify our behaviour towards it. If it were the moral equivalent of a hamster, our concern would be less, or of a different order, arising from views on the moral claims that animals — non-humans — may make on us. Our intuition tells us that a human fertilized egg or embryo should not be regarded as if it were a hamster, that this is offensive. The reason may well lie precisely in the fact that it has the potential to be human, regardless of whether it can or will realize it.

The argument can be tested another way. Let us accept for the moment the minimum criterion of humanness now commanding agreement in some quarters: namely, the capacity for sentience, or the development of the central nervous system. Let us further imagine that a technique has been developed which could inhibit or prevent the development of the brain or nervous system, but otherwise allow for normal development of the embryo. Would it be morally licit to experiment on embryos intentionally crippled so that they can never meet the criterion of humanness? The response would undoubtedly be one of moral outrage. On analysis, such outrage would be seen to rest on the wrongness of interference with the potentiality of the embryo to develop further.

Indeed, such a sense of moral outrage may provide the final validation of the argument. There is, many would argue, a deep sense of moral disquiet about research on early embryos. Admittedly, it is a non-rational reaction, but this does not mean that it should be ignored. There is a perfectly proper place for intuitive response in the sum total of moral views and values.

Equally, there is a perfectly respectable argument for taking account of a strongly held and widely held sense of moral outrage or repulsion when considering any scheme for ordering affairs. Furthermore, the fact that such moral outrage can draw on some reasoned argument as well as intuition makes it doubly valid as a ground for objection.

The argument from potential is not short of critics.[3] The principal objection raised against it is that it reduces to the argument that there exists a duty to regard an entity as if it were now what in fact it has only the potential to be. And, it is said, attempts to generalize this proposition will show its implausibility. Is a father, it can be asked, morally obliged to treat his 6-year-old son as if he were already a concert pianist merely because he has, on present reckoning, the potential to become one? The answer, in a crude sense, must be that no such duty exists. But in a more subtle sense, it can be said that at the first inkling of his son's potential to be a pianist, the father may indeed be morally obliged not to thwart this possibility. He may indeed have a duty not to prevent his son's potential from having a chance to be realized. This is the potentiality argument being used here.

Arguably the case is stronger when the potential in question is that of becoming a human person. We should all be slow, it could be urged, to thwart the chance the entity may have, not only because it is a real chance for a real entity, but also because of what denying the chance may say about our sense of responsibility to future generations.

Furthermore, it is not the case, as some maintain, that the argument from potential ultimately takes us back to primeval slime. An ovum and a sperm do not, on their own, have the *potential* to become a human person. They do not separately have the necessary and sufficient conditions for such potential. Once united, there is a new entity which, for the first time, at least has the chance to become a human person. Admittedly, even this new entity does not have the sufficient conditions to become a human person, since it still needs a welcoming womb. But, if this is available, nothing more is required of the entity itself, except that it develop.

A further point can be made. There are those who reject the argument from potential here, because, perhaps, they favour embryo research on utilitarian grounds. But, at the same time, they are content to use this very argument about potential in other contexts. Take, for example, support for selective abortion where a pregnant woman has been exposed to rubella and there is a risk that the child will suffer from a congenital disability. The justification for abortion here can be based only on the argument from potential. The foetus is harming no one. The abortion is not sought because of the present state of either the mother or the foetus. And, let us assume,

---

[3] These critics are, however, fairly comprehensively seen off by Professor Richard Hare in his 'Abortion and the Golden Rule?' *Philosophy and Public Affairs* (4), 1974–5, 201.

the foetus is not suffering hardship while still *in utero*. It may not, indeed, be disabled. Once born, of course, the baby may be a burden to itself and, perhaps, to others. So, the argument goes, it may be permissible to abort it.

But is that not to respond to the foetus by reference to its potential rather than its current reality? Is this not to treat the foetus as if it were already the disabled child it may become, and to argue that there is a duty to save it from a miserable life, quite apart from any rights or duties the mother may have? It strikes me that if the argument from potential is valid here—and it would appear to be—then it can be validly applied elsewhere, in particular in the case of the embryo.

Holbrook, in an interesting paper, argues cogently that rejection of the potentiality argument comes from an approach to medicine and science which he calls 'mechanistic Darwinism'.[4] Explanation and understanding of life and being are reduced by this approach to mere discussions of 'molecules'.[5] In the process, he urges, much that goes into the understanding of being and living and the potential for these is lost. This mechanistic approach and the accompanying nineteenth-century utilitarianism are, in his view, responsible for our losing our way as we grapple with issues such as the moral status of the embryo.[6]

One manifestation of what Holbrook would term a mechanistic approach is the appearance of the term 'pre-embryo' to describe the entity for about the first 14 days of its existence, after which it becomes an embryo proper. This may look like a mere linguistic ploy, designed to make a moral issue go away by defining it out of existence.[7] Its adherents claim otherwise. They argue[8] that the term is necessary to take account of the scientific facts that for the first 14 days of embryonic development, more or less, there is no more than a mass of cells, some of which will become embryo, some of which will become placenta. Until it is clear which cells will become the embryo, it cannot, they claim, be plausibly said that this mass of cells constitutes an embryo. From this, they deduce that research is licit on the 'pre-embryo'. A number of responses can be made. The first and most obvious is that if it cannot be known which cells will become the embryo, but it is known that

---

[4] D. Holbrook, 'Medical ethics and the potentialities of the living being', 291 *British Medical Journal* 459 (1985).   [5] Ibid.

[6] See further the lively exchanges between B. F. Scarlett and P. Singer and H. Kuhse, 'The moral status of Embryos' 10 *Journal of Medical Ethics* 79 (1984), and 'Correspondence', 10 *Journal of Medical Ethics* 217 (1984). It will be clear that I regard Scarlett as having the better of the argument.

[7] For example, at a meeting in 1986, John Maddox, editor of *Nature*, described the resort to 'pre-embryo' as 'a cosmetic trick', and Dr Robert Edwards remarked, 'I am not sure what scientists or doctors would think about "pre-embryo", but many would question it.' CIBA, *Human Embryo Research: Yes or No* (Ciba Foundation, 1986) p. 150.

[8] See, *First Report of the Voluntary Licensing Authority for Human In Vitro Fertilization and Embryology* (Medical Research Council and Royal College of Obstetricians and Gynaecologists, 1986).

some will do so, then those dealing with it must do so on the basis that all the cells may be the embryo. This must be so, given the reluctance to do research on the embryo once its identity can be ascertained. If there is this reluctance, and if some cells are destined to become an embryo, the conclusion offered seems inevitable.

The second flaw in this approach lies in the reference to a 'mass of cells' some of which will be placenta and some embryo, but which at present is neither. To speak in this way allows for only two ways whereby the embryo can develop as a separate entity. Either it appears by magic on or around the fourteenth day, or the control and development necessary for its emergence was 'inherent in the original mass'.[9] The former solution must be rejected by the scientist. The latter solution destroys the thesis on which he relies.

There is a third objection. The better understanding of embryonic development may well justify terminology such as 'pre-embryo'. But this is terminology about facts. It says nothing about how we should respond morally to those facts. It is not enough, in other words, to say that we now know more about the development of early embryos, and that this, and no more, invalidates any moral objection to research on embryos. This will not do. What has to be demonstrated is what it is about the 'pre-embryo' which marks it off from the embryo in terms of the moral claim it may make on us. And merely to say that some cells become placenta may not be enough, as has been suggested, if we do not know at the outset which cells become what.

THE SPECIAL NATURE OF
HUMAN REPRODUCTION MATERIALS

Quite apart from arguments about potentiality, there is another reason why research on early embryos in the circumstances I have outlined may be said to be morally wrong. This rests on the proposition that there is something special, something commanding moral respect, in human reproductive products. Sperm and ova are not to be regarded in the same way as nail clippings or flaking skin. They are surrounded by taboo and a sense of special respect which lies at the heart of the Jewish and Christian cultural tradition. They have traditionally been the object of moral concern and respect. They must not be wasted or misused. Even greater, then, is the respect due when an ovum has been fertilized by a sperm. Here you have the unique product of reproduction, to which, on this argument, is attached great moral significance. To take this unique product and use it as an object of research

[9] *Supra* n. 4, 461.

is to demean us all by demeaning our respect for that part of us which is uniquely associated with our continuity, and thus with our humanness. Such an argument can, of course, invoke the potentiality argument, but is quite separate from it. It relies not on what these products may become, but on what they already are.

WHERE THE ARGUMENTS LEAD

These then are the arguments about the moral status of early embryos. They have awkward consequences for those who wish to do research on embryos. They face the conclusion that research on embryos is never morally permissible. It has been argued in reply that since the 'spare' embryos have become available, it would be quite wrong not to use them for the purposes of research, to advance the state of knowledge, and to assist in understanding and caring for those embryos which have been or will, in the future, be implanted. The reasoning is made more compelling by the observation that the entity we are discussing is so small and so unlike anything we would recognize as human that to talk in terms of its having any claim on our attention as against, for example, the suffering of a child, who might be cured by the application of knowledge gained through research, is unconscionable.

Two replies are available. The first is that the utilitarian calculus is not so easy. Much depends on the weight you attach to the interests of the embryo and what the protection of those interests may represent as a statement about our commitment to respect for humanness, or the potential for humanness. To prefer the interests of future children or science to those of a minuscule entity just because it is minuscule and immensely vulnerable is to assume what has to be proved, that the interests of the embryo, because it is minuscule, are worth less. To say that, for example, the key to Down's syndrome could be discovered from such research, is, of course, first, to speculate; second, to engage in 'shroud-waving'; and third, to refuse to concede that some things morally may not be discovered if the means of discovering them are morally indefensible. The second response would be that utilitarianism is not the only basis for moral analysis.

REGULATION

Once having taken a position on the morality of conducting research on embryos, there still remains the question of whether any type of regulation should be laid down, and, if so, what the form and content should be. As to form, the options range from professional conscience to professional self-regulation to generally agreed guidelines to appropriately drafted law.

Because of the importance of the questions at stake, because they represent a statement of society's concern for humanness, and because of doubts as to whether the scientific community can restrain itself adequately, I would argue that, whatever moral view is adopted, regulation is called for, and that law must be the appropriate regulatory mechanism. As to which moral view the law should adopt, it is helpful to recall the notion of moral outrage which many in society feel about research on early embryos. Law, as a mechanism for social regulation, if it is to command respect (and therefore obedience), must not stray too far from the collective conscience of society. Thus, if the sense of moral outrage were felt widely enough and were strong enough, this would prove to be an *additional* ground, over and above any reasoned arguments, to outlaw research on embryos. It is equally important, of course, to avoid mere slavish adherence to the majority's view. Whether lawmakers should adhere to a strongly held view or seek to lead opinion in some other direction, is a central issue of democracy. Ordinarily, the law should lead, regardless of popular views, where some fundamental right is involved. Here, the fundamental right asserted is that of the embryo, and popular views and concern for fundamental rights point the same way.

If it is decided that research on embryos should be outlawed, does this mean that any 'spare' embryos must be discarded? It does not. Instead, the arguments already advanced concerning the moral claims of the embryo and the moral wrongness of creating the circumstances in which we have to choose which embryo should continue to live suggest otherwise. The creation of 'spare' embryos should not be facilitated in the first place. This would mean that a woman would have to content herself with the 16-per-cent chance of pregnancy associated with the taking and fertilizing of one egg at a time and the implantation of the resulting embryo. She would also have to accept that she may have to undergo a number of laparoscopies if she is to become pregnant, by IVF. This, however, is the price she must pay if any other course is morally objectionable.

POSTSCRIPT: REPORT OF THE COMMITTEE
UNDER THE CHAIRMANSHIP OF
DAME MARY WARNOCK

Here is not the place for a detailed analysis of the whole range of recommendations made by the Committee. It may be of interest, however, to take note of the section of the Report which deals with experimentation on embryos, in particular, chapter 11.

At the outset of the Report, indeed in the second paragraph of the Foreword, the Committee states its aim as being 'to *argue* in favour of those positions which we have adopted, and to give due weight to the counter-arguments where they exist' (emphasis original). This echoes my own view that argument must try to win the day. Unfortunately, this commitment to argument is not reflected in what is actually contained in the Report. First of all, only a few sentences earlier, the Committee can be seen to be looking two ways at the same time. For, while the Committee accepts that 'reason and sentiment are not opposed to each other in this field', it warns, at the same time, that 'moral indignation, or acute uneasiness, may often take the place of argument', something it apparently disapproves of. The precise weight or validity to be attached to reasoning, or, for that matter, to sentiment, is immediately fudged. This ambivalence, or lack of intellectual clarity, dogs the Committee in the area I shall be considering.

Second, it is a curious feature of the Report that it does not in fact consist of *arguments*, but rather of *conclusions* about arguments. This is a major disappointment of the Report. For, if it is to serve as the basis for widespread public discussion, there should be more of the meat of the arguments, or, to change the metaphor, more of the algebra in the equation before we reach the conclusion. Only in this way can people coming fresh to the issues run the arguments down and test them.

What does the Committee have to say about the moral status of the embryo in the context of experimentation? First, it is important to notice that this was one of the two issues on which some members were prompted to submit an Expression of Dissent (the other being surrogacy, on which two of the sixteen members dissented). The Committee, by a majority (nine members), recommends in paragraph 11. 30 that legislation be passed regulating the use of embryos for experimentation. Such legislation 'should provide that research may be carried out on any embryo resulting from *in vitro* fertilisation, whatever its provenance, up to the end of the fourteenth day after fertilisation'. Seven members dissented. Three took the view that experimentation should not be permitted under any circumstances. Four were prepared to permit experiments on 'spare' embryos, but took the view that 'research should not be permitted on embryos brought into existence specifically for that purpose or coming into existence as a result of other research'.

Clearly, and not surprisingly, the Committee was seriously divided. Seven members agree in whole or in part with the view on experimentation I advanced earlier. Thus, I will concern myself here with the views of the other nine members, the bare majority. And what I am concerned with is not their conclusion, but the thinking and analysis behind it. The more closely you look, I suggest, the more there emerges a picture of ambivalence, confusion, and muddled thinking about the central issue, the status of the embryo, from which the view on experimentation must be derived.

Inconsistencies

Perhaps the best place to start in identifying the confusion in the majority's approach is to look at paragraph 11. 17. It states that 'we were agreed that the embryo of the human species ought to have a special status . . . which should be enshrined in legislation'. It is crucial to remember, by the way, that the Committee is here discussing the status of the embryo quite independently of any question of experimentation or any question of the point at which it may acquire personhood. (The Committee side-steps the issue of humanness (or personhood) by merely stating that the formation of the primitive streak at around 15 days after fertilization is 'one reference point in the development of the human individual' (paragraph 11. 22). So it is, but why is it the reference point chosen as crucial?) In other words, it is discussing the status of the embryo pure and simple. The recommendation made is that 'the embryo of the human species should be afforded some protection in law.' So far, so good. Some protection is better than no protection. The next sentence, however, which opens paragraph 11. 18, is somewhat more equivocal: 'That protection should exist does not entail that this protection may not be waived in certain specific circumstances.' Clearly, it does not mean that the protection can be waived by the embryo. Rather, it must mean that it can be waived by others, and that such a waiver will mean a loss of protection.

Now you will remember that the Committee recommends that experimentation be permissible for the first 14 days after fertilization. Thus 'some protection in law' in paragraph 11. 17 becomes no protection in law for the first 14 days by the time you reach the next paragraph, 11. 18. The justification offered for the waiver of protection is the straightforward utilitarian thesis that 'continued research is essential, if advances in treatment and medical knowledge are to continue' (paragraph 11. 18). The argument that the notion of a special status may not readily be compatible with such rudimentary utilitarianism does not seem to have exercised the Committee. Certainly, the Committee does not see special status as connoting any idea of rights, let alone fundamental rights. Furthermore, the proposition that utilitarianism may not be the only way of looking at the world of right and wrong does not get a look-in. So, the 'special status . . . enshrined in legislation' turns out to be something of a hoax when examined in detail.

Not only is it a hoax, it also indicates the extent of the Committee's desire to look both ways at the same time. Quite simply, the majority wanted to have its cake and eat it too. You can detect the unease with which they approached the issue of experimentation. They wanted to make it clear that embryos were not mere chattels to be regarded casually and used willy-nilly. They realized, however, that if they embraced this view too enthusiastically, it could embarrass them in their obvious desire to support the use of embryos for research. So they settled on what looks like a compromise unless, of course, you regard being used for the purposes of experimentation as being assigned a special status.

The confusion or ambivalence in the Committee's attitude to the embryo is not limited to the recommendations concerning its special status. Nowhere can there be found a considered statement of just what status the embryo should be given. Any statement which is offered is countermanded, either in the same paragraph or subsequently. The reason is, I repeat, that, quite simply, even the majority of the Committee never resolved for itself this central dilemma. It comes as no great surprise, therefore, that its recommendations are contradictory and appear to be ill considered.

Let me offer some proof of my contention. I can do this best by concentrating merely on the recommendation in paragraph 10. 11. The Committee states there that 'the concept of ownership of human embryos seems to us to be undesirable'. It recommends, therefore, that 'legislation be enacted to ensure that there is no right of ownership in a human embryo'. The briefest study of the rest of the Report will indicate that this recommendation represents both a jurisprudential flaw and evidence of muddled philosophical analysis.

The Jurisprudential Flaw

This lies in the fact that while there is to be no right of ownership in an embryo, the very next sentence in paragraph 10. 11 states that a couple who have stored an embryo for their own use may have 'rights to the use and disposal of the embryo'. What, you may ask, is ownership but an abstract concept intended to capture the notion of a bundle of rights which can be exercised over something, and, in particular, the right to use and dispose of something? Thus, while legislating ownership away, the Committee contemplates its reappearance in all but name. It could be said, in response, that paragraph 10. 11 makes no mention of sale, so that at least the embryo is *res extra commercio* if not *res nullius*, and that the rights of use and disposal are limited to the couple. The difficulty with both these points is that the Committee recommends, in paragraph 13. 13, that 'the sale or purchase of embryos should be permitted', subject to appropriate licensing procedures. So, if a couple can have rights to use and dispose of an embryo, and a storage agency or even — and this is not clear — a scientific researcher or establishment can sell embryos, and if embryos may be used for research and thereby (or thereafter) destroyed, it seems to me that you have all the rights and powers commonly associated with ownership — namely, use, alienation, sale, disposal, and destruction. Thus, the recommendation in paragraph 10. 11 seems to be jurisprudential nonsense. That is not to say that the Committee did not know what it was doing. It *is* to say, however, that the means used fail to achieve the desired result. This is not surprising, since the result aimed at — namely, that the embryo shall be special and yet not special, more than a chattel yet the same as one — is impossible to achieve.

Muddled Philosophical Analysis

It is, of course, quite clear why the Committee was opposed to the idea of ownership of an embryo. Ownership is a concept applied to chattels, but not to persons, and an embryo is not a chattel. It has, the Committee agrees, a special moral status, whether or not it has reached the developmental stage at which the Committee recognizes personhood. But, as we have seen, from a legal point of view the Committee's recommendations, in effect, reduce an embryo to the status of a chattel. And, of course, by recommending that it is morally permissible to experiment on an early embryo, the Committee contradicts the very reasoning which persuaded it to recommend that the embryo should not be subject to ownership (that is, because it is something more than a chattel).

The indecision and lack of intellectual clarity do not stop there. In paragraph 11. 24 the Committee recommends that 'spare' embryos may be used for experimentation, but that the consent of the couple for whom the embryo was generated is called for. What is the reason for requiring consent? One reason might be that the couple have rights over the embryo, as over any other thing which is theirs, which cannot be infringed without consent. But this would again suggest ownership, and the embryo is not supposed to be amenable to ownership. An alternative reason could be that the embryo has some special moral status, which, after all, the Committee seeks to assert elsewhere, and that respect for this status is shown by seeking consent before research. After all, requiring consent in everyday medical ethics is a means of protecting individuals from inroads into their right to self-determination. Here, of course, consent cannot come from the embryo. It has to come from another, a proxy. But traditional moral and legal analysis has always held that proxies may consent only to that which is in the best interests of the one who is unable to consent, or at least is not against that other's interests. So, if consent is required out of recognition of the moral status of the embryo, it is a form of consent quite different from other forms, in that, far from being insisted on so as to *protect* the embryo, it allows for exactly the opposite. Both here and in paragraph 11. 18, where, you will recall, the Committee talks of how the protection afforded to the embryo may be waived, you have provisions which purport to recognize the interests and status of the embryo and then vest in others the power to ignore or violate those interests, rendering them nugatory.

Paragraph 12. 5 provides a further example of what I have termed 'philosophical muddle'. In chapter 12 the Committee considers 'Possible Future Developments in Research'. One such development is the use of human embryos for testing drugs or other substances. The Committee notes that 'this is an area that causes deep concern because of the possibility of mass production of *in vitro* embryos, perhaps on a commercial basis, for these purposes'. It concludes: 'We feel very strongly that the routine testing of drugs on human embryos is not an acceptable area of research because this would require the *manufacture of large numbers of embryos. . . .* the testing of such substances *on a very small scale may be justifiable*' (my emphasis).

Leaving aside what amounts to large numbers or a very small scale, this shows once more, I would suggest, the hopelessly ambivalent stance of the Committee. If the embryo can be experimented on until 14 days after fertilization 'whatever its provenance' (paragraph 11. 29)—that is, regardless of whether the embryos were generated specifically for research—why should embryos not be mass-produced for testing drugs? Bear in mind that this could well lead to 'advances in treatment and medical knowledge' (paragraph 11. 18), which is the basis offered to justify experimentation. Can the reason be that the Committee simply baulked at this idea because of some intrinsic sense of revulsion? If this is so, it must be because the embryo, even the early embryo before 14 days have elapsed, *is* to the majority of the Committee something more than an object available for use. But, to follow the argument through, to offer reasons, would seriously expose the inconsistencies between this view and the earlier view on experimentation.

So, the Committee contents itself with 'We feel very strongly' and ignores the obligations to provide arguments and reasons, an obligation they imposed on themselves at the outset. Furthermore, while the Committee feels strongly about the use of large numbers of embryos, it does not baulk at the idea of testing drugs on a very small scale. What principled argument can be offered to support the distinction? The objection to the use of embryos may turn on the moral status of the embryo. If this is so, numbers cannot be relevant, as each embryo would have as much moral worth as the next. Alternatively, the objection may turn on some 'slippery slope' argument that things may go too far. I will ignore the basic objection to such arguments, which is that taking one step does not entail or even imply taking others. Instead, what has to be made clear is why there is a slope down which we may slip; why, in other words, there is an increased risk of moral offence. Surely, if the Committee is convinced of its earlier position, that it is morally licit to experiment on early embryos, then there is no question of having taken a first step towards something morally wrong. Thus, a 'slippery slope' objection seems hard to maintain. The researcher would appear to be on even ground and in no danger of slipping.

The only real objection to the use of even early embryos for drug testing must, I repeat, lie in a sense of revulsion, a 'strong feeling', which is left unargued because of the intellectual embarrassment such argument would entail. And, finally, if strong feelings are a significant basis for opinion at this point of the Report, why are they not elswhere, as regards, for instance, the recommendations regarding experimentation? If the Committee conceded that they are a sufficient basis for reaching a conclusion, the very foundations of the Report are threatened, in that *no* recommendation can be better than another, feelings being as significant a basis for reaching decisions as any other. If, on the other hand, strong feelings are not a sufficient basis, the reasons which are offered to justify the conclusions about experimentation would, if applied to testing drugs, demand that an opposite view be taken.

All this should come as no surprise. In the third paragraph of the Foreword, the Committee pledges itself to 'basing our views on argument rather than sentiment, though we have necessarily been mindful of the truth that matters of ultimate value are not susceptible of proof'. The majority never really solved the matters of ultimate value, so that argument was used when it could be; but feelings, or sentiment, were fallen back on when the Committee wanted to look both ways.

Regulation

Let me make one final comment. I notice with interest the extent to which the Committee relies on the use of law and, in particular, the criminal law, as the appropriate regulatory mechanism to support its recommendations concerning surrogacy and experimentation. To argue that certain conduct is morally wrong does not, of course, entail that it should be made unlawful, far less a crime. Good argument is usually thought to be needed to justify recourse to the law when seeking to regulate the behaviour of people.

Unfortunately, nowhere does the Committee offer any analysis or reason to explain its conclusion. For example, the ideas of free choice and individual liberty identified with Mill must have been rejected, presumably on some notion of a risk of harm to others involved in surrogacy and experimentation. The harm, however, is not always carefully identified. Equally, self-regulation, whether by professional institutions or the scientific and medical community or the individual practitioner or researcher, was also clearly rejected as the appropriate form of regulation, as was resort to some form of Code of Practice or other non-legal device. Equally, use of the civil law was rejected in favour of the criminal law. This happens to be a conclusion I endorse, but it would have been better to see arguments. In particular, it would have been helpful to see arguments on the type of criminal law and on the sanctions which the Committee envisaged. Criminal law covers a lot of ground, from minor administrative crimes such as parking offences, with equally minor sanctions, to major crimes against the State, the person, and property. Where, along this scale, did the Committee intend that its recommended crimes be placed? This question, like many others, goes unanswered. As a document exploring the complex relationship between law and morality, the Report must therefore be counted a major disappointment.

SECOND POSTSCRIPT

It is of interest to note some of the recent developments which have taken place in Australia. By the mid-1980s doctors and scientists, particularly in Melbourne, led the world in research in IVF and embryology. The reaction of the State of Victoria was to pass the Infertility (Medical Procedures) Act 1984, which prohibits the creation of human embryos specifically for the purpose of research. The Act does not, however, define what is an embryo. Professor Wood, Deputy Chairman of the Department of Obstetrics at Monash University, has since threatened to take his research team elsewhere if the law is not clarified. He has suggested a possible definition of an embryo as being a fertilized egg after 20 hours of development—that is, when the male and female nuclei fuse. This, he argues, would at least allow some scope for research on fertility by means of experiments on fertilized eggs.[10]

Meanwhile, in October 1986, the Australian Senate's Select Committee on the proposed Federal Human Embryo Experimentation Bill (1985) issued its long-awaited report.[11] The majority of the Committee decided that there were no objections to therapeutic research, but proposed criminal sanctions against those who engage in 'destructive non-therapeutic experimentation which frustrates the development of the human embryo'.[12] The Committee made it clear that in using the term 'embryo' as 'the fertilized ovum and succeeding stages up to the observation of human form', they meant 'to speak of genetically new human life organised as a distinct entity oriented towards further development'.[13] The Committee went on:

it is in its orientation to the future that the Committee finds the feature of the embryo which commands such a degree of respect as to prohibit destructive non-therapeutic experimentation. While a certain respect may be accorded to the embryo in deference to the 'human and social origins of the sperm and eggs which formed them' (as expressed by the National Health and Medical Research Council [of Australia]) it is this Committee's view that a further degree of respect is due in deference to the embryo's human and social future.[14]

The Government in the United Kingdom, by contrast, has so far been unwilling to propose legislation in the light of the Warnock Report, except in the case of surrogacy. A charitable view could be that this is a justified attempt to allow considered argument and debate. A less charitable view may condemn this inaction as reflecting a lack of political will or courage, since it is inevitable that some people will be deeply offended whatever legislation is proposed. The unfortunate consequence is an absence of legislation, which satisfies no one. To further the consultation process or buy more time, the

---

[10] See 6 *Bioethics News* 1–3 (Jan. 1987).
[11] *Human Experimentation in Australia* (Australian Government Publishing Service, 1986).
[12] Ibid., p. xv.   [13] Ibid.   [14] Ibid.

Government did, however, issue a Consultation Paper in December 1986 asking for news concerning the implementation by legislation of the proposals contained in the Warnock Report. The Paper specifically referred to embryo experimentation, and stated that it was the Government's intention, after receiving submissions, to publish a Bill containing alternative draft clauses on embryo research, so that Parliament could then have a free vote on the issue.[15]

[15] DHSS, *Legislation on Human Infertility Services and Embryo Research: A Consultation Paper* (Cm. 46. HMSO, Dec. 1986).

Ethics in Clinical Decision Making:
The Care of the Very-low-birth-weight Baby*

Given that doctors are called upon to make decisions in the management of patients, what I am concerned with here is what makes these decisions right or wrong, or more right than wrong, in a moral sense. Specifically, I am concerned with decisions involving the care of very-low-birth-weight (VLBW) babies.[1]

Merely to pose this question is to prompt another, more fundamental one. Can we sensibly or profitably discuss the rightness and wrongness of clinical decisions? There are still those, both within and outside the medical profession, who argue that we cannot. They claim that such issues are not amenable to analysis, that they are the product of 'common sense' or experience, or that they depend on the particular facts of each case. I doubt if much persuasion is needed to convince you that this is an unnecessarily pessimistic position to hold. You may also agree that it is, in essence, an untenable one. For, if decisions are in fact made, and if those making them claim to think before they decide, rather than, for example, toss a coin, then they are, indeed, engaging in some sort of rational or reasoned analysis. That being so, there is no reason in principle why this process of rational analysis should be conducted only privately in the head of the decider, with the rest of us then being confronted only with the conclusion. There is no reason why the reasoning should not be articulated and thereby submitted to scrutiny by others, since, unless infallibility is being claimed, there may be times when

---

* This paper was originally presented at the Consensus Development Conference on the Very-Low-Birth-Weight Baby in Sydney in 1985. It appears here in a slightly amended form. Since the Conference was in Australia, I drew on Australian experience. See V. Yu, B. Bajuk, and E. Hollingsworth, 'Neonatal Intensive Care for Extremely Low Birth Weight Infants', 17 *Australian Paediatric Journal* 262 (1981); V. Yu, 'Annotation: Effectiveness of Neonatal Intensive Care', 20 *Australian Paediatric Journal* 85 (1984); idem, 'A Question of Handicap', in P. Singer, ed., *The Tiniest Newborn* (Centre for Human Bioethics, Monash University, 1984); idem, 'Survival and 2-year Outcome of Extremely Pre-term Infants', 91 *British Journal of Obstetrics and Gynaecology* 640 (1984). For a recent English contribution, see A. Whitelaw, 'Death as an Option in the Neonatal Intensive Care Unit', *The Lancet*, 9 Aug. 1986, p. 328. There is, of course, a vast literature on this subject. See, as a start, T. Beauchamp and J. F. Childress, *Principles of Biomedical Ethics*, 2nd edn. Oxford University Press, 1983), and references therein.

[1] A baby who weighs less than 1500 grams at birth.

others can help. And this is quite apart from any right which others may have to participate, a point I shall enlarge on later.

So, I suggest, we can discuss the rights and wrongs of clinical decisions. And, because we can, we must, since by our discussion we demonstrate our commitment to a morally defensible system of medical care.

The next question, then, given that we *can* analyse the ethics of clinical decisions, how do we do it? We do it, surely, by resorting to the same language and techniques of moral reasoning that we use in everyday life as ordinary citizens without having had any special training. All of us have agonized, for example, about whether, in a particular set of circumstances, we should tell someone a lie or keep a secret. We resolve such dilemmas to our own and, we hope, others' satisfaction by reasoning from some general principle, examining its exceptions and limits, identifying any other relevant principle which may run counter to it, and then applying the resulting analysis to the problem at hand. To take an example, the principle 'Love thy neighbour' needs analysis before one can extract from it any guidance in a particular context. Clearly, it invokes charity, but it does not seem to entail the proposition that we cannot dislike someone or that we cannot at times harm someone who, perhaps, is attacking us.

Medical ethics is no different. We identify the moral principles relevant to the issue, and seek to apply them in a concrete way. But it is as well to bear in mind an obvious caveat here. Medical ethics does not consist of a series of answers to all known or conceivable problems. Rather, it involves a process of reasoning whereby a decision-maker can arrive at a morally respectable and defensible position when faced with any problems.

So what are the moral principles which we must have regard to when considering medical care generally? And what are the tools? The notion of reasoning is familiar, but the language in which it is couched may not be. We must come to understand and be comfortable with the principles of beneficence (seeking to do good), non-maleficence (seeking to avoid harm), respect for life, respect for dignity, and respect for autonomy (self-determination). Of course, merely to set them out in this way does not take us much further, since we must then begin the hard work of discovering what they mean and how, if at all, they can be reconciled if, as may be the case, they appear to be in conflict.

When we ask what each of these principles means, we find on examination that this causes us to notice and explore another level of enquiry, and in the process helps us to identify a central issue on which we need to focus. Let me explain.

Beneficence, or doing good, obliges us, analytically, to embark on two further enquiries. The first is obvious: what is good? The second follows naturally from this; indeed, it is an aspect of it, namely, who decides what is good? The same principle becomes, if put negatively, the principle that we must avoid harm; and this again raises the question of who sets the criteria for harm, who decides what is harmful.

Respect for life and dignity both, in turn, oblige us to enquire what are the criteria for such respect, which then invites the question of who decides what is respectful of life or of dignity. Equally, respect for autonomy, or self-determination, proves on examination to ask a subsidiary and yet crucial question: namely, is this a case where respect is due, because, for example, the person involved may be incompetent, may not know his own mind? The question again becomes, who sets the criteria for competence, or decides when someone knows his own mind?

In short, in asking what these general principles mean, we are asking who sets the moral agenda for our society, whether generally or with specific reference to the care of VLBW babies, say. If it is the doctor alone who decides what is good or harmful for the baby, then we must notice what this means. First, we will have declared our commitment to moral principles. But, second, we will then have declared that we are prepared to let the doctor, or doctors generally, be the arbiters or authorities on what those moral principles are and mean, and how they should be translated into action. And if incidentally you decide on the parent rather than the doctor in the case of the VLBW baby, say, the same argument equally applies.

Now I feel strongly that the point cannot be made too often that, ordinarily, we do not regard doctors as the moral arbiters, the moral authorities, in our society. We may regard them as possessed of great skills and blessed with extraordinary qualities of caring. But do we regard them as having the last word on what is right and wrong? I am tempted to think that few would argue this. And this must be equally true as regards any parent whose child is in need of medical care. Of course, the parent is usually deeply caring, and wants to do what is best. It is fair to say, however, that the history of our society's development has been one of setting limits to what a parent may do to, or with, his or her child. The criterion in establishing such limits has been what is thought to be morally right for the *child*, regardless and, in some cases, in spite of what the parent may think.

My submission, then, is that if we are talking about determining what is ethically right in clinical decisions concerning the VLBW baby, we must go beyond, and cannot necessarily be bound by, what a doctor, or doctors in conclave, or a parent, or parents in conclave, may decide. We must look elsewhere to discover the moral agenda, the meaning of the moral principles previously referred to, and how these should be applied. And the only place we can look, in my view, is in the heart of our society, to discover what we as a society hold to be right.

I admit, of course, that this is complicated. It may also appear at first blush to be a recipe for majoritarianism—whereby, if 51 per cent of the population think that something is right, then it is so—or for ignorant primitivism or anarchy. But I am not calling for majoritarianism, since morality is not a matter of numbers. I am demanding that any decisions which are taken must be properly informed ones. I am suggesting, in short, that we should look to the process of debate which has produced considered responses to such moral issues as abortion, capital punishment, and chemical and nuclear warfare, for criteria which will serve as moral guidelines in the treatment of the VLBW baby. Just as with the other issues mentioned, not all will agree on the conclusions reached, though they may accept the principles employed in analysis. But that must be inevitable in moral discourse, as elsewhere, when the issues are of great complexity.

Of course, it will then be for the doctor and parent to decide in any particular case how the guidelines apply. In that sense, decisions are always for doctors and parents. But the crucial issue is not who decides in the particular case, but who sets the moral framework within which such decisions are made.

Having said that, it must be obvious that I do not see it as appropriate to stipulate myself, even if I could do so, the morally appropriate responses to the care of the VLBW baby. Instead, it is my role, as I see it, to make some contribution to the continuing social debate out of which will emerge—indeed, is already emerging—some set of moral guidelines. That may be said to be the purpose of discussions such as this. Their importance lies not so much in what any individual may say as in the gradual raising of public consciousness and the consequent inclining towards solutions that we can all live with.

Let me now move on to the heart of the issue. What do such principles as avoiding harm or doing good or respecting life mean in the particular context of the VLBW baby? It is one thing to say that we must respect the life of a 750-gram baby, but quite another to know what course of conduct, if any, this morally obliges us to adopt. Equally, it is one thing to wish to avoid harm, but quite another to know what this entails when the baby is very small, sick and possibly disabled.

In my analysis, I will discuss two separate issues. The first, and by far the more important, is the care of the child. The second, which I shall look at only briefly, is commonly overlooked. It is the care of the parent. I shall discuss both of them in general terms first, before attempting to apply them in practice.

Finally, by way of introduction, it may be helpful to set the scene by outlining the sort of factual circumstances which are involved. A baby has been born and, in the light of the baby's apparent condition, intensive care has begun. This is what would normally happen. Intensive care would be started unless it was the rare case in which the baby had such a gross malformation as to be obviously incompatible with continued existence. Once care has begun, the baby is assessed. After assessment, the question is asked whether to carry on or not; whether, in the language which I prefer, to treat for living or for dying. The question is whether it is morally permissible in certain cases not to carry on. What does respect for life mean here? What moral stipulation can we deduce from it?

An approach to answering such questions, or at least to providing a mode of analysing them, rests in a formula familiar to all of you. This is that the precise nature of the moral obligation — or, if you like, the operational meaning — of respect for life, or doing good and avoiding harm, turns on the baby's future 'quality of life'. There are, however, two objections which are levelled against this formula. The first is that it is morally unacceptable. The second is that, as a formula, it is meaningless or question-begging, since it leaves unanswered the quality which is the relevant quality as far as moral obligations go. It is this second objection which is more important, but let me deal with the first one straightaway.

Quality of life arguments admit and entail a premiss which some claim to find morally unacceptable. This is that the obligation to respect life does not necessarily, in all circumstances, mean that life must be saved or prolonged. Quality of life arguments call for the measuring of the person's life, in our case that of the VLBW baby, to determine whether the quality is such as to mean that we are morally permitted to choose a regime of treatment for dying. Notice, I do not talk about non-treatment. No baby should be left with no care. The question is only whether the treatment is for living or for dying.

Some deny that any life now being lived can be measured by others as to its quality. They urge that there is an absolute obligation to treat for living each and every baby, no matter what others may regard as the unfortunate consequences of so doing. They may make an exception in the case of a baby who is dying from some condition beyond help from doctors from the moment it is born, but will go no further.

The objection to this position is that it raises to an absolute principle that which, in other circumstances, would be accepted by these same advocates as a principle subject to limitations and exceptions. For, in other contexts, they, like the rest of us, would be prepared morally to defend the right to defend themselves, even if it meant that their attackers were killed. Equally, they and we accept the notion of a just war and the distinction between suicide, to be condemned, and sacrifice, to be praised, although both entail the same end, the loss of one's own life. If, then, in other circumstances, the taking of life, or, as in the case of triage in times of war, allowing to die, is morally permissible, and the preservation of life is not regarded as an absolute, it is proper to ask what special rule might exempt the care of the neonate from the operation of the non-absolutist principle. To argue that the neonate is young or innocent is to clutch at straws, since neither of these attributes will distinguish it from the child locked with its mother in a flooded section of a ship behind the bulkhead. Yet there we would not necessarily condemn the captain of the ship whose only recourse to save the ship and the rest of the passengers was to close that bulkhead and contain the flood.

If this objection to arguments about quality of life is dealt with, the harder one still remains, that the expression, without specific content, is meaningless. This must, of course, be true. Of itself, it only shows the way. It cannot serve as the end-point of any analysis.

So we must try to unwrap this notion of quality of life. The question, properly put, is, can we articulate the criteria for deciding when a VLBW baby's life would be of such a quality that care for dying is morally permissible, or even obligatory?

Let me say at the outset that I am not enamoured of the theory of interests which has recently gained considerable currency.[2] Basically, it is that arguments concerning quality of life may translate into arguments about the baby's best interests. Any judgment about best interests thus depends on the baby's having interests. But since someone may only have interests if conscious of the existence of the interests, the person, to have them, must have reached a certain level of self-awareness. This, in turn, means that certain babies have no interests and, consequently, no interest in, or moral claim to, life-saving or life-sustaining treatment.

One major difficulty is that this view seems to go too far. It supports the notion that, since no baby at birth has the capacity for self-awareness, no baby has a claim to life. Such a view, though perhaps defensible on the logic of the thesis, seems counter-intuitive. Further, it is unhelpful here, since it offers no particular guide concerning any permissible difference in approach to the disabled as opposed to the healthy. Another difficulty is that the word 'interest' is made to do all the moral work by appearing to be a technical term, in that only the self-aware may have them. But this overlooks the argument that others may hold in trust the interests of, for example, a small baby, until the baby reaches the stage of self-awareness. Indeed, if someone did not hold them in trust, wholesale infanticide would be permissible. The trustee, according to this argument, is then morally obliged to make decisions on behalf of the baby, decisions which are intended to bring the child to an enjoyment of its interests at some future date. If the evidence is that such enjoyment is impossible or most unlikely, the beginning of an argument for treatment for dying emerges. Furthermore, these difficulties with the theory of interests are quite apart from the argument that interests may be properties granted by others, rather than something arising of their own accord. It is for these reasons that, in my view, the interest theory seems an unprofitable approach, though its superficial attraction is obvious.

My approach can be stated in a series of propositions. First, the mere fact of handicap in a baby, without more, may not serve morally as a reason for

---

[2] See e.g. M. Tooley, *Abortion and Infanticide* (Clarendon Press, 1983).

discriminating against the baby in terms of the care it receives. Handicap may serve as a justification, however, if it meets criteria to be set out later. Second, avoiding harm, doing good, or respecting life, as moral principles, do not entail that all lives must be sustained or saved. There are circumstances in which it may be morally justified not to do so, since the principle is not absolute. Third, respect for life is, nevertheless, a very important principle, so important in fact that there is a prima facie obligation to sustain or save a baby's life. Fourth, respect for life is so important a principle that no one, particularly one who has the care of another, can depart from it without moral justification based soundly on moral principle itself. Fifth, the moral justification exists where there is a very good reason for not sustaining or saving the life in question. Sixth, we are forced, therefore, to set out what, if any, reasons will serve as sufficiently good reasons.

On analysis, therefore, reliance on quality of life demands that we identify the conditions or circumstances warranting treatment for dying in the case of VLBW babies. The process has two stages. First, there is the moral argument, to find some abstract classification or criterion. Then, there is the medical, factual argument as to what conditions may satisfy this criterion.

As for the moral argument, the key to its resolution, in my view, lies in that aspect of our fellow beings which we would regard as the basic common denominator of humanness in the spiritual, rather than the merely biological sense. And, to me, the common denominator lies in the capacity, or the potential capacity, to interact with surroundings and people, not necessarily intelligently or intelligibly, but in a way which is more than merely vegetating or responding autonomically. This, to my way of thinking, is what marks the person off from the mere living creature.

Some will say that I put it too low, that more should be called for to warrant treatment for living. I can only respond that this is a matter of intuitive belief—a leap of faith, if you will—having to do with what we identify as the core of moral significance in our fellows. And, of course, others may object that the result is a set of vague notions. But they are bound to be vague. They are abstractions, distillations of a concept, not scientific categories or medical conditions.

What has to be done next is to analyse and discover to what extent medical knowledge can help us add reality to these abstractions, by identifying what range of conditions may be met, and the extent to which they allow for what I have called a common denominator of humanness. This, after all, is what most neonatal intensive care units are trying to do every day.

In applying this analysis to VLBW babies, and particularly to extremely-low-birth-weight (ELBW) babies,[3] there is a major difficulty at the outset. This lies in the difficulty of *predicting* the existence of circumstances warranting

---

[3] Babies weighing less than 1,000 grams at birth.

a decision to treat for dying. In the present state of medical knowledge it may not be possible to make any prediction for quite some time in a large number of cases. In such circumstances, doctor and parent may feel obliged, and *be* obliged, to treat for living, since, even if the risk of severe handicap is 25 per cent, the individual baby may be in the 75 per cent group, and, of course, is not itself a statistic, since it has a 100 per cent chance of a healthy life or of handicap.

The ability to diagnose the baby's true condition and, therefore, to predict which category it will fall into may thus be the key to future advances in analysing the questions before us. It is probably the case that in time we shall be able more readily to identify those babies likely to have a healthy outcome. It seems very likely that this will be related to the ability to identify those at risk from peri-ventricular haemorrhage and those who have suffered it already, since it is this condition which seems most associated with mortality and serious handicap.[4] Once it becomes possible to do so, it may be that we will be more able to hazard a prognosis.

At present, however, the absence of such knowledge may trap us in a moral paradox. We may know that some babies will suffer such disabilities that we would think it morally permissible to treat them for dying. Yet, because we cannot know who will suffer in this way, we may be morally obliged, out of an abundance of caution, to treat *all* for living, since each in isolation is a baby with a good prognosis, that is, a 75 per cent chance of doing well.

A second paradox arises here. The only really sound way to discover which babies may have a good prognosis is to engage in research. Indeed, it could be said that all treatment of ELBW babies is experimental, designed as much to gain knowledge for the care of others as to care for the particular child. If such research is to continue — and its results are important, if not essential, for the solution of the dilemma we have posed — it must involve treating some babies, whether as controls or otherwise, as means to the end of knowledge rather than ends in themselves. Such research would, of course, normally be regarded as morally hard to defend.

Perhaps the way out of this particular conundrum is to argue that each intervention, given the existing state of knowledge, is done with the *primary* intention of helping that particular ELBW baby to live and grow up as a healthy baby, if at all possible. Such interventions will also produce data from which, in the future, conclusions may be drawn which will allow more appropriate choices as to treatment to be made, and this can be reckoned as an added benefit.

If this argument does serve to justify the research on ELBW babies that present treatment seems to represent, it may also offer a way to perform

---

[4] See V. Yu, 'Outlook for VLBW Infants in the 1980s' (Paper read at the Symposium on Perinatal Medicine, XVII Singapore–Malaysia Congress of Medicine, Aug. 1984).

what we set as our major task, the identification of circumstances, if any, in which treatment for dying is permissible. It would do so by suggesting that until we have a better basis for making a prognosis, we must treat for living all ELBW babies for whom the prognosis cannot, in all honesty, be said to be clear. Once such data became available, provided that they were accepted as an appropriate basis for judgments as to quality of life, then treatment for living would not be morally obligatory in all cases, and further research not aimed specifically at benefiting the particular baby would, it follows, be impermissible.

That said, that we must treat for living all ELBW and, *a fortiori*, all VLBW babies for whom a prognosis cannot in all honesty be made *as regards that particular baby*, I turn now to the next stage of the discussion. If it transpires that the baby, despite the best efforts of those caring for it, nevertheless subsequently falls into that category of baby which we would mark for treatment for dying, what do we do then?

It may be helpful to distinguish between two types of situation. The first is if the baby is still in intensive care. In such a case, the doctor is morally entitled to discontinue this care. Such care would properly be said to fall into that category of care which commentators have described as 'extraordinary', by which is meant that it is not morally obligatory. However, the baby may not die as a consequence, and it must be remembered that the intention behind ceasing intensive care was that it should.

Three options seem to present themselves. The first is for the doctor to cause the baby to die through some active intervention—to kill it, in more crude terms. While I can see the force in the commonly advanced argument that it may be morally as defensible, if not more so, to bring a baby's life to an end quickly and painlessly as to allow it to die a slow death, when, after all, the desired aim is that it should die, political reality suggests that this will not readily be sanctioned by law, and so is not an option that exists in the real world. The second is to care for the baby with all available means in all circumstances. This would appear to be a morally dubious course, since it may expose the baby to continued suffering or discomfort, and ignores what has been said earlier, that it may be morally permissible to treat for dying if the relevant criteria are met, which is so in this case. The third option is to care for the baby, by which I mean nurse, and give food and fluids and appropriate medication if there is pain, but not to intervene if some infection, or other natural circumstance, threatens the baby's life. This, I suggest, is morally permissible, if the baby meets the stipulated criteria. It is no different from the decision to allow the terminally ill to die without further intervention, when continued existence is, in fact, existence and no more.

The second situation warranting consideration is when the baby is no longer in intensive care. Having survived so far and no longer needing such care, the baby will not ordinarily die if properly nursed, fed, and given whatever else its condition from time to time may warrant. No question of life-support therapy as it is commonly understood arises. Remembering again that the decision has been taken that treatment for dying is, in the circumstances, morally permissible, what may those caring for the baby properly do? They may not kill the baby, as we have seen. Nor, in my view, may they resort to a regime of drugs, which, though represented as intended to ease pain or distress, is, in fact, designed to encourage the onset of death by, for example, suppressing respiration or reducing resistance to infection. Instead, their obligation would seem to be to treat the baby as they would a patient who is terminally ill. This means that their primary obligation is to do whatever will make the patient as comfortable as possible. This will include all necessary nursing care and may involve the provision of drugs, if there is pain or distress, as well as food and fluids, but will not include any active intervention other than that designed to achieve specific symptomatic relief. Each case must be judged on the basis of the individual needs of the individual baby, such that there is no room for laying down any specific regime of treatment, provided the general principle is observed.

Finally, it remains to be asked what the doctor's response should be if, in the situations under discussion, a parent should ask that all available forms of active intervention be employed, despite the hopelessness of the prognosis. In such a tragic case, there are, of course, moral questions about the proper use of resources, both human and financial, as well as concern for the principle of respect for life. I take the view that a parent may not properly make such a demand; or, to put it another way, that a doctor is under no obligation to comply with the parents' wish. The reason must be that resources spent on a child who, on our hypothesis, cannot benefit from what is being done are resources which cannot be spent on a child who could benefit. And this holds true whether we are considering the public or the private sector of health care.

This, then, is the analysis which I would offer. You will notice that in suggesting the moral guidelines to be followed, I have given no place to the wishes of parents or doctors, although they are, of course, important characters in the drama, and as I have said, must translate the guidelines into decisions in particular cases. I have tried to make it clear by my approach, that, in any analysis, it is the baby, and only the baby, whose circumstances are relevant. That the parents may not wish to care for a disabled baby, or that a doctor may feel that such a baby will bring hardship to many and little or no benefit to anyone, are, of course, legitimate observations. They cannot, however, in my view, properly determine the baby's care. After all, others, including institutions, may take the baby and provide for it. Furthermore, it has long ceased to be part of our moral tradition that parents may take it upon themselves to decide that their children should die. The question would not arise if the child were 6 months or 6 years old, rather than only a few days or weeks. Indeed, it is sufficiently serious to be a crime if a parent so much as neglects his child, let alone seeks to take upon himself the authority to opt for treatment for dying.

It would be wrong to conclude my analysis without some reference to the law. So far, I have confined myself to what I see as the moral arguments. These, however, must be seen against the backdrop of the law and the ordinary assumption that there is a prima facie obligation to obey the law. Some argue, somewhat plaintively, that the law is not involved in what is a complex, human tragedy, or that, if it is involved, it ought not to be. Clearly, however, the law is and should be involved in circumstances in which the life or death of a citizen, albeit a tiny baby, is in question. The law represents, if you will, the outer circle of social regulation. Some — indeed, most — matters of social conduct can properly be left to other mechanisms of social control and regulation. Our codes of taste and decency and morals ordinarily do an adequate job of inhibiting those who would break the rules. Some matters, however, are too important, touching as they do the basic liberties and even the lives of the citizenry, to be left to self-control or the sanction of conscience. Instead, the sanction of the law is required. And, by turning to the law, society demonstrates its concern and desire to regulate certain conduct in the most formal way it has, because of the interests at stake.

That said, it is a regrettable fact that the law in the area under discussion is by no means clear. An explanation may lie in the fact that developments in this area of medicine, as in others, have gone ahead of us, leaving us breathless in our attempts to understand them, let alone reflect on them and accommodate them within our existing moral and legal order. Whatever the explanation, however, it is hardly satisfactory to advise doctors and parents that the law is closely concerned with the decisions they may make, and yet not be able to tell them what the law actually requires of them.

Some guidance can, of course, be offered. It is not so much that there is a gap in the law, as that there is considerable uncertainty. To put it another way, a court would lay down what the law is if required to do so in a particular case, but until it actually does so, there is some room for doubt as to what it would decide. It is clear that this may put doctors and those who advise them in an intolerable position.

It is undoubtedly the case that the law in most jurisdictions which have confronted these issues has tended to tread very cautiously. The traditional conservatism of the law persuades the courts to side with the saving or sustaining of life. Legislators have tended to do likewise, with one eye on the opinion polls and the other on the very real problem of writing, in clear terms, a law which will not be liable to spill over, on interpretation, so as to apply to other situations of sick or dying patients when this was either not contemplated or not intended. There is, however, some evidence of a careful movement on the part of the courts. And, if my moral analysis is accepted, more movement in the law will undoubtedly be called for. Nor should this be long delayed. There is every merit in trying to get the law straight, rather than simply muddling through, particularly when some doctor may suddenly find himself in the dock on a charge of homicide. The lawyer who advised him to do whatever is now the substance of a charge, since 'no one will ever prosecute, and anyway, the jury will never convict', will not, of course, be in the dock with him!

There is, then, an urgent need to clarify the law relating to the care of the VLBW baby. It is doubtful, however, that the courts can seriously be regarded as the appropriate agents for change. Depending, as they do, on having the right case before them on which to hang principles of general application, it is obvious that some considerable time could elapse before any coherent body of law emerges. Legislation is the alternative source of law. It is unlikely in the extreme, however, that legislation, in the United Kingdom at least, will be forthcoming. There are no votes to be won, only votes to be lost, in such a controversial area. The only solution may lie, therefore, in what I have called for on a number of occasions, so far in vain, namely the establishment of a set of formal guidelines or a Code of Practice, translating the moral analysis offered above or some other analysis into a formal Code. In this way, doctors, parents, and the general public would have some authoritative source to look to for help and guidance. To those, doctors or others, who may see in my suggestion of a Code some interference in what they regard as their proper area of discretion, I can but remind them that the claimed discretion may be exercised only within the limits set down by the wider society, and that the suggested Code is simply intended to help those who have to face these awful and awesome problems. Things could be left as they are, of course, with everybody muddling through, but this fails to take account of the legitimate right which all of us have to a say in what is done to our fellow citizens.

Such a Code, were it adopted, would not have the authority of law. I would argue, however, that the urgent need for some guidance and the obvious inappropriateness of looking to our other law-making institutions serve as good grounds for stipulating that anyone who observed such a Code of Practice would be assumed to have acted lawfully, such that any challenge to a decision taken or a policy adopted would have to be made against the Code and could not be made against the doctor or parent who had followed the Code's provisions in good faith. If my suggestion of a Code is thought unacceptable; or, if acceptable, its status in relation to the law is not to be as I propose, the implications for current practice are very grave. For, given the present uncertainty in the law, the responsible legal adviser may feel obliged to err on the side of caution in giving legal advice. The consequence could be that those caring for VLBW babies may be inhibited from employing the regime of treatment which, on moral grounds, they feel is entirely justified. The morally proper response to the VLBW baby must, on that latter analysis, await a careful rejigging of the law. If this is so, law reform, or clarification becomes a matter of the highest priority.

May I now, very briefly, advert to the other issue which I said I would discuss, the often-forgotten issue of the care of the parents of VLBW babies. In particular, I wish to draw attention to two problems encountered by parents, both of which, at heart, are ethical in nature.

The first concerns the information available to these parents. It is not uncommon for parents, or one of them, to be unaware of the real circumstances of their child and to be presented, as a consequence, with a series of *faits accomplis* concerning the management and treatment of the child. I do not doubt that this is done with the worthiest of intentions, so as to save the parents from the inevitable distress attending the birth of a baby whose life is in jeopardy. I take the view, however, that parents have a right to know all relevant details about their child. The bond between parent and child should serve as sufficient reason, if reasons are needed. But other grounds exist. Although, as we have seen, parents do not have the right to ignore the moral (and legal) prescriptions of society in deciding what response or course of treatment should be adopted, a parent does, undoubtedly, have the right to *share* in the decisions concerning the child. Further, and perhaps even more important, a parent has the duty to care for a child, from which flows a right to share in any decision on care, whatever the intended outcome of such care may be. It would be putting it too low to say that it would, therefore, be unethical to keep from the parents the facts or circumstances which have given rise to the decision to resort to the particular regime of care adopted. For this could mean that a parent might invest enormous hope in doing that which the doctor has advised, always looking for improvements and often imagining them, when only one outcome, death, was ever likely. This would not merely be unethical, it would be unforgivably cruel.

Having said this, I am anxious to draw the important distinction between the right of a parent to know all material facts and the taxing questions of how best to convey this information, to break the news. The difficulty and anguish many doctors feel in carrying out this unhappy task cannot be denied. They cannot serve, however, as a valid reason for not doing it, for that is to give personal feelings preference over the legitimate rights of others. They do serve, however, as a strong argument for proper training of doctors in the complexities of communication, so that they may be better prepared to carry out what is an integral and very important part of their responsibility as doctors, the duty properly to inform patients or their responsible relatives.

The second ethical problem which concerns parents involves the care and support which is available to parents and child in those cases in which the child has received treatment for living and has survived. The child may be handicapped in some way or may be perfectly healthy, but both parent and child may bear the scars of the anguish, pain, and distress suffered on the road to recovery and health. It is a common feature of our hospital system that while a child is receiving care, both child and parent receive enormous support, advice, and assistance from the hospital staff. The moment the child is discharged, however, the parents often find themselves, or feel themselves to have been, abandoned, with no one to turn to as the hospital staff, quite rightly, turn their attention to the next very frail baby.

No one can seriously doubt the harmful consequences of such a sense of isolation and helplessness, and the very real need to remedy it. In moral terms, I would argue that there is an obligation on all of us to seek to succour and support parents in such circumstances, both for their sakes and for the sake of their children. I detect, however, an almost total lack of political will to translate this moral duty into practical measures. Instead, recent history is a story of repeated reductions in those aspects of public expenditure which would go to provide such help and support. The consequence has been that those who can afford it have been able to buy the help they need, whether in the form of counselling or just help around the house. The rest have been abandoned to their own devices, often inadequate through no fault of their own. The wrongness of this cries out for redress. And this is quite apart from its wrong-headedness. For those who are committed to the notion of the market-place and the value of self-reliance, and who do not share my view of justice and the moral value of communal help, must see that such neglect of those in need is ultimately a wasteful policy. This is because the consequence is that more demands, rather than fewer, are placed on the health and social services, as the family lurches from one avoidable crisis to the next. Regardless of which argument is deployed, however, the fact remains that, as I have said, there seems to be no political will to do anything about the situation. A moral right to help they may have, therefore; but I see little prospect of this right becoming a reality in the case of the VLBW baby and its parents.

8

R. v. *Arthur*, *Re B*, and the
Severely Disabled New-born Baby*

Legal cases involving medical-ethical issues are few and far between. There has suddenly been a flurry of court cases, however. This is an unusual development. It may reflect the lack of clarity felt by many about what conduct is ethically and legally justified, and the need for guidance. It may also reflect the increased visibility of medical-ethical problems: the more people become aware of the existence and complexity of such problems, the less they can be resolved by private arrangement. *R. v. Arthur*, decided in November 1981,[1] was concerned with the treatment of a new-born baby with Down's syndrome, as was *Re B*.[2] I shall also mention at the end *R. v. Reed*,[3] a case concerned not with new-born babies but with the controversy over euthanasia. Because of their very considerable importance, I want to consider them at length. They provoked a great deal of public attention. There was much debate on the issues they raised, the answers arrived at, and the appropriateness of the courts as the medium for deciding. In the long run, this debate can only be a good thing, even if, at the time, not all the debate was informed or considered. It may be that more heat than light was generated. I am convinced, however, that it is wrong to leave questions concerning, for example, the treatment and future existence of a child to be answered in private, behind closed doors. Painful as it may be, we have to turn over this particular stone and examine what is underneath.

Dr Arthur was acquitted on 5 November 1981 of the attempted murder of a 3-day-old baby boy with Down's syndrome. Dr Arthur had consulted the baby's parents. They had indicated that, given his handicap, they did not wish him to live. Dr Arthur then prescribed a sedative drug, DF 118, which also suppresses appetite, and otherwise ordered 'Nursing Care Only'. The baby died within 63 hours of birth. The defence to the charge was that once the baby's disability was known, Dr Arthur had engaged in a 'holding

---

* This paper originally appeared as part of chapter 4 of my book *The Unmasking of Medicine* (Paladin, 1983). As its style indicates, it was written for the general reader. It appears here in an amended form. I append to it a more detailed legal analysis, together with comments on recent writing on the subject. In this way the reader can follow, I hope, a train of thought, from general to more particular and then to critical analysis.

[1] *The Times*, 5 Nov. 1981.   [2] [1981] 1 WLR 1421.   [3] [1982] Crim. LR 819.

operation', keeping the baby comfortable and nursing and even feeding the baby, but otherwise waiting to see whether he would rally and live or whether 'nature would take its course'. This, it was said, was proper conduct, both ethically and legally.

But does the case give us good law and good medical ethics? I think that if it is understood properly, and the passion and drama of the trial are put aside, it can be seen as edging us towards a position as regards the new-born which is ethically defensible, though something of a departure from traditional legal thinking at least, if not from practice. Let me explain. At first blush, it could be said that the case tells us nothing except that a jury was unwilling to convict a much-respected doctor of a very serious crime. And this would tend to reinforce the view that prosecutions of doctors, with all the hullabaloo which surrounds them, are most inappropriate for shaping medical law and ethics. But the jury had to be instructed as to the law on which to base their finding of fact. By studying those instructions, you get a statement of the legal and, to some extent, the ethical duty of the doctor to the handicapped new-born in his charge, as understood by the judge. In my view, Mr Justice Farquharson developed new law in his instructions. He attempted to reshape the law of murder so as to make it sensitive to the moral complexities of modern medicine. He did not do it particularly clearly, nor was his analysis, with respect, all that sound. But he did provide something to build on so as to develop good medical law and ethics.

In his instructions to the jury,[4] Farquharson J. indicated that it was lawful to treat a baby with a sedating drug and offer no further care by way of food or drugs or surgery if certain criteria were met. These criteria appear to be, first, that the child is 'irreversibly disabled' and, second, that it is 'rejected by its parents'. By way of clarification for the jury, the judge drew a distinction between sedating the baby and passively letting it die, 'allowing nature to take its course', and doing a positive act to kill the baby, for example, giving it a death-dealing dose of drugs. The latter, he said, would be unlawful, the former lawful.

A number of serious criticisms can be made of this reasoning. The first concerns the distinction drawn by the judge between allowing the child to die, allowing nature to take its course, and doing some positive act to bring about its death. This distinction between omissions and commissions has, of course, a respectable pedigree in the criminal law, and has provided a full and fascinating life for generations of moral philosophers. But here it is not a good distinction for two reasons. The first is that in both law and ethics, the doctor stands in a special relationship to his patient. Once he has embarked on a course of treatment, once the child is in his care, he has a duty to act affirmatively in the interests of his patient. He breaches that duty if he stands

---

[4] All references to Farquharson J.'s instructions are taken from the official transcript.

by and does nothing in circumstances in which law and ethics indicate that he should act. Second, it may well be possible to argue that certain conduct amounts to an omission; but this in no way determines whether it is justified. It seeks by the use of linguistic or metaphysical sleight of hand to avoid the central issue: what ought the doctor to do, what is his duty?

The court could have arrived at precisely the conclusion it reached by concentrating on the notion of duty and avoiding the unsatisfactory reference to omission and commission. The question should properly have been, what is the doctor's duty to such a child? The court could then have stipulated that in certain prescribed circumstances, the doctor is not under a duty to do anything more than sedate the child and give it 'nursing care only'. The court could have decreed that the law in such circumstances absolves the doctor from a duty to feed or give drugs against infection or whatever. Not only would this have been analytically more sound, but it would also have saved us from a future of interminable wrangles as to whether this or that conduct was or was not properly to be regarded as an omission.

My second criticism refers to the criteria which have to be satisfied before the doctor may lawfully adopt a policy of sedation and nursing care only. The court offered only two. The first was that the child be irreversibly disabled. This cannot be satisfactory. Given the consequences of the decision, it cannot be denied that such a criterion must be much more carefully defined. We must build on the court's decision so as to articulate what disabilities, if any, we think should qualify. Is it, for example, necessary that the child be mentally handicapped? A Down's syndrome baby will be, but what of a spina bifida baby who may be severely disabled physically, but whose mental capacities cannot be measured for weeks or months or longer, and who may turn out to be as bright as a button? Would such a baby qualify for nursing care only? Equally, irreversible disability says nothing about the severity of the disability. Is a Down's syndrome baby with all its handicaps sufficiently seriously disabled to qualify?

The second criterion, that the parents reject the child, seems to me to be most unsatisfactory. The fate of a child, the life of a child, should not, in my view, depend on whether its parents want it. As *The Times* editorial of 6 November 1981 put it:

Parents' wishes in these tragic circumstances deserve every respect, but they must be set against the proposition that their child is not wholly at their disposal: every live-born baby enters civil society and by doing so acquires independent rights, of which the chief concerns life itself.

The previous decision, *Re B*, in August 1981, had already made this point. That case, you will recall, concerned a baby born with Down's syndrome who at birth also had an intestinal blockage. Surgery was needed urgently if the child was to survive. The parents decided not to give their consent for surgery. On an application to the court by the local authority's social welfare service, the parents' decision was upheld by Mr Justice Ewbank. It was subsequently reversed by the Court of Appeal, which authorized surgery, which was then carried out. As *The Times* of 10 August 1981 argued, 'The attitude of the parents, though clearly important as a clue to the baby's prospects of affection in life, cannot be a decisive factor against treatment.'

It has never been part of our law or morality that parents may choose death for their children. Indeed, such a decision in other circumstances would render parents liable to criminal prosecution, and cause the child to be taken into care. This is not to ignore or belittle the enormity of the tragedy suffered by the parents. As a society, we offer parents little or no support, whether in the form of practical help or professional advice, which may persuade them to keep the baby at home despite an initial decision not to do so. And the fate which awaits the baby if it is not kept at home is for the most part one which many parents and others would think was not far removed from a living death, lost in the back wards of some soulless institution. But this need not be, as other countries, such as Sweden, have demonstrated. In my view, to mark the child for death is to bury the problem rather than demand that we do better in terms of the care we provide, whether home support or institutional care.

My third criticism of the judge's instructions concerns his treatment of medical ethics. As we have seen, the duty a doctor owes to his patient is as much an ethical issue as a legal one. Thus it was important for the court to consider what the relevant principles of medical ethics were and to attempt to take account of these in shaping the law. But all the evidence as to what good medical ethics called for in responding to a Down's syndrome baby came from doctors, and, furthermore, from doctors who spoke in Dr Arthur's defence. I refer again to *The Times* editorial of 6 November:

Considered as a test case in medical ethics the proceedings were not entirely satisfactory. All who offered evidence on the ethical question were broadly of one mind. Their evidence was not weighed against the views of paediatricians [and, I would interject, commentators who are not doctors] who are not of that mind, some of whom joined in the public controversy that broke out over another Down's Syndrome case which reached the Court of Appeal earlier this year [the case of *Re B*].

The evidence offered was that it was ethically sound and acceptable to do what Dr Arthur did. No other views were heard. This omission takes on increased significance if you consider the results of the poll conducted by the BBC Television *Panorama* team. They sent out 600 questionnaires to British consultant paediatricians and paediatric surgeons. By 7 November 1981 they had received 340 replies, of which 280 were fully completed. One of the questions was: 'A Down's Syndrome baby, otherwise healthy, requires only normal care to survive: would you give it such care?' Two columns were provided for responses: one for the assumption that the parents wanted the child, the other for when the parents reject the child. Ninety per cent of doctors responding to the situation in which the parents reject the child, which is what happened in the *Arthur* case, said that they would give normal care. Those who said they would not do so were invited to choose between four options: (a) to feed and care for it, but not give it active medical treatment if it contracted a potentially fatal illness; (b) to give it drugs so that it was unlikely to demand food and would eventually die; (c) to give it a quick and painless death; (d) don't know. All the respondents, 8 per cent of the total (allowing for don't knows), opted for (a). None opted for (b).

Recall if you will the facts of the *Arthur* case. The baby was an uncomplicated Down's syndrome baby. Evidence appeared after post-mortem that there was some damage to the child's heart, lungs, and brain, but there is no evidence that this was known at the time Dr Arthur made his decision; nor is it clear that the extent of the damage was necessarily incompatible with the baby's survival, all things being equal. Dr Arthur chose sedation and nursing care only, option (b) of those listed above. Not one of the doctors in the poll, which drew virtually a 50-per-cent response from 600 senior paediatricians, said that he would have done what Dr Arthur did, although I concede that, for obvious reasons, this is an area in which there is not always complete frankness. So it would seem that even if doctors were the arbiters of medical ethics, which I am profoundly convinced that they should not be, none of them in the sample regards what was done by Dr Arthur as appropriate. None the less, evidence was given, and not contradicted, that it was good medical practice and good medical ethics.

Now I come to a fourth criticism, which is of supreme importance. I shall return to it later, but it may help to take note of it here. The case seems to suggest to some—and they have greeted it as showing—that ethical dilemmas of the sort we are considering are best regarded as private matters between doctor and parent. It is said that the case lends support to the proposition that rules, principles, or guidelines—call them what you will—cannot be worked out except in the vaguest, most general way. The situation is too complicated, the argument goes. The doctor and parent must be allowed to judge what to do in the light of the situation or according to the dictates of common sense. The former approach is sometimes called 'situation ethics'; the situation dictates the response. But situations do not dictate responses; people do. The reality is that the person making the decision is bringing certain values and principles to bear, but is either unwilling or unable to articulate them. If he does so, he will have to deal with tiresome problems of resolving conflicts between clashing principles and of dealing rationally with argument and counter-argument. Equally, appeals to common sense are only valid if there *is* demonstrably a *common* sense, and in many of these ethical dilemmas of medicine, there is decidedly no common sense.

Furthermore, whether or not it is realized or admitted, principles and values are being employed already in decision making. It was the court's job to examine these and approve them, or substitute, where necessary, its own rules. It did not do this very well; but there can be no doubt that some rules do have to be laid down and followed. It is a matter of continuing astonishment to me that doctors resist the notion that there can be rules or guidelines stipulating how they ought to act. For again, whether or not it is realized or admitted, doctors are already invoking them when making their decisions. They do not decide in some ethical or legal vacuum. Yet doctors still resist and receive encouragement in holding what is a thoroughly untenable position. The same *Times* editorial, of 6 November 1981, quotes with approval:

Sir Douglas Black, President of the Royal College of Physicians, [who] in evidence put the dilemma like this. The doctor is faced with three variables: the clinical situation of the child, which may range from normal to there being no possibility of intellectual life; the parents' attitude, which may range from loving acceptance to revulsion; and medical management, which may range from no intervention to advanced surgery. For situations governed by three such variables *no predetermined rule and no formula of quantification was any use* (my emphasis).

I reject this emphatically.

Consider, if you will, the following. A policeman has the power to arrest. In exercising that power, he is confronted by a number of variables. The first may be the weather and the time of day; it may be foggy, snowing, icy (he should be careful if running), night, day, and so on. The second variable relates to the person whom he is planning to arrest. He could be a man with a cleaver standing a few feet away, someone with a gun running towards the policeman, or an old lady in a quiet street who is clearly the worse for wear after drinking too much alcohol and could well fall over if touched on the shoulder. A third variable might relate to the circumstances of the arrest. The person to be arrested could be at the head of a mob threatening a riot or on a picket line; or he could be an elderly man on his own on a lonely Dorset road. A final variable may be the experience of the policeman, who may have been on the job for 2 weeks, 2 months, 2 years, or 20 years.

Does this great range of variables persuade us that we cannot establish in advance guidelines which lay down the power of arrest and reflect our ethical commitment to the freedom of the individual? Do we argue that no predetermined rule is of any use? No. We have not only drawn up ethical guidelines; we have gone further and made laws (case-law and statute) setting down carefully and precisely the boundaries of permitted action allowed to the policeman who would arrest someone. The police grumble sometimes, not surprisingly. But we think it of sufficient importance to hold the balance between the supposed needs of the executive and the claims of the individual to tell the policeman that he must accept it. Certainly we would run a mile from any proposition such as 'A policeman may arrest someone whenever he thinks it appropriate.' If a decision which affects the freedom of movement of the individual is thought to be so important as to warrant such attention, *a fortiori*, any decision which affects not freedom of movement, but life itself, must attract the most careful regulation. On such analysis the argument that you cannot regulate the decision of the doctor becomes, in part at least, so much humbug.

A final criticism of the case is that it appears to leave the law in something of a mess. If my view is accepted that the law has been reshaped, it becomes necessary to reconcile it with the law propounded in the case of *Re B*. The baby in that case was more severely disabled than the boy in the *Arthur* case, since, besides being a Down's syndrome child, she had duodenal atresia and needed life-saving surgery. The parents had indicated that they did not want her to live, and the doctors had decided not to operate. The guidance of the courts was sought, and the Court of Appeal authorized the necessary surgery. As *The Times* of 10 August 1981 put it, 'It must almost inevitably be right for the court to come down on the side of life.' Templeman LJ decided in short, that it was wrong that the child's life should be terminated because in addition to being a mongol she had another disability.

It appears that there is a conflict of principle here, and a curious one, since the Court of Appeal's decision came first, and ought ordinarily to be followed by a lower court. The cases can, however, be reconciled, I think, at least in principle. At one point in his judgment in *Re B*, Templeman LJ put the issue:

It devolves on this court in this particular instance to decide whether the life of this child is demonstrably going to be so awful that in effect the child must be condemned to die, or whether the life of this child is still so imponderable that it would be wrong for her to be condemned to die.[5]

Templeman LJ, on one reading of these words, is saying that, in the case before him, of a child with Down's syndrome and an intestinal blockage, the child's life was not 'demonstrably so awful' that surgery should not be authorized. It could follow that cases could arise in which it would be right in law and medical ethics to let the child die. He did not specify in any detail what those cases might be. It could be said that in Dr Arthur's case, the judge based his instructions on these words. The difficulty, of course, is that it is hard to see how they could apply to the baby in Dr Arthur's case, since he was less disabled than the baby in *Re B*. Thus, a new principle may have emerged and been correctly interpreted in Dr Arthur's case, but wrongly applied to the facts.

If we leave aside the particular facts, can we build on this new principle which has emerged from these two cases? Can we develop it into a clearer

[5] *Supra* n. 2, 1424.

rule, or set of rules, for doctors to follow? This is the heart of the matter and the challenge for us. We clearly have to do better than leave decisions to be made on criteria as vague as irretrievably disabled or a demonstrably awful life. We first have to decide what it is about the life of a baby which would make it ethically more justifiable to let it die than to help it to live. To many, this critical criterion would be the capacity to flourish as a human being. Given the amazing number of ways which humanity finds to express itself, despite apparently crushing difficulties, I would have thought that, unless there is very strong evidence, the vote must ordinarily go to life. We must ensure that the class of those marked for death is kept as narrowly and strictly defined as possible. Perhaps the key lies in the capacity to interact with others, to communicate, whether rationally through language or spiritually through displays of feeling and emotion. If this criterion is accepted — and I offer it here for consideration — then we can ask a second question: How do we establish, as a matter of fact, the necessary prognosis? This is a matter of medical expertise. If, for example, we learn that a child will be able to communicate and interact but will never be free of suffering, whether physical or mental, this may cause us to consider modifying our general criterion. But we may in the end decide not to do this, recognizing that suffering in others is hard to assess or predict and can so easily serve as a reason for choosing death for a child rather than as a challenge to our capacity to love and care. Whatever we choose, the doctor's enquiry would then be a legitimate one. He would be seeking to establish something in accordance with principles on which we have generally agreed.

This is what I see as the force of the cases of *Re B* and *Arthur*. There are those who argue strongly, and sometimes stridently, that life is sacred, meaning by this that a child should be cared for and helped to live whatever its disability. To do otherwise, they argue, is to begin to lose respect for the lives of others and, in particular, of the disabled, whom we will more and more push into the shadows of our society. I respect this point of view, but I do not share it. And, unhappily, it is unlikely that we shall ever arrive at a consensus here, just as in a number of other troubling medical ethical issues, such as abortion. Where this is so, we may — indeed, must — choose a position which is rationally defensible, not offensive to the majority, while not, of course, slavishly fitted to what the majority at any one time may wish, and which will work in practice.

A respectable ethical argument can, I submit, be made for not striving to keep alive those babies who soon after birth can be shown to have no capacity ever to flourish as human beings. Modern medicine has brought us to the point where almost all babies are salvageable in some form. But simply because we can salvage them does not mean that we must. We have never as a society regarded the preservation of life as an absolute value in itself. We admit the notion of the just war, and we praise, rather than condemn, the hero who sacrifices his life in a good cause. We also concede that no one has an absolute right to life, since the just war may warrant life being taken, as may capital punishment or the action of a ship's captain in closing bulkheads to save his ship and its passengers, even though some crew on the wrong side of the bulkhead will drown. On the other hand, we do not think that life should be taken lightly. It is something of fundamental value to us. Thus, it should only be taken, or someone should only be left to die, if a very good reason exists. If you apply this reasoning to the new-born, you will see that, while he has no absolute right to life, he should be helped to live unless there is a very good reason to do otherwise. A demonstrable incapacity to flourish as a human being in the sense in which I have indicated would, in my view, amount to such a reason.

Once articulated, these ethical rules would apply equally to other situations in which the quality of life is an issue. For example, in the case of the terminally ill, they would offer a guide to the doctor as to whether he is ethically and legally obliged to intervene if, say, pneumonia or cardiac arrest strikes a patient with advanced cancer. If the patient is unconscious or so drugged, out of necessity, as to be out of contact with the world or is racked by pain, it could be said that his capacity to flourish as a human being has been lost. This would provide the justification for letting nature take its course.

What if someone not yet *in extremis* decides of his own volition that he wishes to die now, rather than await the degrading decline he fears? Do the principles we have begun to map out apply to him, such that if he is asked, his doctor may help him achieve death? The case of *R*. v. *Reed* serves as a caution. The British Euthanasia Society, Exit, is a society which exists to disseminate information to any of its members on how to take his life. In October 1981, the Secretary of the Society was convicted of the crime of aiding and abetting the suicide of several people, all of whom had contacted the Society since they were contemplating suicide, but were fearful that they might make a mess of things. He was sentenced to two and a half years in prison. Undoubtedly he broke the law. There was, however, no effort on the part of the judge to reshape the law, or to interpret it so as to avoid conviction. Further, the sentence was intended as a warning to others. I invite you to stand back and consider what this prosecution and conviction say about our society when contrasted with the case of Dr Arthur. Elderly and, in some cases, ill people formed an intention to kill themselves. They made an autonomous choice, for them, perhaps, the final act of self-determination. They feared, more than anything, ending their days in a hospital bed, shorn of any dignity, prevented from dying, the reluctant recipients of all that modern medicine can deliver. There can be no doubt that this is a very real fear for many, whether it is justified or not. So they sought advice and were given it. They chose to die. And their helper was sent to gaol.

Would it have made any difference if their helper had been a doctor? As a matter of legal principle, it would not. The aiding and abetting of suicide would still have been a crime. But in practice it would have made all the difference in the world. First, there would not have been the fanfare of publicity which surrounded Exit's activities, promoted in part by Exit. Instead, there would have been a discussion between doctor and patient. Second, the means chosen for the comfortable death would have been different: more subtle and more carefully managed. Third, the doctor would undoubtedly have been able to call on medical experts who could show that the dosage of drugs used was not outside the norm of treatment or did not cause or may not have caused the death. And so on. I have no doubt that many doctors have responded to requests for assistance, and have helped such patients ease their way towards death. I am not criticizing them. I believe it can be defended as a humane and caring act in certain, carefully limited circumstances. What is important here is to notice the ethical and legal implications of the Exit case. Surely what happened cannot be explained simply on the basis that in the Exit case there was no doctor. For doctors, as we have seen, enjoy no special privileges. But when a doctor stands by and allows a baby to die, because the child is disabled and unwanted, professionals are tumbling over themselves to defend him and to praise him (at least in public), and he is acquitted. But there was no question of any autonomous decision by the baby. He had no part in the proceedings. If we excuse those who choose death for babies, who cannot speak for themselves, we should, perhaps, be slow to punish those who facilitate the autonomous decision of someone to destroy himself. Alternatively, we must live with the charge of hypocrisy, or even one law for the professional and one for the rest.[6]

I make no apologies for dwelling on this particular problem at such length. Not only is it intrinsically important; it is also necessary to try to tease out the direction in which law and ethics may be going. I can do no better than adopt the words of Mr Justice Kirby, the outstanding Chairman of the Australian Law Reform Commission. In an address to the Royal Australasian College of Physicians in November 1981, he said:

If we are to sanction procedures by which, in certain cases, grossly deformed or profoundly retarded children are not to be given the medical facilities which would be routine and unquestioned in a normal child, we may, in practical terms, be deciding that the deformed and retarded will die. That may be the right decision. The community which has to contribute significantly to the support of such a child may have its own legitimate moral claim to be heard on the subject. But, as it seems to me, these decisions should not be left to the unarticulated judgement of individual

[6] See, now, correspondence between Professor Davis, Professor of Paediatrics, Cambridge University, and this author in 11 *Journal of Medical Ethics* 159 (1985).

medical practitioners. They should not be left to secret in-house rules designed by hospitals or their ethics committees and varying among them. They should not be left to the undefined collective of the Medical Profession, still less should they respond to strident appeals for confidence in medical professionalism. Decisions of life and death, even of a retarded or disabled child, even of an old person on the brink of death, are too important to be abandoned in this way.[1]

Compare, if you will, the words of Dr John Havard, Secretary of the British Medical Association. On 21 October 1981, he delivered a speech at the BMA's annual conference, which he called 'Legal Threats to Medicine'.[8] He gave it in that section of the conference entitled 'Medicine in Jeopardy'. In his somewhat intemperate and casually argued address, which had all the qualities of a rallying call to the besieged faithful, Dr Havard spoke of doctors being 'hounded' by the courts of law, though no evidence of this was offered. He was anxious to alert his members to the 'threat which law presents to modern medical practice'. 'It should be a matter of considerable concern', he said, 'to the medical profession that the courts are attempting, and attempting with considerable success, to influence clinical and ethical decisions, bearing in mind that these decisions have to be taken by doctors at a time when they have no way of knowing for certain what the outcome will be.' Little, if anything, is known for certain. We all work on best estimates. And, in a society subject to the rule of law, we develop guidelines for conduct on the basis of those estimates.

POSTSCRIPT

Let me now reflect briefly on whether, as a matter of law, any *clearer* guide can be obtained, in the light of *Arthur* and *Re B*, as to the circumstances in which a doctor may be justified in opting to allow a baby to die. The starting-point must be Templeman LJ's reference in *Re B* to 'whether the life of this child is demonstrably going to be so awful that in effect the child must be condemned to die, or whether the life is still so imponderable that it would be wrong for her to be condemned to die'.[9] This clearly leaves undecided, however, which circumstances or conditions allow the conclusion that the life meets the criterion of being so demonstrably awful. It is important to notice at the outset that by saying '*still* so imponderable' (my emphasis), the court was clearly indicating that the balance of preference should be for life, if there were still any doubt, though not necessarily any hope.

---

[7] Australian Law Reform Commission, 'The Physician, the Law, Life and Death', C. 86/81 (Nov. 1981).

[8] J. Havard, 'The Legal Threat to Medicine', 284 *British Medical Journal* 612 (1982).

[9] *Supra* n. 2, 1424.

Down's syndrome combined with atresia did not warrant non-treatment (in the sense of non-intervention) in *Re B*. But, are there other cases from which guidance may be drawn? In *Lim* v. *Camden and Islington AHA*[10] Dr Lim suffered appalling damage, 'extensive and irremediable brain damage, which left her only intermittently, and then barely, sentient and totally dependent on others'.[11] Lord Denning remarked *en passant* in the Court of Appeal that 'she suffered what the doctors call a single cardiac arrest. . . . After 25 minutes her breathing was restored to normal. She was brought back to life. The more's the pity of it!'[12] Lord Denning went on: 'We cannot forget, also, that in these days after such an accident as this, the relatives — and the doctors — are faced with an agonising decision: is she to be kept alive? or is she to be allowed to die?' Lord Denning seems, therefore, to be suggesting that in the case of damage such as that suffered by Dr Lim, non-treatment could well be justified in law. Lord Scarman, however, in an extra-judicial discussion of this case stated: 'I am not prepared to advocate that there should be in our society a right or duty to terminate [the] existence of the barely sentient, mobile person, who, given a warm room, regular meals, and attentive nursing, can survive for as long as he could if he were a fully sentient being.'[13]

If these cases and expressions of opinion are of any significance, it is in showing the need to compare and contrast the condition of any baby under consideration with that of, for example, Dr Lim or Alexandra in the case of *Re B*, as far as that makes sense. If sentience, the ability to think and to communicate, and mobility are critical, or, in the case of a new-born baby, the potential for these on any reasonable analysis, then the baby would appear not to be destined for an awful life.

Another expression of judicial opinion which may be relevant is that of Lord Denning in *Whitehouse* v. *Jordan*.[14] 'Seeing this boy's present condition', he said, 'most would say, "what a pity they did not let him die." ' This was said of a baby who was born not breathing and virtually without pulse, on whom 35 minutes were spent on resuscitation before breathing started and who, as a consequence, suffered very severe brain damage.

Any general rule of law will not, of course, offer a checklist of physical conditions or symptoms which would meet the relevant criterion. This raises the question of whether the law should, or will, go further, or whether it is essentially a matter of judgment or personal opinion whether a patient meets the general criterion. I submit that, while virtually nothing by way of further guidance can be gained from existing law, the importance of the issue

---

[10] [1980] AC 174.   [11] Ibid.

[12] *Lim* v. *Camden and Islington A.H.A.* [1978] 3 WLR 906.

[13] Lord Scarman, 'Legal Liability and Medicine', 74 *Journal of the Royal Society of Medicine* 11, 15 (1981).

[14] [1980] 1 All ER 650, 654 (Court of Appeal).

at stake, life or death, will force the courts to develop more specific rules. I offer some here, based on my prediction of what a court would decide today or in the near future, if presented with a relevant case.

It is likely that in any particularization of the criterion of 'so demonstrably awful', a court would adopt the standard of the reasonable doctor. It would say that a patient's life is so demonstrably awful, warranting non-treatment, or, better put, treatment for dying, when any (not every) reasonable doctor would so decide. That this may be a flawed test, leaving to doctors decisions which are essentially moral and legal, is uncontestable, but the recent decisions of *Sidaway*[15] and *Gillick*[16] both demonstrate the willingness of the courts to leave what they perceive to be matters of medical management to doctors.

This attitude is reflected further in *R.* v. *Malcherek*,[17] in which Lord Lane CJ held that 'at some stage the doctors must decide if and when treatment has become otiose'. This, however, can be restricted to its facts, since the issue was the determination of whether the patient was dead; not whether, being alive, treatment should cease on 'quality of life' grounds.

Most significantly, the attitude may also be reflected in the observation of Templeman LJ that in *Re B* there was a difference of opinion among the doctors as to whether surgery was appropriate. Templeman LJ went on to say that 'in this particular case, the decision no longer lies with the parents or with the doctors.'[18] Some take this as authority for the proposition that if the case had not been brought before the court, non-treatment of the child might have been lawful, based on the standard of the reasonable doctor in consultation with the parent, and that if a reasonable doctor could be found who would not operate, that was enough. Two principal responses to this are: first, that non-treatment is, in essence, a legal issue for the courts; and, second, that in deciding as it did, the Court of Appeal in *Re B* indicated that the Court was setting a universal legal standard to be followed thereafter by doctors—that is, the standard of 'so demonstrably awful'—whether a case came before the courts or not.

Notwithstanding the apparent preparedness of the courts to accede to the view of the reasonable doctor, a court could well be willing to hold that the view of the reasonable doctor is subject to certain basic principles to which it must conform. In other words, the courts could be persuaded to hold that the test of 'so demonstrably awful' was a matter of law for the courts; and, as a matter of law, it was for the doctor to determine, but subject to the scrutiny of the court. This, in effect, is the import of the speeches of Lords Bridge, Templeman, and Keith in *Sidaway*, and is the essence of the judgment in *Gillick* (and see further *Re D*,[19] in which Heilbron J. said that

---

[15] *Sidaway* v. *Governors of Royal Bethlem Hospital* [1985] 1 All ER 643.
[16] *Gillick* v. *West Norfolk and Wisbech AHA* [1985] 3 All ER 402.
[17] [1981] 1 WLR 690. [18] *Supra* n. 2, 1424. [19] [1976] Fam. 185.

'evidence of a professional consensus should not be treated as conclusive.') If this is so, the question then becomes, What, in the exercise of such scrutiny, would a court require of the reasonable doctor; or, put another way, what are the guiding legal principles within which the reasonable doctor may exercise his judgment or discretion?

I submit that a court would stipulate that the patient be suffering from or be going to suffer from, on any reasonable assessment of the medical evidence, such *mental* impairment as to allow the conclusion that, on any reasonable view, life could be said to hold out no prospect of enjoyment for the patient. An inability to interact with others or to look after the simplest details of life could well qualify as meeting such a criterion. Alternatively, or in addition, a court would stipulate that the patient's *physical* condition be such, or be likely, on any reasonable assessment of the medical evidence, to be such as to amount to a life of continued pain, anguish, and disability, such that the patient was or would be a burden even to himself. In both or either of these circumstances, the court would also have to be satisfied that the prospect of improvement or recovery from such conditions was, on any reasonable view of the medical evidence, most unlikely, and that the patient's condition could therefore be described as hopeless.

Finally, in both *Re B* and *Arthur*, the courts have also indicated that weight can properly be given to the fact that the parents did not wish the child to survive in deciding whether to cease treatment. As has been seen, this view is wrong, both in ethics and in law, if it means that parents may decide, without interference from the law, that their child should not be treated even if the child does not meet the criteria set out earlier. If, however, the child does meet these criteria, the wishes of the parents are relevant in that they can still decide that the child be cared for. And, if they decide otherwise, they are merely following what are established principles.

POSTSCRIPT 2

It is fair to say that *Arthur* had by 1985 become one of the cases which was all things to all people. Advocates of selective treatment and right-to-lifers all saw in it something for them. They were particularly aided in this by the fact that all the law in the case was in a jury instruction which was not reported.

The debate suffered a bit of a jolt when Professor Smith, one of the most distinguished criminal lawyers, albeit as the junior partner in the enterprise, published with Gunn a short paper.[20] The jolt consisted in a number of their

---

[20] M. J. Gunn and J. C. Smith, '*Arthur*'s case and the Right to Life of a Down's Syndrome Child', [1985] Crim. LR 705.

conclusions which were somewhat surprising When commentators rushed to object, the learned authors replied that it had been their 'limited object . . . to ascertain the effect of the decision, not to express approval of it'.[21] It is proper to ask whether the view they take of the effect of the decision is in all respects sound. If it is not, some response is called for; otherwise it will enter the folklore of the law, given the eminence of one of the authors.

There are two propositions I wish to concentrate on, albeit briefly. The first and central proposition is that they regard *Arthur* as reflecting *Re B* in deciding that 'there is a difference in the content of the duty owed to normal children on the one hand and at least some abnormal children on the other. . . . The question is not whether this distinction exists but how far it extends.'[22] I would respectfully agree with this, as far as it goes. But of course, it does not go far enough. It leaves undecided and unanalysed which children are the 'some abnormal', and what the content of the duty owed to them consists in.

As for the meaning of 'abnormal', Gunn and Smith use the word without further specification in the opening part of their paper, but, by the time they reach their conclusion, it has become a child 'suffering from Down's syndrome (or some other handicap likely to have an equally serious effect on its prospects in life)'.[23] For my part, I would argue that the abnormality that a child must have if a doctor is lawfully to treat it for dying must be far more severe than that suggested by Gunn and Smith, and, in any analysis, must be set out with greater care. Merely to suffer from Down's syndrome should not be, and, in my view, is not, enough to warrant neglect resulting in death, although Gunn and Smith clearly regard it as such.[24] In coming to their view, Gunn and Smith have, I submit, confused the law and the facts in *Arthur*. The law, as stated by Farquharson J., permits a doctor to let nature take its course in the case of a severely disabled child. The facts concerned a child with Down's syndrome. It does not follow that a child with Down's syndrome, *as a matter of law*, fits the description, although this is what the jury decided, since they were given no more precise instructions. In my view, however, the law calls for more precise instructions, and these would exclude the child with Down's syndrome. Thus, although I agree with the learned authors' view as to the general effect of *Arthur* in this regard, I would take issue with them strongly as to the particularization of the general principle.

With regard to the other point I raised in Gunn and Smith's central proposition, the content of the duty owed to those categorized in law as being so severely handicapped that they may be allowed to die, Gunn and Smith, I submit, are somewhat confused and in error. They suggest that in the case of the abnormal child, it is not an offence to decline to perform 'an operation

---

[21] M. J. Gunn and J. C. Smith, 'Comments on Comments', [1986] Crim. LR 390.
[22] Ibid.   [23] *Supra* n. 20, 715.   [24] Ibid. and *supra* n. 21, 390.

or other exceptional treatment which would save the child's life'.[25] Nor is it, they say, an offence, according to *Arthur*, to withhold food. They disagree with this last proposition, however. In their view, it is an offence to withhold food so as to cause death.[26]

Their confusion lies first with the facts. The baby in the *Arthur* case was fed and given fluids. Ordinarily, the route taken to encourage a child to die, to ease its passage, is to prescribe medication which suppresses either respiration or the sucking reflex. The justification offered for prescribing the drugs is usually to relieve any pain the child is suffering. But there is no evidence that a baby with Down's syndrome, for example, routinely suffers pain, although this is the argument used. Gunn and Smith rightly draw the distinction between administration of a drug for the relief of pain and administration to prevent a child from seeking sustenance, describing the latter (rightly) as murder. Unfortunately, this distinction tends to melt away when the medical evidence gets going, as *Arthur* demonstrates. Nevertheless, the justification is offered, as it preserves the appearance of the distinction between killing and letting die which appeals to many and is, perhaps, important as a social precept, while the desired end is accomplished. Babies are rarely starved to death in any event. Even if not sedated, they often succumb to infection which, if not treated, results in death. And the non-treatment would be justified on the same basis.

Gunn and Smith are also confused as to the law. They seem to think that the distinction between ordinary and extraordinary treatment, the former required by law, the latter not, rests on the factual nature of the intervention itself. Operations are, to them, 'extraordinary' or 'exceptional';[27] whereas feeding is ordinary care which the law, therefore, insists on:

> It is submitted that they [the parents] would have been guilty of murder if the child had died of starvation. There is a difference, then, between an omission to take those ordinary steps which are necessary to preserve life, of which the most obvious are the provision of food and some measure of protection from the elements, and extraordinary steps like a surgical operation.[28]

The error in this view is that the difference between extraordinary and ordinary treatment is not a factual one. If examined carefully, it collapses as an analytical distinction, because it can be seen merely to be a substitute for the difference between what *in all the circumstances ought to be done*. Looked at in this way, feeding cannot *always* be required by law, if, for example, a child is so severely disabled that it can be fed only with a naso-gastric tube and has no hope of any successful outcome. Equally, an operation

---

[25] *Supra* n. 20, 715; my emphasis.
[26] Their analysis is couched in the traditional language of acts and omissions, but they still reach the view that 'the omission to provide food . . . ought to be equated with an act causing death' (*supra* n. 21, 390).   [27] *Supra*, n. 20, 711, 715.   [28] Ibid. 711.

may in law be called for—that is, a doctor may owe a duty to perform one—where a child has, for example, a spina bifida lesion which, if corrected, will give the child a chance of a good life, but if not, will mean that the child suffers severe disablement.

In short, Gunn and Smith cannot beg the questions by talking of ordinary and extraordinary. Nor can they insist that a particular treatment such as feeding is always required by law, whereas another may not be. This is not only to misunderstand the law, but to rob it of the flexibility which Gunn and Smith say—and I agree—that it has now acquired.

The second proposition that I wish to consider is that concerning the role of the parents of an 'abnormal child'. Gunn and Smith regard *Arthur* as having decided that where a doctor and a child's parents decide jointly to let the child die, then no offence is committed. They are anxious to point out that they do not argue that 'parents would not commit an offence if they unilaterally decided to starve a child, however badly handicapped, to death'.[29]

This is a most difficult point. I am inclined to agree that *Arthur* may, indeed, decide what Gunn and Smith set out. I am anxious, however, to examine closely whether *Arthur* can be right in law, and what Gunn and Smith have to say on the matter. According to them, neither a doctor nor a parent may *unilaterally* decline treatment, whether it be surgery or merely feeding the child. But together they may do so, which Gunn and Smith think is correct in law as regards the surgery, though not the feeding. I have already shown the weakness in the distinction between types of treatment, so will not repeat it; but it is important to bear it in mind.

What intrigues me is why the doctor and parents can lawfully do together what they cannot lawfully do on their own? The answer must surely be that their agreement or otherwise is irrelevant in law, and that if *Arthur* decided it was relevant, then it is wrong, and so are Gunn and Smith to repeat it. What *is* relevant in law must be the legal principle by reference to which the treatment decision is made. On this basis, who makes it is of no concern, save that whoever does make it—and in the case of a new-born child, it is ordinarily the parent who is responsible for the child—must abide by the relevant legal principle. This principle is that severely disabled new-borns are not owed the same duty of care by those responsible for their care as that owed to other children. Indeed, the child may be so severely disabled that those caring for it may lawfully permit it to die, and decline treatment which would seek to prevent or postpone death. This is the content of the parents' and the doctor's duty. It is, first, a matter of legal principle as to how the child may be categorized, and then a matter of medical evidence. It is decidedly not for the doctor or the parents to decide for themselves,

[29] *Supra* n. 21, 390.

apart from or outside the parameters set by the law. Any agreement between them, therefore, must take account of and be in accordance with what the law allows.

Gunn and Smith seek to distinguish the decision in *Re B* from that in *Arthur*. Prima facie the cases do seem to be in conflict. Gunn and Smith say that *Re B* may merely have decided that, on the facts, the parents had a discretion to treat; but that once they brought the issue to the court, the *court* opted for treatment. The implication, supported to some extent by the judgments of both Templeman and Dunn L JJ, is that if they had not come to court they could have agreed lawfully to allow baby Alexandra to die. But, if this is correct, it simply means that, in the view of the court, baby Alexandra qualified for the category of those who may be allowed to die. Thus, the parents had a discretion. But whether or not the child is in that category is still a matter of law in the first instance.

On this reasoning, it does not follow that the baby in *Arthur* cannot, as a matter of law, be in the category of those to be allowed to die, just because baby Alexandra's condition was worse; it could be said that *Re B* merely represented the opinion of the court and nothing more. And this is what Gunn and Smith say. But, in my view, the law was wrongly applied in *Arthur*, since I do not regard it as good law that a baby with uncomplicated Down's syndrome is, without more, in the category of those not to be treated. Indeed, neither do I regard a baby with Down's syndrome and atresia, as in *Re B*, as being in that category.

Does it follow from what went before that, if the child is properly categorized as belonging to the class of babies who may be allowed to die, the parents *may* unilaterally decide not to let the child be treated, even to the point of withholding food? In principle it would seem to; but there is little doubt that a parent may not do this. This may seem odd, in that a mother may wish to take the baby home and wait with it until it dies, and yet may not do so lawfully. She may only do so together with a doctor, so that, to this extent, Gunn and Smith appear to be right. The reason cannot be that the law looks to doctors as the approved bringers of death. It must be because the determination of whether the child belongs to the class of children who can be permitted to die depends on medical evidence, and that, once the determination has been made, the death ought to be supervised by doctors trained in the management of infections, medications, and whatever. This latter point is not, however, a particularly strong one, in my view. If a child is categorized as so severely disabled that it may be allowed to die, and if feeding the child is a form of treatment which, in the circumstances, may be unwarranted, there seems no reason in principle why a parent should not in law be entitled to allow the child to die through want of food, supported if possible with proper medication. So, on reflection, Gunn and Smith may be wrong. Perhaps, however, there are practical reasons why this should not be contemplated.

It remains to be said that, although the title of their paper refers to the 'Right to Life of a Down's Syndrome Child', there is very little mention of the rights of the child in the body of the text. Only in the conclusion do the child's rights appear, and then in a form which suggests that for a Down's syndrome child they are fairly limited. In my view, it is unfortunate that the paper is largely concerned with what parents may do, rather than with the rights of the child. After all, the former is qualified by, and contingent upon, the latter, as *Gillick* made clear. It is particularly unfortunate that the view is taken that a child with Down's syndrome (*simpliciter*) has 'no right not to be treated with a drug which is reasonably considered by a doctor to be necessary to prevent it suffering, but which will accelerate its death, *i.e. kill it*'.[30]

In the absence of clear evidence that the child is suffering at the time, I regard such a proposition, in so far as it relates to a child with Down's syndrome, as morally objectionable and not supportable in law whatever *Arthur* may have said (see *Re B*). This, of course, takes us back to what was said earlier. The child's rights in law certainly depend on the degree of disability from which it suffers. In fact, the child either has all the rights to protection enjoyed by everyone or none except the right not to be killed. But it cannot be the law that merely to suffer from Down's syndrome means that a child forfeits all other rights save that of not being killed, particularly when we know from *Arthur* how narrow the line is between being killed and being sedated to death. A much greater degree of disability is called for, in my view, before the law would say with Templeman LJ in *Re B* that life was going to be so demonstrably awful that the child may be allowed to die.

My conclusion, therefore, is that Gunn and Smith's contribution, while helpful in establishing the important central premiss, is in other respects less helpful. To the extent that it may encourage some to have less respect for the rights and lives of those born disabled, it is to be regretted, even though, as the authors make clear, this was certainly not their intention.

Against this background of theoretical discussion, it is important to keep an eye on the real world. For this reason, I turn now to another recent paper. Whitelaw, writing in *The Lancet*,[31] contributes the latest of a series of studies of decision making in the neonatal intensive care unit, in this case the unit at the Hammersmith Hospital. His paper is of interest both in the view it takes of how institutional decisions concerning very sick babies should be made, and in terms of the operational criteria for decision making which it offers.

---

[30] *Supra* n. 20, 715.

[31] A. Whitelaw, 'Death as an Option in Neonatal Intensive Care', *The Lancet*, 9 Aug. 1986, 328.

For Whitelaw and his team, as for other paediatricians, it is clear that life goes on, largely untouched by consideration of the law. In one sense this is no bad thing, since no one wants doctors looking over their shoulders for 'the law'. In another sense, it perpetuates the idea so often encountered that the law is an irrelevance, an intrusion, something that gets in the way. 'Paediatricians have recognised a need for selection,' says Whitelaw. 'But the law in England has tended to the view that handicap (certainly Down's syndrome) is no reason for allowing a baby to die untreated.'[32] It will be immediately clear that these two propositions are not, in fact, in opposition to each other, but may happily coexist, depending on the criteria chosen for selection for non-treatment. Indeed, Whitelaw's aloofness towards the law allows him to get both his propositions of law wrong.[33]

This is unfortunate, because it is clear from the paper that the Unit has an extremely caring and thoughtful policy, appears to carry it out admirably, and could serve as a model for discussion as to what the content of the law should be in managing severely disabled new-born babies. Whitelaw argues for decisions to be made by doctors and parents. There is no need, he says, to invoke legal procedures. On both these points, the law would, of course, support him, provided that the criteria by reference to which decisions are made meet with the approval of the law. It may be, therefore, that Whitelaw conflates the two levels of decision making. If he were to separate them, he would see that the law does leave decisions to parents and doctors, but, in my view, insists that the criteria for decisions are for the law to determine. If Whitelaw then examined the criteria which have emerged in law so far, he would discover that the criteria by which he and his team, together with parents, are guided, are well within those required by law.

This takes me to the second point of interest raised by his paper. The operational criteria proposed by Whitelaw follow in the tradition begun by Lorber and carried on by others.[34] They have a general conceptual starting-point, which is then translated into factual conditions which serve to indicate the presence of what is contemplated as the conceptual basis. The starting-point for Whitelaw is that non-treatment may be contemplated if there is a 'near certainty of death or no meaningful life'.[35] He gives substance to this second phrase by defining it as 'a virtual certainty, not just of handicap, but of total incapacity—for example, microcephaly, spastic quadriplegia, and blindness'.[36] Although it is not articulated as such, this is clearly an attempt to define in more concrete terms the notion of a minimal condition of humanness, which I have described as an incapacity to interact and

---

[32] Ibid. 329.

[33] The Court of Appeal did not *order* that an operation be carried out in *Re B*. The Court merely consented on behalf of the baby girl, provided a doctor was willing to operate. And Dr Arthur was not ultimately charged with murder, but with attempted murder.

[34] *Supra* n. 31, References, 331.   [35] Ibid. 330.   [36] Ibid. 328.

flourish. From this starting-point, Whitelaw then lists the range of conditions which in his experience meet this criterion, ranging from trisomy-13 to anencephaly to congenital muscle disease with chronic ventilator dependency. Such an attempt to specify factual details carries further the process begun by Lorber, and can be of great assistance to doctors, parents and others, provided, of course, that the underlying criterion is acceptable, which, in my view, Whitelaw's is.

Finally, the procedure adopted in the Unit is worth noting. The baby's condition is verified. There must then be a unanimous decision on the part of the medical team that the baby should be selected for non-treatment. The parents are then brought in, and discussions are held. If the parents accept non-treatment, this is the policy followed. If, however, the parents ask for treatment, the baby is treated. Of the 51 babies selected in the 4 years of the study, 4 were treated at the request of the parents. Of these, 2 died subsequently, and 2 survive very disabled. Subject to the proviso that scarce resources should not always be expended even if a parent requests treatment, if the case is clearly hopeless, this procedure has much to recommend it.

Whitelaw warns that 'advances in life-support techniques are likely to increase the number of infants for whom this dilemma has to be faced'.[37] Indeed, many of the babies who were not treated had been born after extremely short periods of gestation (25 weeks or less). Whitelaw's paper makes a most useful contribution to the consideration of this dilemma. It moves us all a little nearer to being able to translate principle into practice in the care of the severely handicapped new-born baby.[38]

---

[37] Ibid. 331.

[38] This is not the place to explore the very considerable developments which have taken place in the United States, particularly since the Baby Doe controversy and the Child Abuse Prevention and Treatment Act Amendments 1984, 42 USC 5101–5 (1985). See L. Gostin, 'A Moment in Human Development: Legal Protection, Ethical Standards and Social Policy on the Selective Non-Treatment of Handicapped Neonates', 11 *American Journal of Law and Medicine* 31 (1985); J. Moskop and R. Saldanha, 'The Baby Doe Rule: Still a Threat', 16 *Hastings Center Report* 8 (1986), and G. Annas, 'Checkmating the Baby Doe Regulations', 16 *Hastings Center Report* 29 (1986).

9

The Patient on the Clapham Omnibus*

Medical law used to be fun. All you had to do was read lots of strange American cases, the odd Commonwealth decision, and maybe some English nineteenth-century cases on crime; then you could reflect that none of these was relevant and get on with the fun of inventing answers. Suddenly, in the last few years, the courts have got into the act. Cases have come rattling along; medical law is beginning to get a corpus of law. Medical lawyers are having to do homework.

This is not an unimportant point. It suggests that the parties involved in the practice of medicine—not only patients, but doctors, nurses, parents, pressure groups, and social service departments—are concerned to clarify the relationships they have with each other and their respective rights and duties. The reasons for this pressure for clarification are too many and too complicated to pursue here. They include the introduction of complex technology, a more informed and better educated population, which is more likely, therefore, to ask questions and expect answers, and a changed attitude among the products of the Welfare State towards the medical profession, whereby the doctor is expected to see his patients as partners in the enterprise of health care. This last point is now reflected more and more in the education of doctors and in their attitudes, particularly in the case of GPs. You may be forgiven for not noticing this trend, however, if you listen only to those who claim to speak for the medical profession. It would not be the first time that trade-union leaders have lost touch with their members and have continued to defend barricades long since abandoned as indefensible (morally or practically) by the rest.

This pressure for clarification concerns both medical ethics and medical law. As regards the law, it is the courts that are being asked to provide the answers. Whether this is the right way to go about things is another question for another place. There are lots of disadvantages to waiting for a tenacious litigant to appear, then letting a court decide, and hoping that the court will get the right facts on which to build a ruling of general application. The arguments in favour of a more liberal use of declaratory judgments seem.

* This paper was originally published in 47 *Modern Law Review* 454, and is reproduced here with a postscript which takes account of and seeks to analyse the subsequent decision of the House of Lords, [1985] 1 All ER 643.

overwhelming in medical law, this would allow a coherent body of doctrine
to be developed, and doctors and patients would not then find themselves
in a legal vacuum. Perhaps the best way is to follow the lead of the Australian
and Canadian Law Reform Commissions or the President's Commission
for the Study of Ethical Problems in Medicine in the United States. These
bodies have examined both the ethical and legal dilemmas posed by modern
medicine, and have suggested solutions which, to the extent that proposals
are made to change the law, need further action by the legislature, but
otherwise take the form of recommendations for the profession and the public
and suggested Codes of Practice which thereafter serve as guides to what
is good law and good ethics. In the United Kingdom, apart from the odd
ad hoc committee, we seem happy to stumble along; so doctors, patients,
nurses, and their advisers often seek in vain for guidance.

INFORMED CONSENT

The nature of the consent which a doctor must obtain from his patient
has been a classic area of difficulty for some years, particularly in the
light of the changing nature of medical practice and of the doctor–patient
relationship. In an attempt to take stock, to make sense of the cases and arguments and to offer a way forward, the Canadian Law Reform Commission
published an excellent study paper on law and ethics in 1980.[1] In the United
States in compliance with its brief, given by Congress, the President's Commission published its three-volume report, *Making Health Care Decisions*,
in 1982, charting a path for the future development of law and practice.[2]
This is a brilliant work, not least because two volumes are dedicated to
examining, through careful research, the various anecdotes about informed
consent, and to comparing the evidence with the myth.

In England, it was left to Mrs Sidaway to follow the path of several
others,[3] and go to court to clarify her legal position.[4] Her complaint was that
she was not given certain information about the surgery she was to undergo
and that, had she been given it, she would not have had the operation.
Skinner J. found as a fact, at first instance,[5] that she would not have had
the operation had she known of the possible risk of severe disablement. He

[1] Law Reform Commission of Canada, *Consent to Medical Care*, 1980.

[2] President's Commission for the Study of Ethical and Legal Problems in Medicine, *Making
Health Care Decisions*, (US Government Printing Office, 1982).

[3] For example, *Chatterton* v. *Gerson* [1981] QB 432; *Hills* v. *Potter* [1983] 3 All ER 716;
Sankey v. *Kensington, Chelsea and Westminster AHA* (2 Apr. 1982, unreported).

[4] *Sidaway* v. *Governors of the Bethlem Royal Hospital and the Maudsley Hospital and
Others*. Reported in *The Times* 24 Feb. 1984. Now reported at [1984] 1 All ER 1018 (Court
of Appeal).

[5] Ibid. 1020, per Donaldson, MR.

held, however, that her doctor's obligation in law was to give her whatever information a reasonable and responsible member of the medical profession would think it proper to give. Since the medical evidence was that a reasonable doctor would not have imparted information about the risk which materialized, Skinner J. dismissed her claim. In so doing, he fell in line with approved previous judgments at first instance, *Bolam* v. *Friern Hospital Management Committee*[6] and *Chatterton* v. *Gerson*;[7] and his judgment was later followed in *Hills* v. *Potter*.[8] Mrs Sidaway appealed. The Court of Appeal upheld Skinner J.'s decision.

The crucial holding for the medical lawyer is seen as being that the transatlantic doctrine of informed consent is not part of English law. Instead, the court opted for the standard of the reasonable member of the medical profession. What the particular patient wanted to know about her treatment, or what a prudent, reasonable patient may wish to know, is not, they held, the legal standard by which to measure the doctor's duty. This decision, I submit, is insupportable, both in principle and on its own reasoning.

Consent in Medical Ethics

Before examining the judgments in the Court of Appeal, it is as well to recall briefly the significance and purpose of consent in the context of medical care. It is, of course, not a legal, but an ethical, doctrine. It flows from the Kantian imperative of respect for others, respect for each person as a person in his own right.[9] One of its crucial consequences is that we should respect each person's autonomy, his power to make his own decisions and to act on them. Consent is one aspect of respect for autonomy. In the context of medical ethics, it means that a doctor may not touch or treat a person without his consent, always assuming that the person is competent to make an autonomous decision. The unconscious person is, by definition, incompetent. The immature, the mentally ill, the overwrought, or the over-anxious may well be. In such a case, any purported consent would be invalid, and ethically may not be relied upon, but rather may be ignored, just as refusal of consent may be overriden. This is ethically justifiable because, in fact, to ignore it is not autonomy-reducing, but autonomy-enhancing, in that the incompetent person is prevented from doing that which deleteriously affects his ability subsequently to come to an enjoyment of autonomy free from avoidable harm. On this reasoning, taking a six-year-old to the dentist against his kicks and screams is autonomy-enhancing and therefore justified paternalism, in

---

[6] [1957] 1 WLR 582. [7] *Supra* n. 3. [8] *Supra* n. 3.

[9] Good medical ethics would not distinguish between a paying and a non-paying patient, but see Donaldson MR: 'At the same time the patient received a letter from Mr. Falconer asking her how she was getting on. Bearing in mind that the plaintiff was not a private patient, it is a great tribute to Mr. Falconer's compassion and interest that he wrote as he did' (*supra* n. 4, 1020).

that he will then come to maturity able to chew his food. Thereafter he has the choice of whether to neglect his teeth.

Clearly, then, the commitment to autonomy represented by the requirement of consent is respected by having a notion of incompetence; but it can also be undermined by it unless the criteria of incompetence are articulated as clearly as possible, and the inquiry as to their presence is conducted with total integrity. The doctor, therefore, ought ethically to begin with an assumption of competence, and must defend a determination otherwise. This way of ordering the analysis is crucial to good medical ethics, and will find its echo subsequently in the discussion of the law.

The need for consent may be an ethical imperative, but what does consent consist in? Emphasis on the doctrine of informed consent may blind some to the fact that consent has two equally important aspects; it must be voluntary, as well as informed, as was discussed in the recent case of *Freeman* v. *Home Office*.[10] To be informed, a person needs to know not only about risks but also about alternatives. This latter requirement is often overlooked, but is of central significance. A woman with breast cancer is entitled to know not only what radical mastectomy may do to her, and its attendant risks, but also that other forms of treatment exist, such as chemotherapy, radiation therapy, or lumpectomy. Without knowing this, she is not sufficiently·informed to make a reasoned and comprehending decision. As regards the amount of information the doctor is obliged to give, the ethical principle can only be that she be given that information which *she* would regard as material in reaching a decision consistent with her views and values.

Consent, in short, is an ethical doctrine about respect for persons and about power. It seeks to transfer some power to the patient in areas affecting her self-determination, so as to create the optimal relationship between doctor and patient, which is the same as that between any professional and his client—namely, a partnership of shared endeavour in pursuit of the client's interests. Good medical ethics strives for a relationship which is neither one of 'medical paternalism' nor 'patient sovereignty', but one of 'shared decision-making'.[11] Some, of course, do not see medical care as involving such a partnership, either because they believe patients do not want this or because doctors may not find it appropriate.[12] Neither of these arguments is sound: the first, because whatever evidence there is suggests otherwise; the second, because it is not for professionals to set the moral agenda for their relationship with those they serve. They have only extra duties, not privileges.

---

[10] [1984] 1 All ER 1036.   [11] *Supra* n. 2, 36.

[12] Interestingly, the President's Commission found that while 72 per cent of the public wanted to make a shared decision, 88 per cent of doctors said that the public wanted them to choose (*supra* n. 2, 43–4).

Enter the Law

It would be nice if the law reflected and gave effect to good medical ethics to the greatest extent possible, having due regard to matters such as evidence and the burden of proof and the extent to which these may give unfair advantage to one party or another. Indeed, some pretty good reason would have to be found if it did not. As Lord Coleridge CJ put it in *R.* v. *Instan*: 'It would not be correct to say that every moral obligation involves a legal duty; but every legal duty is founded on a moral obligation. A legal common law duty is nothing else than the enforcing by law of that which is a moral obligation without legal enforcement.'[13] The Court of Appeal in *Sidaway* appeared to endorse the view advanced earlier as being good medical ethics. As Browne-Wilkinson LJ observed, 'I start from the basic proposition that in the ordinary case it is for the patient and not for the doctor, to decide whether he wishes to run the risk of an operation.'[14] Unhappily, the court also seems to have persuaded itself that there were good reasons why good medical ethics should not become law. The Master of the Rolls and Browne-Wilkinson LJ, if not Dunn LJ, did so, it is submitted, somewhat sheepishly, aware that good reason and good ethics were tugging them one way, while what they saw as good policy pulled them another way.

The policy which the court endorsed is, I submit, both unjustified and inappropriate. This is so not for the cynic's reason that this is one more case in which the legal profession protects the medical profession. It is so because, tragically, most doctors and patients do not want such a policy; and good medical practice, in the changed environment in which we live, will be sadly damaged by it. This is the significance of the case. It cannot be overstated. The future development of medical practice as a partnership of shared decision making was at stake. The court voted, for reasons which, it will be argued, are at best based on anecdote and largely on myth, for a type of doctor–patient relationship in which the patient is seen as having only those rights granted by the profession. Make no bones about it, this is how the case has been received. Yes, of course, the Master of the Rolls said that 'the law will not permit the medical profession to play God,'[15] with the implication that consent was for the courts and not for doctors to regulate. But those who see their task as defending doctors against what they perceive to be a hostile world will nod gently, and then feel tempted to follow Holmes J.'s dictum and look not at what the court said, but at what it did.

Any critical examination of *Sidaway* must, of course, put aside Holmes J.'s aphorism, valid though it may be, and analyse the respective judgments, remembering that they are not intended to be read as a tax statute, so that

---

[13] [1893] 1 QB 450, 453.   [14] *Sidaway, supra* n. 4, 1034.   [15] Ibid. 1028.

a touch of realism is not out of place. All three members of the court agreed that, as Dunn LJ put it, 'there is no English decision binding on this Court which compels us to answer the question posed in this appeal in one way or another.'[16] The most interesting and, with respect, the most thoughtful, and, therefore, the most troubled and troubling, judgment is that of Browne-Wilkinson LJ. In effect, he does three things: he analyses the North American doctrine of informed consent, the English law, and the, to him, relevant policy considerations.

The Transatlantic Doctrine of Informed Consent

As regards North American law, Browne-Wilkinson LJ concluded that he 'receive[d] no assistance from the transatlantic cases in the determination of this appeal'.[17] He held, as did the other members of the court apparently, that the North American doctrine of informed consent neither was nor should be part of English law. The arguments warrant close analysis. The doctrine in the United States, from which the later Canadian cases[18] drew their inspiration, has been described as drawing upon trespass, negligence, and fiduciary obligations.[19] Not every jurisdiction endorses the doctrine by any means,[20] and several different juridical bases have been laid for it. Nevertheless, the near universal trend, which started in 1972, is to regard it as a doctrine in the tort of negligence. The reasons for this are undoubtedly pragmatic. The rules on limitation of actions and on causation were thought to be too oppressive to the defendant; and the crucial fact that intentional torts are usually not covered by insurance tipped the balance in favour of basing the action in negligence. But, as Browne-Wilkinson LJ rightly observed,[21] the foundations of the duty to disclose lie in the tort of trespass and its assertion of the right to be free from touchings that have not been consented to. The task, then, for the courts in the United States, in developing the doctrine, was to justify the creation of a duty in negligence to disclose information, in addition to the duty to take reasonable care in treatment. The method chosen was to describe the relationship between doctor and patient as a fiduciary relationship, casting on the doctor a fiduciary duty to disclose,

---

[16] Ibid. 1029.   [17] Ibid. 1033.

[18] *Hopp* v. *Lepp* (1980) 112 DLR (3*d*) 67; *Reibl* v. *Hughes* (1981) 114 DLR (3*d*) 1; and *White* v. *Turner* (1981) 120 DLR (3*d*) 269.   [19] *Supra* n. 2, 22.

[20] Although the Master of the Rolls regards *Canterbury* v. *Spence*, 464 F. 2*d* 772 (1972) as the 'leading authority' in the United States (*Sidaway, supra* n. 4, 1024), it is interesting to note that it may not even have reflected the law of the District of Columbia, in which it was decided, let alone United States law, until it was affirmed in the District of Columbia Appeal Court in *Crain* v. *Allision*, 443 A 2*d* 558 (1982). See further O. J. Sharpe, S. F. Fiscina, and M. Head, *Law and Medicine* (West Publishing Co., 1978), p. 203. On United States law generally, see D. Louisell and H. Williams, *Medical Malpractice*, vol. 2, (Matthew Bender, 1983).

[21] *Sidaway, supra* n. 4, 1021.

failure to comply with which amounted to negligence. This has some intrinsic appeal, since the basis of the notion is some kind of potential for undue influence, or, more generally, an imbalance in the power of decision making, deriving from the status of the doctor or of his being better informed. Browne-Wilkinson LJ chose to regard fiduciary obligations as limited to dealings with the property of clients or patients, and refused to extend it further. Dunn LJ was of the same view: 'This doctrine has been confined to cases involving the disposition of property, and has never been applied to the nature of the duty which lies upon a doctor in the performance of his professional treatment of his patient.'[22] 'Has never been' is accurate. But the question can be asked whether it could be so applied in the future. Browne-Wilkinson LJ, however, could not see 'any policy reason to make such an extension'.[23] This was because, having identified trespass as the real source of the right to be free from touchings that have not been consented to, he felt that 'the concept that carrying out an operation constitutes a battery to the plaintiff does not accord with common sense.'[24] Like it or not, however, this is how the law has always analysed medical treatment involving any touching, that it is a battery unless consented to.

Thus, it was open to the court, in the absence of authority against it, to find that for a doctor to behave lawfully, he needed consent for his touching, and that the relationship with his patient was such that the law cast on him a fiduciary duty to disclose all material information concerning the treatment. The court could have then gone on to hold that failure to disclose vitiated any purported consent, and rendered the doctor liable in trespass. All three judges, however, were categorical in their affirmation that trespass did not lie, once a general consent had been given. In doing so, they endorsed the view taken previously in *Chatterton* v. *Gerson*[25] and *Hills* v. *Potter*.[26] Indeed, Hirst J. in *Hills* v. *Potter* agreed in 'deploring reliance on these torts [assault and battery] in medical cases of this kind'.[27] The reasons are undoubtedly similar to those influencing North American judges in the same direction; the stigma which attends a finding of battery in the context of a therapeutic relationship, connoting, as it does, an intentional and offensive or harmful interference, and the difficulties to which it might expose a doctor in defending a case, particularly as the plaintiff need not prove damage and the rules of causation are less restrictive. Notice that these reasons of policy, which do not include insurance considerations, reflect, in essence, a desire not to expose the doctor to a burden of litigation on terms which may not conduce to the maintenance of good relations between doctors and their patients and to the good image of the profession. As will become clear, these same arguments were also used to bar the plaintiff's claim in negligence.

---

[22] Ibid. 1029.   [23] Ibid. 1032.   [24] Ibid.
[25] *Supra* n. 3.   [26] *Supra* n. 3.   [27] Ibid., 728.

It is accepted that the arguments may well tell against allowing an action in trespass, though they are by no means as overwhelming as Dunn LJ would have it, in his stark assertion that 'this is not the law of England.'[28] To clinch his argument, Dunn LJ relied, with the Master of the Rolls, on *R.* v. *Clarence*.[29] This is, perhaps, to invest that case with more significance than it deserves. Indeed, Fleming savages the reasoning in the case and argues:

Doctors frequently fail to make a full disclosure to patients concerning proposed surgery. If not justifiable by genuine concern over the patient's health, half-truths or 'soft' answers today run the risk of being condemned as either negligent mis-representation, deceit, or even vitiating consent. The modern patient has the 'right to know'.[30]

The court, however, thought otherwise, at least as regards the tort of trespass, and by implication—though it was not argued—also as regards misrepresentation and deceit. And it did so largely for policy reasons. These reasons may, indeed, justify the court's refusal to extend the law, and thereby create the necessary legal infrastructure to support the North American doctrine of informed consent. But they do not, it is submitted, apply in the context of a home-grown basis of liability arising out of the traditional tort of negligence, to which we must now turn.

Negligence and the Duty to Disclose

Browne-Wilkinson LJ began 'by considering the general duty of care which the law would impose on anyone who in the course of business has undertaken to give advice'.[31] Stop at this point for a moment and notice the word 'advice'. It can lead the unwary astray and seems to have done so, with respect, in the case of Dunn LJ. To him, the doctor's functions include 'diagnosis, advice and treatment'.[32] There is no doubt that the standard of care for diagnosis and treatment is that of the ordinary skilled practitioner in the circumstances. But what of advice? To Dunn LJ, 'in the realm of advice the standards of his profession are also to be applied.'[33] *Saif Ali* v. *Sidney Mitchell and Co.*[34] is cited in support. But there are difficulties with this. Advice giving is to a solicitor what diagnosis and treatment are to a doctor: namely, what their skill consists in. Indeed, the advice which is the pro-fessional preserve of the doctor is that which is involved in treatment—advising as to what, if anything, can be done. The advice given by the doctor, in the context of informed consent, is not the same sort of advice as that given by the solicitor. Rather than *advice*, what is really involved is

---

[28] *Sidaway, supra* n. 4, 1029.   [29] (1889) 22 QBD 23.
[30] Fleming, *The Law of Torts*, 5th edn., (Australian Book Co. Ltd. 1977), p. 79.
[31] *Sidaway, supra* n. 4, 1033.   [32] Ibid. 1029.   [33] Ibid.   [34] [1980] AC 198.

information. Thus, Dunn LJ's conclusion, that the standards of the medical profession are to be applied, begs the question by assuming that information giving is the same as advice giving. This mis-analysis is clear when Dunn LJ goes on to argue that 'in giving advice the professional man will normally refer to the advantages and disadvantages of the course which he recommends.'[35] But this is precisely to misstate what patient self-determination is about. Advantages and disadvantages are evaluations which only patients can make. What doctors must give is information about alternatives and consequences, including risks, thereby enabling the patient to judge for him- or herself. For example, a woman has breast cancer. Only she can decide whether the risk of not eliminating the cancer by opting for radiation treatment is a disadvantage as against undergoing maiming surgery.

The next step for Dunn LJ is to argue that advice cannot easily be distinguished from warning, which, at least on the above analysis of advice, must be right. This, then, allows Dunn LJ to square the circle, and conclude, with suitable brevity, that '*since* his advice as to the advantages of a particular treatment is to be judged in accordance with the standards of his profession, . . . his advice as to disadvantages, including any warning or lack of warning of the risks, should be subject to the same standard.'[36] But substitute 'information as to consequences, including risks', for 'advice as to disadvantages', and the proposition that it is for the profession to set standards becomes hard to sustain.

Browne-Wilkinson LJ reached this same conclusion and, thus, by implication, rejected Dunn LJ's analysis by another route. He simply states as his opening premiss that, 'in the absence of special circumstances', a person who has undertaken to give advice '*would* owe a duty to disclose any unusual and material risks of which he knows or ought to know and which will be run if the advice he tenders is adopted'.[37] Here, Browne-Wilkinson LJ seems to be using the term 'advice' in the way I have suggested that it ought to be understood. He cited the example of 'a hotel brochure which represents that there is sea swimming but fails to point out that there are sharks in the sea'.[38] The 'failure to disclose the risks of sharks would', he concludes, 'be a breach of an obvious duty of care'.[39] He goes on to hold that if this is the case generally as regards advice-givers, it is surely the case where the person is a professional, such as an engineer, and holds himself out as having a special skill. And, he emphasizes:

Once it was established that there was such a risk and the engineer either knew, or in the exercise of reasonable professional skill, ought to have known of such risks . . . *the duty to disclose the risk and the answer to the question whether there had*

---

[35] *Sidaway, supra* n. 4, 1030.   [36] Ibid. my emphasis.
[37] Ibid. 1033; my emphasis.   [38] Ibid.   [39] Ibid.

been an adequate disclosure would be determined by the general law, not by the standard of the profession.[40]

Well, you may say, that does it. The reasoning makes the conclusion inevitable. The standard for disclosure to the patient is for the court, not for the medical profession, to decide. But Browne-Wilkinson LJ chose to ask himself another question: are there 'factors peculiar to the medical profession which demonstrate that the general rule applicable to other professions is inappropriate to that case?'[41] He found that there were. So what are these policy factors?

Policy

Two factors distinguishing the doctor's position from that of other professionals were held by Browne-Wilkinson LJ to be fundamental. They flow from the doctor–patient relationship. The first is that 'the patient goes to the doctor to be cured'[42] (or, more accurately, to be treated). The second is that the doctor–patient relationship depends on the patient having confidence in his doctor. 'If the disclosure of the risks results in prejudicing the ability of the doctor to cure and the confidence of the patient in the doctor, the existence of a duty to disclose such risks would probably militate against the main purpose of the relationship.'[43] This, of course, is sound common sense. No one—not even the wildest court in the United States—has ever held that a doctor must in *all* circumstances disclose material risks. *Canterbury* v. *Spence*,[44] *Cobbs* v. *Grant*,[45] and *Wilkinson* v. *Vesey*,[46] the three landmark decisions in 1972, all spell out what has come to be known as the 'therapeutic privilege', that 'situations may be envisioned where the disclosure of a risk would be detrimental to the patient. The existence of such a situation is a matter of defense for the doctor. . . . Included are mental incompetence, emergencies and potential physical trauma or mental disturbance to the patient.'[47]

It is most important to notice how Browne-Wilkinson LJ describes this problem. 'There are undoubtedly cases where the emotional state of the patient is such that disclosure of the full risks . . . would be medically harmful.'[48] Notice that the word 'full' may beg some of the questions. 'Some patients', he continues, 'may not want to be told of the risks.'[49] Clearly, therefore, Browne-Wilkinson LJ regards the cases calling for non-disclosure as *exceptions*. As he remarks later, 'most people want to

---

[40] Ibid; my emphasis.   [41] Ibid. 1034.   [42] Ibid.   [43] Ibid.
[44] *Supra* n. 20.   [45] 502 P. *2d* 1 (1972).   [46] 295 A. *2d* 676 (1972).
[47] *Miller* v. *Kennedy*, 530 P. *2d* 334 (1975).
[48] *Sidaway*, *supra* n. 4, 1034.   [49] Ibid.

know the material risks in taking a particular course of action before they take it.'[50] Well, that does it again. Surely, then, Browne-Wilkinson LJ must adopt the doctrine of informed consent endorsed in the North American cases. He edges even nearer when he states that 'in general the doctor is under a duty to take such steps to ensure that the patient has such information relating to the benefits and material risks of the operation as is reasonable in the circumstances.'[51] All that has to happen now is for Browne-Wilkinson LJ to hold that reasonableness is for the patient or the court, and contains the notion of reasonable non-disclosure; then a sensible and sensitive doctrine of informed consent would be part of English law.

There is, however, one step still be to taken. 'If', Browne-Wilkinson LJ continues, 'the duty is as I have formulated it . . . the crucial question will be whether the steps taken are in all the circumstances reasonable.' His next sentence reads: '*This, being a matter of professional judgment*[52] and the balancing of risks and benefits, must essentially be determined by reference to the practices of the profession.'[53] What happened? Browne-Wilkinson LJ suddenly persuaded himself, apparently, that the exceptions relating to justified non-disclosure, which are matters for professional judgment, rather than the norm, which would be for the court, should dictate the legal principle. He even hints that he recognizes this and is not entirely convinced by his own reasoning when he further refines the doctor's duty to disclose as governed by the practice of the profession only so long as this practice relies on 'the circumstances of the particular patient'.[54] What does this mean? The only way that this can be consistent with his ruling that disclosure is to be judged by the standard of the profession is if 'the circumstances of the patient' are also a matter for professional judgment. But this is hardly consistent with his previously stated 'basic proposition that in the ordinary sense it is for the patient, not for the doctor, to decide whether he wishes to run the risk of an operation',[55] and that most people want to know the material risks. On this basis, professional judgment should only be relevant as regards the exceptional case. Where does that leave Browne-Wilkinson LJ's general ruling? The problem is compounded when, in a final attempt to be seen to be furthering patient self-determination, he points out that the effect of his decision is that 'there is a *prima facie* duty to inform.'[56] So there is, but if it is only to inform to the extent considered proper by the medical profession, it clearly is not the assertion of patient self-determination which Browne-Wilkinson LJ would have us believe.

The policy factors, then, which Browne-Wilkinson LJ identifies as fundamental do not necessarily entail the decision he reached. On the contrary,

---

[50] Ibid.   [51] Ibid.
[52] My emphasis. Reminiscent of Dunn LJ's 'Since . . . '; see *supra* n. 36.
[53] *Sidaway*, *supra* n. 4, 1035.   [54] Ibid.   [55] Ibid. 1034.   [56] Ibid. 1035.

it is submitted, they demand a rejection of the professional standard rule. Admittedly, the issue is not clear-cut. It calls for balance. It is submitted, however, that entirely the wrong balance was struck.

The Master of the Rolls's Judgment

The judgment of the Master of the Rolls follows the same pattern. While he asserts that a patient is ordinarily entitled to that information which will enable him to make a reasoned decision, he too is persuaded that disclosure is to be judged by professional standards. 'What information should be disclosed and how and when . . . is [sic] very much a matter for professional judgment.'[57] Having said this, like Browne-Wilkinson LJ, he also seems anxious to retain some sense of patient self-determination in the final test he proposes. 'The duty', he states, 'is fulfilled if the doctor acts in accordance with a practice *rightly* accepted as proper by a body of skilled and experienced medical men.'[58] In other words, the standard is for the medical profession, provided they get it right, or, in the Master of the Rolls's language, unless a judge was satisfied that the medical view was 'manifestly wrong and the doctors must have been misdirecting themselves as to their duty in law'.[59] It is at least doubtful whether doctors will feel encouraged by this ruling. If the legal standard was unclear before, such a rule can hardly be said to have enhanced its clarity. Doctors, it seems, must comply with their legal duty, which, on consulting a lawyer, they will be told consists in setting a standard which is right. When they ask what rightness consists in, they will be further advised that it involves setting a standard which conforms with their legal duty and which a judge does not subsequently think is wrong![60]

More Policy

This is not the end of the story. What are, perhaps, the real reasons for the decision emerge at the end of the judgments of both Dunn and Browne-Wilkinson L JJ. They consist in the now familiar litany of horror stories should a rule other than the professional standard rule be adopted. Patients'

---

[57] Ibid. 1027.   [58] Ibid. 1028.   [59] Ibid.

[60] One hint of what 'rightly' may amount to appears in the Master of the Rolls's judgment and is fairly alarming. After stating that the doctor must, *inter alia*, take account of a patient's true wishes, he observes that 'while I recognise that the patient has an overriding right to as little or as much as he wishes and can absorb, it by no means follows that the expression of a wish for full information either generally or specifically represents the reality of the patient's state of mind' (*Sidaway, supra,* n. 4, 1031.) Does the Master of the Rolls really intend to hand over such power to the doctors, giving them the authority to second-guess and veto the expressed views of the patient, because that is what the decision in practice would amount to? Reading a patient's mind is hard enough for psychiatrists. The Master of the Rolls would make all doctors into psychiatrists.

trust in doctors would be undermined, and the practice of medicine would be adversely affected. There would be an increase in claims against doctors, and 'defensive medicine' could follow. In short, the American disease might break out. These, undoubtedly, are the real reasons for the Court of Appeal's decision. If, therefore, they can be shown to be lacking in real substance, the reasoning advanced so convincingly by Browne-Wilkinson LJ would have to prevail, and a non-professional test for disclosure adopted.

Therapeutic Privilege

The first argument in rebuttal of the 'look where it will take us' school of thought invokes the development of the defence of therapeutic privilege in the United States. The doctrine explicitly responds to the fears voiced by the Court of Appeal. It allows the doctor proper discretion in the exercise of his duty to disclose. It does, however, require that the doctor show good cause (since the onus is on him) why information was not disclosed. Such a defence could well be incorporated into English Law. If it were, then any law which aimed to be sensitive to the interests of both patient and doctor should probably stipulate that the general categories of circumstance in which the privilege may be invoked should be a matter for the court. As the Canadian Law Reform Commission paper suggested, the privilege should not be a 'wide doctrine and probably only applies when to disclose the information would cause recognized physical and mental harm to the patient'.[61] It would then be a matter of professional judgment and evidence whether the particular patient came within one of these categories. Clearly, the principle behind the doctrine is the same as that justifying informed consent: namely, respect for the person. What the doctrine makes clear is that the balance is best and most fairly struck if a presumption is made in favour of disclosure, which can be rebutted by good evidence. Indeed, some argue that unless that which can amount to good evidence is carefully stated, the defence can, in effect, swallow up the principle. The doctrine equally makes it clear that the circumstances in which the patient will not wish to be informed are the exception and not the norm. So, if the balance is struck in favour of therapeutic privilege, not as a defence but as a rule, by making disclosure a matter for the medical profession, this inevitably means that a doctrine developed for exceptional circumstances will result in diminishing respect for the patient as a person in the majority of cases.

Confidence and Trust

The second argument relates to confidence and trust. It is important here to tread warily. Is there a real danger? Or is it a case of the medical profession,

[61] *Supra* n. 1, 16.

like any profession, being anxious to preserve the status quo, anxious to guard what it sees as its territory from any sort of interference, and in that anxiety engaging in a form of 'shroud-waving'? It is submitted that it is the latter. In saying so, there is no intention of questioning the integrity of doctors. It is simply to suggest that they have succeeded in persuading themselves, as well as others, that trust and confidence will wither if they, as doctors, are asked to disclose more than they wish to. Instead, the opposite is true. Confidence and trust can only prosper if the patient is treated as a partner to be taken into confidence by his doctor, to be trusted to participate in the enterprise called treatment. What empirical evidence there is confirms this unreservedly. The studies undertaken for the President's Commission in the United States demonstrated clearly that people wish to be given information by their doctors and resent being ill informed.[62] The picture is the same in the United Kingdom.[63] Even more compelling is the evidence which any medico-legal analyst will vouchsafe, that the vast majority of complaints made against doctors, whether or not resulting in litigation, arise precisely from the doctor's failure properly to communicate with his patient, particularly by withholding information.

So far from enhancing doctor–patient trust, the affirmation of a professional standard for disclosure is, therefore, more likely to corrode it. This is so particularly in the case of hospital care. It is common knowledge that when a number of doctors are involved in treating a patient, the incidence of complaints rises. With one doctor, the patient can become a friend, but it is hard to establish such a relationship with several doctors sporadically. And while someone may be reluctant to sue a friend, he will be more willing to complain in the latter case. Openness and a sharing of information, therefore, become even more important, if the patient is to trust and have confidence in his doctors. Finally, if further proof is needed, the debates on the reform of the law relating to the treatment of the mentally ill and the wishes of the people expressed by Parliament in the provisions on consent ultimately incorporated into the Mental Health Act, 1983, should surely be of the greatest weight.

Floodgates?

Third, will litigation against doctors increase if the professional standards are not adopted? Or is this a case of the medical profession's hyperbole being translated into the judiciary's much-loved floodgates argument? Again, it

---

[62] *Supra* n. 2, ch. 4.

[63] See, e.g. *Report of the Royal Commission on the National Health Service* (Cmnd. 7615, HMSO, 1979) ch. 5, and I. E. Thomson *et al.* 'Learning about Death', *Journal of Medical Ethics*, 62 (June 1981).

is submitted that it is the latter. There has already been an increase in litigation on this issue, with the several cases noted earlier. This is merely part of the phenomenon of seeking to clarify the patient's relationship *vis-à-vis* his doctor. But what of the United States experience? Surely that proves that litigation will increase. Again, the facts may not wholly sustain the fears.[64] Undoubtedly, there was a great increase in malpractice claims in the 1970s.[65] But the reasons for this are very complex, and largely relate to factors not present in the United Kingdom. Gerald Robertson may be right,[66] that such litigation is a method of compensating injured parties in the absence of a developed social welfare system and a National Health Service. But he may have been too persuasive, and caused some to conclude that there is no need for such a doctrine here, despite his expressed view to the contrary. There *is* still room for an English doctrine of informed consent, which would not need to serve the ends it serves in the United States, and, therefore, would not promote litigation. Furthermore, if the evidence, rather than the myth, is examined, informed consent cases form a very small part of malpractice litigation in the United States.[67] Now that the standard has been established, it seems, the number of cases has settled down. Of course, this has not necessarily satisfied the medical and insurance lobbies, which have successfully persuaded a number of state legislatures to take action to change the law.

Regardless of what happens in the United States, it is fair to observe that, far from ensuring that claims against doctors will not increase, the Court of Appeal's judgment, if left as it is, is likely to invite further claims against doctors. The Master of the Rolls's judgment, resting as it does on the single, undefined, and undefinable word 'rightly', could well persuade unhappy patients to take proceedings, as could Browne-Wilkinson LJ's insistence that the doctor must take account of the patient's 'particular circumstances'. Because the court could not bring itself whole-heartedly to endorse a professional standard, it gave any number of hostages to fortune. One such hostage is that the whole thesis of the court rests on an obvious fiction. In the context of the disclosure of information, the very notion of a professional standard is something of a nonsense. *There simply is no such standard*, if only because the profession has not got together to establish which risks should be disclosed to which patients in which circumstances. That the

---

[64] See generally C. Wood (ed.), *The Influence of Litigation on Medical Malpractice* (Royal Society of Medicine, 1977), esp. pp. 45–56, 184. Hart reports, e.g., that the National Malpractice Commission set up in the mid-1970s found that lawyers accepted only approximately one in eight claims on which their advice was sought.

[65] See e.g. *The Economics of Medical Malpractice* (American Enterprise Institute, 1978), esp. pp. 125–55.

[66] G. Robertson, 'Informed Consent to Medical Treatment', 97 *LQR* 102, 109.

[67] 'The number of successful claims . . . appears to be relatively small' (*supra* n. 2, 21, n. 22). A national survey of claims in 1975–6 showed that informed consent was raised as an issue in only 3 per cent of cases (ibid.).

profession has, by contrast, got together and established which treatment should be attempted for which patients under which circumstances is, if you will, strong evidence of what their sphere of competence is and should be. Furthermore, in the absence of a professional standard, the likelihood exists of doctors affirming that Dr X's conduct was, in the circumstances, proper, out of some sense, misguided or otherwise, of professional solidarity.[68] If such a state of affairs were to occur, it would do nothing for patient confidence, and could well foster a sense of bitterness or frustration, out of which might grow further litigation.

Defensive Medicine

A fourth argument to be addressed is the commonly rehearsed spectre of 'defensive medicine'. Doctors may, in Dunn LJ's words, 'inevitably be concerned to safeguard themselves against . . . claims, rather than to concentrate on their primary duty of treating their patients'.[69] Is defensive medicine a real possibility, or another example of hyperbole? Again, it is the latter. To begin with, one doctor's defensive medicine may well be another's idea of good practice. In other words, it may simply be a term to describe that kind of careful medicine which ought to be practised, but which some find irksome. Next, to engage in a dialogue with a patient, in which the doctor explains the nature and implications of treatment, can hardly be called defensive medicine. It can only be described properly as good medicine. The legal test need only be that the doctor does what is reasonable in disclosing risks, just as he is required to do in the case of treatment and diagnosis. If sensitive guidance were available on what may be reasonable — what, for example, a prudent patient in a particular patient's circumstances might wish to know, and what amounted to justifiable exceptions — there need be no more defensive medicine than there is now. It is uncertainty about what is ethically and legally called for which may cause doctors to act defensively. Finally, references to alleged defensive medicine in the United States do not carry great weight. Most critically, there is no hard evidence to sustain the claims which are made.[70] Also, in a fee-for-service form of medical care, defensive medicine may well be a method whereby fee-splitting or generating income, by, for example, ordering further diagnostic tests which may otherwise be uncalled-for, can be justified by being blamed on the legal system!

---

[68] Also, 'there are strong biases in medical practice and training against making disclosure' (Ibid. 22, n. 25). These factors would combine to make a plaintiff's task of obtaining experts willing to testify on his behalf even harder than it now is in the context of alleged malpractice in diagnosis or treatment.

[69] Sidaway, *supra* n. 4, 1031.

[70] See e.g. Hart, *supra* n. 64, 52.

There is, however, one lesson to be learned from the United States, if the courts in England are to develop their own informed consent doctrine. This is that disclosure can become formalized and routinized through the use of consent forms. Here is not the place to explore the theory and practice behind consent forms. Suffice it to say that good patient care is not achieved by courts or laws or lawyers drafting forms. It depends on training, understanding, education, experience, and guidance. All that the law can do is to set the framework of what is right within which medicine is to be practised. It is then for other social mechanisms to take over. If this were to happen, we would be saved from the formal incantations often associated with consent forms. This is the basic thrust of the recommendations of the President's Commission, and must be right.[71]

The Way Forward

If the arguments set out above are accepted as demonstrating that the standard for disclosure should not be for the profession to set, it only remains to sketch what approach English law should adopt, in what can only be the briefest outline.

A doctor should be under a duty to disclose any unusual and material risks inherent in the proposed treatment, and any feasible alternatives. Whether a risk and/or an alternative exist and ought to be known by the doctor should be a matter for expert evidence. Whether a risk is material should be decided by the court on the basis of the prudent patient test; that is, a risk is material if it is one which a prudent patient in what the doctor knows to be the patient's position would regard as significant in deciding on the proposed treatment.[72] It is admitted that, ethically, the test for disclosure ought, optimally, to be measured by the needs of the particular patient. Such a standard would, however, pose great problems in law; and, since hindsight is always an exact science, would weigh the scales unfairly in favour of a complainant. Whether the disclosure had been carried out adequately would also be for the court. The manner in which disclosure should be made is one calling for skill and sensitivity. It should not consist in presenting the patient with an indigestible lump of information. It may, for example, take more than one session. Written consent forms could provide useful evidence, but may not be regarded as a substitute for real disclosure. Some patients may not comprehend what is being said, despite the doctor's best efforts. To adopt a standard demanding comprehension, as has been hinted at in, for example, Canada,[73] is to set a standard which is both too high and impractical. All that can be demanded

---

[71] *Supra* n. 2, 2–6.   [72] See e.g. *Miller* v. *Kennedy, supra* n. 47.
[73] See *Kelly* v. *Hazlett* (1977) 75 DLR 3d 536, 556; *Reibl* v. *Hughes, supra* n. 18; and, generally, *Consent to Medical Care, supra* n. 1.

of the doctor is that he makes his best efforts in a sensitive and appropriate manner, and records his conclusion carefully if he forms the view that the patient is not able to comprehend what is being said.

Once the basic duty to disclose is understood, there are specific points which call for attention. First, the duty would be subject to the defence of therapeutic privilege. Next, if the patient waives his right to disclosure, the doctor is absolved in most circumstances. And, of course, waiver may be express or implied. Equally, there can be no justification, ethically or legally, in forcing unwanted information on a patient. If the patient remains silent when his treatment is discussed, or says, for example, 'Whatever you say, Doctor,' the doctor must judge by sensitive appraisal whether this is out of a desire not to be informed or for some other reason, which may create in the doctor the duty to disclose. Such sensitive appraisals, properly noted by the doctor, take time, of course, but they are part of many doctors' regular practice. But time taken is not time wasted.[74] Not only is it part of the treatment, since it mobilizes the co-operation of the patient; it also heads off problems which could arise later.

A further question is whether the doctor needs to disclose the ordinary risks of treatment. Browne-Wilkinson LJ observed that 'it is of course obvious that the doctor is not under a duty to give information as to the ordinary risks normally attendant upon any operation.'[75] With respect, it is not so obvious. Surely, it must depend on the particular circumstances of the patient, and his awareness of what others may regard as ordinary risks. Probably the rule is better stated that, prima facie, the doctor is under no such duty, and strong evidence will be needed to show that the particular patient warranted special consideration.

It follows from the analysis put forward so far that telling a patient something which is untrue cannot be justified, except, perhaps, rarely in the context of the therapeutic privilege. Thus, Denning LJ's judgment in *Hatcher* v. *Black*[76] must be open to the most serious doubt, particularly his aphorism that 'the law leaves this question of morals to the conscience of the doctor,' which, after all, is the antithesis of the sort of disclosure rule being proposed.

Finally, the patient in a negligence action must always show that the defendant caused him damage. The first question to be faced is what is the proper rule of causation. Bristow J. in *Chatterton* v. *Gerson*[77] seemed to favour a subjective approach, which looks to what the particular patient claims he would have done had he known then the risks and alternatives which he knows now. Many United States jurisdictions and the leading Canadian

---

[74] Interestingly, the President's Commission recommended that the time for such discussion should be taken account of when setting the price for the treatment, so as to give an incentive to doctors (*supra* n. 2, 5).

[75] *Sidaway, supra* n. 4, 1034.   [76] *The Times*, 2 July 1954.   [77] *Supra* n. 3.

case of *Reibl* v. *Hughes*[78] favour an objective approach which looks to what a reasonable person in the patient's position would have done. The latter approach, I submit, is to be preferred, if only again because, with the best will in the world, an aggrieved patient is not unlikely to claim, after the event, that he would never have undergone the treatment had he known. The second question concerns what amounts to damage. Must the unwarned-of risk have materialized, or is it sufficient, in a negligence action, for the patient to say that his interests were invaded without real consent? Since negligence is fundamentally concerned with risk-creating behaviour, it seems that the former view is to be preferred; and this has been the approach in the United States and elsewhere.

With this framework, English law could make a major contribution to the development of a doctor–patient relationship based on shared decision making. It would then be for the educators, the trainers, the doctors, and the patients to ensure that the idea became a reality. The courts would have done their task, and litigation would be needed only, as now, in the rare case of malpractice.

POSTSCRIPT: THE HOUSE OF LORDS' DECISION

The above has, in part, been overtaken by the decision of the House of Lords. I reproduce it here only because some of the analysis, I venture to suggest, is valid, and may be relevant to further developments in the law. I append now, however, an analysis of the House of Lords' decision, to bring the discussion up to date.

The House of Lords considered Mrs Sidaway's appeal in December 1984. They announced in February 1985[79] that the appeal was lost.

The Result

Let us start at the end. All five members of the court, Lords Scarman, Diplock, Bridge, Keith, and Templeman, found against Mrs Sidaway. They did so principally because there was simply not enough evidence of what had passed between her and her long-dead doctor by way of advice or warnings. It was not possible, therefore, for the House of Lords to draw any conclusion as to whether, if a duty to warn or disclose information existed, it had in fact been breached. Her case was, as Lord Scarman put it, at best 'non-proven'.[80] So, eleven years after the operation and after three years of litigation, Mrs Sidaway lost her case.

---

[78] *Supra* n. 18, followed in *White* v. *Turner*, also *supra* n. 18.
[79] [1985] 1 All ER 643.　　　　[80] Ibid. 645.

This was not, however, the end of the matter. Their Lordships proceeded to treat the issue raised as a pure issue of law and to give their view of what that law is or should be.

The Law

Four of the five Law Lords made speeches in which they offered their analysis and views of the law. Lord Keith did not, being content to agree with Lord Bridge. It will come as no surprise to learn that, although unanimous that the appeal must be dismissed, their Lordships were anything but unanimous in their legal analysis. Each had his own line of reasoning. None, incidentally, referred to the reasoning offered by the Court of Appeal. To gauge the impact of the case and predict the future development of the law, we must examine each speech in turn, given the diversity of views on offer.

Perhaps we should let Lord Scarman set the scene:

The case is plainly of great importance. It raises a question which has never before been considered by your Lordships' House: has the patient a legal right to know and is the doctor under a legal duty to disclose, the risks inherent in the treatment which the doctor recommends? If the law recognises the right and the obligation, is it a right to full disclosure or has the doctor a discretion as to the nature and extent of his disclosure? And, if the right is to be qualified, where does the law look for the criterion by which the Court is to judge the extent of the disclosure required to satisfy the right? Does the law seek the guidance of a medical opinion or does it lay down a rule which doctors must follow, whatever may be the views of the profession?[81]

Before embarking, however, there are a couple of preliminary matters to be disposed of.

The existence and legal basis of the duty to inform

Leaving for a moment questions of the content of any duty to warn, it first has to be settled whether, in law, such a duty exists, which must be complied with before the patient's consent is valid. Further, if it does exist, what is its legal basis? Lord Scarman asked himself: 'Is it a cause of action in negligence, i.e. a breach of the duty of care, or is it based on a breach of a specific duty to inform the patient which arises not from any failure on the part of the doctor to exercise the due care and skill of his profession but directly from the patient's right to know?'[82] He concluded 'that there is room in our law for a legal duty to warn a patient of the risks inherent in the treatment proposed, and that, if such a duty be held to exist, its proper place is as an aspect of the duty of care owed by the doctor to his patient'.[83] Subsequently, he found that the duty does indeed exist: 'I think that English

---

[81] Ibid. 646.   [82] Ibid.   [83] Ibid. 652.

law must recognise a duty of the doctor to warn his patient of risk inherent in the treatment which he is proposing, and especially so if the treatment be surgery.' On this, the rest of the House was with him. All assumed or expressly stated that a doctor owes a duty to advise and warn his patient of certain matters. Difficulties in identifying such a duty in the fabric of English law, which had occupied the Court of Appeal, were shrugged off. Given that a doctor owes his patient a duty to exercise proper care and skill, the duty to inform, they all agreed, was an aspect of the doctor's duty to exercise proper care on his patient's behalf, since no lack of skill was alleged.

This does not tell us, of course, what is the legal test of compliance with this aspect of the duty of care. This is the heart of the matter, and it is to this that we must now turn.

Standard of care

It may be helpful to make a general point first. The question before us is not whether the House of Lords accepted the need for informed consent. There can be no doubt that the House reiterated that a doctor needs the valid consent of his patient before he may treat (in the sense of touch). This has always been English law. Equally, the House recognized that such consent must be informed to the extent deemed proper. The question for the House, in short, was who does the deeming? This is where the *doctrine* of informed consent, as opposed to the recognition of a general need for it, comes in. The question for us here is whether the House accepted or rejected the doctrine of informed consent as advocated earlier in this paper and recognized in the United States and Canada in varying forms.

Let me offer an answer which, I hope, will not pre-empt discussion and which will be borne out by what follows. Lord Diplock rejected the doctrine. Lord Bridge, with whom Lord Keith agreed in a concurring judgment, apparently rejected it, but offered something of his own, by way of a realignment of the law, in its place. Lord Scarman accepted it. As for Lord Templeman, it is not entirely clear; but, from the words he uses, he can probably be said to adopt some variant of it, similar to that adopted in Canada, while appearing at the same time to suggest that he was not doing so.

This said, I think it important to consider the various speeches in turn. The importance lies in the apparently simple need to know what the law is. As we all know, what the law is can only be answered by predicting what a future court will make of what the House of Lords has said. So, I must do the same and offer my predictions.

Lord Diplock's speech

This is the speech most obviously committed to the professional standard of disclosure:

To decide what risks the existence of which a patient should be voluntarily warned and the terms in which such warning, if any, should be given, having regard to the effect that the warning may have is as much an exercise of professional skill and judgement as any other part of the doctor's comprehensive duty of care to the individual patient, and expert medical evidence on this matter should be treated in just the same way. The *Bolam* test should be applied.[84]

The *Bolam* test[85] is that, as Lord Scarman put it succinctly, 'a doctor is not negligent if he acts in accordance with a practice accepted at the time as proper by a responsible body of medical opinion even though other doctors adopt a different practice. In short, the law imposes the duty of care; but the standard of care is a matter of medical judgement.'[86] Lord Diplock took this rule to apply to all aspects of a doctor's exercise of his duty of care, diagnosis, advice, and treatment. Indeed, he refused to recognize that the law could, or should, separate these various activities: 'This general duty is not subject to dissection into a number of component parts to which different criteria of what satisfy the duty of care apply, such as diagnosis, treatment and advice (including warning of any risks of something going wrong however skilfully the treatment advised is carried out).'[87]

Lord Diplock's speech was, then, essentially a recital of the traditional paternalistic arguments captured in the aphorisms 'Doctor knows best' and 'Leave it to Doctor'. and they were supported by the usual warning that if 'unsought information'[88] was volunteered, the patient might not agree to the treatment. The difficulty with the word 'unsought', of course, is precisely that it fails to comprehend the imbalance in power between the patient and the doctor. Information may be 'unsought' because its existence or relevance is not suspected, or because the patient is too nervous to ask. Lord Diplock may have been prepared to play his part in moulding the law towards a greater equalization of power between consumer and seller. But the demise or modification of *caveat emptor* offers no example for him when he comes to *caveat patiens*.

There is, however, one matter of general concern in his judgment. One of the principal reasons offered by Lord Diplock for rejecting the doctrine of informed consent was his unwillingness to accept the notion that an objective test based on the 'prudent patient' could be part of English law. Consent is a 'state of mind'.[89] Being so, it does not make sense, nor is it the law, he urged, that a doctor should be entitled to assume that a patient knows some things—namely, what the reasonable patient knows—but does not know others, of which the doctor must inform him. This fundamental attack on the prudent patient variant of the doctrine of informed consent is central to the opposition of many legal commentators and must be borne

---

[84] Ibid. 659.   [85] *Supra* n. 6.   [86] *Supra* n. 1, 649.
[87] Ibid. 657.   [88] Ibid. 659.   [89] Ibid. 658.

in mind when considering the speeches of Lords Scarman and Templeman. It is reflected in the speech of Lord Bridge, which I consider next.

Lord Bridge's speech

The speech of Lord Bridge, with which Lord Keith concurred, is most interesting. It displays the same signs of anguish and distress, of being drawn one way by the head and reason, and another by the heart and tradition, which were evident in the judgment of Browne-Wilkinson LJ in the Court of Appeal. Lord Templeman displays them also, as we shall see, to perhaps an even greater degree.

Lord Bridge recognized from the outset that the case is about a patient's right to decide whether to agree to treatment; and he stated clearly that a patient (whom he describes with typical precision as 'a conscious adult patient of sound mind')[90] does indeed have such a right in law. For example, in dismissing the view that a doctor need not volunteer any information, Lord Bridge remarks that this 'would effectively exclude the patient's right to decide in the very type of case where it is most important that he should be in a position to exercise that right'.[91]

Lord Bridge then 'recognise[s] the logical force'[92] of the doctrine of informed consent, as giving effect to this right to decide, set out in *Canterbury v. Spence*.[93] But, he goes on, and here we meet the first 'but', he regards the doctrine as 'quite impractical'.[94] Consequently, he rejects it 'as a solution to the problem of safeguarding the patient's right to decide',[95] for 'three principal reasons'.[96]

It may be as well to look at these reasons. If, as I submit with respect, they are found on examination to be without real substance, a later court may be persuaded, perhaps, to disregard them, and to consider anew the validity of the *Canterbury* doctrine. The first reason given is that the doctrine 'gives insufficient weight to the doctor/patient relationship'.[97] Doctors cannot, he asserts, educate patients to their own standard of medical knowledge. But this is a red herring. The doctrine calls for adequate, not full, information. Further, Lord Bridge warns, some patients may be put off, especially by warnings of remote risks. But *Canterbury* recognized the existence of the 'therapeutic privilege' precisely to meet the problem of upsetting the nervous patient. The reference to remote risks is another red herring. The doctrine does not insist that these be disclosed.

The second reason is that it would be 'unrealistic'[98] to allow medical evidence on 'primary medical factors'[99] and yet 'deny the court the benefit of evidence of medical opinion and practice on disclosure'.[1] This seems an

---

[90] Ibid. 660.   [91] Ibid. 661.   [92] Ibid. 662.   [93] *Supra* n. 20.
[94] *Supra* n. 1, 662.   [95] Ibid.   [96] Ibid.   [97] Ibid.   [98] Ibid.
[99] Ibid.   [1] Ibid.

odd criticism. Whether it is 'unrealistic' or not is beside the point. The issue is whether such evidence is relevant. The doctrine makes it clear that it is not, since what is at stake is the patient's right to be informed, not the doctor's (or doctors') alleged right to give or withhold information, subject to the therapeutic privilege.

The third reason is that the objective test in the *Canterbury* doctrine is 'almost meaningless'.[2] Individual judges would have to decide what a 'reasonable person in the patient's position' would decide, and this would lead to unpredictability in litigation. This, you may think, is again an odd criticism, or at least unduly pessimistic. Are not courts routinely asked to solve questions by reference to the ubiquitous 'reasonable person'? And do not standards soon emerge from the courts which set the boundaries, or at least suggest them, so that legal advisers may make sensible decisions about litigation? In short, therefore, the three reasons offered cannot be regarded as overwhelming, and the 'logical force' of the *Canterbury* doctrine remains relatively unscathed.

Lord Bridge, having dealt to his own satisfaction, however, with the doctrine of informed consent, does not then follow Lord Diplock into the view that *Bolam* is the only other view and thus represents the law. His approach is more subtle. He asks whether the patient's right to decide is 'sufficiently safeguarded by the application of the *Bolam* test *without qualification*'.[3]

In *Reibl* v. *Hughes*,[4] the Supreme Court of Canada decided that the *Bolam* test was not enough. Lord Bridge recognizes 'the force of this reasoning'.[5] *But*, (yes, you knew a 'but' was coming) he none the less accepts the test subject to a qualification. Again, his reasoning is not allowed to have its head (if you will forgive the metaphor).

The qualification, or proviso, which Lord Bridge offers is fascinating. The degree of disclosure 'must *primarily* be a matter of *clinical* judgement'.[6] So, it is not the *Bolam* test completely, but only 'primarily'. It is not entirely a professional standard. The courts also have a role. But just as one's head swam when Donaldson MR introduced the notion of 'rightly',[7] so the word 'primarily' gives one pause. After all, it is the word which sets the limit to the role of the court. It is hard to see how Lord Bridge can criticize the use of the concept of reasonableness, which is well known to the law, and then introduce a term, the parameters of which, in law, as elsewhere, are completely uncharted. In what follows, however, Lord Bridge does seek to offer some guidance to its meaning. He concedes that since the degree of disclosure is 'primarily' a matter of clinical judgment, the question of whether a doctor is in breach of his duty to disclose is 'primarily' a matter of expert

---

[2] Ibid.

[3] Ibid.; my emphasis.

[4] *supra* n. 18.

[5] *Supra* n. 1, 662.

[6] Ibid. 663; my emphasis.

[7] *Supra*, p. 186.

evidence. But, he asserts, this does not mean that the standard of care and whether it has been met are handed over to the profession entirely. He then, in what is the crucial part of his speech, seeks to demonstrate both that the law is the ultimate arbiter of the standard of disclosure and how a court can carry out that role:

Even in a case where, as here, no expert witness in the relevant medical field condemns the non-disclosure as being in conflict with accepted and responsible medical practice, I am of the opinion that the Judge might in certain circumstances come to the conclusion that disclosure of a particular risk was so obviously necessary for an informed choice on the part of the patient that no reasonably prudent medical man would fail to make it. The kind of case I have in mind would be an operation involving a substantial risk of grave adverse consequences, as for example the 10% risk of a stroke from the operation which was the subject of the Canadian case of *Reibl* v. *Hughes* (1980) 114 DLR 3*d* 1. In such a case, in the absence of some cogent clinical reason why the patient should not be informed, a doctor, recognizing and respecting his patient's right of decision, could hardly fail to appreciate the necessity for an appropriate warning.[8]

It may help to consider this critical passage in stages. First, on the principle that the greater includes the lesser, if, according to Lord Bridge, the court can set its own standard and insist upon disclosure when the profession is uniformly committed to non-disclosure, or at least does not condemn it, it must follow that the court can do so where there is a division of opinion within the profession. The court can prefer one view to another, thereby setting its own standard. Significantly, in doing so, the court will not be violating the principle laid down in *Maynard* v. *West Midlands RHA*,[9] that where there is a conflict of medical evidence on a matter of diagnosis (or, *semble*, treatment), the court may not prefer one body of medical evidence to another so as to justify a finding of negligence. For the basis of the test in *Bolam*, on which *Maynard* relied, is that a doctor is not negligent if what he does can be supported by a body of responsible medical opinion. In stipulating that the court can decide among competing bodies of opinion, therefore, Lord Bridge confirms that he is rejecting the *Bolam* test *simpliciter*, as regards the issue of the patient's right to be informed.

Second, Lord Bridge states, in the passage just cited, that the criterion to be employed by the court in preferring to ignore the professional standard and set its own is exemplified by 'an operation involving a *substantial* risk of *grave* adverse consequences' (my emphasis). I say 'exemplified' because Lord Bridge clearly intends this to be an example. How such an example is to be generalized into a principle of wide application — outside the context of surgery, for example — is not clear. One way of doing so, and a way which Lord Bridge clearly found attractive, would be to take the words 'substantial' and 'grave' and seek to quantify them, the form of quantification being in terms of percentage risk. This has the apparent merit of lending a measure of certainty to the test. It thereby appears to give doctors and their advisers something to bite on, and removes the need to examine what a prudent patient in the patient's circumstances might consider material.

In my view, the recourse to probabilities that a risk may materialize is an unfortunate feature of what is otherwise a measured rejection of the professional standard test. First, it creates the impression that the law can produce a standard of care which would substitute mathematics and probability theory for the uncertainties of words such as 'reasonable' or 'material'. Such an impression is not only an illusion which ignores the fact that the law exists by words of general application and needs their very generality to retain its flexibility and capacity for development; it could also have serious practical consequences for the further development of the patient's right to be informed. This is because in medicine there may well be disagreement as to the precise number to be assigned to the chance of a particular risk materializing. Lord Bridge himself referred to the 'marked and understandable reluctance'[10] of expert medical witnesses to commit themselves to measuring the risk in Mrs Sidaway's case in percentage terms. In any given case, some may say 2 per cent, others 3 per cent, and others 4 per cent. The variety of estimates may depend on the presence or absence of data, or on how the data are interpreted. A case could then be won or lost on an argument about numbers in which the real issue of the plaintiff's legitimate complaint was lost.

This is not, I think, a fanciful point. In *Sidaway*, Lord Bridge cites the 10 per cent risk in *Reibl* as being substantial, but apparently finds the 1–2 per cent risks in *Sidaway* not substantial. Leaving for a moment the merits of this conclusion—and one risk was the risk of spinal cord damage—what, on Lord Bridge's test, will a court say about a 4 per cent risk or a 3.5 per cent or a 5 per cent risk? We will see later that Lord Templeman regarded a 4 per cent risk of death as being something a patient should be told about. But would this apply to a 4 per cent risk of disfiguring scars? Would such a percentage risk persuade experts to advise an anguished and disfigured patient that she should not seek redress, when she had not been told of the risk and is now facing a shattered life? I submit that we should accept that the law must perforce be uncertain, and not seek to incorporate tests which have a spurious certainty but could be invoked against the interests of patients.

Thus, if Lord Bridge is, or is taken to be, advocating that the meaning of 'substantial' can be reduced to quantifiable risks, this would be most regrettable. Even if he is not, the use of the words 'substantial' and 'grave' is still open to exception. For do they not beg the central question: 'substantial'

---

[10] *Supra* n. 1, 664.

and 'grave' to whom? The answer cannot be to the medical profession, because this would take us back to the wholly professional standard which Lord Bridge rejects? It cannot be to the patient, because this would call for a wholly subjective standard which no court anywhere (with the exception of Oklahoma[11]) has accepted. It must, therefore, be to the court. But if this is so, Lord Bridge cannot be very far from the reasonable or prudent patient test which he previously found unattractive. In my submission, this in fact is the only proper interpretation of Lord Bridge's speech. He differs from those who advocate the prudent patient test only in the emphasis he would place, prima facie, on medical evidence as to what the professional standard of disclosure should be.

Lord Bridge's speech, therefore, represents a major development in the law on informed consent, and is to be welcomed as such. The resort to the language of percentages is to be regretted and should have been avoided, but this is a minor theme. The speech rejects the *Bolam* test, and substitutes a test which requires that substantial risks of grave adverse consequences be disclosed, except where there are sound clinical grounds for not doing so. It insists, in other words, that the standard of disclosure is ultimately a matter of law for the courts, due attention having been paid to the view of the medical profession. It may not go as far as to provide for the prudent patient test, but there can be no mistaking that, in Lord Bridge's view, the law has changed.

Lord Scarman's speech

In Lord Scarman's view, the time had come to reject the *Bolam* case as applying to the disclosure of information, if it ever did, and to incorporate into English law the doctrine of informed consent developed in the *Canterbury* case. And this is what he does. He was not able to carry the other members of the House with him in adopting explicitly the formal doctrine of informed consent. As will be clear, however, save for Lord Diplock, they undoubtedly introduced a variant of their own, which constitutes a rejection of the *Bolam* test (*simpliciter*). To that extent, it would be wrong to regard Lord Scarman's as a dissenting speech, although this is how it is characterized in the *All England Law Reports*. Rather, Lord Scarman has, perhaps, taken two steps forward, whereas Lords Bridge, Keith, and Templeman have taken only one.

In large measure, the views expressed earlier in my comment on the decision of the Court of Appeal coincide so closely with those of Lord Scarman that there is little need here for any detailed analysis. Given the importance of the speech, however, I will mention here what I take to be the major points.

Lord Scarman began by drawing attention to the implications of continuing to adhere to a professional standard as regards the duty to inform:

---

[11] *Scott* v. *Bradford* 606 P. 2d 554 (Okl. 1979).

The implications of this view of the law are disturbing. It leaves the determination of a legal duty to the judgement of doctors. Responsible medical judgement may, indeed, provide the law with an acceptable standard in determining whether a doctor in diagnosis or treatment has complied with his duty. But is it right that medical judgement should determine whether there exists a duty to warn of risk and its scope? It would be a strange conclusion if the courts should be led to conclude that our law, which undoubtedly recognises the right in the patient to decide whether he will accept or reject the treatment proposed, should permit the doctors to determine whether and in what circumstances a duty arises requiring the doctor to warn his patient of the risk inherent in the treatment which he proposes.[12]

Such a conclusion would indeed be strange once the language of patients' rights is used. And, as Lord Scarman puts it, 'the doctor's duty arises from his patient's rights.'[13] This is a view echoed by Lords Bridge and Templeman, and represents a crucial shift of emphasis in the law. But, for Lord Scarman, it is not enough merely to use the language of rights. To him, what is involved is a 'basic human right',[14] which he sees as protected by the common law: the right to make one's own decisions. To talk of human rights is of immense significance. It recognizes that here, and in many other areas of medical law, what is at stake for the courts is the protection of human rights. Examples range from the detention and treatment of the mentally ill to care of handicapped neonates to research on human subjects to care of the elderly. It thus makes clear that the law and the courts will be particularly vigilant in the protection of these rights, such that very good reasons will be needed before an encroachment on them will be contemplated. With such a commitment as his backdrop, it is hardly surprising that Lord Scarman did not regard the view of the medical profession of what was right for a patient to be a sufficiently good reason for encroachment.

If, then, the standard of disclosure was for the law, through the courts, to set and to supervise, what was the appropriate legal device? Lord Scarman had no doubt that some device had to be found. And, in the absence of statute, the common law could do the job. Here is a favourite theme of Lord Scarman's: that basic human rights exist and need protection, that we have no Bill of Rights to protect them, and that, therefore, the courts must do so. And they can do so by having recourse to the principles of the common law (Lord Scarman's Bill of Rights by another name). One such principle is *ubi jus ibi remedium*, and it is this principle which was properly to be invoked. The remedy lay, Lord Scarman held, in a proper development of the law of negligence. The law had not been set in stone by the *Bolam* case. When a case such as *Sidaway* came before them which 'raises a question which has never before been considered by your Lordships' House',[15] there was:

---

[12] *Supra* n. 1, 649.   [13] Ibid. 645.   [14] Ibid.   [15] Ibid. 646.

no reason why a rule of informed consent should not be recognised and developed by our courts. The common law is adaptable; it would not otherwise have survived over the centuries of its existence. The concept of negligence itself is a development of the law by the Judges over the last hundred years or so. . . . It would be irony indeed if a judicial development for which the opportunity was the presence in the law of a flexible remedy should result now in rigidly confining the law's remedy to situations and relationship already ruled on by the Judges.[16]

You may think that Lord Scarman is making a great deal of what is merely an adjustment or refinement of the existing law of negligence and the duty of care owed by a doctor to his patient. This would be a mistake. By building on first principles and pointing out that what was before the House was an issue of human rights, Lord Scarman has both established the framework within which medical law, one of his interests,[17] may develop, and provided a legal analysis which it will be hard for other courts to ignore.

Having set himself to find a remedy in negligence, Lord Scarman found one in the *Canterbury* doctrine, which he had 'no difficulty in accepting'.[18] In his own words:

English law must recognise a duty of the doctor to warn his patient of risk inherent in the treatment which he is proposing: and especially so if the treatment be surgery. The critical limitation is that the duty is confined to material risk. The test of materiality is whether in the circumstances of the particular case, the court is satisfied that a reasonable person in the patient's position would be likely to attach significance to the risk. Even if the risk be material, the doctor will not be liable if on a reasonable assessment of his patient's condition he takes the view that a warning would be detrimental to his patient's health.[19]

It should be added, by the way, that although Lord Scarman talks only of risks in this particular section of his speech, he makes it clear at the outset that the patient's right to information extends both to warnings as to risk and 'the options of alternative treatment'.[20]

One further point should be noted. You may recall that earlier I considered and ventured to disagree with the view of Browne-Wilkinson LJ that a doctor need not disclose the ordinary risks of treatment.[21] This is an issue which, you may remember, also troubled Lord Bridge, and which plays a significant role in the speech of Lord Templeman. It is, in truth, a question of the meaning of materiality. And, true to the logic of his argument, Lord Scarman refuses to attach legal significance to any distinction, real or otherwise, between 'general' and 'special' risks. Special risks are 'more likely to be

---

[16] Ibid. 650.
[17] See e.g. his extensive review in *Gillick* v. *West Norfolk and Wisbech AHA* [1985] 3 All ER 402, and Scarman, 'Legal Liability and Medicine', 74 (1) *Journal of the Royal Society of Medicine*, 11 (1981).   [18] *Supra* n. 1, 653.
[19] Ibid. 655.   [20] Ibid. 645.   [21] *Supra*, p. 192.

material'.[22] But, Lord Scarman was at pains to point out, general risks, by which he meant risks which would ordinarily be a matter of common knowledge, were not necessarily excluded. 'It is not difficult to foresee circumstances particular to a patient in which even the general risks of surgery should be the subject of a warning by his doctor, e.g. a heart or lung or blood condition.'[23]

To Lord Scarman, the merit of the approach adopted in *Canterbury* lies in the relative roles allocated to medical evidence and to the court. The court is the ultimate arbiter, preserving and protecting rights. But medical evidence, and thus the views of the profession, are not ignored by the prudent patient test. Indeed, they are essential. Their significance, however, is limited to establishing matters of medical fact. While the materiality of a risk is for the court, therefore, to decide, the probability of the risk materializing and the seriousness, in factual terms, of possible injury if it does are for medical evidence. The therapeutic privilege is also a matter of medical evidence. This is a most important point. For the therapeutic privilege is the mechanism whereby Lord Scarman, while requiring that the law judge the patient before the court by reference to an objective or prudent patient standard, allows the doctor to bring to the court's attention the particular circumstances of the particular patient being treated:

The prudent patient cannot . . . always provide the answer for the obvious reason that he is a norm (like the man on the Clapham Omnibus), not a real person; and certainly not the patient himself. Hence there is a need that the doctor should have the opportunity of proving that he reasonably believed that disclosure of the risk would be damaging to his patient or contrary to his best interest. This is what the Americans call the doctor's therapeutic privilege.[24]

---

[22] *Supra* n. 1, 654.

[23] Ibid. See further on the concepts of 'material' and 'special' risks, E. Picard, *Legal Liability of Doctors and Hospitals in Canada*, 2nd edn. (Carswell, 1984), pp. 95–8. She refers in particular to the outstanding judgment of Mr Justice Linden in *White* v. *Turner*, (1981), 120 DLR (3d) 269. Linden J. described 'material' and 'special' risks as follows: 'the meaning of "material risks" and "unusual or special risks" should now be considered. In my view, *material* risks are significant risks that pose a real threat to the patient's life, health, or comfort. In considering whether a risk is material or immaterial, one must balance the severity of the potential result and the likelihood of its occurring. Even if there is only a small chance of serious injury or death, the risk may be considered material. On the other hand, if there is a significant chance of slight injury this too may be held to be material. As always in negligence law, what is a material risk will have to depend on the specific facts of each case.

As for "unusual or special risks", these are those that are not ordinary, common, everyday matters. These are risks that are somewhat extraordinary, uncommon and not encountered every day, but they are known to occur occasionally. Though rare occurrences, because of their unusual or special character, the Supreme Court has declared that they should be described to a reasonable patient, even though they may not be "material". There may, of course, be an overlap between "material risks" and "unusual or special risks". If a special or unusual risk is quite dangerous and fairly frequently encountered, it could be classified as a material risk. But even if it is not very dangerous or common, an unusual or special risk must be disclosed.' [24] Ibid.

Notice, however, that Lord Scarman recognizes the dangers implicit in adopting a defence of 'therapeutic privilege'. As has been argued, if it is not tightly confined, it can readily run away with the principle of respect for the patient's right to be informed. Lord Scarman covers the point neatly, although in general terms, by stipulating that 'it is a defence available to the doctor which, if he invokes it, *he must prove*'.[25]

This, then, is the approach adopted by Lord Scarman, an approach which, I submit, undoubtedly represents the law as it will be, if not as it is at present. One final point is worth making. What does Lord Scarman have to say about the spectre of 'defensive medicine' which certain opponents of the doctrine of informed consent wheel out to frighten or subdue opponents. As you may recall, I doubt the intellectual validity of the notion. To me it is bogus, borne of a combination of misunderstanding, fear, and propaganda. Lord Scarman, however, was too wise to be drawn into the debate. He relied instead on one of his favourite analytical devices. He was concerned, he said, with legal principle. If there was any danger of defensive medicine as a consequence of the decision, this was a matter of policy. As such, it was for the legislature, not the courts.

Lord Templeman's speech

In a sense, Lord Templeman's speech is the most intriguing. Lord Scarman's view is clear. He rejects *Bolam*. Lord Diplock accepts it without demur. Lord Bridge edges carefully away from *Bolam*. Lord Templeman's speech is significant, therefore, not only because of the intrinsic importance of what he says, but also as being a sign of the direction which the law is taking and the speed with which it is likely to move. The closer he is to Lord Bridge, the more circumspect the law will remain and the more weight will be given to the professional standard. The closer he is to Lord Scarman, the nearer we shall be to a fully-fledged doctrine of informed consent, on the model of *Canterbury* or *Reibl* v. *Hughes*.

Lord Templeman's speech is a relatively short one, and is entirely devoted to statements of principle. Indeed, as in his speech in *Gillick* v. *Norfolk and Wisbech AHA*,[26] he refers to only one decided case, *Reibl* v. *Hughes*. The principle which he finds to be central to the case before him is as follows:

In order to make a balanced judgment if he chooses to do so, the patient needs to be aware of the general dangers and of any special dangers in each case without exaggeration or concealment. At the end of the day the doctor, bearing in mind the best interests of the patient and bearing in mind the patient's right to information which will enable the patient to make a balanced judgment, must decide what information should be given to the patient and in what terms that information should be couched. The Court will award damages against the doctor if the Court is satisfied

[25] Ibid.; my emphasis.   [26] *Supra* n. 17, 431.

that the doctor blundered **and that** the patient was deprived of information which was necessary for the purposes I have outlined.[27]

There are a number of points here which need to be spelled out. First, Lord Templeman makes it clear that the language of rights is appropriate. The patient has a 'right to information'. It follows that Lord Templeman places a duty to inform on the doctor, a duty which is derived from and forms part of the duty of care which each doctor owes to his patient and which is remediable through the tort of negligence. Second, you will notice that Lord Templeman draws the distinction between 'general' and 'special' dangers. Two observations are in order. The first is that it is unfortunate that Lord Templeman sees the right to information only in terms of risks or dangers. As has been said, information on alternatives is equally important. Second, we have seen already that Lord Scarman, while noticing the plausibility of such a distinction, did not let it bully him into adopting two separate rules of law, one for general and one for special risks or dangers. But what does Lord Templeman make of the distinction?

As for general dangers or risks, Lord Templeman's analysis is as follows. Where a patient is to have a surgical operation—or, one assumes, *pari passu*, any other form of treatment—'a simple and general explanation of the operation should have been sufficient to alert [the patient] to the fact that a major operation was to be performed'.[28] If we stop there for a moment, we learn that for all operations, and *semble* other treatment, there must be—that is, the doctor has a duty to offer—a simple and general explanation. This must be obvious, but it cannot hurt to repeat it. We also learn that, armed with the explanation, the patient may be assumed to appreciate the nature, in terms of the seriousness, of the intervention. This is not so obvious (compare here Lord Scarman's view). But Lord Templeman at least seems to hold to the view that, after the explanation, at least as regards general dangers, the patient is on her own. She may ask questions, and if she does, she has a right to straight answers; but otherwise she may not complain.

This may be said to offer less than complete protection to the right to information which Lord Templeman recognizes as a legal right. It assumes a level of awareness which not all may have, and a preparedness to interrogate their doctors which few patients would be willing or able to adopt. But, of course, much turns on what 'a simple and general explanation' consists in. And here Lord Templeman offers some guidance. 'In the case of a general danger the courts must decide whether the information afforded to the patient was sufficient to alert the patient to the possibility of serious harm of the kind in fact suffered.'[29]

---

[27] *Supra* n. 1, 666.   [28] Ibid. 664.   [29] Ibid. 665.

This guidance clearly tempers the apparent harshness of the more general principle and, I submit, goes a long way to providing the kind of respect for the rights of patients which has been the theme of this paper. It represents, if you will, the kind of reasonable and pragmatic approach which characterizes the response of the English courts in so many areas of law. Clearly, doctors should not be made to explain more or less everything to everybody. They may assume some knowledge—indeed, they must be entitled to do so—if they are ever going to get on with their job. And, as Lord Templeman recognizes elsewhere, they must have the benefit of the therapeutic privilege if they can show that it was applicable in a particular case. But, that said, Lord Templeman in his guidance makes it clear that the assumption of knowledge is only valid with regard to general dangers, and that it is subject to major provisos which must not be overlooked. First, the information must be sufficient 'to alert *the* patient' (my emphasis). Lord Templeman does not say '*a* patient'. Second, it is the court, not the profession, which will judge the sufficiency of the information.

Thus, on general dangers, Lord Templeman's view of the law can be said to be very close to that of Lord Scarman. The standard of disclosure is set by the law, not the profession. The law may assume that most patients, on receipt of a simple explanation of the procedure proposed, will be put on notice as to whether it will expose them to some general danger common to all such procedures. If they wish to know more, they can ask and must be answered. But the doctor must always take account of his patient's particular circumstances. The court will be vigilant to see that he does; but if he 'conscientiously endeavours to explain the arguments for and against the major operation and the possibilities of benefiting and the dangers',[30] the law will be slow to interfere.

Turning now to special dangers, there is, as far as Lord Templeman is concerned, 'no doubt that a doctor ought to draw the attention of a patient to a danger which may be special in kind or magnitude or special to the patient'.[31] So far, so good, you may say; but does Lord Templeman go any further in telling us what a special danger is, so that we can distinguish it from a general one? 'Special in kind or magnitude' does not tell us a great deal. Like Lord Bridge with his 'substantial', Lord Templeman seems to be saying that, like the elephant, he knows a special danger when he sees one. But, as we have observed, it is entirely in the tradition of the law to regulate in general terms, and it is no bad thing that the words are so general. It makes clear that, since the presumption is that the patient has the right to know, any doctor who thinks a risk may be judged by the court to be special in kind or magnitude would do well to inform his patient, unless he has a very good reason for not doing so.

---

[30] Ibid.   [31] Ibid.

Unfortunately, Lord Templeman goes on to refer to the percentage risks involved in *Reibl* v. *Hughes*. This could suggest that he is playing the numbers game, something I suggested was an inappropriate exercise on which to base future findings. I would, therefore, prefer to think that Lord Templeman referred to percentages only by way of example, since they can be helpful pointers, and that he did not intend them to be of any definitive legal significance. It is fair to say, however, that in reaching his conclusions on the facts of Mrs Sidaway's case, Lord Templeman did seem to regard the fact that the risk was only 1–2 per cent as enough to show that it was not such as to call for further explanation, unless Mrs Sidaway had specifically asked for it. This could lead to the unfortunate and, I hope, unwarranted view that 'special in kind or magnitude' was to be, or could be, defined in terms of percentages.

Even more interesting is Lord Templeman's reference to a danger as being special if it was 'special to the patient'. This, I submit, is the crux of his decision, the point around which all else revolves. How is a doctor to know that a danger is special to his patient? Put simply, this drags us back to the central question: who decides what is 'special to the patient'? If it is the patient, then the doctor must tell the patient all that she may need to know in order so to judge. This is clearly not what Lord Templeman intended, since, as he put it, he does not 'subscribe to the theory that the patient is entitled to know everything'.[32]

It must, then, be the doctor who decides what is 'special to the patient'. But does this not reduce Lord Templeman's rule to the following: the doctor must tell the patient what the doctor thinks the patient ought to know? Does not Lord Templeman thereby usher in by the back door the professional standard? I submit that, although it is far from clear, a case can be made for the proposition that he does not do this. For Lord Templeman makes it clear that the doctor's decision is subject to review by the courts. It is to be made, in other words, against the knowledge that it will be accepted only if it puts the patient in the position to make his own balanced judgment as to whether to go ahead or not. Ultimately, Lord Templeman asserts, 'it is for the court to decide.'[33] And a court's decision will presumably be made against the backdrop of Lord Templeman's central observation that 'the doctor is not entitled to make the final decision with regard to treatment which may have disadvantages or dangers. Where the patient's health and future are at stake, the patient must make the final decision.'[34]

It would be wrong, however, to assert that Lord Templeman's speech makes this argument conclusive. Far from it. Indeed, it is fair to say that on the critical question of the role allowed for professional paternalism, Lord Templeman is, with great respect, equivocal. The final paragraph of

---

[32] Ibid.   [33] Ibid.   [34] Ibid. 666.

his speech has all the signs of a judge agonizingly seeking a compromise, and, when he is unable to find one, retreating into propositions which, read in isolation, offer clear guidance, but which, when put together, seem only to contradict each other. Look again at his conclusion:

At the end of the day, the doctor, bearing in mind the best interests of the patient and bearing in mind the patient's right to information which will enable the patient to make a balanced judgement, must decide what information should be given to the patient and in what terms that information should be couched. The court will award damages against the doctor if the court is satisfied that the doctor blundered and that the patient was deprived of information which was necessary for the purposes I have outlined.[35]

For my part, I regard the section of Lord Templeman's speech which is concerned with 'special dangers' as meaning the following. A doctor must recognize a patient's right to be informed and, subject to the therapeutic privilege, may only, at his peril, fail to inform her of risks of which a court would think she would want to know. In deciding whether a patient would have wanted to know something, a court will ask itself whether the risk was special in kind or magnitude or special to the patient. The court will, in other words, apply the standard of the reasonable or prudent patient in the particular patient's circumstances.

My conclusion is, therefore, that as far as both general and special dangers are concerned, Lord Templeman rejects, without referring to it, the *Bolam* test, and adopts as the standard of care a set of principles broadly similar to those adopted in *Reibl* v. *Hughes*. I accept, of course, that there may be other interpretations which suggest themselves to other commentators.

A final point is worth noting. I hazarded the view much earlier[36] that Lord Denning's dictum in *Hatcher* v. *Black* that a doctor could even in law be justified in lying to his patient should no longer be regarded as good law. Both Lord Templeman and Lord Bridge make it clear that if a doctor is asked for information, he must reply truthfully. To that extent, Lord Denning's view is no longer law, if it ever was. It may still be the law, however, that, within the context of the therapeutic privilege, the doctor need not always volunteer the whole truth and may, perhaps, even tell the occasional 'white lie'.[37]

---

[35] Ibid.　　　　　　　　　　　　　　　　　　　　　[36] *Supra*, p. 192.

[37] And see now the decision of the Court of Appeal in *Blyth* v. *Bloomsbury HA* (unreported), which has considerably muddied the waters. It is not clear from the complicated facts whether the case was one in which the doctor involved failed to answer Mrs Blyth's question concerning the side-effects of the long-acting injectable contraceptive drug Depo-Provera, or whether he merely failed to inform her of these. In any event, the doctor involved was absolved from liability by the Court of Appeal, having been found liable at first instance.

CONCLUSION

The decision in *Sidaway* was awaited with great interest. Would the House of Lords opt for *Bolam* and medical paternalism, or develop law which gave greater respect and protection to a patient's autonomy? I have sought to suggest that, on careful analysis, the law relating to a doctor's duty to inform his patient has been cut free from *Bolam*. Lord Scarman is in the vanguard in recognizing the need for, and validity of, a doctrine of informed consent. Lord Bridge and Lord Templeman in their own ways, and perhaps falteringly, are not so very far behind. The transatlantic doctrine may not have been embraced, but an English variant is certainly in the process of being constructed.

There are those who have welcomed *Sidaway* as rejecting informed consent and as endorsing the 'right' of doctors to decide for patients what they need to know. Not only is such a view unwarranted on a proper reading of the case; it also fails to take account of the fact that the law is a dynamic social institution, developing and moving in step with, even if several paces behind, social changes.[38] The message of *Sidaway* is clear. Those who advise doctors already know it. Medical paternalism has had its day. Whether it can be replaced by a system of rules which promotes the welfare of patients, while preserving a proper respect for the skills and discretion of doctors, is a task for all of us in the future.

That it is a considerable task is clear in the light of the extraordinary and regrettable decision of the Court of Appeal in *Gold* v. *Haringey HA*,[39] which was decided as I prepared this book for publication. My confidence in my analysis of *Sidaway* remains intact, but I must say that the decision in the *Gold* case does somewhat take one's breath away. Mrs Gold brought an action for damages when she became pregnant after having had a sterilization operation. It was admitted that the operation had failed, and that she had not been advised either that this was a possibility or that there was an alternative to sterilization—namely, that her husband could have had a vasectomy. Her action was successful at first instance, but, on appeal, she lost.

To read the judgment of the Court of Appeal is to imagine that *Sidaway* had not happened. Admittedly, Lord Justice Lloyd refers to *Sidaway*, but only to the speech of Lord Diplock. Lloyd LJ represents Lord Diplock as speaking for the House when, on any reasonable interpretation of *Sidaway*, it can be said that none of the other judges agreed with his deeply conservative view. Lloyd LJ states that in *Sidaway*, 'the House of Lords applied the same

---

[38] For a recent analysis of the empirical evidence concerning attitudes among patients and doctors to informed consent, see Institute of Medical Ethics, *Bulletin: Supplement No. 3* (Dec. 1986).

[39] *Gold* v. *Haringey HA* [1987] 2 All ER 888.

test' as in *Bolam*. On that basis he was able to find that Mrs Gold's action failed, as there was a responsible body of medical opinion which did not believe women should be warned that sterilization operations might fail. This was enough to satisfy the *Bolam* test and rebut liability.

The duty to inform the patient of any alternative treatment, which commentators have for some time identified as part of the general duty to inform, was rejected without really being recognized as a legitimate argument, let alone analysed. This is hardly surprising given the court's adoption of Lord Diplock's approach to the whole notion of the duty to advise and warn, that it is a matter of what a responsible body of medical opinion would have accepted as proper.

Clearly, the Court of Appeal cannot have been referred to a speech delivered by Lord Scarman to the Royal Society of Medicine[40] soon after *Sidaway* was decided. The speech makes somewhat poignant reading in view of what the Court of Appeal has made of *Sidaway*. Lord Scarman set himself the task of discussing the way in which the law and the doctor–patient relationship will develop after *Sidaway*. He paints a picture of himself forging ahead while his brother judges trod more carefully. Is the so-called doctrine of informed consent, he asks, part of English law? 'Scarman said "yes"; Diplock said "no"; Bridge, Keith and Templeman said "yes, with reservations".'

'We can ignore Lord Diplock's opinion,' he goes on, 'as he was in a minority of one; the other three opinions were perhaps truer to the spirit of English law than I was, since they knew they must advance more slowly towards a doctrine of the patient's right to informed consent.' Whatever the pace of the advance, Lord Scarman has no hesitation, however, in drawing one implication 'which I can deal with extremely quickly. Medical paternalism is no longer acceptable as a matter of English law; that has gone.'[41] The Court of Appeal in *Gold* seems not to have been convinced!

Furthermore, the Court of Appeal in *Gold* could have profited from reading what Lord Scarman had to say on the meaning of the word 'advice', given that a doctor has a duty to advise. It is 'not limited to the recommendation which the doctor makes to the patient, but [includes] also *advice about alternative courses of treatment*, their advantages and disadvantages. That is to say, "advice", when it is used in the Law Reports by judges, means *information as to options* as well as the doctor's recommendation.'[42]

It is to be hoped that the *Gold* case is speedily consigned to the history books. That women in the late 1980s should not be entitled in law to information about the risks and alternatives to a procedure such as sterilization without having to ask is, frankly, an appalling state of affairs.

---

[40] Lord Scarman, 'Consent, Communication and Responsibility', 79 *Journal of the Royal Society of Medicine* 697, (Dec. 1986).   [41] Ibid.   [42] Ibid.; my emphasis.

Women patients have put up with this kind of nonsense from doctors for far too long, and it is time that the courts realized this. If the courts think that by such decisions they are saving the medical profession from litigation and thus doing us all a service, they are tragically wrong. Far worse consequences will befall the doctor–patient relationship if patronizing paternalism is legitimized as the appropriate mode of communication between doctor and patient.

Indeed, those who fear that the floodgates of liability will be opened by admitting the doctrine of informed consent should examine the evidence from Canada.[43] It already demonstrates that the judicial recognition of the duty to inform is not, in the event, resulting in any significant increase in the liability of doctors. This is because the doctrine of causation is being used by the courts to check any untoward growth in liability. The courts are deciding that, even though a patient was not informed of a material risk which subsequently materialized, he may not succeed in his action unless he can show that if he had been so informed, he would have refused the treatment. And, since most reasonable patients would not refuse what is otherwise reasonable treatment, having been advised of any material risks, the patient's case will ordinarily fail. The effect is interesting. Litigation and liability are controlled, while the important principle of a patient's right to information is recognized and enforced.

[43] See A. Dugdale, 'Diverse Reports: Canadian Professional Negligence Cases', 2 *Professional Negligence* 108 (July 1986).

10

The Law and Ethics of Informed Consent
and Randomized Controlled Trials*

The controlled clinical trial, and particularly the Randomized Control Trial (RCT), has come to be regarded over the past two decades as 'the paradigm source of information on which to base . . . therapeutic decisions'.[1] RCTs can be described as clinical trials to compare treatments in which the division of patients into groups is done by some method independent of human choice—that is, by the use of random numbers, without regard to the particular characteristics of the patients. 'In this way, the characteristics of the patients are randomised . . . and it is possible to test the hypothesis that, for example, one treatment is better than another and express the results in the form of the probability of the difference found being due to chance or not.'[2]

My concern in this paper is to identify the relevant legal and ethical rules pertaining to the conduct of RCTs, with particular reference to consent.

CONSENT IN GENERAL TERMS

Although it is common to talk of 'informed consent', it is, of course, well known that the concept of consent has three discrete and equally important aspects: first, consent is valid only if the person giving it is competent to do so; second, the consent must be properly informed; and third, the consent must be given voluntarily. All of these aspects are involved and warrant consideration when deciding whether to embark on an RCT. Since it is the question of information which provokes the greatest discussion and raises the most difficult problem, I shall largely confine my remarks to this aspect, although it may be necessary to make passing reference to voluntariness.

INFORMED CONSENT

As we saw in the last chapter, the law relating to the information which a doctor must give his patient was considered extensively in a recent decision

---

* This paper was prepared for and delivered at the First International Conference on Philosophy, Methodology, Ethics and Economics in Clinical Cancer Research, held at Kos, May 1986.
[1] Editorial, 9 *Journal of Medical Ethics*, (1983), 59.
[2] A. Cochrane, *Effectiveness and Efficiency* (Nuffield Provincial Hospital Trust, 1972).

of the House of Lords, in the case of *Sidaway* v. *Bethlem Royal Hospital Governors*.[3] Here, I want to look at the salient points with regard to RCTs and to do so from the point of view of what the law may be at present, while recognizing that this is a somewhat difficult objective, particularly given the dynamic nature of the law in this area.[4]

As we have seen, a doctor owes a duty of care to a patient whom he is treating. This duty also includes the duty to give the patient information about the treatment to be embarked upon. The nature and extent of the information to be provided is to be determined, ordinarily, if not exclusively, by reference to what a reasonably conscientious doctor, with the skill and experience professed by the doctor in question, would choose to provide. The doctor may, therefore, in the light of the above consideration, decide not to give a patient certain information; and this will ordinarily be seen as justified if it is done in what the doctor perceives to be the interests of the patient, and if other responsible doctors would do the same. The doctor must respond truthfully, however, and tell a patient what he wishes to know if the patient specifically asks to be informed on some matter. The discretion granted by the law to doctors as regards informing patients is subject to supervision and review by the courts, such that a court may not endorse a particular decision if, under the circumstances, it is thought that 'disclosure of a particular risk was so obviously necessary to an informed choice on the part of the patient that no reasonably prudent medical man would fail to make it'.[5] Should a doctor be found to have breached his duty to inform his patient, the patient may recover damages if he can prove that, had he been given the information, he would not have consented to the treatment, and that he has suffered harm as a consequence, in that a risk that he was not warned of materialized.

As we have seen already, the law as stated above is far from satisfactory. There is no doubt that in the next few years further cases will come before the courts which will serve to clarify the law. In the interim, however, it is difficult for the doctor to know with any degree of certainty what his legal obligation may be, and his legal adviser will be no better off in advising him.

The principal criticism of the present state of the law in the United Kingdom is that it fails to give proper recognition to the ethical principle of respect for autonomy, which in this context translates as the right of any competent patient to all information material to the decision of whether to consent to a particular treatment. It sets a standard for disclosure which reflects the views of the doctor as to what the patient ought to know, rather than what the patient may actually wish to know. It thereby favours paternalism, albeit subject to an ill-defined power of review, over autonomy, at a time when

---

[3] [1985] 1 All ER 643.

[4] Note that the strictures against *Sidaway* here are to be read against what I predict will become of the law.   [5] Lord Bridge, in *Sidaway*, p. 663.

paternalism is increasingly seen as morally unacceptable, and when the law in other contexts is increasingly recognizing and enforcing the civil rights of citizens. If consent is seen as a key factor in protecting the civil rights and liberties of patients, the case of *Sidaway* will be regretted as unjustifiably restrictive.

By contrast, the courts in Canada[6] and in a large number of jurisdictions in the United States[7] have developed the law somewhat differently, so as to give greater recognition to the principle of respect for autonomy as reflected in the law on consent. The courts have developed the rule that the doctor must—that is, has a duty to—give a patient that information which a reasonable patient in the particular patient's position would wish to know. Although not fully recognizing the principle of respect for autonomy, this is, in my view, an acceptable compromise.

It must be remembered, however, that the law in the United Kingdom is not static; and there is no doubt that the *Sidaway* case represents a small, but significant, step along the path to recognition of the patient's right to information. Such a view is justified in the light of the words of Lord Bridge already referred to, which were echoed in three of the other four speeches in the House of Lords.

LAW RELATING TO RCTs—AN INTRODUCTION

It is crucial to notice that the *Sidaway* case is concerned with *treatment*, and says nothing about the legal rules governing the conduct of RCTs. There is no law in the United Kingdom which specifically regulates the conduct of trials, whether therapeutic or non-therapeutic. For that reason, it would be wrong to conclude that the legal regime established in the context of treatment is also applicable to RCTs.

Any RCT concerned with testing a particular therapy or with comparing therapies necessarily involves the doctor in using the patient for the purposes of gaining information. In so far as this may affect specific decisions as to the treatment the patient may receive, it is my view that the law requires that, to the extent that this treatment differs in any way from that which the patient would receive if a trial were not being conducted, he is entitled to such information as will enable him to decide whether he wishes to take part in the trial or not. I submit, therefore, that the law set out in *Sidaway* does not apply to the conduct of trials in general, nor to RCTs in particular.[8]

---

[6] See e.g. *Reibl* v. *Hughes* (1980) 114 DLR 3*d* 1.

[7] See e.g. *Canterbury* v. *Spence* 464 F. 2*d* 772 (1972).

[8] Support for this view can be found in *Gold* v. *Haringey HA* (unreported) *The Times*, 17 June 1986, at first instance. The distinction between the duty to inform in non-therapeutic and therapeutic circumstances was, however, rejected by the Court of Appeal, [1987] 2 All ER 888,

The following considerations, among others, seem to justify the position I take. The patient is under no obligation to volunteer for a trial. To the extent that his treatment may be different from, or more or less than, that which he would otherwise receive, his consent would seem to be essential. And for it to be effective and real consent, it must be that the restrictive approach to informed consent adopted in *Sidaway* does not apply. This is because the question is not whether the patient is to receive treatment at all, the issue with which the *Sidaway* case was concerned and as regards which the restrictive approach was developed, but whether the patient is to receive treatment under special circumstances in which he is asked to submit to that which other patients in his position would not be asked to submit, and which carries no obvious benefit to him and, indeed, may have disadvantages.

Furthermore, it may follow that the North American legal doctrine of the 'therapeutic privilege', which also found favour with Lord Scarman in *Sidaway*, and which extends to doctors the discretion not fully to inform patients if the information would so alarm the patient as to cause him unwisely to refuse a particular treatment, even when ordinarily the doctor is obliged to give that information which a reasonable patient would wish to have, should not apply to the conduct of trials. The reasons are similar to those already given. There may be some justification for making inroads into the principle of respect for autonomy when treatment is in question. There seems no justification for it when the patient is being asked to volunteer for, and may be exposed to, that which is not directly in his interests. Indeed, if this were not so, there would be no reason why patients should not simply be

and see further, p. 210. *infra.* Compare the view of Lord Scarman, speaking extra-judicially: 'Even before *Sidaway* I was troubled — and I remain now very puzzled — as to the ethical and legal implications of the so-called randomized clinical trial, where, *ex hypothesi*, the doctor does not know, and is "using", to put it baldly, his patient for the purposes of very worthwhile experimentation. . . . As the law stands at the moment, I would have thought that any doctor who allows his patient to go into a randomized clinical trial without telling him runs a very real risk if things go wrong and the patient suffers injury or damage. . . . One can see the value of this form of experimentation . . . but I am bound to say that I think there is danger for the doctor in going ahead with subjecting, if that is the correct word, his patient to a randomized clinical trial without warning him' ('Consent, Communication and Responsibility', 79 *Journal of the Royal Society of Medicine* 697–8 (Dec. 1986)).

A leading Canadian case, decided in 1965, is even more categorical. In *Halushka* v. *University of Saskatchewan* (1965) 52 WWR 608 (Sask. CA), Hall J. A. stated that 'There can be no exceptions to the ordinary requirements of disclosure in the case of research as there may well be in ordinary medical practice. The researcher does not have to balance the probable lack of treatment against the risk involved in the treatment itself. The example of risks being properly hidden from a patient when it is important that he should not worry can have no application in the field of research. The subject of medical experimentation is entitled to a full and frank disclosure of all the facts, probabilities and opinions which a reasonable man might be expected to consider before giving his consent.' See further, E. Picard, *Legal Liability of Doctors and Hospitals in Canada*, 2nd edn. (Carswell, 1984), pp. 118–20.

conscripted into trials, and international declarations such as the Declaration of Helsinki[9] would then be unnecessary.

WHAT INFORMATION SHOULD BE GIVEN FROM THE STANDPOINT OF ETHICS?

If the legal analysis offered above is accepted, it follows that the patient has a right to more information about his proposed treatment than is contemplated in the *Sidaway* case, and that the doctor *pari passu* has a duty to supply it. The question then is one of stating in more precise terms the extent of the doctor's duty, once its nature, to preserve and protect the patient's autonomy, is understood. The most appropriate way to do this, in my view, is to set out first the doctor's ethical obligations, since in this area, the law ought to follow and to be led by ethics.

Let me, therefore, outline what I take to be the relevant ethical rules, as this will also involve, in large part, a description of the law, at least, as it ought to be.

In principle, it would seem that there is no valid moral objection to RCTs provided the patients involved in them are fully informed of what participation implies for them. Then it would seem to be merely a question of defining what 'fully informed' means, and the ethical problems would be solved. But it is not as simple as that. Some argue that, quite apart from any questions of information, RCTs may be unethical as a mode of medical research in all circumstances. It is important, therefore, to take account of these arguments before going any further.

Are RCTs Unethical?

The first objection is scientific, or at least technical, and, therefore, I will merely mention it here, without considering it in any depth. It can be found in the writings of, for example, Burkhardt and Kienle.[10] It is that RCTs are inevitably flawed in that the sample on which any study is based is inevitably unrepresentative of the general population with a particular condition and does not serve, therefore, as a sound basis from which to draw conclusions of a general nature. 'Any group of patients comprises a highly selected *non-random group*,'[11] because random selection of trial subjects is not ordinarily possible. Conclusions cannot, therefore, 'be generalised to apply to particular

---

[9] See T. L. Beauchamp and J. F. Childress, *Principles of Biomedical Ethics*, 2nd edn., (Oxford University Press, 1983), p. 339.

[10] R. Burkhardt and G. Kienle, 'Basic Problems in Controlled Trials', 9 *Journal of Medical Ethics* 80 (1983); and see this volume generally; also Beauchamp and Childress, *supra* n. 9.

[11] *Supra* n. 1.

patients outside the trial group',[12] save by the process of induction which is anathema to current scientific thought and which RCTs are designed to render unnecessary. If this point is valid, it deals a death-blow to RCTs, since, if they are not scientifically valid, they are necessarily unethical.

The second objection is that when a doctor conducts RCTs, his duty to care for his patient, which is his primary and most important duty, is inevitably compromised by his concurrent duty to carry out the RCT with all due scientific rigour. There must be occasions, the argument goes, when the doctor refrains from doing what he recognizes to be in his patient's best interests, because to do so would, in some way, impinge on the scientific validity of the RCT. The reply to this objection is that no ethical problems exist if the patient is asked whether he wishes to take part in the RCT, is informed what RCTs are, and specifically that his treatment will be randomized, and agrees to participate. This reply is not a complete answer to the objection raised, however, in that the issue is far more complicated than such a reply would suggest.

For a third objection then arises. It has to do with the proposition that the doctor's primary duty is to his patient. A doctor may persuade himself that he is not in breach of this duty when he describes the difference between two proposed forms of treatment or between treatment and a placebo as insignificant, such that the patient is in no way worse off by agreeing to take part in a trial in which neither he nor even, perhaps, his doctor will know which treatment he will receive. The difficulty lies, however, in the patient's approach to probabilities as compared with the doctor's. What a doctor may represent as an insignificant difference between treatments may be of great significance to the patient.

The key lies in the notion of significance. The doctor engaged in research may assert that significance is an objective and neutral term of art in statistics. Such a view should not pass without comment. A significance level is that level at which experimental evidence will be accepted as validating a scientific hypothesis, so as to justify acting on the evidence. Thus, it is an arbitrary point, chosen to satisfy scientific convention, but not necessarily relevant to the balance of evidence on which an individual, here a patient, would be prepared to act. A patient who is dying, for example, may be prepared to grasp at straws and take a 1 in 10,000 chance if the alternative is death. Such a chance may, however, be insignificant on the particular statistical approach adopted, and, thus, not a valid reason for action in the eyes of the researcher. Thus, if the patient is to be properly informed, account must be taken of what I will call 'the problem of probabilities'.

The fourth objection is similar. It again brings into question the compromise in duties into which the doctor may be forced by taking part in RCTs.

---

[12] Ibid.

A doctor may be involved in a trial which is designed to compare two treatments, both of which have their supporters. The doctor may have a preference for one form of treatment, although he has no evidence of a scientific nature to justify his preference. It may be based on experience, hunch, or some other reason; but whatever the reason, he has a preference. Now, if it is accepted that the therapeutic relationship between doctor and patient is most successful when the doctor has faith in the treatment he is giving his patient, and this faith is reflected also in the trust which the patient has in the doctor, it will be clear that by adopting a form of treatment in which he has less confidence, the doctor may be aiding the pursuit of knowledge, but doing so by opting for a less than optimum relationship with his patient. The only ethical course open to the doctor in such a case would seem to be to tell the patient of his preference, and then leave it to the patient to decide what to do. Even this, however, is not free from ethical problems, as I will show later.

If the doctor genuinely has no preference, then the problem does not arise, although I would submit that this would be a comparatively rare occurrence. In such a case, it would seem safe to argue that, here at least, the doctor may be excused from the obligation which I have suggested applies in the context of trials, fully to inform his patient. He may also take advantage of the therapeutic privilege. Certainly, the law would probably support him in this. The reason is that in such a situation, there is, in effect, no question of a conflict of obligations. The doctor is merely engaged in treating his patient, and the existence of the trial has no bearing on the decisions he makes, subject to any other objection raised. Except in this situation, however, the ethical problem remains; and it should not be ignored or underestimated. I shall call it 'the problem of doctors' preferences'.

A fifth objection may now be noted. As a trial progresses, a trend in the evidence may appear, suggesting that it would he harmful to patients to continue with a particular form of treatment which is the object of the research. Such a trend may appear, of course, before any statistically valid conclusions can be drawn from the research which would demonstrate whether the trend was real or not. This is particularly possible if sequential analysis is part of the design of the trial.

The problem is obvious. Is it ethically justifiable to continue a form of treatment in the face of such a trend; and equally, is it ethical to terminate a trial for this reason, when there is no valid scientific evidence to justify termination and, if the trial is ended, it will prevent the acquisition of the requisite information? In my view, the answer must be that the trial must cease, despite the unfortunate consequence this may have for medical science. To argue otherwise and insist that the trial go on is hard to defend in any ethical system which takes seriously the principle of respect for autonomy. It would put the interests of others, at present unknown, and the interests of science and scientists above the interests of the patient whom the doctor has undertaken to treat. There is, after all, no obligation on patients to allow themselves to be guinea pigs; and usually it is not part of a doctor's duty to treat patients as such. Indeed, the Physician's Oath, as set out in the Declaration of Geneva, states that 'the health of my patient will be my first consideration.'

It can be argued that a doctor need not end a trial when faced with a trend of the sort I have suggested, if the patient has agreed beforehand that trends shall be ignored. But this, in turn, raises the question of whether a patient may properly absolve his doctor from doing what the doctor thinks best for his patient. I shall return to this later; but let me say here that it *may* be morally permissible for the patient to do so. An example might be where a patient asks a doctor to treat him as best he can, while refusing to submit to a particular test or examination. It is another question whether a patient would be prepared to agree to this. I would have thought it unlikely. And, of course, the fact that it is unlikely is not a good reason for going ahead without consent, on the ground that otherwise it will be impossible to do the research. This is to prefer the interests of others to those of the patient, which I suggested earlier was morally impermissible.

This objection raises, therefore, very serious ethical problems *vis-à-vis* RCTs, and I shall call it 'the problem of trends'. One way out of the difficulty is the suggestion that there be an independent review committee which could examine the evidence as it emerges and advise doctors accordingly. I am not persuaded that this offers any real assistance. It shifts the responsibility of decision making, but does not resolve the dilemma which the doctor is faced with, since the doctor is still bound by his duty to put his patient first.

The sixth and final ethical objection which can be made to RCTs is that no account may be taken of a particular patient's preferences as a consequence of his being involved in a trial. For example, if the patient is elderly, he may well prefer a form of treatment in which the short-term risks are low while the long-term risks are higher, and yet be placed in a group receiving treatment which has the opposite risks, the purpose of the trial being to determine the precise nature and extent of these risks. And there may be numerous other instances in which the patient may have what to him are important preferences which may be ignored for the benefit of the trial. This objection is easily remedied, obviously, by informing the patient of this possibility before seeking his consent. It has to be said, however, that it is unlikely that many patients, thus informed, would be prepared to consent. This I shall call 'the problem of patients' preferences'.

My conclusion, therefore, is that, in the face of these objections, it must be recognized that the pursuit of scientific rigour represented by RCTs inevitably involves the doctor in conduct the ethical propriety of which is open to serious challenge. This is because the doctor seems unavoidably involved in doing that which, if he had only his patient's interests at heart, he would not do.

The Ethical RCT?

Let us assume that satisfactory answers can be given to all the objections raised above. We can then turn to the next question, that of what information a doctor must give his patient so as to comply with his ethical duty to him? I would suggest that he must tell the patient the following: that he is to be involved in an RCT; the material risks of the various forms of treatment which may be adopted, the definition of materiality being that which the particular patient would wish to know, given the doctor's knowledge of the particular patient's circumstances; the alternatives open to him, including all other available forms of treatment and the fact that he is under no obligation to take part in the RCT; that, if he agrees to take part in the RCT, he may withdraw at any time and will then receive the best available care; and that the trial is randomized, and what randomization means. With regard to the latter, he must be told that the doctor may do that which runs counter to his (the doctor's) preferences; that he may ignore trends indicating that a particular form of treatment is to be preferred; that the treatment may run counter to his (the patient's) preferences, in that he may be exposed to procedures which he does not like and which would not be necessary if other treatment were used, or that he may have to stay in hospital when otherwise he would be discharged, or that he may be exposed to risks which, from his personal point of view, he would prefer not to run and which he would not incur if other treatment were used; that he may, in fact, receive only a placebo; and that, in short, he may be treated as a member of a set, rather than an individual patient.

If each of these points is made clear to the patient, and the patient consents, then it can be said that he is properly informed and is, therefore, a true volunteer. Does this mean that no further ethical objection can be made? It has to be said that there is still one ethical hurdle to be overcome.

A patient who is asked to consent to treatment which may, or will, involve something which he would prefer was not done, or involves waiving the doctor's obligation to put his interests first, may as a consequence be being subjected to improper pressure merely by being asked. It may well be ethically wrong to ask a patient to make such a decision when he is ill, particularly when it is remembered that a patient is naturally reluctant to displease his doctor, to whom he looks for help, and may regard saying no to the doctor as displeasing him. In short, any consent given under such circumstances may be invalid, on the ground that it is not truly voluntary.

The issue of voluntariness, therefore, takes on very great significance. It may well be that the problem of obtaining truly voluntary consent does not represent an absolute bar to conducting RCTs. But, even if it does not, it constitutes a most important factual difficulty which should not be regarded lightly and will not easily be overcome.

A final comment concerning ethics may be in order. The whole of my analysis presumes that the principle of respect for each person's autonomy is, in this context, the most important ethical principle. It also presumes that ethical problems, such as the one under discussion, are properly analysed in terms of the rights of citizens, whether patients or otherwise. There are, of course, others who will come to different conclusions, because they begin from different premises. In particular, those who adopt a utilitarian approach may argue that it may be proper in some circumstances to favour the interests of society at large over those of any particular individual. This may allow them to argue more persuasively in favour of RCTs. I venture to think, however, that even a utilitarian would ultimately arrive at conclusions quite similar to mine, if only because society has a considerable stake in ensuring that individual rights are respected, such that RCTs which failed to do so would, in the long run, be contrary to the interests of the majority, and so ought not to be defended.

THE LAW ON INFORMED CONSENT AND RCTS

If my analysis of the ethics of RCTs is accepted, and if, furthermore, it is presumed that the law ought to reflect and enforce that which is regarded as ethical, it would follow that the law in the United Kingdom on the conduct of RCTs would take the form suggested above. That is to say, the law would require the doctor to follow the ethical rules I have set out, and that they would be, therefore, the rules of law.

I doubt, however, that the law would be quite so stringent. There is, of course, no law directly in point, so everything I say is speculation. None the less, there is enough evidence of how the courts in the United Kingdom have dealt with medical issues to suggest how they would respond if faced with the need to set down rules to govern RCTs. I say the courts, incidentally, because there is no legislation in this area, nor any likelihood of it.

In my view, a court would seek to establish legal rules which did not do violence to the civil liberties and rights of citizens, and yet did not put wholly insurmountable barriers in the way of a form of medical research regarded as important by the medical community. Thus, it is unlikely that a court would decide that RCTs were inevitably, by their very nature and the premises underlying them, unlawful. On the other hand, a court would be anxious to ensure that any patient in a trial had consented to take part, and that the consent was given freely. The tendency of the courts, as seen in the *Sidaway* case, is to place considerable trust in doctors, such that they would normally be satisfied by the evidence of doctors that consent was properly obtained.

It is an open question whether a court would insist that all the information which I have suggested is ethically called for must be given, as a matter of law, to the patient before his consent could be regarded as legally valid. It is most likely that a court would begin with the presumption that this information must be given, out of a concern for civil rights, but that it might be persuaded to relax a particular requirement if compelling evidence could be produced that it would thwart the whole enterprise of RCTs. I use the word 'compelling' because I do not think a court would be moved by arguments which merely complained of a particular requirement on the ground that it was a nuisance or made life harder for those involved in the research. The courts' commitment to civil rights is too strong for them to be easily persuaded; and they are also not unmindful of adverse public reaction, should they be thought to be offering too little protection to patients, at a time of increasing challenge to any form of medical paternalism.

In particular, it is doubtful that the following two arguments for not adhering to the rules set out would be accepted by the courts. The first is that a patient was not informed either of the fact that he was involved in a trial or of the details of the trial because it was thought appropriate to invoke the therapeutic privilege. For the reasons advanced earlier, when the ethical validity of this argument was considered, I venture to doubt that this argument would be accepted in the context of a trial, even though it may be perfectly acceptable in the context of everyday treatment. The second is an extension of the first. It is sometimes argued that no consent was asked of a patient because, to have asked him, would have involved having to explain the nature of his illness, and, in the case, for example, of cancer, it was thought wrong to tell him this. There are at least three weaknesses in this approach, each of which would be enough to persuade a court to reject it.

The first is that a patient is ordinarily entitled to know what is the matter with him. Indeed, in the *Sidaway* case, the House of Lords stated that a doctor is in breach of his legal duty if he does not reply honestly when questioned by a patient. Second, it is one thing not to tell a patient the nature of his illness; it is another to use that as a reason for further deceiving him, by involving him in a trial without his knowledge. Third, the presumptions involved in the argument are the wrong way round. If it is thought undesirable to inform a patient of the nature of his illness, it cannot be right to assume that the trial should proceed in any event, with the patient kept in ignorance of this fact also. Rather, the correct view must be that, if a doctor is reluctant to inform a patient of his illness, this is a very good reason for not involving him in a trial. To presume otherwise is to put the importance of the trial above the rights of the patient, something a court would be quick to reject.

This, then, is a brief summary of what I take to be the law on informed consent and RCTs. It is, I repeat, entirely speculative, though good arguments can be found to support it. It would follow that any doctor who chose to ignore such advice as to what the law may be could run the risk of being sued either in negligence or in battery.

It may be that what I say does not sit too comfortably with those engaged in RCTs. This is inevitable whenever attempts are made to balance interests which, to some extent, are inevitably in conflict. That it may make the conduct of RCTs difficult is admitted; but this is the price to be paid for respecting the individual's rights. It will not, I submit, make RCTs impossible; and if, in the process, it means that all concerned are reminded that their first duty is always to their patient, only good can come of it.

Pessimists may complain that if they are required to observe the kind of rules I have suggested, they will never get anyone to volunteer for RCTs. I have two responses to this. First, if a patient would not consent if he were fully informed, this is no reason to involve him without his consent; indeed, it is a reason why he should not be involved. Second, many patients are only too pleased to do something which might help others, provided it is not too inconvenient for them. Thus, if they are asked and properly informed, there is no reason why legitimate RCTs should not continue.

11

Further Thoughts on Liability for Non-observance of the Provisions of the Human Tissue Act 1961*

The law regulating the removal of tissue from human corpses for the purposes, *inter alia*, of transplantation is found in the Human Tissue Act 1961. This statute has attracted, particularly since the mid-1960s, regular critical comment and demands for its reform. The principal focus of attack has been on the provisions of section 1(2), wherein it is provided that:

The person lawfully in possession of the body of a deceased person may authorise the removal of any part from the body for use for the said purposes [therapeutic purposes or for purposes of medical education or research, s. 1(1)] if, having made such reasonable enquiry as may be practicable, he has no reason to believe (a) that the deceased had expressed an objection to his body being so dealt with after his death, and had not withdrawn it; or (b) that the surviving spouse or any surviving relative of the deceased objects to the body being so dealt with.

The objections are many, but fall into two categories. First, from the legal point of view, the subsection is vague; for instance, it is not clear who is in lawful possession, or what 'reasonable enquiry' is, or how far 'any surviving relative' extends. Second, from a social-political viewpoint, the subsection embodies a policy, that of 'contracting-in', which prejudices the living, but sick, in favour of the dead. Parliament has been made aware of these criticisms, but has not seen fit to act. The recommendations of the Maclennan Committee[1] have gathered dust ever since the report appeared in 1969.

Little attention in the context of this general debate has been given to a fundamental question: namely, what consequences flow from a failure to observe the provisions of section 1(2)? In view of the growth of interest in, and the importance of, transplantation surgery, this is wellnigh extraordinary. It has been assumed that failure on the part of doctors or hospital authorities to observe the provisions of this subsection of the Human Tissue Act would bring criminal and/or civil liability. In a recent paper, Skegg[2] explored this

---

* This paper was first published in 16 *Medicine, Science and the Law*, 49 (1976).

[1] *Report of the Advisory Group on Transplanting Organs* (HMSO, 1969).

[2] P. Skegg, 'Liability for the unauthorized removal of cadaveric transplant material', 14 *Medicine, Science and the Law* 53 (1974).

assumption, and, after careful analysis, found himself forced to the conclusion that, apart from the provisions dealing with coroners' inquests and post-mortems, there was no recognized tort which would create liability for unauthorized removal of tissue; nor did there appear to be anything but the most tenuous possibility of criminal liability. This is both a startling and a disturbing conclusion, and one which, if valid, should provide the stimulus to provoke Parliament into prompt consideration of the Act in all its aspects. If the provisions laboriously set out in section 1(2) purporting to regulate the conditions under which tissue could be removed from a corpse and put to some use were intended to have any effect, then Parliament should be made to realize that there is no clear way in which this effect can be achieved, and that it remains a matter for conjecture, in fact, whether the provisions need be followed, or whether they can be ignored with impunity.

Until there is some change, however, section 1(2) remains the law. The aim of this paper is to explore further the possibilities of liability for failure to comply with its provisions. Such an exercise is of value, notwithstanding the recent contribution of Skegg, for two reasons. First, it serves to draw attention once again to the problems inherent in the Human Tissue Act. Second, while I am in large measure in agreement with Skegg, I would take issue with him on certain points, and feel that there are other possibilities to explore which he did not deal with.

LIABILITY IN TORT

While reaching the conclusion that there is no established tort which is obviously applicable to conduct amounting to non-compliance with the Human Tissue Act, Skegg does suggest one possible head of liability which could be distilled from general principles. I submit, however, that the theory for liability which Skegg advances is flawed, and is unlikely to persuade the courts, whereas there are at least two other heads of tort liability which could produce a greater chance of success for the potential litigant. Before considering these, Skegg's proposition that an action for damages could lie in tort for the unauthorized removal of tissue from a corpse for transplant purposes at the suit of the person lawfully entitled to possession of the body will be examined. There is no precedent to serve as a guideline, and the argument strains existing principles. The thesis is that, because at law there is always a person who is under a duty to bury a corpse, so there is vested in that person the right to possession of the corpse. Unauthorized removal of transplant material, it is argued, constitutes interference with that right, and such interference is actionable as a tortious wrong. But, it is submitted, the removal of tissue from a corpse immediately after death does not interfere with the right to possession of the corpse for burial. The only ground on which it could be argued that such a right is interfered with is that the right is to bury the complete corpse. Surely, the right to possession derives its existence solely from the prior notion of there being a duty to bury. And this duty cannot be said to extend to the duty to bury a corpse with no parts missing, since, if it did, it would cast on those who bear it the ridiculous burden in major disasters or traffic accidents, for example, of being obliged to gather up each and every part of the corpse for burial. If the duty to bury does not go this far, then neither does the right to possession, surely. Thus, I submit, a tort action argued along these lines will fail before the courts. In support of his argument, Skegg cites the Canadian case of *Edmond* v. *Armstrong Funeral Home Ltd*,[3] where recovery was allowed against a doctor who had conducted an unauthorized post-mortem examination. But the facts of this case show an interference with the right to possession for the purpose of burial by virtue of the detention by the doctor for the unauthorized post-mortem, and are clearly distinguishable, therefore, from the case of a doctor removing tissue for transplant immediately after death.

Let us move to the first of the two actions which may have more hope of success. The first is mentioned, but discounted, by Skegg, whereas it seems to me to merit closer attention. The action would arise out of the tort of negligently causing nervous shock by the removal of tissue without authority. The action would sound in negligence, since it would be very unlikely that recourse could be had to the tort of intentionally inflicting nervous shock as developed in the case of *Janvier* v. *Sweeney*.[4] The doctor removing tissue without consent would not ordinarily have intended thereby to inflict nervous shock. Several courts in the United States have allowed such an action,[5] but it would be unlikely to succeed in this country. Nevertheless, if in removing tissue from a corpse, a doctor could have foreseen that the person whose consent he should have obtained would be affected by his act to the extent of suffering nervous shock, then he may well be liable to that person. The liability arises, in other words, where the doctor goes ahead with the removal of tissue, careless as to the effect his conduct may produce in a person or group of persons whom he could reasonably foresee would be affected. It is not the removal which is careless, but rather the doctor's failure to advert to the likely consequences of doing so.

Three problems exist, but they are not insurmountable. First, the court must decide that the doctor owed a duty to the plaintiff. Given that this is fundamentally a policy decision, it is submitted that when a doctor knows that there are relatives or next of kin whom he or the hospital authorities could contact to determine whether they object to the removal of tissue and, *a fortiori*, when he knows that relatives or next of kin have been in

---

[3] [1931] 1 DLR 676.　　　　　　　　　　　　　　　　　　[4] [1919] 2 KB 316.
[5] See W. Prosser, *Law of Torts*, 4th edn. (West Publishing Co., 1971).

attendance on and shown concern for the deceased, these persons are well within the ambit of 'neighbours' to whom a duty would be owed. Probably the courts would hold otherwise if the person subsequently complaining was not known or could not easily have become known to the doctor or hospital authorities, following the principle in *Bourhill* v. *Young*.[6] Second, the damage suffered must not be too remote. As a matter of principle, nervous shock does not always serve as a basis on which to ground liability. Again, questions of policy are involved, and the law is by no means a model of clarity, since the question really is, should the plaintiff in the circumstances be entitled to recover? In the case of *Chadwick* v. *British Railways Board*,[7] it was held that someone coming upon the distressing consequences of the defendant's conduct and suffering nervous shock thereby was entitled to recover. In that case the consequences were the result of the defendant's negligence. It is submitted that liability would equally flow from the circumstance of a plaintiff coming upon the distressing consequences — that is, the removal of tissue from a loved one — of an intentional act of the defendant doctor committed in a context where he was careless as to these consequences. The third problem is that of nervous shock itself. The cases now show that no action may be maintained for mere grief or sorrow, but will succeed only if the plaintiff suffers some recognizable, psychiatric illness.[8] Since anxiety or depression, *inter alia*, are or can be recognizable psychiatric illnesses, it is submitted that the distinction between mere grief and depression or anxiety is now only perhaps a matter of degree, and crossing the dividing line between the two may not prove too difficult a task for the purposes of successfully maintaining an action.[9]

The second possible area of tort liability has hitherto been overlooked, namely the tort of breach of statutory duty. While it is conceded at the outset that the difficulties in the way of the prospective plaintiff are considerable, an examination of this action may prove profitable. The very first problem to be met — and it may prove fatal — is that there must be a duty imposed on someone by statute, breach of which gives rise to complaint. The duty contemplated here is the duty to observe section 1(2), so that tissue is removed and used only after authority has been given in the prescribed form. Does

---

[6] [1943] AC 92.　　　　　　　　　　　　　　　　　　[7] [1967] 1 WLR 912.

[8] Per Denning, MR, *Hinz* v. *Berry* [1970] 1 All ER 1074, 1075.

[9] [The law relating to recovery in negligence for nervous shock has developed since 1976. The leading case is now the decision of the House of Lords in *McLoughlin* v. *O'Brian* [1982] 2 WLR 982. It extends the ambit of the cause of action, and somewhat strengthens the argument here. Notice that in *Chadwick* (*supra* n. 7), the plaintiff's action was derivative, based on the prior breach of duty by the defendant. There is no need, however, to point to such a breach; 'There can be no doubt . . . that the test of *liability for shock* is foreseeability of *injury by shock*', per Denning LJ in *King* v. *Phillips* [1953] 1 QB 429, 441. See generally, Winfield and Jolowicz, *Tort*, 12th edn. (Sweet and Maxwell, 1984), pp. 90–4. On cases in the United States allowing recovery for shock for the mishandling of corpses, see Prosser, *supra* n. 5, 329–30.]

the Human Tissue Act in fact create such a duty? The author would submit that it does. A duty is imposed upon the person lawfully in possession of a body to make 'such reasonable enquiry as may be practicable' so as to satisfy himself that neither the deceased before death nor the surviving spouse nor any surviving relative objected to the removal and use of tissue. Given a statutory duty imposed on the person lawfully in possession of the body of the deceased, which person in the case of a person dying in hospital is the hospital authority (see section 1(7)), the next question is whether Parliament intended breach of the duty to give rise to a civil action. It is always something of a mysterious exercise to ascertain what Parliament really intended when the courts are unwilling to encourage reference to anything other than the actual words of a statute.[10] Certain presumptions, however, seem to be invoked by the courts, one of which is that where no sanction is provided for breach of a duty, as in the Human Tissue Act, there is a presumption that a person injured by its breach has a right of action.[11] If the above difficulties are overcome, there are still other constituent elements of the tort which must be established. First, only the person to whom the duty is owed may bring an action. If the reasoning above is accepted, then it follows that the only people who may bring an action are those who would have objected to the removal and use of tissue if consulted, namely, the surviving spouse or any surviving relative who could have been contacted on reasonably practicable enquiry. Next, there must obviously be a breach of the duty. Since it is only to make such reasonable enquiry as is practicable, it is not an absolute duty, and the person on whom it falls may avoid liability by showing this standard was met. The onus of proving impracticability, however, would rest on the defendant.[12]

Third, harm of the kind which the statute was intended to prevent must be suffered. This element presents difficulties. The harm complained of would, in the circumstances of the Human Tissue Act be nervous shock of a kind recognized by the law. Was section 1(2) designed to prevent this type of harm? The author would submit that it was. There cannot have been any reason for laying down the obligation of making reasonable enquiry unless it was recognized that there were spouses and relatives who might object to the removal of tissue, and might suffer shock and distress if it were done without their consent. The final element is that breach of the duty must have caused the injury, and on this ground, provided all others are satisfied, no problems are encountered.

This is the basis of the action, and a court could well hold that an action lay at the suit of a surviving spouse or relative who could reasonably have been contacted before tissue was removed, but was not and consequently

---

[10] Winfield and Jolowicz, *Tort*, 9th edn. (Sweet and Maxwell, 1971), p. 133.
[11] Ibid. 130.   [12] Ibid. 133.

suffered shock. Furthermore, if it is accepted that the various principles for establishing liability are guidelines only, and that really the court is being invited to make a policy decision, it is submitted that this is just the sort of area in which, given the possible absence of other means of redress, the court may hold that an action lay.

CRIMINAL LIABILITY

I turn now to the criminal law position: namely, what criminal liability is incurred by failure to observe section 1(2)? Again, Skegg considers this with his customary thoroughness. He has much to say which is instructive on criminal liability in circumstances where the removal of transplant material could interfere with coroners' or police enquiries. I will confine myself to failure to comply with section 1(2). On this, Skegg writes that 'it is not certain that a doctor would commit any criminal offence in proceeding without complying with the Human Tissue Act.' Skegg considers the old common-law offence of disobeying a statute, as in *R. v. Hall*,[13] but seems to rule it out in the context of the Human Tissue Act. The case of *R. v. Lennox-Wright*[14] casts doubt on this and prompts a closer consideration of this particular area of criminal law, the more so because I otherwise agree with Skegg that there is no criminal offence which covers failure to comply with section 1(2). Not even the hydra-like offence of conspiracy—for example, to corrupt public morals or outrage public decency—would apply.[15] In *Lennox-Wright*, the defendant, who had failed medical examinations abroad, gained admission to the ophthalmic department of an English hospital by false representations and forged documents. He removed eyes from a cadaver for further use in another hospital. He was charged, *inter alia*, with 'doing an act in disobedience of a statute by removing parts of a dead body contrary to s. 1(4) of the Human Tissue Act 1961'. Section 1(4) provides that 'No such removal shall be effected save by a fully registered medical practitioner, who must have satisfied himself by personal examination of the body that life was extinct.'

It was argued on a motion to quash the indictment that the Act was regulatory only and created no offence, and that it provided for no punishment for contravening section 1(4). The court held, first, that it was well-settled law that if a statute prohibits a matter of public grievance to the liberties and securities of the subject or commands a matter of public convenience—(for example, repair of the highways), all acts or omissions against the prohibition or command of the statute are misdemeanours at common law punishable on indictment unless such method manifestly appears

---

[13] [1891] 1 QB 747, and see 2 *Hawk. PC* c.25 s. 4.   [14] [1973] Crim. LR 529.
[15] *Law Commission Working Paper* No. 57 (HMSO, 1974).

to be excluded by statute; and, second, that punishment was at large since it was a common-law offence, and hence common-law principles of punishment applied.

This decision may properly be criticized.[16] It appears to go against what has become the prevailing attitude of the courts since the time of *Hawkins* and *R. v. Hall*:[17] namely, that when Parliament intends to create a criminal offence, it should do so expressly and lay down a maximum punishment. If Parliament does not so do, there is now a strong presumption that there was no intention to punish breaches of the statute through the criminal law. Further force is added to this criticism if it is recalled that the effect of the case is that violation of the statute can bring trial on indictment with no limitation on punishment. There are numerous other statutes which impose duties, but provide no sanctions for failure to exercise the duties (see, for example, section 3(1) of the Television Act 1964). It would come as a shock to many to learn that, if a court took the view that such failure was a matter of public grievance to the securities of the subject, open-ended criminal sanctions could be imposed. Admittedly, the Human Tissue Act seeks to establish the boundaries within which removal of tissue will be lawful; but even if non-observance of the Act makes any removal unlawful, this does not mean that the criminal law is necessarily invoked. Skegg mentions this decision briefly, as it was not reported at the time he wrote. He argues that it must be wrong, because section 1(8) of the Human Tissue Act provides that: 'Nothing in this Section shall be construed as rendering unlawful any dealing with, or with any part of, the body of a deceased which is lawful apart from the Act.'

Having demonstrated that it was no offence at common law or under the Anatomy Act 1832 to remove tissue from a body, Skegg concludes that 'a common law offence could not be based *on the Act alone*' (my emphasis). I accept Skegg's position that at common law there is no offence of removing tissue. The only common-law offences having to do with dead bodies seem to have been limited to acts of interference subsequent to burial, and the Anatomy Act merely provided for the regulation of schools of anatomy. The Corneal Grafting Act 1952, the only other relevant statute, was repealed by the Human Tissue Act, section 4(2). Thus, it is not unlawful apart from the Human Tissue Act to remove tissue. And as far as section 1(2) is concerned, subsection 3 merely says that removal shall be 'lawful' if the removal and use is in accordance with an authorization given pursuant to the section. But subsection 3 is specifically made subject to subsection 4. Arguably, this means that failure to observe subsection 4 thereby makes removal *unlawful* according to the Human Tissue Act itself. Thus, with specific reference to section 1(4), the court in *Lennox-Wright* may be correct, subject to the

---

[16] *Supra* n. 14.   [17] *Supra* n. 13.

criticisms already made; and section 1(8) may not apply, despite Skegg's views to the contrary.[18]

But does this necessarily mean that *Lennox-Wright* applies where section 1(4) is complied with, but section 1(2) is flouted? This is the major concern here. Section 1(3) provides that 'removal and use . . . in accordance with an authority given in pursuance of the section shall be lawful.' The situation contemplated is one in which a doctor removes a kidney, for example, without making such reasonable enquiry to determine whether there was any objection to the removal, as is required by section 1(2) where it is practicable to do so. Is the doctor guilty of the common-law offence of disobeying the statute? Two lines of argument can be pursued. First, the words of the common-law offence as repeated in *Lennox-Wright* refer to a statute which commands or prohibits. The Human Tissue Act does neither in subsections 1, 2 or 3. It merely provides that the person in authority *may authorize*. Second, although 1(3) speaks of lawful conduct, so as to imply that all other conduct is unlawful; if, as has already been seen, at common law no offence is committed, then the effect of section 1(8) must be that failure to observe section 1(3) is not unlawful. There are other arguments which meet both these points, however, and which on balance may be more persuasive. First, the words 'may authorize' are conditioned in section 1(1) by the word 'unless', and in section 1(2) by the words 'if he had no reason to believe'. Both these expressions could be said to be prohibitory, so that the requirements of the common-law offence would be satisfied. Second, if the requirements of the common-law offence are satisfied, then section 1(8) will not be relevant because the crime consists in violating a prohibition contained in a statute, and it is not strictly relevant that the conduct is lawful apart from the statute.[19] The crime is addressed specifically to acts contrary to the pro-hibitions of a statute, and this criterion would be met if section 1(2) were not complied with. On balance, therefore, it is submitted that *Lennox-Wright* applies also to breaches of section 1(2).

Throughout this paper, no mention has been made of possible disciplinary action which may be taken by the medical profession against a doctor who acts in defiance of section 1(2). Presumably some action may be taken if the circumstances warrant it, although on many occasions the doctor may well be insulated from responsibility if he can show that he acted only after being given assurances by hospital authorities that section 1(2) had been complied with. In such a case, the only possible liability would be legal liability, which would depend on the authorities discussed.

---

[18] The thrust of this complicated (over-complicated?) argument can be put another way. If 'apart from the Act' in s. 1(8) is read as referring to any dealings with a body, or parts thereof, which is not regulated as to its lawfulness by the Act, then the argument advanced is sustainable.

[19] Again, this argument is posited on the reasoning in n. 18 *supra*.

What has emerged, I hope, is how extraordinarily difficult it may be actually to guarantee that the fundamental provisions of the Human Tissue Act are observed in practice. Such a conclusion should not be allowed to pass unnoticed any longer by those charged with making and changing the law.

ADDENDUM

Since I prepared this paper, there has appeared a report by a subcommittee of the British Transplantation Society,[20] which deals, *inter alia*, with section 1(2) of the Human Tissue Act. It is proposed that the existing section 1(2) be repealed, and a new subsection 2 be substituted, together with a further, entirely new subsection dealing with the interpretation of section 1. The redrafting of subsection 2 and the proposed new interpretation subsection are not without their difficulties, but the effect of the words used, I submit, is to create a legal regime of 'contracting-out' for the purposes of removal and use of, tissue for transplant purposes. The obligations placed on hospital authorities and doctors to make enquiry before removing organs are very much reduced. Despite the fact that the Report notes that some members of the Subcommittee favoured a more radical amendment of the Human Tissue Act than that being proposed, it could be said that the suggested changes are, in fact, radical in effect, although purporting to alter the existing legal position 'only in one respect'. The new section 1(2) would read:

Without prejudice to the foregoing subsection, the person lawfully in possession of the body of a deceased person may authorize the removal of any part from the body for use for the said purposes if, *having made such enquiry as is both reasonable and practical in the time available,* he has no reason to believe that the deceased had expressed an objection (which he was not known to have withdrawn) to his body being so dealt with after his death. *Provided that authorization shall not be given under this subsection if the person lawfully in possession of the body has reason to believe that the surviving spouse or any surviving relative of the deceased objects to the body being so dealt with.*

The 'time available' is defined in the proposed new subsection as follows:

The 'time available', for the purpose of an enquiry under subsection 2 of this section, extends only until the moment at which steps must be taken to remove the part of the body, if it is to be suitable for the therapeutic or other purpose in question.

---

[20] 'Report of the Sub-Committee of the British Transplantation Society', 1 *British Medical Journal* 251 (1975).

Two points are worth noting. First, it could be argued that the effect of these provisions is to make any real enquiry as to the deceased's wishes impossible. The argument is as follows. The Subcommittee accepts the medical fact that organs intended for transplant must be removed within a very short time after death if they are to be of any use. The Subcommittee also accepts the notion of brain-stem death: namely, that the patient on a mechanical ventilator who has permanently lost all brain-stem function, including the ability spontaneously to respire, is to be regarded as dead. A large proportion of donors of organs will have spent their last hours or days on a respirator. Until a determination of brain-stem death is made, it would be premature and inappropriate to discuss with a spouse or relative the possibility of removing organs for transplant. Thus, the hospital authorities or the doctor could always argue that the 'time available' *if the organ is to be suitable for transplant*, was a matter of minutes between the determination of death and the time when the organ must be removed if it is to be viable. Such a short space of time, they could contend, did not allow opportunity to discover whether the deceased had expressed an objection to his body being so dealt with after his death.

Second, the redrafted subsection 2 removes the obligation to enquire whether the surviving spouse or any surviving relative objects to the removal of organs from the body of the deceased. Instead, the burden is cast upon them to make their objection known. If, as would be the case in most instances, they had registered no objection prior to the death of the potential donor, and if what has been said above concerning the 'available time' is accepted, then their views as to the disposal of the body of the deceased can effectively be ignored. For, if the 'available time' can be interpreted in such a way that the hospital authorities and doctors can argue that they really had no time to enquire as to the deceased's wishes from those who would know—that is, the surviving spouse or any relative—*a fortiori*, such a spouse or relative would be given no opportunity for registering their objections. Moreover, even if the spouse or relative were consulted as to the wishes of the deceased, there is no obligation placed by the redrafted subsection upon those consulting them to inform them of their own right to object. Thus, if they were unaware of any objections that the deceased may have expressed, and if, as is likely, they were unaware of their own right to object, they could find that organs were removed from the deceased notwithstanding their own strong (but unstated) opposition to this.

It is not suggested that these two conclusions were intended by the Subcommittee. It is, however, submitted that they are conclusions which the draft law would allow. Admittedly, the draft Code of Practice suggested by the Subcommittee supposes that 'the question of organ removal will be discussed fully with available relatives so that their informed consent is obtained', but this Code is not part of the law. The effective result of these proposed changes in section 1(2), therefore, could be to make it practically impossible to ground any action, whether civil or criminal, on failure to observe its provisions. My view is that the Subcommittee's recommendations as regards section 1(2) would not meet with approval in Parliament. There is still a substantial body of public opinion, particularly among those who hold certain religious beliefs, that the law should be written so as to give proper opportunity for the objection of those opposed to the removal of organs for transplant to be sought out and respected.[21] This being so, it is all the more important to determine whether the existing law not only provides this opportunity, but also provides appropriate legal redress if it is denied.

POSTSCRIPT

Skegg subsequently replied to my paper.[22] I rather think, all told, that he has the better of the argument; although, since we were both dealing with matters of first impression, there is still room for doubt.[23] What is of interest, and why I republish my paper here, is that the issue of non-compliance with the provisions of the Human Tissue Act 1961 was and remains of considerable importance.

There are, principally, two matters on which Skegg takes serious issue. He argues first that I misread the Canadian case of *Edmond* v. *Armstrong Funeral Home Ltd.*[24] Be that as it may, it remains to be seen whether an English court would create a novel cause of action arising from the mutilation of a body and removal of parts of it at the suit of those with the right to possess the body so as to bury it. For my part, I am persuaded that Skegg's argument is to be preferred to my own; but that does not mean that a court would agree.

The second point is the difference of opinion over the relevance of *R.* v. *Lennox-Wright*.[25] On this, I regard the view I expressed as being sound as the law was then, but concede that it is an impossibly difficult point, arising out of a badly drafted statute.

As it happens, *Lennox-Wright* came to be considered *en passant* by the Divisional Court in *R.* v. *Horseferry Road Magistrates' Court*.[26] For our purposes here, it is enough to note that Lloyd LJ found that His Honour Judge Lawson in *Lennox-Wright* had indeed 'held that S1(4) created an

---

[21] See the Report of the MacLennan Committee, *supra* n. 1.

[22] P. Skegg, 'Liability for the Unauthorized Removal of Cadaveric Transplant Material: Some Further Comments', 17 *Medicine, Science and the Law* 123 (1977).

[23] There cannot be too much doubt that between us we produced some of the most boring titles of articles in medical law!

[24] *Supra* n. 3.   [25] *Supra* n. 14.   [26] [1986] 2 All ER 666.

offence'.[27] He went on, however, to hold that the doctrine of disobedience to a statute was never more than a rule of construction.

> In the case of a modern statute it is easier to infer that Parliament does not intend to create an offence unless it says so. There is no longer any presumption, if indeed there ever were, that a breach of duty imposed by statute is indictable. Nowadays the presumption, if any, is the other way; although I would prefer to say that it requires clear language, or a very clear inference, to create a crime.[28]

Thus, it would seem that any argument based on *Lennox-Wright* would now fail. Criminal liability for non-observance of the Human Tissue Act, therefore, would appear to be a non-starter, and the intriguing point which began the exchange between Skegg and myself remains to be made. Here is an Act purporting to regulate matters on which strong views exist, hence the various protections offered; yet no obvious way exists in law of enforcing observance of its provisions or sanctioning those who ignore them.

[27] Ibid. 674.   [28] Ibid.

12

The Donation and Transplantation of
Kidneys: Should the Law be Changed?*

INTRODUCTION

Each year about 2000 people in the United Kingdom between the ages of
5 and 55 fall victim to fatal kidney disease. Most are between 15 and 35.
The pain and anguish suffered by the victim, his family, and friends are
obviously incalculable. The cost is also immense in economic terms, including
not merely the cost of medical care until death, but also the loss of productive
output which the victims would otherwise have contributed. What, it may
be asked, is special about this? What sets it apart from other examples of
fatal accident and illness? The simple answer is that nowadays, to a great
extent, death is preventable. Many of the 2000 need not die.

There exist two established medical techniques for treating those with renal
failure. One is renal dialysis, which became an accepted form of treatment
in about 1965. It involves the use of what is popularly known as a kidney
machine, which does the job of the diseased, non-functioning kidneys. The
patient's blood is passed through the machine, and the impurities which would
otherwise, quite literally, poison him to death are removed. Ordinarily a
patient must be attached to such a machine two or three times a week for
periods of 8 or 10 hours each time. Thus dialysis often takes place during
the night while the patient sleeps. The patient need not necessarily attend
a hospital, as there is a growing effort to make home dialysis available to
more patients. Clearly, there are savings in terms of hospital staff and space
if home dialysis can be organized. Once receiving dialysis, the patient's
condition remains stable, and he may continue to lead a fairly full life.

The treatment is not, however, a bed of roses. It calls for considerable
self-discipline in terms of diet and personal behaviour; travel and movement
are obviously limited by the need to be close to the machine; and nausea,
discomfort, and depression increase as the effects of the last treatment
wane. Because of these factors, some patients are judged unsuitable for
psychological reasons—for example, if they are irresponsible in matters of
diet or in other relevant respects. Other patients are not recommended for

* This paper was first published in 5 *Journal of Medical Ethics* 13 (1979) and appears here
with a postscript.

dialysis for various medical reasons having to do with their physical health. Thus, it is only a proportion of those dying of renal failure who could benefit from dialysis. The number who do in fact benefit from it is even further reduced by the chronic shortage of machines. They are, of course, very expensive, costing around £6000 each, to which a further £3000 per machine per annum must be added to take account of training staff to use them, nursing and medical care, and maintenance; and, of course, it is a long-term financial commitment.

It is a sad, and some would say scandalous, reality that the National Health Service has not attached the necessary priority to this need so as to allocate all the money needed to meet the demand in full. At most, only about 700 people begin dialysis each year. This has forced doctors into the invidious, and to them wholly unwelcome, role of having to choose between patients as to which one shall have dialysis, in the knowledge that a decision against a patient is a sentence of death.[1] To some extent the decision can be based on medical criteria; but there is no doubt that other factors intrude, so that the question has been raised many times as to whether it is appropriate to leave such a decision to doctors alone.

The other form of treatment for those with renal failure, kidney transplant, has been available on a regular basis since about 1967. A kidney is taken from a dead person and transplanted into the donee. Less often, kidneys are taken from living donors, but I shall not consider the separate, complex issues concerned with live donors here.[2] If the operation is a success, the patient is restored to normal good health. However, transplants should not be seen as direct alternatives to dialysis. Often a patient must wait for some time on dialysis before a transplant is available; sometimes the new kidney fails, and the patient will be returned to dialysis, possibly to await a second transplant; and for some, a transplant is not an available option for medical reasons. Thus, transplantation surgery has not replaced, nor could it do without, dialysis. But, at the same time, it offers a far more attractive long-term solution in every respect, whether from the point of view of the individual patient's general health or the comparative costs involved. It is transplantation surgery and the law governing it that I shall concentrate on in this paper.

THE LAW ON TRANSPLANTATION OF KIDNEYS

Let me begin by mentioning that it cannot any longer be argued that kidney transplantation surgery is an experimental procedure, and therefore one to be considered in the light of the special legal regime governing experiments.

---

[1] See e.g. the very recent report from the Office of Health Economics, *Renal failure: A priority in health* (1978), and the comment thereon in *The Times*, 15 Mar. 1978.

[2] See *Human Tissue Transplants*, Australian Law Reform Commission Report No. 7 (1977), ch. 9.

Certainly, there is some surgery which is experimental. Indeed, heart transplants may still be regarded as such. Kidney transplants, however, have passed this point. At the same time, it should be said that the surgery itself is only part—some might say the easiest part—of the treatment. Complicated tissue-matching must be done to ensure the most favourable possible compatibility between donor and donee; elaborate procedures to ensure a sterile environment after the operation must be organized; and a regime of immuno-suppressive drugs must be managed by experts qualified to guide the patient between the twin evils of rejection and over-susceptibility to infection. Thus, although the surgery is not experimental, it is such a demanding therapeutic process that it may only be carried out, in my view, where the procedures I have mentioned can be properly and competently undertaken. Otherwise, to transplant a kidney would be to expose a patient to an unacceptable risk, and would, in my view, attract legal liability if damage ensued. Though in the United Kingdom this is a somewhat academic point, since transplantation is carried out only in designated centres, it could be important if, for example, through NHS cut-backs or inadequacies or whatever, such a centre was no longer able to meet the high standards required, but none the less continued to carry out transplants.

Turning now to the law, for obvious reasons the common law has nothing to say on the proper regulation of such a modern exercise as organ transplantation. As long ago as 1832, the Anatomy Act, an Act which regulated the use of cadavers for medical research and dissection in schools of anatomy, was passed. It thereby facilitated the training of medical students in anatomy. It did not, however, provide for the donation and subsequent removal of parts of the body for transplantation. Long after the discovery that corneas taken from the eyes of dead bodies could successfully be grafted on to the eyes of patients afflicted, for example, with intractable ulcers, Parliament belatedly passed, in 1952, the Corneal Grafting Act. This was the first statute to deal directly with the transplantation of tissue. In 1954 the first human kidney transplant was carried out in Massachusetts. It soon became clear that a new law dealing generally with transplantation was called for if such operations were to be performed in the United Kingdom. Parliament responded in 1961 with the Human Tissue Act, repealing the Corneal Grafting Act and making provision generally for the removal of tissue from cadavers for transplantation, without reference to any specific tissue or organ. Despite the fact that it was passed while transplantation surgery was very much in its infancy, despite the criticism levelled at it, and despite numerous attempts to amend or repeal it, the Human Tissue Act is still the only law there is.

CRITICISM OF THE ACT

The criticisms made of the Act are basically of two kinds. The first concerns the obscurity of its principal provisions and difficulties of meaning and interpretation.[3] The second relates to the political and social premiss upon which the Act is based, the notion that tissue should not be taken from a cadaver if either the deceased in his lifetime or his spouse or relatives after his death have objected to its removal. I am more concerned here to draw attention to this second criticism. Let me, in passing, point to some of the problems arising from the language used in the Act, always remembering, of course, that these problems are themselves, in part at least, the product of differing views as to the proper scope and aim of the Act.

Interpretation

It will help if I first set out Section 1, Subsections 1 and 2.

S 1(1) If any person either in writing at any time or orally in the presence of two or more witnesses during his last illness has expressed a request that his body or any specified part of his body be used after his death for therapeutic purposes . . . , the person lawfully in possession of his body after his death may, unless he has a reason to believe that the request was subsequently withdrawn, authorise the removal from the body of any part or, as the case may be, the specified part, for use in accordance with the request.

S 1(2) without prejudice to the foregoing sub-section, the person lawfully in possession of the body of a deceased person may authorise the removal of any part from the body for use for the said purposes if, having made such reasonable inquiry as may be practicable, he has no reason to believe
a) that the deceased had expressed an objection to his body being so dealt with after his death, and had not withdrawn it: or
b) that the surviving spouse or any surviving relative of the deceased objects to the body being so dealt with.

The first subsection provides for what has become known as 'contracting-in', whereby the deceased may express his wish that his kidneys be used for transplanting. The second subsection provides for the circumstance in which the deceased has not expressed any wish. It would not be an exaggeration to say that some of the words and expressions used here have virtually defied all efforts at clarification. A full treatment of these problems of interpretation is inappropriate here.[4] Two obvious examples are, who is 'the person lawfully in possession of the body' of the deceased? and what does 'having made such reasonable inquiry as may be practicable' really amount to? There

[3] I. Kennedy, 'Alive or Dead: The Lawyer's View'. 22 *Current Legal Problems* 102 (1969).
[4] For a thorough discussion, see G. Lanham, 'Transplant and the Human Tissue Act 1961', 11 *Medicine, Science and the Law* 16 (1971); and R. M. Dworkin, 'The Law relating to Organ Transplantation in England', 33 *Modern Law Review* 353 (1970) and British Transplantation Society, 'The Shortage of Organs for Clinical Transplantation, 1 *British Medical Journal* 251 (1975).

are also other problems which have bedevilled commentators, such as whether donor cards carried by motorists and others in fact have any legal force, on which even the DHSS took a contradictory stance, saying in 1973 that they did not, but in 1975 that they did. For a long time too, of course, the vexed issue of the legal definition of death, crucial to the question of when kidneys could be removed, was a major medical-legal preoccupation, since to be of use, a kidney must be removed within half an hour, or an hour at most, of death.

The Policy of the Act

Once the political decision was taken that the removal of kidneys for transplantation was to be encouraged and facilitated, Parliament had to decide how to act. In particular, consideration had to be given to what opposition there might be to the removal of kidneys, and what, if any, weight should be given to the interests of this opposition. It is often represented that there existed for Parliament two alternatives: the policies of contracting-in, whereby kidneys are removed only from those who have requested this during their lifetimes, and contracting-out, whereby kidneys may be removed from all except those who before death indicate their objection. In fact, a range of options existed for Parliament: first, that doctors on behalf of the National Health Service should have the right to salvage all kidneys deemed suitable, regardless of consent, objection, or opposition (subject only to coronial veto); second, the other end of the spectrum: that kidneys be removed only if the prior consent of the deceased and his spouse and relatives has been obtained; third, a modification of the first: that kidneys be removed unless the deceased has indicated during his lifetime his objection; fourth, a modification of the second: that only the prior consent of the deceased be required; fifth, a modification of the third and fourth: that as regards the third, the spouse and relatives should have the right to object and/or that, as regards the fourth, the consent of the spouse and/or relatives be required if the deceased had not objected, but had not consented.

It was self-evident that the policy adopted by Parliament would have a crucial effect on the future of transplantation. If the most far-reaching scheme of contracting-out were adopted, many kidneys would become available each year, doubtless more than the number needed. If, however, the most limited form of contracting-in, with wide scope for objections, were enacted, kidney transplantation as a viable alternative treatment would be in danger of failing for want of kidneys. The scheme which Parliament eventually adopted in the Human Tissue Act is a perfect example of political compromise. Various interests received the protection they sought. The only casualty, the committed observer may remark, is transplantation surgery itself, for there can be no doubt that, quite apart from difficulties of interpretation and other factors, the policy of the Act represents a less than energetic endorsement of transplantation.

What are the competing interests? There are at least five. First, there is the deceased (should he have a say in the disposal of his body?); second, the spouse and relatives (should their views prevail, even as against the deceased, for example, if they oppose donation while he has requested it?); third, the potential donee, dying at an early age while the kidney which could save him is being buried or cremated; fourth, certain groups who have strongly held views on how the body of a deceased person should be treated; and fifth, society at large, which must bear the economic and emotional burden of 2,000 people each year contracting fatal kidney disease and the cost of dialysis as an expensive alternative to transplantation, and yet must seek to respect the views of religious groups and others so as to avoid the 'tyranny of the majority'.

What Parliament decided on was a two-tier approach. First, there was section 1(1), a contracting-in scheme, whereby the request of the deceased, if expressed in the correct form, prevails, subject of course to the fact that it may be revoked and that the ultimate discretion lies with the person lawfully in possession. The second tier, in section 1(2), covers the circumstances in which the deceased has not made a request. In this case, Parliament seems to have opted for a contracting-out scheme, that the kidneys could be taken unless there were objections, but subject to two reservations. The first is the power of the spouse or relatives to object. The other is that Parliament, in considering on whom to place the burden of recording objection, chose to place it on the hospital authority (if it be judged the 'person lawfully in possession'), rather than the relative. Thus, it becomes contracting-out with very wide limitations.

It is possible, then, to put in order the priorities respected by Parliament. First, there is the deceased's expressed view. Then the spouse and relatives, in the absence of a view expressed by the deceased, have a power of veto. The existence of a veto also means that groups opposed to taking organs from the dead have succeeded in safeguarding their particular views. The dying and society at large very much play third fiddle as regards having their interests and needs satisfied, which is rather surprising, given that the stated aim of the Act in the long title was to 'make provision with respect to the use of parts of bodies of deceased persons for therapeutic purposes'.

An Irony

After taking so much trouble to strike what it conceived to be the right balance in the Act, Parliament then did something very strange. It failed to provide for any sanctions if the provisions of the Act were ignored! The irony is compounded in that, as I will seek to show, were it not for the policy of the Act, not to mention the difficulties of interpretation, a sufficient supply of kidneys could be obtained. So what is to stop doctors and hospital authorities from ignoring the Act which they feel reluctantly bound to observe every day? At least two things come to mind.[5] First, it may be that a sanction *does* exist for non-observance, even though the reasoning required to discover it is tortuous at best. The assumption on the part of hospitals and doctors that, since it is a statute, the Act must be complied with, coupled with the fact that some sort of legal liability for non-compliance could be conjured up, persuade them to observe it, out of a sense of its being best to err on the side of caution, if nothing else. Second, whatever the law, it is probably the case that it is good — indeed, required — ethical conduct to observe the Act, so that non-observance would invite professional sanction. Notwithstanding this, it is the greatest irony that practically all those who have for so long criticized the Act and pressed for its reform have concentrated on its alleged faults and overlooked the potentially fatal flaw that it may be unenforceable.

Kidney Transplantation: The Reality

More than 6,000 people are killed in the United Kingdom each year in road accidents. From these (and I do not include the additional 2,000–3,000 who die each year from strokes and cerebral tumours), more than enough kidneys could be salvaged for transplantation, though, of course, by no means all of these 6,000 will be placed on respirators. Of the 2,000 who annually fall victim to fatal kidney failure, most could benefit from a transplant. Amazingly, in 1977 in the United Kingdom only 706 transplant operations were carried out, and this figure represents a massive improvement of more than 22 per cent on the 1976 figure. In 1969 there were 200; in 1970, 274; in 1971, 315; and in 1973, 465. Why are so few transplants carried out? Before I try to answer this, let me recall other relevant facts so that a considered judgment may be made. Renal dialysis, the alternative therapy, is very expensive, and being long-term treatment, the financial commitment is recurrent and growing. For this and other reasons, there has always been a chronic shortage of machines. Under the terms of the Finance Act 1978, the Secretary of State for Health and Social Security has indicated that he will allocate £3.5 million of the NHS's promised additional £8 million for the purchase of 400 extra machines and for associated costs.[6] This is both an admission of the existing shortage and, by all accounts, a less than adequate

[5] P. Skegg, 'Liability for the Unauthorised Removal of Cadaveric Transplant Material', 14 *Medicine, Science and the Law*, 53 (1974); and chapter 11.
[6] *The Times*, 6 Apr 1978.

response to it. For, on average, only 650–700 patients begin dialysis each year. Thus, until the new machines are in service, the maximum number treated by dialysis or transplant was approximately 1,440 in 1977. The figure for previous years was much lower, and even with the proposed new machines, will only be 1,800 at the very most. Thus, at present, there are at least 600 people each year who contract kidney disease and who are told they will die because no treatment is available. This is so notwithstanding the fact that we, as a society, are burying several thousand healthy kidneys each year, and that a mere £3–5 million (a comparatively insignificant figure in national terms) would provide all the dialysis machines needed. Finally, it is not the case here, as it may be in other areas, that there is not the specialized staff available in NHS hospitals to deal with treatment if all were to be offered dialysis or transplantation. On the contrary, the fact is that even in these days of financial stringency in the NHS, not one of the 40-odd units set up throughout the country to provide dialysis or any of the transplant teams is working to its full capacity. In other words, doctors are underused and patients are dying through lack of machines, lack of kidneys, and lack of political will to do anything about it.

But is there any link between the Human Tissue Act and the lack of kidneys? I will suggest, in company with most commentators, that although there are other factors, the Act plays a prominent role in bringing about this shortage. What are these factors? At least eight can be identified, four unrelated to the Act and four related thereto.

FACTORS UNRELATED TO THE ACT

Apathy in the Medical Profession

Remarkably, one of the principal reasons for a shortage of kidneys is that doctors working in hospitals—for example, in accident units—do not appear to be at all active in obtaining kidneys from patients who are dying there. Tam Dalyell, MP, who has campaigned vigorously for modification of the Act, pointed out in a speech to the House of Commons in December 1974 that 'many of the largest teaching hospitals, with active transplantation units, including some of the most prestigious in Britain, have provided not a single kidney for transplantation.'[7] He contrasted this with 'one small district general hospital, where keen, young medical staff have transplantation in mind, which provides an average of half-a-dozen donors a year'.

[7] R. Y. Calne, *et al.*, 'Transplantation, 1 *Journal of Medical Ethics* 61 (1975).

The Extra Work Involved

To prepare a patient for kidney donation after death takes time and effort. A team of doctors and nurses may have spent a night and a day (or several) trying the save a patient's life, and may view with something less than enthusiasm the prospect of spending another night doing all the careful work required before a kidney can be removed.

Ignorance of the Success Rate of Transplants

The chances of a transplant being a success have improved markedly as tissue typing and immunological expertise have developed, and a national and international registration scheme, listing potential donees and their relevant medical histories and requirements, has been developed, so that selection of donees and donors is from a wider pool. The success rate reported in the 1975 report of the Committee of the British Transplantation Society was that 50 per cent of cadaver transplants were still functioning after two years, and that 70 per cent of the patients in whom transplant failed were still alive, back on dialysis and perhaps awaiting another transplant. This figure has improved somewhat since then. (It must be recalled that the operation had only been routinely performed for about five years at that time, so that data on greater life expectancy were not available. Also, of course, this success rate has to be judged against the background of the poor quality of the kidneys obtained.) The British Transplantation Society felt that these figures were very encouraging, particularly when it is recalled that a successful transplant means restoring the patient to the community as an active member. Nevertheless, it is alleged, many doctors not directly involved in the field are unaware of these improvements, and still view transplantation as experimental, or as an alternative to dialysis which is to be avoided.

Adverse Publicity

In 1967 heart transplants attracted massive publicity. Acclaimed at first, they were soon attacked as being, *inter alia*, a failure therapeutically, done for national prestige and an unjustified expenditure of scarce resources. There was also a good deal of concern about the definition of death as the Press in particular ran stories of beating hearts being taken from the chests of donors.[8] Whatever the validity of these arguments, there is no doubt that this bad odour affected all transplant surgery, including kidney transplants, and tended to turn public and doctors alike away from such surgery.

[8] See Kennedy, *supra* n. 3.

FACTORS RELATED TO THE ACT

Framework of the Act

The very framework of the Act, calling for contracting-in and providing wide veto powers over contracting-out, limits the number of kidneys available. The number is made even smaller when account is taken of the numerous doubts and difficulties involved in its interpretation, which make doctors understandably err always on the side of caution.

Coroners

The interpretation which some coroners put on the Act further limits supply.[9]

The Need to Approach the Spouse or Relatives

If no request has been made under section 1(1) an approach has to be made to the deceased's spouse or relatives. This task falls on the doctors who have been caring for the one who has died. They find it a distasteful task for two reasons. First, they have just lost a patient and, for psychological reasons cannot easily move on to think in terms of removing the patient's kidneys. Second, since time is of the essence, the relatives must be approached at the time when they have just heard of the death, which, even if they may have been prepared for it, will still leave them unprepared to listen to overtures concerning kidney donation, and may even cause them to be resentful of what they may see as a tasteless intrusion on their grief.[10]

There is a rather bleak postscript to the point that the need for urgent action tends to conflict with consideration for the feelings of a spouse or relatives and the need to comply with what is seen to be the meaning of the Act. The quality of the kidneys obtained has often been poor. Problems do not arise if a donor is on a respirator, as the machine can facilitate the continued supply of oxygenated blood after death. But in the past many donors have been taken off respirators, the doctor preferring the old notion of death—the absence of heart-beat—to the notion of brain-stem death. The sad, and even shocking, fact is that in 1975, for example, as many as $17 \cdot 3$ per cent of all kidneys transplanted never functioned at all because, during the time taken to remove them, they had already become irretrievably damaged. The transplantation of a useless kidney which has then to be removed is, of course, doubly tragic; the patient has to undergo two useless and dangerous operations, and false hopes have been raised. This does not include the waste

---

[9] Ibid.　　[10] See Calne *et al.*, *supra* n. 7.

of resources in time, money, and effort, and the anguish caused to those close to both donor and donee. Indeed, so notorious did the poor quality of British cadaver kidneys become that many European transplantation centres, though linked with the United Kingdom through the European Register in Leiden for the purposes of exchange of kidneys throughout Europe, would often not, in fact, take British kidneys when they were offered for transplantaion.

Adverse Publicity

The adverse publicity mentioned earlier may also have had the further effect of dissuading people from donating their kidneys for transplantation under section 1(1).

REFORM OF THE LAW

It does not necessarily follow from what has been said that the law should be changed. Some might argue that while it is accepted that not enough kidneys are becoming available under the existing statutory scheme, this is an unfortunate, but inevitable, price to be paid for giving proper weight to all competing interests. Others, however, would argue that if we have a law the purpose of which is to facilitate transplantation, it makes no sense at all for hundreds to die unnecessarily each year. Of these two positions, I confess that I find the second more persuasive. Thus, in this final section, I shall consider various ways in which the law might be reformed. Perhaps I should mention that the Secretary of State for Health and Social Security announced in the House of Commons in April 1978 that he intended to publish a discussion paper by the end of the year on the pros and cons of the existing law governing the donation and removal of organs. But so far (January 1979) this paper has not appeared.

I cannot, of course, list every possibility which has been put forward. I will, however, mention briefly what I consider to be the most important ones.

Retain the Existing Law, with Increased Publicity and so on

Those who argue that the existing law strikes a proper balance between the needs of the potential donee and the feelings of the deceased, his spouse, and relatives urge that it should not be changed. What they propose instead is that greater advantage be taken of section 1(1), on the grounds that if it were sufficiently well known, enough requests would be made to meet the annual need for kidneys. First, they accept and endorse the Departmental view announced by Mrs Castle that donor cards meet the Act's requirements, and urge a far more extensive use of them, as well as variations on the theme of cards. For example, the proposal has been made that applications for driving licences should contain a question concerning willingness to be a kidney donor. If the applicant consented, this information could then be stored in a data bank to which hospitals could have immediate access. Another proposal has been that a tattoo could be used, put, of course, on a hidden, but convenient, part of the body (the inside of the lip has been suggested). Of course, the problem immediately arises as to how someone once tattooed is to change his mind, quite apart from the other weaknesses of this idea, that, for example, it is painful, may be unsightly, that certain people have principled objections to tattooing, and, most telling, that it requires rather more positive action on the part of the volunteer than is usually compatible with making voluntary schemes a success. In addition to these and other variants of the donor card idea, it is proposed that a vigorous campaign of public education be undertaken to make people aware of the circumstances of kidney failure, and urging them to become future donors, by written request or whatever. However, quite apart from whether the Government would be prepared to finance such an educational campaign, the evidence of previous such campaigns—for example, for the voluntary wearing of seat-belts in cars—is that they are of minimal success at best.

The plain fact is that these proposals are well-meaning, but most unlikely to have any real effect. Only a very few will be persuaded to volunteer. It is a sad fact, which transplant surgeons report with a hint of irony, that it is very rare indeed that people who carry donor cards actually become donors. By their nature, they are public-spirited, conscientious people, and are less likely, therefore, to become the victims of road accidents and other traumas. The prime candidate, the young, healthy motor-cyclist, who by his youth and choice of transport is clearly convinced of his immortality, will be just the person not to have volunteered as a future donor.

Amend the Act

The most recent and well-known examination of kidney donation was a report published in 1975 by a Committee of the British Transplantation Society, called 'The Shortage of Organs for Clinical Transplantation'.[11] A number of recommendations were made therein. The principal proposal, and one echoed by others, was for the Act to be amended in particular details. The aim appears to have been two-fold: first, to retain the underlying policy of the Act—that is, contracting-in (section 1(1)) plus contracting-out with limitations (section 1(2)).—while, second, redrafting these two subsections

---

[11] See *supra* n. 4.

so as to remove existing uncertainties, thereby facilitating a greater supply of kidneys. In particular, a new form for section 1(2) was proposed, as well as an interpretation section for sections 1(1) and (2). In the proposed interpretation section it would be made explicit that the hospital authority is the person lawfully in possession of a body lying in a hospital, at least until such time as someone with a greater claim demands it. It also provides that printed donor cards or other such documents are 'in writing' for the purpose of section 1(1).

The revision of section 1(2) is crucial. It concerns the question of what inquiry must be made, and proposes the following version:

Without prejudice to the foregoing sub-section, the person lawfully in possession of the body of a deceased person may authorise the removal of any part from the body for use for the said purposes if, *having made such inquiry as is both reasonable and practicable in the time available*, he has no reason to believe that the deceased had expressed an objection (which he was not known to have withdrawn) to his body being so dealt with after his death.

Provided that authorisation shall not be given under this sub-section if the person lawfully in possession of the body has reason to believe that the surviving spouse or any surviving relative of the deceased objects to the body being so dealt with.

The Committee notes that only 'in one respect' is any change made in the existing law: that, by the new section 1(2), the person lawfully in possession 'would no longer be under a duty to make inquiries' as to whether a spouse or relative objected to removal. The proviso to the proposed section 1(2) merely refers to having 'reason to believe', without the requirement of an obligation to inquire. This has to be understood, however, in the light of the proposed definition of 'the time available' in the interpretation section, as meaning only that period of time 'until the moment at which steps must be taken to remove the part of the body, if it is to be suitable for the therapeutic . . . purpose'. It is my view that the Committee somewhat understates the significance of its proposal. It may alter the law only in one respect; but, on one reading of the proposal, that respect involves a virtual abandonment of the central thesis of the Act (which the Committee claims to accept), the spouse's or relatives' power of veto. For, if it is conceded that, optimally, kidneys should be removed as soon as death is pronounced, 'the time available' may, by reference to the interpretation section, be made to mean a mere matter of seconds or minutes. Given that no obligation is cast on the hospital authority to discover objections, unless a spouse or relative is both aware that death is imminent and on the spot when it takes place, he may be presented with a *fait accompli*: that the kidney has been removed. Admittedly, the Committee argues that the doctor would 'invariably approach the closest available relatives', but he is not *required* to do so. Thus, the Committee's recommendations are far from satisfactory, in that they either provide for one course of conduct while recommending another, thereby writing uncertainty back into the Act; or they provide for a radical shift of policy towards what has the potential for being an almost full-scale contracting-out scheme, though masquerading as maintaining the existing policy. If the Committee had thought that contracting-out, though the right approach, was politically unlikely to be adopted, then it should, perhaps, have said so and confronted the issue more openly.

The Sale of Kidneys

If kidneys from cadavers are not available in sufficient numbers, one radical way to make up the deficiency, which would respect all existing objections against removing them from the dead, would be to allow the living to sell one of their kidneys.[12] Nature provides us with two kidneys, but we can live perfectly well with one. Why should someone not be able to sell the other? Such a proposal is hardly voiced in Britain; and when it is, the response is prompt and hostile. Yet, in the United States, the sale of kidneys and other organs has been much discussed and is not unknown.[13] There are several interconnecting levels on which to consider this issue. The first is the purely legal one. Would such a sale be considered valid and enforceable, or be judged to be contrary to public policy? Would the whole apparatus of products liability and exemption clauses surround such sales? The possible answers to these questions lead to deeper philosophical issues, such as whether we as a society think it right to condone a traffic in human parts or regard it as fundamentally degrading; or, put another way, whether a society acting paternalistically should deny an individual his right to self-determination, to do with himself as he pleases, to engage in unorthodox, but perhaps profitable, commerce, when the exercise of such a right involves a mutilating operation. Further, should a society committed to a national health service contemplate the possibility that kidneys become available only to the highest bidder, leaving the poor to die? Then there are medical-ethical issues, such as whether the person's consent to the removal of his kidney for sale is real, or one induced by financial need or other stress. Also, the history of the sale of blood in the United States may caution us against supporting the notion of selling kidneys. As Titmuss pointed out in his classic study,[14] blood donors in the United States who sell their blood, more often than not, are poor and often unhealthy. Their medical histories, which would be even more critical if it were kidneys that they were giving, may be fabricated so as to suppress unfavourable facts and thus ensure they are not refused as donors.

---

[12] See the full discussion in the Australian Law Reform Commission Report, ch. 15.

[13] J. Dukeminier, 'Supplying Organs for Transplantation', 68 *Michigan Law Review* 812 (1970).

[14] R. Titmuss, *The Gift Relationship* (George Allen and Unwin, 1970). See also R. Plant, 'Gifts, Exchanges and the Political Economy of Health Care', 3 *Journal of Medical Ethics* 4, 1970, pp. 166–73; and 4, 1 (1978), 5–11.

Finally—and this could be the most crucial objection if kidneys were involved—testing procedures may not be carried out with all the proper rigour. For the doctor removing the blood is often a middleman who resells his product; and the greater the desire for profit, the less inclined he is to reject a donor.

There are, of course, counter-arguments. Some see nothing wrong with the market-place playing its part here as elsewhere. They need not take the more extreme position widely held in the United States that health care is a commodity, to be bought and paid for, rather than a service to be made available to all, rich and poor alike. Instead, they may argue that those who can afford to should pay, always assuming there are sellers, and that those who cannot should have the kidneys which have been donated under the existing law. Further, they can point to psychological arguments which have it that this provides gratification to the donee and an enhanced feeling of well-being, rather than possible guilt at having taken something from the dead, or at having been given a kidney while others have been allowed to die. They may argue also that any method of increasing the supply of kidneys is to be welcomed in the light of the existing state of affairs. Finally, the point can be made that, if the idea of cash for kidneys is deemed too objectionable, there are, of course, other methods of payment. It can take the form of future priority treatment for the donor and/or relatives in case of illness, or some form of indemnity insurance against future illness.

These are some of the arguments. They are rarely aired. I must say that I am firmly opposed to the sale of kidneys, and think it most unlikely that such sales would be tolerated here in the United Kingdom. Some indeed go so far as to propose that they be outlawed, as does, for example, the recent 1977 Report of the Australian Law Reform Commission on Human Tissue Transplants.[15] I am inclined to think that such legislation is unnecessary.

Contracting-out

As was seen at the outset, a spectrum of choices was, and is, available to Parliament as to whose interest should weigh most heavily in any law governing transplants. In the light of the past ten or so years of kidney transplantation, it can be concluded that the present mixture of voluntary contracting-in and contracting-out subject to veto has weighted the scales heavily against those dying of kidney failure. Partial reforms, such as giving the spouse or relatives less power, may be the answer. Indeed, the Australian Report, after some equivocating, opts for this. My view is that if we really care about helping those afflicted by kidney disease, who, it will be recalled, are often young people who have much to offer, then piecemeal, bitty

---

[15] *Supra*, n. 2, 187.

reforms should be seen for the partial solutions they are, and abandoned. Instead, Parliament should take the positive step of introducing a pure contracting-out system. Even this would not go far enough for some, since it gives the deceased a power of veto, by registering his objection before death; whereas they would advocate removal regardless of anyone's wishes. Donald Longmore put it strikingly, as follows: 'We can either preserve the ancient laws that guarantee the inviolability of the dead, and the present rights of the next-of-kin, or we can rewrite those laws in favour of the living.'[16]

That Parliament has not introduced contracting-out despite considerable pressure over ten years should suggest that powerful arguments exist against it. But it is not clear what these arguments are. None the less, the past ten years show a record of complete failure of *any* attempt to change the law. In 1968 Sir Gerald Nabarro introduced a bill providing for the removal of kidneys unless the deceased had, during his life, indicated his opposition. The bill failed in 1968, and again in 1969, the Government of the day opposing it on the rather spurious ground that it dealt only with kidneys, whereas any law should deal generally with all transplants. In 1969 the Government's own Advisory Group[17] set up to consider the working of the Act recommended, albeit by a bare majority, contracting-out, but its views were completely ignored. It is true that in 1970, a British Medical Association committee advised against contracting-out; but, in part, its opposition was the result of a general antipathy to transplantation at the time, created by the failures of various heart transplants, which, of course, had nothing to do with kidney transplants. The Bar Council in its Report in 1971[18] was also against contracting-out, principally because it invaded the rights of the individual; but this is patently question-begging, as it depends on which individual is considered, the deceased, his spouse or relative, or the dying patient. On nine occasions, culminating in his Transplantation of Organs Bill in 1974, Tam Dalyell, MP, has sought to introduce the system of contracting-out, each time to be met with no support from the Government. Finally, the Report of the British Transplantation Society I referred to earlier[19] certainly edges towards contracting-out; but it failed to provoke any response from the Government, despite the distinction of the members who wrote it.

I ask again why successive Governments have not changed one word of the 1961 Act. I can find no satisfactory answer, save the exertion of pressure by those who claim they are safeguarding freedom, and a wholly unjustified timorousness on the part of the DHSS concerning public opposition, which, if the views of those involved in the area are to be trusted, is completely

[16] D. Longmore, *Spare Part Surgery* (Aldus Books, 1968).

[17] Advice from the Advisory Group on Transplantation Problems on the question of Amending the Human Tissue Act of 1961, (HMSO, 1969)

[18] Report of the Law Reform Committee on the Law relating to Organ Transplantation, adopted by the Bar Council, 20 July 1971.   [19] *Supra* n. 4.

unfounded, since the consensus of informed opinion is that the vast majority of the public do not share the misgivings attributed to them by the Government and Parliament.

Mahoney,[20] in a careful examination of contracting-out, presents a number of ethical objections. He reaches the conclusion that voluntary service is better in such matters than conscription, because of what it says about the society and the respect given to differing viewpoints. Voluntary donation, he says, may be less efficient, but is more humane. Again, the question is begged, since I imagine that Mahoney would also at the same time deny that it is humane to stand by and let hundreds of people die each year when their lives could be saved.

Certainly, there can be no argument against contracting-out based on cost, as it is obvious that, as between dialysis and transplant, the latter is much cheaper. Finally, there is no lack of examples in other countries of contracting-out laws. France, Czechoslovakia, Hungary, Sweden, Norway, and Israel all have contracting-out.[21] Indeed, while somewhat perversely recommending a scheme like the Human Tissue Act, the Australian Report inclined to the view that contracting-out would be the accepted model within five years.

If the DHSS does not, in its proposed consultation document, offer a reasoned and compelling argument against contracting-out, the Government should, in my view, introduce it as soon as possible. Furthermore, if the Department, with or without reasons, opposes contracting-out, it must quite clearly face the fact that it is condemning many suffering from kidney failure to die for want of resources, given that an adequate number of dialysis machines is not available. Also, given that resources are, as a matter of policy, being restricted, the Department must suggest criteria according to which these scarce resources should be made available. To leave these harrowing decisions to doctors is grossly unfair. Of course, the Department would not dream of entering that particular lion's den. But, in failing to lay down guidelines, while condoning, through inaction, the circumstances which demand them, the Department and the Government are being both callous and less than honest.

POSTSCRIPT

Perhaps I should point out that my views in the above paper did not go unchallenged. The distinguished transplant surgeon Mr Robert Sells wrote a response[22] to which I published a reply.[23]

---

[20] J. Mahoney, 'Ethical Aspects of Donor Consent in Transplantation', 1 *Journal of Medical Ethics* 67–70 (1975). [21] See *supra* n. 2, chs. 7 and 10.
[22] R. Sells, 'Let's Not Opt Out: Kidney Donation and Transplantation', 5 *Journal of Medical Ethics* 165 (1979).
[23] I. Kennedy, 'Kidney Transplants: A Reply to Sells', 6 *Journal of Medical Ethics* 29 (1980). In recent conversations with me, Mr Sells has indicated that he is now persuaded that

Obviously, most of the facts and figures referred to above have changed; for example, the number of transplants performed in the United Kingdom had reached 1,500 by 1986.[24] More significantly, the number of those receiving treatment for end-stage renal failure had risen by 1986 to about 2,000. The situation complained of, however, remains, particularly as the number who could possibly benefit from such treatment is considerably greater than 2,000, if the arbitrary age limits of 15–55 are ignored. But there is now evidence that the Government may be considering amendments to the Human Tissue Act. The last time 'opting out' was seriously proposed (and staunchly supported by the redoubtable Mr Dalyell), in 1984, the Government declared that it 'did not support amending the Human Tissue Act in such a way at present'.[25]

For whatever reason, the Government appears to have changed its mind. The reason may be cost. This would not be surprising given Mrs Thatcher's government's 'commitment' to public-sector health care. The costs of treatment for end-stage renal failure by 1986 were: for transplant, £10,000 in the first year and £4,000 per annum subsequently; for home dialysis, £12,000 in the first year and then £8,000 per annum; and for hospital dialysis, £15,000 per annum.[26] The form of amendment currently under consideration by the Government is that which has recently gained currency in the United States. This is the 'required request' procedure. This involves a change in the law whereby an obligation is placed on the doctors caring for a dying person, or the hospital administrators, to ask the relatives of the person for permission to remove the organs for the purposes of transplantation, before turning off the patient's ventilator, or to demonstrate that the circumstances made such a request impracticable.[27]

It is impossible to say what effect, if any, this would have on transplantation. It can be predicted, however, that doctors would not welcome it. And, in my view, it would be a most unfortunate step to take. If, as I have contended, the problems of kidney transplantation have a lot to do with the burden which the present Act places on doctors, it seems most unfair, as well as counter-productive, to try to remedy the problem by increasing the burden on doctors and, presumably, attaching a sanction for breach. I say 'on doctors', since although administrators may be nominated in any proposed law, they will presumably establish a system whereby their decision

'opting out' may be the only way forward, since all other means of increasing the supply of kidneys have been less than a complete success.

[24] Pers. com. Dr Gwyn Williams, King's College Hospital.
[25] *The Times*, 14 Feb. 1984.
[26] *Supra* n. 24.
[27] For a brief summary of the developments in the United States, where, by the autumn of 1986, 27 states had adopted some form of 'required request' legislation, see Institute of Medical Ethics, *Bulletin* no. 22 (Jan. 1987), 11.

is delegated to the doctor. For my part, I see a change to 'required request' as representing a less than charitable attempt on the part of the Government and the rest of us to slough off this particular problem on to doctors, thereby assuaging our guilt; and it should be condemned as such. I remain convinced, therefore, that a change to 'opting out' is the only real solution.[28]

One further point which may be worth noticing is that when I discussed the question of the sale of kidneys, I did so largely to dismiss it. Well, we live in changed times, in which the market-place is considered by some to be the solution to all problems. Thus it was that reports appeared in the Press[29] alleging a traffic in kidneys from live donors, whereby donors were recruited in the Indian subcontinent and were persuaded for about £3,000 or less to represent themselves as close relatives so that wealthy Middle-Easterners could receive kidneys in transplant operations in London.

I have already touched on some of the objections to which this kind of traffic could give rise. Not least is the very real fear of exploitation of the donor and the possibility of fraud surrounding the exercise. These objections and others persuaded the General Medical Council to respond. It published a strongly worded statement in November 1985 which was incorporated into the Rules on Professional Conduct and Discipline. It stated, *inter alia*, that it was unethical for any doctor to be involved in any way in trafficking in human organs.

Equally, the Council of the Transplantation Society, in an important paper,[30] announced that it was against the sale of kidneys by live donors and laid down guidelines incorporating this view. Guideline 6 states that 'It should be clearly understood that no payment to the donor by the recipient, the recipient's relatives, or any other supporting organization can be allowed. However, reimbursement for loss of work earnings and any other expenses related to the donation is acceptable.'[31] The British Transplantation Society has also issued guidelines which reflect this view.[32]

Such was the immediate and hostile reaction to the idea of the sale by unrelated donors of their kidneys. It remains to be seen whether the Government will respond with any revision of the law to clarify the issue, or whether

---

[28] Note the introduction of 'opting-out' in Belgium in 1985.

[29] *Mail on Sunday*, 12 May 1985.

[30] 'Commercialisation in Transplantation: The Problems and some Guidelines for Practice' in *The Lancet*, 28 Sept. 1985, p. 715.

[31] Ibid. 716.

[32] See Institute of Medical Ethics, *Bulletin*, no. 17 (Aug. 1986), 10. For the sake of completeness, it should be noted that the Council of Europe Resolution (78) 29 recommended that governments, in harmonizing their laws relating to transplantation, stipulate that, as Article 9 puts it, 'No substance may be offered for profit.' Compare, however, the recent paper by L. Andrews ('My Body, My Property', 16 *Hastings Center Report* 28 (Oct. 1986)) in which she argues for the operation of the market as regards body parts, including the sale of kidneys by live donors.

it is thought that professional self-regulation is enough. After all, once the Government legislates on one aspect of the law relating to transplantation, it will find it extremely difficult to avoid a thoroughgoing examination of the whole law, which would necessarily include a consideration of the merits of introducing an 'opting-out' scheme.

13

Transsexualism and Single-sex Marriage*

'We all know when someone has died, it is perfectly obvious.' 'We all know whether someone is a man or a woman. How can there be any doubt?'

Such certainty is reassuring. Some things may change, but at least fundamental truths remain. They are, after all, laid down by Nature. The chink in this otherwise disarming argument is that Nature exists only to the extent that we comprehend it. Our comprehension, however, based as it is on observation, intuition, and guesswork is always only partial. From time to time evidence appears which challenges received notions of the truth. It is received with fear; for it threatens that comforting security and certainty which hitherto have shaped our actions. It is denounced, and scorn and more is poured on its protagonists. But ineluctably it gains acceptance. It infiltrates our conception of things, sometimes slowly, sometimes with dramatic rapidity. A further dimension is added to our understanding. In this way there are always fundamentals, but they may change.

Until very recently, death was an issue which we could be certain about. No doubts existed as to our comprehension of it. It could be recognized with ease, and the criteria for its presence were precise and immutable. Then suddenly (in historical terms) this traditional conception was challenged. A hitherto unthinkable question was asked: 'What is death?' The dramatic development of transplant surgery brought this issue out of the restrained polemics of academia into the hurly-burly of public discussion. No final answers have yet appeared. All that is certain is that the old certainty no longer exists.[1]

The purpose of this paper is to examine a similar issue, the nature of sex determination, and the implications which attend a rethinking of the old certainties. What, it may be asked, has this to do with the law? Is it not a matter for scientists? The law and legal rules incorporate and build upon perceptions of reality. Of themselves, of course, the rules are normative, and

---

* First published in 2, *Anglo-American Law Review* 112 (1973).

[1] A voluminous literature has appeared on this subject in the space of a few years, particularly since the development of transplantation surgery. See e.g. G. Dworkin, 'The Law Relating to Organ Transplantation in England', 33 *MLR* 353 and citations therein; I. Kennedy 'Alive or Dead', 22 *Current Legal Problems* 102; idem, 'The Kansas Statute on Death—An Appraisal', 285 *New England Journal of Medicine* 946 (21 Oct. 1971).

their validity is thus unaffected by issues of fact. But since they operate in a real world, their force and the respect they can command depends to a very considerable extent on the degree to which they take account of the real world. Equally, concepts, the stuff of rules, cannot exist in a vacuum as mere semantic toys. They represent conclusions of social policy. Thus, to retain their value, they must be seen not as rigid dogma, but as sufficiently flexible to accommodate a changing social scene. The concept of sex, its nature and quality, is currently under systematic and meticulous examination by medical scientists. The old verities are being challenged. Questions such as: what is a man? what are the essential criteria for determining sex? are being asked. They would not have been contemplated just a few years ago.

Whenever an issue arises which turns on sex determination, the law (what is really meant is those who make the law) is asked to rethink a classification system. The position is put that the existing system (here the method of dividing people into one or the other sex) produces unfortunate consequences and should be abandoned. Recourse is had to the growing body of scientific knowledge to demonstrate that the traditional classification no longer reflects the external realities of life. But, of itself, such empirical evidence does not compel the abandonment of the classification. For classifications involve considerations of reason and policy over and above mere empirical data. Instead, the more legitimate approach is to demand that those who maintain the existing system in the face of scientific development must justify their position by pointing to these considerations of reason and policy. This will be a recurring theme in the paper. To this demand, at least two responses can be made. Scientific development can be taken as an overwhelming criterion for reclassification, with a consequent rethinking of legal rules and concepts. That this will bring doubt and uncertainty, at least temporarily, is undeniable. It may also bring in its wake the danger of a too-ready acceptance of that which is not yet proven. But the ultimate dividends in terms of continued responsiveness to a changing world are considerable. Alternatively, the rule-makers can set their faces against the pressures for change. They can prefer the certainty and security offered by rigid rules. They can find their justice in what has always been decided. But their reasons will have to be good!

The dilemma of sex determination may at first seem to be far removed from the real business of the legal world. But the recently decided case of *Corbett* v. *Corbett* explodes this myth.[2] That there is a real and pressing problem was made clear by that case. What was made equally clear was that a solution which is realistic, lasting, and just is still awaited. Since the case, the Law Commissioners have considered the matter and dismissed it in terms which raised doubts as to whether the full implications of the issues were

---

[2] [1970] 2 All ER 33.

understood.[3] The House of Commons saw fit to incorporate a provision in the recent Nullity of Marriage Act[4] to deal with the problems raised. An issue with real social ramifications does exist.[5] But the particular circumstances of *Corbett* are not the only, or the real, problem. What are equally challenging and will be considered here are some of the wider issues implicit in the case.[6]

What did *Corbett* v. *Corbett* decide? In short compass, it was held that someone who by reference to purely biological criteria is undoubtedly of the male sex at birth remains a male, notwithstanding a diagnosis of transsexualism, medical and surgical intervention to alter external sexual characteristics, and adoption of a female role or gender identity. Second, the court held that marriage as an institution is, by definition, the association of someone of the male sex with someone of the female sex, gender having no relevance. From these two premises, the judge proceeded to find that there was no marriage between April Ashley, the surgically operated transsexual who led the life, quite successfully,[7] of a female, and Mr Corbett.

Both of these premises warrant careful examination. My own position is that the first finding of the judge, that April Ashley was a male, was in the light of available information unfortunate and unnecessarily conservative.[8] I will go on to argue that the finding as to 'maleness', though regrettable, should not have precluded a finding that there was a marriage. I shall suggest, in other words, that marriage as a legal institution implying certain mutual rights and obligation is capable of being extended, and should be extended, to cover single-sex relationships.

Traditional wisdom has it that there are two sexes. Every human being belongs to one sex or the other, the two categories existing as separate, mutually exclusive units. Contemporary opinion, however, has moved towards the view that there exists, even on the physiological plane, a spectrum of sexuality, ranging from the definite, polar positions of male and female through a whole series of indeterminate conditions where one sex prevails

---

[3] The Law Commission, *Report on Nullity of Marriage*, (Law Com. No. 33, HMSO, 1970) paras. 30–2, pp. 15–16. [4] 19 and 20 Eliz. 2, c. 44 s. 1(c).

[5] The *New Law Journal*, in welcoming a paper by David Green, 'Gender Identity — Some Legal Problems', remarked: 'Mr. Green's contribution . . . on a subject still considered esoteric and certainly far-removed from the obvious realms of law, is particularly commendable because, as the now more familiar but once equally esoteric phenomenon of transplant surgery has shown, delay in the proper recognition of the legal implications of developments of this kind may have very harmful results, both for the particular practice concerned and for the law itself' (31 July 1969, p. 726). See also the literature cited hereinafter.

[6] For a recent review of the law in this area (one of the very few), see Comment: 'Transsexualism, Sex Reassignment Surgery and the Law', 56 *Cornell Law Review* 963–1009, which is comprehensive and magnificently well documented. [7] *Supra* n. 2, 47.

[8] As early as 1945, a Swiss court concluded that gender identity was the proper legal standard for determining the sex of an operated transsexual (*In re Leber*, Neuchâtel Cantonal Court, 2 July 1945). See further, Comment, *supra* n. 6, 971–2.

but coexists with features of the other, or where neither sex prevails and the individual is either of both sexes or no sex.[9] Rapid and dramatic developments in the medical sciences,[10] particularly in the area of biochemistry and genetics, have demonstrated that the previous certainty which surrounded thinking in this area is an illusion. New attitudes need to be forged in the light of the evidence which has been gathered. The criteria of sex are, we learn, many; and none of them itself is definitive. Decisions as to sex may depend in difficult cases on following a preponderance of factors and ignoring or correcting inconvenient anomalies.[11]

This area is further complicated by the dilemma concerning the importance which should be attributed to factors which are not physiological, but psychological. For psychologists would rate as a very important factor in sex determination the role a person plays and seeks to play, and the image that the person may have as regards the sex he or she belongs to. Put shortly, they urge that sexuality is a combination of sex and gender.[12] They point to the existence of abnormal psychological conditions which demonstrate varying degrees of ambivalence towards the apparent biological sex, showing itself in deviant patterns of behaviour or dress. These anomalies are separate from those the root of which is biological, for they are found in individuals who are otherwise without doubt members of one sex according to biological criteria. The most extreme of these psychological disturbances is transsexualism. The transsexual is one who utterly and completely rejects his biological sex, seeing personal fulfilment and even survival as possible only

---

[9] See generally, R. Green and J. Money, eds., *Transsexualism and Sex Reassignment* (Johns Hopkins Press, 1969), the major work in this area; R. Stoller, *Sex and Gender* (Science House, 1968), an extraordinarily profound and humane book which raises many issues of philosophical, as well as medical, worth; Comment, *supra* n. 6, which coins the striking phrase 'parameters of human sexuality' (p. 95); The Report of the Committee on Homosexual Offences and Prostitution, which talks of a 'continuum' of sexuality, referring to the work of Dr Kinsey, *The Sexual Behaviour of the Human Male* (Cmnd. 247, para. 22, p. 12). See also the report which four Danish scientists sent to the International Olympic Committee objecting to sex tests for female competitors in the Olympic Games. They objected that the tests were unreliable; 'a few individuals cannot be unambiguously assigned to either sex. According to one set of criteria they may be male; according to another, female.' Second, 'appalling psychological damage could be done to somebody like this by the sudden revelation she is a male' (*Sunday Times*, 6 Feb. 1972).

[10] Stoller (*supra* n. 9, preface) talks of advances made over the last 15 years in allied scientific disciplines as contributing to a 'crescendo of interest and information'.

[11] This paper will not deal with the many complex difficulties created by people born with physiological abnormalities, e.g. hermaphroditism, pseudo-hermaphroditism, and Klinefelter's and Turner's syndrome. For a discussion of these and transsexualism generally, from a legal point of view, see *supra* n. 2, *passim*, pp. 44–7; *Hansard* HC 2 Apr. 1971, cols. 1834–6; Meyers, *The Human Body and the Law* (Edinburgh University Press, 1970), p. 50; Comment, *supra* n. 6, 963 *et seq.*; Note, 'Transsexuals in Limbo', 31 *Maryland Law Review*, 236 (1971). And see the medical literature: J. Bowman and B. Engle, 'Sex Variations', 25 *Law and Contemporary Problems* (1960) 293; Green and Money, *supra* n. 9, esp. ch. 5; Stoller, *supra* n. 9.

[12] See Stoller *supra* n. 9, preface, *viii*, and throughout his book; even the title, *Sex and Gender*, is selected to make this point.

through the assumption in as complete a way as possible of the sex to which he feels he really belongs. The classic phrase which describes the plight of the transsexual is that 'he feels he is a woman locked in a man's body'. All his energies are directed towards correcting what he sees as a tragic natural mistake. What is involved here is, in effect, a direct and apparently irreconcilable clash between sex and gender identity, as to which should determine the *sexual profile* of the individual.[13]

In the foregoing paragraph the pronoun 'he' was used, but of course with intent to include, *mutatis mutandis*, the female. For convenience throughout this paper, I shall speak of male-to-female transsexuals. They occur more commonly, and surgery is more frequently practised upon them; but what I say is of equal relevance to female-to-male transsexuals. Also, I shall use the words 'he' and 'she' in describing the male transsexual as it appears appropriate in the context.

There still exists some considerable division of opinion among psychologists and psychiatrists as to the most appropriate form of therapy for transsexuals.[14] Though transsexuals are a rare phenomenon,[15] much attention has

[13] See *supra* n. 2, 42. The Press release announcing and explaining the establishment of the first clinic for transsexuals at Johns Hopkins Medical Institutions is most instructive (Green and Money, *supra* n. 9, 267–9). See further, Comment, *supra* n. 6, 963 *et seq.*; 'Transsexuals are not homosexual. They consider themselves to be members of the opposite sex cursed with the wrong sexual apparatus' I. Pauly, 'The Current Status of the Change of Sex Operation', 147 *Journal of Nervous and Mental Diseases* 460 (1968); Meyers, *supra* n. 11, has a very instructive chapter on transsexualism, ch. 3. I have yet to see an analysis of transsexualism which takes account of *cultural* influences, though such an approach would, I feel, be very revealing. For male and female role playing is to some very considerable extent a function of the degree of importance given to sex-role differentiation. The insights into current Anglo-American cultural patterns in this area provided by the protagonists of Women's Liberation are particularly important. See e.g. Germaine Greer, *The Female Eunuch* (MacGibbon and Kee, 1970), pp. 4–5 and generally.

[14] Stoller sums up his view of the medical dilemma by saying, '[t]he general rule that applies to the treatment of the transsexual is that no matter what one does — including nothing — it will be wrong' (*supra* n. 9, 247). Some psychiatrists argue that the transsexual is a psychotic, and since 'one would not provide a throne for a psychotic who delusionally felt he was a king, is it not irrational to grant the transsexual his request just because he is unhappy?' (Ibid. 248, citing the English psychiatrist Stafford-Clark). See also, Comment, *supra* n. 6, 978. Green, when the Gender Identity Research and Treatment Clinic was set up at the University of California, Los Angeles, sent a questionnaire to 400 randomly selected doctors to discover attitudes to a typical transsexual case history and request for sex reassignment. The majority opposed the request for sex reassignment, even when psychiatrically advised and when suicide was threatened. Reasons for the opposition were fear of malpractice suits, prosecution, or professional censure. The questionnaire provoked a controversy and prompted many outbursts — e.g. 'Dr Green: if you have to select one answer, would you prefer to spit on: A. The American flag; B. The Bible; C. Your Mother. If you don't get the message — forget it!' (Green and Money, *supra*, n. 9, ch. 15).

[15] Dr Randall, an expert witness in *Corbett*, is stated to have treated 190 patients in 12 years (*supra* n. 2, 43). Benjamin, who coined the term 'transsexual', estimated in the absence of reliable figures that there were 10,000 in the United States (Green and Money, *supra* n. 9, 9–10, 85–6, and ch. 26. Pauly suggests 1 in 100,000 males, 1 in 400,000 females (*supra* n. 13)). The number of operations performed in the United States was estimated in 1966 to be 2,000 (Comment, *supra* n. 6 964); see further its n. 5. See also Meyers, *supra* n. 11, pp. 50–1.

been focused on them, not only because of the difficulties encountered in treating them, but also because of the insight a study of their condition may offer into the wider problems of sex determination and gender identity. As the trend in medical thinking has moved towards the view that surgery in conjunction with hormone treatment is a valid form of treatment, particularly as psychotherapy seems to produce no benefits at all,[16] a growing number of legal problems have emerged. For the surgery being considered here, often called 'conversion surgery', involves one or more of several procedures[17] which aim to transform as far as is possible the subject's anatomy so that it approximates that of a member of the preferred sex. Needless to say, it is irreversible. Not all transsexuals undergo surgical treatment, though the number of such operations performed may well rise steadily as the problem of transsexualism gains more attention and becomes more visible, and as clinics are established specializing in treatment and research.[18] For the most part, I will concentrate in this first section on the legal problems facing the transsexual contemplating surgery.

The question here is simply whether the operation itself is lawful.[19] It could be argued that the surgeon could face both criminal and civil liability. Under the criminal law, the position is by no means clear.[20] Without going into the question in detail, I would submit that the operation is lawful if performed by experienced practitioners after very intensive investigation of the mental condition of the patient and the conclusion that there is at least some risk of harm to the patient if surgery is not performed.[21]

---

[16] *Supra* n. 2, 42–3. '[N]o-one has ever reported having reached . . . success by any psychotherapeutic technique' (Stoller, *supra* n. 9, 249).

[17] See *supra* n. 2, 36, 42. Green and Money, *supra* n. 9, 249.

[18] See *supra* n. 2, 41: 'There are presently 12 research and treatment teams aiding the transsexual in the United States and Canada' (Comment, *supra*, n. 6, 973).

[19] For a comparison with selected foreign jurisdictions, see Comment, *supra* n. 6, 979–89, particularly the well-known Argentinian cases and the Jorgensen case in Denmark. Meyers (*supra* n. 11, 61–2) has a good summary of the United States position; see also Green and Money, *supra* n. 9, chs. 28–32, on the medical-legal aspects of transsexualism in the United States, England, Sweden, and Denmark over the last 15 years.

[20] A leading criminal law text, after reviewing the law on surgical operations for medical purposes, concludes that the law is 'in an uncertain state and one depending very much on the views of the judge as to what is desirable, and what is undesirable, conduct' (Smith and Hogan, *Criminal Law*, 1st edn., Butterworths, 1965), p. 268. Cf. specifically on conversion surgery the view of Professor James in Green and Money, *supra* n. 11, ch. 30, with that of G. Williams in 'Consent and Public Policy' (1962) Crim. LR, 154.

[21] This is the standard I would also impose in such surgery as sterilization or lobotomy. It is indeed the practice followed by all the reputable centres specializing in this treatment. Dr Randall of Charing Cross Hospital requires his patients to have lived in the new sex role for at least 6 months. '[H]e does not consider the surgery justified unless there is an "unequivocal demonstration that they are markedly better adjusted in the role they desire than the role they have left"' (Comment, *supra*, n. 6, 974). See further, Stoller, *supra* n. 9, 250–1; Green and Money, *supra* n. 9, chs. 16 and 17, wherein the cautious steps taken to set up a research project at the University of Minnesota are described, particularly the elaborate screening of individuals

The civil law position is less problematical. The situation at present is still that any operation performed by a surgeon is, prima facie, a battery rendered lawful by the consent of the patient. Perhaps this is not the place to repeat the plea made elsewhere that such a legal approach to standard medical procedure is somewhat barbaric.[22] It could well and easily be replaced by a doctrine which has it that the surgeon's act carries liability only if good faith and due care and skill can be shown to be lacking. There is no doubt that, superficially at least, the transsexual consents, is indeed very anxious that surgery be carried out. But is the consent valid, coming as it does from someone who is under severe mental stress? Further, the law requires that the consent be informed, and whatever that may mean, it certainly raises questions about whether the transsexual is fully able to comprehend the implications of surgery, both because of the uncertainty always contingent upon such an operation, and also because of the supervening anxiety which operates to play down, at least before surgery, any consequences which may be inconvenient. Basically these problems attend many surgical operations,[23] and the question resolves itself into whether the transsexual *should be allowed to consent*; whether, in other words, the state has an interest in striking out such consent, and thereby rendering the surgeon who goes ahead liable in tort, on the ground that he cannot rely on such consent. If the matter is dealt with purely on the basis of the doctrine of consent, then I submit that there is no room here for invalidating the transsexual's consent. While the courts should not be slow to protect the unwary from possible error, the transsexual is usually well able to understand what is involved in surgery, and is usually operated on only after careful screening. If these factors were absent, the question would be more difficult. If the law concerned itself instead with the good faith of the doctor, consent would be only one of several relevant criteria. On this view, a doctor could avoid liability only if he could show that, apart from consenting, the patient was carefully studied and examined in a context where specialist medical and psychiatric facilities were available, that the consensus of expert opinion was that surgery was called for, and that this was explained to and understood by the patient before he gave his consent.

---

before surgery. Legal advice was taken, and the view was expressed that the absence of a mayhem statute in the state was 'pivotal' in allowing the project to be established. One very important condition laid down following the example of the Johns Hopkins Gender Identity Committee is that married patients are not accepted until they have obtained a divorce, thus avoiding the confusion created by having two women in a house, mentioned by Ormrod J. (*supra* n. 2, 49). Unfortunately, unscrupulous doctors are always ready to treat transsexuals without imposing conditions if the price is right.

[22] Kennedy, 'Alive or Dead', *supra*, n. 1.

[23] A striking parallel is the removal of a kidney from a live donor who is closely related to the donee and whose 'consent' may be gained through family pressure or temporary altruism; see *Ethics in Medical Progress, A Ciba Foundation Symposium* (Churchill, 1966), p. 78 *et seq.*

The next set of legal problems which falls for discussion concerns the situation of the transsexual once operated upon. The desire to pass as a member of the preferred sex has been in part satisfied by surgery. The person who emerges from such treatment is usually superficially, and often on close examination, convincing in the new sex role. What is still required, however, is recognition of the 'changed' sex by 'officialdom'. For it cannot be emphasized too much that the transsexual, even after conversion surgery, continually seeks reassurance that she is now accepted in her new sex role. It follows that this quest for reassurance will cause her to seek out situations in which some sort of official sanction will be given to her change. In other words, two forces operate to raise the problems to be discussed: first, the natural desire to avoid awkward, embarrassing, or unmanageable social situations, situations which challenge the perception of the new role; and second, the almost perverse and in a way contradictory claim to be accepted totally and without reservation.

The question which serves as a starting-point is why there should be legal obstacles to the recognition of the transsexual's change. What business is it of the State if someone now wishes to be known as a woman, where previously she was considered a man? Obviously the State has an interest in regulating the behaviour of its citizens.[24] So, equally obviously, the question becomes, what disruption to normal regulation would be caused by recognizing the change, always bearing in mind the rarity of the situation, and that even if some disruption were shown, it might not be sufficiently serious to warrant withholding recognition?

Recognition can operate at various levels. Mere documentation of the new identity may be sought through changes in various papers.[25] Further, some of the privileges incident to membership of the new sex may be sought. These privileges may range from the relatively inconspicuous one of being treated differently for insurance purposes to the ultimate extreme of contracting a

---

[24] 'The fundamental purpose of law is the regulation of the relations between persons, and between persons and the state or community' (*supra* n. 2, 48).

[25] This in itself may be a major difficulty. April Ashley failed to obtain a changed birth certificate, though she successfully obtained an insurance card as a woman and a passport (*supra* n. 2, 38). See Comment, *supra* n. 6, 992–1003, which lists 15 states in the United States which permit post-operative change of sex designation on birth records by statute. Of particular interest is the practice in Minnesota, not specifically sanctioned by statute, whereby a new birth certificate is issued with a code number which indicates that a previous certificate exists. This latter practice prevents the possibility of fraud if the code number is known to relevant agencies. It could well be adopted in the United Kingdom. See also Green and Money, *supra* n. 9, on a similar practice adopted in Baltimore (p. 261), and ch. 29 for a general survey of the United States position; compare, however, the decision in *Anonymous* v. *Weiner*, 270 NYS 2d 319 (1966) refusing an application for a new birth certificate, criticized in a later New York case, *In re Anonymous*, 293 NYS 2d 834 (1968), which, however, directed only that a copy of the court order recognizing the petitioner's new sex be attached to the birth certificate—wholly inadequate relief. A Scottish Court in 1957 likewise refused to change the original sex registration of a proven transsexual (Meyers, *supra* n. 11, 55).

'marriage with a member of the opposite sex'—opposite, that is, to the adopted one. To the layman, logic might seem to compel that acceptance by the State of a person as a female for one purpose or at one level would necessarily mean acceptance of the person as a female for all purposes, on the simple reasoning that acceptance means what it says. This, indeed, was the view taken by counsel for Miss Ashley.[26] But the law has never felt obliged to follow such rational simplicity if there are good reasons for doing otherwise.[27] The reasons advanced in *Corbett* therefore become critical. Ormrod J., noting that this was 'the first occasion on which a Court in England has been called on to decide the sex of an individual',[28] felt constrained to find that 'legal relations can be classified into those in which the sex of the individuals concerned is either irrelevant, relevant or an essential determinant of the nature of the relationship.'[29] Whatever view is taken of this analysis, and it will be discussed more fully below, it seems to state quite clearly that the determination of sex is a matter for lawyers and courts; that the law, in other words, must establish methods for determining sex which may or may not correspond to medical opinion. That the court is entitled to establish its own classification system has been seen already. But it has been further seen that strong justification is needed for adopting a system at variance with prevailing medical views. How does Ormrod J. justify his decision?[30] He sets down some, though not all, of the medical criteria for determining sex,[31] and resolves that these criteria, while relevant, 'do not necessarily decide the legal basis of sex determination'.[32] Fundamentally, therefore, he implies that other factors, or criteria, are of heavier weight in making the classification. But then he proceeds to limit his enquiry to the medical criteria put before him. In other words, rather than introducing other,

---

[26] *Supra* n. 2, 47.

[27] Edward Lyons, MP, talks of society dealing with the problem of transsexuals 'on an ex tempore *ad hoc* basis . . . Mr. Justice Ormrod . . . came down to this test—that the sex of the parties at birth must be looked at . . . other Departments of State have taken a different view'; e.g. the Ministry of Social Security, 'Society is faced with a choice of continuing to deal with this matter on various different bases or regulating the law to insure that there is a uniform code for transsexuals, that they must behave according to their original admitted sex or that they can in certain circumstances behave as members of the opposite sex. I would favour, because it is more humane, this latter view' (*Hansard, supra* n. 11, 1845–6). Compare the different treatment of minors in terms of their legal capacity to engage in different activities.

[28] *Supra* n. 2, 47.　　　　　　　　　　　　　　　　　　　　　　　　　　[29] Ibid. 48.

[30] Five distinguished experts gave evidence before Ormrod J., and it must be admitted that their conclusions did not all point one way. But, I submit, this can be explained by the fact that they were asked to concentrate only on biological sex, a point which will be taken up later (*supra* n. 2, 41–3).

[31] *Supra* n. 2, 44, cites five criteria. Others list eight factors (Comment, *supra* n. 6, 965); Money lists nine variables (Green and Money, *supra* n. 9, 91–3). The point, however, is not how many there are, but the fact that they may not all point one way; the more criteria one recognizes, the greater the likelihood of divergence, and the stronger the case for allowing the psyche of the individual to prevail in difficult cases.　　　　　　　[32] *Supra* n. 2, 24.

more persuasive factors, he merely sets up the court as the arbiter of a medical issue, and decides that, of all the criteria involved, the crucial ones for determining how the individual is to be regarded by the law are the biological criteria. Psychological criteria are thus given no weight, despite the fact that the medical evidence is that where the two sets of criteria clash, the only effective treatment is to try to reconcile the clash in favour of the psychological. Ormrod J., in ignoring the psyche of the individual, seems to assume that the distinction between the criteria is effectively one between what is ordained (biological) and what is chosen (psychological). But this overlooks two points: first, that the transsexual is living proof that, in actuality, the psyche may operate in defiance of biological truths regardless of what the law says it *should* do; second, that the psyche is not necessarily formed by choice, but may instead be determined for the individual by forces operating on him during its development.[33] The judge, therefore, sets up a legal scale for weighing the relative importance of solely medical criteria, without giving any justification for his choice, without advancing sound *non-medical* criteria, and despite the fact that expert opinion would have him avoid such an inflexible position.

Surely if the courts and lawyers limit themselves to medical criteria as justifying their sex classification system, they must follow expert opinion. There are, of course, instances in other areas of the law where such opinion is ignored, and where one searches in vain for a reasoned articulation of justification based on sound policy, but they usually serve as food for the argument that in so doing the law becomes an ass. What possible sense can there be in a legal rule, for example, which has it that a woman is presumed fertile even though she is past menopause or has undergone a hysterectomy operation? The area of medical jurisprudence is replete with such absurdities, which date from an earlier age when superstition was a substitute for knowledge. Attention should surely be directed towards eliminating such anomalies, rather than entrenching them further into the law. The assertion that the courts are now in the business of adjudicating on the complex issue of sex is not a happy development towards this goal. For the courts to take upon themselves the task of making this determination is a stultifying, even a discrediting, exercise.

This is not the same situation as in those areas of the law where there are medical concepts which are not in fact accepted without further refinement by courts; the notion of what constitutes therapy[34] is such an issue, as are,

---

[33] For this reason, some experts point to the 'sex of rearing' as a critical criterion. Stoller demonstrates that a not unusual factor in the aetiology of transsexuals is the perverse desire of the parent(s) to raise the boy as a girl, since a girl was what was desired (or vice versa) (*supra* n. 9, 11).

[34] Ormrod J. states that an operation is lawful 'if . . . undertaken for genuine therapeutic purposes' (*supra* n. 2, 43). This is, with respect, somewhat over-simple. Therapy means more

for example, the concepts of insanity and paternity. Here the courts see themselves as charged with evaluating such concepts further and, when necessary, imposing their own views. The justification advanced—and clearly it has some validity—is that medical opinion is divided, or, more important, that the legal concept is of a *different nature* from the medical, involving considerations other than the mere question of scientific evidence, such as notions of responsibility or the common good. In this way, the legal view of insanity really becomes a view regarding whether someone should be held responsible. If the term 'insanity' were not used, this would be more obvious; for it would show that the purely medical issue of insanity was only one factor involved in the legal determination.

So, the wheel turns full circle, and the question is again asked, if there is a medical view regarding the determination of sex, what arguments exist for having a legal concept which coexists, but is not coextensive? The answer seems to hinge on the analysis of Ormrod J. mentioned above. In situations where sex is not an 'essential determinant' of a legal relationship, he appears to see no reason for denying recognition of the transsexual's change. To this extent, then, he finds that the law will go along with the medical determination. As this medical view is based fundamentally on the gender identity and self-image of the transsexual, he implies that the law is prepared to concede that in most circumstances sex determination is a matter for the individual. But, as will be seen shortly, this individual freedom has limits. This means, then, that the transsexual may obtain the necessary documentation of the new sex, and in many ways carry on as 'normal' a life as possible in the new role. As was pointed out in the judgment, 'In some contractual relationships, for example life assurance and pensions schemes— some aspects of the law regulating conditions of employment, and . . . various state-run schemes such as national insurance',[35] it is ultimately a matter for the parties concerned whether the individual should be treated as a man or a woman. Miss Ashley had in fact, except as regards changing her birth certificate, overcome all these obstacles to acceptance.

---

than curing a physical illness, though how much more depends more on views of social policy than on medical evidence. Extracting a tooth or an appendix is clearly therapeutic; so is removing a wart or fixing a nose, though here no physical illness is involved. Abortions and sterilizations and, *a fortiori*, sex conversion operations raise difficulties. They are performed for the most part on healthy patients. They are justified on the ground not of physical illness, but of mental well-being. The decision is made that the patient needs the operation, that it is 'good' for him. The question is what limits exist on this view of what constitutes therapy. The issue comes down to who should decide what is 'good' for the patient, the patient himself, his doctor, or the public through the courts. As Meyers cautions, 'it is unwise and impossible for the surgeon to solve all psychological urges and needs by physical operation. It is unlawful for a physician to . . . cut off the arm of a patient who wants to stop masturbating' (*supra* n. 11, 67).

[35] *Supra* n. 2, 48.

But the one type of legal relationship closed to her is that in which sex is an 'essential determinant'. In these cases, the individual cannot have his way. Here, according to Ormrod J., the law recognizes a need to impose its own classification and ignore the weight of medical opinion. The examples of such 'relationships' mentioned in the case are certain sexual offences, adultery, and marriage.[36] Now the criminal law makes heavy weather of the issue of sex change only if over-rigid conceptualism is maintained and common sense abandoned. It makes no sense at all to tell an attractive transsexual employed as a secretary, possessed of all the necessary documentation of her sex change and all the physical attributes of her new sex— breasts, female figure, and vagina (albeit a constructed one)—that she can pass as a woman, but cannot be raped because she is a man. A criminal court which admitted such a defence would never hear the end of it. Equally, common sense demands that the operated transsexual should not be able to avoid prosecution and conviction for soliciting or importuning, as the case may be, by suddenly adopting for the duration of the trial the prior and now abandoned sex.[37] The issues become more difficult, however, and more difficult to approach free from emotional bias, when the real problem, that of marriage, is considered.

Since marriage is essentially a relationship between man and woman, the validity of the marriage depends . . . on whether the respondent [Miss Ashley] is or is not a woman. . . . The question then becomes what is meant by the word 'woman' in the single context of marriage, for I am not concerned to determine the 'legal sex' of the respondent at large.[38]

Since marriage has an 'essentially heterosexual character',[39] the criteria used to assess 'womanhood' must, Ormrod J. asserts, be *biological*. For, he reasons, only a *biological* female 'is naturally capable of performing the

---

[36] Ibid; cf. the position of Green: '[i]t is an issue for civil libertarians to consider whether it should be the rightful concern of the law to deny one the right to dress as one wishes, conduct one's life in a preferred gender role, privately conduct one's sexual relationship as preferred by oneself and one's partner and even intermarry in the preferred sexual role' (Green and Money, *supra* n. 9, 472).

[37] See the report in the *Guardian*, 9 June 1970, p. 5. The jury acquitted one Rachel Browne of the charge 'that she, being a man, persistently importuned in a public place for immoral purposes'. Miss Browne was apparently an operated transsexual, and the police, on discovering this, felt constrained to prosecute her as a man. The jury, apparently, was not impressed by the prosecution argument: '[n]o matter how much one might sympathize with people who felt emotionally on the wrong side of the fence, the facts in the case were perfectly plain. If one was born a man, one legally remained a man. The jury would hear that "this unfortunate man" had had a certain operation in 1966, but that made no difference. He remained a man'. See however, the comment of Mr Abse concerning the difficulties encountered by transsexuals who have 'well-founded anxieties that they may fall foul of the Justice of the Peace Act, 1361, which unfortunately is over-frequently used against them' (*Hansard*, *supra* n. 11, 1843). Clearly, therefore, there are still opportunities for the criminal law to be used discriminatingly, without overt reference to sex; see also Comment, *supra* n. 6, 989–92

[38] *Supra* n. 2, 48.   [39] Ibid.

essential role of a woman in marriage'.[40] Besides begging the whole question by using the word 'heterosexual', the tautology of this explanation is striking. All that Ormrod J. is in fact saying is that there has to be a woman in a marriage, because someone has to perform the essential role of a woman in the marriage, and this essential role is to be a woman, biologically so determined. This may be a valid conclusion. Its validity becomes somewhat suspect, however, if the foundation on which Ormrod J. rests his conclusion is examined.

Sex is clearly an essential determinant of the relationship called marriage, because it is and always has been recognized as the union of man and woman. It is the institution on which the family is built, and in which the capacity for *natural*[41] *heterosexual intercourse* is an *essential* element. It has, of course, many other characteristics, of which companionship and mutual support is an important one, but the characteristics which distinguish it from all other relationships can only be met by two persons of the opposite sex.[42]

This is a transparently 'essentialist' approach. Ormrod J. purports to identify the *essence* of marriage as a 'relationship between man and woman'; but to meet the problems implicit in this idea, he must go further and define it in terms of the capacity for 'natural heterosexual intercourse'. If the whole of his decision and, *ex hypothesi*, the whole nature of marriage rests on this thesis, then indeed a fragile edifice has been constructed. For what becomes of the marriage between two 70-year-olds seeking companionship but with no thoughts of sexual intercourse, let alone family? Is it crucial that they still have the capacity for intercourse? What if the ageing man has in fact lost such capacity? What of a marriage of a male severely disfigured and without genitalia as a result of war or an accident? What of a marriage where the parties, though young, want no family and do not engage in intercourse? The logic of Ormrod J.'s decision must cause us to say that the male in these examples is no longer able to perform the essential role of a male—that is, assert his biological maleness—and is not, therefore, a male for the purposes of marriage, and that therefore there is no marriage. Admittedly the examples all relate to men, since it is easier to imagine ways in which a male may lose the 'capacity' for intercourse, but what is sauce for the goose must be sauce for the gander.[43]

---

[40] Ibid.

[41] Note the rejection of the terms 'natural' and 'unnatural' in relation to sexual behaviour by the Report of the Committee on Homosexual Offences and Prostitution, on the grounds that 'they depend for their force upon certain explicit theological or philosophical interpretations, and without these interpretations their use imports an approving or a condemnatory note into a discussion where dispassionate thought and statement should not be hindered by adherence to particular preconceptions' (Cmnd. 247, para. 35, p. 17); my footnote.

[42] *Supra* n. 2, 48; my emphasis.   [43] Or is it vice-versa?

If this is the justification we seek for abandoning medical sex classification and resorting to a legal method, then it cannot defend itself from reproach.[44] Yet Ormrod J. follows his own logic to conclude that April Ashley, in purely biological terms, is not a woman; yet biological terms are all that count, because there has to be someone who can perform the essential role of a woman (remember, the essential role is to be a woman, since marriage is the relationship between a man and a woman): therefore, for marriage purposes, April Ashley by law is a man, and there is no marriage.[45]

No way out of this particular self-made legal thicket is provided, unfortunately, by an amendment to the Nullity of Marriages Act, passed into law as section 1(c). In that section, it is provided that a marriage is *void* if 'the parties are not respectively male and female'. This amendment was proposed and incorporated into the Act as a direct result of the decision in *Corbett*. Its principal avowed aim was to give legislative form to the decision, contrary to the recommendation of the Law Commission,[46] and thereby allow the parties in these 'tragic cases' the dignity of a decree of nullity so that, if thought fit, provision for ancillary relief could be made by the court, and the unsavoury examination of their sexuality, rendered necessary if the only recourse were a declaration of status, could be avoided. But the subsection tantalizingly offers more than it gives. The 'neutral' terms of 'male' and 'female' are used. The justification for this was expressed to be that it would thus be open to a court at a later date to review the matter of sex determination

[44] David Green, in criticizing the decision, makes a further, telling point: 'conversely, where a 'normal' marriage has taken place, and subsequently either spouse is discovered to be a transsexual, the factual adaptation of the individual to the gender with which he identifies is *in itself* apparently of no significance. Despite the fact that in the case one may have effectively two men or two women married to each other the law presumably shuts its eyes and regards the transsexual spouse as he is biologically identified' (*New Law Journal*, 120, 26 Feb. 1970, p. 210).

[45] In defending the decision, Edward Lyons, MP, remarked: '[S]ociety must have a situation where the family comes prominently into consideration. The family is based on the union of man and woman. A woman effectively, I suppose, is thought to have the capacity to procreate. In those circumstances, I support the law as laid down in the *Corbett* case' (*Hansard, supra*, n. 11, 1849). This seems circuitous, if not downright obscure, and what does it have to do with marriage? Compare also the reasoning of Alexander Lyon: '[a] compassionate society ought to be able to allow to exist situations where biological males who believe they are female are treated in circumstances when it makes no difference to anyone else as female. . . . But when such people enter into a relationship with another person which is as intimate and as fundamental as marriage even the most compassionate society should say "Here we cannot go with you; here we must draw the line; although we understand and sympathize with your distress, we find it impossible here to be that compassionate, because *here the relationship also affects intimately some other member of society whose rights and feelings have to be considered*" ' (*Hansard, supra* n. 11, 1854; my emphasis). I confess that the relevance of the words I emphasize is unclear to me.

[46] Law Commission, *supra* n. 3. The view of the Commission was that *Corbett* should not remain law, and that matrimonial relief (possible if a decree of nullity were granted) 'is not appropriate'. It was conceded, however, that 'the question involved is an issue of social policy on which Parliament will be the judge.'

in the light of further evidence, and possibly reach a conclusion other than that reached by Ormrod J.[47] But this deserves closer examination. The legislators are trying to have their cake and eat it too. For two alternative conclusions follow from their position. If they hold the view that by using 'neutral' words, they allow for change in the future, they ignore the fact that the only change, at least from the medical viewpoint, will be a further confirmation of the existing medical opinion that in certain individuals there may be a conflict between sex and gender, which conflict can be resolved only by allowing gender identity to prevail. They must, then, accept the possibility that gender identity will come to be considered as the *primary* sex classification index. Thus, someone considering himself a male should be recognized as a male, even for the purposes of marriage. They are thus countenancing precisely the situation in the *Corbett* case, though legislating to declare the union in that case void. In fact, their position must cause them to go further than *Corbett*, and contemplate the recognition of a union of two homosexuals as a marriage if one of the two decides to consider himself a member of the opposite sex for the purposes of marriage. But this is what all who spoke on the bill refused, with varying degrees of vehemence, to countenance.[48] On the other hand, if gender identity is *not* to prevail, the dichotomy of male and female can only find its reflection in the dichotomy of biological male sex and biological female sex. If this is the case, then section 1(c) of the Act, for all its vaunted progressiveness and liberality, entrenches the law as found by Ormrod J. in *Corbett*; for the court refused to look at Miss Ashley's gender identity to discover her maleness or femaleness. The courts in future will thus remain the arbiter of the issue of sex determination, though admitting that it is a medical issue and offering no good reason for ignoring medical opinion.[49]

---

[47] *Hansard, supra* n. 11, 1832, 1852.

[48] See e.g. *Hansard, supra* n. 11, 1829, 1837 (the Solicitor-General considered it 'out of consonance with reality'), 1838 (Leo Abse, MP, did not, however, 'boggle at the idea of a marriage between homosexuals', but agreed that it should not be introduced 'as a side effect of a Nullity Bill'), and 1844.

[49] See *Hansard, supra* n. 11, 1832–3; Mr Lyon, MP, demonstrates clearly the confusion in the minds of the legislators: '[T]he way that a Judge decides the sex of a particular person is and always will remain a question of fact. It is a question of fact which will change with the change in medical opinion. . . . If medical opinion were that the mere sex-change operation was enough to change a person from a man to a woman or a woman to a man, that would be the end of the case. . . . If in the end medical opinion is able to state with greater certainty who is male and who is female on tests which were not applied in the *Corbett* case, then some new court can apply those tests because the evidence will have changed and the question of fact, therefore, will also have changed.' In other words, the courts must maintain the *biological* distinction betweeen male and female. But doctors in the case of transsexuals are not concerned· with *changing sex*. They cannot. (See the statement on the consent form: 'I understand that it [the conversion operation] *will not alter my male sex* and that it is being done to prevent deterioration in my mental health' (*supra* n. 2, 42; my emphasis)). The courts ask the wrong question — has the person changed sex? The doctors are not concerned with sex; they want to be asked — what is the gender identity of the person? A hopeless impasse between the law and medicine is thus created. Transsexuals will continue as Mr Abse, MP, suggested, 'to live under

Ormrod J.'s decision, much cited and approved of in the House of Commons debate,[50] evidently will remain the law.

Instead, the following submission may be advanced. First, April Ashley should have been recognized as a female. This would have involved giving the criterion of gender identity precedence over physiological criteria. Since this is the rationale behind treatment of the operated transsexual — namely, causing the physiological profile to conform as much as possible to the gender identity — it is not of itself outrageous.[51] Second, the union of two people who have the same biological sex, but one of whom is an operated transsexual with a female gender identity should be recognized as a marriage.[52] Section 1(c) of the Nullity of Marriage Act should, therefore, either be repealed or be given the wide, radical, but unintended, interpretation outlined above.

Immediately, problems present themselves to the fertile legal mind, and the final part of this paper will concentrate on exploring the implications of this submission.

a law which is too hidebound, too rigid and, perhaps, too frightened to acknowledge that not all the human race can be neatly divided into two — and only two — separate compartments. Nature does not obey man-made laws, and although this may be inconvenient to the lawyers, law commissioners, and legislators, we would be unjust and unfair if we persist in continuing to believe that Nature is not often shamelessly untidy. We have in our community a small group of people on whom Nature has played a tragic trick and, because of this, they live in a twilight world and our laws can do little to rescue them from their fate. We would indeed be an insensitive Parliament if we allowed the passing of this Bill without amendment, for that would push these people yet further into a bewildering limbo' (*Hansard, supra* n. 11, 1834). Mr Abse's own amendment (*Hansard, supra* n. 11, 1827) which went some way towards meeting my own objections was, however, withdrawn.   [50] See *Hansard, supra* n. 11, 1830, 1846, 1850.

[51] As Mr Abse argued, 'I do not believe that we as lawyers should be trying to have law which sabotages the work which surgeons and psychiatrists are doing to enable a person happily to become reconciled to her fate. . . . If a person believes she is a woman, even if the biologically male characteristics are present, such a person should be acknowledged as a person and should not be placed in this limbo' (*Hansard, supra* n. 11, 1842).

[52] This appears to be a position acceptable to Mr Abse (*Hansard, supra* n. 11, 1837). The prevalence of already existing 'marriages' cannot be estimated. Two have come before the English courts (*supra* n. 2 and *Talbot* v. *Talbot*, 111 *Sol. J.* 214, 17 Mar. 1967) but many more may exist, though it is generally conceded to be a rare phenomenon. The figures in the United States seem far greater. Stoller (in a telephone conversation) confirmed that many of his patients subsequently 'marry', in that they go through a ceremony in which a judge thinks that he is marrying a biological female to a biological male, often in Las Vegas, Nevada, or in other states not requiring a birth certificate prior to issuing a marriage licence — e.g., Florida (see Bowman and Engle, *supra* n. 11, 308, for discussion of a Florida marriage) — or in Mexico. The validity of such marriages has yet to be challenged in the United States. In one extraordinary case a court *ordered* a conversion operation on a 17-year-old transsexual boy with a record of delinquency after hearing evidence from experts at Johns Hopkins University, reported in Meyers, *supra* n. 11, 61. Should this person later wish to marry, it would be hard to deny her that right. Meyers also writes: 'Dr. Harry Benjamin, reporting on the performance of 44 conversion operations, notes that 12 . . . had since been married, some divorced, and one granted a legal child adoption' (ibid). Green and Money report that patients have married and adopted children (*supra* n. 11, 336). Stürup reports an odd case of a male-to-female transsexual marrying a female and then undergoing sex-change surgery. The court, for reasons which are not clear, declared the marriage void as the husband 'was no longer a male' — the converse of the *Corbett* decision (ibid. 459). See Comment, *supra* n. 6, 1003–9.

The first and most obvious question which can be asked is, why call the union between a man and an operated transsexual a 'marriage'? The question as to what is involved in the marriage relationship deserves a study in itself. Reasons of space alone demand that what may appear to be a contentious response to this question be suggested, rather than developed. First, marriage as a legal institution developed, I submit, as an essential legal first step towards amassing wealth and power by uniting partners with these attributes and endowing with legitimacy their heirs so as to guarantee inheritance according to articulated and certain principles. In other words, doubts as to the proper division of property at death, as well as rights between living partners, were resolved by having legal rules prescribing a formula, but only applying within the context of a sanctioned, and thereby state-controlled, relationship. Side by side with such unions existed, and still exist, unions not sanctioned by law. It is not a coincidence that these unions are most common among the poor, for what do they care about legitimacy and inheritance?[53] Besides this materialist aspect, marriage in Western society developed a complex overlay of social connotations. These involve the intangible, yet very real, personal and spiritual qualities the institution has come to represent. For it has come to pass that through marriage certain feelings are communicated by the partners to each other and, more important, to society at large. By going through a particular formality, a qualitatively different posture is presented by the parties. They represent to the world that theirs is a relationship based on strong human emotions, exclusive commitment to each other, and permanence. Put another way, they wish to say, and indeed advertise, that there is nothing transient, superficial, or casual in the way they view each other *and wish to be viewed*. The world is invited to see their relationship in a very special way. The crucial importance of this point will be seen later. Only two developments are worthy of note, both of which serve to substantiate further the notion of the institution as formalizing and legitimizing property arrangements: first, the gradual recognition of the right to end the relationship (with greater ease as social mobility increases and old class structures requiring protection of their pedigree collapse) on the condition that the more vulnerable party economically be protected; and the corollary idea that, given the possibility of separation and divorce, while the relationship subsists, certain mutual rights of support exist for the partners. This overall picture of the marriage relationship would not be complete, however, without some reference to its role as a device imposing 'decency and respectability' by regulating 'indiscriminate child-bearing'. Intercourse,

---

[53] See e.g. such writings of Oscar Lewis as *Children of Sanchez* (Random House, 1961); *La Vida* (Random House, 1965). The notion of the 'common-law marriage' known to some states in the United States further reinforces my thesis. For, although the legal formalities of marriage are absent, a long-standing relationship is given partial recognition through the use of the concept of marriage, just so that certain property rights can be recognized as between the parties.

since it usually produced offspring, was only to be tolerated in a controlled and formalized context. Clearly, this policing role, giving legal form to religious doctrine, and generally making for an ordered and 'tidy' society, was never successfully performed. Changes in the values of society, the status of illegitimates, and the advent of reliable birth-control devices robbed the institution of marriage of much of its regulatory quality in the area of sexual behaviour.

If this analysis of marriage, though no doubt over-simple and lacking subtlety, has some validity, then an argument clearly exists for extending it to relationships previously outside its scope. For other types of relationship do exist in which the parties may desire the system of rights and duties which flow from the legal concept of marriage, while—and this is a critical point—the common law is singularly lacking in alternative forms of institutionalized and legitimate union. If marriage exists to create some kind of secure relationship, from which flow mutual rights and expectations, and to provide a stable environment for raising children, if there be any, but is not predicated solely on the opportunity for intercourse, then it can legitimately be extended to cover the union of two persons, one of whom is an operated transsexual. Instability, with its consequent social and personal price, haunts the lives of the socially abnormal. The pressures and prejudices which attend their activities and relationships only exacerbate their instability. To offer a means of institutionalizing their relationships (which, if given the opportunity, would perhaps be as stable as the average 'normal' modern marriage), thereby guaranteeing some rights of continued support between the parties, would thus serve as a valuable method of ameliorating a particular social ill. Children would not be a natural product of such a union, so that objections directed at the welfare and support of a family would not apply.

The issue has been considered so far in the narrow context of a union between an *operated* transsexual and another. Such unions are so rare that, of course, they pose no real problem or threat for the legal system. Clearly the real difficulties begin, and the issue becomes of real concern, when the argument so far advanced is taken further. If the skeletal analysis of marriage proposed above is accepted, why should relationships between *unoperated* transsexuals and others be excluded? More fundamental, and not to be avoided, is the question of whether homosexual unions should be excluded. This, a particularly wide and extraordinarily far-reaching implication, obviously lurks within the interstices of the decision in *Corbett*. Ormrod J. was no doubt acutely aware of what a decision in favour of Miss Ashley could be construed as meaning, even if in fact it were limited, as it can be on the arguments advanced above, to its particular and very unusual facts. The classic common-law dilemma presented itself. A hard case calls for decision. But, in a precedent system, any decision becomes a springboard for further litigation. The lid of Pandora's box could be wrenched off or tightly sat upon.

To decide for Miss Ashley in this context could be, therefore, to question a vast area of social values and philosophy. It is little wonder that Ormrod J. considered this the task of others in other places, and chose to sit firmly on the lid.

Let us examine first the situation of the unoperated transsexual. He may have received psychotherapy, but has not yet undergone conversion surgery even if he is contemplating it. First of all, the problem exists of determining whether in fact the 'condition' of transsexualism exists. If it does not, and the person is merely displaying sexual ambivalence short of transsexualism, then the issue is really one of giving recognition to what amounts to a homosexual union, and will be discussed below. The second difficulty involves the question of fraud. This is a problem whether the transsexual is operated on or not, but is seen in greater relief if he is not. The possibility exists of a friendship developing between a transsexual and someone else, which eventually leads to thoughts of marriage.[54] Even in these days of permissiveness, it may be that the one party has not had, or has been denied, the opportunity of discovering the anatomical characteristics of the other. It is not difficult to imagine the shock which would attend such discovery after being deceived into marriage. In the case of the operated transsexual, the discovery may never be made. If this possibility of fraud is not to be an insurmountable barrier to recognizing such unions as marriages, what is the solution? Any purported marriage contracted in a context of improperly gained consent is, since the Nullity of Marriages Act 1971, voidable. The party thus deceived would therefore be able subsequently to avoid the marriage. Is this enough, particularly in the case of the operated transsexual, remembering that proceedings for a decree of nullity must now be instituted within three years of the date of the marriage? There is no denying that this is a severe problem. But it must be addressed. Let me repeat the thesis being developed: namely, that marriage as an institution should be extended, on the basis of the argument presented, not only to the transsexual, but also to homosexual unions. If it is conceded that the really explosive issue concerns the homosexual, and that the situation of the transsexual is a rare phenomenon, then difficulties which arise within that spectrum of rarity should not be allowed to defeat the whole force of the thesis. The following therefore is suggested. It is in the nature of a marriage relationship that partners once married discover things about each other that were previously unnoticed or concealed. No partner has a guarantee that the other will turn out exactly as he or she would wish. Therefore, in the unlikely event that

---

[54] For an incredible, yet pathetic, example of fraud, maintained for over three years of marriage by a female-to-male transsexual, see Green and Money, *supra* n. 11, 69. Interestingly, in the light of what has been said above, in this case, after discovery and diagnosis, conversion surgery was recommended, but the hospital administration refused to sanction it, fearing the legal complications which might ensue. See further ibid. 186–7.

a ceremony of marriage is performed between an unoperated transsexual and someone who is unaware of the partner's condition, the remedy of a petition for nullity must suffice, grounded on the fact that the marriage is voidable because of the fraud of the other and the consequent lack of valid consent of the innocent party. This would mean that a marriage did exist; but doubtless it would not be beyond the wit of the courts to arrange things so that the question of ancillary relief received short shrift. It would also mean that the Nullity of Marriages Act, section 2(c), must be interpreted so that this type of fraud comes within its terms. Section 2, (a) and (b), of the Statute[55] is not relied on here, for reasons which will be obvious later.

Where the fraud is perpetrated by an operated transsexual, the innocent party will have the same remedy until the expiration of three years. If the extremely unlikely event transpires that in three years he has discovered nothing of his partner's past, then why should he complain? The only reason must be the absence of a family. The most cursory testing would explain why no children have been produced. If he undertakes such tests and discovers the truth, should he then be able to jettison his partner, otherwise presumably to his liking? In many ways, he is in the same position as a husband who finds that his wife is infertile. The route of divorce may ultimately be open to him, but to give him more may, in the context of this argument, be unfair. In addition, however, he will undoubtedly experience considerable psychic shock, for he will have discovered that his wife is a biological male — that, in crude, popular terms, he has married a man. The fact that this revelation would doubtless be made in a context of privacy and confidentiality so as to insulate him as far as possible from the prying eyes of scandalmongers may not reduce his desire to put actual and legal distance between himself and his spouse. Therefore it is suggested that for the husband whose outrage forecloses the possibility of a mere divorce proceeding, a clear case exists for having the courts carve out an exception to the three-year rule so as to allow a suit to be brought for nullity through fraud or mistake.[56] To the protesting reader who may feel that this spurious reasoning leads us into the realm of nonsense, the only answer is that it is the purpose of this paper to provoke a re-examination of certain fundamental values and ideas.

Another way out of the problem of fraud could be to require from both parties the presentation of a birth certificate as a prerequisite for the issuing of a marriage licence, as is done in some states in the United States. The registrar could be obliged to report the matter to one party when there appears to be some irregularity between the registered sex and the appearance of the

---

[55] A marriage shall be voidable on the ground: S. 2(a) 'that the marriage has not been consummated owing to the incapacity of either party to consummate it; (b) that the marriage has not been consummated owing to the wilful refusal of the respondent to consummate it.'

[56] See further on the question of fraud, Law Commission Report, *supra* n. 3, para. 32, p. 16.

other party. This would be obvious from the birth certificate if unchanged; and if, as has been proposed,[57] an amended certificate has been granted, the code used to signal this fact would alert the registrar. It is a matter for debate whether the introduction of further administrative duties is justified in terms of the dimensions of the problem being dealt with.

What, then, of the homosexual union? Should such a union be called a marriage? This, after all, is the real issue lurking in *Corbett*. As has been said, technically, it need not be raised in disagreeing with Ormrod J., but surely it cannot be avoided. The Sexual Offences Act 1967[58] removed some of the aura of instability and guilt which hitherto surrounded the lives of homosexuals. Partnerships could henceforth be established between consenting adults so that 'two men could live permanently together without fearing prattling informers bringing down the criminal law upon them'.[59] Where, then, is the need to harness the concept of marriage to suit their needs? Why not invent some other legal concept or, for example, use the legal notion of partnership? To this latter suggestion, the homosexual can simply reply that he wants his relationship to be a marriage and nothing short of this, and can see no reason to justify the denial of his request. A partnership connotes a *business* relationship, whereas what is being sought is institutionalization of a *domestic* relationship.[60] Only marriage has for him the required social connotations, expressing the kind of personal and social commitment mentioned earlier. Furthermore, as regards the former suggestion, a new institution analogous to, but not the same as, marriage, would lack the very special connotations inextricably involved in the marriage union of two people who feel strongly for each other and desire to bear witness to this feeling to the world. Marriage is the institution which suggests this quality; and is the only type of domestic relationship known to the common law from which flow rights and expectations prescribed by law. If this is the case, rather than attempt to invent a new conceptual framework, there is much to be said for turning to marriage as the one, already existing legal concept which has the obvious potential for expansion so as to provide the institutional framework for such a union.

But, the argument runs, this apparently attractive reasoning offends us. Marriage, even if it does not rest for its validity on the capacity for 'normal heterosexual intercourse', has an intrinsic quality of bisexuality. Granted, hypothetically, that it may be a flexible legal concept, it nonetheless is of a nature which does not extend to the union of two people of the same sex.[61]

---

[57] See *supra* n. 24.   [58] 15 and 16 Eliz. 2, c. 60.   [59] *Hansard, supra* n. 11, 1837.

[60] See *Pheasant* v. *Pheasant*, where Ormrod J. (as it happened) pointed out that 'Parliament has not yet completely assimilated the law relating to marriage with the law of partnership,' in [1972] All ER 587, 589.

[61] Cf. the intuitive reasoning of Alexander Lyon, MP, that a homosexual relationship 'would be contrary to any understanding of the Churches about what is the *nature* of marriage. It would certainly counter what I regard as the *proper* basis of English marriage' (*Hansard, supra* n. 11, 1829; my emphasis).

Here, Ormrod J.'s view may be recalled. Given that he may have fallen victim of an essentialist fallacy, is he not right in asserting that marriage as always understood is a relationship involving a man and a woman, commonly so defined? Am I not guilty of the same essentialist fallacy if I tear down Ormrod J.'s thesis simply to erect my own property based 'essence' which conveniently allows me, then, to advance my argument concerning homosexual unions? My reply is that I have sought to identify some of the congeries of qualities of the legal institution of marriage, not to identify its 'essence'. As a legal device, it exists for a number of purposes which I have sought to set out. It is true that it has only been considered in the context of people of opposite sex; but that may be primarily because its materialist aspect was developed to *regulate the consequences of such unions*. I am, in this regard, simply challenging received wisdom as to which is the chicken and which the egg.

I am acutely aware of a further objection. While Ormrod J.'s attempt to identify a single definitive criterion for the notion of marriage may falter, there must still be certain *negative* definitive criteria setting the proper limits of the concept. Such a negative criterion could be that the parties should not be of the same sex, as could be the notion that one party should not be an animal. To this I would respond as follows. My analysis of the particular qualities of the institution shows that it may well extend to cover a homosexual union. For, besides the materialist qualities, the spiritual quality of commitment and feeling is as present between homosexual as between heterosexual partners. Equally, I am prepared to advocate that, in historical terms, the time has arrived, in the absence of other viable legal institutions, to forsake the requirement of bisexuality and thus abandon the negative definitive criterion of homosexuality, if indeed it is such a criterion.

Another argument I must meet is that while it is one thing to tolerate behaviour and remove criminal sanctions, in this case concerning homosexual activities, it is quite another thing to facilitate and give recognition to unions built on such activities. It is submitted in response that the gradual movement of social history is towards such a position of recognition and facilitation, and that this position should indeed be adopted. The task becomes one of persuading people that earthquakes will not follow,[62] and that this step is merely another in the gradual process of acceptance and tolerance of varied social and sexual behaviour begun by the Sexual Offences Act, 1967; that there is nothing harmful or threatening in institutionalizing, and thereby recognizing, a relationship which some fear, many object to, and most still misunderstand. The reasons for such fear, opposition, and misunderstanding are many and complex. Though they cannot detain us here, an examination

---

[62] It was Justinian, I think, who suggested a causal link between earthquakes and homosexuality.

of them could well be a step towards dispelling them for ever. It is indeed a salutary (and exceedingly difficult) exercise to attempt to analyse them in the security of a solitary armchair. The more rigorous the enquiry, the more elusive become the real grounds for opposition. My own, much attenuated view, for what it is worth, is as follows. Fundamentally the whole complex of hostility towards homosexuality is a reflection of a biological imperative to procreate, in which the homosexual is seen as a threat to the species, 'unnatural', and therefore worthy of condemnation. Introduce intellectual reasoning, and of course this threat is seen as harmless. The species continues to survive and multiply. A small aberrant group endangers no one. But this does not prevent the threat from being felt as very real, with all the consequent aggressive reactions.

Whatever the truth of this, the proposition is repeated that homosexual unions should be recognized as marriages with all the rights and duties this may imply. For instance, on a down-to-earth, but very real, level, one partner to a homosexual union may forsake his work to look after house and home, or may become financially dependent on the other. Is it not hypocrisy to say that the new tolerance accepts the union, but gives no security or protection to the injured party if the other suddenly decides to leave? Clearly, such a drastic change in the law could be undertaken only by the legislature. No doubt it will sorely test the liberal and progressive credentials of certain members. Also in its wake will follow countless problems in rewriting the law related to marriage and divorce. However, I have no doubt that it will occur, later if not sooner.[63]

Two final issues among the host remaining for consideration will be touched upon.[64] First, should the couple in the type of marriage unions discussed

---

[63] The attempts of two homosexuals to obtain a licence to marry in the State of Minnesota has become something of a *cause célèbre* in the United States, reaching even the hallowed columns of *Time Magazine*, 6 Sept. 1971. Their request for a licence was rejected by the Clerk of the County District Court, and the Supreme Court of Minnesota affirmed this by refusing to issue a writ of *mandamus*. The petition claimed that the absence of statutory prohibition against single-sex marriage evinced a legislative intent to authorize such marriages; and that prohibiting a single-sex marriage denied the petitioners their constitutional rights under the Ninth and Fourteenth Amendments to the United States Constitution. Both claims were rejected in a short decision which echoed the views of Ormrod J.; e.g. 'The institution of marriage as a union of man and woman, uniquely involving the procreation and rearing of children within a family, is as old as the book of Genesis' (*Baker* v. *Nelson*, 191 N.W. 2d 185 (Minn. 1971)). Baker, a top-ranking law student at the University of Minnesota Law School, then countered by establishing another legal relationship with his partner, McConnell: he was formally adopted by McConnell. Subsequent reports indicated that later he went through a ceremony of marriage in another county (*Los Angeles Times*, 8 Sept. 1971). Goodness knows what effect this has on his status as an adopted son! This unseemly legal mess results from the energetic efforts of the Gay Liberation Movement, of which Baker is a member (correspondence with this writer), to gain what are regarded as just demands, including the right to marry.

[64] For example, the author of the Note, *supra* n. 11, ingeniously raises the problem of inheritance caused by the fact that a 'son' named in a will is now a female.

above be able to adopt children, since obviously there will be no natural issue? The matter is raised here as one of principle, since individual decisions must rest with the adoption agency, and ultimately the courts, based upon an assessment of the suitability of the couple involved. As a matter of principle it is submitted that there should not be an absolute bar to adoption in the case of a marriage involving a transsexual. The transsexual, once stabilized in the role long seen as the only natural one, may naturally want a normal family life. Indeed, the desire to succeed in the adopted sex role may make the transsexual a model parent. If careful investigation reveals a secure and successful domestic situation, then there should be no reason why a child should not be adopted and raised by the couple.[65]

Should the case of the homosexual union be treated differently? Consistency with the argument presented earlier would seem to demand that such a couple should enjoy all rights and privileges available to a 'married' couple. Yet, to propose the possibility of adoption by such a couple strikes a discordant note. Again, it is important to try to discover the reasons for this. If a homosexual union is to be accepted as a marriage and yet denied the right to raise children, what is really being said is that the state has an interest in sheltering and protecting children from a homosexual environment. The premiss which serves to justify such a policy is that the young should be raised in a context of 'normality'. The State has the obligation of ensuring this end by guaranteeing that homosexuals, living as they do in an 'abnormal' relationship, do not have the opportunity to influence directly the upbringing of children. The only acceptable environment for children is thus to be in the care of a heterosexual couple, as this is the only 'normal' environment which can provide a 'natural' stable family life. Much obviously hinges on this word 'normal' and the accepted idea of family life. My own view is that perhaps the concept of normality is inappropriate here, since doubtless much of the hostility and prejudice which exists towards homosexuality is a product of this notion. That this means that homosexuals should be able to adopt children is, however, a proposition which I hesitate to advance. It may be that greater understanding of homosexuals is called for and that all measures aimed at countering misunderstanding should be welcomed. Whether children should be in the vanguard of such a movement is another question.

Second, brief mention should be made of the law relating to adultery. Notwithstanding the passage of the Divorce Reform Act 1969,[66] adultery and the case-law governing it are still of relevance in pursuing a divorce action. Clearly it takes on a further significance in the context of the discussion in this paper. Ormrod J. seems to hold in *Corbett* that sexual relations with a woman with an artificial vagina would amount neither to consummation

---

[65] The impression is gained from the medical literature that this position has been accepted in some states of the United States; see *supra* n. 9.   [66] 17 and 18 Eliz. 2, c. 55.

nor to adultery.[67] Clearly, incapacity or wilful refusal to consummate a marriage as presently defined, if it were to be retained at all as part of the law, could only apply to those relationships presently regarded as marriages. In its present form it would have no relevance to homosexual unions and little relevance to a union involving a transsexual. This is not to overlook, however, the fact that the parties to these relationships, may legitimately expect some form of sexual gratification from their partners and should have grounds for complaint if it were denied. Whether this should be called 'consummation' or something else is a question of definition. But what is to be made of adultery? Two alternatives suggest themselves. It could be argued that Ormrod J.'s view of the law is wrong, and that if the transsexual engaged in sexual relations outside the marriage, this would amount to adultery. Considerable difficulty, however, would be met in outlining the degree of sexual conduct which would amount to adultery, even if it were given a much wider connotation where homosexuals were involved. A second solution is advanced here. Besides being far more satisfactory, it is submitted, from a social as well as a legal-theoretical standpoint, it would provide a framework applicable to all unions. It would involve the abandonment of rigid conceptualism: the rejection, in other words, of a formal mechanical set of criteria adding up to the concept of adultery which allows hard problems to be solved with apparent ease by simply referring to a formula without examining the deeper issues of justice involved in the case. It is regrettable that, in legislation basically aimed at facilitating the dissolution of marriages which have failed, the notion of adultery was retained. Emphasis should be — and surely was intended to be — on the fact of breakdown, and not on the formal technicalities of establishing such breakdown. Adultery in effect is evidence of breakdown because it represents conduct, on the plane of sexual behaviour, which is outrageous and offensive to the other partner. The rationale is that such behaviour may make life intolerable; and that, if indeed it does, the offended partner is entitled to say that the marriage has broken down. Conduct on other planes of behaviour may equally produce the same result. Adultery therefore should be seen as having a symbolic quality, amounting to sexual conduct outrageous to the other. This may not be the old rationale of adultery. It is suggested that in the context of a monogamous union, adultery was elevated to the status of a sin (or indeed a crime) and grounds for divorce so as to reinforce this concept of marriage and, in the absence of birth control, to prevent the social 'untidiness' caused by the production of children not the product of a couple married to each other, with all the inheritance and support complications which could follow. This rationale, however, is of considerably less significance now. For this reason,

---

[67] *Supra* n. 2, 49–50, thereby disagreeing with the Court of Appeal's view, expressed *orbiter* in *S. v. S.* (otherwise W.) (no. 2 [1962] 3 All ER 55.

adultery should be seen for what it has become, an act of sexual conduct which takes on a symbolic character if offensive to the other partner. Once this is conceded, then enquiries into the exact details and minutiae of the sexual behaviour[68] so as to announce on its legal pedigree become redundant. They have always been unseemly, since they make a mockery of the moral values they purport to uphold.[69] The eminently more favourable position would be that if one partner engages in sexual conduct with another outside their relationship which the other partner finds intolerable, then this may be cited as evidence that the marriage has broken down. Such a general rule would then have application, regardless of the details, to all unions recognized as marriages.

CONCLUSION

I have proceeded from a narrow premiss: the case of *Corbett* v.*Corbett*. In that case I found questions raised which go to two major issues. First is the issue of sex determination: how the law is to deal with changing scientific opinion which challenges old certainties, and the legality of medical procedures designed to deal with abnormal sexual conditions. Second, the issue of marriage is raised, and I have sought to examine the notion, even though merely to question conventional wisdom regarding its nature already appears to go too far. The suggestions that are made on the basis of the analysis may not suit everyone's palate. The hope is that some will find in them food for thought.

POSTSCRIPT

In the latest edition of his *Principles of Family Law*, Professor Cretney repeats the argument that the use of the words 'male' and 'female' in section 11(c) of the Matrimonial Causes Act 1973 (which repealed and reproduced the provisions of the Nullity Act 1971), suggests that it 'may thus be possible to argue that the terms "male" and "female" refer to a person's *gender* (that is to say, the sex to which he psychically belongs)'. 'If so', he continues, 'the question whether a person is "male" or "female" is not to be resolved (as it was in the *Corbett* case) solely by reference to rigid tests of biological sexuality.'[70] I continue, however, to prefer the view I expressed earlier.[71] The absence of any case-law leaves the question open.

---

[68] See e.g. *supra* n. 2, 49.   [69] See e.g. *Hansard, supra* n. 11, 1845.
[70] S. Cretney, *Principles of Family Law*, 4th edn., Sweet and Maxwell, 1984, pp. 62–3.
[71] *Supra* pp. 270–2.

Since this paper was written, however, there has been one case in English law worth noting. In *R. v. Tan*,[72] one Gloria Greaves was charged with living on the earnings of prostitution contrary to section 30 of the Sexual Offences Act 1956. She had been born a male, but had later undergone sexual conversion surgery and had lived as a woman for eighteen years. Upon conviction, she (I use the pronoun 'she' for the sake of convenience here) appealed on the ground that the statute expressly made the crime one which only a man could commit.

Parker J., giving the judgment of the Court of Appeal, stated that:

It was . . . contended that . . . if the person had become philosophically or psycho-logically or socially female, that person should be held not to be a man for the purposes of [section 30, *inter alia*].

We reject this submission without hesitation. In our judgment both common sense and the desirability of certainty and consistency demand that the decision in *Corbett* v. *Corbett* should apply for the purpose not only of marriage but also for a charge under s. 30 of the Sexual Offences Act 1956.[73]

Pace, in a cogent criticism of Parker J.'s judgment,[74] argues that while consistency in the law may have its merits, there are limits to the extent to which it should be pursued:

It is quite true that *Corbett* has been applied to situations outside marriage, *eg.*, the alteration of birth certificates, unfair dismissal [*White* v. *British Sugar Corporation Ltd.* [1977] 1 RLR 121], and the minimum age for retirement [Dec. CP6/76 (Nat. Ins. Comm.)], [but] there is no obvious reason why the same approach should apply to the criminal law, particularly in view of the different policy considerations which apply in civil and criminal law.[75]

Pace also notes that even if *Corbett* is right, which he does not accept, Ormrod J. 'specifically restricted the scope of his decision'.[76] You will recall that Ormrod J. held that '[t]he question then becomes what is meant by the word "woman" in the context of a marriage, for I am not concerned to determine the "legal sex" of the respondent at large.'[77] Thus, Pace argues, *Corbett* cannot serve as the authority on which Parker J. wished to rely in *Tan*.

Finally, Pace takes the Court of Appeal in *Tan* to task for ignoring developments elsewhere. 'It is a matter of some regret', he writes, 'that the Court did not see fit to investigate civil law developments over the twelve year period since *Corbett* was decided.'[78] He goes on to refer to legislation

---

[72] [1983] QB 1053.   [73] Ibid. 1064.
[74] P. J. Pace, 'Sexual Identity and the Criminal Law', [1983] *Crim.* LR 317.
[75] Ibid. 319.   [76] Ibid.   [77] *Supra* n. 2, 48.   [78] Pace, *supra* n. 74, 320.

in 1980 in West Germany[79] and in 1982 in Italy[80] whereby post-operative transsexuals are deemed to belong to their chosen sex and have the rights and duties of that sex. Canadian provincial legislation in Alberta, British Columbia, Saskatchewan, and New Brunswick allows transsexuals to have even their birth certificates altered, Pace points out.[81] Similar legislation exists in parts of the United States,[82] and Pace could also have mentioned legislative and judicial changes in the law in Sweden, Switzerland, and Norway.[83]

Notwithstanding such criticisms, *Tan* seems to make it abundantly clear that if any change in the law's attitude to transsexuals is to be forthcoming, it will certainly not come from the English courts. Indeed, *Tan* not only confirms *Corbett* at the level of the Court of Appeal, but extends it beyond marriage into, it appears, a case of general application, an outcome which Ormrod J. may not have intended or desired.

But now, of course, the English courts are not the only courts which can develop English law. There is the Court of Human Rights which adjudicates on the basis of the European Convention of Human Rights, of which the United Kingdom is, of course, a signatory. First, a complaint must go to the European Commission of Human Rights. If the Commission regards the complaint as validly demonstrating a breach of the Convention it reports to that effect, and the case proceeds to the European Court of Human Rights unless it is solved in the meantime. If the court finds against a nation which is a signatory, that nation is obliged to bring its law into conformity with the law as stated by the court.

In 1984, the European Commission of Human Rights reported, on the application of one Mark Rees, that the United Kingdom was in violation of Article 8 of the European Convention.[84] The case then went forward to the European Court of Human Rights. If Rees had been successful there, it would have meant that legislation would have had to be introduced into Parliament which would remove those legal disabilities affecting transsexuals which the court may find contravene the Convention.

Article 8 of the Convention, briefly stated, guarantees to a person a right of respect for his private and family life. Rees is a female-to-male transsexual who has undergone sexual conversion therapy. Rees applied to have his birth certificate altered. His request was refused, and attempts to persuade the English courts to order the alteration failed when he was refused legal aid. Rees thereupon complained to the European Commission of Human Rights that, by refusing to alter the recorded sex on his birth certificate, the United

---

[79] See, now, 7 EHRR 433.   [80] Ibid.   [81] Pace, *supra* n. 74, 320.
[82] See e.g. W. Walz, 'Transsexualism and the Law', 5 *Journal of Contemporary Law* 181 (1979).
          [83] See *supra* n. 79.
[84] *Rees* v. *United Kingdom* 7 EHRR 429.

Kingdom, through its law, is depriving him of the legal status corresponding to his actual condition, to which he is rightfully entitled by Article 8.[85]

The Commission referred to its previous opinion in the *Van Oosterwijk* case,[86] 'that a State which refused to recognise the new status of a transsexual after medical treatment resulting in a change of sex failed to respect private life'.[87] It was the refusal to alter the birth certificate which led to the decision against Belgium in the *Van Oosterwijk* case. The Commission could find no compelling reason of public interest which could justify the position of the United Kingdom's government. Furthermore, it found that, although birth certificates were not required by law for any kind of legal transaction in the United Kingdom, there could be occasions on which a birth certificate could be called for by, for instance, an employer or public institution. In such circumstances, the refusal of Rees's request constituted in the view of the Commission a violation of his rights guaranteed by Article 8.

If the European Court of Human Rights had confirmed the view of the Commission, changes in the law would have been called for, at least so as to allow for alteration of all relevant documentation. Clearly, such a law could have consequences going beyond mere changes in documents. Parliament, had it been required to do so by the European Court of Human Rights, could have made a small, interstitial alteration of the law by, for example, merely amending the relevant section of the Birth and Death Registration Act 1953; or used the opportunity to undertake a wholesale revision of the law as it affects transsexuals.

In the event, neither was necessary. In a surprising and unexpected judgment, the European Court of Human Rights rejected the Commission's view, and decided that there was no violation of Articles 8 or 12.[88] As regards Article 8, by a majority of 12 to 3, the court rested its decision ultimately on the notion of striking a fair balance between the interests of Rees and those of the British government. Rees argued that a change in his birth certificate was necessary to give effect to his interest in privacy. The British government argued, first, that such a change would have the effect of forcing them to adopt a type of system for documenting civil status which would have considerable administrative consequences and would impose new duties on the population. This the court accepted. The government could not, it decided, be obliged to alter the very basis of its system of documentation. The fact that some countries who were signatories of the Convention had one system and some another reinforced the court in its view that no single system could be called for. It is fair to say, however, that this is not fatal to Rees's case. His complaint need not be seen as so far-reaching. It can be interpreted more narrowly as merely calling for an

---

[85] Ibid. 434.
[87] Rees, *supra* n. 84, 432.

[86] *Van Oosterwijk* v. *Belgium*, 3 EHRR 581.
[88] *Rees* v. *United Kingdom*, 9 EHHR 56.

incidental adjustment in the form of an annotation of the present birth register. This the court considered next.

The British government argued that if a major change in the system of documentation was not called for, but only minor incidental adjustments, such adjustments would be different in kind from those at present allowed by law. These, it was argued, concern the correction of errors of fact or omissions at the time of birth. The court did not accept this argument. It noted that adjustments are permitted in the case of adoption and legitimation. It pointed out, however, that an annotation of the changed sex on the register would not safeguard privacy because it would reveal Rees's change of sexual identity.

To this, Rees replied that the annotation of the changed sex could be kept secret from third parties. You may recall that I proposed earlier a scheme to do just that—namely, the registration of a new entry, but accompanied by a code known to the Registrar which would alert him in any case of attempted fraud. This, to me, is the crucial part of Rees's case, concerning, as it does, the protection of his privacy without any significant change in policy or practice by government. It is not clear, however, whether a proposal of the sort I have mentioned was put before the court. What is clear is that the court rejected Rees's argument that the annotation could be kept secret, on the basis of a somewhat heavy-handed assumption of what this would entail. The court saw great dangers arising out of such secrecy. Public and private institutions could, it decided, act in ignorance, and great harm could flow as a consequence, and succession and family law arrangements could potentially be prejudiced. But, I would submit, these can be avoided relatively easily. If my proposal was accepted, legislation would not even be needed. All that would be required is a change in practice.

So, Rees failed under Article 8. His complaint under Article 12 received short shrift. He complained that according to English Law he could not marry a woman, and that thus he was denied the right to marry and found a family. The court, without offering any reasoned argument, decided that the right to marry in Article 12 'refers to the traditional marriage between persons of the opposite biological sex'.[89]

This would appear to be the end of the road for transsexuals as far as the law is concerned. They have achieved much of what they sought concerning changes in documents which affect their everyday lives, so as to accommodate their new life-style. But any more fundamental change, which would constitute the ultimate formal recognition of their new identity, is to be denied. Whether this represents a fair balance between the interests of the individual and those of the State I beg leave to doubt.

---

[89] Ibid. 68.

14

The Technological Imperative and its Application in Health Care*

'If it can be done, it should be done.'
'If we can do it, why don't we?'

These are two ways of expressing what is now a widely accepted notion. Technology has its own momentum. To develop new skills and tools is to create the pressure to use them.

This is a familiar enough idea. It has application in a host of contexts. One of them is in health and medical care. As Dr Yu has written, 'Beginning in the 1960s, a great increase in the understanding of neonatal pathophysiology took place. This knowledge was rapidly applied to clinical care by responsible physicians. Since that time, neonatology as a speciality has found its place in paediatrics, with the appointment of full-time neonatal consultants in all neonatal intensive care units. A technology has developed which enabled the growth of the speciality.'[1]

Of course, resort to technology has always been a feature of health care, if we mean by that the development and use of skills and tools. Anaesthesia, vaccines, scalpels, and contact lenses are all examples of technological innovation and development. We live with them relatively comfortably. Yet we are at the same time perturbed by more recent and present-day developments. Are we right to be worried? Or are we just creatures of our time, trapped by our failure to see the solutions around the corner of our life-span?

This, then, is the first question for us. Is there anything different about present-day technological developments which warrants the kind of concern it seems to attract (and warrants this paper!)? The answer is Yes, for three reasons above all others: their cost, the speed of innovation, and their significance at the edges of life. Certainly, when anaesthesia, for example, was first introduced, there were the same debates as there are now over the care of VLBW babies, about its experimental nature and the long- and short-term effects of using it. The difference now, however, is that such

---

* This paper was presented at the Sydney Conference in 1985 (see chapter 7), and appears here in a modified form. Reference again is to the Australian materials cited in chapter 7.
[1] V. Yu, 'Annotation: Effectiveness of neonatal intensive care policies', 20 *Australian Paediatric Journal* 85 (1984).

arguments are multiplied many times over, both by the much more extensive use of technology and the great number of technological developments which appear so quickly and exist at the same time. As for cost, even when we talk of technological development being, in health care, at the service of all who may need it, we realize that, in fact, its supply is limited, and the limitation is expressed usually in terms of cost. The resources, whether material or human, are not there in anything like sufficient quantities, it is said. And, of course, talk of cost must never overlook what are known as opportunity costs: time, effort, and money spent on one thing necessarily means a lost opportunity to spend them on something else, which may be of just as much value. This is a particularly important point to bear in mind when it is realized that many technological developments operate at the edges of life, whether they be ventilators or incubators.

So the special nature of recent technological developments concerns their multiplicity, their speed of appearance, their cost, and the consequent limit on their availability.

Understood in this light, the technological imperative can be seen to pose a central dilemma which can be expressed thus: 'If we can do it, we must. But is there enough of it to go around?'

Here we embark on the next stage of our analysis. To ask the question of whether there is enough presumes that we know what 'enough' is. And that involves the enormously difficult task of allocating resources which are limited among competing claims. 'The technological imperative' meets 'the allocation of resources', two aphorisms which mask an incredibly difficult set of problems. So difficult are they, in fact, that the debate usually begins and ends at the level of aphorism, with lots of commentators wringing their hands and saying that something must be done, while doctors, administrators, and others scramble to make sure that they get a bit of the action.

Let us see if we can do a bit better than this. Here are the issues put starkly, before we try to unravel them. The development of technology creates a momentum towards use. This is as true in health care as elsewhere. Technology in modern medicine poses special problems. There are, and always have been, limits to the amount of resources devoted to any particular technological development. Those limits have created the need to ration what is available, as well as what ought to be developed.

Before proceeding further, let us try to set the context in which the debate must be conducted. There can be no doubt that the introduction and development of technology brings benefits to many. There is equally no doubt that such benefits are bought at a price. The price includes:

(1) the increasing cost of technology, in terms of development, purchase and service, the training of staff, and its operation;

(2) the potential or real imbalance in expenditure which technology introduces into the allocation of resources in health care generally. Money spent on machines or intensive care units or renal dialysis, and on staff for these, is money which is not available for other health and medical services;

(3) the possible distorting effect that technology has on attitudes to, and the availability of, other forms of health care—for example, preventive care and the often forgotten possibility of not *doing* anything;

(4) the fostering of an impersonal approach to health and medical care, where the machine intrudes between the patient and the doctor, and may thereby affect deleteriously the development of caring personal relationships.

Two questions then arise. First, is there inevitably a limit to the resources available. I doubt if anyone would seriously doubt that, now, as a matter of fact, this is the case. Must it be so? If our concern is health, widely defined, not merely medical care, it is probably inevitable in our present society that resources do not exist to meet all the demands that the pursuit of health for all may make.

So, if there are limits to what we *can* do, and if the development of technology brings costs as well as benefits, we now must face the second question: under what circumstances do we either develop or apply a particular technology? Notice that I say 'develop' as well as 'apply', for the thesis is that, once developed, it is extremely difficult to resist its application.

All those involved in health care know how these questions are dealt with at present. First, they are rarely posed as clearly as this; things tend to happen incrementally or interstitially. Second, when they are raised, they are resolved according to the simple criterion of political muscle power. The doctor or unit or hospital that can shout the loudest and wave the biggest shrouds in front of TV cameras on the look-out for 'human interest' stories gets the money and the staff. It needs only a couple of well-publicized mercy flights to the United States and appropriate patriotic breast-beating to ensure that liver transplant units spring up like desert flowers after the rain.

Are we right to think that this system, if system it can be called, is unsatisfactory? Certainly those working with the mentally ill or the handicapped or the senile or in health education may properly think it is. Well, can a better system be devised? This can be answered only by identifying what is wrong with the present system and coming up with an alternative.

What is wrong is that, as a way of ordering our affairs, it is only *dis*order. It is arbitrary, irrational, and does not reflect any principle. It is one of our claims to civilization that we have transcended the level of existence at which survival means making sure you get your nose in the trough and using your elbows to keep others out. Some would flinch at such language as a description of how medical resources are allocated, but would agree with what is behind it, that rational allocation or planning is an illusion, I shall return to this later. But assuming for the moment that we can do better than fight over the trough, how do we do it?

This is best answered by asking what the desired goal is. Some may say that it is efficiency or effectiveness. But although these are attractive and apparently straightforward goals, they are, of course, only half an answer, since they beg the central question: efficient to what end, effective in producing what?[2] So we have to look elsewhere.

The goal on which we would all agree, I suggest, would be one of fairness, whereby resources are distributed and technology applied in the right way. In short, we would wish to order and organize what we do in a morally respectable and defensible way.

But how can this be done? Some may think that you cannot argue—far less, analyse— what is morally right: it is just a matter of personal feeling or common sense. This is a counsel of despair. It is to say that one person's view is as good as another's, which we patently do not accept when it comes to many aspects of our daily lives. We condemn the liar, blame the cheat, and excuse innocent error. In medicine, we talk in general terms of a patient's 'right to know', but also of a doctor's liberty, sometimes not to tell a particular patient for good reason. We analyse both the implications of our general views and the tensions between competing views. We talk, in other words, the language of rights and wrongs.

So it *is* possible to look for ways of ordering our responses to technology and resource allocation in a morally responsible way; and, being possible, it is our duty to do so. And the way we do this is by resort to moral principles, which we identify, weigh, and try to apply to the issue before us.

Two questions then emerge. What moral principles are relevant to resource allocation in the context of the technological imperative? Second, once identified, can they be of any use in helping us solve real-life issues? Or are they no more than generalized exhortations, the playthings of ethicists, who love to pontificate, because that is all they are good for?

Let me answer the second question first. If ethical analysis in this context does not help in the real world, it *is* a waste of time. If we cannot help in the analysis of concrete problems, we should keep our mouths firmly shut. We have, in short, to keep our feet on the ground, to get our facts right, and to remember that we are talking about the real world. We must, therefore, bridge the worlds of principle and practice, move from the abstract to the concrete.

---

[2] G. H. Mooney defines 'efficiency' as 'getting the most out of the resources available' (*Economics, Medicine and Health Care*, (Wheatsheaf Books, 1986)). But 'most' is at least in part a question of values. It is only once the values have been worked out and the goals which are proper to aim for have been agreed upon, that 'efficiency' in its strictly factual sense can be considered.

As for the question of what the relevant principles *are*, debates about the rationing of scarce resources are, in essence, debates about *justice*, about what is fair or right or just. First we have to work out what we think justice is, therefore, before we can decide what justice demands.

This is not the place for any lengthy examination of the concept of justice. All I will say is that I reject as a model of justice the view which has temporarily gained favour in many developed societies: namely, the view that each person is entitled to what he can get, and let the next man look out for himself as best he can. This is not justice; it is not even a theory of morality, since it rejects a consideration of what I take to be central to moral theory, the sense of each person being a member of a community with, inevitably, obligations and duties *to others*, as well as rights.

The notion of justice which I find most convincing is that which tells us that we ought to seek a society in which each person is accepted as of equal moral worth and has equal opportunity to enjoy an equal share of the total sum of society's goods. A particular feature of such a view of what is just is that any attempt to translate it into practice must *begin* by favouring the weakest and the least advantaged, since these are the people least likely to have the opportunity to enjoy an equal share of what we have, and are thus most in need of help.

Notice that talk of caring about the weakest and most vulnerable first may already, even when expressed so generally, have important implications for any consideration of the allocation of scarce technological resources to the care, for example, of neonates.

So, if we are concerned with what constitutes a just allocation of resources, my prescription, at the very least, would call for policies aimed at ensuring, as far as possible, that everyone had an equal opportunity to enjoy an equal share of the total net welfare of society.

One ingredient of the net benefits that a society enjoys is health. It follows that a just society must set its policies and write its laws to ensure that everyone, *beginning* with the least advantaged and most vulnerable, has an equal opportunity to enjoy an equal share of the total net resources allocated to health. Notice, I use the word 'health'. There is no need to remind you that health is not the same as medical care. As you know, health is the product of a combination of factors, among which medical care plays a relatively minor role. Ministries of Health thoughout the world, however, have been converted, largely under the influence of doctors, into ministries of illness, in which policies aimed at the maintenance of health and the avoidance of illness have been ignored or left to others, with little understanding of their true nature. Resources which could be spent on health have been diverted to waiting for ill health and then trying to do something about it, usually with only limited effect.

It will take a complete re-education of the public, as well as considerable political courage and will-power, before 'health' regains its proper meaning, and policies geared to achieving it are accepted.

There seems little likelihood of more resources (in terms of money) becoming available, as a proportion of the total GDP; and perhaps this is as it should be. Therefore, improvements in health can be achieved only if existing resources are re-allocated into policies more productive of health. Such policies would aim, for example, at the provision of education, the elimination of relative poverty, safety in the work place, environmental and ecological protection, diet, the power of the food, alcohol, and tobacco lobbies, transport policy, both in terms of safety and of minimizing isolation, care and comfort of the elderly and adequate housing, employment, and recreation.

Furthermore, these policies must aim at ensuring that everyone has the opportunity to enjoy these aspects of health. Some may choose to neglect their health or to trade it for the freedom to do other things, as does the business executive who opts for a stressful way of life in pursuit of material success. And obviously some compromise must be struck as, for example, in the case of transport, where undoubtedly the need and desire for mobility and the distances involved in travel have to be set against the knowledge that roads pollute and fast cars kill. But such compromises should be made with the larger goal always in view, rather than, as at present, as a consequence of the self-interested lobbying of powerful groups.

As regards care of the neonate, which is our particular concern here, what are important are the criteria whereby resources are allocated. These have to be examined against our bench-mark of fairness or justice; and if unjust, policies must be changed.

We can only identify the proper criteria correctly if we accept that medical treatment in general ought to be divided, for our purposes, into two classes. The first we can call regular, standard, or ordinary treatment, the sort of treatment which any developed, urbanized country should have available for all. The second we can call unusual, or special, treatment, requiring more than ordinary skill, effort, or resources. Arguments will no doubt be made that such a division is unrealistic; but, in my view, not only is it essential for solving resource problems; it is also a division which is made now, albeit not explicitly.

The first point which arises from this division is the necessary implication that ordinary treatment be provided first. One problem which such an approach may pose is that there may be nothing left for special treatment. Third World countries often confront this, and some have opted for 'high technology' (which may be badly delivered) at the cost of ordinary treatment. As regards neonates, even in the developed world, there is a further, special problem. Ordinary treatment may generally include the type of less intrusive, less expensive care we call preventive treatment. More, or even enough, of it may exhaust the allocation of resources for paediatric care. So two questions need to be resolved on my analysis: first, is prevention ordinary treatment? and, second, if preventive care depends on data drawn from special treatment, does this mean that special care may be undertaken only under conditions of limited, controlled research, which is what I suspect is what care of the VLBW baby really is, rather than by adopting the current haphazard approach which may wrongly dissipate resources? We need to think very carefully about preventive strategies, particularly as regards the prediction and detection of, for example, peri-ventricular haemorrhage in the case of VLBW babies.

The issue of allocating resources becomes far more difficult if the treatment under discussion is special, or unusual. Its being so means that more than usual demands must be made on available resources, whether human or material. A neonatal intensive care unit is, on this view, a good example of special treatment. It is not needed for the care of the vast majority of new-born babies, but may represent the difference between life and death in the rare cases.

There are, in fact, at least two separate problems to be solved, both of them enormously difficult. The first is how to choose between the neonatal intensive care unit and one of the many other forms of special treatment which could benefit patients — for instance, a renal dialysis unit or a transplant programme. The second is, if there are to be intensive care units, what share of resources should they have?

As regards choosing between special services, one response may be to argue that if, as will always be the case, there is not enough money to meet all the needs for special care, then the simple answer is to make more available. This, of course, is not a sensible argument. It is impractical, in that raising the necessary revenue would be politically impossible, particularly as needs grow to meet available supplies of resources. It is also unethical, since it would involve far too great an infringement of liberty made in the name of fairness. That a policy may meet the ideal of justice does not necessarily always mean that it is right to adopt it, if in so doing other fundamental values are sacrificed.

Given that more money simply will not be made available as a proportion of GDP, choices have to be made. At present they are made by the politician or the hospital administrator responding to the group which can shout the loudest or bring to bear the keenest political acumen. This cannot be a proper way, not only because it is irrational and unsystematic, but also because it is patently unfair. A case's merit should not have to depend on strong-arm tactics. Thus another, better system must be adopted and translated into policy by planners and administrators. It will be said by many that there is no rational way of doing the job, and that the lobbying and jockeying,

demeaning as they may be, are unavoidable. As I have already said, some
say that planning is just not possible. The answer is that if we find the present
state of affairs unsatisfactory, we have an obligation to try to come up with
something better. What we have to do is to come up with some set of criteria
which relate to the relative value we are prepared, if pressed, to attribute
to a particular form of special treatment. I suppose the sort of factors we
would consider are, first, the number who might benefit. Arguably, the
greater the number, the greater the priority to be given to the service. Then
there are the consequences of not having the service available. They would
range from death to the relatively minor discomfort associated with the
absence of chiropody services. Then you would consider the effect the
treatment would have if available. This would range from total recovery to
the maintenance of a vegetative status quo. Putting these together, it would
mean that a life-saving service would not have by any means the highest
priority if the lives saved were few or were ones of mere existence.

Another of many criteria to be identified could be the subsequent or
continuing costs, economic and social, of proceeding with a particular
treatment. If, for example, to carry out a particular operation meant further
long-term treatment, this must enter the equation; as must also the comparative cost in caring for the patient *without* the particular treatment.

The final stage in the exercise would be to ensure that whatever resources
were made available, they were not dissipated, but concentrated in special
units. The relevant number of skilled personnel could then be trained, and
effective procedures for referral and transfer of patients could be established.

With such a broad framework, a start could be made, through public debate
and discussion, to fill in the details. Involvement of the public would not
only affirm the fact that these are issues for all of us, but would also educate
people as to the range and limitations of existing therapies, and involve them
in the decisions to be made in the light of this. It may mean that a neonatal
intensive care unit, after careful reflection, rather than emotional appeals
and 'shroud-waving', may have to give way to a number of other services,
relating, for example, to the mentally ill, all of which can be financed for
the cost of one such unit, which, in combination, will facilitate a measure
of improvement in the patients' conditions and their integration into society.
It is not, however, for me to judge the issue here, but only to point to what
is involved in such a judgment.

I now turn to the second problem I posed earlier. Let us suppose that some
special service has been given priority, such that it ought to have resources
allocated to it, the question then is what share it should get. Any system of
rational planning must take account of, and answer, two questions. The first
concerns the total amount available for all special services. The answer must
be the amount remaining from the total budget allocation for medical care
services, which, we have seen, is a political decision, taking into account the

need to satisfy other competing claims. The second is the more difficult question. If there are, say, nationally, 100 units of account available for special services, how much should neonatal intensive care units have as against, for example, renal units? Any response is complicated by the fact that calls on resources are different, by being long- or short-term and by being capital- or revenue-intensive. A formula would have to be developed which took account of these differences. In principle, the allocation must be made on the basis of relative priority. This, in theory, is what was supposed to happen in the United Kingdom as regards what are called the 'Cinderella services'. Priorities were fixed in the mid-1970s; but, not atypically, resources did not follow.

The key feature of the exercise I have outlined above is the need for centralized planning. This, of course, is unpopular with all units and levels of administration. It is a feature of modern administration in medical care at any level, whether the team on the ward or the hospital board or any other body, that they assert and seek to defend what they see as a right to autonomy and self-government, while using and distributing to a greater or lesser extent public resources. Clearly, one feature of accountability is the need to show that public money is being spent in publicly approved ways. In this context, it means that the appropriate central planner must decree what total resources on a national or a local scale are to be made available, how much is to be allocated to each special service, and where units offering these services should be established, so as to maximize their effectiveness. Units which sought to establish themselves outside such a plan would not only not receive public money; they would also not qualify for any other public benefits. Obviously, whatever plan was developed would have to be sensitive to regional differences, whether in demographic terms, or in incidence of particular illnesses, or local cultural or political values. This would allow some room for choice, but would not detract from the fundamental notion of a centrally planned service. And those of you who see this as some bureaucratic nightmare or the real face of 1984—that is, State imposition of values and goals—it is perhaps helpful to recall that this is what happens now in an unsystematic, and therefore inefficient, way; and, of course, it is the route accepted by that arch-priestess of free choice, Mrs Thatcher. Under her government, the Health Services, the Social Services, Education, and Local Government have all come under central planning, even more than under previous Labour Governments. I do not hold this out as support for the thesis, but rather as evidence of the direction being taken by governments of whatever political complexion.

Finally, it is clear that centralized planning such as this must be kept under constant review, if it is to respond to changed needs and resources. A mechanism for periodic review after what is deemed an appropriate time must, then, be built into any plan that is devised.

It now remains to ask what to many is the most difficult question whether given that the services are available, albeit on a limited basis, they can properly be denied to certain patients.[3] This raises not only the issue of fairness or justice, but also that of selective treatment and respect for life. This is the particular issue for debate at this meeting, and I do not presume here either to pre-empt discussion or anticipate what I will say later when I consider it in greater detail. Suffice it here to point to what we can call a third, or micro-, level of decision making, the other two being the level of allocating as between health and, for example, defence; and the other, between different sections within health care. Here we are concerned with allocation between different patients. It remains a question of justice or fairness.

The issue for consideration is the selective treatment of disabled new-born babies. As I said, I will resist the temptation to go into detail here,[4] and offer only certain points to weigh as you consider the case. First, I suggest to you that it may be morally permissible to allow a baby to die by non-intervention. It may also be legally permissible to do so. It may even be *morally* permissible to kill the child; but the criminal law neither now nor in the future will countenance this, though it may look the other way from time to time. Second, the basis of the moral argument is that there must be a very good reason not to intervene. The good reason proposed here is the child's future handicap. This is a very taxing issue. Some would say that no degree of handicap warrants being encouraged to die. To them, handicap is never reason enough. I doubt if most would take this view; but if we would not, then we are forced to try to define with care the point at which handicap does become good reason. And in so doing, we must, of course, be aware of the risk of setting a standard which goes so far that it would mean that others — for example, the senile or the mentally handicapped, whom we would wish to treat if they were ill — were also included by it. How far is too far is what has to be decided. If we are not convinced that any standard has been offered, or that what is offered can work, then, I would submit, the principle of respect for life demands that we treat all alike.

My third point is to remind you that fixing a criterion for non-intervention amounts to setting the moral agenda for the treatment of VLBW babies. This task is, in my view, something for all of us, and cannot be left to doctors or parents to determine, unless we decide formally to authorize them to do so by law. You may wish to think carefully about whether you want so to authorize them; whether you are content to leave the principle of respect for

---

[3] For an excellent introduction and for references to the current concern with QALYs, (quality of adjusted life-years) see R. Gillon, 'Justice and Allocation of Medical Resources', 291 *British Medical Journal* 266 (1985), and references therein. See also M. Lockwood, 'Quality of Life and Resource Allocation' (unpublished paper).

[4] See chapters 7 and 8 for my detailed discussion.

life in the hands of doctors or parents, with no check or system of account-ability. You do not do so in any other circumstance.

My fourth point is that some of you may be persuaded to regard as a good reason for non-intervention the fact that the child, if it survives, will so disrupt its parents' lives as to destroy the marriage, or will end up in some institution, in a form of living death. These are important considerations; but you must ask whether they are a good reason to opt for non-intervention, or, rather, a reason to improve the support services available to parents or the institutions which house such children. It is much easier to bury a problem than to consider whether our moral obligation lies elsewhere.

Finally, to return to where we began, you may wonder whether the resources in time, effort, and money which will be involved in treating the child can be justified. I have suggested that it can be shown to be fair or just to do so; but this may not make it right if some other principle of greater weight is involved. You may wish to say that so many more children could be benefited if the resources were diverted to them instead. But this is to introduce a utilitarian calculus, which some may reject as a basis for choosing how to allocate resources. For benefiting others need not be an *overriding* principle, but merely a *competing* principle as to the proper theory of justice.

This scheme assumes, of course, both the desirability and the possibility of planning. Planning, in turn, assumes the existence of a system amenable to planning; a system, that is, which is coherent, consistent, rational, pre-dictable, manageable, and controllable. Some argue that while this may be desirable, it is not possible; it is pie in the sky, since it ignores reality. Reality, they point out, shows us that assumptions about rationality and control are misplaced. This is because, as I said earlier, there are so many different constituencies involved in the process, all of whom have different, and often incompatible, goals. Thus 'process', not 'system', is the correct term, since there is action and reaction, but no system. To talk of planning and decision making is, to these people, to indulge in self-delusion. Things happen. A newspaper story is written about a baby, or a politician is facing an election, or a leading specialist chooses to work in a particular hospital. These are the happenstances from which actions stem, not rational planning and considered decisions.

I am sure there is some validity in this analysis. Perhaps, however, there is a risk of throwing the baby out with the bath water. It may be true that the processes of change and of translating policy into practice are convoluted and very hard to manage. But this is not to say that *no* management is possible, and that the idea is best dropped. A battleship may need a lot of ocean to turn around in, but this is no argument for abandoning our commitment to rudders.

Thus, it may not be a question of a total plan or no plan at all, but rather of *some* planning, aware of the limitations which the nature of the exercise imposes on planning. And, if it is to be some planning, the need, then, is to focus on that approach which will best produce the results desired. Fundamentally this consists in locating the appropriate level of organization at which any issue can best be resolved. For example, the choice of which among several patients should receive a scarce resource is not best tackled in the hurly-burly of political debate; but the ethical ground rules which should guide such a choice may well be the product of such debate initially. The subsequent application of such rules or guidelines must properly be left to those with particular knowledge of the circumstances of the cases in question. Conversely, the ethically proper allocation of funds to health, as compared to education or defence, is quintessentially an issue for political debate, and cannot properly be left for individuals in the trenches to fight over, when they have no knowledge or view of the larger issues.

It will be clear from this that a proper approach will locate not only the appropriate level at which to resolve issues, but also the appropriate problem-solver. This must be the person, body, or institution most qualified to deal with the particular issue. Qualification will depend on the knowledge and expertise possessed and, as important, the extent to which the problem-solver can be held responsible for any decision according to the system of accountability we have; that is, the politician is accountable to Parliament and the public, and the individual to any system which the Parliament may have enacted, whether guidelines or law, and to those immediately touched by any decision.

Given that macro-decisions inherently and inevitably condition micro-decisions, the principal focus of attention must be on the *political* decision-maker. Thus, it is clear that what we are in fact dealing with is an issue of political theory, the proper location of power and responsibility. Any analysis must take account of this, by understanding and responding to the ways in which politicians reach decisions. Fundamentally, politicians in our system are almost always guided by two considerations: first, short-term gains, since their horizons stretch only to the next election; second, public pressure if it is strong enough to suggest that votes depend on their response.

This is not necessarily a recipe for despair, however. It means, by contrast, that when we talk of the technological imperative and resource allocation, we must realize that we are talking about the political process, and understand what this involves. Some clearly do so already; hence the present state of affairs. And, if it is thought that such a state of affairs is, for whatever reason, undesirable, then it behoves those who argue for another approach to learn the lesson of political realities. This, in short, means that they must enter the political arena. They must foster public information and analysis. They must present their arguments to the public, using whatever honest strategies they consider appropriate. This will ensure that the market-place of ideas, which politicians watch so closely, will have all, and not just a few, stall-holders of the truth. The best way to impress politicians is to mobilize public opinion.

I appear to have strayed a long way from our original topic. But it is only against such a background, I submit, that the issue of the technological imperative can properly be understood.

15

The Check-out: A Humane Death?

Produced by David Paterson

ITALIA PRIZE 1978, BBC Documentary Entry

Duration: 49' 50"

Broadcast on 19 August 1977 on BBC Radio 4

The technical accomplishments of modern medicine mean that doctors can often save the life of someone who in previous ages would have died. Consequently, the doctor may appear to play the role of God, the giver and taker of life.

In 'The Check-out', lawyer Ian Kennedy investigates the moral and legal problems created by a group of doctors striving to use the ultimate in medical technology to keep a man alive. Finally, the patient himself asked that the doctors kill him: they did so — through a drugs overdose.

Were the actions of the doctors ethical, moral, even lawful? Should the patient's request to die have been respected or ignored? Even though the case happened in the United States, are the issues it raises the same everywhere?

Ian Kennedy in 'The Check-out' discusses with the doctors involved and also the wife of the patient the principles that guided them in their actions. The responses to his questions are remarkably candid.

(Because of the nature of the subject matter of this programme, the BBC has agreed to the stipulation made by the wife of the patient that if 'The Check-out' is broadcast in the United States, any reference to the family name be deleted or changed. [I have subsequently changed the names of all the parties involved.])

IAN KENNEDY. I'm a lawyer, and during the past year, I've been teaching law in Southern California. It was through this work that I came to hear of the case of Dr Ron Carrington, a 35-year-old psychiatrist. His case raises some immensely difficult issues: issues about death and dying, issues about the appropriate moral and legal responses to be made when a man who has received the best that modern medical technology can offer decides finally that he can take no more. Last December, Dr Carrington asked this question: 'Doctor, will you help me to die?' Was he crazy? How should we, as a society, respond to this kind of request?

From when he was a young man, Dr Carrington had suffered from a chronic lung illness. Pneumonia had followed pneumonia. Despite his crippling disease, he had still managed to practise psychiatry with some success; but finally, the progressive nature of his condition meant that he needed treatment in an intensive care unit with 24-hour-a-day supervision, breathing only with the aid of a respirator. What would you do if you were one of Ron Carrington's doctors? Would you continue to fight for the life of this man who was valued in the community and initially had a strong will to live, even if the odds seemed hopeless?

Would you regard his request to be helped to die as one to be trusted and relied upon? Or was it a request made in a moment of desperation and to be ignored? If you were the wife of this man, what would you want? I'd like to spell out the details of Dr Carrington's case for you. It presents a host of problems — medical, moral, ethical, and legal — that may confront any patient, relative, and doctor when coping with death and dying. Though it happened in California, the issues are of course universal. As you listen to Dr Carrington's wife and doctors, you may be struck as I was by their candour and sincerity, Mrs Carrington takes up the account from the time when her husband was admitted to the intensive care unit.

MRS CARRINGTON. I became concerned when I saw my husband becoming a different person. He had special qualities of sensitivity, patience, rationality, intelligence, and wit; and when those qualities were completely unobservable, I became quite concerned about what was happening to him, you know, what was the meaning of his life at this point. One day when he was extremely unrealistic and euphoric, I really became upset; it was like going in to see a stranger — he was receiving a high dosage of morphine at that time — and I called his pulmonary doctor and requested that something be done or an explanation be given. And I was told that he was going to die shortly, and that if I wished, the measures that they were using with the respirator could be removed at my request, because he was in a terminal stage; it was just a matter of time, and I really felt that I couldn't make that decision myself. I impressed upon the doctor to really talk with Ron, and he said he had, but that Ron didn't seem to hear what he was saying, how ill he really was; and when we hung up, I was really quite shaken.

I had developed an extreme closeness with two of the doctors, and I called them, and they both agreed to go in and evaluate Ron's condition and get back to me, and I said I would abide by their decision. Well, the immunologist from the clinic went in and evaluated Ron and basically told him that he had . . . that he was not going to live more than the most a few weeks, and he could have control over the time of his death if he wished, and that was his decision to make, and he should think about it and talk it over with me. I told Ron that whatever decision he made I would support, and he decided that he would . . . that he would . . . he would die . . . I think it was the following morning after the doctor talked to him. He requested that his parents and a very close friend of ours say goodbye to him, and that I'd be in the room at the time and stay with him when they said goodbye. And I sat with him until he went to sleep, and he really looked peaceful. . . . I decided that I did not want to stay until the moment of his death, I wanted to remember him living . . . but I decided that I wanted to stay just to ensure that he was in a deep peaceful sleep, that he wasn't going to suffer . . . and that's what I did.

KENNEDY. So was Dr Carrington exerting a right — some would say a fundamental right — to self-determination, or was he capitulating under the weight of an intolerable burden?

MRS CARRINGTON. Oh, I don't think you could clearly dichotomize and say it was one thing or the other. I think it was a combination of things. I think Ron needed to feel that he was in control of his fate. He had a stubborn determination about him, and at the same time I think he was really exhausted; he was really exhausted, physically and emotionally.

KENNEDY. You will recall that Mrs Carrington spoke of her husband losing his rationality, and yet that he wanted to retain control over his fate. Clearly, there comes a point when these two must come into conflict. It's not uncommon also for patients in intensive care units to suffer psychological difficulties, such as depression. So you may ask whether it's ever possible to fathom the real wishes of the patient.

One of those assessing whether or not Dr Carrington was able to make rational judgments and to take critical decisions was his psychiatrist Anthony Moore.

MOORE. Dr Carrington was trained as a physician and a psychiatrist; however, particularly as he became more ill, his professional mantle dropped away from him, as is often the case, and he became more simply a sick human. The psychological insights which he might once have applied were no longer applicable; thus, like most people, like all of us would in a similar circumstance, the degree to which he could realistically perceive what was going on within his body and what was becoming of him came and went. On one day he would articulate his awareness that his life-span would be short; on other days he would speak vibrantly to the issue of looking forward to returning to work, to what type of work he would be doing in the future, and so forth and so on. His consistent wish until very very late in his course was that all conceivable medical measures be carried out. Since his primary physicians didn't know to what degree his pulmonary disease was indeed perhaps reversible, there was no reason not to comply with Ron's wish. However, as the medical picture became more clear, there became more and more a sense of underlying tension, with heroic care being delivered by people possessing the knowledge that it wasn't going to work.

KENNEDY. The heroic care Anthony Moore spoke of is only available at a price. Dr Carrington's bill for this particular course of treatment had already reached $48,000, or about £28,000.

There's no health service in California except for the very poor, but most people carry insurance. Nevertheless, it's not uncommon in the United States that families may, for example, have to sell their homes to pay for the medical treatment of a relative. Dr Carrington's insurance coverage was for $50,000 per course of treatment. One of his doctors estimated that each day in intensive care was adding $1,000 to his medical bill.

You may reflect on what influence this financial pressure, in addition to all the other pressures he'd have felt, would have had on his will to live. One doctor delivering 'the heroic care' was Dr John Goode, the lung specialist who was primarily responsible for Dr Carrington's day-to-day treatment. In talking to Dr Goode, I pressed him particularly on how far he felt he could rely on Dr Carrington's ability to assess his prospects.

GOODE. I felt that there were several factors that caused him to want to continue living, and I think they're normal everyday factors. He had a really nice family — he had a very good relationship with his wife — he was very bright, he enjoyed life, he read a lot, he had been teaching up until a month before hospitalization, and he had the will to live . . .

KENNEDY. He had a very strong will to live, did he?

GOODE. I'd say his will to live was extraordinary, it was more than staying alive. He had functioned in the community, not just in his family up until . . . you know, with a lung function that would have kept a lot of people in bed, and he was reading, writing — he had published an article shortly before his hospitalization, and he was a very forceful fellow.

KENNEDY. Was Dr Carrington in considerable pain when he was in intensive care?

GOODE. It's really difficult for me to measure these sorts of things, but if you stop and look at him, he must have been in pain. He had intravenous lines in his arms; he had many blood tests drawn; he had a tracheotomy tube — in other words a breathing tube — attached into his neck, and all these things must be somewhat uncomfortable. Bedpans, not sleeping — these units are very uncomfortable.

KENNEDY. Was he under the influence of medication?

GOODE. At times I would give him more sedation than other times because of the course of the illness. For instance, when one tries to wean a patient from a ventilator, the patient cannot be sedated heavily, because they'll tend to breathe less, and therefore require the ventilator more. However, to get him to the point where he might be weaned from the ventilator, one must allow him to sleep and get stronger, so if it was that kind of day or that kind of period, he might have more sedation than other times.

KENNEDY. We know that Dr Carrington ultimately asked to be allowed to die. What do you think persuaded Dr Carrington to ask that treatment be terminated?

GOODE. I can't be sure; I think it was a combination of events. I think he finally started thinking, for reasons I can't say, about whether or not he could actually leave the hospital, and he finally asked, and he realized that he couldn't leave the hospital alive.

KENNEDY. Do you think he was under any pressure from any source — financial, from relatives, from the staff?

GOODE. I don't know his financial situation. His wife gave me a rough idea of what their insurance situation was. What pressures his wife brought to bear on him to come around to this decision I am not sure. I felt that she may have either directly or indirectly encouraged him to make this decision for several reasons: she was suffering; she knew that he wasn't going to leave the hospital and she accepted that; and she didn't like seeing him talk himself into more suffering for him and for her; and I don't think there's any question that in some sense she must have gotten this across to him that he ought to give up much more than anyone else. The nursing staff definitely did not do that. As a matter of fact, it was one of those cases where the nursing staff had an unreasonable wish for him to live for ever—he was a very charming man.

KENNEDY. Could it be that the decision was taken in a temporary depression from drugs?

GOODE. Drugs may have had an effect. But the thing that always concerns me about these kind of decisions under those kind of circumstances is that it might be a temporary depression: in other words a suicide wish, and this is a terrifically difficult issue that is bantered about a lot under these kind of circumstances, and normally, if someone says 'Kill me,' you figure they're crazy. They must be depressed. Everybody wants to live. So when are you going to say that a man's request to kill him, which is what his request was, is a reasonable request? Personally, I feel it was reasonable under those circumstances. But again, I was closely involved.

KENNEDY. What guarantee did you have that it wasn't a decision taken in a moment of temporary depression?

GOODE. It was a very convincing, not cold, decision which he shared with everyone around him. The other thing is that he asked for his family. He didn't say 'Do it right away, get me out of this.' He listened to me as to what I thought might be a reasonable way to go about it. All of this doesn't mean he wasn't stark raving mad, and just putting on. But it all seemed very appropriate and didn't seem like a headstrong, desperate manoeuvre in any sense.

KENNEDY. Would it be fair to say that you accepted his decision when you thought it was the right decision, regardless of whether he may have been depressed or he may have been under the influence of drugs or some other pressure?

GOODE. No question. I wanted him to make that decision. For several days, maybe up to a week before that, whatever I was doing it was leading him to that decision. He would say, 'How about doing that?' and I'd say, 'Well, I . . . we really shouldn't do that. I don't think that's going to make much difference.' And that might be my only, you know, substantive interaction with him on that day. And my goal was to bring him around to my way of thinking; there's no question that I stopped fooling around when he agreed with me.

KENNEDY. Are you sure that he was totally *compos mentis*? Totally competent in his mind and lucid when he made that decision?

GOODE. Well, to get to my concept of the legal definition in this State, there's no question that he was. I'm sure he was under a terrific amount of both metabolic and emotional stress. You know—he's dying. But as far as . . . could he pass a competency hearing? He would have passed it with flying colours.

KENNEDY. The reason I pressed Dr Goode on the degree to which he could and *should* rely on Dr Carrington's decision is because both morally and legally, such a decision can be relied upon *only* if made by someone who's lucid and fully aware of what he's doing. Since this is crucial in any discussion of a person's right to self-determination, I pursued the question of Dr Carrington's state of mind further with Anthony Moore.

MOORE. Ron was virtually dead physiologically before he achieved a consistent recognition of the severity of his state. At that point, rather late one night, he and I had the last of a long sequence of talks. He began to ask me what the realities were of his medical situation and his prognosis — what could be hoped for in the best of circumstances. I told him. It wasn't anything that he hadn't been told before, particularly by Dr Goode, and yet, it seemed that Ron, at this particular point, was psychologically prepared to hear the information in a way that he had not been before. We talked. We sat. And he said some things like 'And I tried so damn hard.' And I could only say 'Yes'. He said, 'So the most I can hope for would be to be at home on a respirator full-time?' I said 'Yes'. And with some discussion he said, 'That's not for me. That simply is not for me.' And I said, 'Well, Ron, what do you want us to do?' He said, 'You're putting a hell of a burden on me.' And I think I responded with something like 'I think we're trying to share a hell of a burden with you.'

And he thought about that, and he kind of smiled and said, 'Yes, you're right.' Thought a bit more. Said, 'I'd like to have tomorrow morning to say goodbye to my father and to Laura and having done that, I'd like to die tomorrow afternoon.' . . . I said, 'Ron, you've got it.' . . . A lot of pain in that moment. Also about as close and as meaningful a human contact as one could dream of. One that made perfect sense to Ron and made perfect sense to me. I felt immense loss and immense satisfaction at the same time. That was Ron's first clear statement along such lines. It was a sudden shift for him from asking for . . . 'Do everything,' to 'I hear what the realities are and it's no good. You've done what you can; let's quit.'

In the possibility that it might be useful, I documented in his record what we talked about, and my view, as a psychiatrist, that he was absolutely lucid, and that his judgment was not impulsive, but rather a carefully thought through and well-considered decision which I felt should be respected. I spoke to Dr Goode that night as well. Didn't see Ron again. It went precisely as he wished.

KENNEDY. I don't think that anyone would doubt that the treatment Dr Carrington received was extremely caring and humane; but can we be sure that in other cases this will necessarily be so?

Can we be sure that doctors will not continue to force treatment on a patient who has said 'Enough', yet not cease treatment or hasten death too soon? No doubt the good doctor will always do the right thing, but can what the right thing is be stipulated in advance or written down? The doctor has to make choices, and choices should involve principles. Here we meet a central theme: can't we demand that the doctor set out the principles on which he acts for all to see? Is it enough for society in general or the patient in particular to leave decisions over life and death to the doctor? What for example, do we do if we, as relatives or patients, meet the rare case when a doctor is not a good doctor? Should society ask for guidelines? And if so, can satisfactory guidelines or rules, whether in the form of ethics or law, ever be worked out?

The bedrock of medical ethics to many doctors is, of course, the Hippocratic oath. When one looks at this, it's surprising what little guidance in the day-to-day practice of medicine it offers. Significantly, one of the few specific promises called for is: 'I will give no deadly medicine to anyone if asked, nor suggest such counsel.' In addition, can a set of precepts developed in the fifth century BC still retain sufficient vitality and relevance to regulate the practice of medical wonders at the end of the twentieth century AD?

A few moments ago, you heard Dr Moore tell how he assured Dr Carrington that his wish to die the following day would be respected by the physicians. But it was not Dr Moore the psychiatrist who enabled Dr Carrington, in the easy vernacular of California, to 'check out'. That task fell to Dr Goode. I asked him what he did, and what principles guided him.

GOODE. I have certain responses to these things in that . . . I have to live with these responses. And Dr Carrington had particularly asked me to disconnect him from the ventilator. And I said, 'Why do you want that?' And he said, 'I want to die'; and I said, 'Fine', and I said, 'Is there anything else?' And he said, 'I don't want to have any pain. I want to be free of pain.' And I said, 'Well, you know we can accomplish both these things, but I can't remove the ventilator from you—I can't do that, it makes me very uncomfortable.' I said, 'You know I have to stand here and watch you stop breathing if we do that, and as a matter of fact, you'll gasp for air, and you'll be watching us, and you'll see us go away . . . ' I said, ' . . . that's going to be very frightening to you.'

He said, 'But I don't want any pain.'

I said, 'I know.'

And he said, 'I want to die.'

I said, 'I know.' I said, 'But I'm not going to do that. I can't do that because it makes me uncomfortable. It makes . . . it's just too hard for me.' I watched it done before, once, as a student, and it turned my stomach, and it was very distressing to me, and in the end Carrington was going to die, and he did die, but I asked him if he would do it my way. And I said to him—we had a fairly frank relationship—I said, 'Listen, Ron, I'm going to be here tomorrow, and you're not; and I've got to be comfortable.' I said, 'I will accomplish those two goals: that you'll be pain-free and you'll die. But how about this?' And I suggested to him that I sedate him, essentially put him under general anaesthesia with morphine, and let nature take its course. Maybe turn the respirator down slightly, and all the secretions would build up; he couldn't cough, couldn't be suctioned properly, and that without this intensive minute-to-minute care, he would die within hours—even attached to the ventilator. And he said, 'I won't have any pain?'

I said, 'No.'

He said, 'Will I be struggling? Will it be hard for my wife?'

And I said, 'No—none of that.'

He said, 'I will die?'

And I said, 'Yes.'

He said, 'When?'

I said, 'Well, that's tough, but probably today.'

And he said, 'Okay.'

And I said, 'Well, I'll come back in a couple of hours; think it over some more.'

So I came back, and he said, 'Yes, it's still okay.'

And then he talked to his family, and then the third time I asked him again, and he still said it was okay, and so we did it. All on the same day.

KENNEDY. Why wouldn't you be happy just to turn the respirator off?

GOODE. It's for myself. It's totally . . . it's totally, I mean logically and legally, it's a ridiculous distinction; I don't think the distinction is impor-tant—that what comes out in the end is the same thing; I committed or omitted, however you want to put it—it's all the same thing. So what I do is try and think about everybody involved. His wife didn't want to watch him suffer, and she wanted him to die also, and she didn't want to see any suffering. He wanted no pain, and he wanted to die. And I felt like I could satisfy all these requests, plus my own discomfort, which I think is extremely important. I have other patients to care for; I have a day; I have a family; I have . . . you know, I have a life ahead of me, and these things do come up often enough that I saw no contradiction to the . . . not only the needs of the patient but the final ending—what would happen would be the same.

KENNEDY. Do you think you behaved entirely ethically in your treatment of Dr Carrington?

GOODE. Well, . . . I'm not sure. I've gotten away from . . . Let me put this in a less than shocking way, gotten away from thinking of everything in so-called ethical terms, because it confuses me. I know that giving a man on a ventilator morphine in high doses, enough to cause general anaesthesia, is risking his life, and it distracts me to think about whether or not it's ethical. I felt like that there was a . . . a more concrete and unifying decision, that . . . that decision was what are Dr Carrington's chances of being alive in any sense whatsoever, in having any human experiences, away from the hospital and away from this ventilator? And once that decision was made, then I felt that there was sort of humane behaviour that was required.

KENNEDY. What would you say to the commentator who said, 'My, here's another case of the doctor playing God?'

GOODE. Well . . . you see, I don't have a concept of God in that sense. I feel like that the situation in which Carrington was in is what God does and that I'm part of that situation, and that he was going to die, and that there was nothing I could do about it. And as a matter of fact, what got Carrington and myself to that situation on the last day was my giving up trying to play God, and I'd really reject that. I feel that sometimes I do try to play God when I do try and keep people alive beyond reasonable times. But he was to die. I don't think there is any question about that, and I feel like we gave him a good shot at staying alive. I think he got good medical care and was kept comfortable, and God decided he should die, and I couldn't prevent it.

KENNEDY. What would you say to the lawyer who would analyse what you did and what many other doctors, I'm sure, do every day, and would say, 'This looks like homicide — killing by injection.' What would you say to that?

GOODE. I could make no comment.

KENNEDY. Do you think it would be an insensitive response?

GOODE. I think it's a response that has nothing to do with my interaction with Carrington. I think it's looking at a single event out of context. I think his comment is true for what he has to say, in the sense that, you know — I always conceive of interactions with lawyers as answering questions, and that's not a question. All that is, is a comment. And I think his comment should stand for what it is. It's not an important comment as far as I'm concerned.

KENNEDY. But don't you feel uncomfortable, you as a member of the medical profession, don't you feel uncomfortable if there exists in the wider world a set of rules which would condemn as one of the most heinous crimes that which you regard as the most humane of conduct?

GOODE. It's a really uncomfortable thing. It's terribly uncomfortable to be trapped in this situation in the first place. The second place is that probably one of the reasons that physicians feel threatened by these kind of laws is that, without the law, I can cruise along and maintain my patients' comfort and my sanity to the boot of my ability. When the law starts coming along, it brings in another factor that has to be contended with. I trust myself. Now the legal system always thinks that there are people around who shouldn't be trusted, and I think that's right, and that's what there's laws for. Homicide isn't far away from that. But this was not a circumstance of homicide. That's all there is to it. Sure, injecting high doses of morphine, or low doses of morphine in a patient like this, contributes to his demise, but so does turning off the respirator, so I don't think there's any difference really.

KENNEDY. You may feel uncomfortable hearing about Dr Carrington's case. Society at large is naturally uneasy with the notion that doctors — even if acting humanely — may put an end to the life of a terminally ill person, whether young or old, or of a malformed baby with no prospects of survival. Yet we all know that it goes on — under the counter, as it were. Dr Goode's candid responses to those hard questions show, you may think, a doctor acting with great humanity and feeling. But surely we ought to pause before we accept that ethics and law are irrelevant here.

You will recall that Dr Goode specifically regards as unimportant the distinction between omission and commission, between doing something to bring about death, as opposed to standing by and letting death take its course. Yet this distinction is a vitally significant moral distinction to many, and is the linchpin of the law and ethics in this area.

Traditionally, the law has said that allowing someone who is terminally ill to die is lawful, but bringing about his or her death is unlawful, even if he or she consents or requests it. Are these rules unsuited to modern medicine? Is there a real distinction between turning off a respirator and letting Dr Carrington die, and injecting him so as to bring about his death?

If so, do we need our ethical and legal rules to continue to respect and enforce this distinction?

Here and in the United States, most experts now agree that a doctor is *not* obliged either ethically or legally to continue treatment when it's refused or is useless or has become a burden to the patient. But can the doctor do more if the situation calls for it? Dr Goode said he trusted himself, and clearly he is a good doctor; but can we always afford to trust, or do we thereby run the risk of taking a step down the road towards euthanasia, both voluntary and involuntary. Yet again, is the price of having such a distinction doctors who are afraid to act and patients condemned to a lingering death?

It was in part to answer these questions that the California State Legislature in the Autumn of 1976 passed a law called the Natural Death Act. It's the first Act of its kind in the world. It attempts to clarify some of the confusion I pointed out between that which is called for by law and ethics and what doctors and patients in practice, *think* is called for. Under the Act, a patient who's terminally ill and sustained by mechanical means may sign a directive authorizing the doctor to discontinue treatment and so allow death to take its course. The doctor must do as the patient directs. Should any relative complain, the doctor may rely upon the directive as justifying his actions.

I talked to Assemblyman Barry Keene, who, as Chairman of the California State Assembly Health Committee, wrote the bill and piloted it through the Legislature, and asked him first whether he felt that before the Act there was a grey area of uncertainty surrounding these problems.

KEENE. We found it very much a grey area. We found that practices were very diverse, that people had different impressions, not only of what ought to be done, but what was in fact being done. There were no good rules and regulations, and hospitals and insurance companies felt that they ought not to sit down and make them because, once they made them, they were admitting that these things were taking place and that such decisions were being made and were subject not only to public scrutiny but a threat of medical malpractice suits.

KENNEDY. But you chose to make some rules. In the process of making them, did you meet any opposition apart from that which you said may have come from the medical malpractice fear?

KEENE. We really found two kinds of opposition. One was the philosophic opposition of the Right-to-Life groups in this country; and they said that this was a foot in the door, the first step down the road towards active and involuntary euthanasia, and we had that argument to counter and that group to deal with, and even after countering the argument, we still had the group to deal with.

The other group were the physicians who felt that this was an unwarranted and unseemly intrusion of government into a relationship that is a very private and personal one, the patient–physician relationship.

KENNEDY. What do you think of that argument, you know, that law doesn't really have a place in the intensive care unit?

KEENE. Well, it works for everybody except the terminally ill patient. That's the problem with that attitude; the doctor and the nurse and the hospital and everyone may be convinced that these problems are resolved adequately. The only problem is that the terminally ill patient has in effect lost his autonomy, and it doesn't work for him, and that's what the bill is all about.

KENNEDY. Of course, when it came time to write the bill, there were great problems in choosing the exact words to be employed so that it wouldn't be seen by anyone as a 'Euthanasia Bill'. Originally the bill provided that treatment involving extraordinary medical measures could be refused. These words 'extraordinary medical measures' were replaced by the words 'life-sustaining procedures' which, in turn, were defined so as to be limited to respirators, I put it to Assemblyman Keene that this weakened the bill, and restricted the freedom of action of patients and doctors.

KEENE. It depends in part on how one perceives the function that the Act serves, and it probably serves several. The foremost is to reorient the relationship and the individuals who are party to that relationship in favour of the terminally ill patient and away from relatives and physicians and insurance companies and doctors and priests and others. The operational effect is rather narrow; it operates on a limited group of people who are in a state of physical decline.

KENNEDY. Yes indeed, I mean many argue that in fact a law wasn't required, and that the common law, as it's developed and grown and, for example, in the Quinlan case, says that the withdrawal of treatment, the withholding of consent to treatment, is entirely lawful; and some might argue that, by giving a law like this, which is rather narrowly drawn, you've taken away a lot; in other words, a doctor will feel, this I can do, but the other I can't do.

KEENE. Operationally the law provides a more neutral atmosphere within which the physician may operate. We have tried to make it clear in the law that what we are establishing is a parallel procedure and not an exclusive procedure, so that the other law as it existed, whatever it is, still does exist today, but that here is a prescribed procedure which terminally ill patients may choose to use should they wish to do so. Now some doctors could conceivably still be frightened off, but we must presume, I think, that doctors are literate people, that they can understand what the law is if it is told to them, and the medical societies and other groups are making available to them the workings of this particular Act.

KENNEDY. As you heard, the Act deals with only a narrow and fairly uncommon occurrence. It leaves intact the old law to deal with all the other problems, 'whatever the old law is', as Assemblyman Keene put it. He assumes doctors understand the law and consider it relevant. In the light of this comment I'd like you to hear Dr Goode's observations on the Natural Death Act in the context of Dr Carrington's case.

GOODE. Well this was prior to January 1st, when the Natural Death Act became law. I was aware of its existence, but hadn't read it and didn't know any more about it than that it was about to become law. I didn't know the particulars of it.

KENNEDY. Would Dr Carrington's case have come within the provision of the Act, do you know?

GOODE. It could have. In the sense that myself and another doctor, I think two doctors have to agree that the patient is terminal, and I think that would have been likely; as a matter of fact, I knew of no one who felt we should push ahead, and he had four or five physicians in different roles dealing with him, so he would have fulfilled the definition of being terminal.

The only difference then would have been that he would have had to sign, and then we would have had to wait two more weeks; and I'll tell you, it's interesting, with the bill the way it's written, to put that on the Carrington case would have meant his being alive and suffering two more weeks and honestly, I would have had to do something like that in two weeks, probably because we'd have to work hard on him. The idea of the bill was to keep them going for two weeks, you know, so they can change their mind and . . .

KENNEDY. Is it your understanding then that the bill makes some acts of doctors lawful when they respond to the signing of a directive, but doesn't make lawful what you did thinking it was perfectly good medical technique?

GOODE. The Act does not help the legal standing of what I did.

KENNEDY. Do you think what you did was unlawful?

GOODE. I don't know if it was unlawful; I didn't think about it.

KENNEDY. One couldn't look for a stronger and more candid refutation of Assmblyman Keene's view that doctors think the law is relevant. Despite what Dr Goode and others have said, however, I think the law and ethics governing the situation you've been hearing about are both understandable and quite sensitive to the needs of patients and doctors. But it's a deplorable fact that for far too long lawyers and others have ignored this important area, and have left doctors to wrestle alone with its complexities. Little wonder that the doctor now feels that he can do what he likes with us.

It may help if I explain the legal and ethical position as I see it. As it happens, the only ethical guide which is relatively clear, though still very general, is that contained in a brief statement made by Pope Pius XII 20 years ago. Though a statement of Catholic doctrine, it has received widespread acceptance. In his famous allocution, Pope Pius declared that, morally, a doctor was not obliged to continue treatment, nor was a patient obliged to accept it when such treatment involved extraordinary medical measures. And this has been interpreted as meaning measures which are excessively costly, burdensome, unusual, or which are of no real benefit to the patient. Dr Carrington's treatment could well have been classified as such.

Now the legal position: though I'm referring to England, the law is, in my view, very similar in California. First, a patient who is conscious and refuses treatment must have his wish respected whatever his condition, provided he's mature and lucid enough to make such a decision. If the doctor thinks the patient isn't sufficiently lucid or mature, then the decision should be ignored. Second, when a patient is near death, a doctor is *not* obliged to embark upon or continue heroic treatment which has no prospect of benefiting the patient. Third, a doctor's obligation when he can no longer hold back the approach of death is to make the patient comfortable, including easing his pain. If to ease pain, the doctor must take measures which may hasten death, this is permissible provided the doctor's aim is *only* the relief of pain. Fourth, if a patient is on a respirator and has no prospects of breathing for himself again, then a distinction must be made. The conscious, alert patient, such as the polio victim, must be given treatment for as long as he desires. To switch off the respirator otherwise is impermissible. If the patient is unconscious and will never regain consciousness, or is suffering from a progressive or fatal illness, then the respirator must be seen as heroic treatment and may be turned off, as in the case of Karen Quinlan, when it is no longer of any lasting benefit. Finally, the relatives of patients have no right to make decisions on the patient's behalf. Only a parent has such a right, and even then the parent may only act in the best interests of the patient.

These, then, are some general principles, but you may feel that they still leave considerable scope for discretion and interpretation. So should we pass more laws? Well, I take the view that legislation in a form like the Natural Death Act, although perhaps appropriate for California, should not be adopted in England. Oftentimes, legislation creates as many problems as it solves — limiting flexibility and sometimes even inviting litigation. Also, the constant political process of pressure and compromise may produce a law which satisfies no one. This is not to say that I advocate the status quo. Rather, I would like to see developed a Code of Practice binding on doctors which would grow out of the views of all interested parties: doctors, patients, and the public.

Thus, a whole range of decisions would not be left merely to the instinct of the doctor, good though he or she may be, but would be set down in a form which is at the same time authoritative, yet flexible and able to change if circumstances demand. For we must never lose sight of the fact that the issues involved are moral ones; and that though doctors may be experts in medicine, they are no more competent or qualified to speak on moral issues than you or I.

You will remember that I said that the general principles I proposed still left room for discretion and interpretation. It now remains for you to consider and debate the proper boundaries of such discretion and interpretation. For this is a matter on which not just doctors or lawyers, but all of us, must have our say and our way.

16

The Law Relating to the Treatment of the Terminally Ill*

INTRODUCTION

When a lawyer is invited to comment on the continuing care of those dying from cancer, the first reaction of many is surprise. The assumption is commonly made that the decisions to be taken in caring for such patients, the therapeutic strategy to be adopted, are wholly medical matters, and thus wholly for doctors to make, with or without discussion with the patient. Of course, such decisions are medical matters in that they arise in the context of the professional relationship of doctor and patient, and they are for doctors to make in that the doctor is the professional 'on the spot' caring for the patient. But it cannot be stated too emphatically that the principles by reference to which decisions are made are not within the unique prerogative of doctors to lay down. The word 'strategy', or indeed, 'management', for example, implies that choices are available; and choices, if they are to be rationally defensible, must be made by reference to known and accepted principles. Such principles are those which have been worked out by the larger society, not doctors alone, and which embody the moral, philosophical, and spiritual assumptions of that society. The law is one source of such principles. Indeed, in so far as the law represents the embodiment of those rules deemed so important by society as to warrant setting them out formally with appropriate sanctions for non-observance, legal principles are the most important regulators of doctors' decisions. This is so even though explicit reference to the law is rarely, if ever, made, since the law establishes the pattern with which other normative principles, to which the doctor may more readily refer—his professional code of ethics, his or society's code of morality—by and large conform.

In the case of the dying, as in all other areas of medicine, therefore, the doctor must pay due heed to the law. He must act within the law: he is never

---

* This paper has been adapted from two separate papers: 'Legal Aspects', in R. Twycross, ed., *The Continuing Care of Terminal Cancer Patients* (Pergamon Press, 1980), and 'The law relating to the treatment of the terminally ill, in C. Saunders, ed., *The Management of Terminal Malignant Disease*, 2nd edn. (Edward Arnold, 1982). It contains minor revisions of both papers, together with brief references to more recent developments.

above it. The law or, more correctly stated, those who make the law, have a corresponding obligation to ensure that the principles and rules laid down meet certain criteria. First, the law must be clear. Second, it must be sensitive to the particular circumstances it seeks to regulate—for example, the realities of modern medical practice and the availability and use of new technology and medicines. Third, it must strike an appropriate balance between the interests of the various parties involved, without putting in jeopardy certain fundamental commitments, such as, for example, the protection of the individual and the absolute prohibition on the taking of another's life.

Some argue that the law in England *vis-à-vis* terminal patients does not meet the first of these criteria, and thus cannot satisfy, *ex hypothesi*, the other two. This is because in England there is no statute or code setting out the law governing the continuing care of the terminally ill; nor are there more than a handful of cases that have been decided by the courts.[1] None the less, legal principles undoubtedly do exist and obviously condition the choices made by doctors. The fact that the law is not well documented, however, has produced at least three unfortunate effects. First, it has led to doubts as to the precise legal obligations of a doctor in a particular case. This, in turn, has helped to foster the view that there is really no law at all; indeed, that the law is an irrelevance. Alternatively, the practice has grown up that if the law is not clear, then, given that the possibility of being prosecuted for a crime or sued for damages may exist, albeit as a remote possibility in England, it is better always for the doctor to err on the side of caution and follow the most conservative or restrictive view of the law. This practice, which is much more common in the United States, has acquired its own descriptive term, 'defensive medicine', a term suggestive of the notion that an unnecessary and destructive tension exists between what the doctor thinks is good medicine and what the law requires of him.

All of this can come as no surprise, since one of the greatest difficulties which confronts the medical legal commentator in dealing with the treatment of the terminally ill is that techniques and technology have developed and changed with such rapidity in the past decade or so that it is only *vaguely* that the *problems* are perceived, let alone responded to by developing a general consensus in the form of law. Some general legal rules do exist, but often they assume a set of medical realities long overtaken by events. The recourse to respirators and cardiac pace-makers that has made a legal definition of death based upon the absence of breathing and heartbeat outmoded is a good example. Further, whatever legal rules do exist deal largely with the conventional medical-legal issues of acute and emergency treatment and

---

[1] *In re Potter*, *The Times*, 26 July 1963; *R.* v. *Malcherek* [1981] 1 WLR 690; and, of persuasive authority although not concerned with the care of the terminally ill, *Re B* [1981] 1 WLR 1421 and *R.* v. *Arthur*, *The Times*, 5 Nov. 1981.

with malpractice. These rules are by and large irrelevant in dealing with the terminally ill patient who is, in a sense, in a special class. Such a patient is, by definition, going to die sooner rather than later, and the regimen of care adopted, overshadowed as it is by the mass of available technology, calls for distinct and very sensitive regulation.

To make things more difficult, not only have legal rules failed to develop, but the concepts which provide the stuff of legal rules are equally ill equipped to respond adequately. For example, a legal system which sees the contact of a doctor with his patient as an assault or battery made lawful by consent, and rests so much on the notion of informed consent without showing any real understanding of the dynamics of the doctor–patient relationship, is in danger of losing respect. In the light of the foregoing, an invitation to spell out the legal rules governing the treatment of the terminally ill must be regarded with some trepidation. None the less, the law of England can, in my submission, be stated with sufficient clarity to dispel the various criticisms which have been noted. I further submit that when properly understood, it is sufficiently sensitive to the diverse realities it would seek to regulate to render uncalled-for the criticisms and apprehensions reflected in recourse (now often ritualized) to the term 'defensive medicine'.

PRINCIPLE UNDERLYING THE LAW

Before setting out the law, it is important to discover to what extent there exists any unifying principle or premiss which draws together the individual legal rules. Such a principle would not only add rational coherence to what would otherwise be a set of unrelated rules, but would also supply the reference point whereby novel dilemmas may be resolved. One such principle, often referred to in Continental Europe and the United States, is that of contract, that the relationship between the doctor and the patient is regulated by agreement between the two parties. This is unsatisfactory for a number of reasons. First, in England there is not, as a matter of law, a contract between doctor and patient in the vast majority of all relationships, because health care is made available through the National Health Service. Second, the notion of a contract carries the implication that medical care is a commodity to be bargained for in the market-place, and only available if the price is right, a notion specifically rejected in England. Another unifying principle is said to be the concept of trust. This, it is said, is the key factor governing the doctor–patient relationship. This analysis is equally flawed. First, to argue that each party must trust the other does not demonstrate that each in fact does so. Indeed, oftentimes a doctor may expect trust without himself reciprocating, in that, for example, he will choose not to tell his patient certain facts, on the paternalistic premiss that the patient is better off not knowing.

Second, trust presupposes a conscious and reasoned decision by the patient which, in fact, may be beyond many patients who, through pain, the effect of drugs, or unconsciousness, cannot make such decisions.

If there is a unifying premiss which informs the law, it is to be found, I submit, in the concept of duty. A doctor has expertise. A patient seeks help and is therefore vulnerable. He can only rely on the doctor's skill and good faith. Given this reality, the law imposes duties upon the doctor which exist independently of agreement. The patient may expect and ultimately demand that these duties be carried out.

THE GENERAL DUTY OF THE DOCTOR

So what is the doctor's duty in the case of caring for the terminally ill? The classification of a patient as 'terminally ill' is a decision for the doctor to make, based upon wholly medical criteria. Since, however, the decision carries with it certain significant implications, it is one which must be made in good faith, and on the basis of the exercise of proper medical skill. If arrived at otherwise, clearly legal redress will be available to any patient who suffers harm as a consequence. 'Terminally ill', I submit means that the patient has an illness which has been accurately diagnosed, and which seems certain to bring about his death within a relatively short period of time, since the illness is beyond both cure and palliation. The duty of the doctor in such a circumstance is, stated generally, to use all appropriate medical skills to make the time remaining to the patient as comfortable as possible. This is both his professional, ethical duty and his legal duty.

The primary significance of stating the duty in these terms has to do with the form of caring or treatment the doctor provides. He is no longer under a duty to adopt forms of treatment intended to cure the patient, since, by definition, the patient is beyond cure. Nor need the doctor adopt palliative measures, if 'palliation' is taken to mean the use of measures aimed at modifying pathological processes or their consequences so as to delay or prevent the otherwise inevitable effects of such processes or their consequences. The doctor's duty is limited to the control, to the extent that it is possible, of discomforting symptoms. But even this apparently simple principle requires some clarification before we go further. It is important to notice that although the symptoms displayed by the patient usually relate to the terminal illness, there may be times when they arise from some separate, independent condition. When this happens, the doctor's first duty is to diagnose this fact correctly. Then he must decide on the appropriate response, which is a legal, as well as a medical, decision. There are, perhaps, three principles which must be followed. First, if the new condition has discomforting symptoms, these should be controlled. Second, if it does not, it can be ignored. Third, both these principles are subject to the question of whether the new condition may be cured or palliated. If it can be, and if by so doing, the patient would be able to enjoy a further period of life without increased discomfort, then the cure or palliative measure should be adopted.

This general duty of the doctor, to control symptoms as much as possible and otherwise make the patient as comfortable as possible, has implicit in it two propositions worth noticing. First, medical treatment other than symptom control or management is uncalled-for as a matter of law and, indeed, is inappropriate; not only is it unethical conduct, but the doctor could also be subject to legal sanction. If the doctor's duty is a matter of law, a court could restrain a doctor from continuing such treatment, and he could be held liable to pay damages for any distress or increased discomfort the patient suffered as a consequence, in that his conduct would amount to negligence. It would not be open to a doctor to argue that other doctors did as he did. Medical evidence would be relevant only to establish whether what the doctor did was deemed acceptable medical practice to make the dying patient comfortable. Although this is undoubtedly the law, it often seems to be ignored, particularly in the United States, where pointless efforts are made by doctors, albeit often with the best of intentions. For example, the doctor may fear that if he does not use every technique in his armoury, he will be accused of neglecting his patient; or the doctor may simply not understand the real nature of his obligations. The second implicit proposition is that the diagnosis of a terminal illness does not mean that the doctor's obligations to his patient cease. There is some fear among lay people that this is so, that the doctor gives up and hands the patient over to those nursing him. Furthermore, to the extent that some doctors, especially those recently trained, see themselves as medical scientists solving problems and dispensing cures, rather than fundamentally caring for their patients, they may, in fact, be guilty of distancing themselves from, if not abandoning, their dying patients. This can also happen when a doctor experiences discomfort in the face of death, or an inability to come to terms with his own helplessness. But a dying patient is still a living patient. The law recognizes this and demands that care continue, even if its nature changes. This is an example of the English law's affirmation of its fundamental respect for life.

SPECIFIC DUTIES

Having stated the general duty of a doctor towards his terminally ill patient, it is necessary to examine how this general duty is made more specific and applied in the myriad real-life situations which arise. Analytically, the process is one of deriving more specific principles from more general ones. It is in the nature of the law, however, to be couched in abstract terms. There is not one particular legal rule for each situation which arises or may arise. This would be a system of *ad hoc* law which would suggest that each novel situation warrants the creation of a new rule. Rather, the law works dynamically through the process of analogical reasoning. A principle is enunciated which is intended and designed to regulate a certain real situation *X*. Another principle regulates another real situation, *Y*. When a novel situation *Z* arises for which no principle has apparently been specifically designed, the law is determined by examining the extent to which *Z* is closer to *X* or to *Y*. If it is more analogous to *X*, then the legal principle regulating *X* will ordinarily be invoked. Occasionally situation *Z* may inspire the creation of a wholly new principle, which then serves as a possible precedent for the future. Thus, what is outlined here represents both the existing law and the basis for determining the law in as yet untested or unfamiliar circumstances.

Respect for the Patient's Right to Self-Determination

Perhaps the most fundamental precept of the common law is respect for the liberty of the individual. In a medical-legal context this means that a person's right to self-determination, to deal with his body as he sees fit, is protected by law. The doctor's first duty is to respect this right. This applies as much to the terminally ill patient as to any other. The patient may not be abandoned; but the care given must change from treating for living to treating for dying. Thus, if a patient who is aware of the nature of his condition and competent to make a decision refuses further treatment from his doctor, then continued treatment is unlawful, as constituting a battery or a criminal assault. This is so notwithstanding the fact that the doctor may regard the patient's decision as wrong or ill advised. To abide by the refusal may be difficult for the doctor; but it is required by law, the principle of self-determination overruling any notion that 'the doctor knows best' or some vague notion of there being a public policy in favour of preserving life.

In practice, this situation will arise only very rarely if a regime of symptom control and no more has been adopted. None the less, the importance of the obligation to respect the wishes of the patient cannot be overstated. Of course, the law only recognizes the patient's right to self-determination in circumstances in which the patient is both legally competent (that is, not unconscious or a young child) and sufficiently lucid to comprehend what he is doing. It is obvious that there is some danger that the principle may be swallowed by these exceptions, particularly the second, since the determination of a patient's lucidity is made by the doctor who may well disagree with the patient's expressed wish and want to override it. The decision is made harder by the knowledge that almost all terminally ill patients are receiving medication and may be suffering pain and distress, all of which could affect their mental competence, quite apart from some doctors' reluctance to 'give up.' Ultimately, the good faith of the doctor must guide his actions, since complaints after the event by patients or relatives may founder for lack of proof.

Perhaps the most appropriate mechanism for safeguarding both the patient's and the doctor's interests is for the hospital to document the circumstances fully in the notes, and to have the patient's competence assessed in cases of doubt by a qualified person not otherwise concerned in the case. Thus, in summary, the first duty of a doctor is to listen to and respect the wishes of his patient. It may be noted for the sake of completeness that respect for the patient's right to self-determination is not without its own limitation. A person's autonomous choices call for respect only as long as they do not seriously impinge on another's enjoyment of his autonomy and that other has not agreed beforehand to give up certain of his choices as a condition of practising medicine in, for example, the National Health Service. This allows two further propositions in the present context. First, in the unlikely event that a patient in a hospital refused even nursing care—for example, bathing or changing sheets—different considerations would apply. The hospital's duty to maintain hygiene and protect the health of other patients would entitle the hospital to demand acceptance of such care as a condition for remaining in the hospital. Continued refusal would justify discharging those patients fit enough to be moved and with somewhere to go, and forcing the others to submit. This does not extend to feeding a patient against his will, which I regard as a form of aggressive treatment. Second, although the patient may *refuse* certain procedures, it is doubtful that he can *insist* on procedures which the doctor, in the exercise of reasonable medical judgment, in good faith regards as uncalled-for. Indeed, to the extent that any such request may represent an unjustified use of scarce resources, it would be unethical for the doctor to comply or for the patient to insist that he does so.

The Prohibition Against Taking Life

Having established the point that it is the patient who ultimately may set the limits to the doctor's intervention, it is now necessary to consider the duties which arise in the usual circumstances in which treatment is consented to. The almost trite observation has already been made that the patient, though dying, is still living. This cannot be overemphasized, however, in that respect for life is a cardinal principle of English law. It follows that the taking of a patient's life by some conduct deliberately designed with the primary intention of bringing about his death is unlawful, whether it be at the patient's request or without his knowledge or consent. This is homicide.

The distinction between killing the patient and changing treatment so as to allow death to take place is sometimes a fine one, and taxes philosophers and lawyers. Some see the distinction in terms of a commission which is unlawful and an omission which may not be. I do not adopt this distinction. Though it is part of the general law, I regard it as unhelpful here. The real argument is not how a doctor's conduct can be characterized, but whether under the circumstances he has fulfilled his duty to the patient to care for him in good faith. The principles of good faith reflect professional ethics and general social morality. Neither at present condones euthanasia, so that, to cause the patient's death, whether by omission or commission, would be a breach of the duty to care for the patient in good faith, and hence unlawful. Both, however, contemplate allowing the patient to die, if, under the circumstances, the illness is terminal and no other form of treatment, apart from treatment for dying, is ethically indicated.

Many doctors specializing in the care of the dying consider that the state of modern medicine makes even the need to consider the notion of euthanasia, whether at the request of the patient or otherwise, as an option quite unnecessary, quite apart from its moral repugnance. For the variety of medicines now available to the doctor allow him to relieve the pain, distress, or even agony which could prompt a consideration of euthanasia. While this is so, it is still the case that by no means all hospitals or doctors are yet educated in the pharmacological and other management of the terminally ill, and large numbers of patients outside hospices and centres of excellence may well, by virtue of their condition, continue to pose the problem of euthanasia. The appropriate response, however, is not to alter the law so as to allow euthanasia, and thereby arguably undermine the respect for life enshrined both in the law and medical training. Rather, attention must be directed to ensuring that doctors who care for the dying understand and use the medicines and techniques now available.

To Intervene Or Not

The question which next arises is whether the doctor, while prohibited from doing anything deliberately aimed at causing the death of his patient, may so adjust the treatment that he does not actively intervene and the patient dies. The examples commonly cited are whether antibiotics must be administered if the patient contracts pneumonia, or whether the patient must be resuscitated if he suffers heart failure. As has been seen, the analysis which I prefer is couched in the language not of acts and omissions, but of duties. This approach is superior both morally and legally. The doctor owes the patient certain duties by virtue of the relationship of doctor and patient. The duties which arise in this situation can be set out, as can those arising elsewhere. Moreover, to claim that in allowing the patient to die, the doctor acted lawfully, because he omitted to do anything, rather than committed any act, is to overlook the obvious point that, depending on the particular circumstances, it may be the doctor's duty to act, so that his failure to act by allowing death constituted a breach of duty.

The problem is best analysed in the following stages. The doctor's duty to the terminally ill is centred on making the patient comfortable until death. The doctor is not under a duty to take action to avert death if such action will not aid in the comfort of the patient. Each patient is different in terms of the progress of his disease, his psychological response to it, his will to live or otherwise; and thus the general principle of each patient's comfort is to be judged in the light of these particular facts. Obviously, purely objective criteria such as the patient's age or the particular illness cannot be justified or relied upon. The patient's death is not an evil to be avoided at all costs, but is an inevitable consequence of his condition. Thus, if, in the light of the particular facts, the patient may be discomforted by the doctor's conduct, the doctor is under no duty to act. Equally, if the patient may be comforted by the doctor's conduct, then the doctor is under a duty to act, provided that the conduct is otherwise licit.

Another way of analysing the doctor's duty is to say that, when a patient is near death, a doctor is not obliged to embark upon or continue heroic treatment which has no prospect of benefiting the patient.

An alternative, more common, term to 'heroic' is 'extraordinary'. It was Pope Pius XII[2] who first advanced the view that doctors were not obliged to give, nor patients to accept, 'extraordinary medical measures'. The term has consistently been interpreted as meaning 'whatever here and now is very costly or very unusual or very painful or very difficult or very dangerous, or if the good effects that can be expected from its use are not proportionate to the difficulty and inconvenience that are entailed.'[3] In the 1976 Stevens Lecture, the Archibishop of Canterbury[4] expressed his support for this as a moral principle. I take the view that it is also the legal principle. Indeed, I would go so far as to say that a doctor who continued treatment past this point would be behaving at least unethically, if not unlawfully.

It is important to understand that it is never treatment in the abstract which can be described as 'extraordinary', but only treatment in the context of the particular patient being cared for.[5] It is the particular patient's care which matters. The real question is whether, under the circumstances, it would be wrong to continue intervention. This is often referred to as a consideration of the patient's future 'quality of life'. Once this is understood, it is clear

---

[2] Pius XII, 49 *Acta Apostolicae Sedis* 1027 (1959).

[3] Church Assembly Board for Social Responsibility, *Decisions about Life and Death* (CABSR, 1965).

[4] Archbishop of Canterbury, 'On dying and dying well: Extracts from the Edwin Stevens Lecture', 3 *Journal of Medical Ethics* 57 (1977).

[5] See G. R. Dunstan, 'Life, prolongation of: ordinary and extraordinary means', in Duncan *et al.*, eds., *Dictionary of Medical Ethics* (Darton, Longman and Todd, 1981).

that terms such as 'extraordinary treatment' or 'quality of life' only state the problem. What still have to be worked out are the criteria which would justify not intervening aggressively, or, to put it another way, would amount to a quality of life which was not worth having. There is strong support for the idea that excessive pain, expense, and hardship, together with no hope of benefit, may serve as the starting-points—though obviously words such as 'excessive' need further careful definition. Thus, the term 'extraordinary treatment' is a conclusion rather than a starting-point for analysis. As Dr Gillon argues, 'once the actual criteria of decision are specified, the misleading labels "ordinary means" and "extraordinary means" become superfluous.'[6] I agree with Dr Gillon that it would be more helpful to use the terms 'ethically indicated' and 'ethically not indicated' rather than 'ordinary' and 'extraordinary'.

Applying these principles, pneumonia need not be treated if, on the facts, to do so would mean that the patient recovered to endure a further period of discomfort, pain, or inevitable, distressing deterioration. But if the patient could be restored to a state whereby he could enjoy a further period of life at the level of comfort he previously had, then it should be treated. The same would be true of resuscitation and any similar intervention. Given that the decision calls for considered judgment, it must always be appropriate to consider the matter in the case of each patient before it arises. This avoids the possibility of unwarranted decisions being made in the heat of the moment. It may also be appropriate to record the decision made so that all involved in the patient's case may know. This is not to say that it may not be revised. Indeed, it is appropriate to review it periodically, as the circumstances of the patient may change. Clearly, much room is left for the discretion of the doctor, and this is as it should be, since the assessment of the patient's prognosis is one of his distinct skills. The law lays down the general principle, and the doctor who acts skilfully, reasonably, and in good faith is protected.

This analysis also helps to clarify another issue which taxes some commentators. The realities of modern medical technology have made it possible for doctors to extend the process of dying through the use, for example, of what are colloquially, but perhaps inaptly, called 'life-support' machines. Questions are asked as to how long the doctor must maintain his patient on such a machine before discontinuing its use. Such questions are inappropriate. They stem from an inadequate analysis of the legal and ethical principles involved. Life-support machines are merely one form of interventionist therapy, no different in principle from medicines, surgery, or other treatment. In the case of the terminally ill, their use is ordinarily uncalled-for, since they can readily be categorized as heroic, or extraordinary, therapy, imposing a further burden of discomfort on the patient with no foreseeable benefit in terms of increased

[6] R. Gillon, Editorial, 7 *Journal of Medical Ethics* 55 (1981).

comfort in the future. The key question is not whether their use may be discontinued, once started; rather, it is whether they should be used in the first place. That is, it is not a matter of switching them off, but of whether they should be switched on either initially or again after suitable tests have been carried out. This is, therefore, the same question as whether to give antibiotics when pneumonia occurs, and is resolved by reference to the same principle.

The Doctrine of Double Effect

A doctor's obligation in treating the terminally ill is, as has been seen, to make his patient comfortable, which includes easing pain. There may arise circumstances in which a doctor may use a form of treatment for his patient's benefit aware of the fact that it may have the secondary effect of accelerating (or run the risk of accelerating) the patient's death. This reflects the so-called doctrine of double effect which was incorporated into English law in one of the few cases that have been decided in this area, *R* v. *Bodkin Adams*.[7] The doctor is not in breach of his legal duty to his patient if, by adopting the particular form of treatment, his principal and primary intention is the alleviation of symptoms which are discomforting and irremediable in any less drastic a way. This proposition is not limited to the oft-cited example of the use of increased doses of morphine, a practice which specialists argue is no longer necessary or appropriate, but extends to any treatment decision.

Aiding Suicide

It may happen sometimes that the patient may wish to end his life, rather than wait for death. The specialists again argue that with the right regime of treatment, there is no need for this to happen; but in reality the right

---

[7] [1957] Crim. LR 365. The case of *Bodkin Adams* is, in fact, far more complicated than my brief reference to it suggests. Devlin J.'s direction to the jury, from which the law is drawn, in analytically complex and ultimately unsatisfactory, although on another level it is eminently sensible. There seem to be two strands to Devlin J.'s analysis. The first is that a doctor by administering, for example, morphine does not intend the patient's death in the circumstances under discussion. But any reasonable understanding of intention in law, if not in moral philosophy, would compel the conclusion that if the doctor knows that death will probably follow, he intends to bring that death about, although he may not desire it. Alternatively, the analysis may be that the doctor does not cause the death. The cause is the underlying pathology. But if the drug brings about death sooner rather than later, the doctor does cause the death, on any reasonable view of the word 'cause'.

The better view may be, therefore, that talk of double effect is a legal nicety. What is really at play is the proposition that a doctor may lawfully do an act whereby he intentionally causes the death of a patient in circumstances which the law (the courts) thinks permissible. And it will be found to be permissible, as a matter of public policy, in precisely those circumstances in which life is an intolerable burden, the patient is dying, and the only humane treatment left is one which has death as a likely consequence.

regime is not always available, and even if it were, some patients may wish to retain their independence to choose suicide. By the Suicide Act 1961, section 2, English law makes aiding and abetting the suicide of another a serious crime (see *R* v. *Reed*).[8] Thus, a doctor is under a duty to refrain from any act which may aid his patient in committing suicide. It is, however, a fine line between aiding suicide and making available, for example, certain drugs to relieve pain which, if more than a certain dosage is taken, will cause death. A court would, I submit, be slow to find liable a doctor who merely facilitated the self-determination of someone unable through illness to help himself. This should be contrasted with the situation in which the patient instructs the doctor to refrain from further treatment. As has been seen, the doctor is under a duty to comply with this request, provided the patient is lucid and competent. This is not aiding a suicide, since the patient is not, I submit, committing suicide, but only declining further medical care.

Proxy Decision Making

If the patient is competent, no one else may make decisions for him. Relatives should, of course, be involved; but they have no right to make decisions about treatment. But the patient may not be competent. Thus, the final matter for consideration is the duty owed by the doctor when the patient is unable to participate in treatment decisions, through unconsciousness, lack of comprehension, or legal incompetence, and others purport to speak for him. Is the doctor under a duty to respect treatment decisions proposed by relatives or next of kin? Proxy consent, decision making on another's behalf, is well known to the law. There are, however, certain risks involved in delegating to people other than the patient the power to make what may be life-or-death decisions — for example, the decision to discontinue certain treatment, to control symptoms, or not to resuscitate the patient. English law seeks to avoid these risks.

Where the patient is incompetent, any analysis of the situation should consider children separately from adults. Incompetence (or incapacity) in a child, it should be noted, depends not on age but on maturity and the capacity to understand what is involved in any decision. As regards the incompetent child, only his parents or legal guardian may speak for him, and then only for as long as he remains under their control or until majority at 18 years of age. In speaking for him, they may only act in his best interests. The test of what is in a child's best interests refers to general societal values, rather than the views of the particular parent or legal guardian. Thus, for example, the refusal by a parent or guardian, on the patient's behalf, of a certain treatment need not necessarily be respected, if it is deemed in the patient's

---

[8] [1982] Crim. LR 819.

interests to treat him this way. Equally, a doctor need not respect a parent's or legal guardian's demand that treatment be continued or altered if in his view it is pointless, and the treatment would be categorized as ethically not indicated. This is because the law accepts that it may not always be in the best interests of a patient to receive further invasive, or aggressive, treatment.

Support for these propositions may be found in the case of *Re B*.[9] The Court of Appeal had to decide whether to authorize surgery on a week-old child born with Down's syndrome and duodenal atresia. The child's parents took the view that surgery would be wrong, and wanted the child to be allowed to die. Mr Justice Ewbank endorsed this view. But, on appeal the same day, Lord Justice Templeman, speaking for the court, held that 'the Judge erred because he was influenced by the views of the parents, instead of deciding what was in the best interests of the child'. Earlier in his decision, however, he had posed the question, 'was the child's life going to be so demonstrably awful that it should be condemned to die; or was the kind of life so imponderable that it would be wrong to condemn her to die?' The implication would seem to be that some lives *could* be 'so demonstrably awful' that the doctor's legal duty would be limited to making the child comfortable and allowing it to die. The court does not offer any criteria of awfulness; but it may be that the law will reflect those factors involved in the analysis of the circumstances in which treatment is considered to be ethically not indicated. The significance of the decision here, given that the case concerned a child who was not terminally ill, is its recognition that it may not always be a doctor's duty in law to preserve life, provided certain conditions are met.

As regards others who are terminally ill and whom the law regards as incompetent — for example, the unconscious, the mentally ill, the mentally handicapped, or the seriously confused — it is not clear that anyone has authority in law to consent to or refuse treatment on their behalf. The law's response if the matter were tested would doubtless be that, first, it must be satisfactorily established by the doctor responsible that the patient was in fact incompetent. Second, it must be shown that there was no expression of view made by the person as to what should be done in the event that he became incompetent, or, if there were such an expression of view, that it was made when the patient was already incompetent. Third, the doctor may then decide on the appropriate care according to the ethical and legal principles set out earlier. Fourth, if, having acted according to these principles, he were subsequently challenged regarding the lawfulness of his conduct, the doctor would have the benefit of the defence of necessity if he had intervened, but if he had not intervened, he would not thereby be in breach of his duty to his patient.[10]

---

[9] *Supra* n. 1.
[10] This paragraph must now be read in the light of the decision of the Canadian Supreme Court in *Re Eve* [1986] 2 SCR. The court took the view that the ancient role of the court in

If the patient had expressed a view while still competent as to the treatment he should receive, the precise legal status of such a statement or request is not clear. Such express declarations have come to be known as Living Wills, and have received much attention in the United States and elsewhere.[11] They are not really a case of proxy decision, save that they instruct others to act. They represent, in large part, a reaction to the fear of many, both of being the object of never-ending and useless interventions and of being a burden to others. They represent an attempt to retain autonomy through prior expression of will, after the ability to choose and act on the choice has gone. As with calls for euthanasia, it could be that a proper understanding by doctors of their duties to their patients, both ethical and legal, could obviate the need in large part for such developments.

Returning to the status of such an expression of view, it is probably the case that if the doctor were satisfied that it truly represented the patient's view and was executed while he was still competent, then the doctor ought ethically to respect its intent. In law, however, it has no force, and a doctor must ignore it if it requests him to do that which is otherwise unlawful or is contrary to the duty he owes to any patient. If, for example, a patient expressed the wish that the doctor kill her if she reached a particular point of mental and physical deterioration, or if the request was that she be left to die when she was not terminally ill, then the doctor would be legally obliged to ignore the request.

In other cases, the doctor should, of course, seek to respect the patient's wishes, since, in any event, the patient will be requesting the doctor to do only that which the law already requires and permits him to do, with perhaps some greater specificity as to detail. For example, the patient may have indicated that if her illness has progressed beyond a certain specified point, she should not receive a particular, or any, form of intervention.

Another way in which a patient may seek to achieve control over his fate once he has become incompetent is through the device of an Enduring or Durable Power of Attorney.[12] This *is* a case of proxy decision making,

Chancery to act as *parens patriae* in the absence of anyone else, to protect the interests of those incapable of caring for themselves, was still part of the English common law, and permitted a court to exercise jurisdiction over such a person even though an adult. This is a most significant decision since it offers a way of filling a lacuna in the law which has troubled many for a long time. In the case of *Re B (a minor) (wardship: sterilisation)* [1987] 2 All ER 211 the House of Lords did not have to decide the question, although it was considered in argument. On balance *Re Eve* is to be preferred, if only because of the gap which otherwise remains in the law.

[11] See e.g. President's Commission, *Deciding to Forego Life Sustaining Treatment* (US Government Printing Office, 1983), pp. 136 *et seq.*; Natural Death Act 1976, 7186 California Health and Safety Code; Natural Death Act, South Australia, 1983; Society for the Right to Die, *Handbook of Living Will Laws* (SRD, 1984); and for further information and an excellent analysis, see Areen *et al.*, *Law, Science and Medicine* (Foundation Press, 1984), pp. 1132–47.

[12] See e.g. Durable Power of Attorney for Health Care (New) Act 1983, 2340 California Health and Safety Code. And see further, Bok, 'Personal Directions for Care at the End of Life', 295 *New England Journal of Medicine* 367 (1976), in which it was first proposed that a Living Will should have incorporated into it a provision for a proxy decision-maker.

since it authorizes a named person to make treatment decisions on the patient's behalf, once the patient is adjudged incompetent. The aim, of course, is to delegate decision making to a trusted and close friend or relative who the patient feels best knows him and will speak for him when he cannot speak for himself. No provision exists for such powers of attorney in English law. At common law any power of attorney lapses immediately the person who granted the power becomes incompetent. The Enduring Powers of Attorney Act 1985, although extending powers beyond the onset of incompetence does not cover decisions concerning the grantor's person, which would include treatment, but appears to relate only to the management of his property. Thus, at present, the nominated person would lack any legal authority; and whether he would be listened to in matters relating to the treatment of the patient would depend on the good sense and good faith of the doctor.

CONCLUSION

From this recital of the general and specific duties of the doctor, it can be seen that the law in England, if understood and followed, is sensitive to the needs of patient and doctor alike. It allows the most sensitive care to be practised, because it rests on an understanding of the realities of terminal illness and care. It retains the flexibility necessary to meet changing circumstances, and allows appropriate discretion to doctors without sacrificing its adherence to fundamental principles. Occasionally, disquiet is expressed that the law is not more coherently set out. Indeed, for the majority of these propositions there is no authority in the sense of legislation or court decision. Though I am confident of their validity, it is unsatisfactory for the law to remain a matter of conjecture. It follows that there is a need for some authoritative synthesis of the law. The form this should take, in my view, is a Code of Practice worked out by representatives of the medical profession together with lawyers, theologians, philosophers, and interested laymen. It would not be statute law in the first instance, since it takes so long to get proposed statutes passed into law. Also, there is a danger that in such a sensitive area a statute may well be a clumsy approach initially. A code could serve as a precursor. It would serve as the authoritative guideline, while retaining flexibility and being easier to amend. Since, ultimately, the law has to be stated authoritatively, there is a case for passing a statute, once experience of the working of the Code has had time to show up any problems there may be. An example of the use of Codes of Practice is the report of the working party on the transplantation of organs,[13] produced

[13] Report of Working Party, *The Removal of Cadaveric Organs for Transplantation: A Code of Practice* (DHSS, 1979).

under the aegis of the Department of Health, which itself incorporates an earlier Code of Practice on the diagnosis of death, contained in the Report of the Medical Royal Colleges and their Faculties in the United Kingdom.[14] In this case, in fact, it has not proved necessary to move to the next stage of passing a statute, at least not for the time being.

[14] Report of the Conference of Medical Royal Colleges and their Faculties, 'Diagnosis of brain death', 2 *British Medical Journal* 1187 (1976).

17

The Legal Effect of Requests by the Terminally Ill and Aged not to Receive Further Treatment from Doctors*

The role played by consent in the criminal law warrants careful examination. Particularly challenging to the criminal lawyer is the role played by consent in the medical-legal context. In this article, as the title suggests, I shall deal in detail with a rather specific topic. I hope to show, however, that in concentrating on such a narrow area, issues of wider import can be identified. Indeed, the aim of the article is to raise the question of whether consent is a proper conceptual tool for the analysis of medical-legal problems, by considering its use and usefulness in one particular area.

Medical treatment which involves any touching of a patient is still analysed generally in law as lawful because the patient has consented to what would otherwise be an assault. There are two key concepts involved in such an analysis. The first, which will not concern us here, is that of 'treatment'. The issue, shortly stated, is whether there are touchings which do not qualify as treatment so that consent may be irrelevant. It is arguable that there is a spectrum of touchings, ranging from the obviously curative operation, such as the removal of an infected appendix, to the performance of some-what exotic operations such as silicone breast implants and the removal of 'anomalous' sexual apparatus in sex-change surgery, including *en route* such operations as voluntary sterilization, rhinoplasty, and abortion. The line which the law draws is at the very least indistinct, and turns on such imponderables as *malum in se*, mayhem, degrees of harmfulness, and public policy, and calls for an examination of such unsatisfactory cases as *Donovan*,[1] *Bravery* v. *Bravery*,[2] and *Coney*.[3] The second concept, and the one we are concerned with here, is consent.

If consent makes a touching lawful, then it must follow that if a patient withholds consent, if he refuses to be touched by a doctor, any further

---

* This paper was first published in [1976] Crim. LR 217, and is reproduced here with minor amendments. Clearly, some changes have occurred in the law since 1976, but the debate at the centre of the paper, the proper role and limits of paternalism, continues (see e.g. chaps 5, 9, and 10).

[1] [1934] 2 KB 498.   [2] [1954] 1 WLR 1169.   [3] [1882] 8 QBD 534.

touching will be unlawful, and will give rise to civil and criminal liability. Indeed, this is accepted as a general proposition or principle, and I shall call it 'the general principle' throughout this article. A patient has the 'right to decline operative investigation or treatment however unreasonable or foolish this may appear in the eyes of his medical advisers'.[4] Glanville Williams recently wrote: 'Some doctors seem to fail to realise that if an adult patient has positively forbidden particular treatment, they act illegally if they administer it, and could be . . . prosecuted for assault.'[5]

In the United States, Cardozo J. in the landmark case of *Schloendorff* v. *Society of New York Hospital*, held that 'every human being of adult years and sound mind has a right to determine what shall be done with his own body.'[6]

It should be noted that I am concentrating here on 'further treatment' and therefore assume a pre-existing relationship between the doctor and the patient. I limit my inquiry further by not considering the situation in which the doctor exceeds the norm of accepted treatment—for example, where his treatment borders on experimentation, where other considerations apply. The basic situation which I contemplate is a patient in hospital refusing all but nursing attendance,[7] or the patient at home refusing all care, even if it means that he will be left alone.

The general principle contemplates a model of a patient of an age recognized as endowing him with the competence to exercise a valid choice, and who is lucid in the sense not only that he regards himself as being in control of his mental faculties, but also that he is recognized to be so by others. There are, therefore, two key features: first, that the patient is of an age[8] the law regards as proper, and second, that he is of sound mind. This latter feature has two distinct negative qualities: first, that the patient must not be someone

---

[4] T. A. Grasson J., in *Smith* v. *Auckland Hospital Board* [1965] NZLR 191, 219.

[5] Glanville Williams, 'Euthanasia', 41 *Medico-legal Journal* 4, 24 (1973). Earlier, however, Williams refers with heavy irony to the idea that patients have some right of self-determination in respect of their own deaths as an 'upstart notion', ibid. p. 17. See further, P. Glazebrook, 'The Necessity Plea in English Criminal Law' [1972A] CLJ 87, 98. In Canada, doctors were held liable in the classic case of *Mulloy* v. *Hop Sang* [1935] 1 WWR 714 (Alta. AD), in which the patient's hand was amputated in spite of the fact that he had specifically told the doctors not to do so; and see *Beausoleil* v. *Soeurs de la charité* (1964) 43 DLR (2d) 65.

The American Hospital Association produced a 'Patient's Bill of Rights', provision 4 of which was the right to refuse treatment. This provision has not, however, been included in the Bill of Rights as enacted in Minnesota, the only state so far to adopt it (83 *Yale Law Journal* 1648 (1974)).

[6] 211, NY 125 (1914); and see *Natonson* v. *Kline*, 186 Kan. 393 (1960).

[7] I am not considering the unlikely situation of a patient in hospital refusing even nursing care—e.g. changing sheets, bathing, etc. Different considerations may apply in such a case, including the duty of the hospital to maintain certain standards of hygiene and to care for other patients on the ward. These may well justify overriding the refusal. This does not, however, extend to feeding a patient against his will, which I include as treatment for the sake of this article.

[8] [That is, that he has reached a sufficient level of maturity and understanding. Age on its own, without more, is not, of course, the decisive criterion.]

categorized as chronically mentally unfit, and second, that he must not be someone who is regarded as suffering from temporary unsoundness of mind. The philosophical premiss which underlies the general principle is the right to self-determination. My submission is that the identification and analysis of the two key features mentioned above indicate that it is a right which is far from being the general bulwark it purports to be. I will seek to show that it is confined within narrow, if ill-defined, bounds. For these features have only to be noticed for it to be seen that very considerable scope exists for denying or undermining the exercise of the right. Indeed, there exists an equally strong, and in this context often contradictory, philosophical premiss, that of paternalism.[9] Clearly, the basis of paternalism—that decisions concerning a particular person's fate are better made *for* him than *by* him, because others wiser than he are more keenly aware of his best interests than he can be—conflicts with the notion of a right to self-determination, whereby a person is deemed entitled to make his own decisions concerning himself, within tolerable limits, free from the interference of others.

Paternalism, however, makes its demands, which have to be met. Indeed, it is the purpose of this article to suggest that what was alleged at the outset to be the general principle, that of self-determination, is in fact the exception. I shall suggest that the dominant philosophy in practice is paternalism. Chancellor Garth Moore writes:

Suppose that the patient has said to his doctor, 'I am an old man, I know that cancer will kill me fairly soon. If, mercifully, I get pneumonia first, let it take its course. Do not give me antibiotics. I would rather die of pneumonia than cancer.' Much the same problem would be posed even more dramatically in the case of a polio patient in an iron lung. He might say to the doctor, 'I do not wish to live as a helpless paralytic. Switch off that machine and let me die now.' Less dramatic but equally puzzling would be the problem posed by the patient who deliberately went on hunger-strike in order to end his suffering. Should the doctor and nurses apply forcible feeding? There can be no certain answer in law to these problems. . . . It is here very tentatively suggested

---

[9] A Canadian expert writes: 'While it is clear that Canadian courts have accepted the right of the patient to refuse treatment and have balanced this right with the desirable goal of the health care industry to care for the needs of the patient, there is often considerable disturbance when a patient does exercise his rights to refuse treatment. Mr. Justice Knowles [in *Masny* v. *Carter-Halls-Aldinger Co. Ltd.* [1929] 3 WWR 741] . . . expressed his frustration over a patient who had refused consent to a necessary operation and was, as a result, experiencing an agonizing wait for death. His Lordship said: "Three months ago the medical men knew this would happen, but according to our present legislation, or lack of legislation, they were helpless. The poor immigrant, through ignorance or foolhardiness, or both, forbade them putting forth the hand which would have saved his life. Should not society protect such a man from his own foolishness?" ' L. E. Rozovsky, 'Consent to Treatment', 11 *Osgoode Hall Law Journal* 103, 113 (1973).

Thomas Szasz writes that the attitudes of 'kindness' and 'sweetness' for the 'poor patient' serve the purpose of enhancing the doctor's self-esteem. 'Much of what passes for "medical ethics" is a set of rules the net effect of which is the persistent infantilization and subjugation of the patient' (*Myth of Mental Illness* (1961), p. 188).

that these may be cases in which, as the law now stands, the doctor has a discretion
. . . either to refrain, at his patient's request, from administering life-saving treatments
or to ignore his patient's wishes where compliance is likely to result in death.[10]

In noting such comments, it is appropriate to recall that this discussion
must be seen against a background described with some outrage by many
commentators. Ramsey writes that it is

now possible to deprive many a patient of a fulfilment of the wish to have a death
of one's own, the scene Dr. Rynearson [whose work he is discussing] describes is
one of patients with an 'untreatable' disease being kept alive indefinitely by means
of tubes inserted into their stomachs, or into their veins, or into their bladders, or
into their rectums — and the whole sad scene thus created encompassed within a cocoon
of oxygen which is the next thing to a shroud.[11]

Elkinton writes: 'In his efforts to preserve life and restore health, the physician
sometimes may fail to give enough consideration to his other obligation,
namely to relieve suffering and to allow the patient, if he is to die, to die
with comfort and dignity.'[12]

I further submit that the features of the doctrine of consent which I have
identified, so far from facilitating the patient's self-determination, are in fact
capable of serving as a blueprint for making considerable inroads into, and
even for disregarding altogether, the need for consent. Moreover, the factual
context in which the sort of decisions under review here take place further
militates against the exercise of self-determination. Indeed, the problems
under discussion are in large part by their nature evidentiary problems.
Discussion based on strict legal principle becomes arid and unhelpful if this
is not remembered. Equally, any proposed remedies must be addressed
more to administrative and procedural practice than to changing formal
legal rules.

---

[10] Church Assembly Board for Social Responsibility, *Decisions about Life and Death*,
(CABSR, 1965), p. 44; my emphasis. For a detailed discussion of the moral and ethical arguments,
see P. Ramsey, *The Patient as Person* (Yale University Press, 1970), esp. ch. 3. For a careful
examination of the issues and the law, see P. Skegg, 'A Justification for Medical Procedures
Performed without Consent' 90 LQR 512 *et seq.* (1974), wherein Skegg favours the view that
the general principle warrants modification in several circumstances where the doctor would
be legally justified in overriding the patient's refusal of consent. For an exhaustive survey of
the position in the United States, see 83 *Yale Law Journal* 1632 *et seq.*, where the general premiss
is explored that 'while purporting to apply the basic principle, however, the courts in different
jurisdictions have developed a wide variety of formulations that inhibit the realization of ultimate
control by the patient' (ibid. 1634). The trend seems to be slowly moving towards upholding
the patient's right to refuse, particularly in the light of the development of the constitutional
right to privacy in *Roe* v. *Wade*, 410 US 113 (1973); see esp. *Re Yetter*, cited in 83 *Yale Law
Journal* 1644 (1974); *Erickson* v. *Dilgard*, 252 NYS 2d 705 (1962); and *Re Pogue*, cited in
J. Goldstein, 84 *Yale Law Journal* 691, 695 (1975).
[11] Ramsey, *supra* n. 10, 116.
[12] J. R. Elkinton, 'The dying patient, the doctor and the law', 13 *Villanova Law Review*
740 (1968).

If the philosophical basis for these inroads into the general principle is paternalism, what legal bases or justifications are there? They are somewhat elusive. Because we are dealing with what purport to be exceptions to a general principle, it is sometimes argued that there is no single legal principle of justification, merely a number of disparate responses to the specific factual and legal details of a particular case.[13] Alternatively, a general principle of justification is advanced and given the name of 'necessity'[14] or 'privilege'[15] or some kind of 'comprehensive justification in relation to medical procedures'.[16] Or it is merely called 'public policy'. The latter idea of a general justification may be more welcome and acceptable to lawyers, since it is tidy and fills the need for categorization and easy pigeon-holing. It will be obvious to all, however, that this tidiness is an illusion, because its essence, which is at once its merit and its weakness, is its very indefiniteness and amenability to *ad hoc* decisions based on the 'justice' of the particular facts.[17] Whether there is a general justification or a series of specific legal responses to particular factual situations may well be a sterile debate. If it is necessary for my argument, I am prepared to say that there is, as regards the particular situation under review, a general legal justification, and I will call it 'necessity'. It is one of the two arguments I will examine that are advanced on behalf of the doctor to justify him in overriding or disregarding the expressed view of his patient. It will be noticed that I refer only to those cases where the patient, or someone on his behalf, has made his view known. I do not deal with the equally hard problem of the patient who is admitted unconscious to hospital after a suicide attempt, where the doctrines of implied consent or necessity are used to justify a doctor in treating him. Finally, I urge again that it is of crucial importance to remember the factual context in which these problems may arise. For the set of circumstances in which the patient finds himself is a very great contributing factor to the possible inroads into his right to self-determination.

NECESSITY

The facts are that the patient has requested that the doctor discontinue treatment, and the doctor has ignored this request. What the doctor is saying

---

[13] 'The better view appears to be that a general defence of necessity is not recognised by the English courts at the present time' (J. C. Smith and B. Hogan, *Criminal Law*, 3rd edn. (Butterworths, 1973) p. 159.) See also P. Glazebrook, *supra* n. 5, for a similar view.

[14] See e.g. G. Williams, 'The Defence of Necessity', 6 *Current Legal Problems* 216 (1953); G. J. Hughes, 'Two views on consent in the Criminal Law', 26 *MLR* 233 (1963).

[15] W. L. Prosser, *The Law of Torts*, 4th edn., (West Publishing Co., 1971), 103.

[16] Skegg, *supra* n. 10, 512 *et seq.*

[17] Compare the useful discussion ibid. 514.

is that he *had to continue* treatment, because it was right to do so as a matter of public policy. Stated generally, the fundamental rationale he offers for having to do so is that he, either himself or as the agent of society, knew better than the patient what should be done to or for the patient. He points to several factors supporting this conclusion: first, the patient was incapable of making a rational decision; second, in his clinical judgment, further treatment was called for; and third, the minor harm of proceeding without consent was more than outweighed by the major benefit, in his view, which was gained from his treatment. Stephen refers to a crime being excusable if the defendant can show as one of the requisites that what was done was done to avoid a consequence which could not otherwise have been avoided, and which, if not done, would have inflicted harm on him or on others he was *bound* to protect.[18] The word 'bound' begs a number of questions, and does not appear in other writers' views.[19] Put thus, the doctor's position is arrogant. Does the law support him?

Everything turns on the capacity of the patient and, just as important, who makes the final determination as to that capacity. My position is that the law is so constructed that in all probability, only the lucid, self-assertive patient who has a sympathetic, understanding doctor is able in most circumstances to have his way and be left alone, free from further interference, to die. All other patients run the risk of having their wishes flouted.[20] Consent is represented as the critical feature of the law which ensures the patient's right to self-determination, whereas, in fact, it is referred to and manipulated so as to produce the opposite result.

A number of legal and extra-legal factors combine to produce this result. First, the determination of capacity to consent or to withhold consent is not made by the patient, but by those treating him. It is as if there existed a right to free speech, but that, before exercising it, one must submit to someone with a practically unchallengeable power of censorship a copy of one's proposed speech for approval. Second, the presumption made by the healthy is that no one really wants to die. When these two factors are put together, it is readily understandable that a request that treatment should cease should be seen as not really meant, but as merely the response to either a passing mood[21] or

---

[18] J. F. Stephen, *A Digest of the Criminal Law* 1st edn. (Macmillan, 1977), p. 9; my emphasis.

[19] E.g. Glazebrook, *supra* n. 5. I note in passing that the doctor cannot justify his disregard for the patient's refusal on the basis that the refusal is uninformed, for just as consent must be informed, so must refusal, and it is the duty of the doctor to inform the patient to the extent necessary to allow a reasoned decision; see generally, P. Skegg, 'Informed Consent to Medical Procedures' 15 *Medicine, Science and the Law* 124 *et seq.* (1975).

[20] *Pace* Williams, who asserts that 'the doctrine of necessity does not override the patient's right to self-determination'; 'Euthanasia', *supra* n. 5, 31.

[21] It is conceded that the issue is not always clear-cut. G. Schreiner reports a case in which a patient wished to withdraw from dialysis. He was nevertheless dialysed, and then said, 'Don't

a loss of mental fitness. Thus — and this is a critical point — refusal of consent is seen not as an assertion of will, but rather as a symptom of unsoundness of mind.

The right to refuse should, of course, be upheld, even though the patient's view is deemed irrational or unreasonable by the doctor or is based on what seem to be poor grounds. Hughes takes the view, however, that 'exotic' or 'unreasonable' views need not necessarily be respected.[22] Initially, the view in the United States was that the refusal had to be based on good grounds — for example, religious beliefs strongly held — but the position now is moving towards the idea that 'individual freedom here is guaranteed only if people are given the right to make choices which would generally be regarded as foolish ones'.[23] In the case of *Re Pogue*,[24] the court declined to make the patient's refusal based on her belief as a Jehovah's Witness a basis for declaring her incompetent to decide for herself. Goldstein nevertheless warns of the bias in therapeutic transactions towards perceiving refusals as uninformed: 'refusals may therefore be used as a justification for challenging the capacity of the citizen to decide what is best for himself.'[25] Third, it must not be overlooked that a doctor is a professional whose training predisposes him to 'save' lives and treat the sick. Furthermore, modern medical training may well encourage him to see himself as a scientist applying particular skills to solve a problem, rather than as dealing with people. This takes on an added significance when it is remembered that geriatrics and the terminally ill are regarded as the failures of the health service and are often consigned to the young and inexperienced who, as one doctor recently put it, 'do strive very officiously to keep people alive because they are interested scientifically and they want to use every method they can as part of their training'.[26] Finally, there is a group of patients who are considered mentally unfit to make decisions concerning themselves. These are the chronically

---

listen to me, that's my uraemia talking, not me. I want to stay on the programme.' At the same time, another patient's decision was accepted because '*I became convinced* that this was an intellectually free decision on his part and *we allowed him to withdraw*' (*Ethics in Medical Progress*, G. E. W. Wolstenholme, ed. (Ciba, 1966), p. 129; my emphasis). Such a view illustrates the narrow ground allowed to self-determination.

[22] Hughes, *supra* n. 14, 233.

[23] 83 *Yale Law Journal*, 1648 (1974). [This remains one of the most difficult issues. I prefer the view which says that a patient's decision is to be respected, even if deemed irrational in the eyes of those around him, if it reflects and conforms to a set of values and beliefs which the patient has consistently lived by. Some argue that when the belief is based on a demonstrably false assumption of fact (as could be the case with someone who suffers hallucinations), any decision based on this belief may properly be ignored. I accept this, but regard it as distinguishable from my view, since there is no consistency of view over a period of time in this latter case. See further, editorial, 'Impaired Autonomy and Rejection of Treatment', 9 *Journal of Medical Ethics* 131 (1983)].

[24] Unreported; cited by Goldstein, *supra* n. 10, 695.

[25] Ibid. 691.

[26] Cited in Williams, 'Euthanasia', *supra* n. 5, 19.

mentally ill and minors,[27] and, if the above is accepted, also include those whose judgment, others assert, cannot be relied upon.

Once a patient is deemed incapable, having been assigned to one of these categories, his powers of self-determination are taken from him. The law, as ever in these areas, is unclear. Some state categorically that the fact that a patient is judged mentally unfit does not mean that he can therefore have treatment forced upon him against his will and despite his express refusal. But the problem is not so simply solved. I take the law to be that someone mentally unfit may not necessarily be incapable of reaching a rational decision as regards further treatment. It would depend both on his precise mental state, whether he was capable of lucid moments at the particular time, and the particular treatment involved; for instance, refusal of therapeutic drugs prescribed to control dangerous behaviour would not be regarded in the same light as refusal to have a tooth extracted. To ignore the latter refusal could well be unlawful.[28] The point, however, is that abstract legal discussion must pay some regard to the reality of situations. The real problem here, because of the nature of the legal framework, is not so much a legal one as one of evidence. For it is the doctor who makes the determination that the view expressed by the patient is unreliable and that the particular treatment is called for. Once this determination has been made, two consequences follow. First, the way is made clear to invoke the plea of necessity; and, in the majority of cases, such a determination is, as a practical matter, virtually impossible to overturn. Second, the patient's right to self-determination, in other words, becomes not a matter of legal principle, but rather a consequence of the degree of paternalism exercised by the doctor, supported by societal attitudes which reinforce such paternalism.

In the light of the above, provided the doctor is of the opinion that the patient's mental faculties are such as to make his refusal of treatment unreliable, I take the view that, in the case of an incompetent child, if there is a parent or guardian who can be consulted, the doctor can rely on their consent to treatment, despite the expressed wishes of the patient.[29]. There continues to be some doubt as to whether anyone has authority to consent to treatment in the case of an adult, in the absence of statute. Where there

---

[27] [The word 'children' is now to be preferred, and should be taken to mean a child who lacks the maturity and capacity to understand so as to decide for himself].

[28] Cf. the views of a Canadian expert: 'Canadian mental health legislation by and large creates a vacuum in the matter of consent to treatment, especially where the patient in a psychiatric hospital must be transferred to a general hospital for non-emergency treatment and where such a person has not been declared legally incompetent'. Rozovsky, *supra* n. 9, p. 111. See also his discussion of attempts to meet the problem. In the case of *Re Yetter*, *supra* n. 10, a Pennsylvania court held that a 60-year-old schizophrenic was competent to refuse life-saving surgery even though, in the view of some, her reasons were irrational — she opposed the operation (for breast cancer) on the ground that it would prevent her from pursuing a movie career.

[29] As regards a minor, Skegg argues that 'a legally effective consent can sometimes be given even when the minor is capable of consenting but refuses to do so' ('Consent to Medical Procedures on Minors' 36 *MLR* 370, 376 (1973). See also *S. v. McC, W. v. W.* [1972] AC 24, 45.

is no parent or guardian available, the doctor will be protected if he proceeds to treat. Williams argues that:

Even if the patient is compulsorily admitted under the Mental Health Act, and can therefore be deprived of his liberty, there is no authority that I know of to justify medical treatment against his express refusal. But doctors and nurses do from time to time brush aside the protests of aged, dying or mentally affected patients. It is tempting for them to assume guardianship and disciplinary powers that they do not possess.[30]

With reference to the mentally unfit patient, I would respond that there is no authority which forbids such treatment apart from the general principle which, as has been seen, presupposes a 'sound mind' and is, therefore, a weak basis on which to rely.[31] Indeed, Williams then goes on to discuss the propriety of treating children against the wishes of their parents, and states that 'the legal authority for this rests on the doctrine of necessity.'[32] This seems in principle to be an equally available justification as regards the mentally unfit, even though it may well be deplored. The Medical Defence Union, in its pamphlet entitled 'Consent to Treatment', advises that 'a patient who is compulsorily detained under the Mental Health Act must submit to treatment for his mental disorder whether or not he agrees', but that 'if a compulsorily detained patient develops a condition unrelated to his mental disorder, then only such treatment as is immediately necessary to preserve his life and health may be given without his consent.' The advice concludes, however, with the observation that 'this situation should be looked at sensibly and the prohibition outlined above *must not be allowed* to jeopardise the patient's health. It is unlikely that the courts would criticise a practitioner who had acted *in good faith* and in the interests of his patients.'[33] Goldstein in the United States, a strong advocate of the patient's right to self-determination, argues that a person involuntarily incarcerated in a mental hospital, for example, is in no different a position from a free person, except that incarceration affects volition, not the patient's capacity to make a choice. This logic compels him to criticize the case of *Kaimowitz* v. *Michigan Department of Mental Health*,[34] in which an inmate was offered the choice between experimental surgery with the possibility of release and continued

---

[30] Williams, 'Euthanasia', *supra* n. 5, p. 24.

[31] *Bracknell JJ., ex p. Griffiths* [1975] 3 WLR 140, seems to support my argument and to provide Williams with the authority he seeks. [32] Ibid., p. 25.

[33] Medical Defence Union, 'Consent to Treatment' (MDU, 1974), pp. 7–8; my emphasis. On this question of consent to treatment by the mentally unfit, see the discussion in Report of the Committee on Mentally Abnormal Offenders (Cmnd. 6244, HMSO, 1975), pp. 47–55. See now, Mental Health Act 1983, ss. 56–63, whereby, broadly, consent to treatment for mental illness in the case of a person compulsorily admitted under the Act may be dispensed with, save in the case of psychosurgery and a regime of hormone therapy. The Act makes no provision for treatment for illness other than mental illness, so the common law, as set out, applies.

[34] Michigan Circuit Court 10 July 1973.

incarceration, and the Court held that consent could not be given by an involuntarily detained mental patient. Goldstein argues that if a patient is capable of consenting to ordinary therapy, and if both incarceration and experimental surgery are approved social practices, a person should not be denied the choice.[35]

Alternatively, the doctor may seek the concurrence of a relative who is neither a parent nor a guardian. If the doctor desires to treat the patient, he is often in a strong position to persuade such a relative to concur. After all, the relative will usually be ignorant of the processes involved and will doubtless begin with the presumption that the doctor knows best. From a legal point of view, however, such concurrence from a relative is of no effect, since there is no power vested in a relative to consent to the treatment of another.[36]

What is the position where, the patient being incapable, the parent or guardian refused to sanction further treatment? I shall consider this issue again later on. As regards the present argument, the law seems to be that a parent or guardian can consent only to treatment which is in his charge's interest. It may be that the converse also holds, namely, that he may refuse only when such refusal is in his charge's interest. The point then again arises, as with unsoundness of mind, that it is the doctor who initially defines and outlines these interests. He may prefer his own assessment of the patient's interests, and ignore that of the parent or guardian. Since the question is — or is made to be — one of his clinical judgment, his view will later be respected unless shown to be wholly unreasonable. Skegg, though putting it differently, argues that there is a justification available to the doctor, provided two conditions are satisfied: 'first that the procedure is necessary to save the life of the child, to prevent permanent injury to his health, or to prevent prolonged pain and suffering. Secondly, that despite the fact of the doctor having made all reasonable efforts to obtain consent, consent has been unreasonably withheld.'[37] As an alternative, he proposes that the test be 'whether it would have been unreasonable for the doctor not to have proceeded'.[38] The conclusion is the same: provided the doctor can argue that he was seeking to prevent pain and suffering, the other criteria proposed by Skegg allow for a sufficient degree of subjective assessment as to offer no real barrier to the exercise of the doctor's paternalism. For the sake of completeness, if a *relative* refuses further treatment on behalf of a patient, this can be ignored, for the reasons advanced above.

It must be stated at this point that it is not intended here to suggest that there is a conspiracy on the part of doctors to deprive patients of their rights,

---

[35] Goldstein, *supra* n. 10, 696.

[36] Cf. the Canadian practice of obtaining consent from relatives, so as to stop the relatives from subsequently taking action against the hospital or the doctor; Rozovsky, *supra* n. 9, 111.

[37] Skegg, *supra* n. 10, 522.   [38] Ibid.

or that doctors act out of ill will. Rather, it is conceded that they doubtless act out of a well-meaning desire to treat. What is suggested is that the supposed right to self-determination may not be the creature it is thought to be. It is admitted that there is no evidence to support this view, except the total lack of prosecutions, which, of course, cuts both ways. It is worth considering, however, just how flimsy this supposed general principle is. Though it may be the last right remaining for the terminally ill or the aged, it is remarkably easy to undermine it. Its theoretical weaknesses are implicit in the fact that it rests on the vague and easily manipulated notion of consent. Once such theoretical weaknesses are identified, it is but a simple step to weaken the right as it operates in practice. The persuasive power of paternalism supplies the motive for this step to be taken. Paternalism in the guise of 'The doctor knows best' or 'You don't really mean that' provides the social justification, and necessity the legal justification.

THE RISK OF LIABILITY

A second line of argument advanced on behalf of the doctor to justify his failure to accede to the request of his patient is that the doctor must continue treatment because to do otherwise would render him criminally and/or civilly liable. The doctor is saying that he had to continue treatment as a *matter of legal obligation*. He is saying that it would have been unlawful to honour the patient's request, even if he had been willing to do so.

Two principal heads of potential liability are cited to justify this position and call for consideration.

Suicide Act 1961, Section 2

Though suicide is not a crime, it is an offence under section 2 to aid, abet, counsel, or procure the suicide of another. The argument advanced is that the doctor is not obliged to respect the request of the patient — indeed, he is obliged to disregard it — since otherwise he would be guilty of an offence under section 2. There are clearly a number of objections to this. First, the term 'suicide' calls for some elucidation. It is by no means clear whether the omission/commission dichotomy which applies to (and some would say, in the medical-legal field, bedevils) the crime of murder applies to suicide. If 'suicide' is defined as the doing of a positive act with the intention of ending life, then there would be no question of suicide in the case of patients who refuse treatment, but otherwise do no positive act, merely allowing death to occur. Thus, in the case of a patient who did nothing more than refuse further treatment, there could be no liability on the part of the doctor for aiding and abetting under section 2. But the issue may still arise in either of the following two cases.

First, the patient's failure to take care of himself in the knowledge that death will result sooner rather than otherwise — and this would apply to the aged as well as to the terminally ill — *may* be treated as suicide, despite what has been said. An objection to liability in this case, advanced by Williams, is that the doctor who fails to treat has not done something; he has merely failed to act, and an omission cannot amount to an abetment.[39] There are those who argue that the doctor in this situation is, in fact, under an obligation to ignore the patient's request, and to prevent him, under the protection of the plea of necessity, from adopting a course of conduct which would lead to self-destruction.[40] The much cited case of *Leigh* v. *Gladstone*[41] is invoked in support. This case has become all things to all men. I would prefer, at the risk of offending the purists, to take a robust attitude, and simply say that it is a decision made at a particular time in response to a particular situation against a particular political background, and is poor material on which to build any general proposition.[42] It is best seen as an anomalous departure from the general principle of self-determination. Unless it is submitted that prisoners have, on entering prison, surrendered all rights over their own bodies, in which case medical experimentation on them would be equally lawful, the case cannot stand as authority for the proposition that there exists a duty, even as regards prisoners, far less at large, to prevent someone from refusing food and, *a fortiori*, medical treatment.[43] The second case which raises the issue of liability under section 2 is where the doctor, in honouring the patient's request, in some way facilitates the suicide by, for example, leaving around an extra quantity of tablets in the knowledge or with a strong suspicion that they will be taken in such a dosage as to produce fatal consequences. This is rather more problematical. *Fretwell*[44] may avail the doctor, but is somewhat discredited by the decision in *N.C.B.* v. *Gamble*.[45] Alternatively, the doctor may argue that he gave the pills to ease pain or for sleeping, and invite the court to believe him. The very few cases in point suggest that his confidence would not be misplaced.[46]

---

[39] Williams, 'Euthanasia', *supra* n. 5, 31.   [40] Smith and Hogan, *supra* n. 13.
[41] [1909] 26 TLR 39.

[42] See the criticism of the case in Skegg, *supra* n. 10, 525–6. Glazebrook remarks that the case 'is based on considerations of prison discipline and is not authority for any wider principle that injury may lawfully be caused to save a person from himself' (*supra* n. 5, 99).

[43] See further the view of Chancellor Garth Moore, that while the law is unclear it is probable that the doctor would not in these circumstances be guilty under the Suicide Act, s. 2 (*Decisions about Life and Death*, *supra* n. 10, 44).   [44] (1862) Le. & Ca. 161.

[45] [1959] 1 QB 11. [See also *Attorney-General's Reference* (No. 1 of 1975) [1975] QB 773, and discussion thereof in G. Williams, *Textbook of Criminal Law*, 2nd edn. (Stevens, 1983), pp. 337–43].

[46] Parry Jones shows, in a study of the period 1961–70, that 80 cases had been reported to the Director of Public Prosecutions, and that criminal proceedings had been instituted in 12 under section 2. All but two of the cases in which proceedings were taken involved a suicide pact, in which the suicide was facilitated at the request of the deceased. Neither involved a doctor,

One case which may cause problems is where the doctor's facilitation takes the form of switching off a necessary mechanical aid, such as a ventilator or an artificial kidney machine. This may be considered by some to be an invitation to explore the issue of whether the switching-off is an act or an omission; for if it is an act, it may be an abetment. I offer the following three alternative arguments. First, Williams's admittedly artificial argument may be accepted that it is an omission, a failure to treat, so that there is no liability.[47] Second, the doctor has aided and abetted the patient only in his refusal to undergo further treatment. No one is obliged to endure treatment for ever. The switching-off facilitates the decision, not the suicide. Third, mechanical aids such as ventilators and the like may be classified as 'extraordinary measures' in so far as they involve excessive pain or other inconvenience.[48] The doctor is arguably under no duty to continue treatment (as will be seen later) that is 'useless' or a 'burden'. The fact that the aid is an extraordinary measure and that the patient has indicated that it is a burden absolves the doctor of his duty to continue treatment, and he may therefore discontinue it by switching off the machine.

A final point which ought to be considered is whether the doctor may be liable under section 2 in the case that the patient expressing the wish to die is mentally unfit. There is some authority to suggest that a doctor is under a duty to prevent the suicide of such a patient in so far as there is a duty to control the patient.[49] Whatever the strength of this reasoning, it seems to apply to cases where the patient commits some act to achieve his end, and would not apply to the situation being discussed here.

All in all, it is submitted that the claim that there is a risk of liability under section 2 of the Suicide Act does not serve as a valid justification for ignoring the request of the patient that treatment be discontinued.

Neglect

An alternative, and in some ways overlapping argument advanced in justification of the doctor is that his duty to his patient, once he has embarked on treatment, is to continue to care for him until he dies. It may be that with a patient who is terminally ill or aged, the doctor's obligation does not extend to anything more than the relief of pain and making the patient comfortable. But, the argument goes, the doctor cannot abandon the patient altogether. The simple response to this is to recite the general principle that

and the penalties were probation for three years and binding-over for two years respectively ('Criminal Law and Suicides', 13 *Medicine, Science and the Law*, 110 (1973)); Williams, 'Euthanasia', *supra* n. 5, 27–31.

[47] Williams, 'Euthanasia', *supra* n. 5, 20–1; and see G. Fletcher, 'Prolonging Life', 42 Wash. L. R. 999 (1967).

[48] See e.g. Ramsey, *supra* n. 10, 120–3.   [49] Williams, 'Euthanasia', *supra* n. 5, 27–31.

no treatment is warranted, or indeed lawful, without consent, and that if consent is withdrawn, nothing need be done. We have already seen that the doctor may well honour this principle more in the breach than the observance if he is so minded. The question here is whether he need feel compelled to continue treatment, especially since he may know that if he does continue, his actions will, if reasonable (and it will be hard to prove otherwise), qualify as being justified. What reasons may persuade him that he is so compelled or obliged?

The first reason is really the other side of the view already considered, namely, that a patient's express wish may be disregarded on the ground that he was not of sound mind. Here, this view becomes converted into the argument that the refusal of treatment may not have been a rational decision or may not appear to others to have been so. Thus the doctor will be persuaded to err on the side of caution and to disregard the expressed view of his patient; that is, just as earlier we noted the possibility of the patient's view being overriden by an excess of zeal, now we see the same result produced by an excess of caution. This caution is reinforced by a second reason, which in practical terms may be of paramount importance, the fear of being the object of a legal action at the suit of parents, guardians, or relatives, who might allege that the patient was neglected, and would urge that the patient's refusal should not have been relied upon.

Given the doubts and uncertainties surrounding this area of law, it is not surprising that doctors may feel insecure in adopting a course of conduct which they otherwise may feel to be the most desirable. Moreover, this sense of insecurity and consequent bias towards caution may be further reinforced by the fact that very often the sort of decisions we are discussing are made in hospitals, where doctors are made aware of the views and reactions of another interested group, the nursing staff. The involvement of nurses in every stage of medical treatment may on occasions serve as a salutary check on possible excesses by doctors. It may also, however, particularly in the situation under discussion, be another factor obstructing the doctor even if he were to desire to give effect to a patient's wishes. The nurse is committed, both professionally and personally, to the care of a patient, and may well, out of well-meaning but misguided concern, mistake respect for a patient's wishes for neglect.[50] The prospect of unwelcome publicity, particularly in the popular press,[51] not surprisingly may further persuade the doctor that his interests lie elsewhere than in following his patient's instructions.

---

[50] 'The advent of the National Health Service, combined with the great influx of Irish Catholic nurses, has made it far too dangerous for doctors to continue taking the law into their own hands' (a medical journalist's view cited in Williams, 'Euthanasia', *supra* n. 5, 15).

[51] See e.g. 'Neasden Affair', referred to in Williams, *supra* n. 5, 25.

Is there any legal foundation for this concern? Is the doctor in breach of his duty to his patient if he discontinues treatment? Provided that the doctor is satisfied that the patient, when forbidding further treatment, was aware of what he was saying, the short answer must be that he is not in breach of his duty. There is no doubt that his duty extends to informing his patient, if asked,[52] of the nature of his illness and its likely prognosis. He thereby puts the patient in a position to make a decision which is informed. Once the decision has been made, he is obliged to respect it. Thus, the doctor, on this reasoning, incurs no liability under the civil law; nor can he be accused of any crime.

To consider the issue in greater detail, the only circumstance under which his omission to treat his patient further could render him guilty of manslaughter is where he has failed to act in a situation where the criminal law imposes on him a duty to act and death has ensued.[53] The case of *Instan*[54] seems to be authority for the proposition that a common-law duty was imposed upon the defendant to continue to care for her aunt, having once undertaken this responsibility.[55] It would seem to follow from the fact that a relationship has to be created for the duty to arise that if the relationship ceases by one party releasing and absolving the other of his obligations, the duty also ceases. Once expressly absolved, then by operation of the general principle of the right to self-determination, the other would incur no liability for the consequences of the absolution.

The words used in the case are, however, that the duty was 'imposed' by law. Does this mean that absolution by the patient is ineffective in relieving the doctor of his duty? Elliott takes the view that 'although most persons are not liable for omissions a doctor is so liable *vis-à-vis* his patient, unless he can justify his failure to give treatment on the grounds that such was useless.[56] Williams has said that the doctor is 'probably exempted from that duty if life has become a burden to the patient'.[57] There is no authority for these propositions, and a leading critic in the United States has taken a contrary view,[58] as did the court in the case of *The Application of the President and Directors of Georgetown College Inc.*, holding that 'death resulting from failure to extend proper medical care, where there is a duty of care, is manslaughter.'[59] This obviously begs the question of when a duty

---

[52] [And, of course, the law is now gradually recognizing that, even if not asked, the doctor ought ordinarily to inform a patient about his condition. This is certainly the view of good medical ethics, and may become law before too long. See further, chapter 9].

[53] Smith and Hogan, *supra* n. 13, 40   [54] [1893] 1 QB 450.

[55] Smith and Hogan, *supra* n. 13, 41.

[56] D. W. Elliott, *Medicine, Science and the Law*, 77, 78.

[57] G. Williams, *The Sanctity of Life and the Criminal Law* (Faber and Faber, 1958), p. 291. He has recently noted, however, that the 'idea that it was the duty of the medical man to continue to struggle for his patient's life has been reinstated' ('Euthanasia', *supra* n. 5, 15).

[58] Y. Kamisar, 42 *Minnesota Law Review* 969 (1958).   [59] 118 U.S. App. DC 80, 1964.

exists. If necessary, I am content to rely on the propositions advanced by Elliott and Williams, although the words 'useless' and 'burden' are not very helpful. I think the stronger point, however, is that the arguments to the contrary revolve around questions of voluntary euthanasia as opposed to the situation I am discussing. If a patient dismisses his doctor, the criminal law would not lightly regard as manslaughter the act of a doctor who respected the wishes of a dying or aged patient.[60]

All this assumes, of course, that the doctor's duty demands that he first satisfy himself that the patient is capable of making a rational decision. What if the patient is mentally unfit or is a terminally ill minor?[61] Will the doctor be neglecting his duty if he respect this patient's expression of will? Ultimately this is a question as to the proper limits of self-determination, as well as turning on the specific lucidity of the individual patient. It is also an immensely difficult decision for the doctor, who will have established over time a relationship of confidence with all but the most severely unfit of his patients (who anyway are unlikely to have expressed a view), which confidence will be shattered if the patient's request is ignored, thereby adding, if possible, to the unhappiness of the patient. If my view that a doctor incurs no liability if he ignores the request to discontinue treatment made by the mentally unfit and minor is correct, it does not of course follow that he would also be free from liability if he complied with their requests.[62] It may again turn on the evidential issue of unsoundness as determined at the moment by the doctor. But it may be that even where there is evidence that the patient was mentally unfit or too young, the doctor would still avoid liability, not so much on the basis of the patient's refusal as on the proposition of Elliott that further treatment was useless, or that of Williams that life had become a burden to the patient. These may even prevail when a parent or guardian, learning of the patient's request, has instructed the doctor to continue. On the other hand, the doctor would probably be in breach of his duty if it could be shown that the patient's request was made at a time when he was demonstrably and predictably suffering from a temporary condition which made his judgment unreliable.

Finally, what is the position if, in the case of a terminally ill minor, incapable himself of making any request, the doctor is asked by the parent or guardian to discontinue treatment? I have considered this previously in the context of necessity, and have suggested that necessity may provide an adequate ground for ignoring such a request. The question here, however,

---

[60] See further for an excellent comparative review, D. W. Meyers, *The Human Body and the Law* (Edinburgh University Press, 1970), ch. 6, esp. pp. 147 *et seq.*

[61] ['Child' is to be preferred].

[62] See *Bonner* v. *Moran* (1941) 126 F. 2d 121 (DCCir.). For an assessment of the legal position in the United States, see W. Wadlington, 'Minors and Health Care', 11 *Osgoode Hall Law Journal* 115 *et seq.* (1973).

is what are the consequences for the doctor if he should honour the request. It could be argued that the propositions considered earlier as regards the patient so requesting would be applicable, since all that has changed is that the relevant legal decision-maker is the parent or guardian, so that the doctor would be absolved from his duty. But is this so, even in a context, which we assume throughout, in which the parent or guardian has been fully informed and can make a rational decision? What would be the relevance of section 1(2)(a) of the Children and Young Persons Act 1933, which makes it a criminal offence for the person legally liable to maintain the child not to provide, *inter alia*, medical care? I take the view that the doctor has a choice here in the absence of any clear guide, either to continue to treat or to stop. If he were to discontinue treatment and merely make the child comfortable, the courts would not find him guilty of manslaugher. The ground would either be that he was expressly absolved from his duty, or the wider ground of Elliott's, that further treatment was useless.[63]

These exceptional cases apart (and it must be recalled that they are not really examples of the situation under discussion), it has been seen that there is no good ground for arguing that the doctor breaches his duty to his patient when respecting the patient's wishes to be left to die. Asserting this, however, as cold legal doctrine may well fail to convince the doctor who has to make his decision in the real world and must weigh all the arguments advanced above.

CONCLUSION

What I have tried to show, in a very narrow context, is the vulnerability of the principle of self-determination, contrasted with the persuasive power of paternalism. Consent, which lies at the root of self-determination, should be the conceptual mechanism whereby the right is guaranteed and safeguarded. I have suggested, however, that it is equally capable of being manipulated to defeat the right. If this is accepted, it is of value to move from the narrow base of this article to consider whether it is so in other areas. Further, it may even be appropriate to debate again whether consent is appropriate as the governing concept in the medical-legal context. Daube argued several years ago that 'it is time to revise our legal construction . . . of surgery in general',[64] and criticized the fact that it was still considered an assault rendered lawful by consent. The intervening years have not seen any revision,

---

[63] Williams, in discussing the failure to treat spina bifida children, argues that if parents 'forbid action to be taken [by the doctor], that should be conclusive' ('Euthanasia', *supra* n. 5, 23).

[64] D. Daube, 'Transplantation: Acceptability of Procedures and the Required Legal Sanctions', in *Ethics in Medical Progress*, *supra* n. 21, 193.

but this is not to say that it is not both necessary and desirable.[65] Ultimately, however, what may be needed is a set of proper procedural guides and guarantees which would ensure that whatever the legal rules may be, they are observed in practice.[66]

[65] For a tentative outline, see my 'Alive or Dead, The Lawyer's View', 22. *Current Legal Problems* 102, 122 *et seq.* (1969).

[66] [See further the discussion in chapter 16, and particularly the reference to Living Wills and Enduring Powers of Attorney as a reaction to the imagined or real risk of being 'over-treated'].

18

Switching Off Life-support Machines:
The Legal Implications*

In this paper I am concerned with whether the termination of the use of artificial 'life-support' machinery on which a person is being maintained (particularly a ventilator) ever involves a violation of the criminal law amounting to homicide. I shall discuss three situations in which the issue is typically presented: the much publicized, widely known case of the unconscious, dying patient connected to a ventilator; the case of the chronically dependent, conscious patient whose condition is stable—for example, a polio victim; and the temporarily dependent, emergency patient.

THE UNCONSCIOUS, DYING PATIENT

A patient lies in the intensive care unit of a hospital. He is attached to an artificial ventilator which ventilates his lungs, and his heart is beating. His doctors reach the conclusion that his condition is hopeless. Under what circumstances may the doctors switch off the ventilator? This apparent problem has attracted considerable attention in recent years. The Press has introduced into common speech such expressions as 'pulling the plug' or 'switching off the machine'.[1] The intent has been not only to describe the activity, but also to surround it with the appropriate drama. An assumption has been made by everyone. It is as follows: that the decision to turn off

---

* This paper first appeared in [1977] *Crim. LR* and is reproduced here with minor amendments and a postscript in which I comment on more recent developments.

[1] *The Times*, 19 Nov. 1975, reported Dr Miriam Stoppard as saying on a television programme concerning the case of Karen Quinlan that she 'confessed last night that she had ended a man's life'. 'I was not killing the patient; I was simply turning off the mechanism which was keeping him alive [*sic*].' See further my letter, *The Times*, 25 Nov. 1975. My complaint was with the language used and the extent to which careless use of words may prevent careful analysis. A very recent example in the United States was reported under the headline 'Court Allows Removal of Life-Support Device', *San Diego Union*, 12 Feb. 1977. Chancery Court Judge Franks in Chattanooga, Tennessee, is reported as outlining the steps to be followed 'to make the removal of the life-support systems a "lawfully compelled act" rather than murder'. See also *The Times*, 12 Nov. 1976, commenting on the publication of a Report on the Diagnosis of Brain Death by the Royal Colleges. The press coverage throughout the world of the Quinlan case is a prime example; see e.g. *Newsweek*, 12 Nov. 1975.

a ventilator is, in fact, a decision to terminate the life of a patient or to remove from a patient the last thread by which he held on to life. For this reason, because of its apparently crucial importance as regards the life and death of the patient, turning off the machine has attracted to itself an enormous significance, and has already spawned its own folklore. A recent editorial in the *British Medical Journal* criticizes past 'muddled thinking' on the matter, and calls for 'an end to uninformed comment on the topic'.[2] It is therefore ironic that the report which it unreservedly endorses and which appears in the same issue should perpetuate the thinking I seek here to expose as muddled and erroneous. This report, of the Medical Royal Colleges and their Faculties in the United Kingdom, concerns itself with the diagnosis of brain death, but at the outset acknowledges that *'the dilemma of when to switch off the ventilator* has been the subject of much public interest.'[3]

Clearly, if the assumption were correct, turning off a ventilator raises thorny problems for the criminal lawyer. Why is it not homicide to turn it off if, as is assumed, the patient is alive? Those who imagine that they see the spectre of euthanasia raising its head look with particular misgiving at the doctor's decision to discontinue ventilation.[4] Those lawyers who have given the issue their attention have accepted the common factual assumption that turning off a ventilator is significant, and have then sought legal arguments by which to justify it.[5] For they have had to recognize both that it is a common medical practice, and that it is one which prima facie calls for some justification. They realize, without necessarily evaluating the implications of the realization, that patients cannot be kept on a machine for ever.

The most common justification offered is elaborate and unsatisfactory. Turning off the ventilator, 'pulling the plug', the argument goes, is an omission, rather than a positive act. It is an omission because it represents a failure to continue treatment. The doctor, to use George Fletcher's language, merely 'permits' the patient to die.[6] Criminal liability, the argument continues, ordinarily attaches only to commissions which *cause* consequences not omissions whereby consequences are *permitted* to occur. It is conceded, however, that liability may follow some omissions, when there is a relationship between the victim and the defendant imposing on the defendant a duty to act. The doctor–patient relationship is just such a relationship. Thus the question of liability, whether for manslaughter or murder, turns on the duty of the doctor in the particular situation. Fletcher resolves this by saying that

---

[2] 2 *British Medical Journal* 1157 (1976).

[3] 'Diagnosis of Brain Death', 2 *British Medical Journal* 1187–8 (1976); my emphasis.

[4] See the discussion in G. Williams, 'Euthanasia', 41 *Medico-Legal Journal* 14 (1973). For an up-to-date review of the position in the United States, see 51 *New York University Law Review* 285, 293 (1976); 10 *John Marshall Journal of Practice and Procedure* 148 (1976).

[5] See e.g. G. Fletcher, 'Prolonging Life', 42 *University of Washington Law Review* 999 (1967); Williams, 'Euthanasia', previous note. [6] Fletcher, previous note, 1007.

'[I]t all depends on what doctors customarily do,'[7] so that if doctors customarily switch off ventilators in the circumstances under discussion, then this of itself makes it lawful to do so. This is obviously unsatisfactory, for it suggests that what is a matter of policy and values—namely, whether the doctor ought to treat—is within the special competence of doctors, whose expertise, in fact, is not in policy, but only in medical science. The question of criminal liability cannot be relegated to a matter of medical consensus.

Furthermore, ignoring the weaknesses of this conclusion, to describe turning off the machine as an omission does some considerable violence to ordinary English usage. It represents an attempt to solve the problem by logic-chopping. Such an approach may demonstrate to the satisfaction of some that no crime is involved, but it is surely most unsatisfactory to rest the response of the law to what is seen as a testing moral and philosophical issue on some semantic sleight of hand. Finally, and fatally, it rests on a flawed understanding of the relevant medical facts.

The justification, or analysis, which I propose here proceeds differently. It seeks to take account of the facts. It involves no recourse to sophistry, and it demystifies and strips of sensationalism the termination of the use of artificial support. Its major aim, as will appear, is to demonstrate that *the crucial medical-legal decision is not switching off a ventilator, but rather, switching it on, either initially or after having once turned it off.* My argument is as follows.

There is no doubt that the ventilator may be turned off when in fact, the patient is already dead. Once dead, treatment obviously is no longer called for. If not dead, the question becomes one of whether the patient still needs the ventilator in order to breathe; and, if so, whether, from the point of view of ultimate benefit, there is any longer any point in turning it back on. As regards the patient already dead, the reasoning is that although the patient displays outward manifestations of life, in that, by virtue of the ventilator, breathing and heartbeat are maintained, these manifestations are mechnically induced and are not sustained nor will ever again be sustainable by the patient.

This, of course, merely moves the debate a step further back, because it implies an understanding of what death is. Prompted by the rapid development of medical technology over the past decade or so,[8] the medical community has come to reject the notion that death is associated exclusively with breathing and heartbeat, the 'vital functions'. The view has been accepted that the state which has traditionally been regarded as death in a human being is reached when the brain, including[9] the brain-stem, is

---

[7] Ibid. 1015.

[8] 'Developments in medical technology have obfuscated the use of the traditional definition of death' (*Re Quinlan* (1976) 70 NJ 10, 355 A. 2d 647, 656).

[9] More correctly, 'particularly'.

destroyed.[10] A person will not breathe, nor will his heart beat, without a functioning brain-stem; and if this is destroyed, he will never recover the ability to do so, since, once destroyed, brain cells do not regenerate. A machine may well perform these tasks for him for some considerable period of time, but it has come to be accepted that once the brain[11] can be shown to be dead, the machine is not keeping the patient 'alive' in any accepted sense of the word; it is merely ventilating a corpse. Thus has emerged the medical concept of 'brain-stem death'.[12] The crucial feature is the irrecoverable loss by a patient of the ability ever again to sustain his own breathing and heartbeat, as a consequence of the total destruction of a functioning brain-stem. The reaction of the law was rather circumspect. Once convinced, however, that no major philosophical change was involved, but merely the identification by reference to more sophisticated criteria of what has always been regarded as death, medical lawyers have increasingly come to accept brain-stem death as the legal description also.[13] Legislation has put the matter beyond doubt in eight jurisdictions in the United States[14] and elsewhere—for example, in France.[15] In the United Kingdom, although some advocate legislation, it is likely that the new description will merely be incorporated into the law without more.[16]

The acceptance of brain-stem death may resolve a number of problems, but there is still the problem of how it is to be established in a particular case. Fundamentally, this is a matter for doctors, although the lawyer has

[10] The seminal paper was the Report of the *Ad Hoc* Committee of the Harvard Medical School, 'Definition of Irreversible Coma' 205 *Journal of the American Medical Association* 337 (1968). At last there has appeared an equivalent statement in the United Kingdom: 'Diagnosis of Brain Death', *supra* n. 3.   [11] [More correctly, 'the brain-stem'].

[12] [See C. Pallis, *The ABC of Brain Stem Death* (British Medical Journal Publications, 1983)].

[13] R. M. Veatch suggests that I fail to realize that the question 'What is death?' is a normative one, and not one for the medical profession alone. (*Death, Dying and the Biological Revolution* (*Yale University Press*, 1976, pp. 64 *et seq.*). A careful reading of what I have consistently written is that if what is being determined (brain-stem death) is the state always heretofore regarded as death, then the medical profession is merely continuing to reflect the normative consensus of society, albeit by means of more complex techniques, and is not developing some new concept of death. If a new concept of death were being advanced, then clearly it would no longer be a matter to be left just to doctors. See further, Kennedy, 'A Legal Perspective in Determining Death', 236 *The Month*, 46 (1975).

[14] Alaska, California, Kansas, Maryland, New Mexico, Oklahoma, Virginia, and West Virginia. There has also been a scattering of cases; *Wm. E. Tucker Admr. etc.* v. *Dr. Lower et al.*, Law File 2831, 25 May 1972, Law and Equity Court, Richmond, Virginia; *People* v. *Lyons*, No. 56072, California Superior Court, 1974, unreported; *New York City Health and Hospitals Corpn.* v. *Sulsona* (1975) 367 NYS 2d 686; *Re Quinlan*, *supra* n. 8. Since this paper was written, there has, of course, been considerable further activity, in both the courts and the state legislatures. See, generally, J. Areen *et al.*, *Law, Science and Medicine* (Foundation Press, 1984), pp. 1065–77.

[15] Decree of the Council of Ministers, 27 Apr. 1968.

[16] See Skegg, 'The Case for a Statutory Definition of Death', 2 *Journal of Medical Ethics* 1905, and my reply in 3 *Journal of Medical Ethics* (Mar. 1977).

a role to play in ensuring that the strictest possible safeguards attend the measures taken to establish it. At this point the theme of this paper re-emerges. The need to determine whether the patient has suffered brain-stem death arises only if the patient is on a ventilator. Only in this case can breathing and heartbeat continue independently of the patient's own ability to sustain them. At some stage in this process of determination, the ventilator must be turned off. Only thus can there be confirmation that the patient cannot in fact sustain his own vital functions. The Report of the Royal Colleges makes this explicitly clear. One of the six proposed tests for confirming brain-stem death is that 'No respiratory movements occur when the patient is disconnected from the mechanical ventilator for long enough to ensure that the arterial carbon dioxide tension rises above the threshold for stimulating respiration.'[17]

Here lies the key to the argument being presented. First, if the patient meets the criteria of brain-stem death in that, *inter alia*, he shows no sign of brain-stem activity and, in particular, does not breathe spontaneously, then the diagnosis that the patient is dead can be confirmed. *The machine need not be switched on again.*[18]

Second, if the patient breathes, however weakly and albeit without the regularity or strength to sustain himself, or otherwise demonstrates some sign of brain-stem functioning, then the question arises as to *whether or not to switch the machine on again.* On this analysis the medical-legal dilemma is properly identified as being one of determining whether, and if so, for how much longer, further treatment should be continued. Much has been written on this, and it need not be repeated here.[19] Basically this determination must first take account of what prospect the patient has of advancing along the

---

[17] 'Diagnosis of Brain Death', *supra* n. 3, 1188. Hypoxia (insufficiency of oxygen supply) is avoided during disconnection 'by delivering oxygen . . . through a catheter into the trachea' (ibid.).

[18] Indeed, my view is that to do so amounts to unethical practice by a doctor, except in the relatively rare case where an organ is wanted for transplantation and the ventilator is turned on to keep the organ viable. It could also bring criminal liability if the ventilator were turned on again for dishonest reasons. See the recent case in Kansas in which Herbert Smith Jr., struck his 19-month-old daughter and caused harm resulting in brain death. He failed in an attempt to require the attending doctors to keep the girl on a ventilator despite the diagnosis, so as to enable him to avoid prosecution for murder by arguing that she was alive according to the bizarrely drafted Kansas Death Statute, Kansas Session Laws, 1970, ch. 378; *San Diego Union*, 1 Mar. 1977.

[19] See the report of the Archbishop of Canterbury's Stevens Memorial Lecture before the Royal Society of Medicine and editorial comment thereon, *The Times*, 14 Dec. 1976. See further, Veatch, *supra* n. 13 ch. 3 for an up-to-date discussion of the literature, albeit somewhat idiosyncratic; Fletcher, *supra* n. 5; P. Ramsey, *The Patient as Person* (Yale University Press, 1970), pp. 113–44. For recent judicial views and comment thereon, see *Re Quinlan*, *supra* n. 8, esp. pp. 666–9 and the wealth of citations therein (particularly 667); I. Kennedy, 'The Karen Quinlan Case: Problems and Proposals', 2 *Journal of Medical Ethics* 3 (1976); the case of Saikewicz, Massachusetts, 1976, discussed in 17 *Medical World News*, 9 Aug. 1976; [and now, *Superintendent of Belchertown* v. *Saikewicz*, 370 NJE. 2d 417 (1977)].

line from hopelessness to improvement to recovery. The less the prospect and most cases which reach this point will be hopeless — the less the obligation to continue treatment, including the use of the ventilator, which is thus seen as only one factor of many which have to be considered. Chief Justice Hughes, writing for the New Jersey Supreme Court, put it well when he wrote, resting his decision on the fledgling constitutional doctrine of privacy but addressing the wider issue: 'We think that the State's interest [in the preservation of life] weakens and the individual's right of privacy grows as the degree of invasion increases and the prognosis dims.'[20]

Third, if the patient breathes on his own so as to sustain himself successfully, then the ventilator is not needed and *need not be switched on again*. Difficult problems may, of course, still remain. For example, breathing may fail again, and the decision will have to be taken whether to put the patient back on to the ventilator. The patient may still be irreversibly comatose, despite the ability to breathe spontaneously. Thus, the problems just considered may soon arise again — namely, how much more care in terms of time, resources, and energy is called for. Karen Quinlan falls into this third category, despite initial medical and popular views to the contrary. She has now survived more than nine months without the aid of a ventilator. Of course, she would die very quickly if she were not to receive intensive and expensive round-the-clock treatment from the staff of the nursing home where she is now a patient. How long this can and should, go on is the question which has to be asked, and answered.[21]

In none of the three alternative situations described above does switching off the ventilator have any significance, of itself, from a medical-legal point of view. 'Pulling the plug' is not an event to tax the criminal lawyer. The language of analogies, such as 'cutting the last thread of life', is both inaccurate and unhelpful. Provided he acts with good faith and all due care in the context outlined above, the doctor[22] who turns off the ventilator does

---

[20] *Re Quinlan, supra* n. 8, 664.

[21] She is fed a closely monitored high-protein diet by tubes leading directly into her stomach. Another tube delivers antibiotics directly into her kidneys. The tubes are routinely examined for infection. Padding prevents her contorted limbs from bruising and wounding themselves. Bedsores are so deep, despite careful nursing, that her hip-bone is visible under dressings. [Miss Quinlan subsequently died, but not until 1985].

[22] As the setting would always be a hospital, I have presumed that a doctor or other member of the medical team (including a nurse) would switch off the machine. If the switching-off were done by some other person who had gained access to the patient, without the doctor's authority, the question of criminal liability could be different. It would turn on whether brain-stem death had yet been established. If it had, there may or may not be an *attempted* homicide depending on the knowledge and intent of the person; but there is no question of homicide. If brain-stem death had not been established, then the answer as to liability could depend on post-morten reports. If the patient could be shown incontrovertibly to have suffered brain-stem death before the machine was turned off, then there is at most the possibility of an attempted homicide. If this could not be shown, the assumption must be made that the patient was alive, and thus, depending on knowledge and intent, there would be liability for murder or manslaughter. See further, the discussion *infra*.

nothing to warrant criminal sanction. A further benefit of this analysis is that it causes attention to be focused on the real medical-legal issue; whether, and if so, what, liability (criminal or civil) ever attends the decision which is significant, namely turning, or failing to turn, the ventilator *on* again. This is the really thorny question, but only relatively recently has it begun to receive the attention it merits.

THE CHRONICALLY DEPENDENT PATIENT

There are some patients who are permanently maintained on ventilators because of illness. No question arises as to whether they are alive or not; they clearly are. Their brains function; they are conscious and are able to do a variety of things; but they have been struck down, for example, by polio.

In the case of the chronically dependent patient (the polio victim, say), if the ventilator is turned off, he will die. He is receiving long-term life-sustaining treatment. 'Pulling the plug' in such a case *is* significant from a medical-legal point of view. Its significance, in terms of the legal consequences which would follow, can be assessed, however, only by drawing a crucial distinction between the situation where the patient requests that further support be terminated, and that where the ventilator is turned off without the consent of the patient.

What law governs the situation when a lucid adult whose continued existence depends on a ventilator decides that his existence is no longer tolerable and that he wishes to die? Strictly speaking — and this is important analytically — he is asking for treatment to be discontinued. The distinction has to be noted (because traditionally thinking in criminal law seems to regard it as important) between a request by the patient that treatment be discontinued which is complied with and a request by the patient that someone stabs him to death which is complied with. The former, on my analysis (*infra*) would not attract criminal liability, whereas the latter, on traditional analysis, would be homicide, often categorized in appropriate circumstances as voluntary active euthanasia. I do not wish to argue that stabbing the patient should not be homicide. But this obliges me to explain why different criminal law consequences follow compliance with the same request made in different ways.

To say that the patient cannot demand to be stabbed because he cannot suspend the operation of the criminal law and absolve the other of liability begs the question, depending as it does on a determination of what the criminal law is. I do not wish to argue that one is an act of killing and the other an omission to treat, or that there is active, as opposed to passive, conduct. I find such arguments distinctly unsatisfying. Neither can reasons of motive or intention be relied upon if, for the sake of argument, I admit that good faith and the best of intentions prevail throughout.

Perhaps the distinction between the response of the criminal law to a request that treatment be ended and to (figuratively) taking a knife to the patient rests on four basic and interrelated premisses. First, there is the libertarian premiss that a person's position should not be *irremediably* worsened by another's conduct. Stabbing to death offends this principle. Turning off a machine lets other factors intervene, and thrusts the ultimate decision back to the patient who can still (in theory, at least) change his mind. Causation thus also plays a part. Second, there is what some philosophers call the red-light rule. It may not be necessary for all cars always to stop at a red light at a crossroads, but to have any other rule, such as 'stop when reasonable to do so', or 'stop unless the road is clear', invites chaos. Thus, it is better to have a clear, if crude, rule and invite leniency in the case of justifiable transgression, such as passing through a red light in an emergency. Equally, a crude general rule condemning all acts of killing is preferable to any other possible rule. Third, there is an evidential point. Recourse to stabbing is at least potentially more open to abuse. The criminal law, if faced with two alternative ways of achieving a similar end, may well prefer that which raises fewer issues of proof and potential abuse. Fourth, a patient on a machine making such a request is a comparatively rare phenomenon. The criminal law can respond to it as a tolerable and justifiable exception to basic criminal law rules developed long before ventilators ever existed. Stabbing consenting patients goes beyond such narrow confines, is less manageable as a practice, and makes too many inroads into these basic criminal law rules.[23]

I discussed the law on this problem of requesting that treatment be discontinued recently in this *Review*,[24] and reached the conclusion that the patient who is mature, lucid, and informed may validly withhold consent to further treatment, and that treatment thereafter would be unlawful. It follows that the person—doctor, nurse, or other—who complied with the request that treatment be withdrawn, provided he acted in good faith, would not be acting in violation of the criminal law.[25] There should be no difference in principle between the patient diagnosed as having irreparable kidney failure who refuses to submit to dialysis on an artificial kidney or who refuses to continue such treatment[26] and the polio victim on the

[23] See further Ramsey, *supra* n. 19, 144–56; *supra* nn. 13 and 19.

[24] I. Kennedy, 'The Legal Effect of Requests by the Terminally Ill and the Aged not to Receive Further Treatment from Doctors' [1976] *Crim. LR* 217; reprinted as chapter 17 above. See also Veatch, *supra* n. 13, 116–63; *Re Quinlan*, *supra* n. 8, 656, 662–4, 669–70.

[25] See the detailed discussion in *Re Quinlan*, *supra* n. 8, 669–70.

[26] Ernie Crowfeather became the centre of attention in the United States for a short while when he walked away from the kidney dialysis programme in Seattle. Unknown to him, he was about to be dropped from the programme anyway, as an unsuitable patient, by the recently appointed committee appointed to allocate scarce medical resources among competing (and dying) patients; Veatch, *supra* n. 13, 173. See also Schreiner's case reports in *Ethics in Medical Progress* (Ciba, 1966), p. 29.

ventilator who requested that the machine be switched off. No one doubts the right of the patient with kidney disease to decline treatment. The polio patient's equal right to self-determination should not be denied merely because he is helpless. Whether a court would grant a patient an order requiring a doctor or whoever to cease treatment, to 'pull the plug', is not yet known in England. But, it is submitted, the law is as stated above.[27] It should be noted in passing, however, that where a patient is deemed for whatever reason legally incompetent, the law is less clear. It probably requires that treatment continue, even if a request is made by the patient or another that it should cease.[28]

It is conceded that not all may accept this view of the law. Some support for it, however, can be gained from the legislation which came into effect on 1 January 1977, in the State of California.[29] Generally speaking, the law in California in this area developed in the same way as it did in England. By 1976, it had reached a similar degree of complexity and confusion. The legislation, which is the first of its kind in the common-law world, was seen as clarifying and putting the law beyond doubt, rather than making new law. It can therefore serve as a helpful guide. In its preamble, the Natural Death Act 1976 states that 'adult persons have the fundamental right to control the decision relating to the rendering of their own medical care, including the decision to have life-sustaining procedures withheld or withdrawn in instances of a terminal condition.' '[M]odern medical technology', it goes on, 'has made possible the artificial prolongation of human life beyond natural limits.' Further, 'there exists considerable uncertainty in the medical and legal professions as to the legality of terminating the use or application of life-sustaining procedures where the patient has voluntarily and in sound mind evidenced a desire that such procedures be withheld or withdrawn.'[30] The Act thus provides that an adult may execute a duly witnessed 'directive' in a form laid down, 'directing the withholding or withdrawal of life-sustaining procedures'.[31] *Ex abundante cautela*, the Act goes on to provide that 'no physician' or other who complies with the directive 'shall be subject to civil liability therefrom' or 'shall be guilty of any criminal act or of unprofessional conduct'.[32] Clearly the range of the Act is very limited,

---

[27] [But compare the California case of *Bouvia* v. *County of Riverside*, Docket no. 159780, Superior Court of California, 16 Dec. 1983].

[28] For a more detailed discussion, see chapter 17.

[29] Sections 7185–95, California Health and Safety Code, 1977. See *The Times*, 1 Sept. 1976; *Los Angeles Times*, 2 Oct. 1976; *San Diego Union*, 20 Dec. 1976.

[30] Section 7186, California Health and Safety Code, *supra* n. 29, 'Life-sustaining procedures' are defined in section 1786(c) as 'any medical procedures or intervention which utilises mechanical or other artificial means to sustain, restore or supplant a vital function, which, when applied to a qualified patient [as defined] would serve only to prolong the moment of death and where, in the judgment of the attending physician, death is imminent whether or not such procedures are utilised'.

[31] Ibid., s. 7188.   [32] Ibid.

applying only to lucid adult patients connected or about to be connected to a ventilator who are suffering from a terminal condition (as defined) and who execute the appropriate directive.[33] A first step, however, has been taken in clarifying the law. Both the particular rule it lays down and, more important, the general principle it enshrines should be accepted as part of the English law also, though it may be debatable whether there is a need for it to be put into statutory form.[34]

Next, what is the law governing the situation when the respirator is turned off without the knowledge and consent of the chronically dependent patient? It is important to distinguish the situation of the patient here from that of the patient who is unconscious and terminally ill. Here, the patient, though chronically dependent on the ventilator is a conscious, sentient person. Although his condition is in one sense hopeless, in that he will not recover, it is not hopeless in the sense that he is in imminent danger of dying. He is stable and, all being well, will remain so for some considerable period of time.[35] The motive for turning off the ventilator in this situation may be evil, or it may be good, as, for example, in the case of involuntary euthanasia intended to bring about an end to misery and suffering. There is no doubt that in such a case, given the necessary knowledge and intent, the person turning off the machine would be guilty of murder. Some may seek to argue that a lesser crime is committed, because they would like the law to be sufficiently flexible to allow the 'mercy-killer' to avoid facing a charge of murder. But murder it is, and whatever leniency is called for must find itself reflected either in a verdict of not guilty by a jury, despite the facts, in the sentence of the court (though in England the sentence is at present fixed by law), or in the exercise of some executive discretion.[36]

---

[33] Two further provisions are worthy of note. Section 7192(a) provides that compliance with the Act by a patient shall not constitute suicide. Section 7192(b) then goes on to provide that life insurance policies shall not be invalidated by the patient's action; nor may those selling health care insurance require that buyers execute a directive.

[34] See, now, the discussion in chapter 17.

[35] An argument could be made on economic grounds that the ventilator should at some point be turned off. Where complicated medical technology and intensive care are involved, the question must always be faced as to whether the scarce resources of health care are being appropriately allocated. It could be said that the chronically dependent patient's prognosis is hopeless in the long term, if hopelessness is judged in terms of recovery. In his recent lecture (*supra* n. 19] the Archbishop of Canterbury touched on the theme of resources. This was, with respect, a brave decision. It brought him considerable criticism e.g. from the editorial columns of *The Times*, but he was right in my view to bring into the open for public debate what is a hidden, but often critical, factor in decisions about medical care. It is a subject which warrants extensive treatment elsewhere. In the present context, few would support the termination of care to the chronically dependent purely on grounds of resources.

[36] In the section of their recent working paper on Offences Against the Person dealing with 'mercy killing' (at pp. 31–4), the Criminal Law Revision Committee proposed no change in the relevant law. See the discussion in *The Times*, 29 Sept. 1976, and in the correspondence columns thereafter.

Others, for the same reasons or for what they believe are reasons of legal principle, may argue that no murder is committed, on the basis of the reasoning noted earlier that the ventilator is 'prolonging life', and turning it off is an omission permitting death, not a commission causing death. This argument, however, is clearly untenable as a simple analogy will illustrate. For example, a tightrope-walker balances on a high wire strung sufficiently far above the ground and without a safety net; hence a fall would ordinarily be fatal. Anyone who cuts the wire with the necessary intent and knowledge would be guilty of murder.[37] No amount of talk about only permitting the tightrope-walker to fall will persuade otherwise. For the same reason the doctor, medical attendant, or other who turned off a ventilator in this situation would be guilty of murder.

THE TEMPORARILY DEPENDENT, EMERGENCY PATIENT

The patient referred to here is one who needs to be connected to a ventilator to cope with a crisis or emergency. It will be assumed for the sake of argument that this patient had not indicated or is unable to indicate a desire that treatment on the ventilator be terminated.[38] Provided the ultimate prognosis were one of improvement or recovery, it is submitted that anyone—doctor, medical attendant, or other—who turns off the ventilator with knowledge that death will result and an intent to bring this about is guilty of murder. If the prognosis for the patient, though initially favourable, becomes poor, then the question becomes the same as that already considered, for how much longer treatment must be given. The extent to which treatment on the ventilator must be continued is determined, I submit, by reference to the extent to which recovery or improvement is possible. At some point, treatment becomes futile. At this point, the ventilator, along with other forms of treatment, can and should be discontinued.

POSTSCRIPT

Beynon, in a paper snappily entitled 'Doctors as Murderers',[39] responded to my views concerning the unconscious dying patient and declared herself

---

[37] Of course, granting for the moment that turning off the machine could be an omission, if it is the doctor who turns it off, he would still be liable since the special relationship he enjoys with his patient obliges him to render aid. The doctor would have to argue that his duty was to turn off the machine; and if it were done without the knowledge or consent of the patient, such an argument, even if advanced in all good faith, would founder. If, however, the machine were turned off by someone other than a member of the medical team and thus someone who prima facie did not have a duty to render aid, to grant that it is an omission is seen as unwarranted.

[38] If he has indicated such a desire, the arguments advanced earlier apply.

[39] H. Beynon, 'Doctors as Murderers' [1982] *Crim. LR* 17.

unconvinced. She set herself the task of considering 'the withholding of treatment',[40] and did so first through the traditional language of acts and omissions, since she did not regard as satisfactory the option of concentrating analytically on duty which I propose. In a sense, of course, her phrasing of the problem conditions her subsequent approach. To talk of 'withholding treatment' is already to invite consideration of the language of omissions. If the doctor's conduct were described as *changing* treatment, from treatment for living to treatment for dying, as I contend it should be,[41] any subsequent analysis might proceed somewhat differently.

By saying that the doctor is changing treatment, attention is drawn to the fact that while he may stop doing one thing — for example, by turning off a ventilator — he may still be doing other things — for example, monitoring heartbeat and respiration. Of course, the immediate reply is that the criminal law is concerned with causation, and is thus interested in isolating what, if any, conduct caused death, so as to enquire whether there is any conduct which can give rise to criminal liability. And Beynon would reply that turning off the ventilator caused the death of the patient, in that otherwise he would have gone on breathing, at least for a while, and his heart would have continued to beat. This being so, she would say, you cannot escape the question of whether turning off the ventilator is an act or an omission, since if it is an act, it looks like homicide — that is, an intentional act causing death. If, however, it is an omission, no such liability may arise in the absence of a duty to continue to ventilate which the law probably does not impose on the doctor.

Beynon offers a way out of the problem by developing a theory of what omissions really are. The difficulty posed by her solution, however, is that if it is not accepted — and it is not free from difficulties — all is lost, and the criminal law cannot accommodate the doctor's conduct, despite the fact that all, or most, of us would think it right. Let me, therefore, offer a further way out, within the framework of acts and omissions adopted by Beynon, even though it is a framework which I have sought to argue is both unhelpful and avoidable.[42]

The way out is based on a return to the notion of causation which I mentioned earlier. However the doctor's conduct is characterized, the argument goes, he will not be guilty of a crime in changing to treating for dying, where this is justified, because he will not have caused the patient's death in the eyes of the law. To reach this conclusion, we must distinguish

---

[40] Ibid. 18.   [41] See chapters 7, 8, and 16 above.

[42] Beynon seems to misunderstand my position since she soon has me using the language of acts and omissions, when the purpose of my paper was to urge that it be abandoned as an analytical approach. Thus, she proceeds to trump me with her example of the drip. On the analysis I advocate, it poses no problem at all. Whether the bag is taken down or the catheter removed makes no difference, since, in the circumstances, neither would be a breach of duty.

between factual causation and legal causation. The former is qualified by the latter in that, although someone may have caused something to happen in that he brought it about, he will not be held legally responsible for it unless it is considered that he ought to be so held. Legal causation, in other words, introduces into the general notion of causation a normative or prescriptive element.

We can, then, take as given the propositions that death is not always necessarily an evil to be prevented, and that, as a consequence, a doctor may in appropriate circumstances be entitled to embark on conduct which involves ceasing to seek to prevent death and could, as it happens, bring it about. Attention then shifts to the circumstances in which he is so entitled. This, I have already suggested, is when the patient has reached a point such that further intervention is ethically unwarranted as being useless, and even oppressive.

If it is established in good faith that the patient has indeed reached that point, the doctor's conduct in turning off a ventilator is not properly to be described as a legal cause of the patient's death. It may have some factual relationship; but as a matter of law, this would not be regarded as such as to bring liability. I would describe it as a 'non-blameworthy cause'. And, on such an analysis, the debate over acts or omissions, which captivates some, could continue to go on, but would be side-stepped in the real world by a proper understanding of causation. Beynon's insistence that the problem be posed in terms of acts or omissions need not, therefore, prove fatal to reaching the only outcome to the analysis which makes sense.

Support for this view comes from Glanville Williams.[43] *R.* v. *Malcherek*[44] provides further support. It suggests that in a case such as the one under discussion, the court will not enquire into the doctor's conduct, provided it is satisfied that it conforms to what doctors ordinarily do—and, I would add, that there is general approval of what they do. In *Malcherek* a girl was savagely attacked about the head. After several days in the intensive care unit, she was removed from a ventilator and then pronounced dead. Neither the trial court nor the Court of Appeal was prepared to listen to arguments suggesting that the doctors' conduct in ending ventilation was in law causally related to the girl's death.

An alternative form of words to 'non-blameworthy cause', which would produce the same result, is 'minimal cause'. Williams finds authority for this in the case of *R.* v. *Adams*.[45] He suggests that Devlin J.'s instructions to the jury can be taken to mean that, if what the doctor did in providing

---

[43] G. Williams, *Textbook of Criminal Law*, 2nd edn. (Stevens, 1983), pp. 279–85. Compare the 1st edn. of 1978, in which he concentrates more on acts and omissions, pp. 232–7. Williams uses the more traditional language of non-imputable causes (2nd edn. p. 381).

[44] [1981] 1 WLR 690.   [45] [1957] *Crim. LR* 365.

medication for his elderly and very sick patient was approved medical practice, it was not to be regarded as a cause in law, since it plays such a minimal role in causing death that it can be excluded from consideration.[46]

Whichever language is used, both approaches, in my view, are entirely valid. And if more is needed, there is a further way of responding to Beynon's point. Williams again points to *Adams* and finds in it[47] authority for the further proposition that if the doctor was doing what is approved of, the defence of necessity would avail him if any charge were brought. Although I am not entirely persuaded by recourse to this general notion of necessity, it does serve to highlight a major point here. As Williams makes clear, the doctor has to stop treating at some time, once it is agreed that the treatment is both hopeless and useless. Otherwise, scarce medical resources will be needlessly wasted. Whether this gives rise to the defence of necessity or is merely a further demonstration that the doctor's conduct is not blameworthy is, perhaps, a question of impression which need not detain us here.

Thus, returning to Beynon, there are, I think, ways out of the problem she posed, even within the traditional language of acts and omissions. I still, however, prefer my own approach, which turns on the nature and extent of the duty owed by a doctor to his patient. In my view, both criminal and civil law are best analysed in this way. Indeed, the causation argument previously set out boils down in essence to a discussion of the doctor's duty to his patient. Once it is accepted that his duty may consist in ending ventilation, the next step is to describe such compliance with his duty as a non-blameworthy or minimal cause of death.

Beynon also devotes space to criticizing the approach based on duty. This approach, you will recall, obviates the need to categorize conduct as either an act or an omission since, even if it is an omission, it can bring liability if there is a duty to act. Duty, therefore, is the important concept. Beynon has some difficulty in finding a general duty recognized by the criminal law, which requires a doctor to care for his patient. For my part, I find this distinctly odd, and have no doubt that for the criminal, as well as the civil, law the existence of the doctor–patient relationship gives rise to such a duty, such that breach of it leading to death may amount to homicide.[48]

For Beynon, there is no general duty. The duty owed by a doctor depends on the contractual relationship he has with either his patient or his employer. Only in this way, she asserts, can the law reflect 'clinical freedom'; by which she means that 'medical standards' are set by the medical profession.[49] This is such a bizarre proposition that it hardly warrants serious attention.

---

[46] Williams, 2nd edn. *supra* n. 43, 385.   [47] Ibid.

[48] Beynon also has difficulty with the idea that in the case of the mature lucid patient, consent is relevant to the doctor's duty. The answer must be that a patient can waive the duty owed her by her doctor or refuse to have him treat her. Thereafter, on the one hand, the doctor has no duty, and, on the other, any touching would be a crime.   [49] Beynon, *supra* n. 39, 28.

First, if a doctor's duty in law depends on his contractual relationship, it would not be the medical profession, but GPs, hospital doctors, community physicians, and doctors in private practice, all of whom have different contractual arrangements, who would be establishing what *in law* are the nature and extent of the duty owed by a doctor to his patient. Second, Beynon defines 'medical standards' as 'including possibly the definition of a "medical decision" — e.g. withholding of food could sometimes be seen as a medical decision, sometimes not.'[50] This helpful insight does not resolve the question of when it is and when it is not a 'medical decision', nor who decides this question. But whatever the answer, it cannot be that hospital doctors, for example, are the final arbiters of what treatment options they are obliged in law to give or withhold.

And this leads to a third point. If Beynon is right, it means that the courts and the criminal law would lose *all* supervisory power over the conduct of doctors, a position which I doubt that even many doctors would advocate. Imagine, for example, that doctors at a hospital had a policy of not resuscitating patients who were over 65 (as was the situation in the well-known Neasden Hospital case). Imagine further that there was a body of opinion within the medical profession practising in hospitals and among hospital administrators that this was a not unreasonable method of rationing scarce medical resources. Can it seriously be suggested that the duty imposed on doctors by the criminal law is merely that they make sure that the patient is over 65, and that thereafter, resuscitation or non-resuscitation is for them alone?

What if, for example, a doctor treating a bedridden and very sick patient privately at home had a clearly understood agreement by which he was to be paid every week? What if he found that several cheques had not been honoured recently? And what if it were the case that a number of doctors believed that in private practice it was a matter for the individual doctor to decide whether to continue treatment when a patient could no longer pay? And what if the particular doctor decided not to visit his patient? And what if the patient died? And what if the doctor then said that he merely omitted to attend or call an NHS ambulance? And what if he said that such an omission was not a breach of duty since some of his peers in private practice, responsible doctors all, did not think that it was?

It may all be unethical, but on Beynon's argument would the doctor be guilty of a crime? He would appear not to be, except if you massage the definition of omission fairly hard. Beynon clearly regrets the state of the law as she sees it, but has no doubt that it leads to this conclusion. In my view, it does no such thing.

---

[50] Ibid., n. 49.

19

A Woman and Her Unborn Child: Rights and Responsibilities

What I am concerned with here are the relative rights, if any, of a pregnant woman and her fetus. I am concerned with the question, what should, or must, a woman do, or refrain from doing, while pregnant? I shall seek to examine the issues involved from the point of view both of ethics and law. The latter enquiry will necessitate an examination of whether there is a need to make public policy, and if there is what form that public policy should take. Curiously, although the nature of the problem only has to be stated to see how significant it is, there has been relatively little scholarly comment in the United Kingdom[1] in contrast to the United States.[2]

---

[1] See for example, A. Grubb and D. Pearl, 'Protecting the Life of the Unborn Child', *Law Quarterly Review*, vol. 103 (1987) p. 340; B. Dimond, 'Consent, Compulsion and the Rights of the Mother and Unborn Child', *Midwives Chronicle and Nursing Notes*, vol. 99 (1987) p. 1179; J. Fortin, 'Legal Protection for the Unborn Child', *Modern Law Review*, vol. 51 (1988) p. 54, and 'Can you Ward a Foetus', *Modern Law Review*, vol. 51 (1988) p. 768; R. Gillon, 'Pregnancy, Obstetrics and the Moral Status of the Fetus', *Journal of Medical Ethics*, vol. 14 (1988) p. 1.

[2] See, for example, American College of Obstetrics and Gynaecologists, 'Patient Choice: Maternal–Fetal Conflict', *ACOG Committee Opinion* (1987); G. Annas, 'Pregnant Women as Fetal Containers', *Hastings Center Report*, vol. 16 (1986) p. 13, 'The Impact of Medical Technology on the Pregnant Woman's Right to Privacy', *American Journal of Legal Medicine*, vol. 13 (1987), and 'Protecting the Liberty of Pregnant Patients', *New England Journal of Medicine*, vol. 316 (1987) p. 1214; R. Blank, 'Emerging Notions of Women's Rights and Responsibilities During Gestation', *Journal of Legal Medicine*, vol. 7 (1986) p. 441; J. C. Fletcher, 'Emerging Ethical Issues in Fetal Therapy', *Progress in Clinical Biological Research*, vol. 128 (1983) p. 293; J. Gallaher, 'Prenatal Invasion and Interventions: What's Wrong with Fetal Rights', *Harvard Women's Law Journal*, vol. 10 (1987) p. 9; D. Johnsen, 'The Creation of Fetal Rights: Conflicts with Women's Constitutional Rights to Liberty, Privacy and Equal Protection', *Yale Law Journal*, vol. 7 (1986) p. 251, and 'A New Threat to Pregnant Women's Autonomy', *Hastings Center Report*, vol. 17 (1987) p. 33; M. Mahawold, 'Beyond Abortion: Refusal of Cesarean Section', *Bioethics*, vol. 3 (1989) p. 106; D. Mathieeu, 'Respecting Liberty and Preventing Harm: Limits of State Intervention on Prenatal Choice', *Harvard Journal of Law and Public Policy*, vol. 8 (1985) p. 19; L. Nelson and N. Milliken, 'Compelled Medical Treatment of Pregnant Women: Life, Liberty and Law in Conflict', *Journal of the American Medical Association*, vol. 259 (1988) p. 7; N. Rhoden 'The Judge in the Delivery Room: The Emergence of Court Ordered Cesareans', *California Law Review*, vol. 74 (1986) p. 1951; J. Robertson and J. D. Schulman, 'Pregnancy and Prenatal Harm to Offspring: The Case of Mothers with PKU', *Hastings Center Report*, vol. 17 (1987) p. 23; B. K. Rothman, *Recreating Motherhood* (New York: W. W. Norton, 1989); G. Schedler, 'Women's Reproductive Rights: Is There a Conflict with a Child's Right to be Born Free from Defects?', *Journal of Legal Medicine*, vol. 7 (1986) p. 357; B. Steinbock, D. Marquis and S. Kayata, 'Case Studies—Preterm Labor and Prenatal Harm', *Hastings Center Report*, vol. 19 (1989) p. 32.

Consider the following.

1. In the case of *Jefferson* v. *Griffin Spalding County Hospital* in 1981, the Supreme Court of Georgia handed down the following judgement.[3]

On Thursday, January 22nd, 1981 the Griffin Spalding County Hospital Authority petitioned the Superior Court of Butts County for an order authorising it to perform a caesarean section and any necessary blood transfusions upon the defendant, an out-patient resident of Butts County, in the event she presented herself to the hospital for delivery of her unborn child which was due on or about Monday, January 26th.

[The Superior Court found] Defendant is in the thirty-ninth week of pregnancy. In the past few weeks she has presented herself to Griffin Spalding County Hospital for pre-natal care. The examining physician has found and defendant has been advised that she has a complete placenta previa; that the afterbirth is between the baby and the birth canal; that it is virtually impossible that this condition will correct itself prior to delivery; and that it is a 99 per cent certainty that the child cannot survive natural child birth (vaginal delivery). The chances of the defendant surviving vaginal delivery are no better than 50 per cent.

The examining physician is of the opinion that a delivery by caesarean section prior to labor beginning would have an almost 100 per cent chance of preserving the life of the child, along with that of the defendant.

On the basis of religious beliefs, defendant has advised the Hospital that she does not need surgical removal of the child and will not submit to it. Further, she refuses to take any transfusion of blood . . . .

The Hospital . . . seeks authority of the Court to administer to defendant all medical procedures deemed necessary by the attending physician to preserve the life of defendant's unborn child . . . .

The Court has been requested to order defendant to submit to surgery before the natural childbirth process (labor) begins. The Court is reluctant to grant this request and does not do so at this time. . . .

On Friday, January 23, the Georgia Department of Human Resources, acting through the Butts County Department of Family and Children Services, petitioned the Juvenile Court of Butts County for temporary custody of the unborn child, alleging that the child was a deprived child without proper parental care necessary for his or her physical health . . . and praying for an order requiring the mother to submit to a caesarean section.

[T]he Court concludes and finds as a matter of law . . . this child is a viable human being and entitled to the protection of the Juvenile Court Code of Georgia. The Court concludes that this child is without the proper parental care and subsistence necessary for his or her physical life and health.

Temporary custody of the unborn child is hereby granted to the state of Georgia Department of Human Resources and the Butts County Department of Family and Children Services. The Department shall have full authority to make all decisions,

---

[3] 247 Ga. 86, 274 S.E. 2d 457.

including giving consent to the surgical delivery appertaining to the birth of this child. The temporary custody of the Department shall terminate when the child has been successfully brought from its mother's body into the world or until the child dies, whichever shall happen.

Because of the unique nature of these cases, the powers of the Superior Court of Butts County are invoked and the defendant, Jessie Mae Jefferson, is hereby Ordered to submit to a sonogram (ultrasound) at the Griffin Spalding County Hospital or some other place which may be chosen by her where such procedure can be given. Should said sonogram indicate to the attending physician that the complete placenta previa is still blocking the child's passage into this world, Jessie Mae Jefferson is Ordered to submit to a caesarean section and related procedures considered necessary by the attending physician to sustain the life of this child.

The Court finds that the State has an interest in the life of this unborn living human being. The Court finds that the intrusion involved into the life of Jessie Mae Jeffeson and her husband, John W. Jefferson, is outweighed by the duty of the State to protect a living, unborn human being from meeting his or her death before being given the opportunity to live . . . .

The parents filed their motion for stay at about 5.30 p.m. on January 23rd and after hearing oral argument . . . . this Court entered the following order on the evening of January 23:

[I]t is ordered that the Motion for Stay filed in this matter is hereby denied. The trial court's orders are effective immediately.

Hill P. J stated that:

The power of a court to order a competent adult to submit to surgery is exceedingly limited. Indeed, until this unique case arose, I would have thought such power to be non-existent. Research shows that the courts generally have held that a competent adult had the right to refuse necessary life-saving surgery and medical treatment (i.e., has the right to die) where no state interest other than saving the life of the patient is involved. . . . On the other hand, one court has held that an expectant mother in the last weeks of pregnancy lacks the right to refuse necessary life-saving surgery and medical treatment where the life of the unborn child is at stake. *Raleigh Fitkin-Paul Morgan Memorial Hospital v Anderson* (42 N.J. 421) . . . .

In denying the stay of the trial court's order and thereby clearing the way for immediate re-examination by sonogram and probably for surgery, we weighed the right of the mother to practise her religion and to refuse surgery on herself, against her unborn child's right to live. We found in favour of her child's right to live.

Smith J, in a concurring judgement, held that:

[I]n the instant case, it appears that there is no less burdensome alternative for preserving the life of a fully developed fetus than requiring its mother to undergo surgery against her religious convictions. Such an intrusion by the state would be extraordinary, presenting some medical risk to both the mother and the fetus. However, the state's compelling interest in preserving the life of this fetus is beyond dispute.

Subsequent to the court's decision, but before any action was taken, Jessie Mae Jefferson gave birth naturally to her child.

2. In San Diego, California, on 26 September 1986, Pamela Rae Stewart was arrested and charged under a statute of 1872 with causing her son's death by failing to obtain adequate medical care during pregnancy.[4] She had placenta previa, a condition which blocks part of the cervix leading to a risk of haemorrhage and oxygen deprivation of the child. She ignored medical advice to stop taking amphetamines, to refrain from sexual intercourse and delayed going to hospital for 'many hours'[5] after the onset of bleeding and contractions. The baby was born alive but with severe brain damage and died after six weeks. The California statute[6] penalises a 'parent of a minor child [who] wilfully omits, without lawful excuse, to furnish necessary . . . medical attendance or other remedial care for his or her child'. The statute had been amended in 1925 to provide that 'a child conceived but not yet born . . . [is] an existing person'.

The case against Stewart was dismissed. It was held that the statute did not cover the particular situation, in that no proof had been offered that medical attendance had not been sought or furnished.[7] The dismissal did not, however, come before the case had attracted national attention. Equally, it did not come before Stewart had gone through the inevitable trauma associated with the loss of her child and the subsequent prosecution.[8]

3. On 10 November 1987, the Court of Appeals of the District of Columbia, in the case of Angela C.,[9] approved the lower court's order that a caesarean section be carried out on a terminally ill woman with hours or days to live, despite her apparent refusal of permission.[10] The child was in its 26th week of gestation. The mother was heavily sedated and *in extremis* suffering from a metastatic oxygenic carcinoma in her lung. The operation was performed. The child died two hours thereafter. The mother died two days later. The court in upholding the order held that 'the trial judge did not err in

---

[4] See, for a detailed discussion, Annas, 'Pregnant Women', p. 13.

[5] Ibid., citing the police report.

[6] *California Penal Code*, s. 270 (West Publishing, St. Paul, Minn., 1986).

[7] There is some disagreement about the grounds for the dismissal. Compare Robertson's and Johnsen's papers in the *Hastings Center Report*.

[8] Johnsen comments in 'A New Threat': 'By the time Ms. Stewart's criminal prosecution was dismissed five months after her arrest . . . she had spent six days in jail. . . . During her prosecution the most intimate details of her life were repeatedly examined by the news media across the country.'

[9] *Re A. C.*, D.C. Ct. App. 533, A 2d.611 (1987).

[10] 'Before she was sedated, A. C. indicated that she would choose to relinquish her life so that the fetus could survive should such a choice present itself at the fetus' gestational age of twenty-eight weeks. Her physicians never discussed with her what her choice would be if such a choice had to be made before the fetus reached the twenty-eight week point. . . . Shortly after the trial judge made his decision [that the caesarean be performed], A. C. was informed of it. She stated, during a period of lucidity, that she would agree to the surgery although she might not survive it. When another physician went to A. C. to verify her decision, she apparently changed her mind, mouthing the words, "I don't want it done".' Ibid., *per* Nebeker AJ.

subordinating A. C.'s right against bodily intrusion to the interests of the unborn, [but potentially viable] child'. This was particularly so, the court held, because 'caesarean section would not *significantly* affect A. C.'s condition because she had, at best, two days left of sedated life'.[11] Obviously, 'significantly' assumes great significance here.

Commenting on this and other cases, Mahawold reports that out of 15 such applications to court, 14 were granted, although not all of them involved subsequent intervention because the mother was persuaded ultimately to consent, albeit under duress.[12]

4. In the case of Baby R,[13] the Provincial Court of British Columbia, in August 1988, approved the 'apprehension' of a 34-week-old fetus under the Family and Child Services Act which gives the Superintendent of Family and Child Services jurisdiction to 'apprehend' a child 'in need of protection'. The attending doctor took the view that 'a caesarean section was necessary because of the likely complications with a natural birth and the real danger of injury to the child, or death, with a normal birth. The mother declined to consent to a caesarean section.' The Superintendent thereupon decided to proceed with the purported apprehension. This was so as to give some sort of legality to the proposed performance of the caesarean section, contrary to the wishes of the mother who was already in labour. In the face of the order the woman subsequently agreed to the caesarean section, 'practically at the door of the operating room', but it would be hard to argue that she did so voluntarily. The Supreme Court of British Columbia subsequently overruled the decision, relying for their reasoning on the English case of *Re F (in utero)*.[14] '[T]he powers of the Superintendent to apprehend are restricted', the Court decided, 'to living children that have been delivered. Were it otherwise, then the state would be able to confine a mother to await her delivery of the child being apprehended.'[15]

---

[11] *Re A. C.* (supra n. 9) *per* Nebeker AJ. *Re A. C.* was subsequently reheard *en banc* and the Court of Appeals issued a second judgement on April 26, 1990, No. 87–609. . . . The Court vacated its prior order on the grounds that there had not been a proper finding of fact whether A. C. was competent, or, if she was not, how 'substituted judgement' was to be applied. The Court did, however, decide that the decision of a competent patient or substituted judgement should prevail, even if surgery was refused, in 'virtually all cases' unless there are 'truly extraordinary or compelling reasons to override them,' by taking account, for example, of the State's interest in protecting life. At the same time the Court did not dissent from, or overrule, a previous decision (1986) of the Superior Court in *Re Madyun* (unreported: published as Appendix to *Re A. C.*). In *Madyun*, the Court authorised surgery on a woman who objected for religious reasons. 'All that stood between the Madyun fetus and its independent existence was, put simply, a doctor's scalpel [sic]. In these circumstances, the life of the infant inside its mother's womb was entitled to be protected.'

[12] Mahawold, 'Beyond Abortion', p. 113. She notes that, '[I]n the majority (88%) of reported requests for court orders, the order has been obtained in less than six hours, 19% have been granted in less than one hour, and at least one order has been granted by telephone'.

[13] *Re Baby R* (unreported), No. A872582, Vancouver Register (Supreme Court of British Columbia).

[14] [1988] 2 All ER 193, and see following discussion.

[15] *Re Baby R* (unreported), No. A872582, Vancouver Register, *per* Macdonell J.

5. Dawn Johnsen writes that the San Diego case was

only the most recent manifestation of a broader trend in which the state and other third parties increasingly are asserting what they perceive as the interests of the fetus in an attempt to use the law to dictate how women must behave during pregnancy .... A New Jersey statute seems to allow [she goes on] the state to seize custody of an 'unborn child' on the ground that the pregnant woman's behavior is endangering her fetus' welfare. A Los Angeles juvenile court did just that when it ordered that a woman who allegedly had an undiagnosed mental illness be detained for the last two months of her pregnancy. On appeal, a higher court found that the detention was improper: the statute on which the juvenile court had relied applied only to children. . . . By then, however, the woman had given birth and been released, and the court dismissed the case as moot.[16]

Nancy Rhoden equally expresses alarm at 'The potential for far-reaching state control of pregnant women . . . suggested by the frightening array of prenatal interventions that some proponents of fetal protection advocate.'[17]

6. And lest you think this is a peculiarly North American phenomenon at the level of public action, recall first the warning of Nigel Lowe in 1987 that the use of wardship jurisdiction to limit the *mother's* behaviour could involve her being ordered, for example, 'to stop smoking or imbibing alcohol and indeed any activity which might be hazardous to the child' and could even involve the court in being faced with saving the fetus rather than the mother.[18] Then, recall the case of *D* v. *Berkshire CC*,[19] which concerned a baby girl born with drug withdrawal symptoms to a mother who was dependent on drugs. The House of Lords held that Berkshire Social Services Department were entitled to take the child into care *at birth*, because of the mother's prior neglect coupled with the threat of future neglect. As Fortin writes,

The child's physical state at her birth which had necessitated her reception into intensive care for several weeks was the direct result of her drug-addicted mother's persistent and excessive use of drugs during her pregnancy.

Such a short summary of the case, Fortin goes on

should not disguise its importance. Thus, whilst doctors will be unperturbed by the suggestion that a child's existence does not commence at birth and that its antenatal development should not be ignored, it is a well-established principle of law that a child does not obtain an independent legal status until it is born. Nevertheless, the House of Lords' willingness to consider the mother's antenatal behaviour was a clear

[16] Johnsen, 'A New Threat', p. 34.

[17] Rhoden, 'The Judge', p. 2027.

[18] N. V. Lowe, pp. 29, 30, cited in Fortin, 'Can You Ward a Fetus', *Law Quarterly Review*, vol. 96, p. 772.

[19] [1987] 1 All ER 20.

acknowledgement that in certain circumstances, the law may quite properly concern itself with the appropriate treatment of unborn children.[20]

In *Re F* (*in utero*),[21] another social services department attempted to *ward* a child *in utero* because of fears concerning the mother's capacity to manage her pregnancy safely. The local authority sought an order from the court under wardship jurisdiction *inter alia* directing that the court's tipstaff seek out the mother and request that she reside in a particular place and attend a particular hospital during pregnancy. An order was also sought giving the local authority care and control of the child when it was born. The mother was well-known to the local authority. She had a history of mental illness and drug use. Her first child had been subjected to a care order, was living with foster parents, and was due to be adopted. She had previously lived a nomadic existence and her disappearance when pregnant again prompted the local authority to take the unprecedented step of seeking to persuade the court to ward the unborn child. Hollings J refused to extend the wardship jurisdiction in this way. His decision was affirmed by the Court of Appeal. Balcombe and Staughton LJJ based their rejection of the application largely on the potential consequences of deciding otherwise, not least the limitations it would place on the mother and the difficulties of enforcement of any order. May LJ, however, was far more bullish: 'this is a case in which, on the facts, I would exercise the jurisdiction if I had it, [but] in the absence of authority I am driven to the conclusion that the court does not have the jurisdiction contended for'.[22]

A third English case we should notice is *Re P*.[23] Here again was a mother known to the local authority. She had had five children. Four were in care. The fifth had died soon after birth, after the local authority, under a Place of Safety Order, had removed it from the mother. The mother was pregnant again and was told that the baby once born would also be made subject to a Place of Safety Order. Anxious to prevent this and thereby keep the child, the mother started wardship proceedings while still pregnant, seeking thereby to outflank the local authority. Ewbank J dismissed the mother's application on the basis that *Re F* had established that 'as a matter of principle there is no jurisdiction at the present time in the High Court to make an unborn child a ward of court'.[24]

A PARADIGM FOR ANALYSIS

To complete the scene-setting, let me add to the circumstances which have already attracted the attention of the law, some indication of the breadth

---

[20] Fortin, 'Legal Protection', p. 54.   [21] [1988] 2 All ER 193.   [22] Ibid., 196.
[23] Unreported: a decision of Ewbank J., 28 March 1988. See, further, Fortin, 'Can You Ward a Fetus', pp. 773–4.   [24] Ibid.

and range of factual circumstances which can pose the problems we are interested in. Only when we have seen these and understand them can we begin to understand the nature of the analysis which we must embark upon. Robertson and Schulman, in a very important paper in the Hastings Center Report in 1987[25] (a paper which I gratefully rely on), uses as a paradigm for analysis the case of a mother with maternal PKU. This involves the following: a mother, when a newborn, is born with PKU, which involves the inability to metabolise phenylalanine. If untreated, severe retardation will follow. If placed on a diet low in phenylalanine for at least five to seven years, retardation is prevented. When such a woman reaches adulthood and becomes pregnant she is at great risk of having a baby who will become severely retarded while still *in utero*. The risk arises because the phenylalanine which she continues to produce, but cannot metabolise, crosses the placenta. The fetus does not lack the enzyme necessary to metabolise its own phenylalanine but cannot deal with the mother's as well. Hence, the fetus is overwhelmed with phenylalanine and harmed *in utero* as a consequence. If the woman, before, or as early as possible after pregnancy, resumes the special diet low in phenylalanine which she had as a child, evidence suggests that the problem can be avoided. But this means that she must adhere strictly for nine months to what is an unpleasant diet. Most women will, of course, gladly do so, but what of the woman who is feckless or simply refuses? As Robertson reminds us, 'the mother's normal diet acts like a toxin on the fetus, damaging it just as ingesting alcohol, cocaine, heroin or other drugs might'.[26] What, to remind you of our opening question, are the mother's rights and responsibilities in such a case?

There are, of course, other factual circumstances which are more familiar to us. Avoidable prenatal injuries or death may arise from the abuse of alcohol, heroin, or other substances, from exposure to environmental hazards, particularly in the workplace, from contraction of herpes, syphilis, or HIV infection, and, of course, from refusal to undergo prenatal medical or surgical treatment, e.g. blood transfusion in the case of rhesus negativity or a caesarean section.

Indeed, surveying such a scene and recognising the potential extent of the limits which could be placed on a mother's freedom of action, John Robertson was moved to write eight years ago that pregnant women

may also be prohibited from using alcohol or other substances harmful to the fetus during pregnancy, or be kept from the workplace because of toxic effects on the fetus. They could be ordered to take drugs, such as insulin for diabetes, medications for fetal deficiencies, or intra-uterine blood transfusion for Rh factor. Pregnant anorexic

---

[25] Robertson and Schulman, 'Pregnancy and Prenatal Harm'.
[26] Ibid., p. 24.

teen-agers could be force fed. Prenatal screening and diagnostic procedures, from amniocentesis to sonography or even fetoscopy could be made mandatory. And *in utero* surgery for the fetus to shunt cerebroventricular fluids from the brain to relieve hydrocephalus, or to relieve the urethral obstruction of bilateral hydronephrosis could also be ordered. Indeed, even extra-uterine fetal surgery, if it becomes an established procedure, could be ordered, if the risks to the mother were small and it were a last resort to save the life or prevent severe disability in a viable fetus.[27]

THE SIGNIFICANCE OF THE PROBLEM

These examples set the scene of our discussion. They pose, as you realise, very difficult problems which will only multiply as time goes on. In seeking to resolve them, we must notice three things. First, the problems posed are sometimes characterised as conflicts between the mother and her fetus, whereby they are seen as adversaries. It is important to realise this is not necessarily so. As we have seen, the mother may insist on a course of action which she realises is against her own interests as well as the interests of the fetus but which she feels she is obliged to follow. Thus, an analytical model which assumes that mother and fetus are *ex hypothesi* adversaries may be unhelpful. The second point to notice is that clearly the issue is not trivial. Indeed, it is likely to grow in importance and significance. Developments in medical technology and knowledge make this inevitable as do the changes in society's concern for the fetus and consequently the political climate concerning, for example, abortion. Thirdly, it is also clear that the issue is very charged. George Annas, writing a paper in the Hastings Center Report, critical of the San Diego case, used the title 'Pregnant Women as Fetal Containers'[28] and quoted Margaret Atwood's, *The Handmaid's Tale*, in which one handmaid describes her station as 'we are two-legged wombs, that's all; sacred vessels, ambulatory chalices'.[29] Dawn Johnsen, also in the Hastings Center Report, wrote of a 'New Threat to Pregnant Women's Autonomy'.[30] And many feminists (not, it should be remembered, a homogenous group) condemn even raising the issue as being discriminatory, not least because it involves considering women's rights in terms of their child-bearing capacities. Obviously, the arguments about the 'woman as chattel', or 'the

---

[27] J. Robertson, 'The Right to Procreate and *in utero* Fetal Therapy', *Journal of Legal Medicine*, vol. 3 (1982) pp. 333, 358. It is important, however, to notice, by way of counterpoise to Robertson's warnings, the recent dramatic increase in the US of infant mortality due to maternal drug use. In the first half of 1989 there was a 50 per cent increase in infant mortality because of a surge in babies born to cocaine-addicted women. The rate was 32.3 deaths per 1000 live births, compared with 23.2 per 1000 in 1988 in Washington DC and 9.9 per 1000 in the USA overall. *Minneapolis Star Tribune*, 1 October 1989.

[28] Annas, 'Pregnant Women'.   [29] Ibid.

[30] Johnsen, 'A New Threat'.

woman enslaved by society once pregnant' are just as much to the fore here as in the context of abortion.

So, with these points in mind, how should we proceed? An examination of the facts suggests that we can identify at least five variables or points for analysis, as being critical if we are going to conduct a careful enquiry. They are:

(a) The nature of the risk, or threat, to the fetus. Clearly, there is a wide variation. It may be death or it may be disability, and if the latter, it may be serious or less so.

(b) The causal link between the conduct of the mother and the risk to the fetus. The facts suggest that the link may be more or less tenuous, (alerting us to arguments about slippery slopes).

(c) The time-frame involved. This can be extensive or short. In the case of maternal PKU, the restriction on the mother's choice lasts for nine months. By contrast, in the case of a caesarean section, it will be a matter of hours.

(d) The stage of development of the fetus. The facts indicate that a problem may arise at various stages of fetal development. The fetus may have a gestational age of only a few weeks, it may be viable, or it may be virtually at full term.

(e) The degree of limitation on the woman's choice, (I avoid here the language of 'freedom' as it may affect the subsequent analysis). It is clear from the facts that the degree of limitation may fall to be assessed both in terms of length of time (as suggested above), and of what the mother is called upon to do, e.g. undergo surgery or deny her religious convictions.

ANALYSIS

Let us now begin our analysis. Analyse we must, as a first step to arriving at policy options. This, you will recall, is my concern: the making of good public policy in the face of real medical-moral dilemmas. I intend to ask what the woman is morally entitled, and obliged, to do and then to ask whether, in the light of this, some public policy is called for and how this policy should be expressed, one form being *law*.

MORAL THEORY

Unhelpful arguments

Let me first consider the issue in terms of moral theory. The question for analysis is whether there is any justification in arguing that a woman is *morally* obliged to submit to a certain regime or intervention, or has a duty to do so. Let me get out of the way two arguments which are unhelpful. The first has it that if we admit, as many do (and the law allows) that abortion, at least in certain circumstances, is permissible, it is contradictory to talk of obliging a woman to submit to a caesarean section or other such medical intervention. Put crudely, if the mother can kill the fetus by abortion, then she must be entitled to do anything to the fetus which amounts to less than killing it. This is a bad argument. It confuses what is at stake. We are not concerned here with the fetus's interest in being born, or society's interest in its being born. We are, instead, concerned with the issue of the fetus's interest in its being born free of avoidable harm when the mother has decided not to abort but to carry the fetus and, all things being equal, to bring it to term.[31]

Now let us turn to the second unhelpful argument. Can we not solve all our questions, it is asked, by saying that the doctor has two patients and that he is justified in protecting his second patient, the fetus (and that we are justified in supporting him). This is unhelpful because it begs the two questions which are central to our debate. The first is, what is the status of the fetus? Is it an entity which is owed duties, i.e. *is* it, or can it be, a patient? The second is, even if it is a patient, why should its interests prevail? How are the duties owed to it to be reconciled with the duties owed to the mother? These are precisely the questions we have to answer.

Fetal rights

With those points out of the way, let us proceed. I take as a starting point the uncontentious proposition that a woman (including a pregnant woman) has a right to autonomy, of which the right to privacy and to be free from unwanted bodily interference is one important aspect. Such a right to autonomy is, of course, only a *prima facie* right. Its enjoyment may, as a matter of principle, have to give way, in appropriate circumstances, to the rights of others. Obviously, the seriousness with which we regard respect for autonomy leads us to be vigilant in demanding justification for any limitations or restrictions. But, none the less, examples are part of our daily life. A woman who poses a threat to the safety of others is an obvious example.

Is the fetus here a relevant other with rights? Does the fetus have rights which may, in appropriate circumstances, limit the mother's right to autonomy? My position is that a fetus *is* a relevant other and that it does have rights. We may call them weak rights, if you will, since they may pertain to an entity not yet (and perhaps never) independent of its mother and whose fate is inextricably connected to hers. We may also recognise that they are

---

[31] See Steinbock *et al.*, 'Case Studies', p. 32.

rights which grow stronger as the fetus develops, since at some point, although still *in utero*, the fetus becomes capable of independent existence. Finally, we may recognise that to state that the fetus has rights is not to deny that until born they may always be defeasible, if 'trumped' by the mother's rights for good reason. Notwithstanding these caveats, I return to my central proposition, that a fetus has rights.

What follows from this? It is my position that, if the fetus does have rights as a matter of moral argument, these rights must include the right of the fetus to be free from avoidable harm, to be free from that which may destroy or damage its potential for being born whole.

Maternal duties

To take the argument a step further, talk of fetus's rights allows us to assert in turn that the mother owes the fetus certain duties. The primary duty is, perhaps, the duty not to interfere with the fetus's rights, including the right to be born free from avoidable harm, save for good reason. In practical terms, this translates into a duty not to expose the fetus to avoidable harm intentionally, recklessly, or negligently, whether by doing something, e.g. dangerous conduct, or by refraining from doing something, e.g. refusing necessary medical care. Robertson helpfully captures the duty as follows: a duty not to engage in 'avoidable conduct that falls below reasonable community standards, after notice and counselling [whereby the] offspring [is] seriously and wilfully harmed'.[32] These latter two conditions are important as indicating that the mother's duty attaches when she is aware of the risk she may pose. I would suggest, however, that there are circumstances in which she may be expected to be aware of the risk, e.g. in the case of abuse of drugs. It is, of course, a question for debate how serious the harm must be, e.g. death, serious disability, or some relatively trivial inconvenience, before the mother is *prima facie* under a duty to limit her conduct. Once she is under such a duty, however, the duty must be observed unless there are good reasons for not doing so.

A calculus

If my conclusion is that limits *do* exist morally to the freedom of action of the mother, the next stage in our analysis must be to ask how this abstract proposition may translate into guidance in dealing with the type of factual circumstances already discussed. Under what circumstances in concrete cases will a mother's freedom of action be limited? This is not, of course, a question to be answered by some sort of checklist, whereby in each case a specific decision, one way or the other, can be reached. The enquiry is too subtle. Instead, the only approach, as in any other enquiry in applied ethics, is to

---

[32] Robertson and Schulman, 'Pregnancy and Prenatal Harm', p. 28.

identify in abstract terms what appear to be the factors which are morally relevant in the light of the competing moral claims which have been set out. The result is not a simple (or simple-minded) either/or system. Instead, it is some sort of calculus. Resort to this calculus will provide guidance for decisions or action, though it will not, of course, resolve any specific case. The elements of the calculus, which you will notice echoes the variables I mentioned earlier, are:

(a) The nature of the harm which the fetus may be exposed to. The more serious the harm, the more compelling may be the mother's duty and the greater the need on the part of the mother to show compelling reasons for not complying with it.

(b) The capacity of the mother to comply with the conduct or regime deemed appropriate to protect the fetus. Account must be taken, for example, of such matters as the availability of medical and other care, access the mother has to such care, the level of her education and knowledge, the relative poverty in which she finds herself, and her capacity to exercise freewill rather than being, for example, dependent on drugs.

(c) A demonstrable relationship between the conduct of the mother (whether it be action or inaction) and the threatened harm to the fetus. This is a matter of medical evidence and advice. The more tenuous the link (e.g. the link alleged between smoking or jogging and early fetal harm), or the earlier in pregnancy the mother engages in a certain conduct, the less the duty can be said to limit the mother.

(d) The relative development of the fetus. The more developed the fetus the greater may be its moral claim and the more limited may be the mother's freedom of action.

(e) The degree of limitation on the mother's choice. The limitation may range from an obligation to undergo a specific diet for nine months, to abstain from smoking, to abstain from some other substance or conduct, to be detained in a specific place under a specific regime, to undergo a medical procedure, or to undergo surgical intervention. The greater the limitation, the greater must be the claim of the fetus.

(f) The risk to the mother's health, e.g. from a proposed surgical intervention. The more serious the risk associated with the proposed intervention or other stipulated regime, the less strong may be the claim of the fetus.

(g) The reasons for the mother's choice or conduct. It may range from mere convenience to religious conviction, concern for her own health or concern for the fetus's or future child's health. That is to say, it may range from the trivial to the serious. The more trivial it is, the less justified the mother may be in seeking to rely on it.

(h) The recognised uncertainty of prenatal diagnosis. The greater the grounds for uncertainty, the less it may serve as a ground for limiting the mother's freedom of action.[33]

The significant features of this calculus are that, first, it allows the fetus to enter the equation and have its interests considered and, secondly, it then offers the means of assessing the competing claims of the mother and the fetus. It entails the conclusion that, when all is taken into account, if the case for the fetus is strong and the reasons for the mother's conduct are weak or less strong, she has a duty as a matter of moral theory to submit to the stipulated regime or treatment. This is so, whether it be a specific diet or drug prescription, abstinence from a particular substance or conduct, or some intervention such as a blood transfusion or even surgery.

ENTER THE LAW

Consequences of requiring maternal compliance

Does this mean, however, that *others* can then *require* the mother to comply with her duty to the fetus, if resort to this calculus indicates that morally she should? To decide that others may require or compel her to do so, has, of course, contingent consequences which go beyond the limitation of the particular woman's choice. These consequences are by no means trivial. The image of 'the woman enslaved' reappears. Grave difficulties exist concerning the enforcement of any limitation. Guilt may be engendered in mothers generally, anxious about the merest deviation from the prescribed norm of conduct. Resentment towards childbearing could equally be engendered. Allegations of unfair discrimination against women could be made.[34] Finally, mothers could become reluctant to seek antenatal care.

Making public policy

These consequences, if thought to be sufficiently serious or real, may have considerable implications for public policy. They may persuade the policy-maker or the analyst not to go beyond the level of moral argument, beyond the assertion that mothers owe a moral duty which they ought to comply with. Alternatively, the policy-maker or analyst may say that these contingent consequences are serious but less serious than the risk to the fetus, and

---

[33] It will be recalled that in the Jefferson case which I began with, Jessie Mae Jefferson gave birth vaginally to a healthy baby while the case was being appealed. See further, Mahawold, 'Beyond Abortion', p. 119.

[34] See, on these points and generally, Mahawold, 'Beyond Abortion'.

consequent unborn child, if no further step by way of formulation of public policy is taken. They may conclude that some further step is called for.

If we are to consider others *requiring* maternal compliance, we are inevitably moving from a moral analysis to a consideration of the law, since interference with the liberties of another is ordinarily impermissible, unless specifically provided for by law. Otherwise it is unlawful. Of course, the first and obvious method whereby others can seek to require maternal compliance is through counselling, education, and persuasion. These are obviously the most desirable routes to take and can represent a significant public policy statement in themselves. Furthermore, they do not call for reliance on the law. But, if we assume that persuasion and education have failed, what then? If we are to consider the law, two questions arise. What does the existing law provide? Secondly, should the law be changed if it fails to strike the appropriate balance between the moral claims of mother and fetus?

In considering these questions, there are obviously two circumstances which the law could address and regulate: while the mother is still pregnant and the fetus is *in utero* and, secondly, when the baby is born. The former more clearly involves the sort of limitation of a mother's freedom of action which we have been discussing. The latter form of regulation, however, by, for example, applying some sort of sanction after birth (as in the San Diego case) could, of course, ultimately have the same sort of limiting effect. If women know, or fear, that once the child is born they will suffer some sanction, e.g. the loss of custody of the child, this will inevitably affect the choices they will make during pregnancy.

So, let us examine what English law has to say about these two potential responses, what Robertson with his eye for the telling phrase calls 'pre-birth seizure' (taking control of the woman) and 'post-birth sanction' (punishing a particular woman and deterring others).[35]

(a) Pre-birth seizure

The pre-birth limitation of a woman's freedom of action, whether by requiring her to do something or refrain from doing something, has its supporters. Keyserlingk argues that,

Unless 'armed' with juridical personality as the basis of his right to care and protection, the unborn child would be (as is now the case) unable to compete on a more or less equal basis with other parties with whom his needs and rights may be in conflict. They would be legal persons and he would remain more or less at the mercy of their ethics, whims or compassions. . . . Since the unborn child has health needs and vulnerabilities analogous to those of healthy children, and since between the child when unborn and after birth there is continuity in all essential respects, then it would

---

[35] Robertson and Schulman, 'Pregnancy and Prenatal Harm', p. 29.

seem logical and just to assign to parents duties to their unborn children analogous (when applicable) to those they have to their children, and to recognise unborn children analogous rights (when applicable) to those already granted to children.[36]

Notwithstanding this view, pre-birth seizure does not appear to be permitted in English law, either by statute or case law.

1. Statute law. At present there is no statute in English law which governs the particular situation under consideration. There are, of course, statutes which permit the seizure of a citizen, for example, for the purposes of arrest,[37] or detention, or even treatment, in the case of mental disorder, provided certain conditions are satisfied,[38] or seizure to recover evidence of a crime.[39] None of these covers the case in question. Nor is it permissible to argue from these statutes by analogy, if only because there is a presumption in law that the liberty of a citizen may not ordinarily be infringed save when specifically provided for by statute.[40]

2. Common law. Recent cases have decided that a fetus has no legal status in English law. Thus, any attempt to seek to persuade a court to protect or enforce a fetus's rights as against those of its mother would not succeed. In the landmark decision of *Paton* v. *Trustees of BPAS*,[41] Sir George Baker P stated that 'The fetus cannot, in English law, in my view have a right of its own until it is born and has a separate existence from its mother.'[42] The subsequent cases of *C* v. *S*,[43] *D* v. *Berkshire CC*[44] and *Re F* (*in utero*)[45] have, as we have seen, reiterated this conclusion. Put another way, echoing the language of state's interests found in the USA, the state in English law has no interest in protecting or preserving the rights of the fetus. Thus, the use of the law relating to child neglect, canvassed in the USA, fails in English law since the fetus is not a legal person, i.e. not a child within the relevant

---

[36] E. W. Keyserlingk, 'The Unborn Child's Right to Prenatal Care—A Comparative Law Perspective.' *McGill Legal Studies*, vol. 5 (1984) pp. 79, 103.

[37] The Police and Criminal Evidence Act 1984.

[38] See Mental Health Act 1983, Part II.

[39] The Police and Criminal Evidence Act 1984.

[40] For a detailed analysis, from the point of view of U.S. law, of statutes authorising 'compulsory bodily invasions', see Rhoden, 'The Judge', pp. 1982–8. She concludes that such laws are designed to promote various state interests of a wholly different order from that under consideration. She refers to compulsory vaccination, intrusions to obtain evidence from criminal suspects, and non-consensual treatment of institutionalised persons, all of which have been held to be constitutional. 'A brief examination of these cases', she goes on, 'will show that in no other area do courts countenance invasions as substantial as caesarean sections', ibid. The same conclusion may be drawn as regards statutes in English law.

[41] [1979] QB 276.

[42] Ibid., 279.

[43] [1987] 1 All ER 1230.

[44] [1987] 1 All ER 20.

[45] [1988] 2 All ER 193.

law. Nor will wardship jurisdiction extend to a fetus, as we have seen. Balcombe LJ put it in the following terms in the case of *Re F*,

since an unborn child has, *ex hypothesi*, no existence independent of its mother, the only purpose of extending the jurisdiction to include the fetus is to enable the mother's actions to be controlled. Indeed, that is the purpose of the present application. . . . [I]t would be intolerable to place a judge in the position of having to make such a decision [to consent to a caesarean section] without any guidance as to the principles on which his decision should be based. If the law is to be extended in this manner, so as to impose control over the mother of an unborn child, where such control may be necessary for the benefit of that child, then under our system of parliamentary democracy it is for Parliament to decide whether such controls can be imposed and, if so, subject to what limitations or conditions.[46]

Is the criminal law relevant here? It does not appear to be a crime in English law to refrain from doing something that may protect a fetus from avoidable harm, or to do something which exposes a fetus to avoidable harm, on the basis that since abortion is allowed, the greater includes the lesser. What of the Infant Life (Preservation) Act 1929? Is it not of some relevance, at least after the fetus is 'capable of being born alive?'[47] Section 1(1) of the Act provides that 'any person who, with the intent to destroy the life of a child capable of being born alive, by any wilful act causes a child to die before it has an existence independent of its mother, shall be guilty. . .'. The obvious difficulties in the way of any successful prosecution of a mother include the need to prove intent, the need for a wilful *act* rather than an omission and the need to show that the act complained of *caused* death. These seem insuperable problems in the sort of factual circumstances which have arisen in decided cases or have been raised by commentators. It is hard to argue that the mother who smokes, drinks alcohol, takes drugs, or continues to engage in sexual intercourse 'intends to destroy the life of [her] child'. Is there a wilful act (leave aside intent to destroy) when a mother refuses a blood transfusion or caesarean section? In any event, whatever the answers to the specific points may be, the Act is only concerned with the viable fetus. Prosecution under the Act does not help the fetus, and it certainly does not allow 'pre-birth seizure'.

The conclusion must be that, as regards the current state of English case law, any doctor who engages in any medical intervention on the mother without her consent, albeit for the benefit of the unborn baby she is carrying, or anyone who, for the same reason, restrains her or restricts her freedom of action would be guilty of a crime and also liable in damages. There would, in other words, be no justification available in law.

---

[46] [1988] 2 All ER 200. [47] Section 1(1).

No contemporary review of English law in this context is complete, however, without reference to the European Convention on Human Rights. Article 2(1) begins, 'Everyone's right to life shall be protected'. Obviously, the applicability of this Article turns on whether a fetus is to be recognised as having a 'right to life' within the terms of Article 2. The European Court of Human Rights has yet to take a view on this point. The European Commission of Human Rights in *Paton* v. *United Kingdom*[48] chose to leave the question undecided. Were the court to decide that the fetus does have such a right to life, albeit not an absolute right,[49] it could go on to decide that, in a particular case, the fetus's right could take priority over the mother's wishes, otherwise protected by her 'right to privacy' under Article 8, save, in the case where the fetus posed a real threat to the mother's life.

Before leaving this discussion of pre-birth seizure, it may be instructive, finally, to notice a striking, and some would say clinching, argument which sums up the legal analysis here and is offered by a number of commentators in the USA. It is as follows. In so far as no one is obliged in law to, for example, donate a kidney or bone marrow to someone else (see *McFall* v. *Shimp*[50]) (although someone may be said to have a moral obligation to do so), it must follow that a mother is not obliged to save the life of a fetus is she chooses not to. There can be no justification, the argument goes, in placing greater obligations on her as regards her unborn child than are placed on others in respect of saving or helping the life of a third party. Rhoden writes of a 'primal revulsion. . . . at a person's or government's sacrificing one person to benefit others'.[51] She cites approvingly the view of the distinguished commentator Professor Tribe, 'that one person's two good eyes, distributed to two blind neighbours, might yield a net increase in happiness on the theory that one blind person will experience less misery than two, cannot justify a governmental decision to compel the exchange'.[52] 'Were there a serious risk of the woman's suffering permanent harm from the [caesarean] surgery', Rhoden concludes, 'requiring it would seem too much like [this example], where our intuitions strongly tell us that such decisions are ethically impermissible.'[53] George Annas makes the point succinctly: 'No mother has ever been legally required to undergo surgery or general anaesthetic (e.g. bone marrow aspiration) to save the life of her dying child. It would be ironic and unfair if she could be forced to submit to more invasive surgical procedures for the sake of her fetus than for her child.'[54]

---

[48] (1980) 3 EHRR 408.

[49] The European Commission of Human Rights in *Paton* v. *UK* (1980) 3 EHRR 408 decided that, whatever the position as regards a claim to a qualified right to life, a fetus could not be said to enjoy an absolute right to life under Article 2.

[50] 10 Pa. D & C 3d 90 (1978). [51] Rhoden, 'The Judge', p. 2002.

[52] L. Tribe, *American Constitutional Law* (Mineola NY: Foundation Press, 1978) p. 918.

[53] Rhoden, 'The Judge', p. 2002.

[54] G. Annas, *Judging Medicine* (Clifton NJ: Humana Press, 1988) p. 122.

It could be said that the vulnerability of the fetus and the lack of any alternative form of possible assistance for the fetus may make the *moral* force of the argument less strong. But these factors should have no weight in any *legal* analysis since the fact that a fetus is not a person in law means its claim is not recognised. Furthermore, if the argument is not to prevail it could be said that the law was adopting a position which was adversely discriminatory towards women.[55]

That said, it is not, of course, a clinching argument in all circumstances. It may argue powerfully against surgical interventions, but it is not clear that it is so persuasive an argument as regards less intrusive limitations on the mother. Its relevance here is to suggest that not only does English law at present not permit pre-birth seizure, but also, should the issue be raised, good arguments exist to reject it.

(b) Post-birth sanction

Does existing English law allow such a sanction to punish the mother and thereby deter her and others?

1. Statute law. I take the circumstances contemplated by post-birth sanction to be that a mother has given birth to her child. The child may, however, have been born disabled or have died as a consequence of the mother's conduct while pregnant. Does the criminal law make any provision for post-birth sanction? Is the mother guilty of any crime in such a situation? Clearly, the Infant Life (Preservation) Act 1929 has no application. Nor, it appears, does any other statutory provision of the criminal law.

What of the Children and Young Persons Act 1969, which allows a local authority by s. 1(2) to take a child into care if the relevant conditions are satisfied? Recall that the question asked is whether this Act may be used by a local authority as a post-birth sanction against behaviour of the mother while pregnant. Superficially, *D* v. *Berkshire CC*[56] would appear to suggest that the Act was used to sanction the drug-addicted mother, and thereby deter others, by taking her child into care at birth. But this is not, in fact, what the House of Lords decided. As Lord Goff was at pains to point out, the child was not being taken into care because of what had happened in the past. Care proceedings could not be justified on those grounds alone. The court had to be satisfied that 'there is an existing likelihood that the state of affairs revealed by those past events *will continue into the future*'.[57] The Children and Young Persons Act 1969 is not, therefore, available as a sanction

---

[55] See Mahawold, 'Beyond Abortion', p. 118.
[56] [1987] 1 All ER 20.
[57] Ibid., 45.

against maternal conduct during pregnancy. Equally, tort law offers no remedy. The Congenital Disabilities (Civil Liability) Act 1976 was passed to provide a remedy to children harmed through negligently caused prenatal injury. But, the Act imposes liability on the *mother* only in the context of driving a motor vehicle.[58] Only in such a case can it be guaranteed that the mother is insured. In all other cases, the mother is immune from liability. Post-birth sanction again, therefore, does not exist.

2. Common law.   There is no precedent at common law for applying a post-birth sanction to a woman, whether by civil action or otherwise. Nor, given the state of the law and the likely response of judges, is there likely to be one.

The conclusion must be, therefore, that the existing state of English law does not allow for either of the two options Robertson identified as ways of giving effect to any moral claims of the fetus.

CHANGE THE LAW?

If the law is to be invoked on behalf of a fetus, if a mother is to be required to do, or refrain from doing, something, the law must be changed. A court, theoretically, could decide to act. But, given the weight of legal argument that the courts have no power to do so, Parliament would have to act. Is this likely?

Undoubtedly, given developments in medical knowledge and technology and the climate of the times, concern over the sort of factual situations we have been discussing will only grow. Calls for some sort of action will become more common. The first response of government should, and no doubt will, be to continue its longstanding commitment to public education and to raising the awareness of women, both as to their responsibilities and to the risks posed by certain conduct. Equally, government could be persuaded, and may be willing, to invest appropriate resources in antenatal care and counselling, and generally to encourage respect for, and the self-esteem of, mothers.

But, these policies, desirable and necessary as they are, may not be enough. We would then have to return to the law.

At one level, there is no doubt that the law *could* be changed to achieve either pre-birth seizure or post-birth sanction or both. At this level it is really a question of drafting. Parliament could amend the Infant Life (Preservation) Act so as to capture and criminalise such conduct of the mother as it thought appropriate. Likewise, the Children and Young Persons Act could be amended to allow a local authority to obtain a care order while the fetus

---

[58] Section 2.

is still *in utero* or at birth, so as to serve as a post-birth sanction. The wardship jurisdiction could be extended to protect the fetus simply by amending s. 41 of the Supreme Court Act 1981, so that the word 'minor' used in that section, was made explicitly to refer to the unborn child.[59] And so on.

But, this is not really the question. While Parliament could make these specific legislative changes, should it do so? We have seen that in terms of moral analysis there is a case, in certain circumstances, for limiting a mother's freedom of action. We have also seen, however, the contingent social consequences which may flow from doing this by means of law. These would perhaps take on even greater significance if the approach adopted was to make interstitial amendments to existing legislation. The weakness of this approach is that it obscures or does not make explicit the process of weighing competing claims which is at the heart of the endeavour. By so doing, it would lend weight to the arguments of those who say that the sole effect of changes in the law is to oppress or discriminate against women.

One solution may be as follows. The calculus advanced earlier by way of moral analysis could just as readily serve as the basis for legal analysis. A judge could hear the arguments, consider the evidence and, having weighed the relative claims of mother and fetus, decide what was to be done in any particular case. A law could be drafted, in other words, to give a judge the power to order pre-birth seizure or post-birth sanction (whether it involves surgery, wardship of the unborn, or a care order at birth) in an appropriate case, i.e. one in which the calculus weighs sufficiently heavily in favour of the fetus's claims.

It is, of course, a matter for legitimate difference whether the undesirable consequences which could flow from such a piece of legislation, not least the perceived oppression of women left to the whim of a mainly male judiciary, are outweighed by the good which may be produced. It must not be overlooked, however, that such legislation, if it were passed, could have a further effect. Unless it was tightly drawn it may be seized on as a legislative precedent for the proposition that a fetus is a legal person. The implications of such a conclusion for the laws of abortion, and for women's rights over their own body, could be extremely far-reaching. Indeed, they may be so problematic that they tip the scales against any change in the existing law. It may well be possible for a judge to do the balancing called for by our moral analysis, provided we could draft a statute sufficiently carefully. It may not, however, be desirable. It may well be that we should continue to leave the fate of the unborn child to its mother and resist the call for legal regulation of her conduct. To do otherwise may cause us to pay just too high a price.

[59] Fortin, 'Can You Ward a Fetus', pp. 769–70.

20

Patients, Doctors, and Human Rights

INTRODUCTION

My concern is with what I will call medical law. The question for consideration is whether there is anything to be gained analytically or practically in approaching medical law in terms of human rights. I will suggest that there is and that a number of recent developments in medical law should properly be seen as involving issues of human rights. I will argue further that if they had been seen in this way, they might well have been analysed and even decided differently.

As a medical lawyer my first task, of course, may be to persuade the doubters—and there are many—that there is a field which can properly be designated medical law. There are still those who regard the law relating to medical practice as merely involving the application of the general law of torts, or criminal law, or family law, or whatever, to the particular facts. To continue to adopt this view is to lose sight of at least two important considerations. The first is that there are certain themes of an ethical nature which run through and underlie medical practice and which must be taken account of in any legal analysis. By contrast, if medical practice is dealt with in an *ad hoc* way, this fact may well be overlooked. A consequence could be (and has been in the past) that legal developments in relation to medical practice lack the kind of internal coherence and consistency of principle which an understanding of the underlying themes would produce. This objection, I may say, is not made out of concern for logical niceties. Rather, it is to say that the law is the poorer and that the interests of patients, doctors, and the community are less well served if such a state of affairs prevails.

Human rights

Secondly, an approach to the law regulating the practice of medicine which treats it as if it were just another application of the law of battery, or negligence, or child custody, seriously neglects a dimension which can broadly be called human rights. It neglects the need to take account of certain broad over-arching legal *as well as* ethical principles against which any proposed legal measure must be tested and approved. And, when I talk of human rights here, I would make it clear that I refer not only to those rights declared in international Conventions or set down in the Constitutions or Charters of particular nations, but also those inchoate rights which are the product of reasoned moral analysis.

It is fair to say, however, that talk of rights or human rights in the context of medical law has often provoked a hostile reaction from those who claim to speak for the medical profession. This is because the rights discussed are asserted as the rights of patients. Such assertions do not sit well with a profession which is, quite properly, educated to think of itself as concerned with the difficult task of caring for the sick and seeking to overcome illness. Talk of rights is often represented to the doctor as if it inevitably involves confrontation, legalism, and strict or rigid restrictions on what the doctor may do. A further impression exists that reference to rights often provokes litigation, with the regrettable consequence of what has come to be known as 'defensive medicine'. Thus, some say, it is far better to avoid such talk of rights. Better to talk in terms of trust, it is said, and let doctors get on with their job.

The weakness of these counter-arguments does not need exposure here. But despite their lack of substance they survive with great tenacity. Trust, for example, has to be earned and is not the birthright of the doctor or any other professional. Equally, the history of mankind, and even of doctors, is that some sort of social system for overseeing the activities of those who enjoy privileges as regards others is appropriate, indeed is essential. Any such system must inevitably consist of principles and rules guiding conduct. It may, of course, be a system of self-regulation, whereby the profession governs itself. Few, however, would now maintain that this is enough and, of course, to do so is somewhat forlorn since the existence of legal regulation of, for example, medicine is a social fact. Further, it must never be assumed that it is only the doctor who is concerned for the interests of the patient, while the lawyer is some interfering wrecker. The lawyer is equally concerned with the patient's interests, is concerned indeed with the patient's human rights. That the two professions may disagree on how these rights should best be protected in any particular case does not entail that the lawyer is necessarily wrong, far less interfering.

However, even when the existence of and perhaps the need for law is granted, there is still the tendency to state and analyse the law wholly in terms of duties, the duties of doctors and perhaps of patients, so as to avoid what is perceived (wrongly) as the more oppressive language of rights. For, to adopt the language of rights—of patients' rights—is, it is argued, to restrict the freedom to practice, the so-called clinical freedom of the doctor. That any assertion of clinical freedom is as much an appeal to rights—the rights of doctors—is sometimes lost on its proponents. And, of course, to argue that patients have rights is not necessarily to deprive doctors of discretion. Rather, it aims to set the framework within which such discretion may properly be exercised.

So, I will adopt here a frank assertion of rights inherent in the doctor–patient relationship. Apart from arguments of principle which elaborate the basis and nature of such rights, I assert them for a further contingent reason. As between the doctor and the patient there is an inevitable imbalance or disequilibrium of power. The doctor has information and skill which the patient, who lacks these, wishes to employ for his benefit. When it is remembered that among the powers possessed by the doctor is the privilege to touch and even invade the body of another and as a consequence exercise control to a greater or lesser extent over that person, it will be clear that, with the best will in the world, and conceding the good faith of the doctors, such powers must be subject to control and scrutiny, from an abundance of caution. This is the role of patients' rights, whereby the permissible limits are set by ethics and law to the exercise of the doctor's power.

Perhaps I should make it clear, before proceeding further, that as a matter of ethical analysis, when I talk of rights in the context of medical practice, I am talking of prima facie rights rather than absolute rights. This is not to deny that absolute rights may be urged by some. Instead, it is to suggest that in the everyday practice of medicine by civilised doctors in a civilised community, such absolute rights, if they exist, are not usually called into play. Thus, the rights we are concerned with are prima facie to be observed, by which I mean that they are to be observed in the absence of any powerful justifying argument which allows them to be overridden. And, of course, any such justification must itself be derived from a morally sound principle.

As a further clarification, I should draw attention to the distinction often made as a matter of law between human rights and civil rights.[1] On this analysis, human rights are those rights recognised by international law, while civil rights are those which translate human rights into the law of particular states. I will use the general term 'human rights' throughout, leaving the context to indicate which meaning is appropriate. To complete the introduction to human rights in the context of medical practice and finally to dispel the doubts of the disbeliever, I should point to their recognition both on an international plane and in other countries similar in most respects to our own. I need only mention, for example, the Nuremburg Code followed by the Declaration of Helsinki[2] concerning the rights of those who may be the subject of medical research. In the United States, the Constitution has been prayed in aid to guarantee, for example, access to contraception by virtue

---

[1] See, e.g., Paul Sieghart (1989) *AIDS and Human Rights*, British Medical Association, pp. 9–11.

[2] For the text of these, see Jay Katz (1972) *Experimentation with Human Beings*, Russell Sage Foundation, pp. 305–6, 312–13.

of the right to privacy under the 9th Amendment[3] and access to abortion, at least in the initial stages of pregnancy by virtue of the equal protection clause of the 14th Amendment.[4] In Canada, too, the Charter of Rights and Freedoms has already seen service in regulating such issues as parents objecting to the treatment of their children on religious grounds, the detention of the mentally ill, and the sterilisation of the incompetent.[5] Nearer to home, we have, of course, the European Convention on Human Rights, a number of Articles of which have been used to assert the rights of patients.[6]

EXAMPLES

So much for introduction. Let me now give you some examples of circumstances of medical practice in which it must be clear that considerations of human rights are involved. In terms of factual circumstances the examples come tumbling over themselves. They include—and I make no judgments here but merely recite examples—the compulsory detention of the mentally ill and the compulsory treatment of them; research on humans, treatment at the end of life which may mean that death arrives sooner rather than later (sometimes referred to as euthanasia in its various forms); the care of the newborn baby and what is perhaps euphemistically called selective non-treatment; contraception; abortion; research on embryos; transsexualism; and the huge issue of resource allocation and access to care. These problems touch on such rights as the right to life, the right to privacy, the right to marry and found a family, the right to the opportunity to reproduce, the right to be free from inhuman treatment, and the right to free movement. As I have indicated, they are, by and large, prima facie rights, such that, for example, compulsory treatment or detention may be justified and may not therefore be a violation of human rights if good, morally sound reasons can be given for imposing them.

ENGLISH LAW'S RESPONSE

Consent

All of these issues have attracted the attention of English law, whether by legislation or judicial decision; the response of English law has been to

---

[3] *Griswold* v. *Connecticut*, 381 US 479 (1965). As is well known, the Supreme Court did not hold that the 9th Amendment, *per se*, created a right to privacy, but such a right was a 'penumbral' effect of the Amendment.   [4] *Roe* v. *Wade*, 410 US 113 (1973).

[5] See E. Picard (1984) *Legal Liability of Doctors and Hospitals in Canada*, 2nd ed., Carswell, pp. 28, 49, 139 and generally.

[6] See, e.g., *Paton* v. *United Kingdom* (1980) 3 EHRR 408, and L. Gostin, 'Human rights in mental health', in M. Roth and R. Bluglass (1985) *Psychiatry, Human Rights and the Law*, pp. 148–55.

consider them as *ad hoc* factual problems to be dealt with by reference to traditional legal frameworks. As I have suggested, however, this may not be satisfactory. It may well cause certain themes and principles to be lost sight of. For example, it is clear that the single most important theme which runs through the examples I have given is the theme of *consent*. And consent is, of course, the legal and ethical expression of the human right to respect for autonomy and self-determination. Lawyers who fail to recognise this and other such unifying themes may find themselves fighting the cause of patients on difficult ground, where everything turns on the meaning of a sub-clause of a statute, and in circumstances in which the court has been mesmerised once again by the spectre of doom which would follow any holding of liability against the doctor. Lawyers who do recognise the central role of human rights argue their cases against a wider background and take their cases further, out of the narrow confines of domestic law and into the more understanding environment of, for example, the European Convention on Human Rights. No one better epitomised this approach than Larry Gostin when Legal Director of MIND (the National Association for Mental Health). Perhaps it was his training in the United States which made him think in terms of an appeal to human rights.[7] In any event, his resort to the European Convention created a minor revolution in mental health law. Perhaps the only English judge who shares this understanding is Lord Scarman, a committed advocate of human rights. His speech in the leading case of *Sidaway* v. *Bethlem Royal Hospital Governors*,[8] for example, made it clear that, when considering the issue of informed consent, he at least could see beyond the narrow issue of who said what, and what doctors thought was good practice, to the fact that when we consider the duty of the doctor to inform his patients we are concerned with a profoundly important human right: the right to control one's own destiny by knowing what it is that will be done by way of treatment, so that one may say no, if so minded.

Seeing and understanding the legal concept of consent as the expression of the right to autonomy provides us with an ever-present example of, and alerts us to the need to recognise and explore, this unifying ethical theme or principle when considering apparently disparate areas of medical practice. First, respect for autonomy, in the form of a requirement of consent before a person may be touched, is contingent on the competence of the person to consent. Autonomy is not respected if reliance is placed on the expression of view of an incompetent person. The treatment of the mentally ill, the mentally handicapped, the senile, or the child, while medically different, each have this in common and prompt a search at the level of abstract analysis for an appropriate meaning of competence and ways of establishing it.

---

[7] Gostin, *supra* n. 6.
[8] [1985] 1 All ER 643.

Secondly, respect for autonomy translated as the legal requirement of consent must also take account of whether the consent is given voluntarily. Out of this grows the notion of vulnerability. It becomes clear that it is not only a violation of respect for autonomy to *compel* someone to be treated, but also to take advantage of, or prey on, the vulnerability of patients to gain apparent consent. In this way, such different questions as whether it is right to treat compulsorily the mentally ill or the pregnant woman who refuses a caesarean section, to offer relief from prison on terms that the sex offender undergo castrating hormone therapy, or to take advantage of the prisoner, the impecunious unemployed, or the patient-anxious-to-please by enrolling them as 'volunteers' in research, are seen as variations on a common theme. Finally, respect for autonomy in the legal form of consent requires an examination of whether the consent is appropriately informed. The whole range of interchanges between doctor and patient, from simple injection or prescription of medicine to life-saving operations, fall to be analysed by reference to this central principle as law and ethics seek to respond to the disequilibrium of power between doctor and patient.

SIDAWAY

This mention of the need for consent to be informed if it is to be regarded as valid takes us back to the case of *Sidaway* which I referred to earlier. As is now well known, the case concerned a claim by Mrs Sidaway that had she known of the risks associated with the proposed surgery to relieve pain in her neck, she would never have consented to it. The House of Lords dismissed her case. It was impossible, they said, to know precisely what had passed between her and her now dead surgeon. But the House of Lords did take the opportunity to comment at length on the law of consent.[9] As I have said, it was only Lord Scarman who saw the case in the wider context of human rights. The implications of the case were not, however, lost on the other members of the House of Lords. All realised it was a landmark decision: a challenge to the conservatism of the medical profession and its continuing validation via the courts. All realised that their analysis of the law could be couched in terms of patients' rights or doctors' duties. All but Lord Scarman chose, with more or less enthusiasm, the traditional analytical model of English law, that of duties. They preferred the safer and more limited ground of doctors' duties. In this way they could at the same time tinker with the scope of a doctor's responsibility to his patient while expressing it in terms of its being a concession to the patient, arising out of a proper understanding of the doctor's duty rather than a legitimate right flowing from the patient's

---

[9] For an extensive and critical examination of the case, see chapter 9.

civic status as a person entitled to control what is done to him by others, even if done in the name of treatment.

The language of patients' rights was lost in the rhetoric of imminent doom which, if those who claimed to speak for the medical profession were to be believed, would follow any weakening of the doctors's control over the doctor–patient relationship. If not quite arguing that lions would whelp in the streets, it would, we were all assured, be a *bad day for medicine*, and with the grand sweep of those unembarrassed by paternalism, for patients. Introduce the right of a patient to be informed, (albeit with carefully crafted provisos) and the excesses of US style litigation (largely imagined) would follow as night follows day.[10] Why doctors should be in a special position goes unanalysed. That the doctor's client is a patient is thought to be sufficient argument. Why being a patient should *ipso facto* weaken a person's claim to have his rights respected goes unanswered. Imagine a solicitor instructed to handle the sale of a house by a client. Imagine then that the solicitor, without informing the client, accepts on the client's behalf a price well below the reserve specified by the client, or purports to sell the contents of the house at the same time. Imagine then that when challenged by the client the solicitor responds that he thought it wrong to consult the client because the client was clearly distraught at the thought of the sale (occasioned, let us imagine, by the death of her spouse) and was in no condition to make a considered judgment. Imagine that the solicitor went on to say that it was indeed his duty to protect the client from such hard decisions in times of distress. Imagine then what a court would do!

Is the patient such as Mrs Sidaway, contemplating elective surgery, i.e. surgery she could take or leave, in any different position? Yes, say the courts. She is a patient. There are different rules for doctors. You may join me in wondering what I have missed in the argument! And the response is all the more regrettable because those who argue for the recognition of the rights of patients are the first to concede that the rights of the patient are only prima facie rights. If the patient really will be terrorised by being told certain things, or is too sick to take in information, it is readily recognised that true respect of the patient's rights may in such circumstances require that he is not informed. Yet still, any expression of the law in terms of patients' rights is vehemently opposed.

The only conclusion has to be that what is being rejected is not the analytical model of rights, but what recourse to the language of rights has traditionally been thought to represent. Rights are subversive. Historically, those who enjoy (in all senses of the term) power have insisted on the language of duty to express the relationship between the powerful and the rest. The assertion of rights, enjoyed by all, is by that token supremely threatening. And, what

---

[10] See, especially, Lord Diplock, *Sidaway* (*supra* n. 8) 657.

has been true historically on a grand scale, is no less true on the smaller stage of medical politics. Recognise that a patient has rights and the days of the hard-won power of the medical profession are numbered. Judges lend a sympathetic ear. After all, is it not the role of one professional elite to protect another?

As if to prove this hypothesis, the first case to apply the decision in *Sidaway* did so in a way which can only be described as deeply disappointing if not perverse. The Court of Appeal in *Gold* v. *Haringey Health Authority*[11] chose to rely on the speech in *Sidaway*, that of Lord Diplock, which had clung most tenaciously to the old 'doctor knows best' approach. It was as if the glosses put on this aphorism, albeit tentatively, by Lords Bridge and Templeman had not happened. Their speeches were certainly not mentioned. Needless to say neither was that of Lord Scarman.

The picture in this particular corner of medical law, is, therefore, rather gloomy. It will have to change. The *Bolam* principle, which (you will recall) has it that 'a doctor is not guilty of negligence if he has acted in accordance with a practice accepted as proper by a responsible body of medical men skilled in that particular art', may have some justification in matters of technical skill,[12] but its application to the question of informing (and thereby empowering) a patient is palpably indefensible.[13] It is quite beyond my comprehension how it can still be regarded as relevant to the law in this most important area of human rights.

NON-CONSENSUAL STERILISATION—THE GREAT CHALLENGE

If the 1980s began in Britain with virtually no developed medical law, and consequently no recognition in medical law of human rights, they certainly did not end that way. *Sidaway* in 1985 represented a major development, a major opportunity (an opportunity lost, many would say). The years 1987 and 1989 provided two cases which proved undoubtedly to be the most significant test as yet of the law's commitment to human rights in the context of medical practice. I refer to *Re B*[14] and *Re F*[15] in which the issue for the courts was, put simply, under what circumstances, if any, is it lawful to sterilise a woman without her consent?

Much has already been written about these cases,[16] and I do not intend any lengthy analysis of their place in medical law. My only concern is what

---

[11] [1987] 2 All ER 888.
[12] *Bolam* v. *Friern Hospital Management Committee* [1957] 2 All ER 118.
[13] *Ibid.*, 122.   [14] *Re B (a minor) (Wardship: sterilisation)* [1987] 2 All ER 206.
[15] *Re F (Mental Patient: sterilisation)* [1989] 2 WLR 1025 (CA) 1063 (H.L.).
[16] See, e.g., M. Freeman (1988) 'Sterilising the mentally handicapped' in Freeman (ed.), *Medicine Ethics and the Law*, pp. 55–84; M. Jones (1989) 'Justifying medical treatment without consent', 5 *Professional Negligence* 178; M. Brazier (1990) 'Sterilisation: down the slippery slope', 6 *Professional Negligence* 25.

they teach us about the prominence given by our highest court to considerations of human rights and the analysis such considerations should provoke.

1. *Re B*

I begin with the case of *Re B*. It involved the question whether it was lawful to sterilise a 17-year-old girl who was mentally handicapped and deemed incapable of giving valid consent to the proposed treatment. Here, if you will, is a classic case for an analyst of medical law. The case *could* be dealt with as if it were no more than a variant of the ordinary run of family law cases which the courts deal with every day. The girl was a minor and a ward of court. The principle that her welfare was paramount could be ritually recited and a decision taken to do that which was in her best interests.

This is how medical law cases, particularly those involving children, have routinely been treated by counsel and judges alike. In so doing, of course, the vital themes which transcend the particular facts of any case go unrecognised and hence unanalysed. The opportunity to develop a body of law, of human rights law, which could be applied in any case of proposed sterilisation is spurned. Each case is said to turn on its own facts. As we shall see, not only is this nonsense as an argument, but it also condemns us to perpetual uncertainty in this most sensitive and highly charged area of medical practice.

The progress of *Re B* through the courts was not auspicious. As a matter of legal analysis the view was taken that the court would not have jurisdiction to enter any consent to treatment in wardship proceedings if the woman was an adult (i.e. 18 or older). At the time of the hearing at first instance she was four months short of her eighteenth birthday. The decision to opt for sterilisation had been taken some time earlier but Sunderland Borough Council, in whose care she had been since she was four, decided that it was proper to apply to make her a ward of court and then seek leave for her to undergo the sterilisation operation. Although the application was made almost a year before her eighteenth birthday, by the time the case came before the court there was a sense of urgency which pervaded the judicial proceedings: an atmosphere somewhat uncongenial, it could be said, to considered reflection on such a significant step. For, it must be remembered, what was under consideration was whether a young woman who was physically healthy, apart from being epileptic and prone to outbursts of aggression, should be sterilised out of a fear that she might become pregnant at some time in the future.

A second criticism of the way the case was dealt with was that it had reached the Court of Appeal before the landmark decision of the Supreme Court of Canada in *Re Eve*[17] was brought to the court's attention. This was a

---

[17] (1986) 31 DLR (4th) 1.

serious omission. The court at first instance, for example, may have rejected the view taken in *Re Eve* but at least it would have had to take account of it. In this way an agenda for analysing and deciding the case of *Re B* may have been set which would have forced the court to consider questions of human rights from the outset.

'Experts' and the 'Dossier'

A further, more subtle, but critically important criticism arises out of this. The court from first instance to House of Lords dealt with B's case on the basis of information compiled by 'experts' beforehand. Largely this was medical evidence. It consisted of descriptions of the girl's mental and physical condition. She was said, for example, to have a mental age of five to six years. Conclusions were expressed as to her inability to understand the link between sexual intercourse and pregnancy (although it was said that she understood the link between pregnancy and a baby), her capacity to cope with childbirth ('the process of delivery would be likely to be traumatic'!) and her lack of 'maternal feelings'.[18] It contained recommendations as to the most appropriate course of action to be taken. The whole of this 'dossier' was, in short, prepared by reference to those factors which the 'experts' thought were important. They had their agenda which they responded to and which reflected itself in the material before the court. Thus, by the time the case reached the courts, all the evidence pointed in one direction. It would have been hard for the court, even if it had so desired, to do other than follow what the 'experts' advised since their advice was based on the evidence they had compiled and the court only had that before it.

The preparation of the 'dossier', therefore, takes on the greatest significance. My point is simple. The 'dossier' constitutes the evidence on which the court decides. If it is prepared by doctors and social workers it will address matters which they regard as important or significant. They may not be the matters which a human rights lawyer would be concerned with. But, in the absence of such a lawyer being present during the compilation of the dossier and able to challenge views and ask appropriate questions, there is no guarantee that consideration of the girl's human rights will be placed before the courts. The courts will be presented with a *fait accompli*. Those who wish to challenge it will have what amounts to a near impossible task. They will have to persuade the court to reject, wholly or in part, the evidence of the 'experts', evidence that is often unanimous and which has all the trappings of expertise. It will be too late to argue that the answers may be wrong because the questions were wrong.

---

[18] *Per* Lord Oliver, *Re B* (*supra* n. 14). 216, 217.

In my view, the court should have recognised this, should have recognised that considerations of human rights were raised by the case. As a consequence, the court should have tested the evidence for itself and, in reaching its decision, should have set down the sort of issues which doctors and other experts must address in any subsequent case in which sterilisation was proposed as an option. Sadly, the court did neither.

Instead, the approach adopted throughout and given the seal of approval by the House of Lords was to treat the case as if it merely raised a question of family law involving a child. As such, it could be dealt with routinely. The principle, that the court was to be guided by consideration of the best interests of the child, was duly incanted. Larger concerns and issues could be ignored.

Best interests

To decide any case by reference to the formula of the best interests of the child must be suspect. To decide *Re B* this way is profoundly to be regretted. The best interests formula may be beloved of family lawyers but a moment's reflection will indicate that although it is said to be a test, indeed *the* legal test for deciding matters relating to children, it is not really a test at all. Instead, it is a somewhat crude conclusion of social policy. It allows lawyers and courts to persuade themselves and others that theirs is a principled approach to law. Meanwhile, they engage in what to others is clearly a form of *'ad hocery'*. The best interests approach of family law allows the courts to atomise the law, to claim that each case depends on its own facts. The court can then respond intuitively to each case while seeking to legitimate its conclusion by asserting that it is derived from the general principle contained in the best interests formula. In fact, of course, there is no general principle other than the empty rhetoric of best interests; or rather, there is some principle (or principles) but the court is not telling. Obviously, the court must be following *some* principles, otherwise a toss of a coin could decide cases. But these principles, which serve as pointers to what amounts to the best interests, are not articulated by the court. Only the conclusion is set out. The opportunity for reasoned analysis and scrutiny is lost.

This critical view of the best interests approach brings two further points into focus. It is crucial to understand both. Together they serve as further evidence of the inadequacy of the current state of the law as represented by adopting a narrow family law approach. First, if best interests is recited without analysis, the very purpose for involving the law is defeated. If the law is to serve any purpose it must be to hold accountable those who propose to carry out medical interventions without consent, to require of them that they render an account to others. This is not because they are not trusted. Rather, it is because what is at stake is sufficiently important for the law to be involved and the law's concern is to examine the reasons and justifications for doing that which ordinarily would not be permissible in the absence of specific statutory authorisation. The best interests approach, however, is not a *reasoned* justification. If any reasoning has taken place, it has occurred prior to arriving at the conclusion that a particular course of conduct is in a person's best interests. If, as is the case, this prior process of evaluation and analysis, and the factors underlying it, go unstated, accountability cannot exist. In effect, the law abdicates its responsibility. Decisions cannot readily be challenged. Discretion becomes virtually unfettered. The disequilibrium of power between patient and doctor (and others) goes uncorrected. In the case of sterilisation, the law fails the woman-about-to-be-sterilised.

Secondly, if best interests is recited without analysis, without any recognition of the need for reasoned justification by reference to established criteria, everything inevitably is made to turn on the facts on which the judgment of best interests is to be made. This is where what I have called the 'dossier' re-enters the argument. What is in truth a complex moral and social question is transformed through the device of the best interests approach into a question of fact. Is it, on the facts of this particular case, in the girl's best interests to sterilise her? And what are the facts? They are the information contained in what I have called the 'dossier'. They are the mixture of fact and opinion compiled by the 'experts'. But, you will recall that these have been compiled without reference to any check-list of *legal requirements*. They are solely matters deemed relevant by doctors, social workers, and others. Thus, best interests becomes nothing other than the views of the 'experts'. Again, the law fails the woman-about-to-be-sterilised. What should be a question of evaluation, a normative issue of prescription, becomes a matter of fact, a descriptive issue.

2. *Re F*

Let me now turn to *Re F*. Obviously, given the criticisms I have made of *Re B*, the question to ask is whether the House of Lords did any better the second time around. The case was more complex than *Re B*. Non-consensual sterilisation again fell to be considered. But F was a mentally handicapped woman of 36. Thus, in addition, the court had to resolve a prior question: under what circumstances, if any, is it lawful to carry out medical treatment on an *adult* who is incapable of consenting. This is clearly a question of the greatest importance to the human rights lawyer. It is also a question which challenges the human rights lawyer to examine carefully what a commitment to human rights entails. The starting point for analysis will, as ever, be a concern to protect the vulnerable from real or potential oppression or exploitation.

In our case, as in most, this will translate as the need to justify any proposed medical intervention by reference to carefully articulated criteria. But, the analysis must not stop at this. Oppression or exploitation may take other forms. It must be recognised that it is equally oppressive to deny an incompetent person treatment which otherwise would be judged appropriate. Whatever criteria are developed to protect the incompetent must, therefore, bear in mind that the cause of human rights is not served by so concentrating on protection of the incompetent that it is forgotten that a significant means of protecting him may be to treat him. One consequence of the failure to recognise this, or of striking the wrong balance, has been the allegation that when a patient is cared for by a human rights lawyer he may well die with his rights on!

How did the House of Lords respond in *Re F*? The first point to notice is that, as their Lordships made clear, the law was remarkably under-developed.[19] It might be thought that an issue of such importance would have long since been settled by the courts. In fact, there was no direct legal authority to guide them, proof of the fact that it is only very recently that law has been evoked as a means of regulating the relationship between doctors and their incompetent patients. (This may, of course, suggest that all was well before and the need for formal legal intervention was, and perhaps remains, unnecessary. I would argue, however, that it shows that those concerned for human rights were slow, far too slow, in establishing and clarifying the rights of the incompetent patient.)

In an effort to put an end to this uncertainty, the House of Lords made a number of significant decisions. The first was that no one in law has authority to consent to treatment on behalf of an adult, albeit an incompetent adult. The authority of parents and guardians extends only to the care of minors. Once a child reaches the age of 16, or 18 if incompetent, parental authority and, as a consequence, the capacity to consent to treatment otherwise in the best interests of the child ceases. It may be common practice to consult and defer to parents, spouses, and relatives but they have no legal authority. What then of the *court's* power as a last resort to act as *parens patriae*, to assert parental authority as the ultimate guardian of the interests of the vulnerable? This power, the House of Lords decided, does not extend to adults. It is limited to minors, expressed through the principle of wardship. Historically, wardship had been merely an example of the exercise of the power of *parens patriae*. But, the House of Lords decided, this ancient power is as a consequence of legislation now limited to minors. The larger power to make decisions on behalf of *all* who need the aid of the court, adults as

---

[19] 'The argument of counsel revealed the startling fact that there is no English authority on the question whether as a matter of common law (and if so in what circumstances) medical treatment can lawfully be given to a person who is disabled by mental incapacity from consenting to it', per Lord Goff, *Re F* (*supra* n. 15) 1082.

well as minors, no longer exists. This led the House of Lords to the conclusion that in law even the court has no power to authorise, to consent to, any proposed medical intervention on an incompetent adult.[20]

To stop at that point, of course, would have left the law even more obscure and thrown medical practice into confusion. It would have left unanswered the question whether, in the absence of any person or institution with authority in law to consent, it was ever lawful to treat an incompetent adult. It would, as a consequence, have gravely endangered the interests of such patients if it meant that those caring for them felt uncertain as to whether they could lawfully treat them. Admittedly, some situations could easily be dealt with. Emergencies have long been recognised as justifying treatment without consent, since it is undoubtedly in the public interest to come to the aid of the person needing medical treatment in an emergency. But, short of extending the meaning of emergency so far that it could serve to justify any medical treatment, and thereby substitute a rule allowing all interventions for one allowing none, the doctrine of emergency cannot provide the answer.

This is not to say, however, that the underlying rationale of the doctrine, the public interest, cannot help us. This is what their Lordships settled on. It cannot be unlawful, it was said, to treat the adult incompetent who needs treatment, even in the absence of an emergency. If it were, the toothache of a mentally handicapped patient must go untreated. This would violate the rights of the patient and cannot be the law. Thus, the House of Lords held, the law must be that treatment is lawful if it is justified on the basis of the principle of necessity[21] or as being in the public interest.[22] And treatment is necessary or in the public interest when it is in the patient's best interests.[23]

So far, so good. The adult incompetent will not go without treatment. But there still remains the crucial question. Under what circumstances will any particular treatment be judged to be in a patient's best interests? This is the central concern for the human rights lawyer. Make it too easy to treat the patient and the danger of abuse re-emerges. Make it too difficult and you deny the patient the right enjoyed by the competent: access to medical treatment.

Bolam

What test does the House of Lords in fact come up with to determine when it is in a patient's best interests to treat regardless of consent? The first

---

[20] The conclusions expressed in this paragraph are argued *in extenso* in the speeches of their Lordships, but encapsulated in the conclusion of Lord Bridge, that 'no court now has jurisdiction either by statute or derived from the Crown as *parens patriae* to give or withhold consent to . . . an operation in the case of an adult as it would in wardship proceedings in the case of a minor', *Re F* (*supra* n. 15) 1063. For the tangled legislative background, see the analysis of Lord Brandon, *ibid.*, 1069.　　　　[21] *Per* Lords Brandon and Goff.
[22] *Per* Lord Griffiths.　　　　[23] All their Lordships were agreed on this.

impression is depressing for the human rights lawyer. Their Lordships seem at first sight to have settled on a most curious rule. The question whether it is in an incompetent patient's best interests to be treated is, it appears, to be analysed and answered by reference to the *Bolam*[24] decision. How extraordinary, you may say. *Bolam* is the leading case in negligence which stipulates the standard of care which a doctor must meet to satisfy his duty to his patient. It establishes that a doctor will not be judged to be in breach of his duty if, on the evidence of peers, he has behaved as a reasonable doctor. *Bolam*, in other words, is a test of competence. What, you may wonder, does it have to do with a judgment whether a proposed medical intervention is in a patient's best interests? Equally, you may wonder whether, if it is relevant to such an inquiry, it means that the House of Lords has decided to reduce to a question of professional opinion by doctors the profound question of the permissibility of non-consensual interventions. If this were indeed what the House of Lords had done it would be a dark day for medical law. In particular, it would represent a severe set back in the attempt to build medical law on a framework of human rights law. The House of Lords, it would be said, had handed over the preservation and protection of the rights of the incompetent adult to the medical profession. If a doctor could show that a number of his peers would have reached a similar view to his, this would be enough to make his assessment of what was in a patient's best interests valid and lawful. Here, if ever there was one, would be an example of the courts' craven acceptance of medical paternalism and their anxiety to slough off hard cases. Here again would be an example of the common law's unease when confronted with the language of rights.

Well, this is how the House of Lords' decision appears at first blush.[25] And, translated into the context of non-consensual sterilisation, its impact is even more troubling for the human rights lawyer. If the law were that treatment is in a patient's best interests when a doctor says it is, the House of Lords would be saying that as regards sterilisation it is permissible in law to sterilise an incompetent adult when a doctor says so, provided other doctors would agree. We only have to state such a startling proposition to realise that it cannot be the law. The House of Lords may make the occasional odd decision but they could never do anything quite this perverse!

And neither did they. In my view, their Lordships' decision, while being far from ideal, is by no means as harmful to human rights as first impressions might suggest. A careful reading of the speeches of Lords Brandon, Goff, and Griffiths suggests that although the starting point was *Bolam*, the analysis is far more subtle than a mere reliance on that case. The House of Lords clearly recognised the significance of their decision and were at pains to show it. How they did so was to attach a series of conditions to the doctor's exercise

[24] *Supra* n. 12.   [25] See, in particular, the speech of Lord Brandon.

of clinical judgment concerning his patient's best interests. In effect the House of Lords established that while the decision to treat without consent was for a doctor to make in accordance with the view of his peers, in making it he must give his mind to certain questions of a general nature. In other words, any doctor must, if he wishes to be judged to have behaved reasonably, give his mind to certain matters. Reasonableness then becomes, as it should be, a prescriptive rather than a descriptive term. And the prescription remains with the court, in that the court can find that failure to take account of one thing or another is unreasonable. Being unreasonable, such a failure would attract liability, arguably in trespass (battery). These matters which the doctor must consider, these questions of a general nature, are undoubtedly relatively simple in the case of a straightforward medical procedure. In the case of a procedure as controversial as non-consensual sterilisation, the questions to be asked and answered satisfactorily are many and complex.

Factors to be considered

So what are the factors which the House of Lords require the doctor to take account of? I say the House of Lords rather than any particular member of the court, since it is important to notice that what I present here is an amalgam of the views of several of their Lordships. In doing so, it could be said that I overstate the concern for human rights which I claim was shown by the House of Lords: in short, the whole which I construct is more than the sum of the parts. My response is that their Lordships were all concerned to make a central point, that the law must play a significant role in regulating a doctor's decision. That they did it in differing ways is inevitable. All I do is to bring the various strands together to make a composite picture.

Procedure

First, we should notice a preliminary point. Although not specifically a factor to be taken account of by a doctor in reaching his decision, it has great consequence as representing a clear signal by the House of Lords of its concern to act as guardian of the interests of the incompetent. The House of Lords was, as I have said, unanimous in deciding that, in the absence of a power of *parens patriae* or statutory authority, the courts in England and Wales have no jurisdiction to approve (give consent to) or disapprove of the carrying out of any medical treatment involving the touching of an incompetent adult. But, they went on, a court does have the power to issue a declaration as to the lawfulness of any procedure if asked so to do. In the case of a procedure leading to the sterilisation of an incompetent adult, because of the special circumstances surrounding such an operation, the House of Lords took the view that it was most desirable in practice to seek the court's view. Lord

Bridge, expressed himself as follows: '. . . the court's jurisdiction *should be invoked* whenever such an operation is proposed to be performed'.[26]

The House of Lords then went on to stipulate the directions which are to be followed in any application for a declaration:

1. Applications for a declaration that a proposed operation on or medical treatment for a patient can lawfully be carried out despite the inability of such a patient to consent thereto should be by way of originating summons issuing out of the Family Division of the High Court.
2. The applicant should normally be those responsible for the care of the patient or those intending to carry out the proposed operation or other treatment, if it is declared to be lawful.
3. The patient must always be a party and should normally be a respondent. In cases in which the patient is a respondent the patient's guardian *ad litem* should normally be the Official Solicitor. In any cases in which the Official Solicitor is not either the next friend or the guardian *ad litem* of the patient or an applicant he shall be a respondent.
4. With a view to protecting the patient's privacy, but subject always to the judge's discretion, the hearing will be in chambers, but the decision and the reasons for that decision will be given in open court.[27]

Finally, the House of Lords then set out the form a declaration should take if the proposed treatment were judged lawful:

(a) It is declared that the operation of sterilisation proposed to be performed on the plaintiff being in the existing circumstances in her best interests can lawfully be performed on her despite her inability to consent to it.
(b) It is ordered that in the event of a material change in the existing circumstances occurring before the said operation has been performed any party shall have liberty to apply for such further or other declaration or order as may be just.[28]

These directions demonstrate, in my view, the House of Lords' commitment to human rights. As a result, the courts may not have the formal

---

[26] *Re F* (*supra* n. 15) 1063 (my emphasis). Lord Griffiths was in the minority in urging that the House of Lords should change the common law so that permission of the court *had to be* obtained. '[O]n grounds of public interest', he stated, 'an operation to sterilise a woman incapable of giving consent either on grounds of age or mental capacity is unlawful if performed without the consent of the High Court', *ibid.*, 1081.

[27] *Per* Lord Brandon, *ibid.*, 1075–6.

[28] *Per* Lord Brandon, *ibid.*, 1076. You will notice the reference to the fact that any order took account only of existing circumstances, which could change in the light, e.g. of further evidence or some medical development. This was stressed by Lord Brandon and is of some significance, as I suggest later (*infra*, pp. 399–401).

power to regulate operations for sterilisation but Health Authorities or doctors act at their peril if they do not seek a declaration. Thus, the House of Lords provides for a formal hearing. Secondly, the House of Lords requires that the patient's interests are always independently represented, usually through the Official Solicitor. Thirdly, the patient's right to privacy is protected.

Factors again

As I have said, once a case is before the court, there are certain factors which the court will need to be satisfied of before it is determined that a proposed operation for sterilisation is in an adult incompetent woman's interests. In my view, when due account is taken of all their Lordships' views, they amount to the following:

1. That her doctors in reaching the view that the sterilisation operation should be carried out are acting in accordance with a respectable body of medical opinion skilled in the care of mentally disabled adult women.
2. That the existing circumstances of the woman which give rise to the need for the operation will continue until and unless the operation is performed and no other less serious intervention is appropriate so as to safeguard her best interests.
3. That her doctors have consulted, where relevant, specialist colleagues.
4. That her doctors have consulted members of the team caring for the woman and relatives and relevant others.
5. That her doctors have taken all due account of such factors as,
    (a) the right of a woman to control her own reproduction and not be sterilised involuntarily without the best of reasons,
    (b) the fact that sterilisation involves irreparable interference with a woman's reproductive organs,
    (c) the fact that the woman's reproductive organs are functioning normally and that the woman is healthy,
    (d) the fact that sterilisation may never be performed as a matter of convenience or to meet the needs of others, or for other improper reasons,
    (e) the fact that sterilisation gives rise to moral and emotional considerations to which many give significance and is an operation concerning which there is disagreement as to its justification among doctors and other experts,
    (f) the fact that the decision to sterilise a woman in such circumstances is a grave decision with considerable social implication.

All of these factors have, I would argue, similar weight, such that a court would need to be satisfied as regards all of them. One to which I draw particular attention is the second, that the existing circumstances of the woman which give rise to the need for the operation will continue unless the operation is performed and no other less serious action is available. Great care should be taken here. Take, for example, the facts in *Re F*. It was alleged that a male patient (P) had formed a relationship with F, a woman of 36 described as suffering from serious mental disability with the general mental capacity of a child of four to five years. The relationship, Lord Brandon stated, 'is of a sexual nature and probably involves sexual intercourse or something close to it, about twice a month. The relationship is entirely voluntary on F's part and it is likely that she obtains pleasure from it'.[29] As it happens, it appears that P had a similar relationship with other patients.[30] In such circumstances, what is striking is that it appears to be assumed that if the relationship between P and F were to continue, it was F against whom preventive measures against her becoming pregnant should be taken. Nowhere is the question raised whether it should not be P rather than F who should be sterilised, or as regards whom some other procedure be adopted to regulate his conduct and thereby reduce the risk of pregnancy to F. Appeals were made to F's right to society, including her right to form a sexual relationship (Lord Brandon's 'it is likely that she obtains pleasure from it').[31] Such appeals are, of course, at least suspect. They can, as arguably they did in this case, serve to justify sterilising F, in the name of protecting and preserving her human rights. They can thereby serve to entrench a male-orientated approach to the management of the institutionalised mentally handicapped.[32] And, of course, those who have recourse to them seem not to be embarrassed by their lack of internal logic: F is entitled to enjoy her rights to society including sexual intercourse (and, as a consequence, should be sterilised) but she is incapable of understanding sexual relationships and their consequences (hence she should be sterilised).

The 'dossier' again

Let me now turn to what I see as the principal significance of the House of Lords' insistence on the need to satisfy certain criteria. You will remember

[29] *Re F* (*supra* n. 15) 1065.

[30] Private communication.

[31] And see Lord Oliver in *Re B*: 'this case . . . is about . . . how best she can be given the protection which is essential to her future well-being *so that she may lead as full a life as her intellectual capacity allows*', *Re B*, (*supra*) n. 15, 219 (my emphasis). Previously, Lord Oliver had stated that she 'is unaware of sexual intercourse' and that 'it was essential in her interests that effective contraceptive measures be taken' because of the 'difficulty of maintaining effective supervision', *ibid.*, 216, 217. I leave it to you to decide whether Lord Oliver's views are compatible with each other.

[32] It was Lord Bridge in *Re B* who remarked that 'the right answer is by a *simple operation* for occlusion of the fallopian tubes' (my emphasis), *Re B*, (*supra* n. 14) 214.

that earlier I referred to the 'dossier' and how the information contained in it, the views of the 'experts', necessarily conditioned subsequent decisions about the best interests of the woman involved. You will remember that my criticism was that if the 'dossier' was prepared on the basis of what doctors and other carers deemed relevant, there was a real danger that the human rights of the woman would not properly be protected. By stipulating the factors to be taken account of, the House of Lords, in essence, has established as a matter of law what it is that those caring for an incompetent woman must give their minds to when considering sterilisation as an option.

The House of Lords has set out the questions which those caring for the woman must ask themselves. The views of 'experts', therefore, though relevant and important are not determinative of the question whether or not to sterilise.[33] In this way, the House of Lords has ensured that considerations of human rights, as expressed in the factors they enumerate, are of central and critical significance.

Official Solicitor's Note

Support for this view was provided by the publication shortly after the House of Lords' decision of what went under the heading of 'Practice Note (Official Solicitor: Sterilisation)'.[34] Such a Note, despite its attempt to clothe itself in the formal trappings of a Practice Direction, does not, of course, have any formal legal standing.[35] None the less, as an expression of view of the Official Solicitor and an indication of the steps which parties proposing the sterilisation of a woman must take and the factors concerning which they should provide evidence, if they are to gain the co-operation of the Official Solicitor in proceedings before the court, it is likely to be of enormous significance. And, of course, to that extent it represents a significant public commitment to respect for human rights.

In paragraph 1 of his Note, the Official Solicitor rehearses the House of Lords' view that 'the sterilisation of a minor or a mentally incompetent adult (the patient) will in virtually all cases require the prior sanction of a High Court judge'. The Note then stipulates, in paragraph 5, that 'prior to the substantive hearing of the application there will, in every case, be a summons for directions which will be heard by a High Court judge' and goes on, in paragraph 6, to say that 'the purpose of the proceedings is to establish whether

---

[33] 'In all proceedings where expert opinions are expressed, those opinions are listened to with great respect; but, in the end, the validity of the opinion has to be weighed and judged by the court. . . . For a court automatically to accept an expert opinion . . . would be a denial of the function of the court', *per* Lord Goff, *Re F* (*supra* n. 15) 1090.

[34] *New Law Journal*, 13 October 1989, p. 1380.

[35] See the subsequent case of *Re C*, *Times*, 13 February 1990, in which it was stated that the Note had no specific legal status and was at best advisory.

or not the proposed sterilisation is in the best interests of the Patient. The judge will require to be satisfied that those proposing sterilisation are seeking it in good faith and that their paramount concern is for the best interests of the Patient rather than their own or the public's convenience'. The role of the Official Solicitor is made clear in paragraph 7: '[T]he Official Solicitor acts as an independent and disinterested guardian representing the interests of the Patient. He will carry out his own investigations, call his own witnesses and take whatever other steps appear to him to be necessary in order to ensure that all relevant matters are thoroughly aired before the judge, including cross-examining the expert and other witnesses called in support of the proposed operation and presenting all reasonable arguments against sterilisation. The Official Solicitor will require to meet and interview the Patient in private in all cases where he or she is able to express any views (however limited) about the legal proceedings, the prospect of sterilisation, parenthood, other means of contraception or other relevant matters.'

Paragraph 8 of his Note is crucial. It states that:

Without in any way attempting to define or to limit the factors which may require to be taken into account in any particular case the Official Solicitor anticipates that the judge will normally require evidence clearly establishing:
1. That (a) the Patient is incapable of making his or her own decision about sterilisation and (b) the Patient is unlikely to develop sufficiently to make an informed judgment about sterilisation in the foreseeable future. . . .
2. That the condition which it is sought to avoid will in fact occur, e.g., in the case of a contraceptive sterilisation, that there is a need for contraception because (a) the Patient is physically capable of procreation and (b) that the Patient is likely to engage in sexual activity, at the present or in the near future, under circumstances where there is a real danger as opposed to mere chance that pregnancy is likely to result.
3. That the Patient will experience substantial trauma or psychological damage if the condition which it is sought to avoid should arise, e.g., in the case of a contraceptive sterilisation that (a) the Patient (if a woman) is likely if she becomes pregnant or gives birth to experience substantial trauma or psychological damage greater than that resulting from the sterilisation itself and (b) the Patient is permanently incapable of caring for a child even with reasonable assistance, e.g., from a future spouse in a case where the Patient has or may have the capacity to marry.
4. That there is no practicable less intrusive means of solving the anticipated problem than immediate sterilisation, in other words (a) sterilisation is advisable at the time of the application rather than in the future, (b) the proposed method of sterilisation entails the least invasion of the Patient's body, (c) sterilisation will not itself cause physical or psychological damage greater than the intended beneficial effects, (d) the current state of scientific and medical knowledge does not suggest either (i) that a reversible sterilisation procedure or other less drastic solutions to the problem sought to be avoided, e.g., some other contraceptive

method, will shortly be available or (ii) that science is on the threshold of an advance in the treatment of the Patient's disability and (e) in the case of a contraceptive sterilisation all less drastic contraceptive methods, including supervision, education and training have proved unworkable or inapplicable.'

These factors are not too dissimilar from those which I set out earlier as my own understanding of *Re F*. Both are derived from and seek to apply in a practical form certain general precepts of human rights found, for example, in the European Convention on Human Rights. Sadly, no mention was made of the Convention either in *Re B* or in *Re F*. You may think this an extraordinary omission. Had the Convention been properly considered, it would have been realised that at least three Articles, 2, 3, and 8[36] were particularly germane to the issues before the court. Whether the House of Lords' decision, as interpreted, represents a proper understanding and application of the Convention is, of course, another question to which I shall turn shortly.

There is, however, a further point to be made about the analysis I have offered of *Re F* which echoes a concern I raised earlier in relation to *Re B*. You will recall that I argued that one of the major weaknesses of the approach adopted in *Re B*, the *ad hoc*, atomising, family law approach, was that it failed to provide any adequate mechanism for holding doctors and others accountable for their decisions and actions. 'Experts' could argue that on the particular facts they formed a view in good faith and that, as a matter of law, would be that. Crucially, by identifying questions which must, as a matter of law, be asked and factors which must be considered, the House of Lords re-established a formal system of accountability, and not just any system of accountability but accountability by law in public to the courts. The significance of this cannot be overstated in terms of human rights. Recourse to discretion is confined and controlled. The rule of law, reflecting the concerns of human rights, is interposed between the incompetent woman and those who would sterilise her.

3. A COUNTER-VIEW

So far, in my effort to demonstrate that medical law is in truth an aspect of human rights law, I have particularly concentrated on two cases involving sterilisation. My point has been that on any analysis the non-consensual sterilisation of incompetent women raises the most profound issues of human

---

[36] Article 2 provides, 'Everyone's right to life shall be protected by law.' Article 3 provides, 'No-one shall be subjected to torture or to inhuman or degrading treatment or punishment.' Article 8 provides, 'Everyone has the right to respect for his private and family life, his home and his correspondence.'

rights. My enquiry has been concerned with the extent to which these issues are reflected in the approach of the English courts. I have suggested that while the decision in *Re B* leaves much to be desired,[37] *Re F*, although not overtly speaking the language of human rights, gets at least an honourable mention. It would, perhaps, be wrong to conclude this consideration of sterilisation, if it really is a paradigm example of human rights in medical law, without asking the ultimate question. The House of Lords took the view that non-consensual sterilisation is lawful subject to certain conditions being satisfied. Is this a valid and correct conclusion, if the question is approached from the perspective of human rights on the basis of first principles?

Let me begin, perversely, with my conclusion. It is that non-consensual sterilisation of an incompetent woman can in my view only be justified if carried out for legitimate therapeutic reasons. Conversely, it is an *unjustifiable violation of human rights if carried out for non-therapeutic reasons and, as a consequence, should be declared unlawful.* To this extent I align myself with the now famous decision of the Canadian Supreme Court in *Re Eve*.[38] Consequently, I regret the decision of the House of Lords in *Re F*, while recognising, of course, the considerable care taken in that case to come to terms with the claims of human rights. I would further argue that Articles 2, 3, and 8[39] of the European Convention on Human Rights could each plausibly compel the view I take, if properly understood and applied.

You will notice that I draw a crucial distinction between therapeutic and non-therapeutic sterilisation. This was the distinction relied upon by La Forest J in *Re Eve*. Therapeutic sterilisation, the Canadian Supreme Court held, is permissible in law. Non-therapeutic sterilisation is not. The distinction, however, found no favour with the House of Lords. Lord Hailsham in *Re B* stated, 'I find the distinction [La Forest J] purports to draw between "therapeutic" and "non-therapeutic" purposes of this operation . . . totally meaningless, and, if meaningful, quite irrelevant to the correct application of the welfare principle.[40] According to Lord Bridge in *Re B*, to say that [the court] can only [authorise sterilisation] if the operation is "therapeutic" as opposed to "non-therapeutic" is to divert attention from the true issue, which is, whether the operation is in the ward's best interest, and remove it to an area of arid semantic debate as to where the line is to be drawn. . . .'[41]

Lord Oliver delivered himself of the following: 'If . . . the expression "non-therapeutic" was intended to exclude measures taken for the necessary

---

[37] Not least that the House of Lords allowed only one day for the whole of the hearing!

[38] *Supra* n. 17. But see the subsequent rejection of the Supreme Court's approach by the Alberta Institute of Law Research and Reform in its report *Competence and Human Reproduction*, Report No 52 (1989) which proposes legislation on the issue. *Sed quaere* the impact of the Charter of Rights and Freedoms?

[39] See *supra* n. 35.

[40] *Re B* (*supra* n. 14) 213.

[41] *Ibid.*, 214.

protection from future harm of the person   then I respectfully dissent from it for it seems to me to contradict what is the sole and paramount criterion for the exercise of the jurisdiction [*semble* wardship], viz. the welfare and benefit of the ward. . . . This case . . . involves no general principle of public policy [*sic*]. It is about what is in the best interests of this unfortunate young woman and how best she can be given the protection which is *essential* to her future well-being. . . .'[42]

Finally, in *Re F* Lord Griffiths put forward the following view: 'In Canada the Supreme Court has taken an *even more extreme* stance and declared that sterilisation is unlawful unless performed for therapeutic reasons, which I understand to be as a life-saving measure or for the prevention of the spread of disease [*sic*].'[43]

With the greatest respect, these views are hard to sustain and bordering on the perverse. The distinction between therapeutic and non-therapeutic is well known to medicine, medical law, and medical ethics. Take, for example, research on human subjects, where a different regime of rules regulates therapeutic and non-therapeutic research. Of course, there are problems at the edges, but when is there not when language is employed? Had the House of Lords approached the question with an open mind, they would have realised that the key determinant in distinguishing between the two is a concept they are entirely familiar with and use every day, the concept of intention. An intervention is therapeutic if treatment (therapy) is intended thereby. It is non-therapeutic when there is no such intention. And, of course, to qualify as treatment, there must be a present intention to benefit the health of the patient. It must be a patient's *health* which is to be benefited. The benefit usually will take the form of remedying or alleviating an existing condition. Less commonly, but important for our purposes, it may (as in the case of a vaccine) protect a healthy person against an event in the future. But it is important to notice here that the difference between a vaccine against a future event and sterilisation is that, in the case of a vaccine, the event is a very real risk and the invasion is relatively insignificant. In the case of sterilisation, the latter is not so and the former may not be. Thus, any benefit in the case of sterilisation will be that much harder to show.

Let me now set out the argument. The question at its most general, and without yet taking any view about the distinction between therapeutic and non-therapeutic sterilisation, is, to what extent does the law permit the violation of a healthy person's (woman's) body without her consent to protect her from a possible future health-threatening event? Arguing from first principles, the first analytical step is to accept that some formal institutional mechanism for answering this question and thereby responding to individual

[42] *Re B* (*supra* n. 14) 219 (my emphasis).
[43] *Re F* (*supra* n. 15) 1079 (my emphasis).

cases is required. Decisions of such gravity cannot be left to private arrangement without the formal involvement of society through some institution. Secondly, such a mechanism must indicate who it is who decides whether or not to sterilise and the criteria governing such a decision. In a sense the latter is a function of the former. If doctors make the decision, then the criteria will be medical and the issue will in essence have been handed over to the medical profession. Thus, I will assert that the criteria must be established by law. This is another way of saying that non-consensual sterilisation is too important to be left to any particular group of 'experts'. The ground rules must be set by society and must take the form of law. Law is the appropriate mechanism, both so as to convey the importance of the issue and also to indicate that no social mechanism other than law is adequate to the task.

If the law should set the criteria governing non-consensual sterilisation, how is the law to do it? There are at least three approaches. The first could be that of family law through the criterion of best interests. We have seen, however, that this approach is bankrupt. It leaves us only with *ad hoc* conclusions rather than an analytical starting point for considering particular cases. A second option could be for the law to rely on what is called substituted judgment. By this a court seeks, in any particular context, to make the decision which, but for her incompetence, the woman would have made. It is founded, however, on the premise that the woman had views on the issue, which she had expressed, but is no longer able to do so because of intervening incompetence. But the cases which concern us involve women who, because of mental handicap, have never been competent. It would be a transparent fiction, therefore, to resort to an approach which claims to be giving effect to their views; they never had any. It would, in truth, merely be a device whereby others could purport to respect the incompetent woman's right to self-determination based on her alleged (but non-existent) wishes, while all the time reaching a decision which *they* want to reach.[44]

A third approach is that of human rights; that in considering the criteria governing non-consensual sterilisation, the law should begin from the position that every person has certain rights which it is the job of the law to preserve and protect. These include, with particular reference to sterilisation, the right to be free from inhuman treatment, the right to privacy, the right to life in the sense of the enjoyment of life unimpaired by the unwarranted intervention of others, and the right to reproduce, as Heilbron J put it in *Re D*,[45] or, as Lord Brandon stated it, 'the right to bear children'.[46]

With these rights as the starting point, it would follow, in my view, that, prima facie, to sterilise someone without her consent, and consequently to

---

[44] See the exposure of the fiction by La Forest J in *Re Eve* (*supra* n. 17) 435.
[45] *Re D (a minor)*, [1976] 1 All ER 326, 332.
[46] *Re F* (*supra* n. 15) 1068.

threaten to violate one or more of these rights, would be unlawful. I stress the words prima facie so as to allow for the fact that there may well be circumstances in which it *is* permissible to carry out sterilisation operations without consent, but that a clear justification must be established in each case, the onus being upon the person proposing the procedure.

What valid justification could be offered? In my view, the doctor or other carer would have to satisfy the following criteria:

(a) That, given the general question posed earlier, there must be evidence that the alleged future health-threatening event would in fact threaten the woman's health. Health would, of course, need to be understood in its widest sense. This would mean, for example, that if a mentally handicapped woman was becoming suicidal because of menstruation and delusions as to what it represented, non-consensual sterilisation may be an appropriate option.[47]

It is as well, however, to notice here certain other circumstances which are advanced as health risks to the woman so as to justify sterilisation but which are much more problematical. La Forest J identifies and responds to them in typically lucid and compassionate fashion.

The justifications advanced are the ones commonly proposed in support of non-therapeutic sterilisation. . . . Many are demonstrably weak. The [Canadian Law Reform] Commission dismisses the argument about the trauma of birth by observing, 'For this argument to be held valid would require that it could be demonstrated that the stress of delivery was greater in the case of mentally handicapped persons than it is for others. Considering the generally known wide range of post-partum response would likely render this a difficult case to prove.'

The argument relating to fitness as a parent involves many value-loaded questions. Studies conclude that mentally incompetent parents show as much fondness and concern for their children as other people. . . . Many, it is true, may have difficulty in coping, particularly with the financial burdens involved. But this issue does not relate to the benefit of the incompetent; it is a social problem, and one, moreover, that is not limited to incompetents. Above all it is not an issue that comes within the limited powers of the courts . . . to do what is necessary for the benefit of persons who are unable to care for themselves. Indeed, there are human rights considerations that should make a court extremely hesitant about attempting to solve a social problem like this by this means. . . .

As far as the hygienic problems are concerned, the following view of the Law Reform Commission is obviously sound: 'if a person requires a great deal of assistance in managing their own menstruation, they are also likely to require assistance with urinary

[47] La Forest J in *Re Eve* referred specifically to such an example, arising in the case of *Re K and Public Trustee* (1985), 19 DLR (4th) 255 (*supra* n. 17) 418–9. At the same time, however, it is as well to bear in mind what the Law Reform Commission of Canada had to say about sterilisation as a form of medical treatment. 'Sterilisation as a medical procedure', their report said, 'is distinct, because except in rare cases, if the operation is not performed, the *physical* health of the person involved is not in danger, necessity or emergency not normally being factors in the decision to undertake the procedure.' Law Reform Commission of Canada, *Sterilisation*. Working Paper 24 (1979), p. 3.

and faecal control, problems which are much more troublesome in terms of personal hygiene'.[48]

(b) There must be a *real* possibility of the health-threatening event occurring. Furthermore, the reality of the risk must be assessed on the basis of a critically important assumption. It must be assumed that the mentally handicapped woman will already be receiving all the care and support to which she is entitled, including all appropriate steps to safeguard and protect her, given her vulnerability and susceptibility to exploitation.

(c) The principle of proportionality should apply such that: (i) there must be no less invasive means available to achieve the desired result, and (ii) the harm done must be proportionate to the risk of harm avoided. And, when considering the harm done, harm must be recognised as referring to and including physical, mental, spiritual, and symbolic harm, in that the law must consider what non-consensual sterilisation may represent to the woman, to us, and as a precedent for the future.

These criteria could, undoubtedly, serve to justify non-consensual sterilisation, the aim and intention of which was therapeutic, to respond to the real health needs of the woman. Can they justify non-consensual sterilisation which is non-therapeutic? In my view, the key lies in the notion of *harm*. If harm is to be defined as I have suggested, there are certain harms, I would submit, which may not be inflicted on a person without that person's consent. The impermissibility of doing some harm, regardless of alleged benefits, without consent is recognised already in medical law in, e.g. the prohibition on psychosurgery on a mentally disordered person without that person's consent in the Mental Health Act 1983.[49]

Does non-consensual, non-therapeutic sterilisation fall into this category of harms, impermissible without consent? In my view, it does, because on the principle of proportionality, the harm avoided will never be as great as the harm done. In reaching this view, I rely ultimately on the spiritual and symbolic nature of the harm done, not merely on the physical (without for a moment ignoring this). I insist that there are things which we may not do to each other without consent, regardless of apparent (or, perhaps, real) short-term benefit. For me, non-consensual non-therapeutic sterilisation involves the destruction of an essential feature of a person's identity, of that which at a very basic level represents a sense of self. A woman may be mentally handicapped. She may have a mental age of four or five years. But if she is 25 she has many of the qualities of a 25-year-old. In particular, she has 25 years of experience[50] and has seen how women and men are treated and

---

[48] *Re Eve* (*supra* n. 15) 430-1.

[49] s. 57.

[50] See the excellent treatment of this point in D. Carson (1989) 'The sexuality of people with learning difficulties', 6 *Journal of Social Welfare Law*, 367-71.

how they react and behave. Some sense that women are different and that the difference lies in the fact that they are women will have been acquired, rudimentary as it may be. Womanness is inextricably identified with reproductive capacity, although this may not be its only feature. To destroy irrevocably this reproductive capacity is, on this analysis, to destroy a fundamental, perhaps the only remaining, element of a sense of self. Institutionalised and ignored, the woman is now to be sterilised.

La Forest J pointed out in *Re Eve*:

There is considerable evidence that non-consensual sterilisation has a significant negative psychological impact on the mentally handicapped. . . . The [Canadian Law Reform] Commission has this to say at p. 50: 'It has been found that, like anyone else, the mentally handicapped have individually varying reactions to sterilisation. Sex and parenthood hold the same significance for them as for other people and their misconceptions and misunderstandings are also similar. Rosen maintains that the removal of an individual's procreative powers is a matter of major importance and that no amount of *reforming zeal* can remove the significance of sterilisation and its effect on the individual psyche. In a study by Sabagh and Edgerton, it was found that sterilised mentally retarded persons tend to perceive sterilisation as a symbol of *reduced* or *degraded* status. Their attempts to *pass for normal* were hindered by negative self-perceptions and resulted in withdrawal and isolation rather than striving to conform.'[51]

In my view, this harm—in part factual, in part symbolic—is something which a civilised community should simply not contemplate. To those who say that this denies the woman the human right to society, including sexual intercourse, I respond, as I said earlier, that there is a good deal of humbug in this view. I would prefer to argue that my approach *further* protects the woman who otherwise might be the object of the sexual gratification of others who may think or be led to think that now it is safe to have intercourse with her since she has been sterilised. I conclude therefore, with the Supreme Court of Canada, that non-therapeutic non-consensual sterilisation cannot be justified in law, on the ground that it violates fundamental human rights.[52] That such a view is discomforting to doctors, carers, and relatives and would make the care of the mentally handicapped more difficult may well be true. These considerations no doubt weighed with the House of Lords. But when

---

[51] *Re Eve (supra* n. 15) 429.

[52] 'The grave intrusion on a person's rights and the certain physical damage that ensues from non-therapeutic sterilisation without consent, when compared to the highly questionable advantages that can result from it, have persuaded me that it can *never* safely be determined that such a procedure is for the benefit of that person' (La Forest J., *ibid.*, 431 (my emphasis)). La Forest J. goes on to suggest that if it is ever to be lawful, it would require action by the legislature. Any legislation, however, would, in my view, violate human rights.

utility and pragmatism collide with human rights it is the former which must give way. If it is otherwise, the game is lost.[53]

CONCLUSION

I have tried in this chapter to persuade you of two things: that medical law is an aspect of human rights law and that within medical law there is no better proof of this than the issue of non-consensual sterilisation. I hope I have convinced you of this, even if you choose to reject the particular conclusions I have reached.

---

[53] See the critical comments of Margaret Brazier on two cases on non-consensual sterilisation decided since *Re B*, both of which are disturbing. They are *Re M (a minor) (wardship: sterilisation)* [1988] 2 FLR 997 and *Re P (a minor) (wardship: sterilisation)* [1989] 1 FLR 182. It is to be hoped that future courts would take account of Brazier's well-argued strictures and the arguments advanced in this paper. See Brazier, (*supra* n. 16).

Bibliography*

American College of Obstetrics and Gynaecologists, 'Patient Choice: Maternal–Fetal Conflict', ACOG Committee Opinion (1987).

Annas, G. 'Pregnant Women as Fetal Containers', 16 Hastings Center Report, 13– (1986).

—— 'The Impact of Medical Technology on the Pregnant Woman's Right to Privacy', 13 American Journal of Legal Medicine (1987).

—— 'Protecting the Liberty of Pregnant Patients', 316 New England Journal of Medicine 1214– (1987).

Areen, J., King, P. A., Goldberg, S., and Capron, A. M., Law, Science and Medicine, Mineola, NY: Foundation Press, 1984.

Aristotle, Nicomachean Ethics.

Bambrough, R. Moral Scepticism and Moral Knowledge. London: Routledge and Kegan Paul, 1979.

Bankowski, Z., and Howard Jones, N., eds. Human Experimentation and Medical Ethics. Geneva: Council for International Organisations of Medical Sciences, 1982.

Bayles, M. D. Reproductive Ethics. Englewood Cliffs, NJ: Prentice-Hall, 1984.

Beauchamp, T. L., ed. Philosophical Ethics: An Introduction to Moral Philosophy. New York: McGraw-Hill, 1982.

—— and Childress, J. F. Principles of Bio-Medical Ethics, 2nd edn.

—— and Walters, L., eds. Contemporary Issues in Bio-Ethics. Encino, Calif.: Wadsworth, 1978.

Berlant, J. L. Profession and Monopoly: A Study of Medicine in the United States and Great Britain, Berkeley, Los Angeles, and London: University of California Press, 1975.

Black, D. et al. Inequalities in Health (The Black Report). Harmondsworth: Penguin, 1982.

Blank, R. 'Emerging Notions of Women's Rights and Responsibilities during Gestation', 7 Journal of Legal Medicine 441– (1986).

Bloch, S., and Chodoff, P., eds. Psychiatric Ethics. Oxford: Oxford University Press, 1981.

Bluglass, R. A Guide to the Mental Health Act 1983. London, and Edinburgh: Churchill Livingstone, 1983; reprinted 'with additional information', 1984.

Bok, Sissela, Lying—Moral Choice in Public and Private Life, Hassocks, Sussex: Harvester Press, 1978.

Bondeson, W. B., Engelhardt, H. T., Spicker, S. E., and Winship, D. H., eds. Abortion and the Status of the Foetus. Dordrecht: Reidel, 1983.

Boyd, Kenneth, ed. The Ethics of Resource Allocation. Edinburgh: Edinburgh University Press, 1979.

* This bibliography draws heavily on one prepared by Dr R. Gillon for the Centre of Medical Law and Ethics at King's College, London and my thanks are due to him.

Bradford Hill, A. 'Medical Ethics and Controlled Trials', 1 *British Medical Journal* 1943 (1963).

Brazier, M. *Medicine, Patients and the Law.* Harmondsworth: Pelican, 1987.

British Medical Association. *Handbook of Medical Ethics.* London: British Medical Association, 1984.

British Medical Journal. 'Teenage Confidence and Consent' (anonymous editorial). 290 *British Medical Journal* 144–5 (1985).

Brody, B. *Abortion and the Sanctity of Human Life: A Philosophical View.* Cambridge, Mass.: MIT Press, 1975.

—— and Engelhardt, H. T. *Mental Illness: Law and Public Policy.* Dordrecht: Reidel, 1980.

Burkhardt, R., and Kienle, G. 'Basic Problems in Controlled Trials' (with critical response from D. W. Vere, and ensuing debate). 9 *Journal of Medical Ethics* 80–9 (1983).

Byrne, P., ed. *Rights and Wrongs in Medicine.* London: King's Fund, 1986.

Calabresi, G., and Bobbitt, P. *Tragic Choices.* New York: Norton, 1978.

Callahan, D. *Abortion: Law Choice and Morality.* New York: MacMillan, 1970.

Campbell, A. G. M., and Duff, R. S. 'Deciding the Care of Severely Malformed or Dying Infants'. 5 *Journal of Medical Ethics* 65–7 (1979).

Campbell, A. V. *Moral Dilemmas in Medicine,* 2nd edn. Edinburgh, London, and New York: Churchill Livingstone, 1975; 3rd edn., 1984.

—— *Medicine Health and Justice: The Problem of Priorities.* Edinburgh, London, and New York: Churchill Livingstone, 1978.

Cancer Research Campaign (CRC) Working Party in Breast Conservation. 'Informed Consent: Ethical, Legal and Medical Implications for Doctors and Patients who Participate in Randomised Clinical Trials'. 286 *British Medical Journal* 1117–21 (1983).

Cartwright, A., and Anderson, R. *General Practice Revisited.* London; Tavistock Publications, 1981.

Catholic Archbishops of Great Britain. *Abortion and the Right to Live.* Abbots Langley, Herts: Catholic Information Services, 1980.

Church of England Board for Social Responsibility. *Abortion: Ethical Discussion.* London: Church Information Office, 1965.

CIBA Foundation. *Law and Ethics of AID and Embryo Transfer.* London: CIBA Foundation, 1973.

—— *Human Embryo Research: Yes or No?* London: CIBA Foundation, 1986.

Code of Practice of the Royal Colleges and their Medical Faculties. 'Diagnosis of Brain Death'. 2 *British Medical Journal* 1187–8 (1976).

—— 'Diagnosis of Death'. 1 *British Medical Journal* 3320 (1979).

Cohen, M., Nagel, T., and Scanlon, T. eds. *Medicine and Moral Philosophy.* Princeton, NJ: Princeton University Press, 1981.

Council for Science and Society. *Expensive Medical Techniques: Report of a Working Party.* London: Council for Science and Society, 1983.

—— *Human Procreation: Ethical Aspects of the New Techniques.* Oxford: Oxford University Press, 1984.

Culver, C. M., and Gert, B. *Philosophy in Medicine: Conceptual and Ethical Issues in Medicine and Psychiatry.* New York and Oxford: Oxford University Press, 1982.

Daniels, N. 'Health Care Needs and Distributive Justice'. 10 (2) *Philosophy and Public Affairs* 146–79 (1981).

Department for Health and Social Security (DHSS). *Report of the Committee of Inquiry into Human Fertilisation and Embryology* (The Warnock Report). London: HMSO, 1984.

Devlin, P. *The Enforcement of Morals*. Oxford: Oxford University Press, 1965.

Dimond, B. 'Consent, Compulsion and the Rights of the Mother and Unborn Child'. 99 *Midwives Chronicle and Nursing Notes* 1179– (1987).

Downie, R. S., and Telfer, E. *Caring and Curing: A Philosophy of Medicine and Social Work*. London: Methuen, 1980.

Dubos, R. *Mirage of Health*. London: George Allen and Unwin, 1960.

Duncan, A. S., Dunstan, G. R., and Welbourn, R. B., eds. *Dictionary of Medical Ethics*, 2nd edn. London: Darton, Longman and Todd, 1981.

Dunstan, G. R. 'The Moral Status of the Human Embryo: A Tradition Recalled'. 10 *Journal of Medical Ethics* 38–44 (1984).

Dworkin, R. M. *Taking Rights Seriously*. Cambridge, Mass.: Harvard University Press, 1977.

Engelhardt, H. T. 'Allocating Scarce Medical Resources and the Availability of Organ Transplantation'. 311 *New England Journal of Medicine* 66–71 (1984).

—— and Spicker, S. F., eds. *Evaluation and Explanation in the Bio-Medical Sciences*. Dordrecht and Boston: Reidel, 1975.

Faden, R. R., and Beauchamp, T. L. *A History and Theory of Informed Consent*. New York: Oxford University Press, 1986.

Feinberg, J., ed. *The Problem of Abortion*. Belmont, Calif.: Wadsworth, 1973.

Finch, J. D. *Health Services Law*. London: Sweet and Maxwell, 1981.

Finnis, J. *Natural Law and Natural Rights*. Oxford: Clarendon Press, 1984.

Fitton, F., and Acheson, H. W. K. *The Doctor/Patient Relationship: A Study in General Practice*. London: HMSO, 1979.

Fletcher, C. M. *Communication in Medicine*, London: Nuffield Provincial Hospitals Trust, 1973.

Fletcher, J. C. 'Emerging Ethical Issues in Fetal Therapy', 128 *Progress in Clinical Biological Research* 293– (1983).

Fortin, J. 'Legal Protection for the Unborn Child', 51 *Modern Law Review* 54– (1988)

—— 'Can you Ward a Foetus', 51 *Modern Law Review* 768– (1988).

Freund, P. A., ed. *Experimentation with Human Subjects*. London: George Allen and Unwin, 1972.

Frey, R. G., ed. *Utility and Rights*. Oxford: Blackwell, 1984.

Fried, C. *Medical Experimentation: Personal Integrity and Social Policy*. Amsterdam and New York: Elsevier, 1974.

—— *An Anatomy of Values: Problems of Personal and Social Choice*. Cambridge, Mass.: Harvard University Press, 1970.

Gallaher, J. 'Prenatal Invasion and Interventions: What's Wrong with Fetal Rights', 10 *Harvard Women's Law Journal* 9– (1987).

General Medical Council. *Professional Conduct and Discipline: Fitness to Practise*. London: General Medical Council, 1986.

Gillon, R. *Philosophical Medical Ethics*. Chichester: Wiley, 1986.

Gillon, R. 'Pregnancy, Obstetrics and the Moral Status of the Fetus'. 14 *Journal of Medical Ethics* 1– (1988).

Glover, J. *Causing Death and Saving Lives*. Harmondsworth: Penguin, 1977.

—— *What Sort of People Should There Be?* Harmondsworth: Penguin, 1984.

Gorovitz, S. *Doctor's Dilemmas*. London: Collier MacMillan, 1982.

Gostin, L. 'Human Rights, Judicial Review and the Mentally Disordered Offender'. 779 (1982), *Criminal Law Review*.

—— *Mental Health Law*. London: Shaw and Sons, 1986.

Grubb, A., and Pearl, D. 'Protecting the Life of the Unborn Child', 103 *Law Quarterly Review*, 340– (1987).

Hare, R. M. *Freedom and Reason*. Oxford: Oxford University Press, 1963.

—— *Moral Thinking*. Oxford: Clarendon Press, 1981.

Harris, J. 'Ethical Problems in the Management of Some Severely Handicapped Children'. 7 (3) *Journal of Medical Ethics* 117–20 (1981).

—— 'In vitro Fertilisation: The Ethical Issues, 1'. 33 *Philosophical Quarterly* 217–37 (1983).

—— *The Value of Life: An Introduction to Medical Ethics*. London: Routledge and Kegan Paul, 1985.

Hart, H. L. A. *The Concept of Law*. Oxford: Oxford University Press, 1961.

—— *Law, Liberty and Morality*. Oxford: Oxford University Press, 1963.

Havard, J. 'The Legal Threat to Medicine'. 284 *British Medical Journal* 614 (1982).

—— 'Medical Confidence'. 11 (1) *Journal of Medical Ethics* 8–11 (1985).

Hoggett, B. *Mental Health Law*, 2nd edn. London: Sweet and Maxwell, 1984.

—— and Pearl, D. *The Family, Law and Society*. London: Butterworths, 1983.

Holder, A. *Legal Issues in Paediatrics and Adolescent Medicine*, 2nd edn. New Haven: Yale University Press, 1985.

Hughes, G. J. *Moral Decisions*. London: Darton, Longman and Todd, 1980.

Illich, I. *Limits to Medicine*. Harmondsworth: Penguin, 1978.

Jackson, R., and Powell, I. *Professional Negligence*. London: Sweet and Maxwell, 1982.

Jakobovits, I. *Jewish Medical Ethics*. New York: Bloch, 1975.

Jennett, B. *High Technology Medicine—Benefits and Burdens*, 2nd edn. Oxford: Oxford University Press, 1986.

Johnsen, D. 'The Creation of Fetal Rights: Conflicts with Women's Constitutional Rights to Liberty, Privacy and Equal Protection, 7 *Yale Law Journal* 251– (1986).

—— 'A New Threat to Pregnant Womens' Autonomy', 17 *Hastings Center Report* 33– (1989).

Katz, J. *The Silent World of Doctor and Patient*. London: Collier MacMillan, 1984.

—— ed. *Experimentation with Human Beings*. New York: Russell Sage, 1972.

—— and Capron, A. M. *Catastrophic Diseases: Who Decides What? A Psychological and Legal Analysis*. New York: Russell Sage, 1975.

Keyserlingk, E. W. 'The Unborn Child's Right to Prenatal Care—A Comparative Law Perspective' 5 *McGill Legal Studies* 79– (1984).

Kirby, M. D. 'Informed Consent: What Does It Mean?' 9 (2) *Journal of Medical Ethics* 69–75 (1983).

Klein, R. *The Politics of the National Health Service*. London: Longman, 1983.

Kubler-Ross, E. *On Death and Dying*. London: Tavistock Publications, 1970.

Lamb, D. *Death, Brain Death and Ethics*. London and Sydney: Croom Helm, 1986.

Law Reform Commission of Canada. *Consent to Medical Care*. Ottowa, 1980.

Lockwood, M. 'Controls or Victims: The Ethics of Non-treatment in Clinical Trials'. 31 (1) *Oxford Medical School Gazette* 29–31 (1979).

—— *Moral Dilemmas in Modern Medicine*. Oxford: Oxford University Press, 1985.

—— 'Singer on Killing and the Preference for Life'. 22 *Enquiry* 157–70 (1979).

Lorber, J. 'Ethical Problems in the Management of Myelomeningocele and Hydrocephalus'. 10 *Journal of the Royal College of Physicians* (1975).

MacIntyre, A. C. *After Virtue—A Study in Moral Theory*. London: Duckworth, 1981.

Mackie, J. L. *Ethics: Inventing Right and Wrong*. Harmondsworth: Penguin, 1977.

Mahawold, M. 'Beyond Abortion: Refusal of Cesarean Section', 3 *Bioethics* 106– (1989).

Mahoney, J. *Bioethics and Belief*. London: Sheed and Ward, 1984.

Mason, J. K., and McCall-Smith, R. A. *Law and Medical Ethics*, 2nd edn. London: Butterworth, 1987.

Mathieu, D. 'Respecting Liberty and Preventing Harm: Limits of State Intervention on Prenatal Choice', 8 *Harvard Journal of Law and Public Policy* 19– (1985).

Maxwell, R. J. *Health and Wealth*. Lexington, Mass.: Lexington Books, 1981.

McLean, S. *Legal Issues in Medicine*. Aldershot: Gower, 1981.

—— and Maher, G. *Medicine Morals and the Law*. Aldershot: Gower, 1981.

Mooney, G. H. *Economics, Medicine and Health Care*. Brighton: Wheatsheaf Books, 1986.

Nelson, L., and Milliken, N. 'Compelled Medical Treatment of Pregnant Women: Life, Liberty and Law in Conflict', 259 *Journal of American Medical Association* 7– (1988).

Nicholson, R., ed. *Medical Research on Children*. Oxford: Oxford University Press, 1986.

Noonan, J. T. *The Morality of Abortion: Legal and Historical Perspectives*. Cambridge, Mass.: Harvard University Press, 1970.

—— *A Private Choice: Abortion in America in the 70's*. New York: Free Press, 1979.

Nozick, R. *Anarchy, State and Utopia*. New York: Basic Books, 1974.

Oken, D. 'What to Tell Cancer Patients'. 175 *Journal of the American Medical Association* 1120–8 (1961).

Ormrod, R. 'A Lawyer Looks at Medical Ethics'. 46 *Medico-Legal Journal* 18–32 (1978).

Pallis, C. *The ABC of Brain Stem Death*. London: British Medical Journal Publications, 1983.

Papworth, M. H. *Human Guinea Pigs: Experimentation on Man*. London: Routledge and Kegan Paul, 1967.

Paris, J. J., and Reardon, F. E. 'Court Responses to Withholding and Withdrawing Artificial Nutrition and Fluids'. 243 (15) *Journal of the American Medical Association* 2243–5 (1985).

Parsons, V., and Lock, P. 'Triage and the Patient with Renal Failure'. 6 (4) *Journal of Medical Ethics* 173–6 (1980).

Picard, F. *Legal Liability of Doctors and Hospitals in Canada* 2nd edn, Toronto: Carswell, 1984.

President's Commission for the Study of Ethical and Legal Problems in Medicine and Biomedical and Behavioral Research. Washington, DC: US Government Printing Office.

—— *Compensation for Research Injuries*, vol. 1, Report. 1982.

—— *Compensating for Research Injuries*, vol. 2, Appendices. 1982.

—— *Deciding to Forego Life Sustaining Treatment.* 1983.

—— *Defining Death: A Report on the Medical, Legal and Ethical Issues in the Determination of Death.* 1981.

—— *Implementing Human Research Regulations. Second Biennial Report on the Adequacy and Uniformity of Federal Rules and Policies and of their Implementation for the Protection of Human Subjects.* 1983.

—— *Making Health Care Decisions*, vol. 1, Report. 1982.

—— *Making Health Care Decisions*, vol. 2, Appendices (Empirical Studies of Informed Consent). 1982.

—— *Making Health Care Decisions*, vol. 3, Appendices (Foundations of Informed Consent). 1982.

—— *Protecting Human Subjects.* 1981.

—— *Screening and Counselling for Genetic Conditions.* 1983.

—— *Securing Access to Health Care*, vol. 1, Report. 1983.

—— *Securing Access to Health Care*, vol. 2, Appendices: Sociocultural and Philosophical Studies. 1983.

—— *Securing Access to Health Care*, vol. 3, Appendices. 1983.

—— *Splicing Life: A Report on the Social and Ethical Issues of Genetic Engineering with Human Beings.* 1982.

—— *Summing up: The Ethical and Legal Problems in Medicine and Biomedical and Behavioral Research.* Washington, DC: US Government Printing Office, 1983.

—— *Whistle Blowing in Biomedical Research: Policies and Procedures for Responding to Reports of Misconduct—Proceedings of a Workshop.* 1982.

Rachels, J. *The End of Life: Euthanasia and Morality.* Oxford: Oxford University Press, 1986.

Ramsey, P. *Ethics at the Edges of Life.* New Haven: Yale University Press, 1978.

—— *The Patient as Person.* New Haven: Yale University Press, 1970.

Raphael, D. D. *Moral Philosophy.* Oxford: Oxford University Press, 1981.

Rawls, J. *A Theory of Justice.* Oxford: Oxford University Press, 1973.

Reich, W. T., ed. *Encyclopaedia of Bioethics.* London: Collier MacMillan, 1978.

Reiser, S. J., Dyck, A. J., and Curran, W. J., eds. *Ethics in Medicine: Historical Perspectives and Contemporary Concerns.* Cambridge, Mass., and London: MIT Press, 1977.

Rhoden, N. 'The Judge in the Delivery Room: The Emergence of Court Ordered Caesareans' 74 California Law Review 1951– (1986).

Robertson J. 'The Right to Procreate and *in utero* Fetal Therapy', 3 *Journal of Legal Medicine* 333– (1982).

—— and Schulman, J. D. 'Pregnancy and Prenatal Harm to Offspring, The Case of Mothers with PKU'. 17 *Hastings Center Report* 23– (1987).

Rothman, B. K. *Recreating Motherhood.* New York: W. W. Morton, 1989.

Royal College of Obstetricians and Gynaecologists. *Report of the RCOG Ethics Committee on In vitro Fertilisation and Embryo Replacement or Transfer.* London: RCOG, 1983.

Schafer, A. 'The Ethics of the Randomised Clinical Trial'. 307 *New England Journal of Medicine* 719–24 (1982).

Schedler, G. 'Women's Reproductive Rights: Is There a Conflict with a Child's Right to be Born Free from Defects?' 7 *Journal of Legal Medicine* 357– (1986).

Searle, J. 'Prima Facie Obligations'. In J. Raz, ed., *Practical Reasoning*, pp. 81–90. Oxford: Oxford University Press, 1978.

Sieghart, P. 'Medical Confidence, the Law and Computers'. 77 *Journal of the Royal Society of Medicine* 656–62 (1984).

Siegler, M. 'Confidentiality in Medicine — A Decrepit Concept'. 307 *New England Journal of Medicine* 1518–21 (1982).

Simanowitz, A. 'Standards, Attitudes and Accountability in the Medical Profession'. 2 *The Lancet* 546–7 (1985).

Singer, P. *Practical Ethics.* Cambridge: Cambridge University Press, 1979.

—— and Walter, B., eds. *Test Tube Babies.* Melbourne and Oxford: Oxford University Press, 1982.

Skegg, P. D. G. *Law, Ethics and Medicine: Studies in Medical Law.* Oxford: Clarendon Press, 1984.

Snowden, R., Mitchell, G. D., and Mitchell, E. M. *Artificial Reproduction: A Social Investigation.* London: George Allen and Unwin, 1983.

Speller, S. R., *Speller's Law Relating to Hospitals and Kindred Institutions*, 6th edn., rev. and ed. by J. Jacob. London: H. K. Lewis, 1978.

Spicker, S. F., and Engelhardt, H. T., eds. *Philosophical Medical Ethics: Its Nature and Significance.* Dordrecht: Reidel, 1977.

Steinbock, B., Marquis, D., and Kayata, S. 'Case Studies: Preterm Labor and Prenatal Harm', 19 *Hastings Center Report* 32– (1989).

Sumner, L. W. *Abortion and Moral Theory.* Princeton, NJ: Princeton University Press, 1981.

Swiss Institute of Comparative Law. *Artificial Procreation, Genetics and the Law.* Zurich: Schultheiss Polygraphischer Verlag, 1986.

Thompson, I. E. 'The Nature of Confidentiality'. 5 (2) *Journal of Medical Ethics* 57–64 (1979).

Thomson, J. J. 'A Defence of Abortion'. 1 *Philosophy and Public Affairs* 47–66 (1971).

Tobias, P. V. 'South African Medical and Dental Council and the Biko Doctors'. 251 *British Medical Journal* 231 (1980).

Tooley, M. *Abortion and Infanticide.* Oxford: Clarendon Press, 1983.

Tribe, L. *American Constitutional Law.* Mineola NY: Foundation Press (1976).

Veatch, R. M. *A Theory of Medical Ethics.* New York: Basic Books, 1981.

Vere, D. W. 'Controlled Clinical Trials — The Current Ethical Debate'. 74 *Proceedings of the Royal Society of Medicine* 85–7 (1981).

Wadlington, W., Waltz, J. R., and Dworkin, R. B., *Cases on Law and Medicine.* Mineola, NY: Foundation Press, 1980.

Warnock, M. 'In vitro Fertilization: The Ethical Issues 2', 33 *Philosophical Quarterly*
238–49 (1983).
Williams, G. *Textbook of Criminal Law*, 2nd edn. London: Stevens, 1983.
World Medical Association. *Handbook of Declarations*. Ferney-Voltaire, France:
World Medical Association, 1985.

Index

Note: Only the more significant cases are entered. These are given in an abbreviated form, e.g. *Bolam* v. *Friern Hospital Management Committee* is entered as *Bolam* case.